knowledge to produce Crowell's Handbook of Contemporary Drama. These contributors are:

Czechoslovakia: Ewald Osers (BBC) and Kurt Arje (formerly manager of the Theatre on the Balustrade, Prague)

Scandinavia: Harry Carlson, Queens College, New York City

Finland: Timo Tiusanen, University of Helsinki

France: Jacques Guicharnaud, Yale University

Germany, Austria, and Switzerland: Jack D. Zipes, New York University

Great Britain: Michael Anderson, University of Bristol

Hungary: George Gömöri, University of Cambridge

Italy: Richard Sogliuzzo, State University of New York at Albany

Latin America: Frank Dauster, Rutgers, The State University

Poland: Boleslav Taborski, BBC

Soviet Union: Arthur Hudgins, University of Minnesota.

Spain and Portugal: E. George Erdman, Jr., State University of New York at Binghamton

United States: Kristin Morrison, Boston College

This critical handbook will be a favorite companion for students, librarians, and all lovers of contemporary drama.

Crowell's Handbook of

Contemporary Drama

*Crowell's Handbook of*

# CONTEMPORARY DRAMA

*by* MICHAEL ANDERSON, JACQUES GUICHARNAUD, KRISTIN MORRISON, JACK D. ZIPES, *and others*

*Thomas Y. Crowell Company*
NEW YORK / ESTABLISHED 1834

97983

# Publisher's Preface

This book is designed to offer a convenient guide to developments in the drama in Europe and the Americas since the Second World War—or, in the case of Spain, since the Civil War. The emphasis is entirely on written drama, not on theater. In a few cases, however, directors, such as Erwin Piscator or Peter Brook, and theatrical companies, such as the Berliner Ensemble or the Living Theater, are discussed briefly because of their influence on the forms of written drama.

Although the handbook is intended primarily as a reference work, the contributors have been encouraged to offer some critical appraisal of both plays and playwrights. As a result, strong points of view are evident in many of the entries. This bias, which in no case extends to factual information, accurately reflects the central importance of social criticism and political ideology in the drama of many nations today.

The choice of playwrights and plays to be given individual entries, in addition to mention in the surveys of national dramas, has been left entirely to the contributors, and the decisions that they have made are often highly personal. This fact is the more apparent because they have chosen, in general, to discuss a very few plays at some length rather than to give only brief descriptions of a large number of plays. In this way they have been able to give a clearer picture of the characteristic qualities of the styles and subject matter of the most important playwrights than would otherwise have been possible.

Because foreign plays are being translated into English every day, and equally because many of these translations are available only in journals, any attempt to provide up-to-date data on readily available translations seemed futile. No distinction is made, therefore, between titles of actual translations and mere translated titles. No translation is offered of a foreign title the meaning of which is reasonably apparent; untranslated titles in unfamiliar languages can safely be assumed to be proper names.

## Contributors

| | |
|---|---|
| CZECHOSLOVAKIA | **Ewald Osers** |
| Czech drama | Specialist in Eastern Europe for the British Broadcasting Corporation, and translator |
| Slovak drama | **Kurt Arje** |
| | Former manager and dramaturge, Theatre on the Balustrade, Prague |

| | |
|---|---|
| DENMARK, NORWAY, and SWEDEN | **Harry Carlson**<br>Department of Speech, Queens College, City University of New York |
| FINLAND | **Timo Tiusanen**<br>Docent in Theater Research, University of Helsinki, and Artistic Director, Helsinki City Theater |
| FRANCE | **Jacques Guicharnaud**<br>Department of Romance Languages and Literatures, Yale University |
| GERMANY, AUSTRIA, and SWITZERLAND | **Jack D. Zipes**<br>Department of Germanic Languages and Literatures, New York University |
| GREAT BRITAIN | **Michael Anderson**<br>Department of Drama, University of Bristol |
| HUNGARY | **George Gömöri**<br>Department of Slavonic Studies, University of Cambridge |
| ITALY | **Richard A. Sogliuzzo**<br>Department of Theater, State University of New York at Albany |
| LATIN AMERICA | **Frank Dauster**<br>Department of Romance Languages, Rutgers, The State University |
| POLAND | **Boleslav Taborski**<br>Editor of British Broadcasting Corporation *Arts Review,* and translator |
| SOVIET UNION | **Arthur Hudgins**<br>Department of Slavic Languages, University of Minnesota |
| SPAIN and PORTUGAL | **E. George Erdman, Jr.**<br>Department of Romance Languages and Literatures, State University of New York at Binghamton |
| UNITED STATES | **Kristin Morrison**<br>Department of English, Boston College |

# A

**Absurd.** In modern philosophy the adjective "absurd" has taken on the sense "devoid of justification, meaning, or purpose." As a noun, the "absurd" designates the general condition of mankind, to the extent that it is experienced and considered as unjustified. This notion, which now has wide currency, is of prime importance in atheistic existentialism, according to which the death of God, proclaimed by Nietzsche's Zarathustra, logically results in the lack of any purpose to man's existence in the universe. On the fringe of existentialism the main exponent of the concept of the absurd in France was Albert CAMUS, who discussed it most particularly in his essay *The Myth of Sisyphus* (1942). For Camus the absurd was most clearly perceptible in the relationship between man and the world, in the profound breach between man's aspirations and his condition, death being its incomprehensible conclusion. The hero of the absurd, according to Camus, is one who, without hope and without illusions, lucidly accepts that breach, refuses to invent gods (as do the totalitarian philosophers), rejects suicide, and assumes his fate like the mythological Sisyphus, who tirelessly pushes his rock up a hill, although it always rolls back. The subject of Camus's first two plays, *Caligula* and *Le Malentendu* (both published in 1944), is precisely that awareness of the absurd and the elementary and erroneous forms of rebellion it entails.

During the first half of this century many other playwrights experienced a feeling of the absurd. Armand SALACROU, Jean ANOUILH, and above all, Jean-Paul SARTRE, in varying degrees, created characters that are haunted by the anguish of meaninglessness, and they constructed their plays around the behavior and modes of action provoked by it. Even before them, the mythology or monsters of Jean Giraudoux and Jean Cocteau were often metaphors or fantasies aimed at filling the vacuum of the absurd.

Nevertheless, the term "theater of the absurd," since the publication of Martin Esslin's study by that name (1961), has been applied to the works of certain specific playwrights who dominated the world of theater during the 1950s and 1960s, and who not only based their plays on the absurd but gave a new and seemingly absurd form to their visions. In the forefront of this group in France are Samuel BECKETT, Eugène IONESCO, and Arthur ADAMOV (until 1955). While they in no way form a "school," they have all contributed to the development of a new aesthetics. In many respects Robert PINGET, Jean Tardieu, Fernando ARRABAL, Boris VIAN, and Roland DUBILLARD are related to this new theater, despite very great individual differences.

In form the theater of the absurd is characterized by an abandonment of the traditional conceptions of what a play should be. Whereas a play by Camus or Sartre unfolds with reasonable and recognizable logic—that is, it has, like a naturalistic play, a plot based on explicable decisions and actions— the works of the theater of the absurd either reduce the plot to zero (Beckett) or construct it out of a juxtaposition of events with no clear causality (Ionesco). As for the characters themselves, they are no longer consistent and rational beings with whom the spectator may identify. Of course, in Beckett they still have some psychological traits that provide a sketchy characterization. But their identities, the permanence of their "selves," are obscure and questionable. In extreme cases (certain plays of Ionesco and Adamov) the characters change identities, completely contradict themselves within the same speech, and, as- tonished at what we consider normal, accept the most fantastic creatures and events without turning a hair; or, when they explain situations, their reasoning is nonsensical and a parody of our logic. On the whole, the spectator is con- fronted with a series of facts that are often contradictory and meaningless, psy- chologically as well as in relation to the events of the play. The effect is gen- erally grotesque: Just as classical farce was a caricatural mirror of the follies of human nature and society, so the theater of the absurd is an equally carica- tural mirror of man's metaphysical condition. With the modern world shaken in its traditional beliefs and in grave doubt as to the meaning of existence and the possibility of communication between men, the theater of the absurd pre- sents exaggerated and clear images of meaninglessness and the absence of com- munication.

Such a theater is essentially poetic. Each playwright draws from his per- sonal obsessions the fantasies that express a feeling of the absurd. Each play is a statement on how things stand, not a reflection on how the feeling of the absurd may be translated into action in the world—a way, perhaps, to accept it or to rise above it, as in Sartre and Camus. Of course, such plays are not altogether "uncommitted": They are often satirical and ridicule the blind good conscience and logical illusions of those who believe that the world has mean- ing. But they do not propose to give it one through the action: They represent it metaphorically, and suggest an aesthetic, not a practical, solution. This solu- tion may be found, for example, in laughter (Ionesco) or in the beauty of form and language (Beckett).

There are some surface resemblances between the theater of the absurd and the poetic theater that succeeded surrealism. Rejecting a rational vision of the world necessarily leads to comparable images: strange coincidences en- countered in reality, fantasies borrowed from dreams and the subconscious, automatic language. But while the surrealistically inclined poetic theater utilizes the fantastic and nonsense to suggest a mysterious reality endowed with a positive existence (love, a magical universe, the Jungian unconscious, demonic or angelic forces), the theater of the absurd presents them as images of the unjustified: Nonsense is not the sign of another world; it is the proof of nothingness.

**Adamov, Arthur** (1908–1970). Russian-born French dramatist. Born in Kislovodsk, in Caucasia, Adamov left Russia with his parents in 1914. He went to school in Geneva (where, as a child, he was familiar with the Georges Pitoëff company), Mainz, and finally Paris. At sixteen he was acquainted with the surrealist group and wrote his first poems. Nevertheless, his literary career did not really begin until after the war. In addition to a confession of personal neuroses (*L'Aveu*, 1945), memoirs (*L'Homme et l'enfant*, 1969), and tales (*Je, ils*, 1969), his works consist essentially of plays and essays on the theater (*Ici et maintenant*, 1964).

The influence of Antonin Artaud, whom Adamov knew well, and his reading of Strindberg led him, in 1947, to write his first play, *La Parodie* (produced 1952). Encouraged first by André Gide and Jean Vilar, for whom he adapted Georg Büchner's *Danton's Death* and who was his first director with *L'Invasion* (1950), then by avant-garde directors, and finally by Roger Planchon, Adamov has written some fifteen plays and several adaptations.

Until about 1955 Adamov's plays were related to both surrealism and the theater of the absurd. Their themes of noncommunication, the instability of identities, incomprehensible guilt, and arbitrary victimization are handled in an obvious and brutal way, with often flat and sketchy dialogue, in an atmosphere of horror and nightmarish humor. (See L'Invasion.) These plays are based on personal obsessions and neuroses, represented concretely on stage, as, for example, the cripple's progressive loss of his limbs in *La Grande et la Petite Manœuvre* (1950), or as the complete depersonalization of a man who feels guilty about an indecent act in *Le Professeur Taranne* (1953). However, even in his very first plays, Adamov places the absurd and horror in a social context and often embodies them in the arbitrary terror inflicted by some police state. With Le Ping-Pong (1955) and especially with *Paolo Paoli* (1957), Adamov has moved toward a theater in which the absurd is considered no longer as a metaphysical absolute but rather as one of the contradictions of a consumer or capitalist society. Roger Planchon's influence and the works of Brecht led Adamov, from then on, to write historical and political plays, which range from the fresco of *Printemps 71* (Spring 71, 1963), in which he explains the failure of the Paris Commune, to the accusation of the United States's current society and politics (Adamov was visiting lecturer at Cornell in 1964) in *Off Limits* (1969). His aim, however, is to combine a theater of neuroses with a theater of political criticism, and he would seem to have succeeded with *La Politique des restes* (The Scavengers, 1962), a play about racism.

**After the Fall** (1964). A two-act play by Arthur Miller. The action takes place in the mind of Quentin, a middle-aged attorney, who remembers the significant relationships in his past life—his parents, his friends, the women he has loved. The sequence of memories, with its sudden shifts in time and space, suggests a process of free association, and the use of an invisible "Listener" to whom Quentin explains himself and in whose silent presence he discovers himself makes the play appear an exercise in psychoanalysis.

This is the first play to appear after the period of Miller's marriage to actress Marilyn Monroe (1956–1961), and the character Maggie is taken to be a portrait of her (Miller's marriage to Miss Monroe was dissolved in 1961; he had already married Ingeborg Morath before Miss Monroe's suicide in 1962). Early in the play Quentin comments, "To admit what you see endangers principles!" He develops this theme as he remembers his mother's scorn for his father, and how she tried to persuade Quentin that he had not heard her call his father a moron; as he remembers Holga's blindness to what was happening in the Nazi concentration camps and the failure of friendships during the McCarthy persecutions; and as he remembers the deadly rigidity of his first wife and Maggie's direct simplicity, her ability to "see it all with [her] own eyes; that's more important than all the books." Miller (and Quentin) clearly admires Maggie; but Quentin's marriage to her is mutually destructive. He cannot appropriate her innocent eyes nor can he assume her suffering. After her suicide Quentin must reckon with his guilt in being a survivor (a theme that appears frequently in this play and in *Incident at Vichy*). His final words to the Listener verbalize what Quentin has discovered through his memory process: Admitting what you see endangers the "principle"—the lie—that we are loving and benign creatures; only when we admit our postlapsarian murderousness can we then, with hope, attempt to love clear-sightedly. Then Quentin goes to meet Holga, with a greeting and a gesture that suggest a beginning. (The final stage direction reads, "The darkness takes them all.")

The play was first performed on January 23, 1964, by the Repertory Theater of Lincoln Center, directed by Elia Kazan.

**Ahlsen, Leopold** (born 1927). West German dramatist, director, and actor. After serving in the German Army during World War II, Ahlsen studied literature, psychology, and drama in Munich. From 1947 to 1949 he acted and directed at various theaters in southern Germany. After this period, he was, until 1960, the director of radio plays at the Bavarian Radio Station. In fact, Ahlsen is best known for plays that he has adapted for the stage from his radio plays. His most successful play is *Philemon and Baukis* (1956), which takes place in the Balkans during World War II. An old couple, Nikolaos and Marulja, take a neutral stand and help both partisans and Germans. When the partisans discover that Nikolaos has helped a wounded German soldier, they sentence him to death. Marulja decides to take the sentence upon herself, too, as a sign of devotion to her husband. The humanity of this old couple, who are not idealized in the least, is contrasted with the intensity of the partisans and Germans, who see the world in terms of black and white. Ahlsen's play, a moving plea for tolerance and sobriety, tends at times to be too stylized. In another drama, *Raskolnikoff* (1960), an adaptation of Dostoevski's *Crime and Punishment*, he presents a metaphysical debate about the existence of God. Raskolnikoff argues that if God is dead, anything is allowed. However, his opponent, Porphyri, refutes his arguments and proves that real freedom lies in accepting one's limitations and maintaining faith in God. As in most of his plays, Ahlsen takes a stand for Catholicism, which he sees as a stand for humanity. His latest plays, *Sie werden sterben, Sire* (You Are Going to Die, Sire, 1964), a drama about the impending death of King Louis XI, and *Der arme Mann Luther* (The Poor Man Luther, 1967), a play about Luther's moral destitution, are also religious in vein. Ahlsen's works reveal good craftsmanship and a strong religious conviction. He is successful with the public, but is not highly regarded by critics, perhaps because his traditional ideas and techniques appear to be out of place in these radical times.

OTHER PLAYS: *Pflicht zur Sünde* (Duty to Sin, 1952), *Zwischen den Ufern* (Between the Banks, 1952), *Kleider machen Leute* (Clothes Make the Man, 1963).

**Albee, Edward Franklin, III** (born 1928). American playwright. Adopted as a two-week-old infant by Reed and Frances Albee, Edward Albee grew up in a millionaire's household. His father's, and grandfather's, chain of theaters provided the child with frequent contact with theatrical personalities and his own emotional needs furnished a motive for writing. At Choate School, where he found a more helpful faculty than he had at Lawrenceville preparatory school and Valley Forge Military Academy, both of which had expelled him, the young man wrote as many as eighteen hours a day. But Albee's early work, through adolescence and into his twenties, was chiefly in poetry and fiction. Not until after a fruitless decade of holding odd jobs, being subtly advised by a poet (W. H. Auden) to give up poetry and by a playwright (Thornton Wilder) to concentrate on playwriting, did the twenty-nine-year-old Albee finally sit down at the wobbly kitchen table in his bachelor apartment and write his first mature play, *The Zoo Story*.

New York producers were not interested in the play; but the young composer with whom Albee had been living for nine years, William Flanagan, sent the play to a friend in Europe, and by a circuitous route—"from New York to Florence to Zurich to Frankfurt to Berlin"—the play reached West Germany, where it had its premier in September 1959. In January 1960 it was produced off-Broadway in a double bill with Samuel Beckett's *Krapp's Last Tape*. Its reception was enthusiastic, and Albee suddenly was seen as a talent to be reckoned with.

In its emotional pattern *The Zoo Story* is emblematic of much that was to come after it: a quiet opening, a slowly growing sense of desperation, an intense and theatrically active climax, an immediate curtain. Its subject, too, is found in other Albee plays: possession as a substitute for communion, violence as the mode of "love." Peter—neat and forty—sits on a bench in Central Park on a Sunday afternoon in summer reading a book; Jerry—a rumpled thirty—enters and says to him, "I've been to the zoo." And the long way to come back a short distance begins. Peter tries to stay in the cage of his own life, not wanting to make living contact with this stranger who has approached him; Jerry asks personal questions, prods, cajoles, offers intimate details about himself, tells stories of his previous attempts at communion—and Peter becomes increasingly more uncomfortable, increasingly more threatened. These two animals have circled each other verbally; now one begins to encroach on the territory of the other: Jerry sits on Peter's bench, tickles him near hysteria, then becomes more aggressive, poking, shoving, insulting, goading Peter into a defensive fight. When Peter picks up the knife Jerry has been threatening him with, Jerry impales himself on it, forcing the frightened Peter to be his executioner. Then, and only then, does Jerry tell the story he began with: "I think . . . I think this is what happened at the zoo." Jerry tells Peter that he has been dispossessed of his bench (and by implication of his privacy, his little caged life) but has defended his honor; Peter has discovered he is not a vegetable, he is an animal, too. Peter flees while Jerry, wiping the fingerprints off the knife, dies.

The play has been variously interpreted: as theater of the absurd, showing the ultimate meaninglessness of life and the impossibility of human contact; or, in the other extreme, as a play of redemption, Jerry as the savior who has agonized in the garden with Peter and who has, by his sacrificial death, brought Peter up from the hell of isolation to the life of communion, however violent, with another. But this play, like *Waiting for Godot*, should not be intellectualized. Its meaning is emotional and, like Beckett's work, lies in the dramatic feeling of increasing desperation. In a single scene Albee has encompassed New York City at its worst: constant physical proximity, body next to body; constant evasion of personal contact, strangers not speaking, eyes not meeting. The play is essentially urban, fear of being alone simultaneous with fear of losing privacy; the cage as its metaphor and violence its atmosphere. Jerry's dying cry "Oh . . . my . . . God" is, as the stage directions require, "a combination of scornful mimicry and supplication."

*The Death of Bessie Smith* (first performed in Berlin in 1960 and off-Broadway the following year) carries on these same notions of possession and violence. Albee wisely shifts the focus of the action away from the famous blues singer who bled to death in 1937 when she was refused admission to a white hospital in Memphis, Tennessee, and concentrates attention on characters implicated in the event. The Admissions Nurse (a southern white girl) owns and enjoys Negro blues records, but she scorns blacks personally. Her passion to dominate extends to the white intern with whom she is carrying on a flirtation. Bessie's comfortable sexuality is contrasted with the tantalizing sex game played by the "honorable" white woman. Against the background of Bessie's significant death, the nurse usurps the attention as she works to a pitch of hysteria, trying to possess rather than love, making contact through violence, keening rather than singing. The climax of the play comes at the moment when the intern slaps her, by his violence repudiating female control and quieting her trivial emotions. Racial hatred, sexual hatred, similar desperations in Albee's zoo.

The American Dream (1961) and The Sandbox (1960) place this desperation in its primal context, the family. Mommy is domineering, querulous, a psychological cannibal; Daddy is passive, acquiescent, negligible; Grandma, spry, eccentric, outspoken, the only parent in this dismal household capable of life; and in their midst Mommy's pet possession, Young Man. (It is difficult not to see Albee's own childhood here: his quiet father; his tall, aggressive mother, whom he remembers wearing riding clothes and carrying a riding crop; her mother, the only one with whom he felt he could communicate.) What Mommy and Daddy want is the American Dream: "Clean-cut, midwest farm boy type, almost insultingly good-looking in a typically American way. Good profile, straight nose, honest eyes, wonderful smile . . ." They had bought a baby before but did not get their money's worth; the more they pruned and clipped the child—gouging out its eyes, cutting off its "you know what"—the less it resembled their ideal; finally the "bumble" up and died. Just as Mommy and Daddy are negotiating for a replacement, the ideal Young Man arrives at their door looking for work. In the only really personal conversation in the play, Young Man tells Grandma that he had had an identical twin who must have suffered terrible mutilation because Young Man now bears those deprivations within himself: Though he looks ideal, inside he is incapable of love or feeling. As Grandma leaves the family, to die in her independent way (celebrated by The Sandbox), the incomplete Young Man joins the group, an empty shell whose appearance makes Mommy very happy. The inane and highly accurate middle-class idiom (an American equivalent of Ionesco's dialogue) reinforces the fusion of comedy, desperation, and meaninglessness that links this work with Continental theater of the absurd.

Albee's most successful play, both commercially and dramatically, is his first of several full-length Broadway dramas, WHO'S AFRAID OF VIRGINIA WOOLF? (1962). Here idiom, situation, character, and mood snap together flawlessly; and in that join the American public recognized something true about itself. This play, like most of Albee's work, has been subject to homosexual interpretation; but despite the cryptic meanings that may or may not be there, what accounts for the play's popularity is the intensity and accuracy of its image of something that is part of the "normal" American scene: games people play in order to make life possible, not just Hump the Hostess and Get the Guests, but more deadly maneuvers like using children for parental satisfaction (which makes an illusion of even real sons) and substituting talk for touch between sexually attracted couples (guaranteed to subvert even a loving relationship). The total dramatic coherence of *Who's Afraid of Virginia Woolf?* makes this play the clearest of all Albee's statements that possession is no substitute for communion, and violence is not the true mode of love.

With *Tiny Alice* (1964) Albee's work took a new turn. Brilliance and turgidity combined to tantalize critics and Broadway audiences. The basic metaphor of a small castle inside a large castle (one so exact a duplicate of the other that an accidental fire occurs in both buildings simultaneously) raises the metaphysical question which is the model and which the "real thing." This dizzying suggestion of nested levels of being moves in many directions: Is sanity inside or outside the asylum where Julian took refuge? Is God big and enveloping or small and contained? Is love to be directed toward the abstract or the concrete, the remote or the immediate, Tiny Alice, Miss Alice, or— even—Big Alice? The character caught in this puzzle is Brother Julian, secretary to a worldly-wise Cardinal of the Catholic Church who has sent him to collect a large donation from a wealthy old woman called Miss Alice. "Sold" by his church to suffer a dark night of the soul, Julian is seduced by Miss Alice, who has become an elegant vampire, and is manipulated by the Lawyer and the Butler, her companions, until finally he does not know whether he has been delivered *from* illusions or *to* illusions. His confusion is shared by the audience, caught by the theatricality of the final scene but not enlightened by it: a crucified man, darkened lights, a resounding heartbeat that grows louder and louder like approaching steps, massive doors prominently in view. What is behind them, something or nothing? The play is overweighted with symbols and allusions; and however genuine the philosophical problem of inadequate images may be, *Tiny Alice* seems intellectually pretentious. Albee's crisp American idiom gives way to an imitation British that only heightens pompousness.

None of Albee's plays since *Who's Afraid of Virginia Woolf?* has had a Broadway run longer than four or five months. *Tiny Alice* was searched for occult meanings, but the audience of interpreters was soon exhausted; his adaptation of a novella by Carson McCullers, *The Ballad of the Sad Café* (1963), dealing with a bizarre Southern Gothic situation, was not dramatically distinguished; and *Malcolm* (1966), adapted from the novel by James Purdy about a fatherless boy who gets mothered and sexed to death, mercifully closed after a few days.

*A Delicate Balance* (1966) was rather erratically awarded the Pulitzer Prize that had been denied to *Who's Afraid of Virginia Woolf?* This play, like much of *Tiny Alice*, rings with echoes of Eliot's *The Cocktail Party;* and, like theater of the absurd, hints at disaster lurking within the banal. But the delicate balance between safety and disaster, sanity and madness, daylight and darkness, neighbor and stranger that is the thematic subject is not achieved dramatically and the play appears to be only derivative, commercially competent entertainment.

With *Everything in the Garden* (1967) Albee attempted adaptation not of a fictional work, as he had done before, but of another play. Giles Cooper's *Everything in the Garden* had been successfully produced in Britain in 1962, a brittle little comedy about dirty money and clean hands. Albee's revisions focus the play more around domestic issues—how the husband adjusts to his wife's prostitution and the extra money it provides for their comfortable suburban life—and it loses the sharp point of Cooper's play that contemporary society considers itself not guilty of what does not show: prostitution, murder, nuclear stockpiling—all quite innocent if unnoticed. This want of values on the individual level contributes to the collective danger.

*Box* (1967) and *Quotations from Chairman Mao Tse-tung* (1968) bring Albee back to his beginning, experimental one-acts obliquely related to theater of the absurd; the visually static quality of *Box* (a giant cube that emits voices for ten minutes) and the self-revelatory counterpointed monologues of *Quotations* are reminiscent of Samuel Beckett's work. Albee described these experiments as attempts to apply "musical form to dramatic structure."

Albee has written seven or eight short articles and given a few published interviews. In addition to a large number of essays and articles on Albee, there are five books dealing with his work, among the most useful being Christopher Bigsby, *Albee* (1969), and Michael E. Rutenberg, *Edward Albee: Playwright in Protest* (1969), as well as the University of Minnesota pamphlet by Ruby Cohn, *Edward Albee* (1969).

OTHER PLAYS: *Fam and Yam* (1960).

**Alfred, William** (born 1922). American scholar, teacher, and playwright. Born in New York City and graduated from Brooklyn College (B.A. 1948) and Harvard University (M.A. 1949, Ph.D. 1954), Professor Alfred has been a popular teacher at Harvard since his appointment in 1954. His verse play *Agamemnon* was published in Rome in 1953 and in the United States in 1954. His first play to be given professional production was *Hogan's Goat,* a vigorous dramatization of Irish Catholic passions and politics in the Brooklyn of the 1890s, presented at the American Place Theatre in 1965. A musical version of the play, adapted by Alfred, had a brief run on Broadway in 1970 under the title *Who to Love.*

**alienation effect (Verfremdungseffekt).** A dramatic theory developed by Bertolt Brecht. Brecht insisted that the actor maintain distance from the role he plays so that the spectators, and the actor as well, are aware of the difference between illusion and reality. Brecht used all possible means of contrast and counterpoint to smash the traditional illusionary devices of drama, for he believed that a play should educate and enlighten an audience by making it conscious of distinctions between fact and fiction in a sociopolitical con-

9

text. He coined the term *Verfremdungseffekt* about 1935. The theory was most clearly outlined in the essays *Die Strassenszene* (The Street Scene) and *Neue Technik der Schaulspielkunst* (The New Technique of the Art of Acting). To alienate the spectator does not mean to offend him but to cause him to detach himself so that he may see familiar objects in a new light. The spectator is to be induced to experience the excitement of a scientist who discovers new truths. Here the emotions are involved, but they are not to cloud one's thinking. The spectator who is aware that he is in a theater and that the play is not real will, in Brecht's view, be able to draw parallels to his own reality and seek ways to change society. See also EPIC THEATER.

**Alonso Millán, Juan José** (born 1936). Spanish dramatist. Alonso Millán learned the mechanics of the theater during his university days in Madrid when, as a student of law and philosophy and letters, he directed both the Teatro Español Universitario and the Teatro Popular Universitario. The twenty-odd plays that follow *Las señoras primero* (Ladies First, 1959), his first commercial success, depend for their appeal on fast-paced dialogue, appropriate to farce, both irrelevant and irreverent, tending toward black humor. But at the hands of Alonso Millán, such fare is more cordial than corrosive, its sole intent being "to provoke hilarity and surprise in spectators of simple habits, clear conscience, and good intentions." *El cianuro . . . ¿solo o con leche?* (Cyanide—Black or With Cream? 1963), of the arsenic-and-old-lace school, achieves just that through the confrontations of a dealer in shrunken heads, his mad child bride, an octogenarian on his deathbed but planning elopement, and a gigolo making off with the wife of the man he carries with him in matching suitcases. *Mayores con reparos* (Adults Only, 1965) is typical of Alonso Millán's comedies of manners; a type is planted in a situation likely to elicit revelatory action and dialogue. In this instance, each act is a variation on the theme of a pickup on the boys' night out. Critics were relieved to see in *La vil seducción* (The Seduction, 1967) a deviation from the formulas of farce and comedy-mystery. Here, the playwright sympathetically delineates the interaction not of types but of individuals. *Estado civil: Marta* (1969) is his first serious drama, a departure from the comic theater which *Amor dañino o la víctima de sus virtudes* (Harmful Love, or The Victim of Virtue, 1969), a parody of rural drama, proves to be but temporary.

OTHER PLAYS: *La señora que no dijo sí* (The Lady Who Didn't Say Yes, 1962), *El ex-presidente* (1963), *Carmelo* (1964), *El crimen al alcance de la clase media* (Crime for the Middle Class, 1965), *Pecados conyugales* (Conjugal Sins, 1966), *Marbella, mon amour* (1967), *El alma se serena* (The Soul Finds Repose, 1968).

**Altendorf, Wolfgang** (born 1921). West German dramatist, novelist, and poet. After returning from the Russian front, where he was wounded several times, Altendorf tried various jobs while writing plays and novels in his spare time. In 1950 he decided to devote full time to writing, and soon after he drew critical acclaim with his one-act play *Der arme Mensch* (The Poor Creature, 1952). The play, based on his war experiences, depicts the helplessness of two men sentenced to death by the army. One soldier has killed a commanding officer, who has committed atrocities; the other has deserted his regiment out of fear. Altendorf's focus is on the desperate situation of humane men who are accused of crimes by criminals. This theme runs throughout most of his plays, all of them realistic dramas, which deal with social problems from an ethical point of view. A prolific writer, Altendorf founded his own publishing company in 1962 and publishes most of his works. Of late he has done more writing for television and radio.

OTHER PLAYS: *Die Mücke und der Elefant* (The Flea and the Elephant, 1953), *Der Puppenspieler* (The Puppet Player, 1953, revised as *Circulus Vitiosus*, 1961), *Die Feuer verlöschen* (Extinguishing the Fires, 1954), *Das Dunkel* (The Darkness, 1956), *Partisanen* (Partisans, 1956), *Thomas Adamsohn* (1956), *Die Wettermaschine* (The Weather Machine, 1956), *Schleuse* (The Sewer, 1957), *Die Stunde der Mutter* (The Hour of the Mother, 1957), *Weg durch den Sumpf* (The Way Through the Marshes, 1958), *Die Vogelinsel* (The Island of the Bird, 1960).

**Amante anglaise, L'** (The English Lover, 1968). A play in two scenes by Marguerite Duras. It was first performed December 16, 1968, in the Salle Gémiez of the Théâtre National Populaire, under the direction of Claude Régy. The title, *L'Amante anglaise*, is an allusion to a mistake in language made by the main character, Claire, who confuses *la menthe,* or mint (*la menthe anglaise* means peppermint), a fresh and healthful plant that interests her in the midst of her somber existence, with *l'amante,* or a woman in love. The play's subject matter is based on an actual news item. It had already been treated twice by Duras—once in another play, *Les Viaducs de la Seine-et-Oise* (1960), another time in the form of a novel of the same title.

In a suburb of Paris, Claire Lannes has freely admitted that she killed her deaf-mute cousin, Marie-Thérèse, and cut her into pieces. She hid the head of the corpse and got rid of the other pieces by throwing them from a bridge into trains leaving for the four corners of France. The play has only three characters and consists of two static interviews conducted by the Interrogator, whose only motive is to try to understand the crime and the murderer herself, but whose perversely insistent questions gradually provoke the two main characters, Claire and her husband, Pierre, into self-awareness. Thus, in the first scene, there is the gradual revelation of the distress of a husband who has never really known his wife, who has little by little allowed her to slip into what he calls madness out of his own inadequacy or negligence, and who, without understanding the murder, does understand that he himself might well have been the victim. In the second scene the interview with Claire confirms certain indications of Scene 1: Before her marriage she had had a great love that went wrong and because of which she nearly committed suicide; for her,

Pierre doesn't count, but she has been fascinated by a Portuguese workman who seems to understand her from afar. One gradually discovers that the ordinary motives for murder (hate for her cousin, for example) have no meaning whatever in this case. Her way of getting rid of the corpse may be ascribed not to sadism but to practical good sense. The actual form of the crime had developed within Claire before she had the intention of committing it. By dissecting, one after another, the details of behavior and various psychological factors, the dialogue goes around in circles until it finally discloses the absolute nature of this antisocial and destructive act.

The almost clinical investigation—circuitous, interrupted by long pauses, shot through with shattering revelations—is characteristic of the art of Marguerite Duras. The language, which constantly aims at greater precision, discloses, or meticulously re-creates, a past reality of which the characters become aware as they talk. Claire, a woman crushed by unhappiness and boredom, telling about her withdrawal and the inexpressible discoveries of her solitary and despondent meditations, who has committed an irremedial and apparently monstrous act, is the best of Marguerite Duras's creations, along with the mother in *Des Journées entières dans les arbes* (Days in the Trees, 1965). Both parts were first played by Madeleine Renaud.

**Anderson, Maxwell** (1888–1959). American playwright. Anderson was born in Atlantic, Pennsylvania, and spent his childhood and adolescence there and in various places in the Midwest where his father, a Baptist clergyman, held pastorates. He was graduated from the University of North Dakota in 1911. In 1914 he was a teaching assistant at Stanford University, where he received his M.A. degree. After a year on the faculty of Whittier College in California, Anderson turned to journalism, working on newspapers in North Dakota, California, and New York (from 1918 to 1924 he was on the editorial staffs of the New York *Globe,* the *World,* and *The New Republic*). At the age of thirty-five he turned to playwriting. In 1924, with the great success of *What Price Glory?* (written with Laurence Stallings), an anti-war play about World War I, Anderson began to devote himself entirely to the theater.

A prolific writer, Anderson produced thirty-two more plays in the next thirty-four years. A number of these—such as *Elizabeth the Queen* (1930), *Mary of Scotland* (1933), and *Anne of the Thousand Days* (1948)—were attempts at restoring poetic drama to the stage, but Anderson's twentieth-century blank verse never reached the heights of the renaissance period he so admired, nor equaled the modern achievement of his British contemporaries T. S. Eliot and Christopher Fry. Anderson's interest in historical subject matter is seen in these plays and also in *Winterset* (1935), based on the Sacco-Vanzetti case; *Joan of Lorraine* (1946); and *Barefoot in Athens* (1951), a study of Socrates and Athenian democracy. He also wrote three plays dealing with World War II: *Candle in the Wind* (1941), *The Eve of St. Mark* (1942), and *Storm Operation* (1944).

A strong moral sense pervades Anderson's work; as he wrote in *Off Broadway* (1947): "the purpose of the theater is to find, and hold up to our regard, what is admirable in the human race. . . . the theater is a religious institution devoted entirely to the exaltation of the spirit of man." Setting off perhaps too directly toward this goal has made his presentation of issues sometimes appear simplistic.

Most of Anderson's work was done in the '20s and '30s. After World War II, despite seeming more and more old-fashioned, several of his productions had successful Broadway runs: *Joan of Lorraine, Anne of the Thousand Days, Lost in the Stars* (1949, a sentimental musical adaptation of Alan Paton's *Cry, the Beloved Country;* score by Kurt Weill), and *Bad Seed* (1954, an adaptation of William March's "genetic" thriller). But *Barefoot in Athens* managed only a short run, and his last two plays, *The Day the Money Stopped* and *The Golden Six,* went unnoticed off-Broadway in 1958.

The best bibliographical guide to Anderson's work is *A Catalogue of the Maxwell Anderson Collection at the University of Texas* (1968), compiled by Laurence G. Avery.

**Anderson, Robert** (born 1917). American playwright. Born in New York City, graduated from Phillips Exeter Academy (1935) and Harvard University (B.A. 1939, M.A. 1940), Anderson had his first play, *Our Town,* produced by an undergraduate group in 1938. A series of out-of-town productions—*Come Marching Home* (State University of Iowa, 1945), *The Eden Rose* (Ridgefield, Connecticut, 1949), *Love Revisited* (Westport, Connecticut, 1951), *All Summer Long* (Washington, D.C., 1953)—preceded his first full-length play produced on Broadway, *Tea and Sympathy* (1953). This play about a sensitive boy accused of homosexuality had a long run that made Anderson's reputation, though in retrospect it is difficult to see the athletic virility of the boy's father and the prep school teacher as anything but grotesque and the boy's own naïveté about sexuality as anything but improbable; least convincing is the emotional climax of the play, with its implication that the young man will be delivered to masculinity by the sexual ministrations of his kindly housemother. *All Summer Long* was given Broadway production in 1954; and *Silent Night, Lonely Night,* another play about sympathy, in 1959. Anderson's popular comedy *You Know I Can't Hear You When the Water's Running* (1967), actually four one-act plays, has been very successful on Broadway. His most recent plays are *I Never Sang for My Father* (1968) and *The Days Between* (1970). He has also worked in film, television, and radio.

**Andorra** (1961). A play in twelve scenes by Max Frisch. In one of his journal entries Frisch remarked that one should not type people and fix their images. This was said in reference to the problem of anti-Semitism in *Andorra.* The problem, as Frisch sees it, is linked to the mechanics of social prejudice that takes on various forms.

Andorra is a small country noted for its justice and purity. It is due to the moral code of the Andorrans that a schoolteacher has raised his illegitimate son to believe that he is an orphan Jew whom he rescued from the anti-Semitic blacks. In actuality, Andri was born in the country of the blacks where the schoolteacher had had an affair that he wanted kept secret. By the time Andri is twenty years old, he has assumed an identity that is very much fixed for him by the townspeople. Everywhere Andri goes, he is taught to act, speak, think, and feel like the Jew that the Andorrans have preconceived. Their prejudices mold and limit Andri's development. In fact, at the beginning of the play Andri is very much an Andorran assimilated Jew, who does not question his role. However, Andri is treated in such a demeaning manner by the carpenter and his apprentices, the innkeeper, and the doctor that he becomes aware of their bigotry and the injustices in the town. He is even forced into the role of a salesman because the carpenter insists that Jews are only fit to handle money. Finally, when Andri asks his father permission to marry his own half sister, Barblin (unaware that she is his sister), the schoolteacher refuses, but without telling him the truth. In despair, Barblin allows herself to be raped by a soldier, and Andri's father takes to drinking.

In the meantime, Andri's real mother arrives from the country of the blacks and desires to see her son. Andri does not accept the strange Señora as his mother, and she is accidentally killed by a stone thrown by Andorrans, who resent people from the country of the blacks. The town minister explains to Andri that the Señora was truly his mother. Yet Andri refuses to give up his Jewish identity, for he has been made into the Andorran Jew, and the Andorrans must learn to accept what they have created.

When the militant blacks invade Andorra as part of their imperialist policy to conquer the world, the schoolteacher pleads with Andri to assume his real identity as an Andorran. Once again, Andri asserts that the only identity he feels is his Jewish identity. The blacks have little difficulty overcoming the cowardly and hypocritical Andorrans, and the Jews are selected for extermination in a scene reminiscent of Auschwitz. Before Andri is executed, his father hangs himself. There is no resistance to the terror of the blacks. The play closes with the deranged Barblin trying to whitewash the town square.

Throughout the play the citizens of Andorra endeavor to whitewash themselves in interpolated scenes in which they take the stand to testify about their involvement in the course of events. Each witness protests his innocence just as the Germans protested their innocence after the Nazi regime in Germany. Here Frisch uses a Brechtian alienation technique to display the complicity of the Andorrans and the credibility gap between their testimonies and their actions. Frisch's parable play is a didactic play specifically condemning anti-Semitism in Germany and Switzerland, and it is also a more general statement about the one-dimensional society that breeds self-righteousness and bigotry. As a model state, Andorra is for Frisch a state that we should all avoid.

**Andres, Stefan** (1906–1970). German dramatist and novelist. Though primarily known as a novelist, Andres has written several dramas that reflect his concern with the social and moral condition of Germany. Reared in a liberal Catholic tradition, Andres studied at the universities of Jena, Cologne, and Berlin. He then embarked on a writing career and produced a series of interesting novels and short stories. Because of his opposition to the Hitler regime, he decided to leave Germany and settle in Rome. He returned to Germany in 1950 for a decade, then returned to Italy. Most of Andres' dramas were written after the war. His best play, *Gottes Utopia* (God's Utopia, 1950), is an adaptation of his novel *Wir sind Utopia*. It deals with a monk and Communist who, during the Spanish Civil War, move closer together in appreciation of each other's viewpoint. His other important drama is *Sperrzonen* (Closed Zones, 1958), a tragedy about German war crimes and the attempt to overcome the past. Andres relies on social realism in all his plays to convey ideas that are linked to Christian socialism. Though he is not an original dramatist, his plays are moral barometers of his times.

OTHER PLAYS SINCE 1945: *Ein Herz wie man's braucht* (A Good Heart When It Counts, 1946), *Tanz durchs Labyrinth* (The Dance Through the Labyrinth, 1946), *Und Zeus lächelt* (And Zeus Smiles, 1957), *Wann kommen die Götter?* (When Are the Gods Coming? 1961).

**Anouilh, Jean** (born 1910). French dramatist. Throughout his life Anouilh's career has been almost exclusively that of a playwright. At the age of thirteen he had already begun trying to write plays. After a very short period of studying law, he worked for an advertising agency, where, according to him, he learned to write effective sentences. At nineteen he wrote his first play, *Humulus le muet* (Humulus, the Mute). In 1930 he became secretary to the director Louis Jouvet and began to write seriously for the stage. His first play to be performed was *L'Hermine* (The Ermine) in 1932. The performances of *Le Voyageur sans bagage* (Traveler Without Luggage) in 1937 and, above all, *La Sauvage* (Restless Heart) in 1938, both staged by Georges Pitoëff, established him as a playwright of the first rank. From 1940 to 1962, with rare exceptions, he turned out one play a season. From 1962 to 1968 he devoted himself to directing. His three most recent plays are *Le Boulanger, la boulangère et le petit mitron* (The Baker, His Wife, and Their Little Helper, 1968), *Cher Antoine* (1969), and *Les Poissons rouges* (The Goldfish, 1970).

At the beginning of his career Anouilh grouped his plays into *Pièces roses* ("Rosy Plays") and *Pièces noires* ("Dark Plays"). The *Pièces roses*, such as *Thieves' Carnival* (*Le Bal des voleurs*, written 1932, produced 1938), are charming fantasies, full of theatrical tricks and superficially Pirandellian effects, each with an essentially comic plot that leads to a happy ending. Yet elements of nostalgia and even, in *Le Rendezvous de Senlis* (Dinner with the Family, written 1937, produced 1941), of bitterness tend to creep in. The *Pièces noires* are somber dramas, sometimes strongly tinged with naturalism (*La Sauvage*, 1934) and often shot through with a bitter and violent cynicism that is in conflict with a passionate but hopeless ideal (*Eurydice,* written 1941, produced 1942; *Roméo et Jeannette,* written 1945, produced 1946). Among the *Pièces noires* is also the tragedy *Antigone* (written 1942, produced 1944) and the painful drama concerning a victim of amnesia in search of his past, *Le Voyageur sans bagage,* which ends boldly with a *pièce rose* fantasy. After the war the distinction between rosy and dark plays became irrelevant: Bitterness and sordidness, as well as the forms of heroism they generate, became Anouilh's subject matter, even in at least one scene of the "rosiest" of his postwar plays, *L'Invitation au château* (Ring Round the Moon, 1947), just as the theatrical fantasy of the *Pièces roses* permeated the most somber of his plots. From then on Anouilh classified his plays as *Pièces brillantes* ("Sparkling Plays"), in which the rose is strongly tinged with black, as in *La Répétition* (The Rehearsal, 1950) or *Colombe* (Mademoiselle Colombe, 1951); *Pièces grinçantes* ("Grating Plays"), in which black and savage comedy prevails, as in ARDÈLE (1948) or *La Valse des toréadors* (The Waltz of the Toreadors, 1952); and *Pièces costumées* ("Fancy-Dress Plays"), that is, with historical subjects, such as *L'Alouette* (The Lark, 1953) or BECKET (1959). Moreover, these categories very often overlap.

Underlying almost all of Anouilh's plays is the conflict between a wish for happiness, without debasing oneself to attain it, and the inevitable compromises called for by the family, society, politics, and life in general. Anouilh's heroes and, especially, his young heroines often prefer death to such compromises. They are thus often presented as champions of purity. Yet Anouilh judges their purity in various ways. While Jeanne d'Arc (*L'Alouette*) towers above her adversaries by refusing either to submit to the vile abstraction represented by the Inquisition or to have the opportunity of becoming a senile old woman, Antigone's total renunciation (*Antigone*) is balanced by Créon's lucid realism. In *Colombe* the pure Julien is responsible for his wife's unhappiness. Occasionally Anouilh exposes the savage and shameful motives behind the lofty demands of justice, as in *Pauvre Bitos* (Poor Bitos, 1956). And Anouilh's sympathy is sometimes with those who, out of a sense of responsibility, courageously submit to compromise as a means of working more effectively, for example, Louis XVIII in *La Foire d'empoigne* (The Free for All, 1962).

In fact, Anouilh's works represent not so much a moral philosophy as the dramatization of a contradiction without any satisfactory practical solution, accompanied by a redemption of that fatality by means of theatricalism, but a theatricalism that has no relation to the new theater and which is presented as an assimilation of the tradition from Molière to the bourgeois theater and the Boulevard. Although Anouilh's characters are very often similar in nature to those of naturalist theater, they are sketchy, simplified, and sometimes even "dressed," so that they may be clearly recognized as theatrical fictions. Often, in dressing his characters in *fin-de-siècle* costumes, Anouilh is alluding to the characters in the dramas or vaudevilles of that period. No matter what happens in his plays, and whatever the bitterness, the satire, or the psychological and moral analyses, they are presented, above all, as *plays,* in which the artifice and tradition of the devices are consciously pointed up. On a deeper level the characters themselves play a part within their part. For example, Antigone seems to be playing the part of Antigone. And the story of Joan of Arc is a Pirandellian performance of that story, in which the characters make every effort to respect the well-known scenario.

In fact, Anouilh's theater has three levels: the level of anecdote (naturalistic, mythical, or historical), where there is a permanent tension between an inevitable evil and a wish for pure happiness; the level of the characters themselves, who are keenly conscious of struggling within a part, which, if accepted blindly or hypocritically, leads to a decline into inauthenticity, but which may be lucidly assumed, sometimes to the point of death; and the level of the play in general, where the playwright is constantly present and kills the reality of his play by transforming it into a theatrical game (to the point of sometimes materializing himself, as the Prologue/Chorus in *Antigone* or as the Author in *La Grotte* [The Cavern], 1961).

OTHER PLAYS SINCE 1945: *Episode de la vie d'un auteur* (1948), *Médée* (1953), *Cécile ou L'Ecole des pères* (1954), *Ornifle ou Le Courant d'air* (1955), *L'Hurluberlu ou Le Réactionnaire amoureux* (The Fighting Cock, 1959), *La Petite Molière* (Molière's Young Wife, 1959), *L'Orchestre* (1962).

**Architecte et l'empereur d'Assyrie, L'** (1967). A play in two acts by Fernando Arrabal. Its first performance, in March 1967, at the Théâtre Montparnasse, Paris, was directed by Raymond Gérome. An airplane crashes on a remote island, whose only inhabitant is an inarticulate creature. The sole survivor of the crash is the Emperor of Assyria. Two years later the first inhabitant of the island has learned to speak and has been named the Architect by the Emperor. Nature (ants, birds, and so forth) obeys the Architect, whereas the Emperor represents civilization and power. The two of them spend their time playing games that are in fact psychodramas—or psychofarces—in which they switch from love to hate and vice versa, and confront, dominate, and humiliate each other in turn. "Happenings"—such as flagellation, the acting out of death, burial, or the transformation of mankind into monkeys after an atomic war—follow one another in rapid succession. In the second act there is a long, chaotic trial, with the Architect trying the Emperor, which reveals the incestuous relationship of the Emperor and his mother and finally his murder of his mother. After his confession the Emperor asks to be killed and eaten by the Architect. In the course of the meal the Architect becomes the Emperor. At the very end of the play there is another plane crash and the new Emperor is horrified to discover that the sole survivor is the Architect. The game must begin all over again.

The language of the play is a mixture of childishness, literary allusions, blasphemy, and bursts of lyricism. And the spectacle itself—farcical, choppy, fantastic, and nightmarish—subjects the spectator to a series of shocks. The general movement corresponds to a long and painful process of the unification of the human being, who is torn apart by a gigantic Oedipus complex. It is typical of Arrabal that the unification can be produced only by means of aggressive, obscene, and scatological games, the exchange of personalities, grotesque female disguises, and, above all, the frightful murder which, here, is accompanied by a concrete representation of ritual cannibalism.

**Ardèle ou La Marguerite** (1948). A one-act play by Jean Anouilh. It was first performed on November 3, 1948, at the Comédie des Champs Elysées, Paris, under the direction of Roland Pietri. The subtitle of this long act, *La Marguerite* (The Daisy), is an allusion to the French version of the game that consists in plucking off the petals of a daisy to discover precisely how much someone loves you. And, in fact, the subject of *Ardèle* is love—but love in hopeless or degrading situations.

The action takes place in the house of General Léon de Saint-Pé, who lives in the company of his ailing and half-mad wife; his hunchbacked sister, Ardèle; his little boy, Toto; his daughter-in-law, Nathalie, whose husband is away. The General has called a family council, consisting of another of his sons, Nicolas, and his other sister, the Countess, who arrives with her husband, her lover, and her daughter, Marie-Christine. The reason for this meeting is the fact that Ardèle (a character never seen by the audience) has fallen madly in love with Toto's tutor, also a hunchback. Closed in her room, Ardèle persists in her love, which the General considers monstrous.

During the first part of the play this situation forces the other characters to face their own loves. The General, constantly watched over and harassed by his wife, has taken refuge in sordid little love affairs with all kinds of women, including the housemaids. Nathalie has made a loveless marriage to the General's eldest son, although she and Nicolas, as adolescents, had pledged their troth. The Countess lives with both her husband and her lover, who out of jealousy acts like a husband, whereas the Count is resigned to the sad masquerade. In the second part, which takes place at night, Ardèle has opened the door of her room and one sees her hunchbacked lover enter. The noise they make causes the General's crazy wife to appear and launch into a frenzied diatribe against the sexuality that is present everywhere—her obsession ever since the General has taken to being unfaithful to her. During the disorder provoked by her tirade, the sound of shots can be heard. The two hunchbacks have committed suicide. The play ends with a scene in which the two children, Toto and Marie-Christine, dressed in grown-up clothing, play at being husband and wife, making great vows of love which finally turn into insults and fierce battles.

At heart, most of the characters yearn for pure and authentic love. Disappointed by life, deceived by others, too advanced in age, or merely incapable of experiencing such love, they are plunged into unbearable solitude, forcing them into makeshift solutions to which they are more or less blind.

The love of the two hunchbacks is a challenge that makes them realize their failures, their compromises, and their degradation. The two cripples, on the other hand, escape from the cruelty of the world and an inevitable decline only through suicide.

Basically cynical and somber, *Ardèle* nevertheless sparkles with humor and spectacular theatricality. The situation of the Countess, for example, constantly accompanied by both her men, is borrowed from *fin-de-siècle* vaudeville, as are the costumes. Classified by Anouilh as one of his "grating plays," *Ardèle* is one of the best examples of his double game of disgust and the laughter provoked by the human comedy.

**Arden, John** (born 1930). English dramatist. Born in Barnsley, Yorkshire, Arden proceeded from education at Sedbergh, a North Country public school, which he has described as one "with less nonsense about it than most," to train as an architect at Cambridge and Edinburgh. *All Fall Down* (1955, unpublished), his first stage play, dates from this time. A radio play awarded a BBC Northern Region prize for original drama brought him to the attention of the English Stage Company, under whose management *The Waters of Babylon* (1957) was given a Sunday-night performance, and *Live Like Pigs* received a full-scale production in 1958. Despite the contemporary setting of these two plays, Arden's treatment of his themes distinguished him from the beginning from the politically engaged school of social realism of which Arnold Wesker was the outstanding member.

Arden's typically uncommitted stance reveals itself in his attitude toward the Polish entrepreneur of the earlier play and the vagrant Sawney family in *Live Like Pigs*. They commit actions that bring them well within the reach of the law, and yet Arden appears to condemn neither them nor the system of morality against which they are in rebellion. "On the one hand," wrote Arden of the disruptions on the council housing estate in *Live Like Pigs*, "I was accused by the Left of attacking the Welfare State: on the other, the play was *hailed* as a defence of anarchy and amorality." Both the Sawneys, he explained, "direct descendants of the 'sturdy beggars' of the sixteenth century," and their reluctant neighbors the Jacksons, "an undistinguished but not contemptible family," uphold "standards of conduct that are incompatible, but which are both valid in their correct context." What appeared as a failure to make his position clear can now be seen as a deliberate ambiguity. A second unfamiliar feature, again characteristic of Arden, was the mixture of verse, written in the English ballad tradition, with the contemporary prose of the dialogue. Arden was later to write of his concern with "the problem of translating the concrete life of today into terms of poetry that shall at the one time both illustrate that life and set it within the historical and legendary tradition of our culture." All Arden's work has included an element of verse introduced by a variety of formal devices but sharing the same function of extending the significance and scope of his drama.

Arden's talents became the subject of public controversy with the first production of SERJEANT MUSGRAVE'S DANCE (1959). Badly received by the critics and defended in the press by its director, Lindsay Anderson, its short run at the Royal Court Theatre was followed by a number of revivals, as well as a television production (1962), which established it as Arden's best known and most successful work. As so often in the work of this dramatist, the action of the play parallels contemporary political events; in this case a vindictive action taken by British troops in Cyprus is echoed in the experience of three deserters from an obscure colonial war in the latter half of the nineteenth century. But while Arden is wholehearted in his condemnation of colonialism, he presents the violent demonstration against it, planned by the half-crazed Serjeant Musgrave, as an action equally repugnant. Arden's many-sided sympathies are wedded in *Serjeant Musgrave's Dance* to a firmly constructed plot that presents the issues in an unfolding pattern of significant action. Against the setting of a North of England mining town Arden exhibits another of his strengths in a strong, supple dialect that slips naturally from prose to verse.

Arden was appointed to the Fellowship in Playwriting at the University of Bristol for the year 1959–60. He evidently welcomed the opportunity for experiment offered by the fellowship. *The Happy Haven,* written (in collaboration with his wife, Margaretta D'Arcy, 1960) during this period, is intended for a "formalized presentation" involving the use of masks and an open stage with an upper level "following roughly the Elizabethan model." The action abounds in stylized devices and direct audience address, and the influence both of *commedia dell'arte* conventions and of the Jonsonian comedy of humors can be discerned in the play. Set in a rest home for the elderly whose director has discovered a rejuvenation formula, the play treats old age and the imminence of death or decay of the faculties as a subject for farcical treatment. The dawning realization of the old folk that death is preferable to a repetition of their lives leads to the grotesque reversal of the final scene. The dramatist's unsentimental portrayal of old age is stimulating, and the defiant preoccupations of the old are vividly expressed in occasional snatches of verse, but in *The Happy Haven* Arden's ambivalent attitudes affect the play with a certain vagueness of overall purpose. Arden's association with Bristol also produced a nativity play, *The Business of Good Government* (1960), written for amateur performance in the village church of Brent Knoll in Somerset and remarkable for its combination of medieval staging techniques with a sympathetic view of Herod as a harassed victim of imperial power politics. The connection also contributed to the writing of *Ironhand* (1963), a free adaptation of Goethe's *Goetz von Berlichingen,* commissioned but not performed by the Royal Shakespeare Company. If this play cannot strictly be termed an original work, it nevertheless marks an important stage in Arden's development. The robber-knight whose rough standards of justice are increasingly out of place in a Germany passing from the Middle Ages into a more sophisticated era engages Arden's complex sympathy as a representative of freebooting liberty at odds with the advancing order of civilization. The themes that first appear in *Ironhand* continue to thread their way through Arden's subsequent work.

*The Workhouse Donkey* (1963), which Arden subtitled "A Vulgar Melodrama," explaining that the term should be taken "in its original sense of a play with a musical accompaniment," takes the corruption of local government in a North Country town as its theme. Alderman Charles Butterthwaite, styled "the Napoleon of the North," is a genially expansive Labour politician with little regard for the petty restrictions of the law. He meets his match in Colonel Feng, a newly appointed Chief Constable with an unbending determination to stamp out corruption. Butterthwaite's downfall is accomplished, but only at the expense of Feng's own career; in typical fashion Arden divides his sympathies between the two. In a preface the author states that he would have preferred the play to have lasted "six or seven or thirteen hours," as part of a Comic Theatre celebrating "the old essential attributes of Dionysus." But the play at its present length sprawls unmanageably, a fault that would be less apparent if its exuberance seemed less contrived. Butterthwaite presents a contradictory mixture of Aristophanic hero-buffoon and defaulting councillor, and the uncertainty as to his dramatic function spreads to the remainder of the characters grouped around him.

*The Workhouse Donkey* was to be followed by one of Arden's most satisfying, and at the same time most difficult, plays. Dedicated to Conor Cruise O'Brien, ARMSTRONG'S LAST GOODNIGHT (1964) explores the subtle dangers of political involvement in terms of the Scottish border disputes of the 1550s. Written in an adaptation of the Scottish lowland dialect that rendered the play almost incomprehensible to its early audiences, the language, once understood, offers the most successful poetic imagery, dynamic and yet precise, that Arden has yet produced. The clash between the anarchic freedom of John Armstrong's marauding adventures and the encroaching exigencies of political order, represented by Sir David Lindsay, is plotted within a structure that links the complexities of diplomatic intrigue with subtle observation of character.

Since *Armstrong's Last Goodnight* Arden has written two more full-length plays for adults, neither of which has rivaled it in strength or subtlety. *Left-Handed Liberty* (1965) was commissioned by the Corporation of the City of London in commemoration of the 750th anniversary of the sealing of Magna Carta. The action explores the immediate consequences of the sealing of the charter, presenting it as a pawn in the struggle for power between the barons and the king, rather than the symbol of freedom from royal interference that history has made it. Arden's King John emerges as an attractive character, warily bargaining from a position of weakness and formulating a policy that shrewdly combines enlightened self-interest with the protection of his country. Arden's interest in the intrigues and maneuvers forming the stuff of politics has produced some scenes reminiscent of Brecht, but the work gives the impression of having been conceived as an illustrated lecture and of having failed to reach full dramatic form. Although Arden's historical instinct was clearly aroused by this commission, he has failed to communicate any sense of the urgency or importance of the issues involved.

No less disappointing is *The Hero Rises Up* (written in collaboration with Margaretta D'Arcy, 1969). The career of Lord Nelson is chosen for this study of heroic public success accompanied by a private life of moral turbulence; the gist of the play's theme is conveyed in Nelson's first song:

> I broke the rules of warfare
> And the nation did forgive:
> But there was no forgiveness when
> I broke the rules of love.

An "asymmetrical authors' Preface," complaining of the distorting effect that any official body dispensing subsidy has upon art, mentions the intention of writing a play "which need not be *done properly*," so long as the audience should be affected with an experience described as "akin to that of running up in a crowded wet street on a Saturday night against a drunken red-nosed man with a hump on his back . . ." In effect the play is a repertory of theatrical devices that in production run the risk of degenerating into an artificially induced anarchy and in which the moral keenness and finely balanced language of Arden's earlier work is wholly overthrown. By reducing Nelson to a pastiche of the hero in a Victorian melodrama, the authors have, for the sake of a dubiously defined theatrical experience, obscured their vision of him as a man who "wasted his extraordinary energy, courage, and humanity upon having men killed."

Arden's dissatisfaction with the conditions imposed upon the contemporary theater has often involved him in work with amateurs and improvisation groups, and expressed itself in a number of plays for special occasions (often written in collaboration with Margaretta D'Arcy). These include *Friday's Hiding* (a one-act play, 1966) and *The Royal Pardon* (1966), two plays for children; the Christmas nativity play mentioned earlier, *The Business of Good Government;* and *Harold Muggins Is a Martyr* (1968), a satirical improvisation presented at the Unity Theatre. *Ars Longa, Vita Brevis* (1964) is a one-act play contributed to the Royal Shakespeare's "theater of cruelty" season, owing something to the absurdist dramatists as well as to Antonin Artaud in its portrait of a rigidly disciplinarian art master whose first lesson leads into a wholesale military operation. The conflict between liberty and order that lies at the heart of Arden's best work finds a new mode of expression in this interesting playlet. Even shorter, *The True History of Squire Jonathan and His Unfortunate Treasure* (a one-act play presented at a lunch-hour theater club in 1968) is an eccentric combination of obscure political allegory and the celebration of total nudity.

For better or worse, John Arden may claim to be the most intellectual of contemporary English dramatists. Perhaps helped by his architectural training, he is aggressively aware of the shortcomings of proscenium-arch naturalism, and draws upon a historical knowledge of the theater to counter it. *The Happy Haven* exploits the virtues of the Elizabethan stage, *Armstrong's Last Goodnight* makes creative use of the emblematic tradition of medieval drama, *The Workhouse Donkey* and *The Hero Rises Up* rely on the tactics of Victorian melodrama. His treatment of historical subject matter in *Ironhand, Armstrong's Last Goodnight,* and *Left-Handed Liberty* not only conveys a rich sense of the period involved but sometimes suggests a mastery of the political issues of the day not unworthy of a professional historian. Arden's sense of historical perspective makes him a conscious, sometimes (as his prefaces reveal) a self-conscious, innovator in dramatic form. His innovations are least successful when theoretically constructed as alternatives to the deficiencies of the contemporary stage and not (as in *Serjeant Musgrave's Dance* or *Armstrong's Last Goodnight*) as organically related to the play's theme. Similar reservations may be made respecting his use of verse, which, while it rarely falls below a level of high competence, sometimes suffers from a relationship to the main action that passes from the oblique to the inexplicable. The obscurity of which Arden must inevitably be accused is a consequence of thinking too much and not too little about significant dramatic form.

Nevertheless, Arden is an impressive poet of the theater, who has demonstrated beyond all doubt that the extension of language beyond the frontiers of naturalistic speech is not exclusively restricted to the preciosity of a Fry or the conservatism of an Eliot. Arden's concern with violence, war, and the encroachment of political necessity upon the freedom of the individual is typical of the postwar dramatist, and yet it is expressed in the ageless language of the popular poet. The variety of themes that Arden has embraced is matched by the diversity of the language in which he has clothed them, ranging from the bluff colloquialisms of *The Workhouse Donkey* to the sinewy precision of his invented lowland dialect in *Armstrong's Last Goodnight.* Arden's North Country background reveals itself in a rich profusion of dialect words and idiomatic expressions.

Among poets Arden is perhaps unusual in viewing man as a political animal. Almost alone among British dramatists, Arden has assimilated the Brechtian technique of "alienation" in its function of setting characters upon the stage inside a sharply defined social and political frame, and his use of ballads to link this to a wider human context is comparable to Brecht's use of verse. But while Brecht (in theory if not wholly in practice) committed himself to a single political doctrine, Arden has refused to distort his art for dogmatic effect. His obstinately disengaged and amoral stance at times makes it seem as if the author has elevated indecision to a virtue, but in his best work it places him among the most humane as well as the most intelligent of contemporary playwrights. Arden skillfully dramatizes the intersecting demands of human passion, full-blooded, irrational, and immediate, and political order calling for the subordination of the personality to cool calculations of advantage for the future. His most effective characters are robustly anarchic characters of heroic stature—leaders of men overtaken by a stricter civilization, such as Goetz, Johnny Armstrong, and Charles Butterthwaite—and their antagonists, the rational politicians swimming with the tide of history, ironically aware of their own limitations and the finite quality of morality, such as Weislingen, Sir David Lindsay, and King John.

Arden is a dramatist more respected than imitated in a theater distrustful of the intellect, and more than any other dramatist of his stature he has found difficulty in attracting the notice of the general public; but his experimental approach to his craft has placed him at the forefront of contemporary theater practitioners and has justified, in the face of hostile criticism, the support of his early work by the English Stage Company, which established *Serjeant Musgrave's Dance* as a key play in the late 1950s revival of the English theater.

Arden is also the author of two television plays, *Soldier, Soldier* (1960) and *Wet Fish* (1961), and a play for radio, *The Life of Man* (1956). Arden's essay "Telling a True Tale" appears in *The Encore Reader* (1965), edited by Charles Marowitz, Tom Milne, and Owen Hale. An interview with Arden by Milne, Clive Goodwin, and Simon Trussler appears in *Theatre at Work* (1967), edited by Marowitz and Trussler. His work is discussed by William Gaskill in "Comic Masks and *The Happy Haven*," published in *Encore*, Vol. VII, No. 6 (1960) and "John Arden: A Survey," *Encore*, Vol. XII, No. 5 (1965); Richard Gilman in "Arden's Unsteady Ground" in *Modern British Dramatists* (1968), edited by John Russell Brown; John Russell Taylor in *Anger and After* (1969), and Trussler in "Political Progress of a Paralyzed Liberal: The Community Dramas of John Arden," in *The Drama Review*, Vol. XIII, No. 4 (1969). Ronald Hayman has written a short critical study, *John Arden* (1968).

**Argentina.** The principal factor in Argentine theater is the solid organization of the experimental or "independent" theater. Although its origins are in the reaction against the collapse of a decadent commercial theater and the military coup of 1930, these groups flourished after the second world war. The Peronist movement and its fall and the tensions between extreme conservative and leftist groups have given a marked radical tone to most of the independent movement. Although open to diverse formal influences, the movement has also attempted to develop an authentic dramatic form rooted in such past tradition as the *sainete*, a brief popular musical play often using extreme melodramatic elements. Many of the formal characteristics of the *sainete*—integration of music, dance, and drama; mixture of farcical and serious; a strong grotesque note—coincide with recent European currents, and younger playwrights, under the influence of Roberto Arlt, a little-known dramatist of the

1930s currently being reevaluated, have sometimes achieved a happy blending of the two tendencies.

Although such longtime professionals as Conrado Nalé Roxlo and Samuel Eichelbaum turned out sporadic new works, Nalé Roxlo's best plays are from the early 1940s, except for the subtly ironic *Judith y las rosas;* Eichelbaum's dramas of profound spiritual conflicts have not achieved the stature of his earlier works. Other older dramatists include Pablo Palant, author of a series of realistic psychological dramas, which, at their best, are tense and intelligent, and Aurelio Ferreti, creator of delightful ironic farces.

But the new movement in Argentina can be dated from 1949 with the simultaneous production by professional and independent companies of Carlos Gorostiza's *El puente* (The Bridge). Although *El puente* is characterized by a somewhat populist tone and imaginative use of internal structure, the author's later plays have been intellectual, often metaphysical. Sometimes static, their best moments are strikingly human, as in *El pan de la locura* (The Bread of Madness, 1958). In *Los prójimos* (The Neighbors, 1965), based on the Kitty Genovese murder, Gorostiza examined man's eagerness to avoid responsibility, and ¿*A qué jugamos?* (What Shall We Play? 1969) raises a parlor game to ritual in the same search for meaning.

Osvaldo DRAGÚN is probably the best known of this generation outside Argentina; *Historias para ser contadas* (Tales for the Telling, 1957), a group of agile farces with shifting roles, is a staple of the university theater in Spain and Latin America. Dragún's work is always human, and only his tight control keeps the emotion in check. *Tupac Amarú* (1957) is a moving tragedy of the rebellious Inca of 1781; later works have become in the main increasingly social and less orthodox structurally. *Y nos dijeron que éramos inmortales* (And They Told Us We Were Immortal, 1962) employs Brechtian and music-hall techniques to present the case for an alienated youth, and *Heroica de Buenos Aires* (1966) is a conscious variation on *Mother Courage,* in which Dragún typically uses alienation techniques to establish contact with his audience. Two other dramatists closely connected with the independent movement conceive of theater as a social weapon: Andrés Lizárraga and Agustín Cuzzani. Lizárraga is best in his *Trilogía sobre Mayo* (Trilogy About May), and especially in *Santa Juana de América* (1960), an "epic theater" version of the War of Independence in Peru from 1809 to 1825. Cuzzani is a playwright of great vitality and imagination but of limited discipline. The result is a series of works that are sometimes brilliant, always stimulating, often sentimental, and usually overtly political. In *Para que se cumplan las escrituras* (That the Scriptures Be Fulfilled, 1965) he broke this pattern to create a complex parable of Man, God, and the Computer.

Many of the most impressive younger dramatists have abandoned the Brechtian, socially oriented ambience of the independent group in favor of a more traditional, if no less bitter, realistic idiom. Roberto Cossa was highly successful with *Nuestro fin de semana* (Our Weekend, 1964), whose stripping away the frivolous cover that hides human frustrations, failures, and hysteria clearly touched a nerve in Argentine society. Ricardo Talesnick achieved international success with a comic version of the same theme, *La fiaca* (Down in the Dumps, 1967). Although the last act fails to follow up the implications of the first, urban Latin America has responded overwhelmingly to Talesnick's protagonist, a man so sorely disgusted by the demands on him that he drops out of normal relationships. Germán Rozenmacher explored the generation gap in a Jewish family in a touching first play, *Requiem para un viernes a la noche* (Requiem for a Friday Night, 1964). These dramatists and others, such as Julio Mauricio, Abelardo Castillo, and Ricardo Halac, are absorbed in the stresses of modern society, but a substantial number of authors continue to try to work out the meaning of the Argentine past, both thematically and formally. Sergio de Cecco, among others, concentrates on the meaning of the past to understand the present; Alberto Rodríguez Muñoz and Pedro Orgambide explore the urban Buenos Aires of sixty years ago and experiment with the form of the *sainete* as a viable expression for today, a search that has preoccupied older dramatists such as Juan Carlos Ghiano.

Some of the most interesting work in Argentina is being done by a group of avant-garde directors and playwrights based at the Instituto di Tella. Mario Trejo has been heavily influenced by such American groups as the Living Theater. Griselda Gambaro is the best of Argentina's younger dramatists. *El desatino* (The Blunder, 1965) and *Los siameses* (The Siamese Twins, 1967) explored human indifference on a one-to-one basis; they are extremely effective, theatrical works. *El campo* (The Camp, 1968) opens her concern to humanity, as she presents all existence as a concentration camp. One of the most effective aspects of *El campo* is its rejection of overt horror and brutality in favor of smaller frustrations, inconsistent behavior, and random violence. In spite of the promise of Gambaro and others, it is impossible to judge the future of the theater in Argentina, given the nation's political climate and the severe limitations on artistic freedom.

**Armstrong's Last Goodnight** (1964). A play by John Arden. Perhaps the only play in which Arden completely fulfills the promise held out by *Serjeant Musgrave's Dance*, this play was written after Arden had read Conor Cruise O'Brien's *To Katanga and Back* and is dedicated to its author. The confused events of recent African history provided a point of inspiration and "a basic similarity of moral" rather than an exact parallel for this drama set on the border of sixteenth-century Scotland. Arden takes some liberties with history in involving the poet and diplomat Sir David Lindsay with the execution of the marauding chieftain Johnny Armstrong, but re-creates the atmosphere of the period with an exactness matched in few historical dramas. Subtitled "An Exercise in Diplomacy," the play is concerned with the subtle intrigue upon which Lindsay embarks in his attempt to insure peace along the troubled Scottish border. Entrusted by the Scottish King James V with the delicate task of restraining Armstrong's embarrassing raids into English territory, Lindsay goes beyond his brief ("I did ever tak pleisure in ane devious activity," he observes) and enters into secret negotiations with the English in his search for a wider solution to the problem. Only by an act of dishonesty that destroys Armstrong does he restore himself to favor with the king. If a moral is to be extracted from the intricacies of the plot, it is that "ane man of rhetoric and discreet humanity" who puts his talent at the service of a troubled world must learn that the material of his "devious activity" is human life. A victim of the action is his secretary McGlass. "Ye did tak pride in your recognition of the fallibility of man," the dying McGlass tells Lindsay. "Recognize your ain, then Lindsay: ye have ane certain weakness, ye can never accept the gravity of ane other man's violence. For you yourself hae never been grave in the hale of your life!"

In Arden's typical style sympathy is divided evenly between the two main characters. The unlettered border chieftain and the courtly poet both have a keen appetite for life, and each displays a mixture of moral excellence and human frailty. Armstrong's abuse of the code of hospitality in the murder of his rival Wamphray is matched by Lindsay's deceit. Armstrong's wary appreciation of the forces plotting against him eventually gives way to simple gullibility; Lindsay's insistence that the presence of his mistress is "ane absolute necessity—at unpredictable intervals: but absolute" upsets his delicate plans when Armstrong predictably seduces her. Armstrong falls, not because he is a lesser man than Lindsay, but because his freebooting life is an anachronism in a world of increasing political sophistication.

The subtle demands of the plot are served by a setting of effective simplicity. Arden employs the medieval staging convention of "simultaneous mansions" in which an unlocalized central area is flanked by symbolic units representing Armstrong's castle, the king's palace, and a forest, which forms a natural background for the darker pattern of sexual passion and violent murder that parallels the exercise of diplomacy. The influence of medieval conventions may also be discerned in Arden's insistence on the hierarchical aspect of costume, which is linked to a recurrent insistence on the contrast between the naked man and his badge of office. Stripping off his official livery, Lindsay declares:

> The rags and robes that we do wear
> Express the function of our life
> But the bawdy body that we bear
> Beneath them carries nocht
> But shame and greed and strife.

Arden's model for the language of his play was Arthur Miller's adaptation of early American speech in *The Crucible*. As a *tour de force* it rivals its model, and in wit and ingenuity it is the equal of any prose dialogue for the contemporary stage: "You are ane lovely lion to roar and leap," says Lindsay's mistress to Armstrong, "and sure wad gratify all submissive ladies beneath the rampancy of your posture. You are indeed heraldic, sir." The ballads in the lowland dialect that recur throughout the play contain some of the finest and most dramatically appropriate poetry to be found in Arden's work.

By writing a play whose very vocabulary presents problems to the English ear, and whose complex patterns of intrigue require some perspicacity in their unraveling, Arden produced in *Armstrong's Last Goodnight* a play that did not court popularity. As a glittering exhibition of intellectual power it has already achieved respect.

**Arrabal, Fernando** (born 1932). Spanish-born French dramatist. Born in Melilla (formerly Spanish Morocco), Arrabal as a child witnessed the Spanish Civil War and police persecutions, of which his father was a victim. He himself, during a recent trip to Spain, was imprisoned. Settled in France since 1954, he became a writer in the French language and produced novels, tales, and a great number of plays. In 1968 he founded a review, *Le Théâtre*, devoted to avant-garde and political theater.

His first plays were published in 1958, before being performed. In 1959 *Pique-nique en campagne* (Picnic on the Battlefield) was his first play performed in Paris. Although early in his career he was better known in Germany and the United States, since 1966 he has become one of the most performed and discussed avant-garde writers in France. In 1969 he was awarded the Prix de l'Humour Noir.

Arrabal's dreamlike universe was at first peopled by childish characters— that is, characters that are both tender and murderous, loving and perverse, chaste and given to voyeurism, poetic and scatological, and constantly threatened by authoritarian figures that are maternal or related to the police. They are in some respects reminiscent of Charlie Chaplin and the Marx brothers, and somewhat resemble the characters of Beckett and, most of all, Adamov, although their sadomasochistic imaginations are far more horrible (*Le Tricycle*, 1961). Since about 1965 Arrabal's works have gradually evolved toward a theater of ceremony and, finally, into what he himself calls *Théâtre Panique*. The childish ritual of frightful games has become gradually more formal, complex, and spectacular, with an increasing number of profanations of the Catholic rites, which are inseparably linked to a pathological sexuality, including castration, rape, and necrophilia (*La Communion solennelle* [The Solemn Communion], 1966).

Arrabal has explained his conception of panic theater: a mixture of tragedy and a Punch and Judy show, of bad taste and refinement, of sacrilege and the sacred—a kind of *opera mundi* made up of unbearable ritual scenes, a theory that to some extent recalls those of Antonin ARTAUD. Actually, in these works all sorts of avant-garde techniques, from surrealism to pop art, are applied to psychodramas through which runs a constant theme: the difficulty of childhood continued into adulthood, the torture of the transition from child to man. Arrabal tries to exorcize a huge backlog of sexual and religious terrors by means of scenic ceremonies and a series of initiations that are meant to be all the more barbarous as the childish complexes take on gigantic proportions. In his most recent play, *Et Ils passèrent des menottes aux fleurs* (And They Handcuffed the Flowers, 1969), Arrabal combines his favorite themes (cruelty, scatology, pornography, coprolalia, castration, profanation of the cross, and so forth) with effects taken from the new American theater: nudity and an invitation to the spectators to become actors and undress—not to have a love-in, however, but rather to flog one another. (See L'ARCHITECTE ET L'EMPEREUR D'ASSYRIE.)

OTHER PLAYS: *Les Deux Bourreaux* (The Two Executioners, published 1958), *Oraison* (Orison, published 1958), *Orchestration théâtrale* (1959), *La Bicyclette du condamné* (The Condemned Man's Bicycle, published 1961), *Le Labyrinthe* (published 1961), *Guernica* (1961), *Le Cimetière des voitures* (The Automobile Graveyard, 1964), *Fando et Lis* (1964), *Cérémonie pour un Noir assassiné* (Ceremony for a Murdered Black, 1965), *Concert dans un œuf* (Concert in an Egg, 1965), *La Couronnement* (The Coronation, 1965), *Les Amours impossibles* (1966), *Le Grand Cérémonial* (1966), *La Princesse et la communiante* (The Princess and the Communicant, 1966), *Strip-Tease de la jalousie* (1966), *Dieu est-il devenu fou?* (Has God Gone Mad? published 1967), *La Jeunesse illustrée* (Illustrated Youth, published 1967), *Les Quatre Cubes* (The Four Cubes, published 1967), *Une Chèvre sur un nuage* (A Goat on a Cloud, published 1967), *Le Jardin des délices* (The Garden of Delights, 1968), *Bestialité érotique* (Erotic Bestiality, published 1969), *Groupuscule de mon cœur* (Groupuscule), *Tous les Parfums d'Arabie* (All the Perfumes of Arabia), and *Sous les pavés, la plage* (Under the Paving Stones, the Beach), in *L'Aurore rouge et noire* (The Red and Black Dawn, 1969), *Une Tortue nommé Dostoïevsky* (A Turtle Called Dostoevsky, 1969), *Ars amandi, opéra panique* (Ars Amandi, Panic Opera, published 1970).

**Artaud, Antonin** (1896–1948). French actor and theorist of drama. Although most of Artaud's works were written before the war, it was not until the 1950s and 1960s that he had a really strong influence on many Western playwrights. Artaud's life itself was physical and psychological hell. At nineteen he began to feel the effects of the mental disease that was to grow steadily worse throughout his life and was responsible for his being confined in sanitoriums for nine years (1937–1946). Arthur Adamov and other friends managed to have him released in 1946. Still under psychiatric observation, he died of generalized cancer in 1948.

At the age of fourteen Artaud began to publish his poems. Later, in 1923, when his poems were refused by *La Nouvelle Revue Française*, he felt obliged to explain them in what turned out to be a lengthy correspondence with one of the editors, Jacques Rivière. The correspondence was subsequently published and constitutes an extraordinary and revealing document on self-analysis, the creation of poetry, and the most profound psychological mysteries. During the mid-1920s Artaud was involved in the surrealist movement, but he finally broke with André Breton in 1926.

Theater was Artaud's primary concern. As an actor, he worked with Lugné-Poe, Charles Dullin, and Georges Pitoëff, and also appeared in films (Abel Gance's *Napoléon*, 1926; Carl Dreyer's *The Passion of Joan of Arc*, 1928). As a theorist and director, he wrote numerous essays on theater, most of which are collected in *Le Théâtre et son double* (The Theater and Its Double, 1938).

Artaud's very complex and often obscure dramatic theories are closely bound up with his metaphysical quest and his personal rebellion. He believed that Western civilization, through reason and logical language, has succeeded only in stifling the true driving forces of the universe. These forces still break out at the time of certain collective catastrophes (during a plague, for example) or in certain so-called primitive societies, such as that of the Tarahumara Indians in Mexico, whom he visited in 1936 and whose ritual ceremonies he witnessed. He was convinced that since man is the prey of such forces, they should be known, awakened, and exorcized, and that the rites and arts of the theater are the best means of doing so. Artaud rejected most of Western theater, which to him consisted merely of superficial anecdotes that are falsely "human," are dealt with rationally, and reveal no profound truths. He would countenance only ultraviolent works that transcended logic and, above all, ethics, and in which frenetic characters were under the sway of obscure forces: Seneca's *Thyestes*, John Ford's *'Tis Pity She's a Whore*, and Georg Büchner's *Woyzeck*, for example. He himself contributed a four-act drama to this repertory, *Les Cenci* (1935), inspired by Stendhal and Shelley, and based on the savageness of unrestrained passions, incest, parricide, and torture. He also envisioned a new form of expression in the theater that would replace rational language with spectacular effects, visual and tonal rhythms, and symbols. Here Artaud was influenced by what he had been able to observe in Far Eastern spectacles, beginning with the Balinese dances at the French Colonial Exhibition of 1931.

The dramatic spectacle, according to Artaud, should be a kind of rite or ceremony in which traditional psychology and superficial interests would be exploded and great cosmic and metaphysical themes revealed by means of visual and tonal shock images, fantasies, and monsters represented concretely onstage, and an incantatory recitation of the text, appealing to the emotions, not to reason. Artaud called this dream of his a "theater of cruelty." By this term he did not necessarily wish to suggest the portrayal of torture and bloodshed. To him cruelty meant, above all, that which playwrights and actors inflict upon themselves by very rigorously carrying to the extreme their investigation and evocation of the terrifying forces found in the innermost being of men and the world. It also meant the cruelty inflicted upon the spectator, who would be physically assaulted by visual and tonal images and obliged to do away with his own civilized Western mentality, thus finding himself confronted with the truth about himself, however abominable. All the most subtle and brutal theatrical devices may be used to this effect if they bypass rational intelligence and, by acting upon the spectator's nervous system, put him in contact, almost viscerally, with the realities that have been masked by our civilization. This theater, then, considered an absolutely vital activity, would be similar to a magic ceremony in which collectivities in a state of trance would exorcize their demons and find the true expression of their deepest selves.

Before the war Artaud's theories had no great influence on French theater. And he himself only half fulfilled his dream. *Les Cencis* was performed only seventeen times and was forgotten. From 1927 to 1929 Artaud ran the Alfred Jarry Theater, which put on only a few spectacles, the best of which was Roger Vitrac's *Victor ou Les Enfants au pouvoir* (Victor, or The Children Take Power, 1928), a brutal comedy midway between surrealism and today's theater of the absurd, but nevertheless conventional in its conception as a whole and in its use of language.

Since the war many playwrights and directors have turned to Artaud for inspiration. He has had an obvious influence on Jean-Louis Barrault's spectacles as well as on his theoretical texts. The poetic theater and the theater of the absurd illustrate certain of his ideas, either directly or indirectly. Audiberti's violent poetry and embodiment of the forces of evil, Adamov's actualized nightmares, Jean Vauthier's frenzied visions, Genet's scenic ceremonies, and Arrabal's panic theater all correspond to one or another of Artaud's concepts. Artaud is also considered one of the initiators of audience participation in both American and European theater, with the spectators being invited to give free rein to their impulses by acting them out in the company of the actors. More generally, Artaud's influence is felt in all modern spectacles in which visual and tonal shocks prevail over rational dialogue and put the spectator into a liberating trance.

**Asmodi, Herbert** (born 1923). West German dramatist. A master of the drawing-room comedy, Asmodi relies on the traditional devices of the well-made play and on a macabre sense of humor to satirize postwar German society. In fact, he uses the traditional forms in an original way to comment on the decadence of the forms. In his play *Nachsaison* (Post Season, 1959), the setting is a castle in Austria during the early '50s. Curtis, a naturalized American citizen, returns to his home country, Austria, to buy a castle where he can spend his holidays. In bartering for the estate he uncovers the decadence of the past and present only to cover it again promptly with his money. In *Die Möhrenwäsche* (The Linen of the Moor, 1964) a rich German businessman, who makes great profits by trading with undeveloped lands, becomes furious when he learns that his daughter wants to marry a black. However, he curbs his racism diplomatically when he learns that the black is the Prince of Ombasaland. The play takes an ironic turn when the prince's father comes to Germany to protest his son's proposed marriage to a white girl. After much confusion, the two fathers look upon the marriage as a good business deal and make peace during a Christmas celebration. In *Stirb und werde* (Die and Become, 1967)—the title is a quotation from Goethe—Asmodi depicts the rise of a Bavarian businessman named Xanter, who becomes an elected official in Bonn. Xanter buys and uses all the "cultural goods" that will make him seem respectable, and as he does this, he takes on the form of a monster who is more dangerous and insidious than real gangsters of the underworld. Asmodi has a fine ear for the standard jargon and clichés of people who no longer believe in communication but use language to trade and barter. His plays are realistic portrayals of banal people in a society famous for its economic miracle, and the realism verges on the grotesque because of the accurate reflection of the *nouveau riche* mores and customs. Unlike many other dramatists who criticize German society, Asmodi has no distinct ideological point of view. He does not believe that society can change. His plays are simply a flat denouncement of the hypocrisy and decadence in the reconstruction era of West Germany.

OTHER PLAYS: *Jenseits vom Paradies* (The Far Side of Paradise, 1955), *Pardon wird nicht gegeben* (Pardon Will Not Be Given, 1958), *Tigerjagd* (Tiger Hunt, 1958), *Die Menschenfresser* (The Man-Eaters, 1961).

Aspenström, Werner (born 1918). Swedish poet and playwright. Running through the thirty-odd lyrical, expressionistic short plays that Aspenström has written for the stage, radio, and television is a melancholy theme: the absurdity of the poet living in an unpoetical age, trying to assert the importance of his craft and calling in a world so preoccupied with ideological conflict, economic exploitation, and technological progress that it ignores even the direst portents of imminent catastrophe. In *Arken* (The Ark, written 1955, produced 1959) Noah must endure the hostility of neighbors who fear his vision. In *Poeten och kejsaren* (The Poet and the Emperor, 1956) the Poet refuses to obey an imperial command to write a poem to eternal peace because he knows the hypocritical Emperor plans to go to war. The empty vanity reflected in man's creations is the theme of *Det eviga* (The Apes Shall Inherit the Earth, 1959) and *Den ofullbordade flugsmällan* (The Unfinished Flyswatter, 1963). In *Mattan* (The Carpet, 1966) Aspenström underscores the importance of resignation: Adam and Eve are informed by a schoolteacher who symbolizes God that paradise is a shared solitude and loneliness in which man and woman have the opportunity to quarrel and then comfort each other.

OTHER PLAYS: *Platsen är inhöljd i rök* (The Place Is Wrapped in Smoke, 1948).

Audiberti, Jacques (1899–1965). French dramatist. Born in Antibes (Alpes-Maritimes), Audiberti settled in Paris in 1925 and worked as a journalist, but shortly afterward he gave up that profession and devoted himself entirely to literature. In 1930 he was awarded the Mallarmé Prize for his first collection of poems, *L'Empire et la Trappe*. He is the author of a great deal of poetry and fiction, and his writings for the theater, since the war, include some twenty plays and several adaptations. The first of his works to be performed, QUOAT-QUOAT, in 1946, was ridiculed by much of the public. But in 1947 the performance of *Le Mal court* (Evil Is Spreading), directed by Georges Vitaly, who went on to direct most of Audiberti's works, received the Prize of the Young Theatrical Companies. Despite the constant hostility of conservative critics, Audiberti had the one-act *Les Femmes du Bœuf* (The Ox's Wives) performed at the Comédie Française in 1962, as well as the full-length *La Fourmi dans le corps* (The Itching Body) in 1962, which created a scandal. In addition to the works mentioned above, his best plays are LA FÊTE NOIRE (The Black Feast, 1948), *La Hobereaute* (The Small Falcon, 1958), and *Pomme, pomme, pomme* (Apple, Apple, Apple, 1962).

Audiberti often based his dramatic situations on the encounter of a shy or clumsy man and one or several women who are attractive or formidable, alternatively. These characters change suddenly during the plays, shifting from tenderness to savagery and vice versa, sometimes splitting in two (the two Jeanne d'Arcs of *La Pucelle* [The Maid of Orléans], 1950; Marion and her double in *La Poupée* [The Doll], shown as a film in 1965) or changing identities (Amédée and the *gendarme* in *Quoat-Quoat;* the confusion between Professor Palmas and the Doll or the identification of Coral and the Colonel in *La Poupée*). This is possible since they are not so much traditional characters as unexpected embodiments of deep and obscure forces, sometimes beneficent, sometimes maleficent, according to the situation. Somewhat Manichaeistic, Audiberti presented a world in which evil springs from good and is at the same time necessary so that love may exist. Obsessed by flesh, the Fall, and the Incarnation, Audiberti embodied on stage metaphors of desire, love, Christianity, paganism, magic powers, the poetic imagination, the war of the sexes, or quite simply Good and Evil, by playing on the dual nature—both inner and independently outside man—of those forces and conflicts, in the name of what Audiberti himself called "abhumanism."

These themes might seem banal had they not been poeticized and theatricalized to the extreme by the riotous imagination of Audiberti, who was the most exuberant and original of the postwar poetic playwrights. At first strongly influenced, in his poetry, by Mallarmé's works, Audiberti gradually constructed a fantastic theatrical universe, both farcical and nightmarish. Pure melodrama and even Boulevard theater are mingled with magic spells and agonizing scenes; savagery and even horror are inseparable from a healthy southern vigor and a Rabelaisian sense of comedy. Above all, Audiberti's theater may be considered a "feast of language." His characters, without warning, shift from the most facile puns to long tirades of the most lofty lyricism, from an excessively and strangely picturesque style to the flattest irony. Because of the freedom of his scenic imagination and his extraordinary fecundity, Audiberti's works, despite some tedious, obscure, and incoherent moments, constitute a joyous and generous theatrical ceremony in honor of the most unsettling and primitive of collective obsessions.

OTHER PLAYS: *Sa Peau* (Skin, 1947), *L'Ampelour* (1951), *Les Naturels du Bordelais* (The Natives of Bordelais, 1953), *La Hobereaute* (The Small Falcon, 1956), *Le Ouallou* (1957), *L'Effet Glapion* (The Glapion Effect, 1959), *La Brigitta* (1962), *Le Cavalier seul* (The Lone Horseman, 1963), *La Logeuse* (The Landlady, 1966), *L'Opéra du monde* (1965), *Cœur à cuir* (Jacques Cœur to Be Cooked, 1967). Adaptations: Eduardo de Filippo, *Madame Filoume* (*Filumena Marturano*, 1952); Shakespeare, *La Mégève apprivoisée* (*The Taming of the Shrew*, 1957).

**Austria.** From 1938 to 1944, Austria's theaters were compelled to subscribe to Nazi ideology; at the end of that time they were forced to close their doors. As in Germany, they were permitted by the Allies to reopen in 1945. Austrian theater, unlike the German, quickly found its way back to tradition. The emphasis in Austrian theater has always been on the performance and production rather than content. The lack of talented playwrights in the immediate postwar era did not disturb Austrian directors and audiences. More important was the re-creation of Austrian style, conventions, atmosphere, and charm within the theater. The center of all theater in Austria is Vienna, and Vienna has several outstanding companies: those at the Burgtheater, the Akademietheater, the Theater in der Josefstrasse, and the Volkstheater. These ensembles, along with the state and municipal theaters in the provinces, are financed by public funds. In the period from 1945 to 1965 they produced the standard mixture of classical plays and serious works by modern artists who have been accepted by the establishment. The emphasis is always on light comedy, especially the works of Austrian favorites such as Johann Nestroy, Ferdinand Raimund, Franz Grillparzer, Hugo von Hofmannsthal, and Arthur Schnitzler. After these writers, there is a second generation born about the turn of the century, which is slowly approaching "classical" status: Max Mell, Richard Billinger, Friedrich Schreyvogl, Alexander Lernet-Holenia, Friedrich Bruckner, Franz Csokor, and Fritz Hochwälder. Of these writers, Hochwälder is the most important. Forced to flee to Switzerland in the late 1930s, he has produced a series of works, from *Das heilige Experiment* (The Strong Are Lonely, 1942) to *Der Befehl* (The Command, 1967), which reaveal his unique talent as a classical craftsman and a radical thinker. Hochwälder differs from most Austrian writers of his generation in that he has broken from liberal Catholicism. The tradition of Catholicism still holds most of the postwar writers in its spell: Kurt Klinger, Helmut Schwarz, Kurt Benesch, Kurt Besci, and Harald Zusanek. All these dramatists have written solid works with a strong moral fervor, but they are rather traditional and orthodox in form and thought. The main reason for the conservative nature of these playwrights is undoubtedly the stringent requirements of the bourgeois audiences; another factor may be the neutrality espoused by the government, which took complete control of the country in 1955. Theaters such as the Burgtheater (which may change its course under its talented new director, Paul Hoffmann) and the Theater in der Josefstrasse (supervised by Franz Stoss and Heinrich Schnitzler) have until recently followed a "neutral" policy and produced plays with a high level of acting but a low level of social substance. Only Leon Epp in the Volkstheater has endeavored to stage a significant number of experimental and radical plays, and he has been hindered by lack of funds. The financial situation of Austrian theaters plays an important role in determining the caliber and types of productions. Of late there has been a trend toward encouraging some of the provincial theaters in Graz, Linz, and Innsbruck to become innovative and expand their operations.

The most encouraging sign in Austria is the rise of four interesting playwrights: Peter Handke, Wolfgang Bauer, Hans-Georg Behr, and Thomas Bernhard. Of the four, Handke has drawn the most attention, especially on the international scene. Beginning with his first play, *Publikumsbeschimpfung* (Offending the Public, 1966), Handke showed his flair for creating unusual situations and his ability to play with language. He attacks bourgeois expectations in the theater through his *Sprechstücke* ("Speak Plays"), whittling clichés and euphemisms to nothingness in order to discover the essentials of communication. Handke has also experimented with mime in *Kaspar* (1968) and *Quodlibet* (1970), two plays which seek to break down conventions to free the creative personality. Behr's plays are similar to Handke's. However, instead of creating his own banalities to prove how banal people have become, Behr collects them from newspapers, magazines, and other published sources, as in *Ich liebe die Oper* (I Love the Opera, 1969). Bauer, one of the youngest of the playwrights, has focused more on folk characters and the violence and frustration in Austrian society. His two important plays *Magic Afternoon* (1968) and *Change* (1969) employ a mixture of dialect, High German, and folk types to convey a picture of the brutality of people who can no longer realize their potential. The same theme is used in Thomas Bernhard's remarkable play about cripples, *Ein Fest für Boris* (A Party for Boris, 1969). Bernhard, a first-rate novelist, shows in this his first play a superb ability to create mood through language. All four of these dramatists hark back to the strong tradition in Austrian drama that reacts against false conventions and lack of values. The rediscovery of Ödön von Horváth's works in the 1960s seems to have influenced all of these writers. Horváth had an uncanny knack of using language brilliantly to show how language had become meaningless because of the depletion of values in society. He wrote his best works during a period of inflation and chaos, 1929 to 1935, and there are great similarities between his time and the contemporary period of Handke, Behr, Bauer, and Bernhard. It

# B

**Baierl, Helmut** (born 1926). East German dramatist. More than any other playwright in East Germany, Baierl has endeavored to continue the Brechtian tradition in the theater. He first began studying Slavic languages in Halle and was a Russian interpreter from 1951 to 1955. After a brief period of study in Leipzig and work in a publishing firm, he became a dramaturge at the Berliner Ensemble, where most of his plays have been produced. His first drama, *Die Feststellung* (The Evidence, 1957), was a short, didactic piece reminiscent of Brecht's *Lehrstücke*. A farmer who returns to a collective in East Germany after having fled to the West is given excellent land to farm. The other farmers want to know why he should get a "reward" for returning, and an arbitrator recalls the facts of the case by having people act out the past in different roles. In other words, the reasons for the farmer's departure become more clear through demonstrations and dialectics. In the process of distancing themselves and exchanging roles, the returnee and the farmers of the collective realize their mistakes, and the contradictions are resolved. Baierl's next play, *Frau Flinz* (1961), was modeled on Brecht's *Mother Courage*, except here Frau Flinz has five sons and learns that she does not have to protect them in a socialist state. The action takes place between 1945 and 1952 and reveals the problems that the Communists had to confront in rebuilding the country and orienting the people toward socialism after the Nazi era. In each stage of her development, Frau Flinz loses one of her sons and meets the dedicated party worker Fritz Weiler, who helps her attain a new level of political consciousness. Eventually she becomes the president of a farmer collective and overcomes the traditional resistance of country people toward nationalized farming. In *Johanna von Döbeln* (1969) the heroine is once again modeled after a Brecht protagonist. This time she learns from her experiences in a factory to consider issues from a dialectical point of view and to contribute toward socialist production rather than disturb it. Baierl's utilization of Brecht's characters and devices is an endeavor to portray how revolutionary figures adjust *after* the revolution. He is particularly concerned with determining how the individual can establish his place and identity in a new social structure and be productive. According to Baierl, individualism can be dangerous if it is not channeled and if it questions socialist strictures. Essentially Baierl's point of view is doctrinaire: He emphasizes how the individual must adjust to norms established by the socialist institutions. He rarely suggests that the institutions are in need of change, whereas Brecht was forever suggesting this.

OTHER PLAYS: *Der Dreizehnte* (The Thirteenth, 1962), *Der Lange Weg zu Lenin* (The Long Way to Lenin, 1970).

Baierl translated *The Star Turns Red, Purple Dust, Cock-a-Doodle Dandy,* and *Bedtime Story* by Sean O'Casey.

**Bald Soprano, The** (*La Cantatrice chauve,* 1950). A one-act play by Eugène Ionesco. It was first performed on May 11, 1950, at the Théâtre des Noctambules, Paris, under the direction of Nicolas Bataille. Although not very successful at first, the play gradually became a "classic of the absurd" and has been performed continually in Paris for more than ten years. Compared with traditional theater and even the poetic theater of the '40s, *La Cantatrice chauve* is indeed, as Ionesco calls it, an "antiplay." One evening, in an English drawing room, Mr. and Mrs. Smith begin to converse. They talk about what they have just eaten, about children, about medicine, and about a family, all of whose members are called Bobby Watson. When the maid, Mary, announces the arrival of Mr. and Mrs. Martin, the Smiths leave the drawing room to dress. Enter the Martins, who do not seem to know each other. They begin a conversation and gradually discover, to their great surprise and great joy, that they live on the same street, in the same building, in the same apartment, that they both have a small daughter, that they sleep in the same bed, and that in fact they are husband and wife. Then they have a deadly boring conversation with the Smiths, interrupted by a visit from the fire chief, who is disappointed not to find a fire at the Smiths'. He then recites nonsensical fables. Enter Mary, who kisses the fireman and recites a poem about a fire that burns up the whole universe. When Mary and the fireman leave, the Martins and Smiths launch into an increasingly frenetic conversation comprised at first of clichés, proverbs, and ready-made phrases drawn from conversation handbooks for beginners, which they distort; they go on to associations of ideas or sounds, then to senseless sounds; and finally, in the dark, they shout in chorus, faster and faster: "It's not over there, it's over here." When the lights come on again, the Martins are sitting together exactly as the Smiths were at the start, and the dialogue between them is identical to that in Scene 1.

Apparently absurd from beginning to end, the play is rigorously constructed: Ionesco is vainly trying to find some meaning, some authenticity, behind the dialogue; yet in delving deeper and deeper, he ends by destroying language and reducing his characters to dehumanized and inarticulate puppets. According to him, *La Cantatrice chauve,* despite the laughter it provokes, is a "tragedy of language," derived from a meditation on what appears staggeringly obvious or nonsensical in the sample sentences found in textbooks designed to teach foreign languages.

**Baldwin, James** (born 1924). American novelist, essayist, and playwright.

Born in Harlem, the son of an evangelical minister, Baldwin struggled with the meaning of his humanity in American society until his sense of alienation sent him to Paris at the age of twenty-four. From that expatriate base he established himself as one of America's finest young writers before returning to New York in 1957. His novels include *Go Tell It on the Mountain* (1953), *Giovanni's Room* (1956), *Another Country* (1962), and *Tell Me How Long the Train's Been Gone* (1968); *Going to Meet the Man* (1965) is a collection of short fiction; *Notes of a Native Son* (1955), *Nobody Knows My Name* (1961), and *The Fire Next Time* (1963) are collections of essays; he has contributed to a number of journals and has an essay in *Black Anti-Semitism and Jewish Racism* (1969).

Baldwin's first play, *The Amen Corner*, was written after he finished his first novel, *Go Tell It on the Mountain*, in an attempt to write in a different form and to explore an element in his own life: the tensions between evangelical and artistic identities and the need of a maturing son to break with the safety of his mother's world and go out into the risky life in which his father had lived and perished. The play was first produced at Howard University in 1955 and had a brief run on Broadway in 1965. Baldwin's second play, *Blues for Mister Charlie*, left the domestic sentiment of *The Amen Corner* for a threatening violence and criticism of racist whites that unsettled audiences and, in part, accounted for the shortness of the run on Broadway in 1964.

**Bauer, Friedhold** (born 1934). East German dramatist. After working in a woodworking factory, Bauer studied theater in Leipzig. From 1958 to 1960 he worked at the Theater der Stadt Brandenburg and then moved to Berlin, where he was an editor for the Henschel Publishing Company, which specializes in drama. During this time he wrote his one and only drama, *Baran und die Leute im Dorf* (Baran and the People in the Village), which was performed in 1967. The play centers on the persecution of a Polish prisoner named Baran, who is forced to work on a farm in Germany during World War II. He becomes the scapegoat for a widow and her daughter and is looked upon as a valuable commodity by the jealous neighbors. Bauer brings out the brutality and inhumanity of the self-righteous farmers, who generally like to distance themselves from the perverse city. The moral turpitude of the Germans is shown to be common to the entire country, and only the farmer Feldner, who refuses to be intimidated by the Nazis and works against them, represents a model of humanitarian behavior. Both Feldner and Baran are killed by the Nazis, and their stories are told by three old women, who recall the past and serve as a chorus. Though they seem to be different, the stories of Baran and Feldner are interlocked in such a manner that they show the common fate of all those who were oppressed by Nazism. Bauer weaves the episodes in a dialectical structure that effectively demonstrates the contrast between past and present, superstition and truth, fascism and socialism.

**Bauer, Wolfgang** (born 1941). Austrian dramatist, novelist, and director.

One of the most promising young dramatists in Austria, Bauer began writing plays while studying at the University of Graz. Most of his dramas are written in a mixture of High German and Austrian dialect and concern themselves with characters who have become caricatures of themselves. Bauer uses the folk language—that is, colloquial jargon—to depict the attitude of people who are bored with the conventions of society and themselves. They drop out of the accepted process of acculturation. In *Magic Afternoon* (1968), Birgit and Charly, who are in their twenties, sit in a room and rack their brains for something to do. Their conversation is banal, their frustration great. When two friends, Monika and Joe, visit them, they have really nothing to say to one another. After Joe accidentally breaks Monika's nose and delivers her to the hospital, he returns to Birgit and Charly to smoke hashish. The two men become high while Birgit watches them with disdain. When they joke and try to undress her, she takes a kitchen knife and kills Joe. Charly rolls Joe in a carpet. Birgit takes Joe's car keys and leaves. Charly climbs into a box and closes the lid. The end of the play demonstrates how each of the characters is cut off from the others: They are encapsulated creatures who drift and crash against each other in the emptiness of a bourgeois home. They see no meaning for themselves in society, and as dropouts they see no purpose on the outside for living. Their days are spent seeking ways to alleviate their boredom.

In *Change* (1969), Bauer's most interesting play, an artist manqué named Fery decides to play with life, since he has had little success with art. His friend Reicher, an art critic, has "discovered" a locksmith named Blasi, who has come to Vienna to sell some of his paintings. The sentimental landscapes are atrocious. However, Fery bets Reicher that he can dupe the public into believing that Blasi is a genius. Reicher likes the idea and is even willing to help. He recruits the aid of the rich homosexual connoisseur Antoine, who joins the "sponsors" of Blasi, the painter. Fery's plan is to build Blasi up in the eyes of the public, to change him, but only in order to tear him down and make him commit suicide in the end. Part of the design involves seduction, corruption, drugs, and forgery. As the plan is set in motion, it becomes clear that Blasi will not be changed, but that he will do the changing. Not only does he dupe the public and his "sponsors," but he makes Fery's girl friend pregnant, marries the girl's mother, and drives Fery himself to suicide.

The violence and brutality in Bauer's plays—the characters are constantly erupting and fighting—stem from their frustration at not being able to realize their potential inside or outside of society. Almost all of Bauer's characters range between eighteen and thirty years of age, and not one of them appears able to accept initiation into society. They are dropouts, but even more than that they are "artists" who have become art objects. The language they speak reveals to what extent they have become reified, and the process of reification reflects the manipulative nature of Austrian society. Bauer is not a political playwright, strictly speaking, but, like Ödön von Horváth, with whom he has a great deal in common, he depicts the logical results of a capitalist society that depletes and degrades creativity and offers no alternatives for change.

OTHER PLAYS: *Katharina Doppelkopf* (1967), *Party for Six* (1967).

**Bayer, Konrad** (1932–1964). Austrian dramatist, poet, and novelist. Though Bayer produced very few dramas, most of which were one-act skits, he is important for his influence on other Austrian writers. From 1954 until his suicide in 1964, he was the key figure of the Wiener Gruppe (The Viennese Group), an informal club that included several gifted Austrian writers among its members. Bayer's experiments with language and his use of the prose narrative, begun in the 1950s, are being continued by young Austrian dramatists writing today. The plots of his plays are insignificant. They are composed of puns, fragments, and word associations that reflect the fragmentation of modern technological society. His most interesting play is *kasperl am elektrischen stuhl* (Kasperl in the Electric Chair, 1964), which expresses his pessimistic attitude toward life: "One has to kill oneself to do away with illusions and hope." Here Kasperl throws his woman out of a window, reports himself to the police, and prefers to die when he is offered the chance for mercy. Kasperl is disconnected from himself and society, as are most of the figures in Bayer's plays. The broken language they utter reveals in effect the hopelessness and despair of their author, who could not connect with the society he criticized.

OTHER PLAYS: *ein abenteuer des lion von belford* (An Adventure of the Lion of Belford, 1954), *der analfabet* (1956), *bräutigall & anonymphe* (1959), *idiot* (1960), *der berg und der see* (The Mountain and the Lake, 1961).

**Bayr, Rudolf** (born 1919). Austrian dramatist, poet, essayist, and short-story writer. One of the foremost translators into German of Greek drama, Bayr received his doctoral degree from the University of Vienna in 1948, after writing his dissertation on the problems of the art of translating. Bayr also began writing theater criticism at this time and eventually became the director of literary programs at a radio station in Salzburg. Bayr has become more and more politically concerned in his writings. Aside from his superb translations of Sophocles and Aeschylus, he has used Greek themes in such plays as *Königslegende* (The Legend of the King, 1949) and *Sappho und Alkaios* (1952) and drawn political parallels with the present-day social situation.

OTHER PLAYS: *Lass wehen die Zeit* (Let Time Fly, 1957), *Die Teestunde* (The Tea Hour, 1962), *Ein heiliger Abend* (A Holy Evening, 1965).

**Becher, Johannes R.** (1891–1958). East German dramatist, poet, novelist, and editor. Appointed the first East German Minister of Culture in 1954, Becher had a long history of service in the cause of socialism. After studying in Berlin, Jena, and Munich, Becher rebelled against his authoritarian parents and took an interest in socialist movements. He refused to serve in the German Army during World War I. Instead, he joined the Communist Party. During the 1920s he edited various radical journals and wrote poetry and short stories. He was also an elected representative to the government as a Communist. Charges of treason were brought against him but were proven to be false, and he continued working for revolutionary movements in Germany until 1933. At this point he was forced to leave the country and went to France. There he attempted to organize resistance groups until 1935, when he was expelled from the country. From 1935 to 1945 he worked in the Soviet Union as an editor for a German exile journal. When he returned to East Germany in 1945, he continued his writing. In 1949 he and Paul Wiegler founded *Sinn und Form*, one of the best literary journals in German-speaking countries. After his death in 1958, an institute for creative writing and literature was named after him in Leipzig.

Becher's dramatic works, all written in verse, are closely connected with his political beliefs and actions. They are not of the same caliber as his poetry, but they do reflect his ability to make a trenchant analysis of social situations. His best play, *Winterschlacht* (The Winter's Battle, 1942), depicted the defeat of the German Army outside Moscow in the winter of 1943. In a postwar drama, *Der Weg nach Füssen* (The Way to Füssen, 1956), Becher displays the hardships endured by a proletarian family from 1933 to 1942. In his dramas Becher shied away from socialist doctrine in favor of portraying the human dilemma of oppressed peoples caught in the class struggle.

OTHER PLAYS SINCE 1945: *Das Führerbild* (The Picture of the Führer, 1945).

**Becher, Ulrich** (born 1910). German dramatist and novelist. After completing his studies at the gymnasium in Berlin, Becher studied graphics with George Grosz and then law at the universities of Berlin and Geneva. Since he made his opposition to the Nazi party clear in his first collection of short stories, *Männer machen Fehler* (1932), he was declared a decadent author, and his books were banned in Germany. His first play, *Niemand* (No One, 1934), was a mock medieval mystery play, which parodied Hugo von Hofmannsthal's everyman play. Since Christ was portrayed as a revolutionary, the play could not be performed in Germany, nor in Austria, where Becher lived until 1938. When Austria was annexed by the Nazis, Becher commenced his years of wandering and lived for several years in Brazil and New York City. In 1948 he returned to Europe and settled in Basel, Switzerland.

Most of Becher's works are satires that condemn totalitarianism and depict the difficulties confronting outsiders who are maltreated by the Philistines of society. In the immediate postwar years, he collaborated on a series of plays with the Viennese actor Peter Preses. The most important is *Der Bockerer* (The Stubborn Mule, 1949), which satirizes the Austrians who blandly accepted the Nazi annexation. Some of his plays are autobiographical, such as *Samba* (1951), which is a satirical treatment of German emigrants in Brazil. His latest works, *Die Grossen und die Kleinen* (The Big and the Small, 1956), *Der Herr kommt aus Bahia* (The Man Comes from Bahia, 1957), and

*Biene, gib mir Honig* (Bee, Give Me Honey, 1960), are caustic comedies about the petty bourgeoisie. Becher's plays are not light comedies. Their satire reflects the pitiful state of people who cannot see their own predicament.

OTHER PLAYS SINCE 1945: *Das Märchen vom Räuber, der Schutzmann wurde* (The Fairy Tale of the Robber Who Became a Policeman, 1945), *Der Pfeifer von Wien* (The Piper from Vienna, 1950, with Peter Preses), *Das Spiel vom lieben Augustin* (The Play about Dear Augustin, 1950, with Peter Preses), *Feuerwasser* (Firewater, 1952), *Mme Löwenzorn* (1953).

**Becket ou L'Honneur de Dieu** (1959). A four-act play by Jean Anouilh. It was first performed on October 8, 1959, at the Théâtre Montparnasse, Paris, under the direction of Anouilh and Roland Pietri. For this play Anouilh drew freely from the story of King Henry II (1133–1189) and Thomas à Becket (1118–1170), in order to confront two types of men bound by deep friendship but diametrically opposed in their aims and their conceptions of life. The play begins and ends with short scenes depicting King Henry doing public penance after Becket's assassination. The actual adventure of Henry and Thomas, which makes up the body of the play, is thus a flashback consisting of the vital encounters of the two men.

Fascinated by the intellectual superiority of his favorite, the deacon Thomas à Becket, who shares his life of pleasure, the king makes him chancellor. Becket thus devotes his whole mind and all his ability to reinforcing the royal power by subduing the clergy and putting down the rebellions in France. Through his active loyalty, Becket, in his own terms, "improvises his honor." When the Archbishop of Canterbury dies, Henry imposes Becket as his successor, with the idea of thus definitively dominating the Church through his friend. But Becket then discovers another loyalty or honor—what the play's subtitle terms "The Honor of God"—to which he devotes himself body and soul. Henry tries to check Becket's politics by every means possible. His rage and his sufferings are caused, first of all, by Becket's opposition to his authority as king, but more especially, and increasingly, by the fact of his friend's betrayal. As tortured and exasperated as a lover by Becket's estrangement and obstinacy, Henry finally delivers him over to the barons, who assassinate him in the cathedral.

Anouilh presents Becket as a man who is isolated and detached. In a simplified England, where the Saxons are oppressed by the Norman conquerors and their king, Henry Plantagenet, Becket is a Saxon who "collaborates" through his friendship with the king. Actually, he is only half-Saxon, his mother being a Saracen. A traitor in the eyes of many, a profligate along with the king, Becket is in search of a moral absolute. His ruling principle is to be faithful to his word, which leads him to sacrifice even his mistress when the king asks for her. As chancellor, he does his job "absurdly" but perfectly. Once he is archbishop, the honor of God prevails over his loyalty to the king. Indeed, Becket plays his part so completely that he ends by identifying with it.

The actor in him is now indistinguishable from himself as a man. The price of his conquest of the absolute is his death, which he accepts.

To confront Becket, who is not too different from certain characters in the theater of the existentialists and Camus, Anouilh set up, in the person of the king, a creature greedy for power and pleasure. While Becket is an agonized intellectual seeking moral integrity and identity, Henry, who is often compared to a little boy, is all of a piece—not only greedy but brutal, spontaneous, and passionate. His greatness comes from his refusal of mediocre beings—whence the highly comical scenes of rage in which Henry tells a few home truths to his mother, his sons, and his wife (called the "young queen," and in no way resembling Henry's real wife, Eleanor of Aquitaine), whom he reproaches with their mean souls, their cowardice, and their conventions. Becket is an exceptional being whom the king has trouble understanding but whose depth and strength attract him and have aroused his passion. In fact, his love for Becket is almost Racinian, in that the beloved's betrayal leads fatally to his murder by the forsaken lover.

Around this tragedy of a couple, Anouilh constructed a fast-moving and picturesque play. The one setting, consisting of columns which, from scene to scene, become the pillars of a church, trees in a forest, the framework of a palace, and so forth, is the background for a historical fresco—somewhat naïve, full of contemporary allusions ("collaboration," for example) and touches of satire (for example, showing up the tortuous politics of the Vatican). Moreover, the play abounds in theatrical effects, the most striking of which is toward the end when one hears the sound of a tom-tom signifying the beating of Henry's heart while his barons are on their way to assassinate Becket.

**Beckett, Samuel** (born 1906). Irish-born French dramatist and novelist. Born near Dublin, Ireland, into the Protestant middle class, Beckett began his studies at a school directed by a Frenchman. He continued to study French at the Portora Royal School and then at Trinity College and was also very active in sports. Having received his B.A. in French and Italian in 1927, he was sent to the Ecole Normale Supérieure in Paris as a lecturer in English. He became friendly with James Joyce in Paris and began to write articles and poems. Back in Dublin in 1931, he received his M.A. and became an assistant professor at Trinity College. His remarkable little book *Proust* dates from that year. Since he found it hard to bear the moral and literary constraints of Irish life, Beckett resigned from his job in 1932 and, after traveling in France, Italy, and Germany, settled definitively in Paris in 1937. During the Nazi occupation Beckett, still an Irish citizen—in other words, a neutral—did nevertheless join the Resistance. In 1942, threatened by the Gestapo, he hid in the Vaucluse and worked there as a farmhand. At the end of the war he worked for the Red Cross. Since then he has devoted himself entirely to writing and lives very discreetly in the company of his wife. Beckett, since 1947, has generally written his works in French—for example, his trilogy of novels *Molloy, Malone*

*Meurt* (Malone Dies), and *L'Innommable* (The Unnamable), published from 1951 to 1953, as well as his two major plays, *Waiting for Godot* (*En Attendant Godot,* 1953) and *Endgame* (*Fin de partie,* 1957). He himself then translated them into English. A few of his works, however, were written directly in English. Two examples are *Happy Days* (1961) and *Play* (1963), which Beckett himself translated into French as, respectively, *Oh! Les Beaux Jours* and *Comédie.*

Beckett's dramatic works consist of seven plays, two pantomimes, and a few radio plays written for the B.B.C. He became known as a playwright in 1953 with WAITING FOR GODOT, which seemed to initiate an altogether new genre of theater. From that point on, and despite the attacks of certain critics who are unable to bear the closed and despondent aspects of Beckett's works, his popularity has continued to spread throughout the world.

Beckett's plays are based not on plot but on a situation which, without changing in nature, becomes worse every minute. The place of the action, even if it is open—such as the plain in *Godot*—is in fact a prison that the characters are unable to leave. In *Happy Days* and *Play* they are physically immobilized: Winnie, in the former, is sinking into the earth; the three characters in *Play,* apparently dead, are enclosed in urns, with only their heads showing. The worsening of the situation is irreversible. Each character has a past, if not glorious, at least one that must have seemed livable (love, adultery, work, travel, and so forth). When the play beings, this more or less normal life has, for a long time, become no more than a memory. In the course of the play either the memory becomes increasingly obscure or, if precise, discloses some sin or reason for guilt which, in the last analysis, perhaps consists quite simply in the fact of having been born.

The deterioration itself, while reducing life to one single minute containing both birth and death, seems interminable. The characters react by playing, trying to tell about their memories, affirming the value of life, giving exaggerated importance to trivial objects, and, above all, trying to find words that will glorify and give permanence to their pasts and presents. All this forces them to make great efforts, for the objects are deceptive or irritating, their games and gestures come to nothing, and the right word eludes them. They merely go on and try all over again, with growing exasperation—which makes for both comedy and pathos. This theater is comic because the characters are ludicrous. Clumsy clowns, they are constantly colliding with a hostile universe and making continual blunders. The pathos stems, on the one hand, from the fact that the farce is presented as the mirror of man's condition, and, on the other, from the characters' despondent awareness of their solitude, the deterioration of their situations, and their increasing physical and moral suffering.

Both farcical masks and three-dimensional human beings, Beckett's characters move about in an eminently theatrical universe. The unreality of the settings, which derive from an expressionism simplified to an extreme, has been combined, since ENDGAME, with a very special frontality: physically immobilized, Hamm in *Endgame*, Winnie in *Happy Days*, and the three characters in *Play* face the audience and are framed, as in a painting by Giacometti or Francis Bacon, by the frame of the stage. Mirrors of the spectator, they are subjected to his gaze just as the spectator is subjected to theirs. Thus the prison, which is man's condition, is not only the stage but the entire theater. Corresponding to the dialogue between characters is the dialogue between the spectator and the characters. In fact, Beckett's theater is a theater of the inseparable couple: Vladimir and Estragon, Pozzo and Lucky, in *Godot;* Hamm and Clov, Nagg and Nell, in *Endgame;* Krapp and his tape recorder in *Krapp's Last Tape* (*La Dernière Bande,* 1960); Winnie and Willie in *Happy Days.* Bound by need, habit, and even a rope (Pozzo and Lucky), they live in the terror of remaining alone, without a voice to answer them (not even that of a tape recorder), without an ear to listen to them, without an eye to watch them, for that is the absolute vacuum, total absurdity no longer masked by anything. As long as Beckett speaks through his characters, the spectator is not alone. As long as the spectator watches and listens to Beckett's characters, they have a reason for being.

Given the irreversible deterioration, Beckett's characters speak less and less, and his plays become shorter and shorter. Life, as it were, is reduced to a voice that hopes it will not speak in the wilderness—whence the anxious quality of Beckett's language, in search of a fundamental mode of expression that is constantly slipping away. At once precise, concise, and musical, it is the murmur of despondent survival.

These works are related, of course, to the theater of the absurd. Yet they differ from other works in the genre—Ionesco's, for example—in that they are devoid of any personal romanticism as well as of any metaphors of dreams or neuroses. Moreover, they are a mine of literary, philosophical, and theatrical allusions. Descartes, Saint Augustine, Dante, Joyce, Charlie Chaplin, and the whole Western tradition of philosophy, great literature, and farce have furnished Beckett with themes, situations, and metaphors. Scholars have not only interpreted those allusions but have explained the meaning of the characters' names (Godot, Hamm, Clov, and so forth), names that are often invented in Joycean fashion. However, all the culture as well as the puns have been absorbed and digested, and the plays are the residuum—in fact, on the verge of annihilation—the meaning of which lies not in the large store of culture but in its reduction to the representation of a pure state of mankind. We must avoid, as Beckett says, "the neatness of identification." One audience understood *Godot* perfectly: the prisoners at San Quentin, who—with no difficulty, probably because of their own situation—explained that the play was quite simply about waiting, waiting for nothing. A theater based on the concrete representation of basic situations, and not on a play of obscure forces, Beckett's works are a unique success in contemporary art.

They are obviously situated at the very opposite pole from those of another master of twentieth-century theater, Bertolt Brecht. They are a closed "statement," not open criticism. Indeed, they are the purest example of pessimism, and not at all "liberation to the oppressed," as the Swedish Academy claimed in awarding Beckett the Nobel Prize in 1969. Beckett has written four radio plays: *Tous ceux qui tombent* (All That Fall, 1957), *Cendres* (Embers, 1959), *Words and Music* (1961), and *Cascando* (1963). He has also written a television play, *Dis Joe* (Eh Joe, 1965), and a film, *Film* (1965).

OTHER PLAYS: *Acte sans paroles I* (Act Without Words I, 1957), *Acte sans paroles II* (Act Without Words II, 1962), *Va et vient* (Come and Go, 1966).

**Behan, Brendan** (1923–1964). Irish dramatist. After a childhood spent in the tenement slums of Dublin, Behan joined the Irish Republican Army in 1937 and in 1939 was sentenced in an English court to three years in a Borstal Institution for young offenders for political offenses. In 1942 he was sentenced, again for political offenses, to fourteen years' imprisonment in Dublin and served nearly six years of his sentence. *The Quare Fellow* (1956), his first play, was staged in London by the Theatre Workshop Company under Joan Littlewood's direction, and marked the beginning of the rise to prominence of that company. Set in an Irish jail on the eve of an execution, *The Quare Fellow* is an intensely felt evocation of prison life, observed with a wit and humanity that is extended with equal sympathy to warders, inmates, and the hangman. The firm structure of the play, relying on the mounting tension as the moment of execution approaches, presents a moving condemnation of capital punishment in effective dramatic terms.

After a memorable television appearance and some extensively reported public incidents, Behan's drinking habits became something of a popular legend, and the success of his second play, *The Hostage* (1958), was enhanced by his own impromptu curtain speeches. The kidnapping and subsequent death of a young English soldier in Dublin, while a member of the Irish Republican Army awaits hanging in Belfast, form the plot of *The Hostage,* but these events are often forgotten in the bawdy and uproarious scenes of low life in an Irish brothel, interspersed with the ballads, dances, and direct address to the audience in the music-hall tradition that were fast becoming the hallmarks of a production by Joan Littlewood. Only spasmodically does the theme of an Ireland that has become a victim of its own revolutionary past emerge with dramatic clarity from the action. In fact, the undisciplined vitality of *The Hostage* owes as much to its director, using the text as a basis for improvisation, as it does to its author (the original version, written in Gaelic, is a third of the length of the published text); and despite its theatrical exuberance the play represents a coarsening of the fine perception of life disclosed in *The Quare Fellow.*

Increasingly incapacitated by alcoholism, Behan worked on *Richard's Cork*

*Leg*, a third full-length play, which was incomplete at the time of his death in 1964. He was the author of *Moving Out, The Garden Party*, and *The Big House*, short plays for radio (1958), and of *Borstal Boy*, an autobiography. Two biographies of Behan are *Brendan Behan: Man and Showman* (1966), by Rae Jeffs, and Ulick O'Connor's *Brendan Behan: A Biography* (1970).

**Behr, Hans-Georg** (born 1937). Austrian dramatist. One of the more unusual young dramatists in German-speaking countries, Behr writes plays without using his own words. He incorporates quotations from advertisements, news reports, books, speeches, articles, and other plays to expose the emptiness of accepted forms of communication. In *Ich liebe die Oper* (I Love the Opera, 1969), which bears the subtitle "A Bourgeois Life in Two Acts Including Two Overtures and a Tableau," he tells a gruesome story of a young couple who marry in good bourgeois fashion. In the second part of the play, the husband kills the wife in effigy and is brought to trial. Throughout the play strange characters race through the scenes using banal speech, which makes them into caricatures. Another of Behr's plays, *Das himmlische Peloton* (The Heavenly Firing Squad, 1969), is a semidocumentary piece about the Auxiliary Bishop Matthias Defregger, who delegated a firing squad during World War II to execute seventeen Italian civilians in retaliation for actions by Italian partisans. Behr's drama is based on factual information and involves the audience by asking spectators to decide whether the civilians should be shot at the end. Behr's plays hark back to Hannah Arendt's theory about the banality of evil, and his experiments with language and fact are attempts to confront this banality.

OTHER PLAYS: *Werbung um Antigone* (The Courtship of Antigone, 1969).

**Behrman, S[amuel] N[athaniel]** (born 1893). American journalist, short-story writer, playwright, and biographer. Born and reared in Worcester, Massachusetts, Behrman graduated from Clark University, then worked with Harvard's famous teacher of playwriting, George Pierce Baker. Most of his best plays, comedies of ideas, were produced in the late '20s and '30s. Since World War II he has occupied himself mainly with adaptations, such as *I Know My Love* (1949), based on a play by Marcel Achard, and *Jane* (1952), taken from a short story by Somerset Maugham. His latest plays, *The Cold Wind and the Warm* (1958), *Lord Pengo* (1962), and *But for Whom Charlie* (1964), which was presented by the Repertory Theater of Lincoln Center, lack the quality of his earlier work.

**Bellow, Saul** (born 1915). American novelist and occasional playwright. Born in Quebec of Russian émigré parents, Bellow went to high school in Chicago, where his family had moved, and then attended a series of midwestern colleges, finally getting a degree in anthropology from Northwestern University (1937). A job with a W.P.A. writers' project began his career. His most important publications are the novels *The Adventures of Augie March*

(1953), *Seize the Day* (1956), *Henderson, the Rain King* (1959), *Herzog* (1964), and *Mr. Sammler's Planet* (1970).

Bellow's first one-act play, *The Wrecker*, was published in *New World Writing 6* (1954). Encouraged by Lillian Hellman, he produced one full-length play, *The Last Analysis* (1964), which ran for a short time on Broadway. Despite theatrical failure, the play in its printed revised form is poignantly and successfully comic about "a clown driven to thought." Bellow denies that it is simply a spoof of Freudian psychology and asserts its real subject "is the mind's comical struggle for survival in an environment of Ideas —its fascination with metaphors, and the peculiarly literal and solemn manner in which Americans dedicate themselves to programs, fancies, or brainstorms." In this play and in two broad little one-acts—*A Wen* and *Orange Soufflé*, which were produced in a double bill at the Traverse Theatre, London, in 1965 and failed in New York City in 1966, along with *Out from Under* —Bellow utilizes aging heroes, wizards of some sort, in the grip of a humorously grotesque passion, like Dr. Solomon Ithimar, Nobel Prize-winning physicist, whose entire career has been inspired by the sight of Marcella Menelik's soft little apricot-colored . . . which she showed him when they were children. A wen, slightly to the left, has seemed to him, in Bellow's glorious excess of language, "a fixed star, an electromagnetic potency" and four decades later makes him risk everything, his own security clearance and the cause of world peace, in order to see it again, buried among the rolls of fat. Always, under the intellectual absurdity and farcical actions and mixed in with zesty distortions, lies some painful human truth—such as *Orange Soufflé's* "If wives can hustle, whores can bake"—in an earthy idiom that is typical of the New York Jewish characters in his novels.

Saul Bellow has genuine dramatic talents, reminding more than one critic of Chekhov, and could contribute a significant comic note to contemporary American theater should he decide to spend his energies on a public rather than a private art.

**Benesch, Kurt** (born 1926). Austrian dramatist and novelist. After his release from a prisoner of war camp in Italy, Benesch returned to Vienna, where he studied drama and wrote a doctoral dissertation on Ibsen. Since leaving the university, he has been successful in writing both novels and dramas. Benesch attempts to expose the masks and disguises that people use to protect themselves from themselves. In *Ein Boot will nach Abaduna* (A Boat Wants to Travel to Abaduna, 1951) the passengers on a ship seek a Utopia in Abaduna, but when they arrive in the real Abaduna, they are unable to cope with the contrast between their dreams and reality. In *Der Weg nach Samaria* (The Path to Samaria, 1961) a lawyer discovers that even the flight into his own petty legal work cannot free him from a troubled conscience. All of Benesch's works are dramas of psychological realism. They do not experiment with form but rely on the careful study of the actions of people in a dilemma who move toward self-recognition.

OTHER PLAYS: *Valère* (1960), *Akt mit Pause* (An Act with Intermission, 1961), *Gespräch am Fluss* (A Conversation at the River).

**Berger, Raimund** (1917–1954). Austrian dramatist. Disabled by a ski accident in 1932, Berger was bedridden for many years. He was also plagued by financial problems during his lifetime, and his plays show signs of his attempt to master these difficulties. The central theme of his dramas, most of them comedies, concerns the limitations of people and how they cause their own downfall when they do not recognize these limitations. In the course of his plays, people learn to accept their own foibles and eccentricities, and in accepting themselves, they learn how to cope with the world around them. Berger was not an innovator as a dramatist. His plays draw on the tradition of folk comedy. His most popular play, *Jupiter und Jo* (1951), is an amusing piece, which exposes the provinciality and hypocrisy of small town officials. Berger writes a mock version of *Amphitryon* and reduces Jupiter and Mercury to a thief and a prostitute, who blackmail the town officials because of their illicit affairs. In the end, after everyone is exposed, the thief and the prostitute promise to go straight, and the townspeople have come to see how ridiculous they are. Berger is a master of the short scene, which he endows with a dance tempo. His characters are constantly moving and testing themselves, searching for a joyous recognition of their real talents.

OTHER PLAYS: *Der Rattenfänger von Hameln* (The Pied Piper, 1947), *Ein Papierblumenfrühling* (A Spring of Paper Flowers, 1949), *Mogens* (also, *Der verwandte Engel*, The Sympathetic Angel, 1951), *Zeitgenossen* (Compatriots, also *Die Helden von Granville*, The Heroes of Granville, 1951), *Die Ballade vom nackten Mann* (The Ballad of the Naked Man, 1952), *Der Nachsprecher* (The Mimic, 1952), *Das Reich der Melonen* (The Realm of Melons, 1953), *Der Fremdenführer* (The Guide, 1953), *In einem fremden Land* (In a Foreign Country, 1953).

**Berliner Ensemble.** A theater company established in East Berlin by Bertolt Brecht in 1949. This repertory group is considered one of the finest in the world. Brecht gathered about him some of the best talent of the pre-Hitler years: his wife, the actress Helene Weigel, the director Erich Engel, and the set designer Caspar Neher. With their help, and with a crop of exceptional actors and young directors (Manfred Wekwerth and Peter Palitzsch), he began to work out his theories on the stage. Brecht worked for months in preparing the production of each play, and the Berliner Ensemble became noted for its remarkable precision and cohesion. In the early productions of *Mother Courage and Her Children* (1938–39), *Herr Puntila und sein Knecht Matti* (1940), and an adaptation of J. M. R. Lenz's *Der Hofmeister* (1950), the ensemble practiced Brecht's theory of gesture: Each movement of an actor was to imply a social attitude. In 1954 the company, which had been performing in the Deutsches Theater, moved to the Theater am Schiffbauerdamm. In 1956 it made its first tour outside East Germany and received great critical acclaim. Unfortunately Brecht was not alive to see this success. Since his death in 1956, the company has continued his work and produced mainly his plays. However, in recent years, the theater has shown signs of becoming more of a museum than an experimental stage. Brecht, who was forever making experiments, would certainly have deplored such stagnation. It would seem that the Berliner Ensemble must go beyond Brecht or be unfaithful to Brechtian precepts.

**Bernhard, Thomas** (born 1931). Austrian dramatist, poet, novelist, and journalist. After working as a reporter, critic, and librarian at the end of World War II, Bernhard studied music in Vienna and Salzburg. He first drew the attention of critics with his poetry, and today he is primarily known as one of the leading novelists in Austria. Among his best works are *Frost* (1963) and *Die Verstörung* (1967). In his novels and short stories Bernhard evokes moods that reflect the isolation and loneliness of mutilated human beings. His one play, *Ein Fest für Boris* (A Party for Boris, 1969), is also a mood piece about the desolation of crippled souls. In three scenes (the Prelude, the Ball, the Party) Bernhard portrays the desperation of a quarrelsome, rich, old woman who has lost her legs in an accident. Known as *die Gute* (the good one), she lives in a mansion and is waited on by a taciturn servant named Johanna. In the prelude, she bickers with Johanna about nothing and reveals how she decided to marry Boris, the ugliest of the cripples without legs, who had lived in an asylum across from the mansion. In the ball scene, she is wheeled about by Johanna, pretends to be a queen, talks about the various dignitaries in the empty room, and then berates Boris. In the party scene, thirteen cripples from the asylum, all without legs, are invited to a birthday party for Boris. At one point, while Boris plays on a drum, they complain about the conditions in the asylum, especially about the small beds. They talk about collective suicide and their dreams of wish fulfillment. *Die Gute* promises to donate larger beds, and as the party draws to a close, the cripples realize that Boris has stopped his drumming and is dead. They leave *die Gute* alone with her dead Boris, and she breaks out into terrifying laughter.

Elements from the "theater of the absurd" and the "theater of cruelty" are used effectively in the play. Bernhard's focus is on modern man as a cripple. Neither language nor action can provide the crutches to change the oppressive conditions. Death is the only answer, but it is not Bernhard's final answer, for he suggests that the decadence of the present must be exposed by death if life is to take on meaning.

**Besci, Kurt** (born 1920). Austrian dramatist, journalist, and theater critic. Besci began writing plays at an early age and had his first play, *Michelangelo,* produced in 1941. During World War II he served as a soldier, and in 1945 he returned to Vienna, where he received a doctorate in journalism. He has combined his talents as a journalist and dramatist to develop a theory that calls for a revolution of both Christianity and society. Three of his early plays, *Deutsche Passion* (German Passion, 1952), *Atom vor Christus* (The Atom Before Christ, 1952), and *Das Spanisches Dreieck* (Spanish Triangle, 1952), are endeavors to link true Christianity to socialism. The theory in these plays is presented in his book *Das moderne Drama der Völker* (The Modern Drama of the People, 1956). The publication of this tract coincided with the production of his play *Der Salzmarsch* (The Salt March, 1956), which earned him a prize from the United Nations. The drama concerns the march of Gandhi to the sea in order to lift salt and give it to the people as a gesture of protest against the British tax on salt. The English arrest Gandhi and all the leaders of the Congress Party. During this period a British major named Tanner falls in love with the daughter of a Brahman and eventually learns, after she is killed protecting her people, that India's independence is necessary if the world is to be saved—it will be a victory for true Christianity. Besci's drama has good intentions in exposing the contradictions and destructive nature of colonialism and capitalism. Yet the play is much too obvious in its critique and the characters are wooden sociological types. More recently, Besci has switched from social realism to a belated expressionism in such plays as *Russische Ostern* (Russian Easter, 1959) and *Faust in Moskau* (Faust in Moscow, 1963), but his thesis remains the same.

OTHER PLAYS: *Gott im Sumpf* (God in the Swamps, 1946), *Das Spiel von der Stadt* (The Play of the City, 1962), *Die Nacht vor Sarajewo* (The Night Before Sarajevo, 1965), *Party für Propheten* (Party for Prophets, 1965).

**Billetdoux, François** (born 1927). French dramatist. Born in Paris, Billetdoux had close contacts with the theater even as a young man. He worked as an actor with an amateur company, Les Mascarilles, and then was a student at the Charles Dullin School. After the war his interests turned to cabarets, film studies, and, above all, radio. In 1949–50 he was director of the Martinique radio. When he returned to France he wrote and produced a number of dramatic programs. Although continuing with appearances in cabaret numbers, making recordings, and writing a few novels, Billetdoux has mostly devoted himself since 1955 to the theater.

From his very first plays Billetdoux, through the use of black humor, has dealt with the theme that has remained central to his works: Individuals search each other out to put an end to their solitude or unhappiness, but all relationships are, in fact, confrontations and inhuman exploitations. In the comic mode, *Le Comportement des époux Bredburry* (The Bredburry Couple's Behavior, 1960) is quite simply about the sale of an American husband. In a Brechtian mode, *Comment va le monde, Môssieu? Il tourne, Môssieu!* (How Is the World Doing, Sir? It's Turning, Sir! 1964) is concerned with the savage adventure of two escaped prisoners of war who are bound by their reciprocal exploitation, which alone allows them to survive. From *Tchin-Tchin* (1959) to *Il faut passer par les nuages* (One Must Go by Way of the Clouds, 1964), Billetdoux's plays, at first intimate and terse, have become increasingly wordy and ambitious. They have finally been given an epic form and require "orchestrated" stagings, combining Brechtian devices and those of the new theater. Perhaps his most successful play, written midway in his career, is VA DONC CHEZ TÖRPE (Chez Torpe, 1961).

OTHER PLAYS: *A la nuit la nuit* (From Night to Night, 1955), *Pour Finalie* (1962), *Les Femmes parallèles* (Parallel Women, 1970).

**Billinger, Richard** (1893–1965). Austrian dramatist, poet, and novelist. Born in the farm region of Austria and reared for the priesthood, Billinger drew upon this background and his rebellion against it for the material of his plays. After studying at the universities of Innsbruck, Kiel, and Vienna, Billinger devoted himself to the theater rather than to the Catholic Church. Yet in his dramas he continuously portrays the dilemma of those people who break from Catholicism and move toward the cosmopolitan life. In his early works he used expressionist techniques to depict the peasant's struggle against the corrupting forces of industrialization. Another one of Billinger's favorite themes involves the purity of innocent women who fight corruption. All his plays feature in one way or another the conflict between civilization and nature, machine and man, Christianity and paganism, and city and country. His characters are either depraved and bizarre or pure and admirable. His language is poetic (often baroque in style), and the rhythm is sometimes Dionysian in quality. In one of his latest plays, *Bauernpassion* (The Passion of the Peasants, 1959), Billinger incorporates most of his major themes and employs orgiastic rituals in adapting motifs from a medieval mystery play, which has a confrontation between God and the devil. However, the originality that could be noted in his early plays becomes lost here because the advance of the times, which he resisted, had already overtaken the problems of his plays.

OTHER PLAYS SINCE 1945: *Der Zentaur* (The Centaur, 1946), *Der Galgenvogel* (The Scoundrel, 1946), *Das Haus* (The House, 1949), *Traube in Kelter* (A Grape in the Winepress, 1951), *Das nackte Leben* (The Naked Life, 1951), *Der goldene Schatten* (The Golden Shadow, 1951), *Ein Tag wie alle* (A Day Like All the Rest, 1952), *Der Plumpsack* (The Clumsy Lout, 1954), *Augsburger Jahrtausendspiel* (The Augsburg Centennial Play, 1955), *Donauballade* (The Ballad of the Danube, 1959).

**Birthday Party, The** (1958). A play by Harold Pinter. Pinter's first full-length play met with the incomprehension of the critics and the indifference of the public when it was first presented in London; within a few years it had been accepted as one of the key works of the postwar British theater. The success of a television production in 1960 is recognized as a landmark in the introduction of new and supposedly "difficult" authors to a mass audience. *The Birthday Party* exhibits most of the features of Pinter's early work. The first of these to strike an audience is the extraordinary nature of the dialogue. The conversation of Pinter's characters revolves around its subjects like a boxer around his opponent: slow, suspicious pauses are followed by a few feints and a sharp jab at the target, controlled by a rhythm which has enabled critic John Russell Taylor to call Pinter's works "the true poetic drama of our time." While Pinter's themes emerge from these elliptical exchanges, the intimacy with a character's circumstances which a dramatist is expected to establish is deliberately withheld. The structure of *The Birthday Party* allows no place for exposition, and unresolved mysteries confront the audience at every turn. The history of Stanley, the apathetic lodger at Meg's seedy boardinghouse, is left untold; the audience can only guess what truth there is in his story that a promising career as a pianist was cut short after his first concert: "They carved me up. Carved me up. It was all arranged, it was all worked out. My next concert. Somewhere else it was. In winter. I went down there to play. Then, when I got there, the hall was closed, the place was shuttered up, not even a caretaker. They'd locked it up." The natural reaction of one unfamiliar with Pinter's style is to regard this as a riddle to which the answer will duly be supplied, but the existence of the unsolved riddle is the major premise of Pinter's dramatic technique. Thus an adjustment on the part of the audience is demanded which, once accepted, reveals the firm structure controlling the tension and mounting violence of this play.

Pinter's early plays represent the invasion with disastrous consequences of a temporary haven of security (the room which forms the setting of the play) by dark, exterior forces. In *The Birthday Party* the invaders are "two gentlemen," Goldberg and McCann, who take a room in Meg's dreary boardinghouse. From the first casual announcement of their visit Stanley senses danger. He frightens Meg to a pitch of hysteria by warning her that "they" are coming in a van with a wheelbarrow. "They're looking for someone. A certain person." The sinister nature of the two visitors soon becomes apparent; they talk of 'doing a job" and make suspiciously detailed inquiries about Stanley to the unsuspecting Meg, and when she tells them it is his birthday they plan a "party" for him. In the second act their assault upon Stanley begins. He is subjected to a meaningless barrage of questions and accusations which leaves him screaming incoherently. The climax of the act, and perhaps of the play, develops during an eerie game of blindman's buff in which Stanley, taking advantage of a failure of the lights, is discovered crouching over the spread-eagled form of Lulu, the attractive girl next door, and is then pinned giggling against the wall by Goldberg and McCann. In the last act the two visitors, McCann now expressing some distaste for his role, remove a Stanley cowed into total submission and apparently deprived of speech to an unknown destination. To the ineffectual protests of Meg's husband they reply that he "needs special treatment."

*The Birthday Party* resists attempts to place it within an existing literary tradition. The nightmare interrogation of Stanley suggests a link with Kafka, while its meaningless, staccato dialogue that borrows its rhythm from music-hall patter is reminiscent of Beckett's in *Waiting for Godot*. Critic Martin Esslin has interpreted Pinter's work as an English variant of the European "theater of the absurd," while others have explained the play as an allegory of the pressures of conformity or a commentary on twentieth-century violence. But whatever Pinter may have derived from earlier authors (and he acknowledges the influence of Beckett) he redeploys in a wholly individual manner, while his repeated assurances of the intuitive basis of his work make it clear that he had no allegorical or symbolic scheme in mind. "I think it is impossible—and certainly for me—" he has stated, "to start writing a play from any kind of abstract idea." *The Birthday Party*, he has claimed, was "sparked off by a very distinct situation in digs" encountered during his days as a touring actor. But he has also stated that his characters are presented "at the extreme edge of their living, where they are living pretty much alone"; and the accuracy of his dialogue is matched by an accuracy of psychological perception in the outfields of human behavior, which lends force to Pinter's claim that he is a "realist" despite the apparently unnatural situations of his drama. Recognizing that the conventional pattern of exposition, crisis, and denouement had become an obstacle rather than an aid to psychological truth, Pinter replaced it with another pattern, more essentially theatrical and less susceptible to academic analysis but no less strictly disciplined. *The Birthday Party* occupies a position of permanent importance in the history of contemporary British drama as the first full-length play in which this new technique was displayed.

It is noteworthy that while Pinter's later plays leave a character's background as unverifiable, and his actions as unpredictable, as does *The Birthday Party*, they dispense with the mysterious intruders of his first works for the stage and avoid scenes like the savage reactions provoked by Meg's present of a toy drum to Stanley, where the undeniable theatrical effect seems at variance with the developing structure of the play. *The Birthday Party* revealed Pinter's distinct talent, while some of the features in the play which critics have been most concerned to defend have been rejected in the author's later work.

**Bjørneboe, Jens** (born 1920). Norwegian playwright, poet, and novelist. Bjørneboe made his early reputation as a classically-oriented poet, but soon turned to polemical writing, satirizing the shortcomings of the Norwegian educational system in his novel *Jonas* (1955), and of the penal system in his novel *Den onde hyrde* (The Bad Shepherd, 1960). The latter was adapted in 1965, with the help of playwright Helge Krog (1889–1962), into the music-drama *Til lykke med dagen!* (Congratulations!). This play was performed successfully in several Scandinavian countries and helped pave the way for wide public acceptance of another satirical play, *Fugleelskerne* (The Bird Lovers, 1966), with music by Hans Dieter Hosalla. Showing the influence of Brecht and Dürrenmatt, *The Bird Lovers* is set in Italy and depicts how a group of bird-loving German tourists use economic pressure to force their will on the inhabitants of a small, poor town. The Italians give up their preference for roasted birds after the tourists intimidate them by offering to help turn the town into a profitable resort. At the end of the play a Volkswagen stands beside every cottage.

**Black Theater in the United States.** In the time between William Wells Brown's *Escape, or a Leap to Freedom* (1858), the first known play by a Negro playwright in the United States, and Charles Gordone's *No Place to Be Somebody* (1969), the first play by a Negro playwright to win the Pulitzer Prize, there has been a slow but radical change in both the image and the activity of Negroes in American life. Legal slavery has given way to a struggle for genuine civil rights, the white man's label of "Negro" has in many quarters been supplanted by a proud assertion of "black," avenues of accomplishment have been opened and roles of leadership taken. In the theater this means that the minstrel shows of the nineteenth century (written by whites and played by white actors in blackface before white audiences) have been replaced by serious drama written by blacks, directed and acted by blacks for blacks. Although the Harlem renaissance of the '20s and '30s saw an efflorescence of black theater—groups such as the Ethiopian Art Players, playwrights such as Jean Toomer and Langston Hughes, actors such as Paul Robeson—social pressures and prejudices were still too great to allow this display of talent to be anything more than a temporary novelty (the senseless destruction of Paul Robeson's career is a sign not so much of American fear of Communism as of a deeper unwillingness to admit blacks to full membership in success, with all the leverage of power and influence that that entails). Not until the 1960s did black theater really establish itself, but then it quickly assumed a position as one of the most potent forces on the contemporary American stage.

The second world war marks the division between the older Negro theater, with its struggle to provide jobs for black actors and its attempt to deal in an integrated situation with a more realistic presentation of Negro life in America, and the new black theater that asserts itself as revolutionary, superior, and apart. A number of important "firsts" antedate the war: in 1903 the first play written by a Negro to see print was published (Joseph Cotter's *Caleb, the Degenerate*). In 1916 the first successful play written and acted by Negroes was produced by the N.A.A.C.P. (Angeline Grimke's *Rachel*, a social document about lynching). The next year saw Negro actors for the first time in serious drama on Broadway (in three one-act plays by the white poet Ridgely Torrence, *Granny Maumee, The Rider of Dreams,* and *Simon the Cyrenian*). In the 1920s some of the first experimental theater groups comprised of Negroes and concerned with real Negro life were founded. In 1925 the first play by a Negro was produced on a Broadway stage (Garland Anderson's *Appearances*). The first long-run Broadway hit by a Negro playwright was Langston Hughes's *Mulatto* (1935), which ran for 373 performances. In the 1930s for the first time Negroes had access to certain kinds of technical training through the

Federal Theater Project. The period after World War II had its firsts, too—for the first time theaters generally did not segregate audiences and for the first time Negroes began to be cast in non-Negro roles—but the time of novelty was over and developments rather than first hurdles took the energies of young black writers, some of whom were intent upon making it in the white artistic world and some in forging a distinctive black art of their own. Protest had always been present in Negro theater, but after World War II it became increasingly more pronounced and its style grew increasingly militant.

The Committee for the Negro in the Arts, founded in 1947, and the Council on the Harlem Theater, 1950, were both instrumental in fostering postwar black theater and in helping to achieve, as the C.N.A. states, "the integration of Negro artists into all forms of American culture on a dignified basis of merit and equality" and to destroy racial stereotypes in various arts. One way of doing this was through Harlem revues making use of genuine folk elements, such as Alice Childress' adaptation of Langston Hughes's "Simple" (under the title *Just a Little Simple*), which played to thousands in 1950, and *Gold through the Trees* (1952) with its African dances and American blues. Serious drama provided another avenue for the black theater's assertion of dignity: In 1951 William Branch's *A Medal for Willie* dealt movingly with the black soldier who fights and dies for an America that discriminates against him. Branch's *In Splendid Error* (1954), a play about Frederick Douglass and John Brown, did well off-Broadway. Loften Mitchell's *A Land Beyond the River* (1957), dealing with an actual struggle over segregation in South Carolina, had an extended run off-Broadway and then toured the East Coast. Broadway, too, was the scene of a number of successes for the black theater in the 1950s. Louis Peterson's *Take a Giant Step* (1953) and Lorraine HANSBERRY's *A Raisin in the Sun* (1959) were serious studies of the twin problems of black identity and integrated housing, and both focused on the particularly painful problem of maturation for a black man in a society bent on humiliating him.

These were competent plays, honest plays, written by playwrights who wanted dignity for blacks in an integrated society, with peace and justice for all. But they were plays that lacked hatred, and as such missed how deep the roots of prejudice go in both groups that define each other in terms of color. Several decades of theater had shown blacks suffering the hatred of whites; it remained for the 1960s to reveal theatrically the corresponding hatred that blacks have for whites.

Along with plays more traditional in structure and attitude—Ossie Davis' *Purlie Victorious* (1961), Douglas Turner Ward's *Happy Ending* and *Day of Absence* (1965), Ronald Milner's *Who's Got His Own* (1966), and various plays done by the Negro Ensemble Company since its first season in 1968—there exploded on the New York theater scene a first-rate and very angry talent in the person of LeRoi JONES, whose Obie-winning play *Dutchman* (1964) exposed in an exact myth the demonic exploitation of blacks by whites. Since then, and very much under the influence of Jones, there has developed a militant and separatist movement among younger black playwrights, represented by an anthology such as Ed BULLINS' *New Plays from the Black Theatre;* the arrangement of plays and their summary sentences sketch the climax in feeling and idea that this group had reached by 1969: *"The Death of Malcolm X* by LeRoi Jones. The white conspiracy to murder Malcolm. *The Rise* by Charles H. Fuller, Jr. Brother Marcus' bold attempt to rouse Black consciousness in America. *In New England Winter* by Ed Bullins. A study of Black life style and survival. *El Hajj Malik* by N. R. Davidson, Jr. The dramatization of Malcolm X's life. *Family Portrait* by Ben Caldwell. The generation gap between yesterday's Uncle Toms and today's militants. *Growin' into Blackness* by Salimu. Life dedicated to building the Black nation. *Sister Son/Ji* by Sonia Sanchez. An appeal for solidarity against the white community. *The King of Soul* by Ben Caldwell. Otis Redding's plane crash plotted by a white man. *The Man Who Trusted the Devil Twice* by Herbert Stokes. The whites will sell you out every time. *The Black Bird* by Marvin X. Loyalty to whites means that you, too, will Burn Baby Burn. *We Righteous Bombers* by Kingsley B. Bass, Jr. The Black revolution to liberate all Americans."

Besides the group of conventional Negro playwrights and companies and the group of separatist black radicals, there are a few blacks, such as Adrienne KENNEDY, who operate quite individually in elitist off-off-Broadway circles (a route Jones had open to him in the early 1960s and chose not to take), and whose theatrical concerns seem to be rather exclusively artistic, even when using racial and social issues. James BALDWIN has managed with *The Amen Corner* (1955; 1965) and *Blues for Mister Charlie* (1964) to provide one work for either group without ever reaching the literary heights of his novels and essays. What direction Charles Gordone will take after receiving his Pulitzer Prize (1970) remains to be seen.

Of the many books and articles now being written on black theater Doris E. Abramson's *Negro Playwrights in the American Theatre, 1925–1959* (1967) is heavy with summary of individual plays; Loften Mitchell's *Black Drama, The Story of the American Negro in the Theatre* (1967) is interesting and useful, and Lindsay Patterson's *Anthology of the American Negro in the Theatre: A Critical Approach* (1967) is direct and informative. The *Negro Digest* regularly has articles relating to blacks in the theater, and Ed Bullins' New Lafayette Theatre publishes a *Black Theatre Magazine.*

**Boeck, Johann A.** (born 1917) Austrian dramatist, journalist, and short-story writer. Boeck's youth was spent in Rumania and Yugoslavia. His bitter experiences during World War II shaped his pessimistic view of the world. He has not written many plays, but those he has written reflect the breakdown of values in Central Europe. In *Das Nest* (The Nest, 1962) he depicts how members of a family lose their lives in a concentration camp because they cannot decide whether party or family loyalty is more important to them. In

*Jeanne 44* (1966) he presents a modern version of Joan of Arc in the resistance, and here again the problem of political commitment is the major theme. As a journalist and a political realist, Boeck relies on social realism to show the ambiguity in situations that call for firm political decisions.

OTHER PLAYS: *Mario und Sulla, Die Herberge* (The Inn), *Das Purpurzelt* (The Purple Tent), *Der Spion* (The Spy), *Guter Bruder* (Good Brother).

**Bolt, Robert** (born 1924). English dramatist. Bolt was educated at Manchester Grammar School and Manchester University, his studies being interrupted by three years of military service (1943–1946). From 1950 to 1958 he worked as a schoolmaster. During this time he discovered his talent as a playwright, progressing from radio drama to writing for the stage. He has confessed that *The Critic and the Heart* (1957), his first stage play, has a plot consciously modeled on the disciplined form of Somerset Maugham's *The Circle*. *Flowering Cherry* (1957), his next play, is viewed by the author as a move away from naturalism. However, this study of a businessman who dreams of his escape from the city remains, despite some uneasy formal experiments, a naturalistic portrayal of ineffectual aspirations in the manner of Chekhov. *The Tiger and the Horse* (1960, written before *A Man for All Seasons* although presented later) is also a combination of the traditional and the innovative. Its university setting and its portrait of the humane, articulate master whose family crises impinge upon college politics are familiar features of West End drawing-room drama, but by introducing the issue of nuclear disarmament and presenting a stark picture of Gwendolin Dean's mental breakdown Bolt aligned himself with contemporary dramatists.

In *A Man for All Seasons* (1960) Bolt turned to a historical theme. The life of Sir Thomas More was treated in an episodic fashion before formalized units of scenery, with scenes introduced by a "common man" speaking directly to the audience. The rising interest in Brecht was undoubtedly the effective cause of these formal devices, but the substance of the play did not depart radically from the tradition of historical drama. More's growing isolation and eventual death are presented in a subtle and intelligent character study against a background of diplomacy and political maneuver. Bolt's historical sense was sufficient to allow the natural inclusion, in certain passages, of More's own words. With its rich opportunities for the actor and its powerful dramatization of the conflict between individual conscience and political pressure, the play was an immediate success in London and New York, where it won the New York Drama Critics Circle Award in 1962. But it was a success which owed little to the movement initiated by Osborne, Arden, and Pinter. "I do accept the given audience," Bolt has said; "that is to say a largely middle-class, West End, theatregoing audience." The timing of Bolt's major success obscured the fact that he is a serious dramatist in the tradition of Terence Rattigan and N. C. Hunter rather than of the younger dramatists who formed his contemporaries.

In the years following *A Man for All Seasons* Bolt's main successes were scored in his work for motion pictures. *Gentle Jack* (1963), his next work for the stage, failed to find favor with London audiences. This fantasy sets out to display the gentle and the destructive aspects of man's nature by inserting a figure invested with the supernatural powers of Pan into a modern landscape. It was described by the author as an attempt "to combine all the elements of ritual, dance, and music in a specific modern context." *The Thwarting of Baron Bolligrew* (1965), a play for children, was successful in its more limited aims; *Brother and Sister* (1967), a revised version of Bolt's early play *The Critic and the Heart*, failed to reach the London stage. *Vivat! Vivat Regina!* was produced in 1970.

As well as adapting *A Man for All Seasons* for the screen, Bolt has written the screenplays for *Lawrence of Arabia* and *Doctor Zhivago*. An interview with Bolt appears in *Theatre at Work,* edited by Charles Marowitz and Simon Trussler (1967); there is also a study of the dramatist by Ronald Hayman, *Robert Bolt* (1969).

**Bond, Edward** (born 1935). English dramatist. A writer who has been hailed as "the most important new British playwright to emerge in the sixties," Bond left school at fourteen to work in factories and offices. His spare time was devoted to theatergoing and writing plays. He had completed some fourteen or fifteen plays before *The Pope's Wedding* (1962) was given a Sunday-night performance at the Royal Court Theatre. This production, together with his membership in the Royal Court Writers' Group, gave him a more formal introduction to the dramatist's craft; but it was not until 1965 that Bond exchanged obscurity for notoriety with *Saved,* a play banned by the Lord Chamberlain and greeted with vituperation by all but a handful of critics when it was presented, in defiance of the Theatre Licensing Act, by the English Stage Company. "There comes a point," wrote J. W. Lambert in the London *Sunday Times,* "when both life and art are irretrievably debased, and Edward Bond's play, in this production, is well past that point." But from the beginning the play was not without its defenders, notable among them Sir Laurence Olivier. SAVED has been presented abroad, and revived in England since the abolition of stage censorship, with a minimum of controversy and has quickly taken its place as one of the key plays of the mid-1960s. There can be no doubt that the scene in which a baby is smeared with his own excrement and stoned to death by a group of youths in search of excitement is an integral, and justifiable, part of a play that extends the bounds of realism to present a bleak and profoundly personal view of the human condition.

Three years' silence was followed by two plays performed in quick succession. *Early Morning* (1968) was one of the last plays to be banned by the Lord Chamberlain before the abolition of his licensing function, and in its first production received only two performances under clandestine conditions. Against a background of casually amoral crime, watched over by a perverted and vindictive judiciary, Prince Albert and Disraeli plot to unthrone a Queen Victoria whose primary consolation is her Lesbian relationship with Florence Nightingale, while the succession is complicated by the fact that Victoria's eldest sons are Siamese twins. A simple legend introduces the printed text: "The events of this play are true." In fact, they are merely impertinent. The unhistorical, comic-strip extravagance of this fantasy was never likely to endanger or even offend the institution of the monarchy. If the play's point is that behind the grand statements and recorded policies of recent history there lies only a welter of meaningless events, it is weakened rather than strengthened by the gross distortions imposed upon historical personages. But despite the dubious premises of the play Bond succeeds—particularly in its second half, where internecine strife conveys the characters to a heaven which is the scene of eternally gruesome but nevertheless painless cannibalism—in conveying something of his vision of a world in which evil and corruption are the inescapable norm. "Heil Hitler! Heil Einstein!" cries Prince Arthur, whose frustrated love for Florence Nightingale is a feature of the plot. "Hitler gets a bad name, and Einstein's good. But it doesn't matter, the good still kill. And the civilized kill more than the savage. That's what science is for, even when it's doing good. Civilization is just bigger heaps of dead." A perverse glimmer of hope for humanity in the midst of these atrocities is preserved by Florence's love for Arthur, whose living head she preserves about her person while the rest of his body is gnawed into oblivion. The play received the George Devine Award.

*Narrow Road to the Deep North* (1968), written rapidly as an oblique supplement to a conference on city planning held in Coventry, was presented at Coventry's Belgrade Theatre in June 1968. Set in Japan "about the seventeenth, eighteenth, or nineteenth centuries," the play weds an adaptation of Brechtian techniques to a terse, formal dialogue of great effectiveness, portraying the ebb and flow of savagery as rival factions war for mastery of the city. The arrival of the colonial powers in the shape of an English naval commander and his missionary "sister" complicates the issue, but the play is not a simple tract on the evils of imperialism. In fact the Commodore and Georgina, for all their posturing as representatives of a superior civilization, become pawns in the subtle political maneuvers of Shogo and his rivals, whose callous brutality is blended with an ironic intelligence that is more than a match for the Commodore's naïveté. Neither the discipline imposed by Shogo's iron hand nor the perversion of Christian ethics adopted by Georgina ("instead of atrocity I use morality") prevents the city's order from collapsing in a welter of bloodshed. The play ends with an image of violence characteristic of Bond: A man who has narrowly escaped drowning clambers ashore to upbraid a Buddhist monk for failing to come to his rescue. But the monk is in fact dying from a self-inflicted wound, and while the other has his back turned he "lurches forward on to his back and stretches his legs. His robe is vivid red where the bowels

have fallen." "The message is clear," wrote critic Martin Esslin. "Not in speculation about moral principles lies salvation, but in one man's active help for
another." But there is little support for this tone of brisk humanism in the
events depicted by Bond, for "one man's active help for another" is a concept
which circumstances, psychology, and the failure of communication conspire
to prevent his characters from formulating.

Bond's dramatic method has differed in each of his three major plays, but
his work displays a remarkable consistency in its preoccupation with violence
and its refusal to offer facile remedies to the problems so starkly presented, in
its terse yet expressive language, and in its feeling for the physical nature of
dramatic situations expressed in hard, precise stage directions. Bond has spoken
of "the possibility of a total cruelty" created by twentieth-century technology:
"We are now face to face with the fact that Man is a very violent creature, and
the problem of violence is the problem which is going to concern our society
for the next ten, fifteen years, just as in the earlier part of the century society
was concerned with the problem of sex. The battles of sex have been won.
What we have to face now is the problem of violence." Although his plays may
be thought to negate his own words, Bond has stated that he does not consider
this violence an innate element of human psychology: "People are not born
violent by nature. The natural condition in which people are born is love, the
aptitude for loving and being loved. . . . Children are made competitive,
aggressive—society does not control the beast in men, it makes men animals
in order to control them." And indeed there is a distant element of respect for
the human species in the dogged determination with which Len mends a
broken chair in the final silence of *Saved*, Florence holds on to Arthur's head
in *Early Morning*, and the gentle Kiro preserves his innocence in *Narrow Road
to the Deep North*.

Bond's opponents attribute an element of gratuitous violence to his writing,
and his struggle for a right to express himself in his chosen manner has perhaps
obscured the dramatic justification for the scenes most objectionable to conventional taste—and indeed may have tempted Bond to ignore such justification
in the ghoulish excesses of *Early Morning*. But Bond is undeniably a dramatist
of the '60s in his implied suggestion that man's distinction from the animal
world is marked less in reason or in high ideals than in blind, destructive violence toward his own species. For Bond there is no simple socialist panacea,
which might restore the lost dignity of man; his excellence and originality lie
in his uncompromising, pitiless view of man that strips him of his last shreds
of nobility without recourse to the dubious symbolism of earlier writers. At this
stage in his career he has expressed himself most successfully in the unmerciful
realism of *Saved*, but *Narrow Road to the Deep North* shows that his talent is
not limited to a re-creation of the bleaker aspects of working-class dialogue.

Bond has written a number of film scripts, which include that of Antoni-
oni's *Blow-Up*. He contributed to "Discussion on Contemporary Theatre"

in *New Theatre Magazine*, Vol. VII, No. 2 (1967). Ronald Dryden discusses his work in "Society Makes Men Animals," *Observer Review*, February 9, 1969, as does John Russell Taylor in "Edward Bond: Beyond Pessimism?," in *Plays and Players*, October 1970. William Gaskill discussed and interviewed Bond for *Gambit* (No. 17, 1970).

**Borchert, Wolfgang** (1921–1947). German playwright, actor, and poet. Despite the fact that he was crippled in the war by the Nazis, Borchert never gave up the hope that something new and great might spring from the ruins of Germany. He had a vision that a new man might be reborn from a cripple. This flicker of hope resided in the mutilated Borchert to the very end of his short life, and it is the motivating force behind the verse that served as the motto to his first collection of poems in 1946:

> I would like to be a lighthouse,
> in night and wind,
> for the smallest of fish,
> for every boat,
> and yet I myself am but
> a ship afloat.

Borchert began writing verse and short stories in the fall of 1945 after escaping from an American prisoner of war camp. During this period he also did a great deal of stage work and was instrumental in founding a small theater in Hamburg. However, in December 1946 he was compelled to curtail his theater activities and was confined to his bed as a result of a liver disease. It was perhaps the realization that his days were limited which contributed to Borchert's writing his best prose works. His only drama, *Draussen vor der Tür* (The Man Outside, 1947), was composed in eight days in January 1947. When the play was first heard over the radio, Borchert was recognized as the voice of the German conscience, as a spokesman for the ravaged German generation.

*The Man Outside* is a tragic, surrealistic play that portrays the experiences of the infantryman Beckmann, who returns home to find that he has no home. Beckmann's wife has deserted him and his parents have killed themselves. In despair, Beckmann, too, decides to kill himself. However, "the Other" (his conscience) and the River Elbe will not permit Beckmann's suicide because he has not tried hard enough to find his place in postwar Germany. Once again, he begins a quest to secure a job, find love, and assume the responsibility for his actions in World War II. However, Beckmann learns that he is merely a mutilated being surrounded by savages in a wasteland. In the end, he refuses to live in a society which demands that he be a murderer and accept being murdered at the same time.

Like the *O Mensch* dramas—written by the German expressionists after World War I—*The Man Outside* protests against the corruption and decadence in a postwar Germany. Borchert's pregnant, repetitive phrases give birth to a total mood of anguish. His images seek to blend and form a universal canvas portraying a cripple who yearns to become part of a chiliastic future. Though not a great work, *The Man Outside* is extremely significant because it was the first drama written after World War II to speak for a generation that had been devastated by the war. The quality of the play bespeaks the quality of his times, and Borchert's achievement emanates from his sensitivity, which was akin to the temper of his times.

**Bowen, John** (born 1924). English dramatist and novelist. Bowen was born in India and brought up in Britain; after military service with the Indian Army he went to Oxford. He had already made his mark as a novelist and television dramatist before writing for the stage. Although his first play, *I Love You, Mrs. Patterson*, was staged in 1964, his viewpoint is by no means that of the younger dramatists of the anarchic left who emerged contemporaneously with him. He has described himself as "one of those middle-aged liberals in this country, who voted Labour until Hugh Gaitskell died, and have been politically directionless ever since." The style and content of his articulate exercises in dramaturgy, however, display an interest in current theatrical developments. *After the Rain* (1966), a reworking of material from an earlier novel of the same title, demonstrates the author's avowed preoccupation with myth. In a future in which our present civilization has been destroyed by flood, a group of prisoners on a bare stage reenacts, as therapy for themselves and instruction for the audience, the creation of a new mythology that binds the survivors from disaster into a new society. Although at the end the reality of death impinges upon the performance of the play-within-a-play, Bowen's interest centers on the process by which the group's leader assumes the attributes of supernatural power to assert his divinity and demand a human sacrifice from the mixed bag of rational atheists and conventional Christians who comprise his fellow survivors.

The double bill *Little Boxes* (1968) presents two plays, *The Coffee Lace* and *Trevor*, in a more conventional mode, sharing the theme of social isolation. Two other plays of the same period were first performed under the author's direction by students at the London Academy of Music and Dramatic Art. In both Bowen adapted powerful dramatic traditions from the past to accord with contemporary theatrical techniques. *The Fall and Redemption of Man* (1967) is a selection of scenes from the medieval mystery cycles rendered into modern English verse as close as possible to the original, for performance by twelve young actors with a minimum of properties and costume. *The Disorderly Women* (1969) is a more ambitious and not entirely happy updating of *The Bacchae*, in which passages of Bowen's own writing jostle with scenes created by directed improvisation and recourse to Euripides' text. In a foreword to the printed edition Bowen defends his equal division of sympathy between Pentheus, in this version a tolerant, liberal administrator devoted to the running of the "orderly city" of Thebes, and a Dionysus who represents an "anti-social and anti-logical" philosophy dependent upon hallucinatory drugs.

Three of Bowen's television plays have been published under the title of *The Essay Prize* (1962).

**Brazil.** One of the most original and impressive movements in drama in South America is the Brazilian. A staple output of commercial plays varied by some experimental activity was revolutionized in 1943 by Nélson Rodrigues' *Vestido de noiva* (The Wedding Dress), which stunned theatergoers with expressionist techniques and a Freudian theme. Os Comediantes, which produced *Vestido de noiva*, was, like many of the experimental groups, deeply influenced by the many Europeans who had fled to Brazil to avoid the war. During this same period São Paulo began to emerge as the theater center, although Rio de Janeiro continued substantial activity. A serious effort to create theater out of the colorful Brazilian historical and ethnic panorama resulted in a black theater, which lasted until the mid-1960s. All these factors produced a movement of great excitement and activity during the 1950s and 1960s. Unfortunately, it has been progressively more frustrated by the extremely difficult internal situation and the arbitrary censorship to which Brazilian theater is subject.

A number of dramatists have achieved considerable international reputation, among them Pedro Bloch, with his one- and two-character theater of passion, and Guilherme Figueiredo, author of a theater of ideas, but best known for *A rapôsa e as uvas* (The Fox and the Grapes, 1953). Jorge Andrade, profoundly influenced by Arthur Miller in both technique and content, has portrayed the sources of modern Brazilian society, and especially the sociological history of São Paulo. Despite his orientations, Andrade's theater is neither historical nor sociological; his best works, such as *A moratória* (The Moratorium, 1955), are both dramatic and theatrical. The arid, backward northeastern region of Brazil, the subject of a whole cycle of novelists, has also been dramatized. Ariano Suassuna's *Auto da compadecida* (The Rogue's Trial, 1957) is a splendid fusion of popular elements and social criticism, and it is the source of virtually all the theater in the Northeast today. Alfredo Dias Gomes has had great success following this line. *O pagador de promessas* (The Given Word, 1960) shows the frustration of a simple man dehumanized by an uncomprehending society; in *O Santo Inquérito* (The Holy Inquisition, 1966) Dias Gomes took a historical incident of an innocent girl executed by the Inquisition on circumstantial evidence and created an attack on hypocrisy and narrow-mindedness. With a strong social bent and his roots in the popular culture of the Northeast, Dias Gomes is one of Latin America's most powerful dramatists.

The economic and political difficulties of the Brazilian theater have led to such innovations as *Liberdade, liberdade* (Freedom, Freedom) by Flávio Rangel and Millôr Fernandes, a satire composed of a collage of struggles for freedom. Gianfrancesco Guarnieri, a dramatist of the generation gap and the economic struggle since his great success in 1958 with *Êles não usam black-tie* (They Don't Wear Tuxedos, 1958) and *Gimba* (1959), has formed a repertory company, Teatro Arena, with the dramatist and director Augusto Boal. Boal had created in São Paulo the *ferias de opinião*, musical and theatrical montages on social and political themes. In Arena, they have collaborated to produce choral or group works, most notable of which is *Arena conta Zumbi* (Arena Tells Zumbi, 1965), based on the black Republic of Palmares (1605–1695), which was destroyed by whites in what *Arena conta Zumbi* presents as a parallel to recent events in Brazil.

**Braun, Felix** (born 1885). Austrian dramatist, poet, essayist, and novelist. After studying art history and German literature at the University of Vienna and receiving his doctorate, Braun moved to Berlin and worked for a newspaper. He was a close friend of Hugo von Hofmannsthal and Rainer Maria Rilke and was encouraged by them to write poetry. Braun soon gave up his newspaper work and concentrated on both poetry and drama, which reflect a strong interest in classicism. In 1928 he moved to Italy, where he taught German literature and wrote plays, poetry, and essays until 1938. He traveled to England and remained there for the next thirteen years. In 1951 he was offered a position as professor of dramatic literature at the Reinhardt Seminar and returned to Vienna.

Braun's plays are filled with Greek motifs and themes. Most of them are adaptations and draw parallels between the past and present. The compact structure of his dramas and the graceful style show his concern with a harmonious universe that corresponds to the Judeo-Christian view of the world. Braun argues against despair in his dramas, and in such a play as *Orpheus* (1957) he depicts the suffering of the creative individual who nevertheless is placed by God among the stars in the end. This argument for humanity in the name of Christian civilization is characteristic of all his plays.

OTHER PLAYS SINCE 1945: *Rudolf der Stifter* (Rudolf the Patron, 1952), *Der Schäfer im Wald* (The Shepherd in the Woods, 1956), *Josef und Maria* (1956), *Irina und der Zar* (Irina and the Czar, 1956).

**Braun, Volker** (born 1939). East German dramatist and poet. After several years with the Berliner Ensemble as a dramaturge, Braun began working as a professional writer on an independent basis. He is best known for his volume of poetry *Provokation für mich* (Provocation for Me, 1965). His best play, *Kipper Paul Bauch* (The Dumper Paul Bauch, written 1962–1965), has yet to be produced because the East German censors believe that it reflects a negative picture of factory life. The drama concerns the workers at a coal-mining plant who dump the carts of sand that is discarded from the coal. Essentially these men represent the lowest class of workers: They are unskilled garbage men who receive little compensation for their work. One of the dumpers, Paul Bauch—his last name means stomach and symbolizes his gargantuan appetite— is a remarkable individualist with a great deal of imagination but no sense of responsibility. The administrators in the firm make him leader of the dumper brigade in order to encourage him and the other workers to become more productive. The central problem of the play centers on transforming the dirty work of the dumpers into dignified labor and increasing their productive potential without exploiting them. When one of Bauch's experiments to improve conditions fails, and a worker loses a leg, Bauch leaves the firm. He returns, however, only to realize that he cannot help the dumpers in his individualistic way but that the technological revolution itself must find ways to change the working conditions and workers so that the essence of humanity is preserved. Bauch finally leaves the firm for good, and the situation of the dumpers remains essentially the same as at the beginning of the play. It is for this reason that the East German censors have not viewed kindly the problem of the play. Braun has touched upon a sensitive area in East Germany, and he has asked how the socialist state can best use the enormous energy of the individualist and feed his appetite so that he can contribute to the development of the socialist state. Here he follows other East German playwrights in using a "gargantuan" hero whose enormous potential is not recognized. Bauch's energy must be harnessed and his integrity must be protected if the state is to grow. The fact that Bauch must resist exploitation suggests that even the proletarian state is beset with a class problem, and Braun suggests ways to resolve it.

OTHER PLAYS: *Hans Faust* (1968).

**Brecht, Bertolt** (1898–1956). German dramatist, poet, essayist, novelist, and director. In 1968, Manfred Wekwerth, who assisted Brecht as a director at the Berliner Ensemble, made the following remark: "Brecht is a classical writer who is effective through success. Brecht as a fashion is over and done with. Let's begin now to work with Brecht." Wekwerth was referring to the academic quarrel about whether Brecht has ironically become a classical writer. He implies that the entire question has been answered by Brecht himself and that the academicians are wasting their time in trying to find the answer. One might go further than Wekwerth and argue that it is *not* ironical that Brecht has become popular and classical. This is what Brecht hoped might happen. To be sure, he saw himself as a classical writer in a socialist tradition in opposition to the very bourgeois academicians and critics who regard him as the most important dramatist of the twentieth century.

Brecht was born into a bourgeois family in Augsburg. His father owned a paper factory, and Brecht appeared to be headed toward a respectable bourgeois career. After completing his studies at the gymnasium, he went to Munich to study medicine and the natural sciences. But the war, which interrupted his studies, made him rethink his position *vis à vis* society and his choice of career. After writing theater reviews for the *Augsburger Volkswille* he returned to Munich and soon became an apprentice actor with the remarkable German comedian Karl Valentin, who taught him a great deal about both irony and mime. Brecht's early plays demonstrated his great zest for learning from such writers as Valentin, Frank Wedekind, and Georg Kaiser. All of them are passionate accounts of the violent attempts of outsiders to find a link to a society they ostensibly detest.

In 1924 Brecht moved to Berlin and became dramaturge at the Deutsches Theater. There he came in touch with the leading radical writers, critics, and directors of his time and began to turn to Marxism. The play *Mann ist Mann* (A Man's a Man, 1926) showed definite signs of Brecht's conversion to Marxist thinking. Moreover, the drama is structured along lines that anticipate Brecht's EPIC THEATER.

In 1928, the year of *The Threepenny Opera*, Brecht began attending the Marxist Proletarian School, and his plays written between 1928 and 1933 took on a more pronounced didactic tone. The aim of his short plays called *Lehrstücke* was to teach socialist tenets, and the enjoyment was to be provided in the development of a new consciousness both on the part of the audience and the actors.

Two longer plays, *Saint Joan of the Stockyards* (1929–31) and the adaptation of Gorki's *Mother* (1930–31), an adaptation of Gorki's novel, also have strong didactic elements. These two plays show Brecht's optimism about the outcome of the socialist struggle in Germany. This optimism was dimmed by the events of 1933.

With the advent of the Nazi dictatorship in Germany, Brecht began a period of wandering and hardship. In 1933 he emigrated to Austria, then to Switzerland, and finally to Denmark, where he remained until 1940. After 1940 he made his way to Finland and thence to the United States in 1941. During this difficult period many of Brecht's finest plays were written: *Galileo* (1937–1939), *Mother Courage and Her Children* (1938–1939), *The Good Woman of Setzuan* (1938–1942), *Herr Puntila und sein Knecht Matti* (1940), *The Resistible Rise of Arturo Ui* (1941), and *The Caucasian Chalk Circle* (1943–1945). He also wrote important theoretical essays on realism and the ALIENATION EFFECT. All the plays of this period dealt with a new concept of ethics. Working in exile, Brecht endeavored to show that justice is a matter of power, and that one of the most important virtues for members of the working class is cunning. This is also the chief virtue of the exile plays: their cunning in language and idea. Not only did Brecht use the alienation technique in these plays to demonstrate the distinction between reality and illusion, but he used alien settings sufficiently distant from the lives of spectators that they would not be moved by false emotions. This did not mean that Brecht was against moving the emotions of the audience. Indeed, he was forever trying to provoke his spectators to act—but to act with clear minds.

It was with a clear mind that Brecht opposed the House Committee on Un-American Activities on October 30, 1947. Within twenty-four hours he departed from America for Switzerland. There he worked in Zurich with the Schauspielhaus, and in 1949 he moved to East Berlin where he established the

BERLINER ENSEMBLE with his wife, Helene Weigel, and Erich Engel and Caspar Neher. Until the time of his death in 1956, Brecht worked constantly with the company and made it into one of the finest repertory groups in the world. Many critics like to believe that Brecht lost his creative talent, or was prevented from exercising it, when he moved to East Germany. The fact is that Brecht had always been first and foremost a practitioner. Once he was given his own theater and group of actors he concentrated all his energies on working out his theories and compositions onstage. Not only did he constantly rewrite his plays for production in the postwar years, refining them and sharpening the social criticism, but he wrote important adaptations that reflect his great creative talent. Sophocles' *Antigone* (1947, as *Die Antigone des Sophokles*), J. M. R. Lenz's *Der Hofmeister* (1950), Shakespeare's *Coriolanus* (1951–1953), Molière's *Don Juan* (1952), and George Farquhar's *The Recruiting Officer* (1955, as *Pauken und Trompeten*) were brilliantly revised in a way that stressed the class antagonisms both in the peculiar historical situation and in the analogous contemporary situation. The adaptation of "classical" works was part of Brecht's aim to reutilize all that was of value in the bourgeois tradition and make it serve the socialist cause. In the last years of his life, as can be seen in his important theoretical work *Kleines Organon für das Theater* (Short Organon for the Theater, 1948), Brecht was working toward a dialectical theater, which would be appropriate in the scientific age. He sought an object-subject relationship between the actors and the audience, and he believed that the theater would have to seek out the workers if it was to become progressive. This need for collaboration with the workers was part of a dialectical process of creating a new socialist aesthetic that would give audiences pleasure in making scientific discoveries and gaining a sense of liberation. In keeping with his theory of dialectics, Brecht believed all solutions to be imperfect and provisional. This is the reason he never cared to complete a definitive edition of his works, which he was constantly changing. In fact, many of his plays imply that the next generation will provide answers to the aesthetical and social questions he raises.

More than any other twentieth-century playwright, Brecht as a classical writer has exercised a dominating influence over postwar dramatists, not only in Europe, but in North America, South America, and the Far East. His theories of epic theater, alienation effect, gesture, and dialectics have given new impulses to contemporary playwrights. His plays, which draw on biblical language, English themes and language, Japanese *nō* plays, Chinese acting, Villon's poetry, Wedekind's plays, Valentin's comedies, Marxism, and sporting techniques, have a universal appeal. Because of Brecht's insight into history and the class struggle, his plays are extremely relevant today. Throughout the world scholars are publishing treatises on Brecht's work. Recent editions of his works reveal that he was not only a great dramatist but a superb poet and literary critic. He certainly is not a passing fashion, as some critics have argued earlier. On the other hand, it is still an open question whether his classical status can work, as Brecht wanted it to work, for radical changes in the theater and society.

OTHER PLAYS SINCE 1945: *Die Tage der Commune* (The Days of the Commune, written 1948–49, produced 1956), *Herrnburger Bericht* (Report from Herrnburg, 1951), *Turandot oder der Kongress der Weisswäscher* (Turandot, or The Congress of the Whitewashers, written 1953–54), *Der Prozess des Jeanne d'Arc zu Rouen 1431* (The Trial of Jeanne d'Arc at Rouen 1431, 1952).

**Bridie, James** (1888–1951). Scottish dramatist. A Glasgow doctor, and for a time a professor of medicine, whose real name was Osborne Henry Mavor, Bridie had established a modest reputation in Scotland before *The Anatomist,* a dramatized history of the Scottish body-snatchers Burke and Hare, was presented on the London stage in 1931. *Tobias and the Angel,* aptly called by the critic J. C. Trewin a "venture in the colloquial-ironical-poetical," followed, also in 1931, and thereafter the majority of Bridie's plays were seen in London as well as his native Scotland. Most of his plays have a Scottish background, and a favorite device of the dramatist is to present the incursion of the supernatural upon an otherwise homely, straightforward, and everyday setting. A playwright who would tantalize audiences with the startling ingenuity of his opening scenes, he was often criticized for the weakness of his final acts, but his failures, like those of Shaw, were the failures of a good-humored, tolerant intellectual impatient with the petty requirements of drama, and not those of an incompetent writer of second rank. One of the few writers of his age to attempt to circumvent the limitations of naturalistic drama, Bridie was sometimes referred to as a dramatist of the stature of Shaw; but his work lacks the dialectical edge of the Irish dramatist, and the mixture of whimsy, romance, and irony that characterizes much of his writing has proved to lack the staying power of Shavian drama. Outside Scotland, the past decade has seen few revivals of his work. During his lifetime he was active as chairman of the Glasgow Citizens' Theatre, the foremost Scottish repertory theater.

OTHER PLAYS SINCE 1945: *Lancelot* (1946), *John Knox* (1947), *Dr. Angelus* (1947), *Gog and MacGog* (1948), *Daphne Laureola* (1949), *The Tintock Cup* (with George Munro, 1949), *Mr. Gillie* (1950), *The Queen's Comedy* (1950), *The Baikie Charivari* (1952).

**Broadway.** The commercial theater district in midtown New York City. These theaters have large seating capacities, usually one or more balconies, and traditional stages with a proscenium arch; productions are expensive and theater tickets proportionally high, so that plays are chosen in the hope of their being long-running "hits." Musicals and popular comedy flourish, but some of the best American playwrights, including O'Neill, Miller, Williams, and Albee, have also met with success on the "great white way." (See OFF-BROADWAY and OFF-OFF-BROADWAY.)

**Bronnen, Arnolt** (1895–1959). Austrian dramatist, journalist, and critic.

The son of the Austrian-Jewish playwright Ferdinand Bronnen, who used the pseudonym Franz Adamus, Bronnen led a life of extreme commitments. During the 1920s, he was an expressionist; during the 1930s, a Nazi; during the late 1940s, a socialist, and eventually a Communist. He is best known for his *Vatermord* (Patricide, written 1915, produced 1920), a landmark of expressionism, and for the fact that he was a friend of Bertolt Brecht and wrote about him in *Tage mit Brecht* (Days With Brecht, 1960). Bronnen wrote three plays after World War II, one a comedy about Americans who visit Salzkammergut, *Die jüngste Nacht* (The Recent Night, 1958). However, Bronnen never recovered his expressionist touch. His postwar years were devoted mainly to criticism and dramatic theory. He held positions in Linz, Vienna, and East Berlin where he worked as a theater critic.

OTHER PLAYS SINCE 1945: *Die Kette Kolin* (The Kolin Chain, 1950), *Kaprun* (1955).

**Brook, Peter** (born 1925). English director. Born in London and educated at Westminster, Greshams School, and Oxford (where he founded the Oxford University Film Society), Brook directed his first London production in 1943. He quickly demonstrated his ability to impose a sensitive and original interpretation upon his text, combined with a flair for coaxing outstanding performances out of the actors with whom he worked. While still in his early twenties he was in the forefront of English directors, introducing the work of Cocteau and Sartre to London audiences. From 1947 to 1950 he worked as director of productions at the Royal Opera House, Covent Garden; returning to the drama, he maintained his reputation throughout the '50s in productions of classical and modern authors. His contribution toward the development of contemporary English theater took a distinctively new turn in the years following his appointment as co-director of the Royal Shakespeare Company in 1962 (a post which he relinquished in 1968). His production of *King Lear* in 1962 reflected the influence of Brecht, but by the following year Brook's interest in the alienation devices of the German dramatist was combined with an admiration for the work of Jean Genet and the French theorist Antonin Artaud. In the autumn of 1963 Brook and Charles Marowitz devoted an experimental season to the "theater of cruelty," among the most substantial achievements of which was a production of Genet's *The Screens* in which Brechtian and Artaudian devices were combined. The style evolved by this experimental group was further developed in Brook's 1964 production of *The Persecution and Assassination of Marat as performed by the inmates of the Asylum of Charenton under the direction of the Marquis of Sade* by Peter Weiss (see GREAT BRITAIN). The grotesque techniques adapted for the representation of violence and madness on the stage in the latter production suggested that Brook had taken to heart Artaud's call for a theater that sought to conduct an assault upon the senses of the audience without the intervention of a literary text; and the years following this production saw Brook engaged in the paradoxical search for a play that would be expressive of actor and director rather than of author. Increasingly eager to shock audiences into a sense of the irrational violence, personal and political, which Brook now seemed to see at the heart of the human condition, he worked for four months in 1966 with his Royal Shakespeare Company upon *US*, a passionate denunciation of the American role in Vietnam, which combined the techniques of the "theater of cruelty" with a documentary approach intentionally biased to the point of caricature. Critics, however, were less impressed with those aspects of *US* owing most to collaborative rehearsal than with the more traditional duologue in the latter half of the play between two contemporary intellectuals, aghast and helpless in the face of world violence. For the National Theatre in 1968 Brook produced Seneca's *Oedipus* (in an adaptation by poet Ted Hughes), superimposing ritualized performances and grossly phallic imagery upon the nervous intensity of the text. In the same year he published *The Empty Space*, where he called for a "holy theatre" at the heart of which should be a secular ritual to replace the religious practices of the past.

Brook's constant search for innovation has laid him open to the charge of capriciousness. His productions in the late '60s reflected, as well as the theories of Artaud and Brecht, the influence of the Polish director Jerzy Grotowski and the American Julian Beck's Living Theater company. But while Brook is undeniably more eclectic than consistent in his approach, there can be no doubt that his quest for what is best in the theory and practice of the modern stage has helped to create a theater in which the director replaces the writer as the principal creative force. Since the New York production of *Marat/Sade* his influence upon the avant-garde theater of the United States has been considerable. Charles Marowitz discusses Brook in "Lear Log" and "Notes on the Theatre of Cruelty," in *Theatre at Work*, edited by Marowitz and Simon Trussler (1967); the play *US* is analyzed by Albert Hunt and others in *US* (1967); "Director in Interview: Peter Brook talks to Peter Ansorge" appeared in *Plays and Players* for October 1970.

**Broszkiewicz, Jerzy** (born 1922). Polish dramatist. Broszkiewicz was born and educated in Lwów. He made his literary debut in 1945 and in the first decade after World War II established himself as a short-story author, writer on music, novelist, and author of books for young people. Particularly, his biographical novel on Chopin achieved considerable popularity. Although his debut as playwright belonged to this period, Broszkiewicz's successful career as a dramatist began in 1956 when his play IMIONA WŁADZY (The Names of Power), alluding to current political events, was produced with wide acclaim. Since then he has written more than a dozen plays, which confirmed his reputation as a prolific and versatile author, though he has never quite fulfilled his initial promise. Broszkiewicz was awarded the State Literary Prize in 1951.

In his plays Broszkiewicz experiments with a wide range of subjects and techniques. Though he soon departed from his early socialist realist beginnings, he continued occasionally to write realistic plays—perhaps to fulfill a self-imposed national duty. In a notable example, *Skandal w Hellbergu* (A Scandal in Hellberg, 1961), cast in the form of a thriller set in a small West German town, vestiges of the Nazi past and attitudes are uncovered in the characters' motives and actions. On the other end of the scale *Koniec Księgi VI* (The End of Book Six, 1963), about Copernicus' completing his great revolutionary treatise on astronomy, is a play in the tradition of the historical-biographical school of Polish playwriting of the late '40s and early '50s. *Wesele na osiedlu* (Wedding in the Settlement, 1965) is a contemporary comedy, set in the recently built industrial township of Nowa Huta, which presents a confrontation, and a comment on, the emergence of a new society out of small-town and village elements. Nonetheless, ever since *The Names of Power*, Broszkiewicz's heart has been in searching for new forms and styles. These may vary from a basically straightforward narrative set in a framework of loosely connected scenes, as in *Przychodzę opowiedzieć* (I Am Coming to Tell, 1964), which presents a panorama of an average Pole's wartime destinies, to such symbolic plays as *Bar wszystkich świętych* (All Saints' Café, 1962), where a shady bar frequented by people of doubtful past and occupations undergoes mysterious transformations, representing the many influences that contribute to the demoralization of the play's inexperienced, idealistic heroes. In *Jonasz i błazen* (Jonah and the Jester, 1958), Broszkiewicz considers, under farcical guise, the serious problem of the artist's apparent helplessness in face of authority and force, and sees the solution in the sage's assuming a mask of the fool. This theme is further developed in *Dwie przygody Lemuela Gullivera* (Two Adventures of Lemuel Gulliver, 1961), which is practically a monologue by Gulliver (who also plays the part of narrator), speaking first to an imaginary Lilliputian, then to an imaginary Brobdingnagian—a *tour de force* in which the author probes into relations between the strong and the weak. In *Głupiec i inni* (The Fool and Others, 1959), he comes close to the theater of the absurd; the play's hero accuses himself of perhaps imaginary crimes, and by doing so exposes the hypocrisy of his relatives—the so-called decent people. A similar theme is explored in *Dziejowa rola Pigwy* (The Historic Role of Quince, 1960); the hero's desperate efforts to assert himself emotionally, professionally, or as a public figure turn into repeated failures in an impossible world and end in his suicide. The play begins and closes with his funeral scenes, in which the corpse comes back to life to play out the crucial moments from his past. In the epilogue he revives not so much to assert his immortality as to convince the audience that people who are basically honest and not adjusted to the world's dishonesty are still needed and will reappear among us, for better or worse.

Broszkiewicz is a capable, though uneven, writer. One could say that his very versatility works against him. Wishing to score successes on the front of realistic drama (in his case involving both the "well-made play" and a "panoramic," narrative kind of writing), as well as to join the avant-garde, he may

73

be said to have fallen short of the highest achievements in either form. There is no doubt that his strongest asset is the capacity for writing concise allegorical plays based on monologue directed to a single purpose, as in the first act of *The Names of Power,* or in his *Gulliver* play. Many of his plays reveal also a gift for social comedy and satire.

OTHER PLAYS: *Bancroftowie* (The Bancrofts, with G. Gottesmann, 1953), *Zaczyna się dzień* (The Day Begins, with G. Gottesmann, 1955), *Ta wieś Mogiła* (This Village Mogila, 1966), *Karczma pod czarnym wąsem* (Inn Under the Black Mustache), *Między poniedziałkiem a sobotą* (Between Monday and Saturday, a television play), *Przepis ze starej kroniki* (The Recipe from an Old Chronicle, subtitled "An Opera Libretto," 1968).

**Bruckner, Friedrich** [pseudonym for **Theodor Tagger**] (1891–1958). Austrian dramatist, poet, critic, and director. Since his father was a wealthy Austrian businessman and his mother was French, Bruckner received a cosmopolitan and international upbringing that culminated in his studying at the universities of Vienna, Paris, and Berlin. His early writings were not in the field of drama. He concentrated mainly on poetry, short stories, and essays, and in 1917 he founded the expressionist magazine *Marsyas.* Gradually Bruckner became interested in drama and moved from Vienna to Berlin to establish the Renaissancetheater, which he directed from 1923 to 1929. It was during this time that he assumed the name Bruckner and began writing expressionist dramas that exposed the depravity of the times. He worked closely with Erwin Piscator and other radical directors. After he moved from the Renaissancetheater in 1929, he produced works by such political dramatists as Brecht and Bronnen at the Theater am Kurfürstendamm. During this period he wrote his best play, *Elisabeth von England* (1930), which also marked his move to writing historical dramas under the influence of the *Neue Sachlichkeit* trend in Germany.

In 1933, because of the shift of power in Germany, Bruckner was forced to flee Berlin. After a short stay in France, he traveled to the United States, where his play *Die Rassen* (The Races, 1933), an attack on National Socialism and anti-Semitism, was produced. While in the United States, Bruckner taught, directed, and translated. His plays written during his exile were largely historical and depicted the evils of dictatorship. After his return to Austria in 1948, Bruckner moved toward classicism in an effort to portray the pettiness of man and the bureaucratization of life. His plays make use of classical structure and choruses to comment on the lack of harmony and meaning in modern society. *Pyrrhus und Andromache* (1952) employs classical motifs taken from Sophocles and Euripides to highlight the tragedy of lovers who are frustrated by society. In *Der Tod einer Puppe* (The Death of a Doll, 1956), a woman who is full of life is transformed into a cosmetic doll. In *Der Kampf mit dem Engel* (The Battle With the Angel, 1956), the widow of a rich businessman learns that money will lead her nowhere. Bruckner's final plays were written while he served as dramaturge at the Schiller Theater in West Berlin. His social criticism in these late social dramas is not as devastating as it was in his early expressionist plays. Nevertheless, Bruckner's political perspective, which shaped his dramas from beginning to end, reveals his concern and insights in the reification process of modern man.

OTHER PLAYS SINCE 1945: *Die Befreiten* (The Liberated Ones, 1945), *Fährten* (Tracks, 1948), *Früchte des Nichts* (The Fruits of Nothingness, 1951), *Die Buhlschwestern* (The Courtesans, 1954, adapted from J. M. R. Lenz's play), *Das irdene Wägelchen* (The Little Clay Cart, 1957).

**Bruun Olsen, Ernst** (born 1923). Danish actor, director, and playwright. Bruun Olsen made his debut as a playwright in 1956 with a comedy revue *Trylleri i gaden* (Magic in the Street), written with Poul Henningsen (1894–1967). His first big success was the musical drama *Teenagerlove* (1962). An outspoken socialist, Bruun Olsen has used the medium of musical satire to criticize the Danish Social Democratic Party for collaborating with capitalists to build a materialistic "consumer society," thus betraying long-established socialist goals. *Teenagerlove* is about a fading, thirty-five-year-old rock-and-roll singer, Billy Jack, whose grasping efforts to remain at the top include abandoning the girl who loves him. In *Bal i den Borgerlige* (Ball at the Country Club, 1966) a working-class couple are so eager to have their son accepted in upper-middle-class circles that they forget almost entirely the socialist ideals they had shared twenty years earlier during the war, when they first met and fell in love. Bruun Olsen's later works—*Hvor gik Nora hen, da hun gik ud?* (Where Did Nora Go When She Went Out? 1968) and *De fredsommelige* (The Peaceful Ones, written 1969)—have not been as effective as his early efforts, prompting some critics to raise questions about his ultimate importance as a dramatist. Nevertheless, *Teenagerlove* brought to the Scandinavian theater a vigor and excitement that it had not seen for some time. Finn Savery (born 1933), Brunn Olsen's longtime musical collaborator, has composed bold, engaging melodies that have helped to make popular hits of several of their songs.

**Buero Vallejo, Antonio** (born 1916). Spanish dramatist. The wonder of Buero Vallejo's career is that it ever was. He spent some six years in prison for his Republican activities during the Civil War. Yet in spite of the sustained opposition of many critics whose motives were more political than aesthetic, he early gained wide recognition as the most important playwright of the contemporary Spanish theater. The 1949 production of *Historia de una escalera* (The Stairway), his first play and still his most influential, heralded the postwar resurgence of serious drama. In a tenement house in a working-class neighborhood, three generations of four families struggle to determine their individual destinies, and fall into identical patterns of hope, frustration, and defeat. The stairway where over a period of thirty years the characters meet, sometimes in love, sometimes in hate, always in expectation of a decisive moment, is the true protagonist of the play, delimiting the closed horizons of their universe. This realistic portrayal of the everyday existence of the lower class, uncomprised by reversion to picturesque *costumbrismo* or farce, is the formula subsequently adopted by the exponents of the social theater, Lauro Olmo, Ricardo Rodríguez Buded, and Carlos Muñíz. But Buero himself transcends the bounds of the mode for whose life, if not conception, his play is responsible. Unlike its progeny, *Historia de una escalera* emphasizes the characters' flaws as much as society's in tracing the causes of their failure. His later plays, moreover, reveal a metaphysical rather than social preoccupation, developing not typical but unique situations symbolic of man's existential predicament. His theme is man's search for truth about himself; his symbols, light and dark, vision and blindness. In both *En la ardiente oscuridad* (In the Flaming Darkness, 1950) and *El concierto de San Ovidio* (1962) the blind are led by the blind and given insight into the reality of their lives. Man's isolation, his inability to communicate thwarting his attempt to discover the true nature of his relationships with others, is the variation on the theme in *La tejedora de sueños* (The Weaver of Dreams, 1952), *La señal que se espera* (The Awaited Sign, 1952), and *Madrugada* (Dawn, 1953). History, too, offers moments illustrative of man's efforts to rend the veil that obscures individual and collective existence. Velázquez in *Las Meninas* (1960) and Esquilache, a reformer of the eighteenth-century court of Carlos III, in *Un soñador para un pueblo* (A Dreamer for the People, 1958) are individuals in whom Buero discovers eternally valid responses to a hostile environment. In spite of the return to a social orientation in *Hoy es fiesta* (Today's a Holiday, 1956) and *Las cartas boca abajo* (Cards Face Down, 1957) and the political implications of *Aventura en lo gris* (Adventure in Gray, 1963), Buero as resolutely rejects the distortions of a theater committed to a specific sociopolitical position as he does those of the "theater of evasion" and the boulevard comedy. His is a tragic theater in which man's fate is the result of the usually futile struggle to overcome the limitations, both personal and extrapersonal, which hamper the development of full human potential. That man fails negates neither the existence of free will nor the relevance of hope. In fact, rather than succumb to a fashionable nihilism born of doubt without faith, Buero manages the limited optimism of a faith which doubts.

OTHER PLAYS: *Las palabras en la arena* (Words in the Sand, one act, 1949), *Casi un cuento de hadas* (Almost a Fairy Tale, 1953), *Irene o el tesoro* (Irene or The Treasure, 1954), *El tragaluz* (The Skylight, 1967).

**Bullins, Ed.** American playwright. Part of the new black theater, Bullins writes terse, angry plays about blacks and ostensibly for blacks (though occasionally his tell-it-like-it-is idiom and anecdote seem to provide slices of life for a curious white audience rather than genuine drama for a black community that knows how it is). *Goin' a Buffalo* (1968) was given a staged reading at the American Place Theatre. *In the Wine Time* (1968) was first produced at the New Lafayette Theatre, an experimental professional theater for blacks in Harlem. The success of the triple bill *A Son, Come Home, The Electronic Nigger,* and *Clara's Ole Man* at the American Place Theatre in 1968 brought the group a commercial midtown run, billed as *Ed Bullins' Plays. Gentleman Caller* and *How Do You Do* were produced in London (1969) and in New York as part of an evening called *Black Quartet* (1969); *The Pig Pen* was given at the American Place Theatre in 1970. Bullins served as guest editor of the black theater edition of *The Drama Review* (Summer 1968) and is currently a member of the New Lafayette Theatre.

**Buzzati, Dino** (born 1906). Italian dramatist. This distinguished journalist and novelist achieved his first significant theatrical success with *Un caso clinico* (A Clinical Case, 1953). It remains his best play and one of the outstanding dramas of modern times. Although it is scarcely known in English-speaking countries, it has had great success in other countries throughout the world. Many critics consider Kafka to be a dominant influence on Buzzati, but he is also influenced by the legends and fables of the northern mountain country of Belluno in the Dolomites where he was born.

*Un caso clinico* is based on one of his short stories, "Sette piani" (Seven Flights). The play is divided into two parts and thirteen scenes and dramatizes the progressive death of the wealthy, northern businessman Giovanni Corte. Troubled by hallucinations of a female voice beckoning to him from the distance and the specter of a woman apparently haunting his home, Corte is persuaded to consult a famous specialist at his ultramodern hospital. There is something ominous in the cold rationality of the specialist and the super-efficiency of his staff.

Almost unexpectedly, Corte becomes a surgical patient. They assure him at first that his condition is not serious, and he is assigned to a room on the top floor, where the rooms of the healthiest patients are to be found. There is a descending organization in the hospital. Those suffering from serious ailments are to be found on the lower floors, until one arrives at the first floor, the antechamber of death. Corte is helpless against the machine-like efficiency of the hospital. Ultimately, he is brought down to the first floor and discarded amidst the dying. His mother arrives to take him home, but it is too late. The hospital is a metaphor of contemporary society: cold, efficient, uncompromising, and cruel. In such a society, rich and poor alike are hustled away when they are no longer needed.

The same sterile world is created in *Un verme al Ministero* (A Worm in the Ministry, 1960), the drama of a totalitarian revolution. The ministry itself is a bureaucratic nightmare, full of whispers, rumors, and fear. Throughout the early part of the drama the workers of the ministry are unaware that the rumblings in the distance are actually the Morzi, a fanatical sect advancing on the government. Eventually, the Morzi assume power, and the ministry is converted into a paragon of military, machine-like efficiency. The villain and protagonist of the play is Professor Morales, archetype of the deceptive and parasitic bureaucrat, who sacrifices friend and foe alike for his own desires. Morales is determined to possess Flora, daughter of the former chief official, Palesierna. In order to destroy Palesierna, Morales accuses him of worshiping idols, a crime punishable by death. However, Morales' treachery is ultimately revealed. He is brought before a Crucifix. Just as he is about to raise his hand in defiance of the Crucifix to prove his allegiance to the dictatorship, the roar of a hurricane is heard, and a Christ-like figure appears to condemn Morales.

*La colonna infame* (The Infamous Column, 1962), set in Milan of 1630 during a plague, is a less expressionistic play than some of Buzzati's other works, but it is equally critical of man's deceit and treachery. In it two health officials employ nefarious means to discover the individual who is causing the plague, even if it means accusing the innocent.

OTHER PLAYS: *La rivolta contro i poveri* (Revolt Against the Poor, 1946), *Drammatica fine di un noto musicista* (The Dramatic Death of a Famous Musician, 1955), *Il mantello* (The Mantle, 1960), *Don Giovanni* (1961), *L'uomo che andrà in America* (The Man Leaving for America, 1962), *La fine del borghese* (The End of a Bourgeois, 1966), *La famosa invasione degli orsi in Sicilia* (The Famous Invasion of the Bears in Sicily, 1967).

# C

Caligula (1945). A four-act play by Albert Camus. It was first performed on September 26, 1945, at the Théâtre Hébertot, Paris, under the direction of Paul Œttly. Begun before the war, published for the first time in 1944, and then in its final form in 1958, this play devoted to the mad young Roman emperor assassinated in A.D. 41 is a dramatization of the discovery of the ABSURD and the disastrous temptation such a discovery may provoke: that of nihilism.

Following the death of his sister, with whom he has been incestuously in love, Caligula is struck by some elementary but hidden truths: "Men die and are not happy," and "The world, as it is, is unbearable." Caligula rebels passionately against this fate by imitating it, by becoming it in all his purity, that is, by eliminating illusion and carrying logic to its most monstrous extremes. An absolute ruler, he uses his freedom to establish an altogether arbitrary dominion over the Romans. Since death is the absurd event *par excellence*, Caligula aims at destroying everything. Beyond that destruction, he hopes to reach the absolute and accomplish the impossible. Now, as Camus said, "one cannot destroy everything without also destroying oneself." Caligula, carrying his logic to the extreme, does everything necessary to provoke his own assassination, that is, to commit what Camus called "a higher suicide."

*Caligula* is thus the tragedy of a mistake—that of negating man. The play would seem to reflect the period in Camus's career in which he exorcized the temptation of Nietzschean excess. The absurd is a lived experience that must then be assumed by the mind as well as in action. Seeking the absolute is the wrong solution, for the payoff is total destruction. Other possible attitudes, although not solutions, are represented by minor characters: Caligula's mistress, Caesonia, embodies the life of the flesh; young Scipion personifies purity in goodness, just as Caligula personifies purity in evil; Cherea, Caligula's friend, and quite as lucid as he, suggests *life* as a supreme value.

Around an apparently intellectual theme Camus wrote a highly theatrical play. His Caligula is not a madman but the organizer of an experiment: He makes the life of his subjects into didactic theater, but the performances end with real blood and real corpses. The play consists in debates about life and death, shot through with flashes of lyricism and scenes at once burlesque and bloody, in which Caligula humiliates and terrorizes his familiars by his deliberate and extravagant schemes: He organizes a poetry competition in which the bad poets are sentenced to obliterating their compositions with their tongues; he disguises himself as Venus so that the Patricians will worship him; he has a new "treatise on execution" read to the Patricians in which he comically justifies his death sentences in terms of the universal guilt of his subjects; he poisons a Patrician and strangles his mistress, Caesonia, with his own hands. Thus, taken as a whole, *Caligula* is a black feast and the frenzied application of the nihilistic principle, by which, in an absurd universe, everything is permissible.

*Caligula's* success in 1945 was due, on the one hand, to the performance of the young actor Gérard Philipe, and on the other, to the resemblance of Caligula's philosophy, with its disastrous consequences, to that of the Nazi intellectuals.

**Calvo Sotelo, Joaquín** (born 1905). Spanish dramatist. Having completed his law studies, Calvo Sotelo was admitted in 1927 to the prestigious Cuerpo de Abogados del Estado. Always high in governmental circles, active in political and literary organizations, he is a member of the Royal Academy. Calvo Sotelo's earliest plays antedate the Civil War, but his reputation was firmly established only during the 1940s and 1950s. The plays of these years fall within two distinct categories. *La visita que no tocó el timbre* (The Visitor Who Didn't Ring the Bell, 1950) and *Una muchachita de Valladolid* (1957) are representative of his lighter vein, drawing-room comedies not without touches of social comment but designed primarily as entertainment. His dramas, on the other hand, deal with serious moral, social, and political themes. The intent of plays such as *Criminal de guerra* (War Crime, 1951), *El jefe* (The Chief, 1953), and *La ciudad sin Dios* (City Without God, 1957) is to probe problems of the day, positing rather than resolving conflicts, with a view to eliciting socially beneficial controversy. The controversy attendant on the production of *La muralla* (The Wall, 1954) made of it one of the most important plays of the postwar theater. The protagonist, jolted from nominal Catholicism to true faith by a brush with death, determines to right a long ignored wrong that now lies heavy on his conscience. He will restore to its rightful heir the estate, fraudulently acquired, on which his entire fortune is based. Thwarted at every turn by family and friends, who, to justify their opposition, adduce social against Christian dicta, he dies without realizing the restitution, though never deviating from his intent. In spite of the play's terse structure and lively dialogue, its success must be attributed in large part to its relevancy to contemporary problems of the bourgeoisie rather than to its artistic worth.

OTHER PLAYS SINCE 1936: *Milagro en la Plaza del Progreso* (Miracle in Progress Plaza, 1953), *Historia de un resentido* (Resentful, 1956), *La herencia* (The Inheritance, 1957), *Cartas credenciales* (Letters of Credit, 1960), *Dinero* (Money, 1961), *El proceso del Arzobispo Carranza* (The Trial of Archbishop

Carranza, 1964), *El poder* (Power, 1965), *El baño de las ninfas* (The Bath of the Nymphs, 1966), *La amante* (The Lover, 1968).

**Campton, David** (born 1924). English dramatist. A native of Leicester (where he still lives), who worked first for the local Education Authority and later for the Gas Board, Campton had by 1956 begun to build a reputation as the author of one-act plays, conventional in nature and suitable for amateur performance. In that year he took up writing as a full-time profession, contributing scripts under contract to Associated-Rediffusion TV and plays to Stephen Joseph's Theatre-in-the-Round Company at Scarborough. In 1958 he joined that company as an actor.

Little of Campton's work has been seen in London. From 1955 until 1962 he contributed annually to Joseph's program at Scarborough. The characteristic form for his best work is the one-act play and much of his recent work, although published in acting editions, reached its first audience through the medium of radio or television. His neglect on the London stage is an inadequate measure of his quality as a playwright. While he has shown throughout his career that he is capable of returning to the light, conventional comedy of character with which his career began (*Ring of Roses*—1958, *The Manipulator*—broadcast, 1964), Campton's importance among contemporary English dramatists lies in his contribution to the theater of the absurd. As early as 1957 *The Lunatic View* (subtitled by its author "a comedy of menace," a term soon to be applied to Pinter's early work) offered a surreal picture of domestic apathy in the face of encroaching anarchy in the outside world, of murder, and of the aftermath of nuclear destruction. The latter topic was one to which he returned in *Little Brother, Little Sister* and *Mutatis Mutandis,* two of the four one-act plays which appeared in the ominously titled *Four Minute Warning* (1961). Campton's preoccupation with nuclear disaster is a clue to his style. "To my mind," he has written, "the Theatre of the Absurd is a weapon against complacency. . . . The weapon of complacency is the pigeon-hole. Pigeon-hole an idea, and it becomes harmless. (We have a clean bomb.) It is difficult to be complacent when the roots of one's existence are shaken, which is what the Absurd at its best does." Campton's battle against complacency succeeds only partially, however, rarely "shaking the roots of one's existence," because precise, rational ideas can be clearly discerned behind his technique. His characters lack the sinister ambivalence of Pinter's and his dialogue lacks the freewheeling detachment from meaning, casting doubt on the status of language and experience, of Ionesco's early work. When the two diplomats in *Out of the Flying Pan* (1960) mouth nonsense at one another ("My country devours nothing but peas, will never devour anything but peas, has never devoured anything but peas"), the political symbolism is unambiguous. Campton uses the absurd technique to discuss the unspeakable topic of nuclear war, and once the first premises of his plays have been unraveled (that the adolescent innocents in *Little Brother, Little Sister* live in a fallout shelter, their only knowledge of the former world outside derived from the travesties of their cook's fading memory, or that in *Mutatis Mutandis* the husband is gently breaking the news to his wife that their son is a post-nuclear mutant), their intellectual content reveals itself as humane and commendable, but lacking in the darker and deeper exploration of the human psyche characteristic of other writers in the school of the absurd.

Campton's recent work, which has consolidated rather than enlarged his reputation, shows the increasing range of a dramatist who continues to develop. In the one-act play *Two Leaves and a Stalk* (1967) the conversation of two elderly ladies over an ailing potted plant reveals their unspoken fear of death. *Incident* (televised, 1965), a play for women set in a hotel whose management, with all the familiar circumlocutions of racial prejudice, finds no room for guests by the name of Smith, moves beyond the boundary of satire when Miss Jones, a champion of the Smiths, discovers that she unconsciously shares an element of the irrational prejudice against which she fights. Despite some moments of near melodrama, *Where Have All the Ghosts Gone?* (televised, 1969) is a moving portrait of an alcoholic who has made her daughter a scapegoat for her husband's death and is tamed and at the same time dehumanized when the daughter marries a prosaic accountant.

Campton's talents have revealed themselves happily in short revue sketches, which have been seen at the Library Theatre, Scarborough; at the Nottingham Playhouse; and in the West End revues *One Over the Eight* and *On the Brighter Side*. A number of these are published in *On Stage* (1964).

OTHER PLAYS: *Going Home* (one act, 1949), *Sunshine on the Righteous* (one act, 1954), *The Laboratory* (winner of the second prize in the British Drama League one-act Play Festival, winner of the one-act Playwriting Competition organized by the Tavistock Repertory Company; 1954), *The Cactus Garden* (1955), *Dragons Are Dangerous* (1955), *Idol in the Sky* (1956), *The Lunatic View* (*A Smell of Burning, Memento Mori, Getting and Spending*, and *Then . . .* , 1957), *The Gift of Fire* (adapted from *Frankenstein*, 1959), *A View from the Brink* (*Out of the Flying Pan, Mutatis Mutandis, Soldier from the Wars Returning*, and *At Sea*, 1960), *Four Minute Warning* (the plays of *A View from the Brink*, with *Little Brother, Little Sister* replacing *Out of the Flying Pan*, 1961), *Usher* (adaptation, 1962), *Funeral Dance* (one act, 1962), *Silence on the Battlefield* (one act, televised, 1964), *The Life and Death of Almost Everybody* (1970).

An interview with Campton appeared in *New Theatre Magazine* in 1970.

**Camus, Albert** (1913–1960). French dramatist, novelist, and essayist. Born into a very poor family in Mondovi, Algeria, Camus—thanks to a scholarship and various small jobs—was able to complete secondary school and begin advanced studies in philosophy. He published two collections of essays before the war (*L'Envers et l'endroit*, 1937; *Noces*, 1938). Because of tuberculosis, he was not drafted in 1939. After the defeat of France in 1940 Camus not only continued to write (*L'Etranger*, 1942; *Le Mythe de Sisyphe*, 1942) but became a clandestine fighter in the resistance group "Combat." His post-war activities as a political journalist (*Actuelles*, 1950–1956), novelist (*La Peste*, 1947; *La Chute*, 1956), essayist (*L'Homme révolté*, 1951), and play-wright brought him into the foreground of French intellectual life at the same time as Jean-Paul Sartre, with whom he was at first in agreement and then in open conflict. He was awarded the Nobel Prize in 1957 and was killed in an automobile accident in 1960.

At first tempted by Communism and Nietzschean philosophy, Camus sub-sequently became widely known for his reflections on the ABSURD, which led him to reject abstract or totalitarian ideologies and to seek to establish a lucid and coherent line of conduct that would assure human freedom and happiness. His works as a whole are an effort to reconcile a passionate love of life with the demands of truth and justice.

Although his plays are perhaps not as successful as his other writings, Camus was fascinated by theater early in life. In Algeria, during the '30s, he directed the Théâtre du Travail and then the Théâtre de l'Equipe, writing plays for them (in collaboration with some of the members: *Révolte dans les Asturies* [Rebellion in the Asturias], 1936) and even acting for them. The second of his plays to be performed, *Caligula* (1945), was begun as early as 1938. From 1944 to 1960, in addition to writing four original plays, Camus adapted several foreign works, including Faulkner's *Requiem for a Nun* (1956) and Dostoevski's *The Possessed* (1959). His original plays illustrate the main themes of his moral and philosophical thinking. In *Le Malentendu* (Cross Purposes, 1944) and CALIGULA, both published in 1944, Camus cre-ated characters who are at grips with the absurd and who, as the result of a mistaken choice in their line of conduct, end by causing their own destruction. *L'Etat de siège* (State of Siege, 1948) is an allegory of totalitarian thinking and oppression, represented by the Plague, and the different attitudes—de-structive or liberating—taken by the men faced with it. *Les Justes* (The Just Assassins, 1949), derived from actual events in Russia in 1905, is based on the agonized conflicts of the revolutionary terrorists at the time of an assassi-nation.

Given the questions raised, Camus's plays are characteristic of postwar France for the same reason as Sartre's. Traditional psychology is relegated to the background and replaced by situations in which extreme and violent acts point up man's relationship to a universe of absurdity and oppression. In Camus the objective is to find a way to happiness without denying the es-sential truth of the absurd.

By systematically killing off the lonely guests at her inn, in the name of a happiness she passionately desires, Martha, the heroine of *Le Malentendu*, ends as the victim of a trap of fate: She kills her own brother, who himself had made the mistake of playing with the happiness he anticipated by concealing his identity. The terrorists in *Les Justes,* who desire the advent of a happy and just humanity, apply their notion of "everything is permissible" to carrying out a collective plan—as Caligula had done in carrying out his personal plan—and founder in contradictions that destroy the very purpose of their act.

Camus's plays have been criticized as being too intellectual. They indeed often give the impression of being calculated demonstrations and are far more devoid of naturalistic details and circumstances than Sartre's works. Yet behind all the reasoning, one feels the throb of intense passion. In this respect Camus's plays represent an attempt at a rigorous and austere modern tragedy—which does not include variety: *Caligula* is a kind of frenzied orgy of evil, sometimes burlesque, often lyrical; *Le Malentendu* is a somewhat Kafkaesque melodrama, in which the tension is never relaxed; *Les Justes,* in an atmosphere of suspense, is shot through with tenderness and pathos. As for *L'Etat de siège,* it was an attempt to create, with the help of the director Jean-Louis Barrault, a form of total theater in which lyricism, pantomime, and allegory are combined in the great spectacle of men fighting the Plague.

ADAPTATIONS: Pierre de Larivey, *Les Esprits* (The Ghosts, 1953), Calderón de la Barca, *The Devotion of the Cross* (1953).

**Canetti, Elias** (born 1905). Austrian dramatist, novelist, and sociologist. Born in Bulgaria, Canetti traveled throughout Europe as a child, with the result that he is fluent in several languages and cosmopolitan in orientation. From 1924 to 1929 he studied social science in Vienna and came under the influence of Karl Kraus and Hermann Broch. In the following years, he began to study mass psychology and produced the results of his studies in fictional form. His first play, *Hochzeit* (The Wedding), was written in 1932 and his mammoth novel *Die Blendung* (Auto-da-Fé) was completed in 1935. Both deal with man's ability to assert himself and determine his own identity in times of mass conformity. When Austria was taken over by the Nazis in 1938, Canetti made his way to England, which he has since made his home. Aside from his influential sociological study *Masse und Macht* (Crowds and Power, 1960), he has written two interesting plays in the postwar epoch. *Komödie der Eitelkeit* (A Comedy of Vanity, 1950) portrays how a law prohibiting mirrors in a country brings about mass hysteria. *Die Befristeten* (The Doomed, 1956) is a didactic play, which deals with different ways leading to death. Canetti uses characters, which he calls "acoustic masks," that are related to the theories he develops about mass psychology in *Crowds and Power.* In fact, all his dramas stem from his concern over mass movements and the individual's opportunity for development.

**Cannan, Denis** (born 1919). English dramatist. Educated at Eton, Cannan entered the theater as an actor in 1937. After military service he worked in repertory at the Citizens' Theatre, Glasgow, and the Bristol Old Vic Theatre. In his first three plays the theme is the conflict of ideologies, treated as material for tragedy in *Max* (1949) and for intellectual farce in *Captain Carvallo* (1950) and *Misery Me!* (1955). His next two plays, *You and Your Wife* (1955) and *Who's Your Father?* (1958), were farces without the serious undercurrents of his earlier work, and had little except a certain deftness of touch to distinguish them from the normal commercial fare of the '50s. The success of *Captain Carvallo* caused Cannan to be regarded as one of the few dramatists of promise and originality writing for the English theater, but in the years that followed he was not to repeat the success of this work. In 1966 he returned to his interest in the personal consequences of ideological conflict with the original text of *US*, the denunciation of American involvement in Vietnam that reached its final form under the direction of PETER BROOK.

Cannan has written numerous screenplays and has collaborated with Pierre Bost in the impressive stage adaptation of Graham Greene's novel *The Power and the Glory* (1956).

OTHER PLAYS: *Colombe* (translation, 1951), *Ghosts* (adaptation, 1966), *One at Night* (1971).

**Cantatrice chauve, La.** See THE BALD SOPRANO.

**Capitaine Bada** (1952). A play in three acts by Jean Vauthier. It was first performed on January 10, 1952, at the Théâtre de Poche, Paris, under the direction of André Reybaz and Catherine Toth. Some critics believe that *Capitaine Bada* was as important to the creation of the "new theater" as the first plays of Ionesco and Beckett, although it is in no way similar to them.

Bada, alias Badaboum or Dédéboum (and whose real name is René Dupont), is an aspiring poet who is sought in marriage by a childhood friend, Alice. At first he spurns her, since he intends to give himself to God. But at the end of Act I he yields and decides to marry her. The wedding takes place offstage, during the intermission, at which time there is a ballet onstage. At the beginning of Act II Alice and Bada themselves act out a kind of parody of a ballet, during which Alice, still wearing her wedding veil, refuses to give herself to Bada, who pursues her grotesquely, like a faun. During the second part of Act II, in a long scene that is both burlesque and agonizing, Alice, still pursued by Bada, tries to commit suicide, but he saves her and finally physically brutalizes her. Exhausted by their quarrel, both characters, at the end of the act, seem somewhat reconciled. The third act takes place years later, in the disorderly and dilapidated apartment of a penniless writer. Alice has become the slave of the genius Bada: She dresses him, puts on his plumed helmet for him, and is subjected to his insults. Bada, trying to isolate himself completely in order to create more successfully, always keeps the shutters closed and breaks his watch so as to escape from man's time. Their life together is made up of violent quarrels about the banalities of daily life (the cleaning, the badly cooked meals, the bills) and the lyrical explosions of Bada, a misunderstood genius who has undertaken to write an eighteen-thousand-page book. We learn that fragments of this work are actually the precise description of his constant quarrels with Alice. They set about reading these fragments and acting them out, but Bada begins to feel that he soon will die. At the end of the play he starts to hear the music he had been waiting for forever. Trying to figure out where it comes from, he climbs up on a piece of furniture and falls to his death. An undertaker comes to get him and takes him out through the window in the basket of a baloon, which rises into the sky. Alice, now alone, affirms that in spite of his "peculiarities," Bada had managed to imprison beauty and had loved her deeply, and that it was time his greatness was recognized.

On one level this play is a variation on the theme of the war of the sexes, with Alice and Bada constantly caught up in the eternal round of the couple. But they also represent the conflict between a kind of saintliness (Alice) and the monstrous egotism of the artist (Bada). Alice persists in being subservient and is magnified by the suffering that Bada inflicts upon her. She loves Bada because he himself suffers and because she has made him suffer in the second act. For his part, Bada thirsts for the absolute (God, or Love, or Poetry), but in his search for it he never manages to be sincere: He remains a clown, striking grotesque or grandiloquent attitudes. His suffering is exacerbated by the fact that the absolute resists his grasp—or perhaps because of his tragic impossibility of being authentic. Whatever he says or does, he achieves nothing more than a grandiose parody of the language or the gestures he had intended. This frustration increases his bad faith and impels him to torture Alice. His sort of final salvation, affirmed by Alice, is definitely ambiguous.

The play, which is both funny and agonizing, is written in violent language, alternating between insults and explosions of lyricism. The physical action is very lively, with Bada constantly moving about and breaking out into dances and pantomimes. The printed text of *Capitaine Bada*, like the texts of all Vauthier's plays, is especially interesting: The dialogue and stage directions are accompanied by the playwright's detailed comments on the exact tone in which the lines are to be spoken and on everything that is supposedly going on in the characters' minds.

**Carballido, Emilio** (born 1925). Mexican playwright. Carballido is one of the most versatile of Latin American dramatists. His first important success was *Rosalba y los Llaveros* (1950), a delightful comedy that showed the comic possibilities of the provincial theme previously reserved for superficial satire or realistic drama; at the same time, the play helped renovate a theater dominated by sentimental realism and professional comedies. *La danza que sueña la tortuga* (The Dance the Tortoise Dreams, 1955) is another comedy of provincial life, but it contains the germ of the conflict between illusion and reality that fascinates Carballido in most of his later works. *Felicidad* (Happiness, 1955) is an objective but compassionate study of the mediocrity of bourgeois life. After experimenting with horror and nightmare in several unstaged works, Carballido abandoned his previous style, assimilating Brechtian and other methods to his own characteristic humor. *El relojero de Córdoba* (The Watchmaker of Cordoba, 1960) satirizes modern life under the guise of historical comedy; *El día que se soltaron los leones* (The Day the Lions Got Loose, 1963) is an agile fantasy in praise of individualism. In *Medusa* (written 1958, produced 1966), one of his finest works, Carballido presents the process of maturation—that is, of becoming a hero—as spiritual death. Among his many later works, which are increasingly marked by humor with no loss of depth, *Te juro Juana que tengo ganas* (I Swear to You, Juana, I Really Want To, 1967) is a delightful experiment in the farce and *Yo también hablo de la rosa* (I Also Speak of the Rose, 1966) is an attack on the dehumanizing world. Carballido is one of the most prolific dramatists in Spanish and his work continues to show increasing technical range and human profundity.

**Casona, Alejandro** (1903–1965). Spanish dramatist. Casona, a pen name, supplanted the writer's real name, Alejandro Rodríguez Álvarez. During the Republic (1931–1936), he directed the Teatro del Pueblo, an organization of touring players under the auspices of the Patronato de Misiones Pedagógicas, whose mission was to bring culture to rural Spain. One of the short pieces he wrote for their repertory, *La balada de Atta Troll*, was later included in *Nuestra Natacha* (Our Natasha, 1936), his only explicitly social play, which documents the youthful idealism of the reformers of those years. The Civil War drove Casona into exile and theatrical activity in France, Mexico, and Argentina, where most of his subsequent works were first produced. The plays of the late '30s and '40s did not appear on the Spanish stage until the early '60s, causing then no small sensation. Encouraged by their reception, Casona returned to Spain, where he dominated the theater until his death. Fantasy, dream, and illusion play a decisive role in his aesthetics. In *La sirena varada* (The Beached Siren, 1934), his first commercial success, a girl is sustained in the belief she is a siren in order to help her maintain a precarious hold on sanity, and a painter, ostensibly wearing a blindfold to shut out the base reality of the world, hides instead from the world the reality of his blindness. But the play concludes that reality, no matter how harsh, must be faced, and responsible critics reject the charge that Casona's is a "theater of evasion." Rather, fantasy, itself a psychic reality, provides the framework within which the playwright, unencumbered by limitations of time and space, elaborates the fundamental human experiences of love, sin, repentence, fear of death, and hope for salvation. In *Prohibido suicidarse en primavera* (Suicide Prohibited in Spring, 1937), members of a suicide club find cause for hope and continued existence at the climax of a flight from reality. In *La dama del alba* (Lady of the Dawn, 1944), its poetic and folkloric texture as rich as that of the rural tragedies of García Lorca, death the pilgrim comes as consolation, as the serene transition to a sublimated existence, even as the prelude to life and love. *La barca sin pescador* (The Boat Without a Fisherman, 1945), a reworking of the Faust theme with a most sophisticated Satan, assesses the reaches of sin, the consequence of remorse, and the saving grace of love. It is the subtlety of the variation on a theme, though, and not the theme itself that justifies Casona's claim on the contemporary theater, and brief précis cannot pretend to reveal their lyric perfection and depth of perception.

OTHER PLAYS SINCE 1936: *Sinfonía inacabada* (Unfinished Symphony, 1940), *Las tres perfectas casadas* (The Perfectly Married Women, 1941), *La molinera de Arcos* (The Miller's Wife, 1947), *Los árboles mueren de pie* (Trees Die Standing, 1949), *Siete gritos en el mar* (Seven Shouts in the Sea, 1952), *Corona de amor y de muerte* (Crown of Love and Death, 1955), *La casa de los siete balcones* (The House of Seven Balconies, 1957), *El caballero de las espuelas de oro* (The Knight of the Golden Spurs, 1965).

**Cat on a Hot Tin Roof** (1955). A play by Tennessee Williams. It received the New York Drama Critics Circle Award and the Pulitzer Prize. In a bed-sitting room of a plantation mansion in the fertile Mississippi Delta, Maggie and Brick struggle with their sterile relationship. The home is Big Daddy's, not theirs, and it is in the presence of his aging virility that Brick drinks away anxiety about his own possible homosexuality. Both Big Daddy and Big Mama clearly favor Brick over their other son, Gooper, and his wife, Mae; but Gooper and Mae have five children and hope thereby to inherit Big Daddy's kingdom, "twenty-eight thousand acres of th' richest land this side of the Valley Nile!" Maggie and Brick will have no children if Brick continues to refuse to sleep with his wife. Maggie is a cat on a hot tin roof, full of Big Daddy's lusty spirit both for sex and for possessions. She knows if she can produce Brick's child, they will inherit the plantation.

During the summer evening when the action of the play takes place, Maggie tries to get Brick to begin new life in her, as Big Daddy's defeat by cancer is made definite. Maggie lies to the family that she is pregnant: This is her birthday-deathday present to Big Daddy. Whether she will succeed in seducing Brick, and saving him by her love, is not clear in either of two endings of the play. (At the instigation of his director, Elia Kazan, Williams wrote a variant third act for the New York production; both endings are printed in John Gassner's *Best American Plays*, Fourth Series: 1951–1957.)

Maggie and Big Daddy are both archetypal figures of the life force; Brick and his style of drunkenness presents a contrasting mundane realism. Other characters—Gooper, Mae, the five no-neck monsters (their children), Reverend Tooker—are comic distortions. It is only the quality of Maggie's and Big Daddy's talk and the intensity of their desire for life that blends these disparate styles into a unified dramatic impression.

**Caucasian Chalk Circle, The** (**Der kaukasische Kreidekreis**, written 1943–1945, produced 1948). A play by Bertolt Brecht. More than any other drama by Brecht, *The Caucasian Chalk Circle* reveals his great skill in mixing elements from different theatrical traditions and art forms. Essentially the play is a didactic parable, which strives to offer a solution to postwar problems in a socialist country. However, the didacticism is not simplistic. Brecht makes use of the Bible, the Japanese nō-play, American slapstick comedy, Chinese folklore, the cinema, songs, and Marxist dialectics to construct a fable about the people's right to property and justice in a socialist sense.

The initial scene takes place in postwar Russia, where two Soviet collectives debate about the rights to use a valley. After an equitable solution is reached—one that allows for the best possible development of the land—there is a celebration. The famous singer Arkadi narrates the story about the chalk circle while some workers participate as actors. The setting of the story is feudal Georgia (in the Soviet Union), where the governor of a city is dethroned by a group of nobles. The governor's wife, a petty, bickering woman, flees for her life and leaves her infant son, Michel, behind. The good-hearted kitchen maid Grusha takes the infant and protects it, though she knows that her own life will be in danger. When she takes Michel into the country, she is pursued by soldiers. After many hardships, she manages to find refuge with her brother and sister-in-law. She is soon chased from the farm because her sister-in-law does not want their reputation ruined by harboring Grusha and her "illegitimate" child. The brother arranges a marriage for Grusha with a farmer who is supposedly dying. The farmer turns out to be feigning death to avoid the draft. This fact is revealed when the revolt has ended and soldiers are no longer being drafted. At this point, the governor's wife comes out of hiding and claims Michel, who is now three years old. Grusha is forced to return to the city with Michel and appear before the judge Azdak.

In order to explain the significance of the trial conducted by Azdak, the singer narrates Azdak's past. Azdak is a type of picaresque hero. At one time he was a village recorder but was promoted to a judge because of his wit and shrewdness during the recent social upheavals. He is known for making scandalous judgments that favor the poor and the social outcasts. In the final scene of the play, he reviews the case of Grusha and the governor's wife. Though he knows that the governor's wife is the real mother by blood, he also is aware of Grusha's devotion to the child and the sacrifices she has made for him. Azdak decides to settle the case by using the old test of the chalk circle. The child is placed in a circle, and the two women are to pull him. Whoever wins the tug-of-war is supposed to be the real mother. When Grusha refuses to pull, the governor's wife thinks that she has won her son and the property that belongs to him as the governor's heir. However, Azdak awards the child to Grusha because she has shown real maternal affection by refusing to harm the child. He also grants her a divorce so that she can marry the soldier Simon, who has remained loyal to her despite her "marriage of convenience." At the close of the play the singer reports that Azdak disappeared after this, but that his short reign as judge was remembered as a golden age of justice.

Brecht employs an interesting theatrical technique in this play. The singer Arkadi narrates a story that is demonstrated through the gestures of the actors.

The many brief scenes are interrupted and interpreted by the singer, who tries in this way to alienate the audience from the action. The quick scenes have a comic, cinematic effect, and the racy dialogue reveals the chief characters as zany, witty people who know how to define their enemies and how to out-maneuver them. Grusha's goodness is not wasted because she learns to direct it in a social sense. Azdak's justice is not confined to absolute standards, nor does it serve only one class. The virtues of these characters are exhibited in their actions, and the actions demonstrate the possibility of working toward a socialist society with a sense of both *joie de vivre* and political purpose.

**Césaire, Aimé** (born 1912). French dramatist. Born in Martinique, the black poet Césaire got his higher education in Paris, at the Ecole Normale Supérieure. In 1934, along with others, he founded the magazine *L'Etudiant Noir,* with the aim of breaking down the barriers that divided the black students and making them aware of their negritude and their common dignity. Césaire became a *lycée* professor and, in 1945, deputy of Martinique, then mayor of Fort-de-France. At first a member of the Communist Party, he left it in 1956 to head the Martinique Progressive Party.

Césaire's abundant poetic works are closely related to surrealism and are an attempt at finding a black identity by reviving the memory of African forces and culture. But also, by transcending negritude, his poetry aims at a universal definition of man. Césaire has written four dramatic works based essentially on the problems raised by the freedom that has been regained in the colonial countries. His best play is *La Tragédie du Roi Christophe* (1964), which deals with Henri Christophe's assumption of power in Haiti at the beginning of the nineteenth century, his efforts at ridding his compatriots of the image imposed on them by colonization and slavery, his unbounded ambition, his mistakes, and finally, his being destroyed by illness and the rebellion of his subjects. The play has a great lyrical surge of monologues and chants, evoking black aspirations in sumptuous images, and yet is shot through with caricatural scenes satirizing the Blacks imitating the Whites at the King's court. Christophe himself is shown both in his greatness and his tyrannical and grotesque aspects, and his characterization swings from a king of tragedy to a type of King Ubu. *Une Saison au Congo* (1966), centered on the assassination of Patrice Lumumba, discloses the political and tribal contradictions that rent the Congo directly following achievement of its independence, and is a far more didactic play than *La Tragédie du Roi Christophe.* Césaire's most recent dramatic work, *Une Tempête* (1969), is an adaptation of Shakespeare's *Tempest* for a Negro theater. Although the plot follows that of Shakespeare's play, Césaire has made Prospero the type of colonizer who imposes his "illusions" on the people he exploits. He also added a deity: Eshu, a Negro "god-devil," who introduces anxiety into Prospero's order, and he makes Caliban the positive character of the play. An adaptation, not a translation, Césaire's

*Une Tempête* is a vigorous and poetic masquerade, celebrating the liberation of the black people.

**Chayefsky, Paddy** [given name: **Sidney**] (born 1923). American playwright and film writer. Born and educated in New York City, Chayefsky worked briefly in a print shop after his Army service in World War II, then began to write for movies, radio, and television. Many of his scripts have been used in more than one medium; the motion picture *Marty*, which won an Academy Award in 1955, had previously been a successful television drama, and his first Broadway play, *Middle of the Night* (1956), was later produced as a motion picture. Although his career has been chiefly in television and films, Chayefsky has had five plays produced: *Middle of the Night*, *The Tenth Man* (1959), and *Gideon* (1961) were quite successful on Broadway; *The Passion of Josef D.* (1964) and *The Latent Heterosexual* (Dallas, 1968) had only brief runs.

Chayefsky's plays tend to be anecdotal in plot and proverbial in meaning. *The Latent Heterosexual*, for example, is built on a joke about a man "who got married to get the benefit of the joint declaration" and cautions against letting the corporate person usurp individual identity. Even plays using complicated historical material have this capsulating quality: *The Passion of Josef D.* deals with Stalin's passage from belief in a Christian God to belief in an ideological God and shows that in either kind of absolutism human importance is lost. Moments of Brechtian song and chant in *Josef D.* and the comical relationship between God and his fool-prophet in *Gideon*, though adding a certain whimsy, do not sufficiently relieve the monotonousness of long expository passages designed to refresh the audience's memory of historical events.

**Chile.** A fundamental renovation took place in Chilean drama in 1941 with the establishment of the experimental group of the University of Chile, later to be known as I.T.U.C.H. (Instituto de Teatro de la Universidad de Chile). By 1956 both the University of Chile and the Catholic University had professional plants and resident companies. These two centers have been the source of Chilean drama for more than twenty-five years, and from them have come the majority of creative and technical personnel. Over this time, however, both organisms became routinized and bureaucratic, and the crisis of the universities and subsequent reforms of the late 1960s have produced substantial changes. The Catholic University's company, Teatro de Ensayo, has been replaced by a workshop, and I.T.U.C.H. has been altered radically. Now known as the Theater Department of the University of Chile, it has been substantially loosened in structure and the whole operation has been considerably politicized. There are two companies at the university, one in Santiago and one on permanent tour in the provinces and poorer districts; the plays themselves demonstrate a substantial left-wing orientation. The impact of all this has yet to be measured, but Chilean theater, like most Latin American drama, has recently been increasingly social. The picture has been complicated by a general leveling off about 1965, which was caused by the advent of television, by limitations of training, and, to a lesser degree than elsewhere, by usual economic problems. This decline has also made difficulties for other important experimental groups, such as ICTUS, which operate independently of the university and commercial theaters and have a general avant-garde social orientation.

The older Chilean dramatists, born between 1915 and 1922, share a generally realistic line, often with a pronounced social bias. María Asunción Requena and Isidora Aguirre are notable in this connection; Aguirre has written a variety of works, including *La pérgola de las flores* (The Summer House, 1960), one of Latin America's great musical comedy successes, but her most recent work includes *Los papeleros* (The Ragpickers, 1964), a play about those who live in the enormous dumps that have grown up near most Latin American capitals, and *Los que van quedando en el camino* (Those Who Are Left on the Way, 1967), based on a peasant massacre of the 1930s. Fernando Debesa shares the realistic orientation of this group; his plays are basically historical re-creations, although he treats spiritual problems and human suffering with considerable delicacy. A younger group shows much greater cosmopolitanism, although its members share the same social concerns. Luis Alberto HEIREMANS' early death in 1964 deprived Chile of its most versatile and significant young dramatist. Haunted by the theme of the quest, he had essayed a variety of dramatic forms, but his greatest success came in such works as *Versos de ciego* (Blind Man's Poems, 1960), a blending of popular poetic tradition and the theme of the Three Wise Men. Conservative theatergoers protested, unaware that Hieremans had returned to the source of religious drama. *El tony chico* (The Little Clown, 1964) uses the figure of the circus clown in the same fashion, as a metaphor for man's search for meaning. Alejandro Sieveking has concentrated on psychological realism, but Egon Wolff and Sergio Vodanovich have abandoned this approach in favor of increasing social commitment. Wolff is best known for works that utilize apparent realism to underline the irrational in society. Vodanovich first attracted attention with works of overt satire, such as *Deja que los perros ladren* (Let the Dogs Bark, 1959); more recently, he has, like Wolff, shown a social order gone mad, whether through the searing reversal of roles in *El delantal blanco* (The White Apron, 1965) or the indictment of morality which produces immorality in *Perdón, estamos en guerra* (Excuse Me, We Are at War, 1966).

Fernando Josseau, although deeply influenced by Sartre and Camus, had his greatest success with *El prestamista* (The Moneylender, 1956), a three-act monodrama *tour de force* written for the actor Raúl Montenegro. The work's great success—both it and Montenegro have received a number of awards and were hits in Latin America and Europe—depends on the functional simplicity of the setting and dialogue and the excellence of the actor. Enrique Molleto has not yet gone beyond the stage of the highly promising; his symbolic Freudian works hint at obscure horrors behind daily existence, but he has not yet written the work of which he is capable. Best of the Chileans today is Jorge Díaz, who has evolved from a mode close to Ionesco's in tone toward a greater dramatic concentration. Díaz is infuriated by the basic immorality of modern life, and his works are sardonically funny but bitterly angry. *El velero en la botella* (The Ship in the Bottle, 1962) is an acute satire on the generation gap; *El lugar donde mueren los mamíferos* (The Mammals' Graveyard, 1963) disembowels false charity. His best work to date, *Topografía de un desnudo* (Topography of a Nude, 1967), is based on the slaughter of a group of beggars and achieves an angry human idiom that places it among the best of Latin American plays. The extent to which Chilean audiences and theater people have become politicized is visible in two controversial works, Pablo Neruda's *Fulgor y muerte de Joaquín Murieta* (Radiance and Death of Joaquin Murieta, 1967) and Jaime Silva's *La pasión según San Jaime* (The Passion According to Saint James, 1969). Silva, who has worked primarily in children's theater, appears to have attempted a work in a popular idiom; he met with a considerable conservative reaction to what was considered antireligious activity. Neruda, a longtime Communist and the party's onetime candidate for the presidency, as well as a great poet, tinkered with history and perpetrated poor verse in an anti-American diatribe whose theatrical values were lost in the political tone. The play was both acclaimed and denounced, largely on political grounds.

**Chorell, Walentin** (born 1912). Finnish playwright and novelist. Chorell took his M.A. in 1934, majoring in psychology; he has worked as a secondary-school teacher. He is a versatile and prolific writer, and the only internationally known Finnish dramatist since World War II, with translations into English, German, Norwegian, Danish, and Portuguese. He writes in Swedish.

After writing two collections of poems Chorell turned to novels and radio and stage plays. Exceptional individuals, among them underdogs, have been in the center of his interest; he tends to emphasize the value of their absolute points of view, adopted in spite of pressure from the surroundings. His milieu is often in the outskirts of society, his characters are old, adolescent, dreaming, or ill. *Miriam* (1954–1958) is a trilogy of novels; *Fabian öppnar portarna* (Fabian Opens the Gates, 1949) marked Chorell's breakthrough as a live dramatist. *Madame* (1951) is an analysis of an aging actress and her relation to death, while *Systrarna* (The Sisters, 1955), the winning script in a Scandinavian play competition, is a psychological study of two sisters in love with the same man. Another climax in Chorell's career came with *Gräset* (Grass, 1958), based on an incestuous love affair between brother and sister, separated by war, then meeting with fateful consequences. Chorell's technical skill in blending realism and theatricalism is evident. Two examples

93

from the opposite ends of Chorell's scale are *De moderlösa* (The Motherless, 1956), a quick-witted farce, and *Kattorna* (The Cats, 1960), a description of a collective of females in working surroundings. Parts of Chorell's large output (over sixty works for different media) bears marks of tiredness; he sometimes relies rather heavily on childhood experiences and other well-known vehicles of psychological realism. He has also written for the screen and TV; in 1952 a collection, *Åtta radiopjäser* (Eight Radio Plays), was published.

**Cocktail Party, The** (1949). A play by T. S. Eliot. In full accord with Eliot's expressed belief that for poetic drama to reconquer its place in the theater it must "enter into overt competition with prose drama," *The Cocktail Party* adheres with polished irony to the conventions of drawing-room comedy. The skillful plot that charts the affairs of a quartet of lovers, moving from adultery to self-discovery and final reconciliation, was in no way remarkable in the theater of the '30s and '40s. The dialogue, with a few significant exceptions, faithfully echoed the trivial sophistication of upper-middle-class society as represented on the stage. The setting, a fashionable London flat in the first and last acts and a psychiatrist's consulting room in the second, was familiar West End territory. But Eliot employs, in language and structure, a device characteristic of much of his writing. The rhythms and patterns of everyday speech and contemporary experience are placed in an overall context that enlarges their significance. Upon the action that brings a husband and wife together is superimposed Eliot's conception of order in a Christian society. The puzzling alliance uniting Julia, the interfering and omniscient busybody, the well-connected Alex, and Sir Henry Harcourt-Reilly, the psychoanalyst who achieves the reconciliation, is more than a friendly conspiracy. The role of the three as the watchers over society is revealed in the incantation with which they end the second act. While Lavinia and Edward Chamberlayne learn to accept their limited and secular position in society, Edward's lover, Celia, who suffers from "a sense of sin," is capable of a higher order of spiritual experience and is guided toward the lonely road of religious dedication and eventual martyrdom.

To early critics and audiences of the play the role of Julia, Alex, and Reilly appeared enigmatic. (James Thurber recorded the opinion that the play was written so that the women he met at cocktail parties could demand an interpretation of the play and exclaim "My God, how naïve!") There are features of the play that cannot be understood without reference to the body of interpretation that has grown up around it. The relationship between the strange behavior of Reilly in the opening scene and the actions of the gluttonous Heracles before his visit to the underworld was not noticed until Eliot himself indicated that Euripides' *Alcestis* had provided a model for the play. There is an element of deliberate obscurity in *The Cocktail Party*. Eliot hoped that his audience, following a pattern of action and speech close to that of everyday life, would become subconsciously aware of the deeper level of meaning that accompanied it. But Eliot's attempt to present a Christian vision of society in purely secular terms involved him in some unresolved difficulties. The seriousness of the themes that lay behind Eliot's ironic approach sometimes jarred upon the general structure of the play. The account of Celia's death, "crucified/Very near an ant-hill," seemed a tasteless intrusion upon the triviality of its context.

A pattern of spiritual death and regeneration in the play may be interpreted as an echo of the ritual death and rebirth that the Cambridge school of Anthropologists (an undeniable influence upon the poet) discerned in the origins of Greek tragedy. Thus the meeting of Edward and Lavinia in the psychiatrist's consulting room is a rite of initiation into Christian society, and Celia's death is the sacrifice that insures the continued life of the community. But the temptation for students of Eliot's drama is to trace literary influences while ignoring the powerful record of human experience that the plays embody. The confrontation of Edward and Lavinia engineered by Reilly, and the reconstitution of their marriage free from false illusions of their own importance, is a scene indicative of Eliot's deep humanity.

In the years immediately following the appearance of *The Cocktail Party* it seemed that a revival of English poetic drama, predominantly Christian in character, was about to transform the stage. This hope was not to be fulfilled. Eliot's respect for tradition, in religion and literature, was to find little favor with the dramatists of the later '50s. The sophisticated prose drama with which this work entered into "overt competition" was itself to lose its dominant position within a decade. The spontaneity and vigor of the writers who followed *Look Back in Anger* were to make the delicate artifices of this play seem contrived. The principles of dramatic composition that Eliot laid down as general rules in his lectures and essays were part of a purely personal quest for an adequate vehicle of expression. The interest and importance of *The Cocktail Party* lies in its relationship to his development as a poet; its influence upon later writers has been negligible.

**Colombia.** Theater in Colombia is still essentially the story of Enrique Buenaventura and his Teatro Experimental de Cali (T.E.C.), founded in 1955. Unlike most nations, whose theatrical activity is restricted almost exclusively to the capital, the majority of theater in Colombia takes place in Cali, and it is almost nonexistent in Bogotá. Buenaventura's example has led to a whole series of festivals and other experimental groups have followed his lead. During the 1960s some governmental aid was given, and by 1965 30 per cent of all plays staged were Colombian. Although T.E.C. lost its subsidy in 1968 because of official disapproval of a play, Buenaventura continued his work. In that same year he helped set up La MaMa Bogotá, an offshoot of New York's La MaMa Experimental Theatre Club.

Few Colombian dramatists have as yet emerged. Antonio Montaña shows promise and Fanny Buitrago's *El hombre de paja* (The Straw Man, 1964) is

95

a splendid fable of human responsibility, rooted in Colombia's bloody civil war, but Buenaventura is still the most important. He prefers plays of great sweep and scope, and he handles them deftly. *La tragedia de Henri Christophe* (1963) received an award from the UNESCO International Theater Institute. In *Requiem para el Padre Las Casas* and *En la diestra de Dios Padre* (On the Right Hand of God the Father, 1960), Buenaventura handled American themes in an effort to build an American theater, a tack he is now pursuing with a more openly political bent in T.E.C.

**Cooper, Giles** (1918–1966). English dramatist. Born in Carrickmines, County Dublin, and educated at Lancing College and Grenoble, Cooper trained for the stage at the Webber Douglas School of Drama. After military service (1939–1946), he took up a career as an actor, but soon began writing, first for the stage, then for radio, where the B.B.C. Third Programme offered opportunities for experiment free from commercial pressure. In the '50s Cooper's plays for radio, experimental in form and a subtle mixture of the sinister and the comic, anticipated many of the developments that were to be seen on the stage in future years. In such plays from the 1950s as *Mathry Beacon, Unman, Wittering, and Zigo, Without the Grail,* and *The Return of General Forefinger,* Cooper explored the extremities of human experience within the framework of absurdist fantasy. He returned to writing for the stage in 1962 with *Everything in the Garden,* depicting a group of suburban housewives who supplement the family income with afternoon stints of prostitution. More successful than this skillful but somewhat obvious exposure of the hypocrisy of middle-class morality was *Happy Family,* completed before his untimely death in a fall from a train. This picture of a middle-aged family that retains its nursery language and infantile illusions about the facts of life is a compelling image of the tenacity of childhood fantasies in the adult world. The play's absurdist techniques are fundamental to its theme.

Cooper contributed adaptations of Georges Simenon's detective novels to the "Maigret" series on B.B.C. television and was the author of a number of original television plays, which include *The Lonesome Road* and *The Power of Zero.*

OTHER PLAYS: *Never Get Out* (1950), *Haddocks Eyes* (1950), *Out of the Crocodile* (1963), *The Spies Are Singing* (1966).

**Coward, Noel** (born 1899). English actor, playwright, director, and composer. A child actor by the age of eleven, Coward began writing lyrics and composing in his teens. His first light comedy, *I'll Leave It to You,* was staged in 1920. With the success of *The Vortex* in 1924 he achieved notoriety as dramatist, actor, and representative of the youthful philosophy of the '20s, and a succession of plays, in most of which he starred himself, established him as the authentic theatrical voice of the decade. "More clearly than any of his contemporaries," stated St. John Ervine of the figure whom he characterized as "a Savonarola in evening dress," "he expresses the harsh and impatient cynicism of the young who grew to early manhood in the war"; his dialogue faithfully represented the opinions of the "infant atheists" of the period. But Coward's gifts as lyricist and composer insured that his talents were equally at home in revue, and his work has always revealed more the professional hand of the skilled man of the theater than the single-minded devotion of the dramatist of ideas. While *Fallen Angels* (1925), *Hay Fever* (1925), and *Private Lives* (1930) established him as a master of drawing-room comedy, *Cavalcade* (1931), *This Happy Breed* (1942), and *Peace in Our Time* (1947) served to demonstrate that behind the brittle cynicism cultivated in the '20s there lingered in Coward a warm, emotional regard for the traditional values of his native England.

Coward's successes continued into the '40s, *Blithe Spirit* (1941) achieving a record run of 1,997 performances. The '50s saw a decline in his fortunes, with *Nude with Violin* (1956), which appeared in the same year as Osborne's *Look Back in Anger*, being generally accounted among the weakest of his works. Coward found himself opposed to the new brand of social realism characterized by the "kitchen sink" drama of the '50s, which he contemptuously dismissed as the "scratch and mumble" school, and his name was often linked with Terence Rattigan's as typifying the frivolous misuse of talent to which the commercial theater condemned its luminaries. The '60s have brought a more just estimate of Coward's stature as a supreme artist of the theater. The classical qualities of *Hay Fever* were acknowledged in a revival of the play (under the author's direction) by the National Theatre in 1964, and his seventieth birthday in 1969 was celebrated by performances of most of his major plays on B.B.C. television. His reputation as a serious dramatist has been enlarged by *Waiting in the Wings* (1960), a seriocomic picture of life in a home for retired actresses, and by *A Song at Twilight* (1966), in which a famous author's homosexual past haunts the security of his old age. In the latter play Coward chose the severity of traditional technique to deal with a subject which the young dramatists of the '50s and '60s had claimed the right to present on the stage. For its superbly structured exposition and revelation the play has been described as "the first completely convincing, completely serious well-made play in the British theatre for more than half a century."

Coward lives in Switzerland; he was knighted in 1970. He has written the screenplays for *In Which We Serve, Blithe Spirit, This Happy Breed,* and *Brief Encounter.* Coward's plays, with introductions by the author, have been collected in *Play Parade,* volumes I through VI (1934–1962); his autobiography has appeared in two volumes, *Present Indicative* (1937) and *Future Indefinite* (1954). He has been the subject of numerous essays, including "The Plays of Mr. Noel Coward" by St. John Ervine in *Essays by Divers Hands* (1935); his work is discussed by John Russell Taylor in *The Rise and Fall of the Well-Made Play* (1967) and by Raymond Mander and Joe Mitchenson in *Theatrical Companion to Coward* (1957). Two biographies have been published: *Noel*

*Coward* (1968) by Milton Levin and *A Talent to Amuse* (1969) by Sheridan Morley.

OTHER PLAYS SINCE 1945: *Sigh No More* (revue, 1945), *Pacific 1860* (1946), *Ace of Clubs* (1950), *Island Fling* (1951), *Relative Values* (1951), *Quadrille* (1952), *After the Ball* (1954), *South Sea Bubble* (1956), *Look After Lulu* (adaptation from Feydeau, 1959), *London Morning* (a ballet, 1959), *Sail Away* (1961), *The Girl Who Came to Supper* (musical adaptation of Rattigan's *The Sleeping Prince*, 1963), *A Song at Twilight* (1966), *Shadows of the Evening* and *Come Into the Garden, Maud* (double bill, 1966), *Suite in Three Keys* (the three preceding plays presented in repertory, 1966).

**Crucible, The** (1953). A play in four acts by Arthur Miller. The Salem witch trials of the 1690s provide the historical content of this play; its real subject is the damaging rigidity of a repressive society and the price a person must pay for finding his norms and values within himself rather than in "state administration." John Proctor is enough his own man to call the hysteria of his town nonsense. But as the young girls—Betty, Susanna, Mary, Mercy—follow their leader Abigail in paroxysms of "diabolic" torment, eventually accusing all the most respected women of the town of witchcraft, their power over the lives of others increases to such an extent that no one can oppose them. Officials of church and state, most importantly Deputy Governor Danforth, share the girls' sense of violent righteousness and bring many innocent people to trial and execution.

As the number of hangings escalates, the emotional need of this "good" society to justify its persecution grows: The more who have died, the more the initial principle cannot have been wrong.

In the midst of all this John Proctor wrestles with his own conscience. In the past he had a brief sexual affair with Abigail; this has crushed his wife and still stings his memory (and accounts for Abigail's vindictiveness against Elizabeth Proctor). Faced with hanging for witchcraft, Proctor for a moment takes the only avenue of escape available, one many in the community have made use of: He "confesses." But then, realizing he has lost thereby not only his soul but his name, he retracts the false confession. In this moment he realizes that he must hang, not because he is a totally innocent person, like Rebecca Nurse, and not because his wife once again sees him as good (though she does), but because finally he sees "some shred of goodness" in himself: "Not enough to weave a banner with, but white enough to keep it from such dogs." Goodness lost through lust with Abigail is regained as he affirms himself against an insane society proclaiming itself moral.

Explaining the relevance of this play to the American political scene of the 1950s, Miller writes in the Introduction to his *Collected Plays* (1957): "It was not only the rise of 'McCarthyism' that moved me, but something which seemed much more weird and mysterious. It was the fact that a political, objective, knowledgeable campaign from the far Right was capable of creating not only a terror, but a new subjective reality, a veritable mystique which was gradually assuming even a holy resonance."

**Csokor, Franz Theodor** (1885–1969). Austrian dramatist, director, poet, and novelist. Born in Vienna, Csokor was part of an Austrian generation of writers known for their precocity and despair. He published his first collection of poems at twenty and his first play, *Thermidor*, at twenty-two. After serving in the Austrian Army during World War I, he went through an expressionist phase under the influence of Wedekind and Strindberg. From 1922 to 1928, Csokor was a director and dramaturge at the Raimundtheater and the Deutsches Volkstheater in Vienna. He gradually turned toward realism and became part of the *Neue Sachlichkeit* movement in the late '20s. Since Csokor had taken a stand against Hitler, he was forced to leave Vienna in 1938. He was in constant danger until the end of the war and traveled in Poland, Rumania, Yugoslavia, and Italy under the protection of partisan groups. His wartime experiences are described both in his plays and in his memoirs. After returning to Vienna in 1946, Csokor moved toward Christian socialism. Most of his postwar dramas, particularly *Caesars Witwe* (The Widow of Caesar, 1952) and *Hebt den Stein ab* (Pick Up the Stone, 1956) are either traditional historical plays or call for a return to Christian thinking. These dramas are essentially neoclassical in form and deal with social themes about rebuilding European civilization from a liberal point of view.

OTHER PLAYS SINCE 1945: *Medea postbellica* (1945), *Treibholz* (Driftwood, 1959), *Die Erweckung des Zosimir* (The Awakening of Zosimir, 1960), *Das Zeichen an der Wand* (The Mark on the Wall, 1963).

**Cuba.** As in most nations, the relative calm in international relations just after World War II brought new life to the Cuban theater. Small groups flourished and some governmental aid was forthcoming. This activity was soon frustrated by the worsening political situation; the professional theater nourished itself on commercialism and a pseudo-pornographic popular tradition fallen on evil days, and more serious efforts consisted of irregular performances by small companies. Between 1954 and 1958, professional and semiprofessional companies in Cuba staged thirty plays, many of them vulgar farces. The new government after 1958 made clear its interest in theater, and federal and other governmental agencies have been extremely active in stimulating theater. The national and international drama festivals are the most interesting in Latin America; there is a steady dramatic activity and serious efforts are made to carry theater to the provinces and to poorer areas. Until recently, Cuban theater appeared to be free of significant censorship problems, although anti-revolutionary works, if written, were not staged.

Several of the principal prerevolutionary playwrights are active, notably Carlos Felipe and Virgilio Piñera. The former still suffers from extreme verbalism, and has written little of late. Piñera has successfully followed dramatic fashions. His pre-1958 works, such as *Electra Garrigó*, and *Jesús* (1958), are violent but often fascinating examinations of what Piñera conceives to be the Cuban psyche. *Aire frío* (Cold Air, 1958) is a realistic and highly uneven denunciation of prerevolutionary middle-class life. More recently *Dos viejos pánicos* (Two Old Men in a Panic, 1968) is a moderately successful effort in a Genet-Beckett line. Other prerevolutionary playwrights are generally inactive; many of the most promising, such as Matías Montes Huidobro, René Buch, and Ramón Ferreira, have left Cuba. Others, including Nora Badía and Eduardo Manet, have abandoned playwriting for direction and production. Still others, like Fermín Borges, are simply silent.

The interest of Cuban drama today is chiefly in a group of younger playwrights who have appeared since 1958: Antón Arrufat, José Triana, Abelardo Estorino, and Manuel Reguera Saumell. Estorino and Reguera Saumell are basically realists, although far from restricted. Estorino's *El robo del cochino* (The Stolen Pig, 1961) was one of the earliest successes of post-revolutionary theater. Like much of this group's work, it examines the role of the generations and the decay of family life, without falling into propagandizing. Although Estorino has experimented with other techniques, this realistic approach, repeated in 1964 in *La casa vieja* (The Old House), serves him best in his examinations of human frailty. Reguera Saumell is also focused principally on the family in disintegration, but his best work is a moving study of an aging carnival dancer, *Recuerdos de Tulipa* (Memories of Tulipa, 1962).

José Triana is the best known of the group because of his *La noche de los asesinos* (The Night of the Assassins). Like his earlier works, *Medea en el espejo* (Medea in the Mirror, 1960), *El Parque de la Fraternidad* (Brotherhood Park, 1962), and *La muerte del Ñeque* (1963), *La noche de los asesinos* lifts the irrational to a mythic level; the whole play is a ritual structure raised to exorcise random violence. The three murderous adolescents scheming the archetypal murder of their parents are directly related to Genet's *Les bonnes,* but they are more closely related to the savage types of the earlier works, in all of which Triana seeks some understanding of the violence he sees all about him. Arrufat has been highly successful in his efforts to create viable modern theater from the elements of the nineteenth-century *teatro bufo,* a popular form based on stock types. In other works he has dealt with the incoherence of daily life, the inevitable, cyclic nature of daily defeat. His most ambitious play, *Los siete contra Tebas* (Seven Against Thebes, 1968) touched off a major controversy with international repercussions. Based on the Greek theme but with some clear parallels to recent Cuban history, the play was awarded the Writers' Union prize by an international jury over the protests of two members who rejected its alleged anti-revolutionary bias. Arrufat and the poet Heberto Padilla, whose volume of poetry suffered an identical fate, were severely criticized and there appear to have been economic reprisals against them. Both books were published, but never circulated. The play hardly seems to justify such actions, since it is a plea for tolerance and compassion within a severe framework sometimes reminiscent of the model.

A number of other dramatists are of interest, although none has achieved the stature of those mentioned. José Brene is a successful author of vigorously political works in the tradition of the vernacular theater. Nicolás Dorr, Ignacio Gutiérrez, Héctor Quintero, and José Milián have all had successful productions, but none has yet emerged as a dramatist.

**Czechoslovakia.** The end of World War II in 1945 saw not only the reopening of all the Czech theaters, which the German occupation authorities had closed a year earlier, but also the opening of a number of new ones. Before very long, Czechoslovakia had more theaters in relation to its population than most other countries. Prague alone, with a million inhabitants, had twenty-six permanent theaters, and a great many more existed in provincial centers and lesser towns.

*Czech drama.* The most important figures in the Czech theater in 1945 were E. F. Burian and Jan Werich. Burian, a playwright and director, had survived the German concentration camps, where he had been held for his Communist ideas. On his release he was at once appointed director of Prague's three biggest theaters. There he staged several of his prewar productions; he did not, however, contribute anything new to the Czech theater after the war. Werich, also a man of the left, had spent the war years in the United States. After his return to Prague he produced not only some of his prewar musical comedies, but also several foreign (mainly English) plays in his own translations. He was deeply involved in the Czech liberalization movement of 1968, but because of his great popularity it proved impossible for the authorities, even after 1969, to ban him from appearing on the stage.

The large number of theaters had great difficulties in finding new, original Czech plays for their repertories—especially as the country's cultural life was extensively controlled by the Communists and "socialist realism" was regarded as the only appropriate style in literature and the arts. The first postwar play by a Czech author to be staged by the National Theater in 1946 was Jan Drda's *Hrátky s čertem* (Jesting With the Devil). Drda was a Communist Party member of long standing and was later to be imposed by the party upon the Czechoslovak Writers' Union as chairman, but, strangely enough, this popular novelist's first dramatic effort was lighthearted and almost escapist. Fifteen years later, in his second play, *Dalskabáty—hříšná ves* (The Sinning Village), Drda again managed to get away with a play that entirely avoided the political issues of the day. But Drda's position was privileged and therefore exceptional. Other playwrights of the immediate postwar period had to earn the approval of the all-powerful censors if they wished to see their work produced. They chose their subjects mainly from the history of the working class's struggle. Typical examples are two plays by Vojtěch Cach, *Duchcovský viadukt* (Duchcov Bridge, 1950) and *Mostecká stávka* (Miners' Strike in Most, 1954). The subject of Vašek Káňa's topical comedy *Parta brusiče Karhana* (Cutter Karhan's Gang) was the clash between old and young workers over the introduction of new socialist working methods. Miloslav Stehlík dealt in his plays mainly with the problem of the socialist transformation of the Czech countryside, with the class struggle between landowners and farm laborers; the best known are *Mordová rokle* (The Hollow, 1949), *Jarní hromobití* (Spring Thunderstorm, 1952), *Vysoké letní nebe* (High Summer Sky, 1955), and *Selská láska* (Peasant Love, 1956). In *Nositelé řádu* (Award Winners, 1953), Stehlík portrayed exemplary workers, well schooled in Marxist-Leninist-Stalinist doctrine.

Milan Jariš belongs to the same group, even though in his first few plays he chose subjects from Czech history. *Přísaha* (The Oath) deals with the dilemma of Czechoslovak Army units ordered after Munich to hand over their arms to the Germans without a fight. His second drama, *Boleslav I*, written in verse, is concerned with the rise of feudalism seen from a Marxist viewpoint; in *Království boží* (Kingdom of God) he glorifies the Czech Hussite revolutionary movement of the fifteenth century. His plays *Inteligenti* (Intelligentsia, 1957) and *Šerif se vrací* (The Sheriff Returns, 1961), set in the present day, deal with the problem of responsibility in the realization of Communist ideas and aims, and the difficulties caused by this to the older generation not educated in the Communist spirit. Strangely enough, Vítězslav Nezval, one of the leading prewar poets, also wrote a socialist-realist play, *Dnes ještě zapadá slunce nad Atlantidou* (The Sun Still Sets Behind Atlantis), which was produced by the National Theater in 1955 and taken by it to the first World Theater season in London. Both play and performance were rightly condemned by critics and audiences.

All these playwrights were typical products of the Stalinist era, true socialist realists; their stage characters were either black or white, good or bad. Needless to say, the good ones were always Communists, opposed to capitalist exploiters or ideological subversionists. Socialism was portrayed as the glorious era of absolute freedom, the Communist Party as the bearer of all that was progressive; nothing the party did was ever wrong. This crude stereotype was alien to the Czech public, brought up in the spirit of Thomas G. Masaryk, the first humanitarian President of the republic, and accustomed to playwrights such as Karel Čapek (whose plays were banned at that time), František Langer, Jaroslav Seifert, and Jaroslav Hašek, the author of the *Good Soldier Schweik*. The theaters remained empty even after the Trade Unions started organizing "voluntary" mass visits of workers. Most of these "lost their way" and awaited the end of the performances in nearby bars.

In 1956 Jelínek's *Skandál v obrazárně* (Scandal in the Picture Gallery) was produced—the first postwar satirical play criticizing certain aspects of Communist dictatorship. Admittedly, its criticism was mild and confined to those aspects of party policy which the party itself condemned. Nevertheless, the staging of such a play caused a sensation and marked a real turning point in the postwar Czech theater. An equally important factor was the foundation of the first "small-stage theater" in Prague, the Theater on the Balustrade (Divadlo na Zábradlí). This experimental theater consisted of two companies, the Theater of the Mime, led by Ladislav Fialka, and a dramatic-satirical group led by the playwright, director, and actor Ivan Vyskočil, assisted by the composer-actor Jiří Suchý.

Fialka, as a solo mime, may not have attained the standards of Marcel Marceau or Sami Molkho, but his group has no equal anywhere in the world. His full-length mime plays, though not "drama" in the accepted sense, occupy an important place in the postwar Czech theater and were instrumental in reestablishing its international position. The first of these plays was *Cesta* (Clowns), the second *Blázni* (Fools), and the third *Knoflík* (The Button). Fialka's plays had several hundred performances in Prague, and soon the group started giving guest performances abroad. In time it took part in practically every theater festival in the world. The fact that there was no language barrier helped the company to be successful everywhere on its worldwide tours, both with sophisticated theatergoers and with people who had never seen a performance before.

The dramatic group of the Theater on the Balustrade opened with Ivan Vyskočil's play *Kdyby tisíc klarinetů* . . . (If a Thousand Clarinets . . .), an experimental comedy with songs. With the exception of Ljuba Hermanová, a well-known prewar entertainer, the actors were all young people in their early twenties. Their enthusiasm infected the audiences, and the play was performed nearly three hundred times. In 1962 Jan Grosman took over the leadership of the Balustrade's dramatic group, which at the same time was joined by the young playwright Václav Havel. From then on until 1968, the Balustrade was Prague's leading dramatic ensemble. Grosman, a well-known drama critic, theoretician, and translator of German and English plays, held exceedingly nonconformist views and was employed by the Balustrade management in spite of the fact that, by party order, he was at that time banned from public theatrical work. He introduced to Prague the "theater of the absurd," by producing, in 1964, his own adaptation of Alfred Jarry's *Ubu Roi*. This production became a European hit. It had almost five hundred performances in Prague and was performed in Czech at several important foreign festivals. Grosman was rehearsing *Ubu Roi* at the time the Communist Party of Czechoslovakia had just published a statement criticizing the anti-socialist activities of certain Czech cultural workers—a statement in which more than two thousand words were devoted to the condemnation of Grosman himself. The play was performed in spite of the fact that the Soviet Cultural Attaché in Prague several times "informed" the Czech authorities of his displeasure. The tremendous success at home and abroad made it impossible for the authorities to ban the play. The Theater on the Balustrade also presented other foreign works of the theater of the absurd, such as Ionesco's *The Lesson* and *The Bald Soprano* and Beckett's *Waiting for Godot*. More importantly it staged Havel's first play in the absurdist manner, *Zahradní slavnost* (The Garden Party).

Václav Havel has so far written three absurdist plays, all of which had their world premieres at the Theater on the Balustrade. *The Garden Party* was followed in 1966 by *Vyrozumění* (The Memorandum) and in 1968 by *Ztížená možnost soustředění* (Concentration Made Difficult). The main subject of Havel's plays is the inherent conflict in the relationship between man and system. This is demonstrated in the first two plays by the exposure of social institutions designed not to serve the people but to operate in effect for their own sake. In his third play he analyzes the personal life of a typical helpless and frustrated intellectual who endeavors to find an acceptable way of existence in his stereotyped environment. Havel accentuates in his plays the curse of modern civilization, where people stubbornly cling to pseudo-values and vainly try to shake off the tyranny of social mechanisms. His plays have been translated into several languages and have become regular repertory productions in many Western countries. After the British premiere of *The Memorandum* the London *Times* literary critic wrote: "Havel's achievement is that he has created a play that works very effectively on two levels. On the one hand he amusingly satirizes the idiocies of any bureaucratic system in which form becomes more important than content, regulations more significant than actual communication. But this is also a political play in that it shows that one of the first instincts of an autocrat is to tidy up the variety, color and expressiveness of language. Nothing in the play strikes one as more truthful than the attempt to justify the inhumanity of the new language on the grounds of its fundamental helpfulness; equally the attempt to rewrite history by pretending the language never existed, once it has failed, has a manifest political relevance."

Grosman's last major production at the Balustrade, his own dramatization of Franz Kafka's *Proces* (The Trial), will remain an unforgettable achievement of the Czech theater. It was performed at the world's most important festivals and in several West European countries. The Balustrade's dramatic group has never been invited to perform in any country of the socialist bloc.

In 1968, after the Soviet invasion of Czechoslovakia, both Havel and Grosman left the Theater on the Balustrade. They were both barred from all public artistic activities, but in spite of many offers to continue their creative work in the West they decided to remain in Czechoslovakia. A part of Havel's fourth play reached the West in 1969, but he has since disappeared from the public scene.

In a political system with a strongly centralized "cultural establishment" and strict state control over the major "official" theaters, a particularly important part—much more so than in a "free enterprise society"—is played by small and experimental theater groups. The proliferation of original and inventive "small-stage theaters" in Prague and the Czech provinces between 1956 and 1968 was so typical of the country's cultural life and so vital for the development of the younger generation of Czech playwrights that the most important ones shall be named here. At the Paravan Ivan Vyskočil and J. R. Pick staged their satirical sketches; at the Reduta young playwrights and aspiring actors tested their talents; at the Viola, a small stage-cum-discothèque, well-known actors gave poetry recitals, including such full-length poetical "compositions" as Antonín Bartušek's *Červené jahody* (Red Strawberries). Very popular also were the Semafor, where the playwright-composer-director Jiří Suchý was joined by the composer-actor-painter Jiří Šlitr, whose New York exhibition in 1968 was acclaimed by the critics, and the Rokoko. Practically all the artists associated with these small theaters were supporters of the Czechoslovak liberalization movement in 1968, and some of them were barred from public work in 1969.

An entirely different kind of experimental theater is the Laterna Magica, invented and founded in 1958 by Alfred Radok, who had been barred from work in the National Theater in 1957 because of his nonadherence to socialist realism. His Laterna Magica, a combination of living theater with polyécran and film, was one of the main attractions at several world's fairs. Jiří Srnec's Black Theater (Černé Divadlo) is another Prague specialty: On an entirely blacked-out stage, invisible actors clad and masked in black perform sketches with illuminated objects or parts of their bodies. Like the Laterna Magica, the Black Theater has toured most countries, including the United States and Australia. Jaroslav Hybner's Alfred Jarry Mime Theater was founded in 1967 and was a great success at the 1969 Prague Mime Festival.

Otomar Krejča's Theater Behind the Gate (Divadlo za Branou), another repertory theater, was founded in 1966. Like Radok, Krejča had been barred from working at the National Theater in 1957. At the Theater Behind the Gate he was joined by several leading actors from the National Theater and by the playwright Josef Topol, whose first drama, *Půlnoční vítr* (Midnight Breeze), written in verse and dealing with the origins of Czech history, had been produced in 1956 when Topol was only twenty-one. In his play *Jejich den* (Their Day, 1959) Topol examined the younger generation's attitude to topical events, attacking in particular the empty political phraseology used at that time. In his next play, *Konec masopustu* (Carnival's End), he dealt with the life of the younger generation in the new conditions of cooperative-farm villages. His comedy *Kočka na kolejích* (Cat on the Tracks), again about the problems of the younger generation, was performed by the Theater Behind the Gate at the 1969 World Theatre season in London. Topol's latest play is *Hodina lásky* (Hour of Love), produced in 1968.

Another popular small stage in Prague was the Drama Club (Činoherní klub), which opened with a play by its resident author, Alena Vostrá, *Na koho to slovo padne* (Whose Turn Next?). Her second play, *Na ostří nože* (On the

Knife's Edge), was produced at the Drama Club in 1968. This company represented Czechoslovakia at London's World Theatre season in 1970 with Vostrá's *Whose Turn Next?* and Machiavelli's *Mandragola,* directed and produced by Jiří Menzel, known for his Oscar-winning film *Closely Watched Trains.*

The best-known provincial small stage is Brno at Nightfall (Večerní Brno), founded in the Moravian capital by the Brno State Theater director Evžen Sokolovský and dedicated from its very beginning to sharp political satire. Its adaptation by Milan Uhde of Karel Havlíček Borovský's *King Lávra*—a political satire written in the first half of the nineteenth century and then aimed against the Habsburg monarchy—now called *King Vávra (Král Vávra),* ridiculed Czechoslovakia's totally uneducated President and First Party Secretary, the neo-Stalinist Antonín Novotný. It was certainly the most courageous theatrical production of the '60s, and people traveled to Brno from all over the country to see it. When the production moved to Prague it was banned by the censors after a very few performances. Small-stage theaters existed also in Ústí-on-Elbe, Karlovy Vary (Karlsbad), and other provincial centers.

The Czech cultural "thaw" saw the revival of several previously forbidden prewar plays, notably those of Karel Čapek, for which the now internationally famous stage architect Josef Svoboda designed the sets. This period also witnessed the introduction to the Czech stage of the works of Friedrich Dürrenmatt, Günter Grass, Max Frisch, Jean Genet, Harold Pinter, Arthur Miller, Edward Albee, Eugene O'Neill, Jean-Paul Sartre, Rolf Hochhuth, Albert Camus, Félicien Marceau, and other Western authors.

The majority of Czech progressive authors at that time fought against the "deformations" of the neo-Stalinist regime in the country by writing satirical plays. The most successful playwright of this kind was Vratislav Blažek with his comedy *Tři přání* (Three Wishes, 1958) and his play *Příliš štědrý večer* (An Over-Generous Christmas, 1960), in which he attacked the formalism and falsehood of life under Communism. František Pavlíček, who at the time of the liberal Dubček regime represented Czech creative artists in the Communist Party Central Committee and was expelled from the party in 1969, had in his youth written the drama *Chtěl bych se vrátit* (I Want to Return); its subject was the problem of political emigration. Pavlíček was only twenty-three when this play was first produced in 1956. His second play, *Labyrint srdce* (The Heart's Labyrinth), was produced in 1959. Although his early works, up to a point, still expressed orthodox Communist ideas, they cannot be put in the same category as the above-mentioned stereotyped, dogmatic plays. In his third play, *Zápas s andělem* (Wrestling With Angels), which describes life in a corrective institution for juveniles, Pavlíček clearly showed where he stood in the struggle for freedom of thought and expression. One of Pavlíček's most important achievements is his dramatization of the Soviet author Isaac Babel's story "Sashka Christ." Babel was executed in Stalin's purges and to this day most of his works are banned in the Soviet Union. Pavlíček's dramatization, produced in 1968, was thus an unreserved condemnation of Stalinism and a great avowal of freedom of speech; it was received with particular enthusiasm by the younger generation. In 1969 his dramatization of Karel Čapek's novel *Život a dílo skladatele Foltýna* (The Life and Work of the Composer Foltýn) was successfully produced under the title *Posedlost* (Obsession).

Another progressive author and playwright is Ludvík Kundera, whose very first play, *Totální kuropění* (Total Submission), opposed the unrealistic ideas governing official thinking in the '60s. In his series of sketches *Historie velkého okresního kýžala* (History of the Big Boss, 1963), Kundera satirically portrayed the life of a dogmatic party functionary and ridiculed people who were too frightened to express their own independent ideas. This progressive and liberal group of playwrights also includes the well-known novelist Ivan Klíma, whose play *Zámek* (The Castle), based on Franz Kafka's novel, was produced in 1967. Klíma's second play, *Porota* (The Jury), completed after the occupation of Czechoslovakia in 1968, was banned from production. His third play, *Ženich pro Marcelku* (A Bridegroom for Marcelle), met with the same fate.

Milan Kundera's first play, *Majitelé klíčů* (The Owners of the Keys), was produced at the National Theater in 1961; after several novels lampooning Communist dogmatism he wrote a second play, *Ptákovina, čili Dvojí uši— dvojí svatba* (Double Wedding), in which he exposed the corruption and hypocrisy of party officials. This play was produced at the Balustrade in 1968. Ladislav Smoček, co-founder of the Drama Club, author of *Bludiště* (The Maze), *Podivné odpoledne dr. Zvonka Burkeho* (Dr. Burke's Extraordinary Afternoon), and *Piknik*, as well as Jaroslav Gillar, the new leader of the Balustrade's dramatic ensemble, author of *Život jaký milujeme* (The Life We Love), should also be mentioned among this group of authors.

One of the most important playwrights of this group is the poet František Hrubín, who in his *Srpnová neděle* (August Sunday, 1958) and *Křišťálová noc* (Crystal Night, 1961) described the internal dilemma of the intelligentsia at that time. The first of these plays is concerned with a self-centered attitude, reflected by the meeting at a holiday resort between an unsuccessful poet and a married couple, whose emptiness of thought and boredom Hrubín contrasts with the lively activity of the younger generation. His second play, dealing with a similar problem, is somewhat reminiscent of Chekhov in the creation of atmosphere and the buildup of dramatic conflict. Hrubín's latest play, *Oldřich a Božena*, is set in the eleventh century. Its subject is the love of a Czech king for a peasant girl and the conspiracy of the nobility, who try to prevent the king from getting too close to the people. The play contains clear topical allusions to the new Communist rulers, the technocrats and party bosses, and their total estrangement from the popular masses. It was produced in 1968 and was an outstanding success, enthusiastically applauded after the invasion of Czechoslovakia.

The novelist Ludvík Aškenázy wrote three plays. In his drama *Host* (Guest, 1960), he warns against the dangers of neo-Fascism, in whatever form; his comedy *C.k. státní ženich* (Imperial Bridegroom) is a satire on the personality cult. His latest play, *Pašije pro Andělku* (Passion Play for Angela), was produced in 1968.

The poet Pavel Kohout devoted much of his literary activity in the last fifteen years to the theater. His first two plays, *Zářijové noci* (September Nights, 1955) and *Taková láska* (Such Is Love, 1957), show the influence of the stereotyped manner. They both deal with the conflicts of the younger generation. However, his dramatizations of Jules Verne's *Around the World in Eighty Days* and of Jaroslav Hašek's *Good Soldier Schweik*, as well as his most recent play, *August August, august* (Augustus the Clown), clearly reveal his progressive ideas and have been translated into many foreign languages and produced on a number of Western stages. During the liberalization period Kohout was one of the most involved artists, fighting for a new concept of socialism. He was elected chairman of the Czech Writers' Union Communist Party organization and became a member of the Communist Party Central Committee at the "illegal" Party Congress held in Prague immediately after the entry of the Soviet troops. In 1969 he was expelled from the party and completely silenced. He was offered political asylum in the West, but decided to remain in his homeland, hoping that liberal ideas would ultimately prevail there.

Oldřich Daněk is best known as an author of film scripts, but his comedies *Pohled do očí* (Eye to Eye, 1959) and *Svatba sňatkové podvodnice* (Wedding of a Marriage Swindler, 1968) were both very successful. His latest play, *Vrátím se do Prahy* (I Shall Return to Prague), produced in 1969, was banned in 1970 by the authorities for its "revisionist" ideas.

Milan Uhde, mentioned earlier as the author of *King Vávra*, also wrote a paraphrase of the ancient legend of Antigone, which was produced in 1967 under the title *Děvka z města Théby* (The Harlot of Thebes) and, like his first play, contains topical allusions. *Parta* (The Gang), a script written for Czech Radio and broadcast in 1969, was awarded the first prize in the Czech Radio play competition.

Pavel Landovský, an actor, is a young playwright of the theater of the absurd. His first play, written in 1969, *Hodinový hoteliér* (The Hotel Manager), is clearly influenced by Beckett's *Waiting for Godot*.

In 1966 Evžen Sokolovský, director of the Brno State Theater, for the first time since the war produced a passion play on the Czech stage. It was an adaptation of an old Czech folk play by Jan Kopecký, an orthodox Marxist critic of the contemporary theater. The success of the production was overwhelming; tickets were even sold on the black market. Encouraged by this commercial success, the Prague Realistic Theater staged another old Czech folk passion play with equal success.

A most important contemporary event in Czech cultural life was the

Fourth Congress of the Czechoslovak Writers' Union in June 1967. It demonstrated to the whole country that Czech writers, poets, and playwrights were united in their opposition to the dogmatic leadership of the Communist Party under Antonín Novotný. It was thus one of the principal curtain raisers of the liberalization process that started in January 1968. The short, heady excitement of freedom was not to last: A few months later, in August 1968, the Soviet-led invasion triggered the complete reversal of the process.

Nevertheless, it is a fact that as late as the spring of 1970, about eighteen months after the invasion and a year since Dubček's replacement by Husák, the cultural workers—the writers, artists, and film-makers—were still united in their opposition to the new regime and had so far refused to collaborate with it. Hardly a day passed without some official's or politician's angry attack on the "stubborn" and uncooperative attitude of the cultural workers. In a typical article, *Rudé Právo*, the official Communist Party daily, in January 1970 censured "the responsible officials of Prague's theaters" for proposing to observe the centenary of Lenin's birth not by orthodox Communist plays but with performances of Aleksandr Ostrovski's *The Thunderstorm (Groza)*, Schiller's *Don Carlos*, a number of eighteenth- and nineteenth-century Czech classics, a comedy by Christopher Fry, a farce by the Colombian playwright Enrique Buenaventura, and Shakespeare's *As You Like It*. Not a single Soviet play, nor one by any contemporary author from a "socialist" country!

Another, equally significant, piece of information was broadcast by Prague Radio on February 2, 1970: "The management of the Prague City Theaters has, with immediate effect, withdrawn from the repertoire of the Prague Chamber Theater the production of these three plays: Molière's *Tartufe*, Daněk's *I Shall Return to Prague*, and Albee's *A Delicate Balance*. As has been stated in the announcement approved by the Arts Council of the Prague City Theaters, "performances of these plays have been accompanied by undesirable reactions from the audiences, who reduced to vulgarity the seeming topicality of these productions and thereby impaired their artistic effectiveness. The reactions from the audiences were contrary to the idea and spirit of the plays, as well as to the intentions of their producers and were, fundamentally, of a provocative character." The theater in Czechoslovakia has always been an engaged art form, and Czech playwrights have always considered themselves involved in their nation's destinies. There can be little doubt about where they stand at this moment—but it is impossible to predict how long they will be able to resist the powerful political pressures.

*Slovak drama.* Unlike the Czech lands, which from 1939 to 1945 were under direct German occupation, Slovakia during that period was a "sovereign" state by the grace of Hitler. It was ruled by a Fascist clique, it had a treaty of alliance with Hitlerite Germany, and some of its army units fought side by side with German units. Slovak culture could develop "freely" so long as it supported Nazi doctrines, and Slovak artists were allowed to work if their ancestry was purely Aryan. One might, therefore, have expected the Slovak theater to develop more rapidly than the Czech theater after the reestablishment of the Czechoslovak Republic in 1945. But this did not happen. From 1945 until the Communist take-over in 1948, Slovak drama was characterized by an abstract symbolism. Subsequently, during the late '40s and early '50s, Slovak playwrights produced only one type of play: dogmatic, stereotyped socialist-realist "art," avoiding all real issues of the day.

The organization of the Slovak theater was the same as that in the Czech lands. The center was in Bratislava, with its National Theater companies and an experimental "small-stage theater," founded in 1958, which did not, however, produce anything of major importance. Bratislava also had a Theater of the Mime, founded in 1959 by Chládek and Sládek, but this never reached the standard of Fialka's group in Prague. In the middle '60s a new experimental small stage was founded in Bratislava, the Theater on Main Street—its name an allusion to the Slovak Oscar-winning film *The Shop on Main Street*. Its founders were M. Lasica and J. Satinský, both playwrights and actors, who concentrated on sharp political satire and were the most popular artists in Slovakia until they were banned by the Slovak Communist authorities in 1969.

The most important Slovak playwright was Peter Karvaš, whose first play, *Meteor*, was produced in 1945. It was a symbolical play describing an elemental disaster that almost destroyed all humanity. In 1946 two comedies by Karvaš were produced, *Spolok piatich P* (The Five P's Club) and *Hannibal pred bránami* (Hannibal at the Gates). *Bašta* (Bastion, 1948) deals with Slovak revolutionary history. *Ludia z našej ulice* (People in Our Street, 1951), *Srdce plné radosti* (Heart Full of Joy, 1954), and *Pacient stotrinásť* (Patient No. 113, 1955) are typical stereotyped products of the time. After two light comedies, *Diplomati* (The Diplomats, 1958) and *Zmrtvychvstanie deduška Kolomana* (Resurrection of Grandpa Koloman, 1960), Karvaš wrote three dramas that were to become the most important events in Slovak theatrical art. They were *Polnočná omša* (Midnight Mass, 1959), a ruthless and frank analysis of the attitude and behavior of the majority of the Slovak people at the time of the so-called Slovak State; *Antigona a tí druhí* (Antigone and the Others, 1962), which described life under the inhuman conditions of a concentration camp, and finally *Jazva* (The Scar, 1963), which courageously criticized the persecution of innocent people at the time of the "personality cult." Karvaš' comedy *Veľká Parochňa* (The Wig, 1965) treats the same subjects in a satirical manner. His latest play, *Experiment Damokles* (The Damocles Experiment), was produced in 1968.

Other postwar Slovak playwrights of importance include Štefan Kralik, whose psychological plays *Hra bez lásky* (Games Without Love, 1947), *Hra o slobode* (Play About Freedom, 1948), and *Posledná prekážka* (Last Obstacle, 1956) examine contemporary ethical problems. He also wrote a historical play about the Slovak national revival movement, *Svätá Barbora* (St. Barbara), which was produced in 1953.

During the brief liberalization period in Czechoslovakia a great number of important Slovak writers stood aloof and some even openly criticized the Dubček regime; after the Soviet occupation they firmly sided with the occupation forces. They were duly rewarded in 1969 by the highest state and party functions. An exception was the foremost Slovak theatrical theoretician and critic Pavol Števček, the longtime editor of the now-banned Slovak literary weekly *Kulturný Život*. As early as the middle '60s Števček fought courageously against the Novotný regime and stood unambiguously by the side of the Czech liberal artists during the Prague Spring. In 1969 he was expelled from the party and banned from all public literary activity. Among Slovak playwrights the only exception to the rule was Ladislav Lahola, who had spent his youth in a Nazi concentration camp. He was subsequently kept in prison for many years by the Slovak Communists, and after his release wrote several anti-dogmatic novels and plays: *Bez vetrie v Zuele* (Dead Calm in Zuela), *Štyri strany sveta* (Four Sides of the Earth), *Atentát* (Assassination), *Skvrny na slunci* (Sunspots), produced in 1967, and *Inferno*, produced in 1968. Lahola died suddenly in 1968. Unlike the Czech cultural workers, the Slovaks began to cooperate with Gustav Husák's new pro-Soviet and neo-Stalinist regime.

# D

**Dagerman, Stig** (1923–1954). Swedish novelist and playwright. Immediately following the war, until his untimely death by suicide, Dagerman was one of his country's leading writers. Expressionistic images of guilt and existential terror in his work link him with Strindberg and Kafka. The theme of Dagerman's first novel, *Ormen* (The Serpent, 1945), is that terror must be faced and accepted, honestly and openly, and in the novel *De dömdas ö* (The Isle of the Damned, 1946) he suggested that terror should be nurtured because it can function as a conscience. The central character of his first play, *Den dödsdömde* (The Condemned, 1947), learns a bitter lesson about the fickleness of human emotions. When he is released from prison after having been unjustly convicted of murdering his wife, he finds that the same people who had looked forward to seeing him executed are now full of sympathy for his suffering. He is able to reject their pity because he knows that he faced terror courageously and alone once and can do so again. The play *Ingen går fri* (No One Goes Free, 1949), an adaptation of his novel *Bränt barn* (Burnt Child, 1948), is a psychological study of urban life centering upon a young man with a mother fixation. *Streber* (The Climber, 1949) is a problem play about how the selfish ambitions of a member of a business cooperative betray the working-class syndicalist ideals upon which the enterprise had been founded. Dagerman's last play, *Den yttersta dagen* (Judgment Day, 1954), has a rural setting and is about an old farmer who is racked with guilt because his failure to escort a drunken acquaintance home resulted in the latter's accidental death.

OTHER PLAYS: *Skuggan av Mart* (The Shadow of Mart, 1948).

**Darvas, József** (born 1912). Hungarian playwright and politician. Before the war Darvas was a left-wing populist writer with Communist sympathies. After 1945 he became deeply involved in national politics. Between 1947 and 1956 he was a cabinet minister, first in a coalition and later in successive Communist governments; between 1951 and 1953 and again after 1959 he was president of the Hungarian Writers' Association. Of his plays, *Szakadék* (Precipice, 1942), which portrays the conflict of a provincial schoolteacher with his social milieu and his conscience, is still considered the best; *Kormos ég* (Soot-Covered Sky, 1959) is the apology of pro-Russian Communist intellectuals during the 1956 uprising. *Hajnali tüz* (Fire at Dawn, 1961) and *Részeg eső* (Drunken Rain, 1964) are plays on contemporary social themes. *Zrinyi* is the drama of a Hungarian magnate and military commander of the sixteenth century, a violent and ambitious man who, nevertheless, grows into a national hero in the final hour of truth. *A térképen nem található* (It Cannot Be Found on the Map, 1969) is an interesting attempt to discuss the appalling social conditions still persisting in villages in a part of the country called Hungary's Sicily. Although some of the questions asked by Darvas in his dramas are relevant and central to postwar Hungarian reality, his answers are not satisfactory and his characters are not fully convincing.

**Death of a Salesman** (1949). Pulitzer Prize-winning play by Arthur Miller. These "Certain Private Conversations in Two Acts and a Requiem" take place largely in the mind of protagonist Willy Loman (the play was first titled *The Inside of His Head*), though there is not absolute consistency in this regard. Willy's return home at the beginning of the play, his wife's anxiety that he has smashed the car, his explanation that he is "tired to the death" and "just couldn't make it" foreshadow the end of the play: Willy's suicide and Linda's lack of comprehension (she made the last payment on the house the day of his funeral, but neither she nor Willy has broken out of the trap of finding that important). In between these first and final moments a series of scenes demonstrate the nature of Willy's "death," his failure.

The Lomans live with "a solid vault of apartment houses around [their] small, fragile-seeming home"; and Willy is a small man in a large, demanding world. His failure results from his defining success in the terms of that world rather than of his own possibilities. Not only does he accept the money and personality values of "success" that that world insists upon, he teaches them to his sons, Biff and Happy, ruining their lives as well as his own. When Willy as an old salesman and Biff as a young athlete discover the limitations of "being well liked," they realize the lie inherent in their lives and find they have no grounds on which to like themselves. Willy's response, whether in despair or in a final effort to continue the lie, is suicide. Biff's is to drop out, an apparent failure searching to find himself. Happy, alone of the men in the family, blithely follows the lie, successful in his own eyes but clearly to the audience, and to his mother, the most impoverished character in the play.

Counterpointed against this example of failure are two characters who appear to Willy to have been successful: his brother, Ben, who walked into the jungle at seventeen and walked out at twenty-one, by God, a rich man; and Bernard, Biff's studious schoolmate, who was never "well liked" but who became a lawyer and argued a case before the Supreme Court. Both of these characters—one a recurrent memory from the past, the other a neighbor whose development Willy has watched—tantalize Willy by their very existence. And they tantalize the audience because they are embodiments of acceptable American success stories: the virile adventurer who wrenches money from the land, the hardworking local boy who makes good. Are these legitimate alternatives to Willy's failure, or are Ben and Bernard equally deceived? The answer to this question will determine in part whether or not *Death of a Salesman* is a modern tragedy of a common man or a social drama criticizing the world that common man inhabits.

The final words of the play are spoken by Linda over her husband's grave, as she struggles to understand why he killed himself when for the first time in thirty-five years they were "just about free and clear"; her sobbingly repeated "We're free" is questioned by music from a haunting flute that suggests the great and wild-hearted life Willy never had. Over the darkening stage "the hard towers of the apartment building rise into sharp focus."

**De Filippo, Eduardo** (born 1898). Italian dramatist. De Filippo is Italy's leading contemporary playwright. Most of his plays are set in Naples and many of the characters speak a Neapolitan dialect, yet his plays have universal appeal. His use of Neapolitan has a dual advantage: it creates greater believability and the richness of the dialect gives a lyrical quality to the dialogue.

A variety of influences have determined De Filippo's development as a dramatist. The first and foremost of these is the art and environment of Naples. The Neapolitan music-hall revues and vaudeville theater, which De Filippo attended as a boy and later performed in himself, retained many of the traditions and techniques of the *commedia dell'arte*. Many of these vaudeville skits centered about the antics of Pulcinella, the roguish, clever, indolent servant, who gradually evolved into the stock type of the *piccolo borghese*, the lower-middle-class rogue of Neapolitan comedy. The realistic and farcical events of plebeian life contained in the vaudeville skits were to appear later in De Filippo's comedies.

During De Filippo's early development as a dramatist, naturalism was the dominant theatrical form in Europe. This explains the verisimilitude of De Filippo's characters and settings, the psychological necessity of their actions. However, in contrast to the starkness of naturalism, De Filippo's plays have a certain whimsical quality. Many of his early plays were comedies written expressly for his company, the Teatro Umoristico De Filippo, that featured himself, his sister, Titina, and his brother, Peppino. These were comedies in the *commedia* tradition of the vaudeville theater. De Filippo's postwar plays were more serious, concerned with such themes as illusion-reality, the war years, and the role of the family.

*Napoli milionaria* (1945) is a moving drama of the dehumanizing effects of war. Gennaro, a streetcar conductor, is lost during an American bombing raid and wanders aimlessly for a year. On returning home he discovers that his wife is rich from the black market and living with another man, his daughter is a prostitute, and his son a thief. However, survival of the family takes precedence over pride and revenge. Gennaro blames the war for the family's actions and offers his wife a cup of coffee, a symbol of their former status quo. Life continues, but the scars of war are never healed.

*Questi fantasmi* (Oh, These Ghosts, 1945) is a drama of illusion and reality, but not in an intensely intellectual or Pirandellian vein. Pasquale saves himself from actual tragedy by believing that his wife's lover is a benevolent ghost that haunts his house and leaves him money before departing. His young wife believes that his greed enables him to accept this dishonor and detests him even more, not realizing that he has accepted his fantasy as a reality. Ultimately, the ghost alone realizes the truth and departs forever. Pasquale remains rather contented and hopes that the ghost will return, but the wife considers him a coward and so justifies her adultery.

De Filippo's drama of the role of the family in Neapolitan life, *Filumena Marturano* (1946), was made into a popular film as *Marriage Italian Style*. Filumena, an ex-prostitute, is about to be jilted by the man she has lived with for twenty-five years, a rich parasite who desires to marry a young woman. Filumena attempts to trick him into marriage, but fails. She then announces that he is actually the father of one of her three sons but refuses to reveal which one. The possibilities of fatherhood and family take precedence over the man's personal desire. He marries the middle-aged Filumena, renounces the right to know the identity of his real son, and accepts all three boys as his own.

Throughout De Filippo's drama is a comparison for the plight of his characters and a marvelous sense of theatricality. This, he maintains, derives from his work as an actor-director: "The theater is neither a book nor a literary work: it must always be alive, and thus for one-and-a-half to two hours it must always have elements of surprise. That's why the public comes to see my plays, because they enjoy themselves and carry something home with them as well."

OTHER PLAYS: *S. Carlino* (1947), *Le bugie con le gambe lunghe* (Lies With Long Legs, 1948), *Le voci di dentro* (Voices from Within, 1948), *La grande magia* (The Big Magic, 1949), *La paura numero uno* (Fear Number One, 1950), *Tre atti: Amicizia, I morti non fanno paura, Successo* (Three Acts: Friendship, The Dead Can't Frighten You, Success, 1952), *Carnevalata* (Carnival, 1952), *Pranziamo inzieme* (Let's Eat Together, 1952), *I migliori sono così* (The Best Are Like That, 1952), *Io sono suo padre* (I Am His Father, 1952), *Un pomeriggio intellettuale* (An Intellectual Afternoon, 1954), *Mia famiglia* (My Family, 1955), *Bene mio e core mio* (Dear One and Sweetheart, 1955), *Metamorfosi di un suonatore ambulante* (Metamorphosis of a Strolling Player, 1956), *Sabato, domenica e lunedì* (Saturday, Sunday, and Monday, 1959), *Dolore sotto chiave* (Pain Under Lock and Key, 1960), *Il sindaco del rione sanità* (The Mayor of Sanity Ward, 1960), *De pretore Vincenzo* (Regarding Judge Vincenzo, 1961), *Il figlio di Pulcinella* (Son of Pulcinella, 1962), *Tommaso d'Amalfi* (Thomas of Amalfi, 1963), *L'arte della commedia* (The Art of Comedy, 1966), *Il cilindro* (The Cylinder, 1966), *Il contratto* (The Contract, 1967), *Il monumento* (1969).

**Delaney, Shelagh** (born 1939). English dramatist. Miss Delaney left school at the age of sixteen to find work in the North Country town of Salford where she was born. She embarked upon her career as a dramatist two years later in 1958 when *A Taste of Honey* was presented under Joan Littlewood's direction. Miss Delaney has said that she was spurred into writing the play after the experience of seeing a play by Terence Rattigan had convinced her that she could do better herself. In itself, the contrast between the exuberance of the young girl from the industrial north and the outworn conventions of Rattigan's cosmopolitan style seemed to point to the revivification of the English theater achieved by the English Stage Company and Theatre Workshop, while the very real merits of the play insured that Shelagh Delaney's name would join those of the other young dramatists who had breathed new spirit into the theater of the '50s. The play underwent the extensive modification in rehearsal consistent with Joan Littlewood's style of direction, but a critic who has studied the original script has found it "not so radically different from the version performed as most published comment on the subject would lead one to believe." The author can therefore be credited with the principle achievement of the play, which lies in the creation of the adolescent character of Josephine, explored through her relationship with her errant mother, her Negro boyfriend, and the young homosexual who befriends her during her pregnancy. The play received the Charles Henry Foyle New Play Award. The critical and popular success that attended her first play was not repeated for her second, *The Lion in Love* (1960). A gentle if somewhat formless study of life among a North Country family of market-stall holders, it lacks the sensational and sometimes melodramatic appeal of *A Taste of Honey.* A growing maturity, however, can be seen in the portrayal of the older characters, and a study of the play helps to dispel the illusion that Miss Delaney's reputation owes more to Joan Littlewood's production of her first play than to her own talents.

No further plays have followed *The Lion in Love,* but Miss Delaney has published a book of short stories, *Sweetly Sings the Donkey,* and written the screenplay *Charlie Bubbles* (1968), both of which works suggest that her talent is by no means exhausted.

**Denmark.** Clear evidence of why Denmark is called the most bourgeois of the Scandinavian countries can be found of a summer evening in Copenhagen's Tivoli amusement park: the cheerful but sedate music halls and the fun rides; the comfortable, friendly restaurants; and the open-air pantomime theater that presents elaborately costumed *commedia dell'arte* plays in a sentimentally comic style best described as wholesome family entertainment.

There is a long tradition in the Danish theater of poking fun at the national propensity for the *hyggelig* ("comfy") and the *ovn-lumre dyne* ("toasty-warm quilt") of middle-class idealism. Today the tradition is continued in satirical musical revues that have their roots in the past in the bourgeois comedy of Ludvig Holberg (1684–1754), the vaudevilles brought to Denmark from France by Johan Ludvig Heiberg (1791–1860), and in the present in American musical comedy and the theater of Bertolt Brecht. Rarely as tough-minded as Brechtian drama, Danish satire at its best has wit as well as charm and a flair for theatrical imagery reminiscent of Pirandello.

Kjeld Abell (1901–1961) and Soya (pen name of Carl-Erik Soya-Jensen; born 1896) were two playwrights of the prewar generation who criticized middle-class smugness, notably in *Melodien der blev vaek* (The Melody That Got Lost, 1935) and *Løve med corset* (A Corset for the Lion, 1950), respectively. The second world war produced a change in perspective in Abell. In *Silkeborg* (1946) he probed the problem of bourgeois narrow-mindedness in his story of a wartime provincial family whose desire for respectability and stability is reflected in the father's remark that they can "learn much from the Germans." The meaning of the Nazi occupation comes home to him only after his grandson is killed as a saboteur. Other Danish playwrights dealt with the war—Soya, for example, in *Efter* (Afterwards, 1947)—but they never became as preoccupied with the subject as did the Norwegians.

By the early 1960s the satirical treatment of middle-class values had become sharper and more political. A student revue, *Frihed—det bedste guld* (Freedom—the Best Gold, 1961), by Erik Knudsen (born 1922) with music by Finn Savery (born 1933), was the first of a series of satirical productions that began to revitalize the Danish theater. Knudsen, a poet, teacher, and member of the Danish Academy, is representative of many intellectuals who have criticized Scandinavian Social Democratic Parties for having allowed the development of materialistic "consumer societies" to take precedence over the realization of socialist revolutionary ideals. In this context, middle-class smugness is viewed as a stubborn obstacle to the building of a democratic society.

Criticism of capitalism, however, has not necessarily meant endorsement of Communism. In the musical satire *Nik, Nik, Nikolaj* (written 1964, produced 1966) Knudsen depicts in a gallows humor style how a young painter flees from Russia to the West in order to escape the state directives that prescribed how he was to work, only to discover that profit-oriented capitalism is as great a threat to his freedom of expressionism as was Communism.

In 1962 another student revue, *Gris på gaflen* (Pig on the Fork), by Jesper Jensen (born 1931), Leif Panduro (born 1923), and Klaus Rifbjerg (born 1931), explored many of the hardships and absurdities faced by an ordinary citizen in his journey from the cradle to the grave in welfare-state Denmark. The same year saw an important turning point: the production of *Teenagerlove* by Ernst BRUUN OLSEN with music by Finn Savery. For the first time in the memories of many Copenhagen theatergoers an indigenous work played to full houses at the Royal Dramatic Theater. The earlier student revues had been criticized for being amateurish and sophomoric; Bruun Olsen, a professional actor and director, as well as a playwright, brought to the genre an expertise hitherto lacking.

The target of the satire in *Teenagerlove* is the ruthless economic exploitation practiced by the consumer society in general, and by the popular music industry in particular. In *Baliden Borgerlige* (Ball at the Country Club, 1966), Bruun Olsen's next important musical satire, a wife regrets that the forces of materialistic capitalism have undermined the working-class solidarity she and her husband strove for during the war, and her disillusionment is voiced in a song that expresses a dominant theme of the Scandinavian musical satires of the 1960s:

> We [workers] shared everything: the work, the dirty
> backyards, the poverty, and the workhouse.
> But now times are better; a worker makes money . . .
> Now we've learned from the rich capitalists
> what money means
> Gold is not something you share; you grab it for
> yourself . . .

Knudsen and Bruun Olsen continue to write satire, but they have yet to fulfill their early promise. Director-critic Henrik Bering Liisbjerg has pointed out that while Knudsen has the poetic power and intellectual cogency that Bruun Olsen lacks, Bruun Olsen has the superior instinct for what is theatrically effective.

Several critics believe that Klaus RIFBJERG may eclipse all his contemporaries in the theater. Certainly he has written with humor and sympathy of the uneventfulness and absence of passion in the welfare state. For the central character of his drama with music *Hvad en mand har brug for* (What a Man Needs, 1966), Rifbjerg chose not a Social Democrat from the working classes, as Bruun Olsen did in *Ball at the Country Club*, but a successful engineer who discovers that although he has everything he thinks he needs— all the benefits of the welfare state plus wife, children, automobile, and mistress—his life is empty of meaning.

Leif Petersen (born 1934) and Anders Bodelsen (born 1937) are two younger playwrights who have written about the problems of the welfare state. Petersen, after writing several successful plays for Radio Denmark, finally attracted attention as a serious dramatist in 1969 with his *Alting og et posthus* (Everything and a Post Office), a stage adaptation of two of his radio plays. The setting is the lower-class apartment of a widow, Mrs. Knudsen, and her indolent son, Arnold. The title of the play refers to a hope that these people cherish of one day escaping from their sordid surroundings to a modern housing development that has "everything and a post office." Into the apartment comes a girl whom Arnold proceeds to exploit as he has exploited his mother. At the end of the play he and the girl talk about living together in the apartment after he has done away with his mother. The similarity of Petersen's play to Harold Pinter's *A Night Out* is more than incidental. Like Pinter, Petersen has a gift for suggestive, bitterly humorous dialogue punctuated with ominous pauses.

Anders Bodelsen's *En hård dags natt* (A Hard Day's Night, 1966) won the Prix Italia for the year's best radio play and was subsequently produced in a stage version throughout Europe. The following year he won acclaim for his *Tills Døden os skiller* (Till Death Us Do Part), first written for television and then revised for the stage. The theme of this dramatization of the final hours of the first famous Siamese twins is man's need to recognize how closely his fate is bound to that of his fellow man.

Radio drama continues to provide a valuable proving ground for Danish writers. Among the younger generation, who follow in the footsteps of such accomplished radio dramatists as H. C. Branner (1903–1966), Leck Fischer (1904–1956), and Finn Methling (born 1917), are Sven Åge Madsen (born 1939), Michael Buchwald (born 1943), and the woman poets and novelists Cecil Bødker (born 1927) and Inger Christensen (born 1935).

Useful sources of information on drama in Denmark are *Contemporary Danish Plays: An Anthology*, edited and with an introduction by Elias Bredsdorff (1955); and P. M. Mitchell, *A History of Danish Literature* (1958).

**Dennis, Nigel** (born 1912). English novelist, dramatist, and critic. Educated in Rhodesia and Germany, Dennis has worked as a reviewer and dramatic critic in England and the United States; from 1967 to 1971 he was joint editor of the quarterly *Encounter*. His first play, *Cards of Identity* (1956), was adapted from his novel of the same name in response to the appeal by the recently formed English Stage Company for established novelists with an interest in writing for the stage. His two subsequent plays were presented by the same company. The three plays are satirical in form. Dennis' first play, as its title suggests, is a many-sided satire on the contemporary quest for identity, while *The Making of Moo* (1957), subtitled "A History of Religion in Three Acts," displays the hostility to reason of a progression of religious practices, and *August for the People* (1962) dramatizes Sir Augustus Thwaites's revolt against the hypocrisy and artificial values of contemporary democracy, with short-lived results that are admired by some as the product of courageous honesty and dismissed by others as evidence of insanity. Dennis' outlook is far from typical of those associated with the writers whose plays followed *Look Back in Anger* at the Royal Court Theatre. Containing opinions that are individual sometimes to the point of eccentricity, his plays haughtily dismiss the accepted standards of the twentieth century, and the values they uphold are a curious blend of rationalism and aristocratic conservatism. But Dennis' plays are intellectual celebrations rather than dogmatic statements of opinion. In his own words, "neither the theologian nor the satirist has any interest in everyday justice, fairness, decency, accuracy; each is out simply to make his theme as glorious as possible."

**Deputy, The** (*Der Stellvertreter*, 1963, also translated as *The Represen-*

*tative*). A play by Rolf Hochhuth. The first production of this drama led to
an international controversy about the role of the Catholic Church in World
War II. Interesting essays have been collected in two books, *The Storm over
the Deputy* (1964) and *Der Streit um Hochhuths Stellvertreter* (1964), which
shed a great deal of light on the historical importance of the drama. The play
itself is a traditional five-act drama, which reports incidents relating to the
silence of Pope Pius XII from August 1942 until the end of the war. Hochhuth employs free verse to stress certain points and to vary the tones of reportage and scholarship with which the text is saturated. Still, the drama resembles an urgent report. Gerstein, a German engineer, dashes into the
Nuntiatur in Berlin to describe his experiences at Belsen and Treblinka. The
young priest Riccardo, on hearing this report, leaves Berlin to deliver the
news to the Pope in order to urge the "deputy of God" to protest the annihilation of the Jews by the Nazis. The suspense of the play emanates from
the conflicting interests of the Pope, who compromises his integrity and negates the value of communication by withholding his protest.

In order to establish the causes of this disaster, Hochhuth conceives an
elaborate framework that encompasses a cross section of the three groups central to the drama: the Catholic clergy, the Jews, and the Germans. Acts I, III,
and V have three scenes, while Acts II and IV have one. In the three-scene
acts, Hochhuth centers on the reaction of the Catholic clergy, the Jews, and
the Germans to the Nazi persecution of minorities. Acts II and IV, the most
polemical, are set in Rome. Act II is Hochhuth's inner dialogue on the *Real-
politik* of the Catholic Church. Graf Fontana, a well-meaning, rich layman;
a Cardinal, a shrewd diplomat; and Riccardo, a forthright idealist, argue about
the position of the Church with regard to Jews, Communism, and Nazism.
After each side voices its opinion, Hochhuth concludes that the Church refused to defend the Jews because it feared the Communists more than the
Nazis. In Act IV Hochhuth analyzes those personal failings which led the
Pope to act so reprehensibly during this crucial period.

Gerstein and Riccardo appear in the majority of the scenes. As men on a
holy quest they represent Hochhuth's point of view. Both are passionate in
temperament and act under the assumption that nihilism can be overcome by
moral vigor. Wherever they go, they expose cowardice and perversion—Riccardo by his earnest and righteous appeals, Gerstein by his disturbing and
ironic observations.

The language of the play is formulated as imaginatively as the structure.
Hochhuth uses words to measure moral worth. Decadent language, in which
words are the vehicles of lies and are designed to obscure, not to communicate,
is associated with the decline of Europe. Most discussions in the play are futile
because the speakers do not mean what they say. By transforming rhetoric into
a moral barometer, Hochhuth shows the mettle of his characters. Gerstein mysteriously disappears in trying to save the Jews. Riccardo becomes the real
"deputy of God" by accompanying Jews to Auschwitz.

Hochhuth's original play, which would take close to six hours to perform, has never received a full production. Various abridged productions have been highly successful. This is not so much due to Hochhuth's command of language as to his forceful ideas. His historical perspective is both enlightening and imaginative. Though the play may be classified as melodramatic and didactic by future literary historians, it will still command attention as one of the first documentary dramas in a wave of German plays that have sought to come to terms with the past.

**Déry, Tibor** (born 1894). Hungarian novelist and playwright. Although Déry came from a wealthy middle-class family, his concern for social justice made him a socialist at an early age. Between 1920 and 1935 he changed his country of residence several times: He lived in Vienna, Berlin, Italy, and Budapest. He took part in the 1934 Vienna uprising and, in Dubrovnik, wrote his first important novel *A befejezetlen mondat* (The Unfinished Sentence), which was not published until 1947. Déry translated into Hungarian André Gide's *Retour de l'U.R.S.S.* After the war his talent was at last recognized and he received the Kossuth Prize, Hungary's highest literary award. Official attacks against his novel *Felelet* (The Answer) in 1952 brought him into sharp conflict with the then leading Communist spokesman on cultural matters, József Révai. An important figure in the "writers' revolt" preceding the 1956 uprising, Déry was sentenced in 1957 to nine years' imprisonment for "anti-State activities." He was freed through amnesty in 1960 and a few years later was fully reinstated in Hungarian literary life. His richly woven memoirs, *No Verdict,* was among the most successful books of recent years. His plays published in the volume *Az óriáscsecsemő* (The Giant-Baby, 1967) include his prewar avant-garde play *Az óriáscsecsemő; A tanuk* (Witnesses, 1945), *Tükör* (Mirror, 1946), and *Itthon* (At Home, 1947); the short satirical comedy *A talpsimogató* (The Sycophant, 1954), and *Bécs, 1934* (Vienna, 1934; 1957), a three-act play on the Viennese workers' uprising. All of these *Tükör* is probably the best. It portrays the tragic conflict of a well-intentioned young man crushed between the extreme moral demands of the Judge, his father, and of his Communist girl friend. Déry's talent is basically epic in nature and most of his plays suffer from a lack of dramatic tension.

**Devine, George** (1910–1966). English actor and director. Devine's acting career began in 1932; from 1936 to 1939 he was director and manager of the London Theatre Studio; he was a founder of the English Stage Company in 1956 and remained its director until 1965. This company was founded for the express purpose of discovering and presenting new dramatic writing at a time when the commercial theater boasted few writers of distinction and other outlets for new writers scarcely existed. Responsible for the selection of plays, Devine was the chief architect of the policy that made this company, more than any other, responsible for the revival of the English theater in the latter half of the '50s. Devine began with the hope that established writers in other fields would welcome the opportunity of writing plays for a company free from commercial pressure. With the exception of contributions from novelists Angus Wilson and Nigel Dennis, and later from Doris Lessing, this hope was not realized. Among the new plays submitted by unknown writers, however, was John Osborne's *Look Back in Anger,* and the English Stage Company's production of this play in their first season was to prove a turning point in the history of the English theater. From an intellectual backwater the theater turned in less than five years to a vitally expressive and experimental medium. By the encouragement of young writers as diverse as N. F. Simpson, Ann Jellicoe, Arnold Wesker, and John Arden, the English Stage Company was to play a vital role in this movement.

Universally respected and a tireless worker, Devine combined the abilities of a working actor and director with an appreciation of literary and artistic merit, and it was this combination, rare in the English theater, that guided the English Stage Company during its formative years.

**Diable et le Bon Dieu, Le** (The Devil and the Good Lord, 1951). A play in three acts and eleven scenes by Jean-Paul Sartre. It was first performed on June 7, 1951, at the Théâtre Antoine, Paris, under the direction of Louis Jouvet. Sartre's most ambitious play, it lasts some four hours and has a very large cast and several mob scenes. Situated in Germany during the sixteenth century, the play is very picturesque in its costumes and settings. But the great spectacle is secondary to the main character, Goetz, who dominates the action from beginning to end—an overwhelmingly difficult role played with huge success in 1951 by the actor Pierre Brasseur.

The situation at the outset is extremely complex. Goetz, a bastard and consequently detached from all social strata, is a military leader besieging the city of Worms. The inhabitants of Worms have rebelled and imprisoned all members of the clergy except one priest "who loves the poor," Heinrich. On the other hand, the poor have as their leader a baker-prophet, Nasty. In order to save the priests from being massacred, Heinrich betrays the poor: He brings Goetz the key to a secret entrance to the city so that Goetz and his troops may enter and save the clergy by massacring the inhabitants. Nasty comes to beg Goetz to spare the poor and reproaches him with being merely a tool of the rich and powerful. Goetz, however, is beyond such considerations, stating that he is God's rival. Since God has already done good, Goetz claims that he is inventing evil. He does evil for the sake of evil, whether in massacring the innocent or in making his mistress, Catherine, into a whore. He is delighted with the idea that God sees him, allows him to act, and is thus an accomplice and as guilty as he. Goetz's pride as a great diabolic rebel is shaken when Heinrich, tortured by his own treachery, points out that evil is everywhere on earth and that no one has ever done good. Goetz then decides to do good, which he is told is impossible. In order to "drive the Lord into a corner"—that is, to make God responsible for his decision—he throws dice to determine his action. According to the dice, he is to do good. Goetz, obeying this sign of God, raises the siege on the town. At the very end of Act I we learn that he cheated.

In Act II Goetz has begun to do good by giving his lands to the peasants. But this is hardly a success: The peasants are not much interested in his gift and remain attached to their superstitions and to the Church that sells them indulgences for the salvation of their souls; moreover, the gift provokes a spirit of rebellion among the peasants of neighboring noblemen. Since the people, as Nasty explains, are not yet ready for an effective rebellion, theirs can lead only to massacre. In order to get Nasty to forgive him his betrayal in Act I, Heinrich, who claims to be accompanied by an invisible devil, agrees to help Nasty prevent the rebellion by terrorizing the priests. He is so successful that the priests flee, and the peasants, terrified at finding themselves without the sacraments, give up the idea of rebelling and take refuge in the churches, believing themselves damned. A young woman, Hilda, cares for them with nun-like devotion. She loves them and they love her, which is the sign of Goetz's defeat, for he is hated and alone. Among the peasants in a church is Catherine, Goetz's mistress, who is dying and tormented by visions of Hell. She has never stopped loving Goetz desperately. Goetz decides to put her soul at rest *in extremis* and prays God to let him assume her sins and to show his consent by a miracle: He asks to receive the stigmata. When nothing happens, Goetz pierces his hand with his own knife. Catherine dies in peace, because Goetz has given his blood for her. The peasants, believing it a true miracle, begin to worship Goetz, who announces that he will found a "City of the Sun."

In Act III Goetz's new society, based on love, virtue, and nonviolence, has started to function. His peasants proclaim their happiness. But since their neighbors still live in poverty and oppression, rebellion breaks out. The City of the Sun is destroyed by the rebels when Goetz's peasants refuse to fight alongside their brothers. Faced with this "good" that has turned to evil, Goetz indulges in frenzied forms of saintliness, such as fasting and corporal punishment. One year after the throw of the dice in Worms, Heinrich returns to Goetz to verify his own belief: that good is impossible on this earth. Goetz then reveals what he has learned from his experiment: that he was in fact only playing at doing good and evil, and without a spectator into the bargain, for God does not exist. Heinrich, unable to bear this denial, tries to strangle him, and Goetz kills him. After the murder, which puts an end to his adventure of doing good, Goetz rejoins mankind—that is, the rebellious peasants, who accept him, not as one of themselves, but as their military leader. Goetz is forced to terrorize them in order to drive them into successful battle. He is still a solitary man.

Two basic themes are interwoven in this play: atheism and revolutionary action. Here Sartre's atheism is expressed in violent attacks on the idea of the Christian God and on the Church. The tone ranges from burlesque sarcasm (the scene depicting the sale of indulgences, and that of the leper tired of being piously kissed) to philosophical discourses on the nothingness of Heaven and the equivalence of God to absence and emptiness. The play also says that the love preached by Christianity merely worsens man's situation on this earth. In order to help man and save him, one must join the masses and share their struggles. Yet such action is not easy: On the individual level Goetz, the bastard, will always be isolated from the people, whatever he does; on the collective level no community of men can happily survive while others are being oppressed.

Although the struggle of the poor against the rich is presented in a rather oversimplified manner, the moral and psychological conflicts are, on the contrary, treated with subtlety and vigor. Goetz's diabolical rebellion in Act I, the traitor Heinrich's moral torment as he is pursued by his devil and haunted by the idea of a formidable God, and Goetz's bad faith in his efforts at saintliness all make for highly dramatic scenes.

**Dialogues des Carmélites** (The Carmelites, 1952). A screenplay suggested to Georges Bernanos (1888–1948) by Father Raymond Bruckberger and adapted for the stage by Albert Béguin and Marcelle Tassencourt. It was first performed in 1952 at the Théâtre Hébertot, Paris, under the direction of Marcelle Tassencourt. Inspired by Gertrud von Le Fort's short novel *The Last on the Scaffold, Dialogues des Carmélites* is Georges Bernanos' last work. The action takes place from 1789 to July 17, 1794, and is based on a historical event: the guillotining of sixteen Carmelite nuns from Compiègne. The central character is Blanche de la Force, a weak young girl who is easily terrorized and ashamed of the fear that is consuming her like an illness. She hopes to find peace by submitting to the austere rule of the Compiègne Carmelites. During Blanche's novitiate the prioress of the convent dies in agony, although she had great strength of soul. Young Sister Constance innocently declares that she has probably died another woman's death and that the other woman, when her turn comes, will die with the ease that was denied the prioress. As revolutionary measures begin to threaten the convent, Blanche de la Force gets more and more frightened. She has taken the veil and must soon take her vows and become Sister Blanche of the Agony of Christ. Meanwhile, the persecution of the Carmelites is intensified: The convent is searched, devotional objects are destroyed, the nuns are forbidden to wear habits. The chaplain, a nonjuring priest, is forced to go into hiding. In the absence of the new prioress, Mother Marie of the Incarnation urges the sisters to take the vow of martyrdom—which they do, even Blanche, who seems to have made her decision "as one would toss a coin." However, Blanche flees from the convent and joins her father, the Marquis de la Force, in Paris. When the revolutionaries occupy the La Force house, the Marquis is guillotined and Blanche is forced to become a servant in her own home. In Compiègne the Carmelites are arrested and imprisoned. The new prioress believes she can save them by taking their vow of martyrdom upon herself, although it is a vow of which she disapproves. But they are nevertheless condemned to death—all but Mother Marie, who escaped imprisonment because she had gone to Paris to seek out Blanche. The play ends with a somewhat melodramatic but powerfully effective scene: The Carmelites, one by one, climb up to the scaffold singing the *Salve Regina* and the *Veni Creator*, and their voices die out one after another as the knife falls. Suddenly a new voice is heard from the midst of the crowd—the voice of Blanche, who is being pushed toward the scaffold. She is the last of the sisters to die. Sister Constance's prediction has been fulfilled: By a miracle Blanche's agony had been experienced by the former prioress, and Blanche has overcome her fear and enters tranquilly into death. This miracle is not the only religious mystery in the play. The new prioress, who disapproves of martyrdom, must yield to it, whereas Mother Marie has been refused it.

In addition to being a dramatization of the torturing anguish provoked by life and death, *Dialogues des Carmélites* is marked by the agony of Christ and his anguish, from the Garden of Olives to the Calvary. "Fear is, after all, the daughter of God" is the epigraph of the play, which is both the most human and most mystical of the Catholic postwar repertory.

**Díaz, Jorge** (born 1930). Chilean dramatist. Díaz is akin to Ionesco, but concerned with developing his own idiom and with the social climate of Latin America. His earliest works are in the vein of "theater of the absurd" in their rejection of convention and ordinary logic; they are also bitterly angry with the abuse of man by man. His most recent works have become more specifically social and more tightly structured. *El cepillo de dientes* (The Toothbrush, 1961) is a takeoff on the need for human relationships and the impossibility of developing them; *El velero en la botella* (The Ship in the Bottle, 1962) pillories the generation gap. Later works show greater discipline; *Variaciones para muertos en percusión* (Variations for Dead in Percussion, 1964) satirizes public relations and the publicity industry, and in *El lugar donde mueren los mamíferos* (The Mammals' Graveyard, 1963) Díaz attacks the hypocrisy of charity, which does nothing to eradicate the causes of poverty. In *Topografía de un desnudo* (Topography of a Nude, 1966), the massacre of beggars, based on a specific case, becomes a metaphor for Díaz's total rage.

**Documentary Theater** or **Theater of Fact** (**Dokumentarisches Theater, Dokumentartheater**). A dramatic genre developed in Germany during the 1960s. Documentary theater stems from the *Neue Sachlichkeit* movement of the 1920s. It bears certain similarities to the historical and political play, but it relies more on modern techniques of mass media and reportage to present a version of recent history in a new light. The emphasis is on factual editing with a liberal or radical slant in order to enlighten the audience about social and political problems. To a certain extent, the documentary drama involves a play with and about the facts, for the documentary dramatist wants to rewrite history in a new framework that will give the illusion of authenticity. Critics of the documentary drama have not understood this "play aspect" and have wrongly asserted that documentary dramatists have claimed to discover absolute truth in their plays.

The documentary drama drew international attention in 1963 when Erwin Piscator produced Rolf Hochhuth's *The Deputy* in Berlin. Piscator followed this production with Heinar Kipphardt's *In the Matter of J. Robert Oppenheimer* in 1964 and Peter Weiss's *The Investigation* in 1965. All three of these playwrights have produced other documentary dramas, and they have influenced many such German writers as Rolf Schneider, Fritz Hochwälder, Wolfgang Graetz, Tankred Dorst, Hans Magnus Enzensberger, and Hans-Georg Behr. The trend toward the documentary can also be traced in other countries, such as Great Britain, France, Russia, and the United States, where many documentary plays, as well as novels, films, and TV dramas, have been produced.

**Dorst, Tankred** (born 1925). West German dramatist and screenwriter. After being transported to various camps for prisoners of war in the United States, England, and Belgium, Dorst returned to Germany in 1947 and soon began studying German literature and theater at the University of Munich. He has been greatly influenced by the tradition of the marionette theater, and his first play, *Gesellschaft im Herbst* (Society in the Fall, 1959), reveals how people endeavor to play with one another like puppets in order to gain financial profit. Yet it is not only the marionette tradition but also Beckett, Brecht, Pirandello, and the more recent experimental playwrights who have influenced Dorst in his attempt to make theater out of theater. *Die Kurve* (The Curve, 1960) borrows elements from Beckett and the "theater of the absurd" in telling the story of a junk dealer and a man who delivers funeral orations. They both owe their business to a dangerous curve in the road that causes many deaths. When an investigator is sent to determine where the two get their money, they arrange for his accidental death and then continue their "respectable bourgeois" professions. Absurdity is also at the heart of *Freiheit für Clemens* (Freedom for Clemens, 1960) in which a prisoner adjusts himself so well to prison life that he refuses to accept his freedom when his sentence is completed. Dorst's plays are all parables, and are not as absurd as they seem. Since 1961 Dorst has moved more in the direction of Brecht. His *Grosse Schmährede an der Stadtmauer* (The Great Diatribe at the City Wall, 1961) is a didactic political work that condemns militarism. A woman whose husband has been drafted into the army goes to the wall built by the emperor to demand her husband back. Without him, she will not be able to maintain her livelihood. At the wall she suffers the mockery of soldiers and falls victim to a system that leaves her powerless. Dorst's most recent venture into political drama has been strongly influenced by other German documentary dramatists. His play *Toller* (1968), which concerns the expressionist dramatist Ernst Toller and the collapse of the Munich *Räterepublik* of 1918, is largely documentary in form. Dorst has written an extremely interesting drama, which uses four different play levels to show simultaneous action. The attempt is made to explain why the Munich experiment failed. In doing so, Dorst uses dramatic techniques from the expressionist era to portray Toller as a naïve, idealistic thinker who hoped to make a theater out of politics. Like the political leaders Gustav Landauer and Erich Mühsam, Toller is uncertain of the political demands he must face. In the end, he has no choice but must place himself before the court of those conservatives who brought about the Weimar "restoration."

Despite his eclectic tendencies, Dorst is concerned in almost all his plays with the manipulation of man by man. Therefore, the political themes are rooted not in ideology but in psychology. Some of Dorst's most interesting work has been done in the puppet theater or has been devoted to adapting plays such as Ludwig Tieck's *Puss in Boots* (as *Der gestiefelte Kater*, 1965). It is always with the theater in mind that Dorst seeks to make us aware of the illusions in life that allow us to become deceived and trapped by the absurd.

OTHER PLAYS: *Die Mohrin* (The Negress, 1964), *Der Richter von London* (The Judge of London, adapted from Thomas Dekker, 1964), *Graf Grün* (Count Grün, 1965), *Rameaus Nephew* (adapted from Diderot, 1966), *Wittek geht um* (Wittek Is Going Around, 1967).

**Dragún, Osvaldo** (born 1929). Argentinian dramatist. *Historias para ser contadas* (Stories for the Telling, 1957), a series of extraordinarily agile short works, has become a staple of the university and experimental theaters in the Spanish-speaking world. *Tupac Amarú* (1957) treats the tragedy of the rebellious Inca of 1781 in realistic fashion; the dramatic interest lies in the serenity of the tortured and blinded Inca and his spiritual defeat of his executioner, the Spanish leader Areche. Later works have shown an increasingly social commitment without loss of the humanity that characterizes Dragún. *Y nos dijeron que éramos inmortales* (And They Told Us We Were Immortal, 1963) assimilated Brecht and music-hall techniques to interpret the malaise of youth with bitter irony. *Amoretta* (1964) is reminiscent of Tennessee Williams in its psychological treatment of erotic and family relationships among Italian immigrants. In *Heroica de Buenos Aires* (1966), Dragún used the form of *Mother Courage* to display the misery of the slums, but he is stubbornly original in his use of assimilated techniques.

**Duberman, Martin B.** (born 1930). American historian and playwright. Duberman was born in New York City, educated at Yale (B.A. 1952) and Harvard (M.A. 1953, Ph.D. 1957). He has been an Associate Professor of History at Princeton since 1965. Duberman's documentary play *In White America* (1963) is a white historian's view of "what it has been like to be a Negro in this country." By compiling and editing actual statements made by both blacks and whites from the beginning days of slavery until the confrontation at Little Rock in the late 1950s, Duberman presents a pageant of incidents that is both historically accurate and theatrically moving. As timely social drama, instructing whites and reinforcing the emerging sense of dignity and destiny of the blacks, the play has been widely popular; it was given the Vernon Rice Drama Desk Award for the best play off-Broadway in 1963–64. Duberman's next two plays, *The Recorder, a History* and *The Electric Map, a Melodrama,* were given off-Broadway in 1970 under the title *Memory Bank.*

**Dubillard, Roland** (born 1923). French dramatist. Directly after the war Dubillard, as a student, had several of his short plays performed by friends at the Maison des Lettres in Paris. He then became known as Grégoire, acting in his own radio and cabaret sketches, and has continued to perform in the four plays he has written. A poet as well, Dubillard's collection *Je dirai que je suis tombé* was published in 1966.

Dubillard gained some renown as a playwright with his second play, *Naïves Hirondelles* (Naïve Swallows, 1961), which, after a great deal of hostile criticism, was saved by the enthusiastic support of established playwrights, including Ionesco. In this play two men and two women—part little shop-keepers, part Bohemians—try to live by constantly convincing themselves of the value of their gestures and their undertakings. In fact, they are having great trouble surviving, in a bitter-sweet atmosphere of boredom, instability, self-deception, and an incapacity for really communicating, and they flounder about using a language that is restrained, colloquial, poetic, and hesitant. Following this tenderly pathetic and comically absurd play, Dubillard wrote a more ambitious and difficult work, LA MAISON D'OS (The House of Bones), in 1962. In *Le Jardin aux betteraves* (The Beet Garden, 1969) he uses the theme of a string quartet on tour in a strange foreign land as a means of alternating passages from the Beethoven quartets with a satire on culture and of depicting a vertiginous and fantastic journey (the characters are enclosed in a violin case that becomes, in turn, a train, a submarine, and a rocket), which ends far up in the sky, where the giant Beethoven himself rules supreme.

Dubillard's imagination, especially in the last two plays, derives from the 'pataphysical tradition, which goes back to Alfred Jarry and consists in treating the maddest fantasies with naïve earnestness and putting the extraordinary and the ordinary on the same level, as if they were equally and simultaneously both astonishing and normal. Since the characters find that either their own situation or life in general is beyond them, they obstinately try to seek their salvation in explanatory language, which eludes them or imposes its own clichés. Thus, because of the combined absurdity and earnestness of that language, which they apply just as ineptly to things big and small, they become both poetic and hilarious.

OTHER PLAYS: *Si Camille me voyait* (If Camille Could See Me, 1953).

**Duncan, Ronald** (born 1914). English verse dramatist. Born in Rhodesia and educated in Switzerland and at Cambridge, Duncan worked as editor of *The Townsman* from 1938 to 1946. He was a founder of the Devon Festival of the Arts (1953) and the English Stage Company (1955). He is the author of many books of verse and prose and has written two volumes of autobiography, *All Men Are Islands* (1964) and *How to Make Enemies* (1968).

One of the Christian verse dramatists to be discovered in E. Martin Browne's season of "poets' plays" at the Mercury Theatre, London, Duncan attracted immediate attention with his first play in 1945. *This Way to the Tomb,* "A Masque and Anti-Masque," contrasts a dramatic treatment of the temptation of St. Anthony with a satirical attack upon twentieth-century materialism, employing jazz rhythms and a parody of the liturgy. The most obvious literary influence is that of T. S. Eliot. Although daring for their time, the technical devices of the anti-masque now appear dated and artificial, while the more restrained verse in which the masque explores the ascetic experience seems truer to Duncan's nature as a poet. In the following year he wrote the libretto for Benjamin Britten's opera *The Rape of Lucretia,* an important attempt to return to a greater austerity and clarity of form in musical drama. Duncan's method of work with Britten is described in the published version of the libretto (1948).

Duncan has suffered the misfortune of watching the dramatic movement with which he was associated decline, while his own powers as a dramatist increase. The maturity of the verse and the subtlety of the wit in his later work is by no means negligible, but the Christian experience that lies at the heart of much of Duncan's work seemed increasingly out of place in the theater of the '50s and '60s. Although a founder of the English Stage Company, Duncan became increasingly unsympathetic toward its policy and ended his association with the company in 1965.

OTHER PLAYS: *The Eagle Has Two Heads* (adaptation, 1946), *Stratton* (1949), *The Typewriter* (adaptation, 1950), *Nothing Up My Sleeve* (1950), *Our Lady's Tumbler* (1951), *Don Juan* (1957), *The Death of Satan* (1957), *The Catalyst* (1958), *Apollo de Bellac* (adaptation, 1958), *Christopher Sly* (libretto, 1960), *Abelard and Héloïse* (1961), *Ménage à Trois* (1963), *The Rabbit Race* (adaptation, 1963), *The Seven Deadly Virtues* (1964), *The Trojan Women* (adaptation, 1965).

**Duras, Marguerite** (born 1914). French dramatist and novelist. Born in Indochina, Marguerite Duras, both of whose parents were teachers, arrived in France when she was seventeen and had her first writings published during the war. Beginning her career as a novelist and writer of short stories, in 1956 she had her first play, *Le Square,* performed, adapted from a novel in dialogue form. Since then she has written some ten plays, adapted a few foreign works for the stage, written film scripts (*Hiroshima mon amour,* 1960; *Une Aussi Longue Absence,* with Gérard Jarlot, 1961), and adapted one of her own novels, *Détruire, Dit-Elle,* and one of her plays, *La Musica,* for the screen. She directed both films herself. In May 1968 she began to take an active part in the politics of revolutionary confrontation.

Obsessed by language, its clichés, its treachery, and its deterioration, Marguerite Duras made a great and absurd mockery of it in *Les Eaux et forêts* (Department of Forestry, 1965), *Yes, Peut-être* (Oui, Maybe, 1968), and *Le Shaga* (1968). But generally she makes it into an instrument of subtle torture that reveals secrets or, on the contrary, turns out to be powerless. Duras's best plays, which require restrained and precise staging, are essentially dialogues with a kind of detective-story suspense—confrontations à deux, in which each of the two characters tries to provoke the other into expressing what he thinks, what he wants, what he is. This personal and reciprocal investigation proves to be difficult and painful. It involves some perversity, is punctuated by silences and flashes of sincerity, and alternates between goodwill and bad faith, an intense desire for communication and a craving for complete secrecy.

With the exception of *Un Homme est venu me voir* (A Man Came to See Me, 1968), the mutual confession of a judge and a victim of the Moscow trials, Duras's main characters are women. Each is presented at a point of no return, at the moment she realizes that, because of her situation—the disappearance of the man she loves or the inadequacy of the man she is currently involved with (husband, lover, or even son, as in *Des Journées entières dans les arbres* [Days in the Trees, 1965])—she is faced with nothing but emptiness. The language she uses to explore her situation and her mood causes her gradually to discover herself, and the revelation turns out to be the equivalent of destruction. The adulterous heroines of *La Musica* (1965) and *Suzanna Andler* (1970) are at the point of losing contact with the reality of the surrounding world and with even their own reality. They are well on the road to an inner withdrawal that could lead to suicide. Their rebellions, which consist of antisocial acts, merely drive them into a solitude that is stressed by their language (in L'AMANTE ANGLAISE [The Englishwoman in Love], 1968, the heroine commits the antisocial act *par excellence:* murder). Although in search of psychological explanations for their fall into emptiness and negation, Duras's characters end by calling life itself into question, in a kind of linguistic and metaphysical terrorism.

OTHER PLAYS. *Les Viaducs de la Seine-et-Oise* (1960).

**Dürrenmatt, Friedrich** (born 1921). Swiss dramatist, director, novelist, and critic. Chance has fascinated Dürrenmatt both in his life and in his works. It would seem that his works are all part of a single attempt to explain why chance instead of absolute justice has played such a great role in his life and appears to have determined the course of the world. Born in a small village near the city of Bern, Dürrenmatt never intended to become a dramatist. His father was a minister, and during his youth, Dürrenmatt did not have much acquaintance with the theater, nor did he show an interest in drama. His ambition was to become a painter. After his family moved to Bern in 1935, Dürrenmatt continued to study painting, but he also was exposed to the theater. His interest in drama grew steadily after he graduated from high school and began studying theology and philosophy at the University of Bern and the University of Zurich. As he began to realize that he had limitations as a painter, he wrote his first play, *Komödie*, in 1943, as well as several short stories. It was at this point that he made the decision to abandon both the university and painting to concentrate on drama. Since he was unable to produce *Komödie* and had little success with his first dramatic attempts, he supported himself by writing skits for cabarets, drama reviews for newspapers, and short stories. His first play to be produced was *Es steht geschrieben* (Thus It Is Written, 1946). In this drama Dürrenmatt established a formula that has served as the basis for all of his plays since 1946: the structure of the "normal world" is shattered by indiscernible causes; crimes are committed; justice is needed to restore order, but it is no longer possible because there are no absolutes to guide the people; chance governs all events, and people must learn that they are their own judges and executioners if they are to cope with chance and gain a sense of humanity.

In *Es steht geschrieben,* the Anabaptists conquer the city of Münster in 1533, drive the Catholics from the city, follow Johann Bockelson, a tailor from Leyden, as their king, fail to establish a New Jerusalem, and are eventually defeated by the combined forces of Lutheran and Catholic soldiers. Bockelson is portrayed as a rogue who dupes the richest man in the city, Bernhard Knipperdollinck, and the other Anabaptists. The defeat of the Anabaptists is not proof of the divine will of God, for the Bishop of Münster and his allies are corrupt and hypocritical. It is merely the end of a course of actions that has its meaning in human suffering. Dürrenmatt is not interested in presenting an accurate historical account of the Anabaptist movement but wants to make a farce out of history in order to reveal the human predicament in critical times. He uses the Brechtian alienation technique and draws parallels to contemporary Germany in dialogues that reveal the economic and spiritual poverty of a people exploited by their leaders as well as their enemies.

In *Der Blinde* (The Blind One, 1948) Dürrenmatt treated the theme of suffering again. This play uses motifs from the story of Job. The setting is somewhere in Germany during Wallenstein's campaign against the Swedes (1632). A blind duke's kingdom has been ravaged, but his son has preferred not to disclose the disaster to him. Negro da Ponte, an Italian general in Wallenstein's command, happens upon the duke and plays the role of the devil. His desire is to mock the duke and reveal the truth to him so that he will lose faith in God. However, the duke endures all the humiliations and suffering that da Ponte heaps on him. Da Ponte's profession is to make war, and this has become normal for the times. The duke sees in his blindness that the link to God has been broken and that man must accept all responsibility for his actions to defeat evil. Dürrenmatt's parable play seeks to explore the contradiction between action and words, but both words and action lose their dramatic dynamics in Dürrenmatt's existential exposition.

In *Romulus der Grosse* (Romulus the Great, 1949), an unhistorical comedy in four acts, Dürrenmatt developed a concept of comedy that corresponds to his existentialist point of view. The setting is the villa of the Roman emperor Romulus on the 16th of March A.D. 476, the Ides of March. The Germans have invaded Italy, and the Romans are in a state of hysteria—all except Romulus. His casual air is the dread of his wife, ministers, soldiers, and future son-in-law. They all believe devoutly in the Roman Empire and want to save it. They even attempt to murder Romulus because he is more interested in his chickens, but they are thwarted by the oncoming Germans. They flee, and their flight leads to their death while Romulus, who has resigned himself to death, learns to his surprise that Ottokar wants to keep him alive because he himself fears the barbarism of the Germans under the future leadership of Theodrich. The end of the heroic age is a farce, and Dürrenmatt's play is a sharp condemnation of chauvinism and imperialism. The Roman Empire's final seat is likened to a dirty chicken coop, while the advance of civilization is equated with barbarism. The unheroic antics of the comic Romulus are part of Dürrenmatt's dramaturgical plan to construct a comedy onstage that parallels the comedy of reality.

The radical aspects of Dürrenmatt's concept of comedy have been presented in his provocative treatise *Theaterprobleme* (Problems of the Theater, 1954): "The task of art, in so far as art can have a task at all, and hence also the task of drama today, is to create something concrete, something that has form. This can be accomplished best by comedy. Tragedy, the strictest genre in art, presupposes a formed world. Comedy—in so far as it is not just satire of a particular society, as in Molière—supposes an unformed world, a world being made and turned upside down, a world about to fold like ours. . . . We are all collectively guilty, collectively bogged down in the sins of our fathers and of our forefathers. We are the offspring of children. That is our misfortune, but not our guilt: guilt can exist only as a personal achievement, as a religious deed. Comedy alone is suitable for us. Our world has led to the grotesque as well as to the atom bomb, and so it is a world like that of Hieronymus Bosch, whose apocalyptic paintings are also grotesque. But the grotesque is only a way of expressing in a tangible manner, of making us perceive physically, the paradoxical, the form of the unformed, the face of a world without a face; and just as in our thinking today we seem to be unable to do without the concept of the paradox, so also in art, and in our world, which at times seems still to exist only because the atom bomb exists: out of fear of the bomb."

Dürrenmatt's comedies are either farces or travesties. The extreme situations and distorted forms in his plays stem from the reality he wants to expose. In *Die Ehe des Herrn Mississippi* (The Marriage of Mr. Mississippi, 1952), the state prosecuting attorney Florestan Mississippi punishes himself for murdering his wife by marrying Anastasia, who has murdered her husband for having had an affair with Mississippi's wife. This act is rationalized by Mississippi, who begins to institute the Old Testament laws in the state. He is opposed by the count, Bodo von Übelhohe-Zabernsee, who as a doctor seeks to build a world based on faith and charity, and Fréderic René Saint-Claude, who wants to revolutionize the state along Communist lines. All three are in love with Anastasia, who will prostitute herself for each one of these men and their causes while claiming to have loved only the man she murdered. In the end, the attempts to change the state of the world fail. Anastasia is poisoned by Mississippi, who is poisoned by Anastasia. Saint-Claude is shot. The count is a broken man. The only one who survives with power is the opportunistic minister, who realizes that the "world is bad but not without hope. The world becomes hopeless when one tries to apply an absolute standard to it."

In *Ein Engel kommt nach Babylon* (An Angel Comes to Babylon, 1953) the world does, indeed, become hopeless, for an angel arrives in Babylon with a beautiful young woman named Kurrubi (created by God), who is to be presented to the poorest beggar among mankind. Ironically, King Nebuchadnezzar proves himself in a contest with the remarkable Akki, the only beggar left in his state, to be the poorest beggar. However, after receiving Kurrubi, he exchanges her for the ex-king Nimrod, not realizing that he is placing his kingdom in great jeopardy. The presence of the angel and the cherubic Kurrubi makes the divine visible on earth, and the people revolt against the king in order to make Kurrubi their queen. The king can save himself only by proving that Kurrubi will not marry him. She in turn is saved by Akki, who has realized that it is impossible to live *on* the earth. He has decided to live *off* the earth as a beggar, while Nebuchadnezzar builds the tower of Babel in order to oppose his justice to what he calls the "injustice of God." The conclusion of the play is Dürrenmatt's wry interpretation of the creation of the tower and its consequences for mankind.

The consequences of absolutes are spelled out most clearly in *The Visit* (*Der Besuch der alten Dame*, 1955), Dürrenmatt's most grotesque play and, perhaps because of this, his finest achievement. The drama concerns the sixty-five-year-old Claire Zachanassian, the richest woman in the world, who returns to her native town to demand justice for a wrong done to her when she was eighteen years old by her lover, Alfred Ill. Claire offers one billion dollars to the people of the poverty-stricken town if Alfred Ill is murdered. At first the townspeople refuse, but they gradually turn against Ill and hunt him down like an animal. He is forced to acknowledge his guilt, but in turn forces the townspeople to acknowledge theirs when they execute him at a town meeting. Claire Zachanassian carries his corpse to the Isle of Capri. The townspeople have their money, but have sold themselves like prostitutes.

*The Visit* is Dürrenmatt's answer to Bertolt Brecht, who wrote in the belief that society and man could be transformed. In 1959 Dürrenmatt delivered a speech in Mannheim in which he argued: "The old revolutionary dogma that man can and must change the world has become impractical for the individual and has been taken back. This principle is still useful for the masses, but only as a slogan, as political dynamite, as inducement for the people, as hope for the gray armies of the starving. The part no longer merges with the whole, the individual no longer in the collective, the human being no longer in humanity. For the individual there remains impotence, the feeling of being overlooked and no longer being able to take a step and help decide, the feeling of having to disappear in order to survive. However, there is also the sense of liberation, new possibilities, a sense that the time has come to do one's share in a decisive and brave manner."

Individual responsibility has always been Dürrenmatt's answer to the social upheavals that threaten to engulf mankind. To stress this point dramatically, Dürrenmatt wrote an "opera," *Frank der Fünfte* (Frank the Fifth, 1959), in reply to Brecht's *The Threepenny Opera*. The play portrays the history of a private bank, which exploits both the employers and the employees, who swindle the bourgeoisie, modeling their lives according to bourgeois standards of respectability, loyalty, and sentimentality. Unlike Brecht, who stressed the socioeconomic forces interacting and determining events in a given historical situation, Dürrenmatt sees his characters as completely free to choose their tradition and plot their own world. Naturally, chance plays a significant role in man's destiny, but here, too, man is free to cope with chance. In their freedom the people in *Frank the Fifth* all succumb to the monstrous bank they have built.

In yet another answer to Brecht, this time Brecht's *Galileo,* Dürrenmatt portrays in *Die Physiker* (The Physicists, 1961) a scientist who takes refuge in a mental sanitorium in order to withhold knowledge from a world that will misuse it. Two other scientists follow him there under the guise of insanity, intending to pry his secrets from him as a service to their respective governments. One physicist believes in the progress of science for the sake of science, while the other believes that science must work to develop the power of the state. All three physicists are eventually incarcerated by the director of the sanitorium, Mathilde von Zahnd, a hunchbacked, mad, old psychiatrist, who, like Claire Zachanassian, holds enormous power over the entire world. Dürrenmatt's play illustrates the twenty-one points he makes at the end of it. Three are of particular importance: "The content of physics is the concern of physicists, its effect the concern of all men. What concerns everyone can only be resolved by everyone. Each attempt of an individual to resolve for himself what is the concern for everyone is doomed to fail."

This is a statement that even Brecht might have approved. However, Dürrenmatt is far from taking a Brechtian point of view. In *Der Meteor* (The Meteor, 1966) Dürrenmatt relies on Aristotelian dramatic theory to portray the dilemma of a famous writer, Wolfgang Schwitter, a Nobel Prize winner, who wants to die but continually rises from the dead. After he returns to the atelier where he began his career, friends and relatives visit him to pay tribute, and several meet their own deaths through some accident. During these occurrences Herr Schwitter reveals how he has lived off other people and they off him. He no longer wants this life of artificiality and prostitution. He wants reality, and death is the only absolute real thing he knows. Yet even here chance exerts its power by preventing him from dying and forcing him to face his greatest fear—of life.

The reason why life is fearful is the theme of *Die Wiedertäufer* (The Anabaptists, 1967). Though it is a version of *Es steht geschrieben,* it should not be considered an adaptation; Dürrenmatt has essentially written a new play. The emphasis is now entirely on Bockelson as a frustrated actor who decides to make the entire world his stage. Because the Bishop of Münster is a great patron of the theater, he and the other noblemen who oppose the Anabaptists admire Bockelson's performance and save his life when they take the city. The Bishop at the end of the play cries out that this inhumane world must be made more humane. The question remains: How?

In his twenty-one points to *The Physicists,* Dürrenmatt wrote: "A story has been thought to its conclusion when it has taken its worst possible turn. The worst possible turn is not foreseeable. It occurs by chance. The art of the playwright consists in employing to the most effective degree possible chance within the action." In his notes to *The Anabaptists,* Dürrenmatt has qualified this statement: "The worst possible turn a story can take is the turn to comedy." And, according to Dürrenmatt, the writer of comedies is a moralist, for comedy exaggerates: it exposes all possible extremes and thereby reveals the contradictions in reality. In this respect, the writer of comedies is a social critic who never commits himself to a particular ideology but experiments with all possible means of reflecting human possibilities.

As a social critic, Dürrenmatt has specifically attacked the self-righteousness and hypocrisy of the Swiss. Almost all his plays have settings that recall the provinciality of Swiss towns or the smugness of Swiss middle-class respectability. Like a landscape painter, Dürrenmatt paints with broad strokes and with an eye for details that render a picture of a social milieu that reflects the moral bankruptcy of the Swiss. Dürrenmatt continually revises his plays and adapts them to the temper of the times. His models have been Aristophanes, Nestroy, Shaw, Wedekind, and Brecht. He has developed a theater of paradoxes, which exposes the insane logic of a technological world bent on making crime a matter of course. Along with his dramas and radio plays, his novellas too, such as *Das Versprechen* (The Pledge, 1952), *Der Richter und sein Henker* (The Judge and His Hangman, 1952), *Der Verdacht* (The Quarry, 1953), and *Die Panne* (Traps, 1956), have all been concerned with the question of crime and justice. To a degree, they are all mystery stories in which murders are committed to make us laugh. If we can see the farcical and ludicrous nature of the world, Dürrenmatt believes that we might begin to take life more seriously.

OTHER PLAYS: *Nächtliches Gespräch mit einem verachteten Menschen* (Nocturnal Conversation With a Despised Person, 1952), *Abendstunde im Spätherbst* (An Evening Hour in Late Autumn, 1959), *Der Doppelgänger*

(The Double, 1960), *Herkules und der Stall des Augias* (Hercules and the Augean Stable, 1962), *König Johann* (King John, an adaptation of Shakespeare's play, 1968), *Play Strindberg* (1969), *Porträt eines Planeten* (Portrait of a Planet, 1970), *Titus Andronicus* (an adaptation of Shakespeare's play, 1971).

**Dwa teatry** (The Two Theaters, 1946). A play by Jerzy Szaniawski. The first play to be produced after World War II by the dean of Polish dramatists, *The Two Theaters* went straight to the heart of the audiences in the ravaged country and became Szaniawski's greatest success. Although *The Two Theaters* is a play with a workable plot—the story of a theater director and his enterprise—it is in fact a discussion of two conceptions of theater, and of life, broken by the war and taken up again in the light of the war experience. The theater of bound-to-earth realism, represented by the "Little Mirror Theater" and its director, is contrasted with the "Theater of Dreams," reaching beyond the surface of things to the deeper reality of human emotions, the unexpected and the intuitive. The director is an ambiguous figure who would really like to transcend the "little realism" his theater stands for, and it is his dreams and fantasies that we see presented on the stage as the alternative to the Little Mirror Theater. In the final scene, after his death, the characters of his dreams take over and accept him for their own.

The action of *The Two Theaters* takes place in the theater and contains the device of the middle act consisting of two one-act plays in realistic convention, but with alternative endings presented in the last act, in the imaginary Theater of Dreams. In the first of these playlets, *Matka* (The Mother), an old love affair that may have a chance of revival has to be sacrificed for the sake of present dull stability. In the second, *Powódź* (The Flood), a rescue boat can save from a rising flood only a woman, a child, and a young man needed at the oars. The old father is left behind in the doomed house. The alternative endings of both one-acters go beyond material reality: The shadows of people rejected on the grounds of reason and necessity come back to claim their emotional rights.

*The Two Theaters*, though in no way a political play, contains a significant reference to the war in a scene from the Theater of Dreams showing small boys with wooden swords and paper helmets, as if soldiers in a "children's crusade" on their way to fight a superior enemy. Reason objects to this waste, but the author, in an allusion to the Warsaw Rising of 1944, gives us to understand that the sacrifice of youth in an unequal struggle could not have been in vain. This allusion, in keeping with the overall message of *The Two Theaters*, no doubt contributed to the popularity of the play in the first few years after World War II. The play was not performed in the Stalinist period, as its ideas could not be squared with the concept of socialist realism, but in the '60s it reentered the theater repertory.

**Dyer, Charles** (born 1928). English dramatist, actor, and novelist. After military service as a flying officer navigator in the R.A.F., Dyer began a career as an actor in 1947, and has continued to act on the stage, in films, and on television. He was already the author of a number of successful but unremarkable commercial plays when *Rattle of a Simple Man* (1961) caused his name to be linked with those of the new dramatists of the same period. But this comedy about a forty-year-old man's first sexual encounter with a prostitute is an exploitation of the greater freedom afforded to the dramatist by Osborne and his successors rather than a genuine departure from the commercial traditions of the postwar theater. The same may be said of *Staircase* (1965), despite its appearance in the repertory of the Royal Shakespeare Company. A seriocomic portrait of two bickering homosexuals, it was a theatrical piece well suited to the growing liberalization of the stage in the mid-1960s, but will be remembered rather for its neat observation of homosexual mores than for its psychological perception or its muddled metaphysical overtones. Dyer has written the screenplay for *Rattle of a Simple Man* and a novel under the same title (1965).

OTHER PLAYS: *Clubs Are Sometimes Trumps* (1948), *Who on Earth!* (1951), *Turtle in the Soup* (1953), *The Jovial Parasite* (1954), *Single Ticket Mars* (1955), *Time, Murderer, Please* (1956), *Poison in Jest* (1956), *Wanted— One Body* (1956), *Prelude to Fury* (1959), *Gorillas Drink Milk* (1964), *Mother Adam* (1971).

# E

**Eliot, T. S.** (1888–1965). English poet and dramatist. Born in St. Louis, Missouri, Eliot was educated at Harvard, Paris, and Oxford universities and took up residence in London in 1914. From 1922 to 1935 he edited the quarterly review *The Criterion;* in 1925 he joined the publishing company of Faber & Gwyer (later Faber & Faber), in which he took an active interest for the remainder of his life. In 1927 he adopted British citizenship. He was awarded the Nobel Prize for Literature and the British Order of Merit in 1948.

With poems including *The Love Song of J. Alfred Prufrock* (1917) and *The Waste Land* (1922), Eliot had established himself at the head of a new poetic movement reflecting, in astringent *vers libre,* the fragmented experience of a world that had lived through the Great War. His continuing search for a sense of order led him, to the distress of many of his admirers, toward the traditions of the Christian church, and by 1928 he could describe his "general point of view" as "classicist in literature, royalist in politics, and anglo-catholic in religion." His earlier critical works had given evidence of his interest in dramatic poetry, but (*Sweeney Agonistes* excepted) none of his own work for the stage was written before his profession of Christianity. Underlying it was the attempt to find a dramatic form adequate to the expression of spiritual experience in terms acceptable to a largely secular audience. In effect this led him to prefer the disciplined severity of Greek tragedy to the freer Elizabethan form that had been so influential in the nineteenth century.

It is doubtful whether Eliot ever intended to incorporate within a complete play the fragments of a poem in dramatic form published in 1926–27 under the title of *Sweeney Agonistes,* but they remain as evidence of his early interest in combining the rhythms of the contemporary idiom with the formal requirements of poetic drama. *The Rock* (1934), Eliot's first work written with performance in mind, was a pageant play presented as part of a fund-raising campaign for the Church of England. It was this modest work that began the fruitful collaboration between Eliot and the director E. Martin Browne, which was to last throughout the poet's career as a playwright.

In June 1935 *Murder in the Cathedral* was presented in the Chapter House

138

at Canterbury and described in the London *Times* as "the one great play by a contemporary dramatist now to be seen in England." Eliot himself, however, came to the view that this dramatic treatment of Thomas à Becket's martyrdom, conceived for a special audience and treating a distant historical subject, "had not solved any general problem." "If the poetic drama is to reconquer its place," he observed in a lecture in 1951, "it must, in my opinion, enter into overt competition with prose drama." Audiences must be prepared to accept verse spoken by "people dressed like ourselves, living in houses and apartments like ours, and using telephones and motor cars and radio sets." The setting for all his plays after *Murder in the Cathedral* was a contemporary one. *The Family Reunion* (1939) was in many ways a transitional piece. This version of *The Eumenides* set in an English country house retains vestiges of a chorus and the visible intrusion of the supernatural in the shape of Furies in full evening dress. Ten years intervened before the appearance of THE COCKTAIL PARTY at the Edinburgh Festival of 1949, a play in which (with the exception of the incantation that concludes the second act) Eliot dispenses entirely with the formal devices of his earlier plays; its affinity with Euripides' *Alcestis* remained unnoticed until the poet himself drew attention to it. Borrowing its idiom from the trivial gossip of London society and its theme of marital discord, adultery, and final reconciliation from West End comedy, *The Cocktail Party* presents at a deeper level Eliot's conception of the order and range of experience within the Christian community. *The Confidential Clerk* (1953) must be regarded as a lighter piece; "if you want to say something serious nowadays," remarked Eliot in an interview, "it's easier to say it in comedy than in tragedy." An updated version of Euripides' *Ion*, the play observes the conventions of high comedy with its complicated mechanics of abandoned babies, mistaken identities, and unexpected discoveries. In *The Confidential Clerk* Eliot solved once and for all the formal problems of composing a verse drama that would not alienate a theatergoing audience, but at the cost of making it virtually indistinguishable from the prose drama with which it competed. The dialogue is taut, economical, and witty, but it has the virtues of literate prose rather than verse, and Colby Simpkin's discovery of identity in terms of Christian purpose is so lightly touched upon as to be hardly recognizable as such. *The Elder Statesman* (1959), which proved to be Eliot's last play, appropriately drew upon the *Oedipus at Colonus* of Sophocles. Lord Claverton's confrontation with the ghosts of his past and his final release from guilt, if more obviously schematic than Eliot's preceding work, is invested with a compassion giving added strength to the serenity with which the old man takes leave of his daughter, at peace with himself and at one with nature:

> In spite of everything, in defiance of reason,
> I have been brushed by the wing of happiness.

Eliot described the metrical formula for his dramatic verse as "a line of varying length and varying number of syllables, with a caesura and three stresses. The caesura and the stresses may come at different places, almost anywhere in the line . . . the only rule being that there must be one stress on one side of the caesura and two on the other." Its qualities spring directly from his view of the nature of poetic drama, which should return from "an unreal world in which poetry is tolerated" to "the world in which the audience lives." This world, he hoped, "would be suddenly illuminated and transfigured" for the audience at "the moment of awareness that it is hearing poetry." The language, like the action, of Eliot's drama presents a surface of apparent verisimilitude to that of everyday life, which coincides at its high points with a deeper and more significant rhythm. In *The Sacred Wood* (1920) Eliot defined the contemporary verse dramatist's problem as being "to take a form of entertainment, and subject it to the process which would leave it a form of art." Few critics would deny that some thirty years later Eliot himself had attained success within these terms of reference, but many would regard his victory as a Pyrrhic one. Eliot may have found a solution to his self-imposed problems in the trivialities of *The Confidential Clerk,* but a casualty is the grandeur of design and imagery that distinguishes *Murder in the Cathedral.* Eliot has found few disciples among contemporary dramatists and the hopes of a major revival of verse drama springing from his work and that of Christopher Fry have proved unfounded. In the case of Eliot, it may be suggested that his ironic assault from within upon the conventions of drawing-room comedy lost much of its force when that genre ceased to be the dominant feature of the theatrical scene. His plays from *The Family Reunion* onward are built on the assumption that the English theatergoer would accept complex intellectual fare only if disguised in the conventional forms of entertainment. This argument, always a dubious one, was finally refuted by the work of Osborne, Pinter, and Arden and the elaborate artistic camouflage of Eliot's postwar drama was seen to be unnecessary.

If Eliot was destined not to influence the playwrights who followed him, his contribution to postwar drama was nevertheless a large one. Eliot's respect for tradition, in religion, literature, and politics, has caused his verse drama to be condemned out of hand by a new school of playwrights, but despite their classical severity his plays are as intensely personal as any written since the war. Running through all the plays is a pattern of death and regeneration, on the physical and the spiritual planes. Superimposed upon the ritual structure discerned in Greek tragedy by the Cambridge School of Anthropologists is Eliot's mystical version of the Anglo-Catholic faith: From the death of the martyr the Christian community receives its strength; by the death of the old spirit the sinner takes on new life. But above all these are plays of experience, of the quest for order, or suffering and reconciliation. In them we heard the charitable voice of a man who "after a long and agonizing struggle" had, in the words of his stage director, "found rest in the faith of the English Church."

Eliot's views on drama can be found in "The Possibility of a Poetic Drama" in *The Sacred Wood* (1920) and "Poetry and Drama" in *On Poetry and Poets* (1957). He has been the subject of a number of books, among them, *The Third Voice* (1959) by Denis Donoghue, *The Plays of T. S. Eliot* (1960) by David E. Jones, *T. S. Eliot's Dramatic Theory and Practice* (1963) by Carol H. Smith, and *The Making of T. S. Eliot's Plays* (1969) by E. Martin Browne.

**En Attendant Godot.** See WAITING FOR GODOT.

**Endgame** (*Fin de partie,* 1957). A play in one act by Samuel Beckett. It was first performed on April 3, 1957, at the Royal Court Theatre, London, under the direction of Roger Blin, and first performed in Paris on April 26, 1957, at the Studio des Champs-Elysées. *Fin de partie* is Beckett's harshest and most sarcastic play. This is perhaps why, despite the great success of *Waiting for Godot,* French producers at first hesitated to take it on and it opened in London. The play takes place in a shelter, in a large, grayish room with one door and two high, small windows. A painting is hung near the door, its face to the wall. Two ash cans are covered with a sheet. In the center of the stage a human form, seated in an armchair on castors, is also covered with a sheet. It is Hamm, next to whom stands Clov. Under the sheet Hamm's face is covered with a bloodstained handkerchief; under the handkerchief he wears dark glasses. In the ash cans live Hamm's parents, Nagg and Nell, both legless. We soon learn from the dialogue that outside the room and its adjoining kitchen there is nothing but a desolate and depopulated world, an expanse of water, and lifeless nature.

Clov's work consists in pushing Hamm around the room, giving him a tonic and a pain-killer, making him a stuffed dog, and looking out the windows to keep him up to date on the deterioration of the world. Hamm spends his time ordering Clov around, insulting his father, Nagg, whenever he happens to poke his head out of the ash can, and telling, in an affected literary style, a long story that takes place one Christmas eve. During the play Nell dies and Nagg retires to the bottom of his ash can. Toward the end of the play Clov catches a glimpse of a young boy outside. He decides to leave. The curtain falls on Hamm, who believes he is now alone and again covers his face with his handkerchief, and Clov, dressed to leave but standing motionless next to the door, looking at Hamm.

The first words in the play are Clov's "Finished, it's finished, nearly finished, it must be nearly finished," which is an allusion to the words of Christ on the cross: "It is finished" (John 19:30). At the end Hamm twice calls out "Father," an unanswered cry that recalls Christ's "Eli, Eli" (Matthew 27:46). Throughout the play the sarcastic biblical allusions make *Fin de partie* into a kind of parody of the crucifixion. Some critics see the characters' names as puns on this theme: Hamm = *hammer;* Clov, Nagg, Nell, and Mother Pegg (a character alluded to) = *nail* in French, German, and English respectively. Thus on one level the play likens man's condition to a continuous crucifixion, with no redemption. More broadly, it conveys an image of life and the world as a gradual deterioration, a long progression toward nothingness. As *Fin de partie* unfolds, we learn that there are no more bicycles, no more pain-killers, no more pap, no more coffins. Things are being absorbed into a grayish and empty uniformity. Actually, there is some doubt about the end as such: Hamm, at the end of the play, would seem to think it has come; yet Clov, whom he does not see, is still there; and while it may be the end of Hamm, it may also be a new beginning, given the young boy glimpsed by Clov. On this point the play is deliberately ambiguous.

*Fin de partie* is a grating play, altogether devoid of sentimentality. First of all, the characters do not at all like each other. They are merely bound to one another by reciprocal needs (Hamm would be unable to exist without Clov's services, and only Hamm has the combination to the cupboard containing the crackers on which the characters feed). The father-son relationship is cruelly degraded: Hamm hates his father for having begot him; Clov, who is perhaps Hamm's son, would leave if he could subsist elsewhere; and, of course, this has religious overtones because of the frequent allusions to God the Father. Moreover, Hamm and Clov, who are in the process of experiencing the end of the world, do all they can so that it will not come to life again. Hamm has sarcastically refused any help to those who asked for it; indeed, he is perhaps the one who provoked the beginning of the end. As for Clov, he is bent on killing a rat and, above all, a crab louse and agrees with Hamm that humanity must not "start from there all over again." In fact, Hamm's long and elaborately drawn out story consists in telling how, one Christmas eve, he refused to help a man whose child was dying.

As a spectacle, the play is extremely theatrical. Hamm's almost constant presence in the center of the stage, facing the spectators, gives the impression of being a mirror image of their true selves. Moreover, Hamm and Clov "play" in both senses of the word: they are playing a game and they are acting. Even their names may be seen as allusions to the ham actor (given Hamm's long and intricate speech) and the clown (given Clov's physical activities and gestures).

On the level of language *Fin de partie* is a real *tour de force:* The sentences are short and choppy; the vocabulary is extremely limited and repetitive; yet the play is filled with allusions not only to the Bible and Shakespeare but to most of Western culture. In fact, in a grotesque way, the language of *Fin de partie* expresses, as it were, the minimal residue of a whole civilization on the edge of nothingness.

**England.** See GREAT BRITAIN.

**Entertainer, The** (1957). A play by John Osborne. Like its predecessor, *Look Back in Anger,* this play is a work in which the political confusion of contemporary England (which was brought to a head between the plays by the Suez adventure) is contrasted with an almost nostalgic view of confident, prewar imperialism, but in *The Entertainer* Osborne created a compelling image of this lost vitality in the declining music-hall tradition. Billy Rice, Archie's father, is a lingering representative of the old order. "We all had our own style, our own songs—and we were all English. It was different. We knew what the rules were, and even if we spent half our time making people laugh at 'em we never seriously suggested that anyone should break them." Archie Rice cannot play by "the rules"; his version of Britannia is an aging, helmeted nude posing before the scanty audience of a failing road show. Perhaps surprisingly from a dramatist who had made his reputation as an "angry youg man," the younger members of the Rice household are perfunctory figures; neither the conscientious objector, Frank, nor his sister, Jean, whose love affair ends with her awakening political conscience during the Suez crisis, carries conviction, while Billy and Archie Rice, and even Archie's battered nonentity of a wife, Phoebe, have the ring of observed truth about their characters.

The music-hall image dominates the play's structure: Between the scenes set in Archie's house (where the stage directions demand furniture and properties "as basic as they would be for a short sketch") Archie appears before the footlights and plays out his twice-nightly routine. Osborne envisaged this device as an attack on "the restrictions of the so-called naturalistic stage," but the play achieves naturalism with an added dimension rather than the abolition of naturalism, exposing the tensions in Archie's confused life to the harsh glare of the theatrical follow-spot. The *persona* of the music-hall comedian, timing his punch lines and sighing at the failure of his secondhand repartee, dogs his attempt to communicate with his family, while his solo acts break into compulsive exhibitions of his personal neuroses ("You wouldn't think I was sexy to look at me, would you? Well, I 'ave a go, lady. I 'ave a go, don't I?"). The climax of the play comes toward the end of the second act when Archie, his tongue loosened by alcohol, tells his daughter of the most moving thing he ever heard, an "an old fat negress getting up to sing about Jesus or something like that." Like Jimmy Porter in *Look Back in Anger,* he looks back to a remembered past when emotion was vital and intense. "Billy's heard it. He's heard them singing. Years ago, poor old gubbins. But you won't hear it anywhere now. I don't suppose we'll ever hear it again. There's nobody who can feel like that." But now, "dead behind the eyes," he feels nothing any more—"just like the whole inert, shoddy lot out there."

*The Entertainer* falters toward the end (a not uncommon fault in Osborne's work). The melodramatic news of the death of Archie's elder son in the Suez conflict has remarkably little effect on the development of character or plot, and the action hurries on through the death of Billy, who returns to the stage in a last attempt to revive his son's fortunes, and Archie's refusal to emigrate ("You can't get draught Bass in Toronto") to a strong but sentimental ending in which Archie carries on with his pathetic patter as his world collapses around him, finally to leave the stage for his long-postponed appointment with the Income Tax man, the button-molder of the twice-nightly circuit.

As in *Look Back in Anger,* Osborne's achievement lies less in social comment or new dramatic technique than in the raw theatrical vigor of his hero, here doubly effective in the collision between the entertainer's bravura mask and the real Archie, "dead behind the eyes." In this respect *The Entertainer* marks an advance on the previous play; Osborne has evolved a language for Archie Rice that totally expresses the man. His recurrent imagery is the running gag, the public joke that feeds on a private obsession—draught Bass, the Income Tax man, the two nuns who "quite spontaneously" crossed themselves as he passed them on the seafront. Thus it is Archie Rice, rather than Jimmy Porter, who sets the pattern for Osborne's subsequent development.

**Eörsi, István** (born 1931). Hungarian poet, playwright, and critic. Eörsi studied Hungarian literature and aesthetics at Eötvös Loránd University in Budapest. Although he was a fully committed Communist poet in the early '50s, he spent three years in jail after 1956 for the publication of an anti-Russian poem. His two plays *Sírkő és kakaó* (Tombstone and Cocoa) and *Hordók* (Barrels), both produced in 1968, are tragicomedies verging on the "theater of the absurd."

**epic theater (episches Theater).** A term coined by Erwin Piscator and Bertolt Brecht during the 1920s. Epic theater designated a type of drama that is composed of a series of scenes that do not have sequential order or reveal causality. Piscator was primarily responsible for developing the practical techniques of this form of theater in his productions during the 1920s of plays ranging from classical to expressionist. Brecht concentrated more on writing dramas that alienated both the actor from his role and the audience from the traditional illusionary theater. Brecht often referred to this conventional form as "culinary theater," implying that people were fed commercial products that they hastily digested and excreted. The epic theater makes use of techniques borrowed from classical and medieval drama, but only to serve the ALIENATION EFFECT. The spectators are supposed to relax and learn from the events of the past as did the people who listened to poets portraying the deeds of heroes in their songs sung in the courts of the Greek nobles. From this analogy Brecht derived the term "epic." However, his theater does not create an illusion of history taking place in the present but compels the audience to realize that the scenes are historical accounts. Each scene is an entity and can be used in unusual arrangements that counter the normal expectations of the audience. In Brecht's view, this disturbance of expectations frees the critical faculty of playwright, actor, and audience alike. The playwright can inform the audience in advance about the outcome of the play. Characters can comment on the action. The audience can learn in this open atmosphere about events and human motives. Pleasure is gained from the exhilaration of developing one's understanding. The montage of contrasting episodes is contrapuntal in structure. It does not seduce, like the theater of illusion, but rather it demands a new mode of audience participation. Epic theater acknowledges the spectator as a "critical creator" who is moved to see more than the usual in the common events of history. Brecht constantly worked on his concept of epic theater, which has influenced most of the leading dramatists throughout the world since 1930. He was never entirely happy with the term and was moving more toward developing a new concept of "dialectical theater" before his death.

# F

**Faulkner, William** (1897–1962). American novelist. Born and bred in the Deep South, Faulkner spent most of his life in the university town of Oxford, Mississippi, writing seventeen novels and six books of short stories about the South as he saw it: a teeming waste where old verities and new exploitations clash around man, who must learn to endure and triumph. He was awarded the Nobel Prize for Literature in 1950 and the Pulitzer Prize in 1954 and 1957.

Always an innovator in technique, Faulkner experimented with dramatic form in *Requiem for a Nun* (1951); acts rather than chapters, dialogue rather than narrative make the novel resemble a play, yet at the beginning of each act is a long nondramatic section, using his typical incantatory rhetoric and inscrutable symbolism, that keeps the experiment basically still fiction. The piece was once presented on Broadway (1959) with the narrative passages shorn away, leaving only the sordid story of Temple Drake, an ex-whore who wants to avoid her responsibility for the past, and Nancy, the black nurse who kills Temple's baby as an act of salvation. The play had only a brief run and has not been revived. Its interest now is primarily as a curiosity, an example of what one of the finest novelists does when he turns to theater.

**Feiffer, Jules** (born 1929). American cartoonist, social satirist, and playwright. Feiffer was born in New York City and has distinguished himself there and nationally as a sophisticated caption-maker for his line drawings that capsulate the absurdities of American life and foreign policy. In addition to his weekly cartoon for the *Village Voice*, Feiffer has produced a dozen or so books of cartoons and one novel, *Harry, the Rat with Women*. His one-act play *Crawling Arnold* was produced at the Festival of Two Worlds in Spoleto, Italy, in 1961. *Little Murders,* a full-length series of comic moments about the violence "out there" (much like James Saunders' *Barnstable*), was given first at the Yale School of Drama (1966). Although it closed after seven performances in New York in 1967, the production by the Royal Shakespeare Company in London was voted by the critics the best foreign play of the year. Given again in New York in 1969, the play was finally a local success. That same year Feiffer's comedy about insurrection in the very heart of government, *God Bless,* was presented at Yale. Another comedy, *The White House Murder Case,* was produced off-Broadway in 1970.

**Ferlinghetti, Lawrence** (born 1919). American poet. Born in Yonkers, New York, graduated from the University of North Carolina (B.A.), Columbia University (M.A.), and the Sorbonne (Doctorat de l'Université), Ferlinghetti found his way to San Francisco's Beat scene of the 1950s, where he set up City Lights, the first all-paperback bookstore in the United States, and published the Pocket Poets Series, including work by Allan Ginsberg, Kenneth Patchen, and Kenneth Rexroth, as well as his own. In the early 1960s he began experimenting with plays; New Directions published his *Unfair Arguments with Existence: Seven Short Plays for a New Theatre* (1963), which Ferlinghetti described as "beat-up little dramas taken from Real Life," and *Routines* (1964), thirteen very short "plays," blueprints for dramatic action to be interpreted and developed by the actors and director. These didactic emblems are interesting chiefly as manifestations of what a contemporary poet considers to be a dramatic form lying midway between HAPPENINGS and conventional theater.

Ferlinghetti's principal books of poems are *Pictures of the Gone World* (1955), *A Coney Island of the Mind* (1958), and *Starting from San Francisco* (1961).

**Fête noire, La** (The Black Feast, 1948). A three-act play by Jacques Audiberti. First performed on December 3, 1948, as *La Bête noire* (The Black Beast) at the Théâtre de la Huchette, Paris, it was directed by Georges Vitaly. In the eighteenth century, in the south of the Massif Central, Dr. Félicien, who is seething with sexual desire but rejected by women because he is foolish enough to idealize them, kills and frightfully mutilates a young peasant girl, Mathilde, who has offered herself to him and then refused him. To exonerate himself, he pretends that he has seen a monstrous beast attack the girl and devour her belly. Everyone believes him, the collective imagination accepts his story, and a gigantic hunt is organized to kill the beast. During a burlesque parody of the Catholic rites, with the participation of a bishop, the beast indeed appears, pursued by the hunters, and is killed. Actually, it turns out to be a poor goat, but the hunters, blinded by the myth of the Beast, are convinced they have done away with a monster. Mathilde's sister, Alice, has understood that the real beast is within Félicien, that it has been produced by a conflict between his sexual desire and the frustration caused by his exaltation of woman's mystery. The rest of the world considers Félicien a hero, while he is making a fortune selling fake relics of the monster throughout Europe. When Alice meets Félicien with the intention of killing him, he gradually makes her understand that it is not by doing away with him that she will do away with the monster, for it exists independently and will go on forever. During the last moments of the play, while an invisible being is creating fantastic and physical havoc onstage, Alice agrees to submit to the beast's power and offers herself to Félicien, despite his warnings of the horror that will ensue. Clasped in each other's arms, they nevertheless escape the horror:

An accomplice of Félicien's fells them with one bullet, which goes through both their hearts.

Inspired by the legend of the Gévaudan beast, this play is characteristic of Audiberti's obsessions and his art. Horror, fantasy, and the most farcical humor are all mixed together. The complex relationship between the creative powers of the imagination, the bad use to which they may be put (the bishop, Félicien's glory in Europe), desire, murder, myth, and reality is presented in an extremely spectacular way and expressed in an overflow of words, loaded with the most unexpected images.

**Finland.** During World War II Finland experienced three separate wars. She lost more than a tenth of her total area and had to resettle 12 per cent of her population. Social and economic reconstruction work was paralleled by fresh orientations in cultural life. Every Finnish generation has opened up new windows to the outer world: This time they were opened toward Sweden, France, England, and the United States. English and American plays, novels, and poems were discussed, produced, or published: The works of Eliot, Fry, Maxwell Anderson, Tennessee Williams, and Arthur Miller were introduced in the late 1940s or early 1950s. The organization of theater life underwent remarkable changes. There was more willingness to cooperate than before; many cities and towns with two professional or semiprofessional theater companies combined these and established city or municipal theaters, subsidized from local and government funds. The support covers some two-thirds of the total yearly expenditure of the theaters. Finland remained a remarkably active theater country: There are more than thirty of these repertory companies, four of them performing in Swedish, for a population of four and a half million and close to two million theatergoers each year.

There was no clear-cut change of generations in the field of native drama. Some of the established playwrights went on writing for the stage; no homogeneous group of the young was formed right away. Maria JOTUNI had died during the war, leaving behind a bundle of works, among them two plays; Hagar OLSSON created two important plays; Kersti Bergroth (born 1886) repeated her prewar success with *Kuparsaare Antti* (1956), another idyllic comedy in the Karelian dialect. Toivo Pekkanen (1902–1957), a fine novelist with a talent for social panoramas, wrote an allegorical play, *Täyttyneiden toiveiden maa* (The Country of the Fulfilled Hopes, produced in 1956). Mika Waltari (born 1908), an internationally known writer of best-selling historical novels, showed his versatility by writing picaresque comedies for the stage.

Among those making new starts rather than writing aftermaths to their earlier works or regarding drama as a side issue were Valentin (the pen name of Ensio RISLAKKI), a writer of serious comedies; Serp (Seere Salminen, born 1894), who has atmospheric historical comedies on her list of credits; and Ilmari TURJA. All three are journalists turned playwrights. Sirkka Selja (born 1920), with her *Eurooppalainen* (A European, 1947), an account of the mental atmosphere in postwar years, was an early and lonely playwright, who did not go on composing plays. Neither did Jussi Talvi (born 1920), the winner of an all-Scandinavian drama prize with his *Ennen pitkääperjantaita* (Before Good Friday, 1955), a play about a soldier sentenced to death for cowardice. The first postwar dramatist to establish himself was Walentin CHORELL, a many-sided representative of psychological realism interested in the conflict between harsh reality and unfulfilled dreams.

Chorell cooperated with Jack Witikka, a stage director of merit both in realistic and avant-garde plays. Arvi Kivimaa, general manager of the Finnish National Theater since 1950 and former vice president of the I.T.I. (International Theater Institute), and Witikka contributed in opening new international vistas for Finnish theater life. This line of development climaxed in the world conference of the I.T.I. in Helsinki in 1959. Witikka directed Samuel Beckett's *Waiting for Godot* as early as 1954, the year in which an intimate stage was annexed to the National Theater, starting the fashion for small stages elsewhere in Finland (in Tampere, Turku, Pori, for example) and shaping the form of native plays.

Beckett, Ionesco, and Adamov gave impulse to a small group of Finnish experimentalists. Juha Mannerkorpi (born 1915), a lonely moralist, was probably independent of these models; the reception of his psychological puzzle play *Pirunnyrkki* (A Puzzle Play, published 1952) and of *Avain* (The Key, published 1955), a grotesque and tragicomic monologue play, did not encourage him to go on. There are grotesque and absurd elements also in the works of V. V. Järner (born 1910) and Mary Mandelin (born 1918), while Paavo HAAVIKKO started his playwriting career with verbal poetry for the stage.

Eino Salmelainen (born 1893), a distinguished theater leader and stage director in Tampere, had worked with the playwright Hella WUOLIJOKI; among his postwar discoveries were the poet Eeva-Liisa MANNER and Kyllikki Mäntylä (born 1907), who described the lot of the refugees from Karelia in *Opri* (1953) and other plays with warm humor and genuine local color. Salmelainen also directed *Viimeiset kiusaukset* (The Last Temptations), by Lauri KOKKONEN.

Tampere is a lively center of theatrical activities. In addition to two regular repertory companies (The Tampere Theater and The Workers' Theater of Tampere), it also boasts The Pyynikki Summer Theater, with its almost unique rotating audience. The audience with eight hundred seats is turned around 360 degrees. Works of Shakespeare and a dramatization of *Tuntematon sotilas* (The Unknown Soldier, 1954), a forceful war novel by Väinö Linna (born 1920), have been produced here. The script was written to fit this exceptional theater. Linna is an interesting case, a potential dramatist who has not written a single play, yet has produced excellent dialogue material for dramaturges and screenwriters in this novel and also in *Täällä Pohjantähden alla* (Here Under the North Star, 1959–1962). Two parts of this trilogy dealing with recent social history have been adapted for the stage.

Side by side with Linna's breakthrough in the 1950s a new generation of novelists announced itself. Finnish writers rarely specialize in drama, although a play begins to turn out greater royalties than an average novel if five or ten theaters produce it. Economic calculations cannot be the only explanation of the fact that some of these novelists turned partly or mostly to playwriting: The stage was, no doubt, also in the direction of their interest. They helped to make the late 1960s into at least a modest flowering period in native drama. Haavikko, Veijo MERI, and Paavo Rintala (born 1930) are the most prominent figures in this group, grown up during the war and trying to settle with the recent past. Rintala, mainly a novelist, adopted strong critical positions, for example in his drama *Rouva sotaleski* (Mrs. War Widow, 1957) and in *Kunnianosoitus Johann Sebastian Bachille* (Tribute to Johann Sebastian Bach, 1963), where the techniques of epic theater are employed to follow the effect of Bach's music on posterity.

In the late 1960s other novelists were induced to try their hands at drama. They include Lauri LESKINEN, a fine writer of tragicomedies, Eeva Joenpelto (born 1921), Eila Pennanen (born 1916), Anu Kaipainen (born 1933), and Christer Kihlman (born 1930). Joenpelto reflected historical events from the last days of czarist Russia to present-day Finland in the fates of two brothers in her drama *Liian suuria asioita* (Too Great Matters, 1968), while Pennanen placed a group of Finnish hippies in the yard of a Philistine family in her *Aurinkomatka* (Sun Tour, 1967), achieving a tragicomic description of the conflict between the generations. *Ruusubaletti* (Ballet of Roses, 1967) by Kaipainen is a satiric fairy tale about small-town life. Kihlman, a talented writer of prose in Swedish, concentrated on the dissolution of the family as a consequence of generation conflict in his stage debut, *Kymmenen askelta kuun pinnalla* (Ten Steps on the Moon, 1970). Having written a few radio plays, Heimo Susi (born 1930) presented a group of young intellectuals in his comitragedy *Elämisen tekniikka* (The Technique of Living, 1967). All of Susi's characters commit forgeries; the most sophisticated of these is a Ph.D. dissertation forged to bring its author a professorship in sociology. *Hyvästi, Mansikki* (Goodbye, Bossy, 1969), by Jouko Puhakka (born 1922) is a chronicle play with songs about the difficulties of small farmers after the Second World War and the resulting movement into towns, cities, and Sweden. The six plays discussed in this paragraph are prizewinners; there are yearly government drama prizes, and several competitions have been arranged to encourage native playwriting. In the Tampere play competition the scripts were judged after production; first prize was given to *Gräset* (Grass) by Chorell.

Haavikko, Manner, Lasse Heikkilä (1925–1961), and Bo Carpelan (born 1926) approached the stage from the opposite edge, so to speak: from the realm of poetry. Heikkilä wrote two modern plays based on classic themes or characters, *Medeia* (published 1953, produced 1958) and *Ofelia* (1955). Carpelan returned to the poetic everyday life of his adolescence in *Paluu nuoruuteen* (Back to Youth, 1970). Kyllikki Kallas (born 1917) made a promising debut with her sharp analysis of the political scene entered by a young idealist: *Herra Puoluesihteeri* (Secretary of the Party, 1958). Jouni Apajalahti (born 1920) dealt with the problems of youth in *Kenen on vastuu?* (Who Is Responsible? 1964). Plays of topical interest or entertainment value have been written by Yrjö Soini (born 1896), Leena Härmä (born 1914), and Inkeri Kilpinen (born 1926).

Both Susi and Chorell started as radio dramatists. Radio plays enjoyed great popularity up to the 1960s, since which time competition with television has made them lose ground somewhat. The Finnish Radio Corporation not only used the talents of established writers but fostered new ones. The theater or play department of the radio network is headed by Pekka Lounela (born 1932), himself a dramatist. His stage play *Mies joka ampui kissan* (The Man Who Shot a Cat, 1970) is a critical analysis of totalitarian character type. Writing for radio has also won Finnish playwrights limited international audiences, always a difficult problem in a country trapped behind a language barrier. *Eros ja Psykhe* by Manner and *Suomen paras näyttelijä* (The Best Actor in Finland) by Meri have been transmitted in several Middle-European countries.

Television has, to a lesser degree, played a similar role of foster parent. Scripts need not necessarily belong to a series to be televised. Reino Lahtinen (born 1918), Liisa Vuoristo (born 1927), and Tauno Yliruusi (born 1927) have made their names mostly as writers for television. A full step from the studio onto the stage was taken by Juhani Peltonen (born 1941), an interesting surrealist. His major work so far is *Päivän sankari* (Hero for the Day, 1968) wherein the "life" of a young suicide case goes on in his grave, a kind of grotesque underworld, visited by his friends and relatives.

Radio, television, and live plays: It is impossible to gather these products of varied creative activities under the title of any single style or ism. As elsewhere in the West, realism and its motley alternatives have governed on the stage. The impression of richness and variety has been further increased by the unorthodox enthusiasms of the young in the theater. Influenced by Brecht, they have been interested in political cabaret and documentary plays. A summing up of these theater forms was *Lapualaisooppera* (The Lapua Opera, 1966) by Arvo Salo (born 1932), who was a member of Parliament from the Social-Democratic Party from 1966 to 1970. Using solo and chorus songs and group movement, documentary materials and caricatures, the play criticized a Fascist movement of the 1930s. The Swedish Little Theater, led for a long while by Vivica Bandler (born 1917), has established a tradition of elegant cabaret plays in cooperation with such writers as Benedict Zilliacus (born 1921), Lars Hulden (born 1926), and Bengt Ahlfors (born 1937).

The postwar period in the Finnish theater was opened with the introduction of a new wave of French and Anglo-American plays. In the 1960s interests were even more catholic. Plays were imported from Poland and Ireland, from Czechoslovakia and Australia, and from East and West Germany. Yet native plays and playwrights retained their position with ease: Every second play produced is by a Finn. Two explanations may help to account for this. On the one hand, Finnish playwrights have been open to stimuli from their foreign colleagues, from the world of Western theater life, now more accessible than ever before. On the other hand, they have been able to add to these impulses their own vision of life as it has been lived in Finland since World War II, their skill, and their knowledge of the workings of the stage. They have spoken to their audiences, a necessary requirement for any and all playwrights. In spite of competition from modern mass communication media, the theater and native drama are far from being peripheral phenomena in present-day Finland.

**Fialka, Ladislav.** See CZECHOSLOVAKIA.

**Fo, Dario** (born 1926). Italian dramatist. This actor, director, mime, and playwright first attracted the attention of the public in 1953 with his production of *Il dito nell'occhio* (A Finger in the Eye), which he wrote and produced in conjunction with Giustano Durano (born 1923) and Franco Parenti (born 1921). The critics were amazed by this political harlequinade, which combined the technique of the *commedia dell'arte* with the Marxist philosophy of Italy's young intellectuals.

Fo's plays have little literary merit. They are essentially theatrical pieces, loosely structured and filled with possibilities for sight gags, songs, and acrobatics. The scenery is extremely stylized, the costume and makeup highly exaggerated. The published script of any of Fo's pieces may have only the slightest resemblance to this work after it has been in repertory for a while, since Fo is continually changing his plays in response to the reactions of his audiences. In his early works his political satire was more concealed. They could be appreciated as pure farce. However, even his broadest farces contain social protest.

*Aveva due pistole con gli occhi bianchi e neri* (He Had Two Pistols with Black and White Eyes, 1960) is an episodic work of confused identities, transvestism, cops-and-robbers chases, and interludes of songs and dances. However, its satire of contemporary Italy is inescapable. An inmate from an insane asylum is released because of his resemblance to Giovanni, leader of a band of thieves. The real Giovanni is killed. His double from the insane asylum organizes a strike of thieves, forcibly causing banks, insurance agencies, police schools, and police dog-training schools to go bankrupt. The police are utterly duped by this ingenious madman, who is ultimately discovered to be a priest.

Throughout all his plays, Fo criticizes the government, the military, the industrialists, and the general superficiality of middle-class morality. His most successful work, *La signora è da buttare* (The Lady Is to Be Removed, 1967), is set in a circus in the United States, where the clowns die and go to an American heaven to find a paradise packed with consumer goods.

In his most recent productions, Fo employs masks and puppets to intensify his social satire. In *Grande pantomima con bandiere e pupazzi piccoli e medi* (Grand Pantomime with Banners and Small and Medium Puppets, 1969) a ten-foot-tall puppet with a bilious, wart-covered face lumbers to the center of the stage and mumbles unintelligibly from an ugly rubber mouth while wielding a black plastic truncheon. A group of men on stage beat the puppet's swollen stomach, shouting, "Kill the dirty Fascist!" Suddenly a shapely brunette in a bathing suit steps out from the puppet's inside, introducing herself as Capitalism. Soon, a thirty-foot-long white and green dragon, symbolizing the Communists, makes its way ferociously onstage. A puppet king, Vittorio Emmanuele, pushes Capitalism toward the dragon, declaring that she alone can save them. The dragon winds itself around Capitalism's body, but ultimately falls victim to her charms, as she moves herself seductively within its coils.

Fo denies having any political affiliation. "We are wedded to the people. They are extremely important. The real theater, not this present museum we call the theater, has always appealed to the masses."

OTHER PLAYS: *Sani da legare* (Lock Up the Sane, 1954, written with Franco Parenti), *La Marcolfa* (1958), *Gli imbianchini non hanno ricordi* (Painters Don't Have Memories, 1958), *I tre bravi* (The Three Wise Men, 1958), *Non tutti i ladri vengono per nuocere* (Not All Thieves Come to Harm, 1958), *Un morto da vendere* (A Corpse for Sale, 1958), *I cadaveri si spediscono e le donne si spogliano* (Cadavers Are Dispatched and Women Undress, 1958), *L'umo nudo e l'uomo in frak* (The Nude Man and the Man in a Tuxedo, 1958), *Canzoni e ballate* (Songs and Dances, 1958), *Chi ruba un piede è fortunato in amore* (Who Robs a Foot Is Lucky in Love, 1961), *Settimo! Ruba un po' meno* (Settimo, Rob a Little Less! 1964), *La colpa* (The Offense, 1965).

**Forssell, Lars** (born 1928). Swedish poet and playwright. Educated in Sweden and the United States, Forssell lives and works in Stockholm. Twelve volumes of poetry and fifteen volumes of plays or play collections have earned him a reputation as one of the outstanding writers of his generation. The title of one of his play collections, *Upptåg* (Pageant, 1967), is fitting. His choice of style and subject matter has been wide-ranging, and includes: a bitter *commedia dell'arte* one-act play, *Narren som tillhörde sina bjällror* (The Fool Who Belonged to His Bells, 1953); a reworking of the Alcestis legend, *Kröningen* (The Coronation, 1956); an absurdist one-act play, *Charlie McDeath* (1962); a lyrical-realistic tragicomic period piece, *Söndagspromenaden* (The Sunday Promenade, 1963); two history plays about Swedish rulers, *Galenpannan* (The Madcap, 1964) and *Christina Alexandra* (1968); and a haunting tragicomedy about a Lenny Bruce-like entertainer, *Geten* (The Goat, 1971).

The central characters in Forssell's plays are bizarre antiheroes who suffer from an inability to give or accept love. Admetus in *Kröningen* is a whining coward who cannot understand the significance of the sacrifice by his wife Alcestis of her life for his. In *Charlie McDeath* a ventriloquist retreats completely from all human demands by changing places with his dummy. Justus Coriander in *Söndagspromenaden* builds a fantasy world where all feelings are artificial, and he is destroyed when he ventures out into the real world. Each of the eccentric rulers in Forssell's history plays, King Gustav Adolf IV (reigned 1792–1809) and Queen Christina (reigned 1632–1654), endures a double tragedy, historical and personal: Their political ambitions are frustrated and their lives are empty of love.

Forssell's strength as a poet-playwright lies in his ability to derive striking metaphors from the interpenetration of the themes of solitude, alienation, and the need for love.

**France.** The 1930s were one of the periods of great achievement in the history of French theater. A movement to revive the dignity of theater and the art of staging, which had begun at the end of the nineteenth century and been insured success by Jacques Copeau between 1913 and 1924, was solidly established by the great directors who, in 1928, joined together to form the Cartel: Louis Jouvet, Charles Dullin, Gaston Baty, and Georges Pitoëff. Chief among the many talented playwrights of the time were Jean Giraudoux, Jean Cocteau, and Armand SALACROU. Jean ANOUILH had already begun his career, and Boulevard theater had been given a new complexion by Marcel Achard. After the defeat in 1940, despite the difficulties created by the German occupation and the death, exile, or retirement of certain great theatrical personalities, French theater remained remarkably vigorous. Not only did the Boulevard entertainments continue to proliferate, but some of the most important dramatic works of the twentieth century were produced: Henry de MONTHERLANT's *La Reine morte* (Queen After Death, 1942), Jean-Paul SARTRE's *The Flies* (*Les Mouches*, 1943), and Anouilh's *Antigone* (1944). Two new plays by Cocteau were performed, and Giraudoux's *Sodome et Gomorrhe* was staged in 1943. However, perhaps the major event in theatrical life during the occupation was the performance of Paul Claudel's stupendous *Le Soulier de satin* (The Satin Slipper, 1943), directed by Jean-Louis Barrault. In 1944, during the last months of the war in France, Sartre had his *No Exit* (*Huis-Clos*) performed, and Albert CAMUS published his *Malentendu* (Cross Purposes).

Immediately after the war, a whole group of new, young directors, most of them trained by the Cartel and including Barrault and Jean Vilar, followed in the wake of the old. Several new developments and trends were notable. First of all, the works of Paul Claudel, written in large part between 1888 and 1940, and until then accepted by only a limited public of Catholics, were revived and widely performed. Indeed, it was clear—from the revival of *L'Annonce faite à Marie* (The Tidings Brought to Mary) in 1946 to the first performance of *Tête d'or* in 1958, by way of *Le Partage de midi* (Break of Noon) in 1948—that Claudel's works were the most imposing dramatic monument in twentieth-century France.

Secondly, the great prewar dramatists continued to be very much in evidence. Three new plays by Giraudoux were staged, although he had died in 1944: *La Folle de Chaillot* (The Madwoman of Chaillot, 1945), *L'Apollon de Bellac* (The Apollo of Bellac, 1947), and *Pour Lucrèce* (For Lucretia, 1953), as well as fragments of an unfinished play, *Les Gracques* (The Gracchi, 1970). Cocteau had two plays performed, *L'Aigle à deux têtes* (The Eagle Has Two Heads, 1946) and *Bacchus* (1951). Georges Neveux (born in 1900), whose reputation had been established before the war with *Juliette ou La Clé des songes* (Juliette, or The Dream Book, 1930), his best play, went on with his career, writing a few strange plays such as *Plainte contre inconnu* (Complaint Against an Unknown Person, 1946) and *Zamore* (1953). As for Salacrou, he may be said to have started all over again, after his long silence during the occupation, becoming a postwar as well as a prewar playwright.

Then, during the period immediately following the war, the public's attention was drawn most especially to a group of plays whose originality lies primarily in the ethical or philosophical ideas they propound. Deeply affected by the war and the social and political state of the world, a number of writers chose to dramatize the problems of conscience raised by situations such as the Resistance, the Revolution, totalitarian regimes, and the fate of humanity. Reflections on man's freedom and the responsibility it creates are at the roots of this theater. The characters, caught in extreme situations that require decisions involving life and death—their own as well as others'—are confronted with the consequences of their acts, for better or for worse. The most representative and most successful of such playwrights are Sartre and Camus. But they are far from being the only ones. Salacrou's theater is permeated with the same concerns (especially *Les Nuits de la colère* [Nights of Anger], 1946). Simone de Beauvoir contributed *Les Bouches inutiles* (The Useless Citizens, 1945), based on the solidarity of men in a besieged city lacking provisions. Needless to say, this type of theater lends itself to politization—by the left (Jean-Richard Bloch, *Toulon*, 1945) as well as the right (Thierry Maulnier, *La Maison de la nuit*, 1954). Besides the plays of Sartre and Camus, and very different from them, the best works—whatever their tendencies—devoted to the moral problems raised by today's world are perhaps Jules Roy's *Les Cyclones* (1954), Emmanuel Roblès' *Montserrat* (1948), Colette Audry's *Soledad* (1956), and, in a much more lyrical vein, Maurice Clavel's *Les Incendiaires* (1946).

At the same time as this "theater of responsibility," directly after the war, a poetic theater began to take shape. On the one hand, Jules Supervielle added a few fantasies to his prewar works (such as *Le Voleur d'enfants* [The Child Stealer], 1949), and Julien Gracq, in 1948, tried his hand at dramatizing the myth of the Grail in *Le Roi pêcheur* (The Fisher King). On the other hand, a whole group of writers, far more original in their conception of poetry in the theater, came to light—writers whose often verbose plays were described by Geneviève Serreau as a "feast of words." The prewar poetic playwrights (Giraudoux, Cocteau) had in general been relatively cautious, trying to fit gods and monsters into the classical mold and keeping their verbal images within the limits of restrained language. The postwar poet-playwrights, brought up on surrealism, suddenly took extreme liberties not only with dialogue but with the very structure of their plays. The 1940s saw performances of plays by Jacques AUDIBERTI (who was already known as a poet and novelist), Henri Pichette, and Michel de Ghelderode. In the case of Pichette, the obscure lyricism of *Les Epiphanies* (1942), later combined with an attempt at total theater in *Nucléa* (1952), finally turned out to be a dead end. Ghelderode, a Belgian whose reputation was established in his own country, had written his best plays during the '20s and '30s, but it was not until 1947 that French audiences were able to witness the turbulent and often grotesque vision of a mystical and violent poet, haunted by death and the degradation of the flesh (*Hop Signor!*, 1947; *Fastes d'enfer* [Chronicles of Hell], 1949). Violent also are the farces of Audiberti, who uses language and spectacular effects to embody the eternal struggle of Good and Evil. During the '50s the group of poet-playwrights continued to grow, the most eminent of them being Jean VAUTHIER, whose works are a frenzied meditation on personal salvation, and Georges SCHEHADÉ, a cruel and delicate maker of metaphors, chiefly concerned with beauty and the vicissitudes of poetic purity. More recently, Romain WEINGARTEN contributed *L'Eté* (Summer, 1966), and René de OBALDIA created works midway between poetry and the Boulevard. What these playwrights have in common, despite great differences in tone, themes, and inspiration, is confidence in poetic language. They replace the analytical and didactic dialogue of the theater of responsibility with verbal invention, which is often obscure but ostensibly possessed of special powers that suggest, reveal, and create profound mysteries.

The term "new theater" has been associated not only with these poets but with writers whose works as a whole constitute the "theater of the absurd," and who had their most striking success during the '50s and '60s. The early plays of Samuel BECKETT, Eugène IONESCO, and Arthur ADAMOV are outstanding in the genre. The trend was then continued by Robert PINGET. The contribution of these playwrights was not only to illustrate the modern theme of the absurd, which had already served as a basis for the works of Camus and Sartre, but also to change the very idea of what a play is. The construction of their works, which are actualized nightmares, is as absurd as the conception of the characters. Also closely related to this theater are the fantasies of Roland DUBILLARD; the perversely erotic and scatological spectacles of Fernando ARRABAL; the apparently more realistic works of Nathalie Sarraute, Claude Mauriac, and Marguerite DURAS, based on solitude and the absence of communication, and the anarchic or tragic farces of Boris VIAN. In plays that are more or less purely absurd and more or less comical or moving, these writers break the conventional rules of theater to dramatize anguished searches for the meaning of life, death, or human relationships that finally lead to nothingness or, at any rate, to silence. Influenced by the sad discoveries of World War II, this theater, unlike that of Camus and Sartre, is devoid of any hope in action as salvation. Whether it deals with daily life, emotional or social relationships, individual neuroses, or a desire for some meaningful transcendency, the new theater—with the exception of the works of the so-called poets—is characterized by the presentation of concrete, often allegorical, images, inexplicably imposed by a cruel and unjustified world, where man is condemned to the solitude of boredom or, far worse, to horror.

Among the playwrights of the new theater are some who, although more difficult to classify, have experimented with form and produced works original in tone and content. In a minor key Jean Tardieu's *Théâtre de chambre* (1953) and *Poèmes à jouer* (Poems for Performing, 1960) are collections of exercises on the possibilities and impossibilities of language, compositions in which the dialogue and movements of the characters are structured as in a piece of music. Of much broader scope are the plays of François BILLETDOUX, which deal with characters who are always ready to exploit one another, carrying their relationships to a logical or absurd conclusion. Doubtless the most independent of the new playwrights is Jean GENET, whose works, performed from 1947 to 1966 and based on a play of mirror reflections in which reality dissolves, are at the same time highly subversive provocations presented in a language that is strangely and shockingly sumptuous, as are the theatrical effects.

The new theater was brought to the public and actually imposed by a whole group of young directors (Roger Blin, Jean-Marie Serreau, Nicolas Bataille, Jacques Mauclair, Georges Vitaly, Sylvain Dhomme, André Reybaz), who at first had to struggle, on small stages, against the reticence of baffled spectators and certain hostile critics. Now Ionesco, Beckett, and Genet are performed on the national stages. At present there is a second wave of young directors who are reacting against the new theater of the '50s. Moreover, the theater of the absurd in particular has been challenged by a number of writers who, although using the techniques of the new theater, believe that drama should express an ideology and represent life not in a metaphysical no-man's-land but as it is or was experienced in a precise historical or sociological context. This has resulted in a somewhat epic, didactic theater often showing a strong influence of Marxism and of Bertolt Brecht, and exemplified in some of the works of Adamov and Billetdoux but more especially in the plays of Armand GATTI, the political and epic writer *par excellence*. On a smaller scale Georges MICHEL questions consumer society. But perhaps the most vigorous expression of this tendency are the works of the French-speaking black dramatists, especially Aimé CÉSAIRE.

Despite all the new trends, more or less traditional theater has continued to thrive. Most representative of it are the sustained efforts of Henry de Montherlant and Jean Anouilh. Montherlant, as rigorous as a seventeenth-century classical playwright, has remained faithful to psychological theater and has created lofty heroes and noble souls only to dissect them, revealing the frightful psychological ambiguities hidden behind all the moral exigencies, religious faith, or contempt for mediocrity. Anouilh is far freer in the composition of his plays. Extremely theatrical and greatly influenced by Pirandello, he plays tricks with traditional devices but does not invent new forms to treat his favorite subject: the intrigues and comical behavior of men greedy for happiness or purity, but faced with a sordid and degrading world. Another exponent of literary theater in traditional form is Marcel Aymé. A rather racy novelist, the author of short stories filled with fantasy, and a merciless satirist of French daily life, Aymé has produced a few interesting plays, including *Lucienne et le boucher* (Lucienne and the Butcher, 1947), a caricature of provincial customs and passions; *Clérambard* (1950), a brutal farce about a modern country squire who victimizes his family in an attempt to become a saint; *La Tête des autres* (Others' Heads, 1952), a satire on the courts and an indictment of capital punishment; and *Les Oiseaux de lune* (Moon Birds, 1955), based on a man's power to change other people into birds.

Also traditional in form is a whole body of religious theater, with the exception of Claudel's revived works and one play by Georges Bernanos, DIALOGUES DES CARMÉLITES (The Carmelites, 1952), which is in fact a film script adapted for the stage. Following François Mauriac, who after the war continued writing more or less successful plays in the Christian tradition, the novelist Julien Green has dramatized the mysteries of souls avid for salvation and pursued by evil. An American by birth, Green situated his first and best play, *Sud* (South, 1953), in the South of the United States: On the eve of the Civil War, a lieutenant falls desperately in love with another man and frees himself of his passion by committing an even more grievous sin—suicide— letting himself be killed in a duel by the young man he loves. Other works that may be included in this genre are the three "Catholic" plays of Henry de Montherlant—*Le Maître de Santiago* (1948), PORT-ROYAL (1954), and LA VILLE DONT LE PRINCE EST UN ENFANT (The City Whose Prince Is a Child, 1967)—which deal less with questions of grace and sin than with the psychology of believers.

Any brief survey of French theater would be incomplete without some mention of the eternal Boulevard theater, which still attracts large audiences despite repeated attacks on its essential mediocrity and the constant recurrence of its particular devices. Actually, some of the best playwrights draw on it for their situations and effects, but manage to transcend them. Often more in the order of entertainment than literature, Boulevard theater has been kept alive by very popular playwrights: Marcel Achard, André Roussin, and the team of Barillet and Grédy. As for Félicien Marceau, he disguises the Boulevard spirit and situations by borrowing certain devices from the avant-garde theater.

The events of May 1968 in France have provoked a serious crisis in the theater. Of course, the established playwrights, whether traditional or avant-garde, are as successful as ever. But the very essence of theater has been brought into question. The combined, although paradoxical, influence of Bertolt Brecht and Antonin Artaud, Julian Beck's short stay in France with his Living Theater, and youth's impatience with a theater that, despite fruitful attempts at popularization, has remained fundamentally bourgeois have led to a proliferation of "happenings" and several experiments in altogether revolutionary theater.

**Fratti, Mario** (born 1927). Italian dramatist. Fratti is more widely known abroad than in his native Italy. He is the only playwright of the younger generation to have his plays translated and performed throughout the world, including India and Japan. He has plays in five major American anthologies of drama and his work has been the subject of four American academic theses. Fratti's characters are universal in their desperate struggle to survive by honesty or deception. He is a modern master of the one-act play form. His dramatic structure is logical and compact. The action usually leads to a sudden but motivated reversal at the end of a play. The dialogue is terse, simple, and direct. The subtext is vital: A gesture often reveals the actual motivation behind the expedient social mask. Fratti is a keen yet benign observer of human error, even when man sacrifices dignity for survival.

*L'accademia* (1963), a one-act play, is Fratti's best comedy. This satire reveals the chauvinism of the Italian male, his vanity, his sexual self-aggrandizement, and his need to feel important in a society where importance is often a matter of tradition rather than achievement. A Fascist teacher attempts to win a Fascist war by maintaining an academy for gigolos in pursuit of American women. An admission fee of ten thousand lire plus the passing of a virility test is required of each student. The one and only test consists in having intercourse with the teacher's "wife," who is actually a prostitute playing this role for the benefit of the boys. This bit of deception is necessary because an Italian will more willingly part with money if he knows he is having his boss's wife.

*La gabbia* (The Cage, 1963) is a powerful study of fear and isolation. Cristiano, afraid and disgusted with life, has locked himself in a cage and communicates with those outside only by quoting lines from Chekhov. Like Chekhov's characters, Cristiano seeks comfort in words, but the words never conceal his loneliness and despair, his inability to cope with life. Ultimately, Cristiano develops a passion for his sister-in-law, Chiara, and makes his first contact with the world outside, but it is brief and deceptive. Chiara pretends to love Cristiano, and urges him to kill her husband, Pietro, so that they may be free to love each other. Cristiano strangles Pietro through the bars of the cage, but Chiara abandons him for her real lover and then accuses Cristiano of murder.

*I frigoriferi* (The Refrigerators, 1965) is an unusual work of Fratti's, a surrealistic parable of America. Nicola, a sincere but ineffectual Italian domestic, is employed in a strange Connecticut household. Irene Flower, heiress to a household-appliance fortune, and her lover, Willy, a scientist, are disguised as twin sisters. This disguise is maintained in order to conceal the fact that they have frozen her real sister, Ines, in one of the three giant refrigerators contained in the house. In the other two refrigerators are Renée, a French nurse, and Gold, an orangutan. Ultimately, the three in the refrigerators are unfrozen. Renée immediately becomes the mistress of the over-sexed Willy, while Ines and the orangutan fall in love. Ultimately, Irene, Willy, and the unfortunate Nicola are trapped in the refrigerators while the others go free. The residents of this quiet Connecticut town remain forever unaware of the mad events that occur within the household.

Most of Fratti's plays are realistic and deceptively simple. Dedicated to the principle of a people's theater, Fratti wishes to be understood by workers and intellectuals alike, maintaining that the primary objective of the theater is to provide a direct confrontation with reality. "I am aware. I believe in the possibility of man becoming aware. By writing plays I hope to communicate my awareness. Because I believe in man, man notwithstanding."

OTHER PLAYS: *Il campanello* (The Doorbell, 1958), *L'assegno* (The Allowance, 1960), *Il rifuto* (The Refusal, 1960), *La liberta* (1960), *Il ritorno* (The Return, 1961), *Gatta bianca al Greenwich* (White Cat in Greenwich, 1962), *La telefonata* (The Telephone Call, 1963), *La menzogna* (The Lie, 1963), *In attesa* (Waiting, 1964), *Il suicidio* (The Suicide, 1964), *Confidenza a pagamento* (The Coffin, 1954), *I seduttori* (The Seducers, 1964), *La partita* (The Game, 1966), *La domanda* (The Questionnaire, 1966), *Eleonora Duse* (1967), *L'amico cinese* (The Chinese Friend, 1969), *Il ponte* (The Bridge, 1969), *Tradimenti* (Betrayals, 1969), *Che Guevera* (1969), *La famiglia* (1970), *Colloquio col Negro* (Dialog with a Negro, 1970), *La Croce di Padre Marcello* (Father Marcello's Cross, 1970).

**Frisch, Max** (born 1911). Swiss dramatist, novelist, journalist, and architect. Throughout his life Frisch has questioned the social forces that have shaped his personality and career, and his works are part of an intense quest to discover his lost self, that is, to define exactly what he is by discovering what he might have become in another social framework. This question and quest have their origins in Frisch's critical attitude toward Swiss society. In his youth in Zurich he was directed along well-defined middle-class lines, which stamped his character with indelible Swiss traits. He did not show any inclination toward the theater until he reached the gymnasium, where he took a special interest in the works of Schiller and Ibsen. After trying his hand at writing dramas, Frisch eventually abandoned these creative efforts to concentrate on German literature at the University of Zurich. In 1933 Frisch's father died, and financial difficulties forced him to leave the university and begin a career as journalist. In addition to writing his first autobiographical novel, *Jürg Reinhardt* (1934), Frisch served as correspondent for various German and Swiss newspapers. From 1934 until 1936 he traveled throughout Southern and Eastern Europe as far as Siberia. In 1936 he returned to Zurich, where he began studying architecture and completed his military service. While he was working for his degree, he drew plans for the municipal swimming pool Letzigraben, which won a prize in 1940. After writing his second novel, *Die Schwierigen oder J'adore ce qui me brûle* (1943), Frisch established his own architectural firm, which enabled him to become financially independent and to continue his writing at the same time.

It was during this period that Frisch returned to the drama. In his first play, *Santa Cruz* (1944), he asks the question, which recurs in all the works that follow: Can man change the course of his destiny which is shaped by societal forces and preconceived patterns of behavior? Frisch sees man's basic potential as infinite, but real social circumstances circumscribe his action and limit his free development. In *Santa Cruz*, the vagabond Pelegrin encounters the cavalry captain and his wife, Elvira, whom he had met seventeen years earlier in Santa Cruz. At that time, Pelegrin and Elvira had fallen in love, and the captain, unaware of this, had wanted to follow Pelegrin on a voyage to Hawaii. Neither Elvira nor the captain had been capable of following their romantic dreams in Santa Cruz. The chance meeting with Pelegrin seventeen years later brings about the death of their illusions. In this romance, Frisch indicates that all dreams must come to an end if we are to live.

Basically, Frisch works toward smashing illusions so that people will realize who they are and be able to deal with the reality of their situation. In *Nun singen sie wieder* (Now They Are Singing Again, 1945), a play strongly influenced by Thornton Wilder, twenty-one hostages are shot by German soldiers during World War II, and in a series of surrealistic scenes, Frisch portrays the effect this has on the German soldiers, their families in Germany who are being bombed by the British, and the British airmen who are doing the bombing. The interconnection between all the killings and inhumanity is clearly demonstrated in contrapuntual scenes, which serve to alienate and shock the audience so that we can see that peace will remain a dream unless we put an end to war.

Frisch's next play also deals with war. In *Die Chinesische Mauer* (The Chinese Wall, 1946), a farce, an intellectual from the present time appears in China during the reign of the Emperor Hwang Ti, who is building the Great Wall. The intellectual, who also plays the role of Min Ko, "the voice of the people," endeavors to turn the course of history by warning the people about the atomic bomb and a world catastrophe. The Emperor, a tyrant, is intent on capturing the intellectual, or Min Ko, who has written poems criticizing his policies. The pursuit becomes entwined with a festive masked ball at the court, where several historical and legendary figures, including Caesar, Columbus, Philip of Spain, Brutus, Cleopatra, and Don Juan, reveal how their lives are fixed roles even though they do not act in accordance with these roles. At one point the intellectual denies that he is Min Ko, "the voice of the people," and when the revolution finally comes, a mute is ironically designated as "the poet of the people." The revolution is led by the wrong forces for the wrong purposes, and the intellectual is forced to realize that he cannot turn the tide of history.

The pessimism in *Die Chinesische Mauer* was an answer to Brecht, whom Frisch met during this period. Frisch borrowed many Brechtian techniques for his plays, but he developed a view of history and society fundamentally different from Brecht's. In essence, Frisch saw man as incapable of changing reality both on the stage and in society, and this accounted for his pessimism. In *Als der Krieg zu Ende war* (When the War Was Over, 1948) his bleak view stems from the postwar situation. Frisch portrays the breakdown of communication between a German couple during the Russian occupation in Berlin at the end of the war. The husband, who has committed war crimes in Warsaw, is hiding in a cellar while his wife tries to pacify a Russian colonel upstairs in the house. The wife falls in love with the humane colonel, even though they cannot speak the same language, and eventually she protects him against her husband, who, she realizes, is a murderer.

The question of guilt and crime has intrigued Frisch, and many of his plays explore the problem of criminality. *Graf Öderland* (Count Öderland, 1951) depicts the dilemma of a state prosecutor who ostensibly falls asleep while reviewing a complex case involving a man who has killed a watchman with an ax for no apparent reason. The murderer's reason becomes apparent in the prosecutor's dreams, which blend with reality. The prosecutor becomes the legendary Count Öderland, a type of Robin Hood, who upsets the established order of society by killing with an ax and stealing from the rich. After leading a successful revolution and freeing himself from the conventions of society, the prosecutor as Count Öderland is asked to form a new government, which actually would mean establishing a new order. The prosecutor wants to rid himself of this nightmare, and suddenly he finds himself back in his own house, where he had begun the dream of Count Öderland. However, there are distinct signs that the dream was a reality and that the revolution is still in the making.

*Graf Öderland* indicates that the conventions of society constrain and repress so as to drive one to crime and revolt. In *Don Juan oder die Liebe zur Geometrie* (Don Juan, or The Love of Geometry, 1952) Frisch offers an unusual interpretation of the Don Juan legend by showing how Don Juan was forced into his "criminal" role by the demands and expectations of society. Don Juan would rather devote his time to the study of geometry, but his father wants to make him into a man and marry him to Donna Anna for business reasons. Out of honesty, Don Juan refuses to marry and is forced into situations that result in adultery and murder. Finally, Don Juan stages his descent into hell in order to fool people into believing that he has disappeared. In actuality, he retires to the castle of the Duchess of Ronda where, along with the freedom to study geometry, he has, for all intents and purposes, a form of bourgeois marriage that is likened to a "prison in the paradisal gardens." Despite the fact that Don Juan has cut himself off from his legend, the truth will not win out. His role in history has been cast for him. He himself realizes that he "shares the fate of many famous men. The whole world knows our acts, but almost no one knows the meaning of the acts."

Frisch constantly accuses society, especially Swiss society, of causing crime by compelling people to play roles that do not fit their natural characters and do not allow for change and creativity. *Biedermann und die Brandstifter* (The Firebugs, 1958) is a parable play about the banality of evil, a didactic play without a lesson because people cannot change their ways. They become functionaries for a social system that thrives on exploitation. Gottlieb Biedermann (the name in German implies a pious and petty good citizen) proves this point. Biedermann is a "respectable" capitalist who drives one of his employees, Knechterling ("Little Slave"), to suicide. Outwardly Biedermann prides himself on his decency and amiability. He orders his life according to the conventions of his society, and therefore cannot believe that anyone will harm him, for he cannot conceive of his harming any individual. When two arsonists, Schmitz and Eisenring, obviously shady characters, force their way into his house, Biedermann complies with their wishes because he is afraid that they will expose his true nature. A chorus of firemen continually warns Biedermann that he will inflict great damage on himself and society, but he pays no attention. Instead he helps the thugs conceal the drums of gasoline in his attic, invites them to dinner, and even provides them with matches to set fire to the house. The lamentation of the chorus falls on deaf ears. Biedermann and his wife remain totally unaware of their evil. In fact, Frisch wrote an epilogue in which Biedermann and his wife appear in hell and protest their innocence. In hell the firebugs are the devils, who are tired of small fry like Biedermann. They are angry at God, who pardons all the great criminals, and because of this, the devils decide to go on strike until God holds to the Ten Commandments. They extinguish the fires of hell and promise that they will make a hell out of earth until God responds to their demands.

There are numerous political implications in this parable play. Frisch based it initially on the postwar situation in Czechoslovakia, when President Beneš, a Social Democrat, invited the Communists to join his government even though he knew that they would eventually pave the way for Russian domination. Yet to limit the scope of the play to this event would be to distort its meaning. The play also addresses itself to Hitler's reign of terror in Germany and the annexation of Austria. It even has a bearing on the war in Vietnam, where the Vietnamese have invited Americans to burn and destroy their country. Essentially the play deals with the evil of self-righteous people who function for and in a socioeconomic system that exonerates criminal acts of oppression and exploitation. The evil is terrifying because it is banal, and the banal people

163

rarely penetrate their own inauthenticity to see how they are used as tools to destroy their own chances to attain humanity.

*Andorra* (1961) is also a play about banality. In fact, the structure of the drama has a resemblance to the Eichmann trial. As the course of events is presented in twelve scenes, various townspeople take the stand during the interludes to recall their connection to the Jew Andri. The witnesses all insist, like Eichmann, that they were not responsible for Andri's persecution and death. Yet the action onstage contradicts their testimonies. Andorra is considered to be a model country. The people pride themselves on their virtues and purity. This is the reason the schoolteacher, who once had an affair with a woman in the country of the blacks, has never told his illegitimate son, Andri, about his origins. Instead he has always pretended that Andri was a Jewish orphan, whom he adopted to protect against the anti-Semitic blacks. As Andri grows older, he finds that the Andorrans, too, are basically anti-Semitic and that they manipulate him. Eventually he suspects even his father, who refuses him the hand of his half sister, Barblin, and cannot give Andri a truthful answer concerning his decision. When war erupts with the blacks, a minister tries to tell Andri the truth, but he has suffered so much as a Jew that he refuses to give up his Jewish identity. The blacks invade the country and persecute the Jews. Andri's father hangs himself. Andri is executed. Barblin becomes deranged and attempts to whitewash the town square.

*Andorra* poses the question of what would have happened if the Germans had invaded Switzerland during World War II. Frisch certainly does not whitewash the Swiss, for the play reflects their prejudices and weaknesses. As a parable, moreover, it illuminates the broader problem of anti-Semitism in regard to identity and freedom. Frisch sees people who accept their society uncritically as likely to commit crimes of oppression, and as incapable of breaking illusions that oppress them as well.

In his most recent play, *Biografie* (1967), Frisch again explores the limitations of social relationships. Kürmann, a forty-nine-year-old Swiss professor of human behavior, whose name means a man who has a choice, asserts that he would live his life differently if he were given a choice. A character called the Registrator (the recorder) offers him this opportunity and begins to play with him. The play is clearly in Kürmann's imagination. The imagination is the stage. The play on the stage reveals that reality cannot be changed—except in the imagination. Kürmann replays his meeting with his second wife, Antoinette, a meeting that had taken place seven years earlier in 1960. Try as he may, Kürmann does not succeed in altering his actions. Only when Antoinette is given a choice is there a possibility for freedom. This possibility is limited by the fact that Kürmann is dying of cancer and would have to die in 1967 no matter how the years between 1960 and 1967 were relived.

*Biografie* recalls the starting point of Frisch's first play, *Santa Cruz*: the impossibility of living a life of illusions. Frisch insists that we accept our social reality and the limitations imposed on us if we are to discover our true potential, if we are to know ourselves. To endeavor to change reality is futile, and Frisch has made his anti-Brechtian position clear in his speech "Der Autor und das Theater" (The Author and the Theater, 1965): "The closer we come to the present and the more familiar we become with the present world, the clearer it becomes to us how it cannot be reflected, the complex reality. A play, even a great one, remains only a play—a narrow passage, and just because of this, salvation for several hours. No matter how the theater may present itself, it is art—play as an answer to the impossibility of reflecting the world. That which can be reflected is poetry. Even Brecht does not show the present world. To be sure, his theater acts as though it did, and Brecht always found new means to show that it showed. But aside from the gesture of showing, what is shown? A great deal but not the present world. Rather models of the Brechtian-Marxist thesis—the desirability of another present world—poetry."

All Frisch's literary works, especially his three novels *Stiller* (I'm Not Stiller, 1954), *Homo Faber* (1957), and *Mein Name sei Gantenbein* (Let My Name Be Gantenbein, 1964), reflect the impossibility of mastering and changing reality. In particular, Frisch wants his dramas understood purely as theater, his novels purely as fiction. Ironically, Frisch has borrowed heavily from Brecht's dramaturgical arsenal and, like Brecht, has worked on revisions of his plays to express his opposition to Brecht. This does not mean that Frisch's plays are nonpolitical or that they totally reject Brecht's political analysis of society. On the contrary, Frisch focuses on many of the same problems in society that Brecht studied, and he uses the parable form to reflect upon concrete reality, especially Swiss reality. Frisch universalizes this reality in order to confront and understand (without illusions) the different roles he has played by choice and the roles that society has imposed upon him.

OTHER PLAYS SINCE 1946: *Die grosse Wut des Philipp Hotz* (The Great Furor of Philip Hotz, 1958).

**Fry, Christopher** (born 1907). English verse dramatist. Born in England and educated at a Quaker public school, Fry experienced at an early age the active influence of a religious belief that his writing was later to display. His father, an Anglican lay preacher who died when Fry was three, had abandoned the profession of architect to work among the poor. Leaving school at the age of eighteen, Fry alternated for a while between teaching and work in the repertory theater. He graduated from acting to directing, and 1940 found him director of the Oxford Playhouse, a post which he resumed in 1944 after four years' service as a noncombatant in the armed forces and held until 1946.

The foundations of Fry's career as a dramatist were laid in the prewar period, when he wrote a number of playlets for the Children's Service of the B.B.C., a musical comedy, and plays and pageants commissioned for religious festivals. In *The Boy With a Cart* (1938), the only work of this period to have been published, the chorus (written for performance by Sussex amateurs) is reminiscent of T. S. Eliot's in *Murder in the Cathedral,* while the dramatized story of St. Cuthman offers a foretaste of the playful dexterity that was to become the hallmark of Fry's later work. *A Phoenix Too Frequent,* a one-act play appearing in 1946 in a season of "poets' plays" presented by E. Martin Browne, established Fry as a playwright of note. With the dazzling success of *The Lady's Not for Burning* in John Gielgud's West End production in 1948, Fry was generally acclaimed as the most promising by far of the postwar dramatists. Until the mid-1950s it was Fry more than any other playwright who held out hope for the revival of an English drama freed from the prosaic shackles of naturalism. Extravagant appraisals of his work were made by critics of every persuasion: "Mr. Fry," wrote Richard Findlater in 1952, "has brought back to the English drama wit, rhetoric, humour, gaiety and colour. . . . The readiness with which audiences accept the eloquence of his characters, the attention with which they follow the convolutions of his rhetoric, and the relish which they show for the subtleties of his wit are, perhaps, signs of a new phase in the drama. He has reinstated comedy as a high theatrical form, and reconciled it with tragedy." Fry's failure to sustain this high estimation is the consequence partly of a radical shift in contemporary taste and partly of a weakness in his dramaturgy that postwar theatergoers had been ready to overlook in favor of the brilliant surface qualities of his work.

Fry's plays may be divided into those with an overtly religious theme and those which, however serious their underlying issues, employ the mode of secular comedy. Within the former category, *The Firstborn* (begun in 1940 and completed after the war, but not seen on the stage until the Edinburgh Festival of 1948) is an ambitious tragedy in which the author fails to dramatize with sufficient clarity the dilemma of his hero, Moses. More effective is *Thor, with Angels* (1948), portraying the arrival of Christianity in a sixth-century Kentish farmstead. Here Fry touches upon the mysteries of faith with a characteristic gaiety that was missing or out of place in *The Firstborn,* and finds scope for his verbal ingenuity in the alliterative pastiche of Old English spoken by his Jutish warriors. But Fry's main claim for consideration as a religious dramatist must be upheld by *A Sleep of Prisoners* (1950). Each of four British soldiers imprisoned in a church during the second world war "is seen," in the poet's words, "through the sleeping thoughts of the others, and each, in his own dream, speaks as at heart he is, not as he believes himself to be." Although its complex structure, shifting from the dreams of the sleeping prisoners to the waking world, may not contain the profundities it seems to offer at first meeting, the play is remarkable for its message of hope and determination in a scarred century:

> The frozen misery
> Of centuries breaks, cracks, begins to move;
> The thunder is the thunder of the floes,

The thaw, the flood, the upstart Spring.
Thank God our time is now when wrong
Comes up to face us everywhere,
Never to leave us till we take
The longest stride of soul man ever took.

It is however upon the series of comedies inaugurated by *A Phoenix Too Frequent* that Fry's reputation rests. *Venus Observed* (1950) was described by its author as "one of a series of four comedies, a comedy for each of the seasons of the year, four comedies of mood." *A Phoenix Too Frequent*, which deftly extracts the last ounce of paradoxical gaiety from the tale of the widow of Ephesus who waits, with all too frail determination, to follow her husband into death in his subterranean tomb, lies outside this seasonal scheme. The remaining three comedies carry progressively deeper overtones, passing from the spring-like exuberance of *The Lady's Not for Burning* to the autumnal melancholy of *Venus Observed* and the wintry sunshine of *The Dark Is Light Enough* (1954). (It was not until 1970 that *A Yard of Sun*, the "summer" play of the series, appeared.) In 1949 Fry wrote of "the two sins of our time: the fear of language, and the fear that no audience can be adult, both of which fears result in condescension." The theme common to these plays is the mystery and ultimate sanctity of human existence, and the purpose of the poet's extravagant language is to startle a delighted audience into an awareness of these qualities. "Poetry," he wrote, "is the language in which man explores his own amazement. It is the language in which he says heaven and earth in one word. It is the language in which he speaks of himself and his predicament as though for the first time." Freshness of vision is most happily maintained in *The Lady's Not for Burning*, in which complicated events catch a world-weary cynic and the rationalist daughter of an alchemist, against the colorful setting of a fifteenth-century market town, in "the unholy mantrap of love." Fry claimed in 1949 that this comedy treats of "the world as I see it, a world in which we are all poised on the edge of eternity, a world which has deeps and shadows of mystery, in which God is anything but a sleeping partner"; contemporary audiences and critics readily accepted this estimate of the play's high seriousness. *Venus Observed* was the object of a more puzzled reception. It was left to the author himself to point out that behind the plot—which concerns an aging Duke who invites three former mistresses ostensibly to watch the sun's eclipse from his observatory (and former bedroom) but in reality to allow his son an opportunity to choose him a wife for his old age—there lay an exploration of the questing loneliness which Fry found to be the unique element of the human condition. *The Dark Is Light Enough*, set in Austria during the Hungarian revolution of 1848, is marked by a clarity of construction which matches a corresponding spareness and discipline in the language. The dying Countess Rosmarin's successive refusal to surrender either the worthless Richard Gettner or, as the tide turns against the rebels, the Colonel who had demanded Gettner's release is a moving testimony to Fry's belief in the inviolable sanctity of human life and the absurd but painful dilemmas that confront the humane pacifist entangled in violent action.

In these "comedies of mood" the most distinctive feature is the dazzling felicity of the verse. Fry's delight in seizing upon colloquial commonplaces and, with a few deft strokes, forcing an extra layer of meaning upon them has some affinity with the method of Eliot's verse drama, but displays an exuberance not shared by the older dramatist. It revels in punning conceits: The Duke in *Venus Observed* is reproached for "coruscating on thin ice." "Where in this small-talking world," sighs Thomas Mendip in *The Lady's Not for Burning*, "can I find a longitude with no platitude?" The following passage from the same play gives some notion of the dexterity with which Fry, touching upon the theme of the Last Judgment, treads the difficult path dividing the solemn from the frivolous:

> No; the time has come for tombs to tip
> Their refuse; for the involving ivy, the briar,
> The convolutions of convolvulus,
> To disentangle and make way
> For the last great ascendancy of dust,
> Sucked into judgment by a cosmic yawn
> Of boredom. The Last Trump
> Is timed for twenty-two forty hours precisely.

But the playful and sometimes precocious nature of Fry's verse has caused the critic Raymond Williams to label his exuberance "not so much intensification as a defect of precise imagination." "A spade is never so merely a spade as the word Spade would imply," remarks Reedback in *Venus Observed*, perhaps echoing Fry's philosophy of language. While the poet's reluctance to call a spade a spade is evident, his ability to distinguish novelty of insight from ingenious paraphrase may be doubted. The superficiality that must be ascribed to his language extends to characterization: Fry's *dramatis personae*, apart from some minor characters drawn from the lower classes to provide broadly conventional comic relief, are hardly differentiated by a purposeful use of rhythm or imagery; nor, in the structure of his plays (*The Dark Is Light Enough* excepted), are they opposed to one another in significant dramatic conflict. Similarly, his picturesque settings, delightful to the eye, often contribute little to the dynamics of the play. Despite his schooling in the theater, Fry often calls upon literary virtues to obscure his basic dramatic weaknesses.

*The Dark Is Light Enough* marked a break in Fry's dramatic output, which was resumed only in 1962 with *Curtmantle*, a dramatization of the life of Henry II of England written in a verse interspersed with passages of prose. The play's theme is described by the author as "law, or rather the interplay of different laws: civil, canon, moral, aesthetic, and the laws of God; and how they belong and do not belong to each other." What Fry's verse has lost in ornamental glitter it has gained in strength, severity, and dramatic fitness, and the play must be accounted among his most successful. But dramatic incident is centered mainly upon the mounting conflict of character and purpose between Henry and Thomas à Becket, and the third act (after Becket's murder) represents a slackening of the tension so successfully sustained over the first two.

A Yard of Sun, the "Summer Comedy" with which Fry at length completed his quartet of seasonal comedies, failed to stimulate a revival of interest in the author's work. Set in Siena shortly after the end of the Second World War against the festive background of the annual Palio, the play is a study of conflicting loyalties and their eventual resolution. The affiliations which had divided an Italian family in the stress of war are linked symbolically with the sharp rivalries among the contestants in the race which forms the climax to the Palio. If the play's language is free from the sometimes facile ingenuity of the earlier comedies, it also lacks the zestful spontaneity which won them their reputation. But Fry's wit and delight in paradox are muted in A Yard of Sun rather than altogether absent from it, and a quality of reflective humanity which runs through the play suggests that Fry's power as a dramatist is not exhausted.

The blemishes in Fry's work cannot of themselves account for the speed of his reputation's eclipse. His demonstration that high art need not be divorced from gaiety was greeted with relief (and consequently overvalued) in a postwar Britain whose pleasures were rationed by an unprecedented program of austerity. The poet's greatest successes date from the period when, against a background of diminishing imperial power, the country set out to celebrate her traditional greatness with a Festival of Britain (1951) and, in the following year, the pageantry of Queen Elizabeth II's coronation ushered in talk of an age of "new Elizabethans." For Fry's values are traditional values, best exemplified in the Church of England—humane, aware of nature, accustomed to a quiet, unquestioning faith and, although tolerant of eccentricity, calmly accepting the established social order. These were values decisively rejected in the theater of the late '50s, and Fry's comedies were to prove an inevitable casualty. Fry was an important figure in the movement to revive religious verse drama that was initiated by George Bell as Dean of Canterbury and Bishop of Chichester in the '20s and '30s, with which Eliot as a dramatic poet and E. Martin Browne as a director were associated. Although he was hailed as the portent of a new epoch in the theater, it is more accurate to view him as the final contributor to a movement that enjoyed a brief revival in the '50s and was soon to be superseded.

Fry's translations from the French of Anouilh (Ring Around the Moon, 1950) and Giraudoux (The Lark and Tiger at the Gates, 1958; Judith, 1962) have been widely acclaimed and extensively performed. His screenplays include *The Beggar's Opera, A Queen Is Crowned* (1952), *Ben Hur* (1959), *Barrabas* (1960), and *The Bible* (1964); he was awarded the Queen's Gold Medal for Poetry in 1962. Fry's contributions are discussed in the following publications: "English Verse Drama: Christopher Fry" by William Arrowsmith in *The Hudson Review*, Vol. III, No. 2 (1950); *The Unholy Trade* (1952) by Richard Findlater; *Christopher Fry* (1954) by Derek Stanford; *The Third Voice* (1959) by Denis Donoghue; and *Drama from Ibsen to Brecht* (1968) by Raymond Williams.

# G

Galileo (**Das Leben des Galilei,** written 1938–39, produced 1943). A play by Bertolt Brecht. Because of the ambivalence in this play, Brecht twice revised the original version, which was first produced in Zurich. The second version was an English translation in collaboration with Charles Laughton in 1949. The final one was made in 1954. Brecht maintained the original starting point—the position of the scientist in society. His changes in the drama were made to sharpen *his* position in regard to that of the scientist. The explosion of the atomic bomb in 1945 made a great impact on Brecht, and he took care to make clear that Galileo's submission to the Church was a criminal act. It was to be likened to a scientist's submission to a state which wants to withhold the truth from the people in order to exploit them.

*Galileo* is an epic play covering the period from 1609, when the scientist, forty-five years old, is living in Padua, to 1637. There are fifteen scenes, and each one moves to illustrate the main thesis of the play: "Whoever doesn't know the truth is simply a blockhead. But whoever knows it and calls it a lie is a criminal." As a brilliant lecturer at the University of Padua, Galileo barely manages to eke out a living. His favorite pupil is Andrea Sarti, the son of his housekeeper. In the opening scenes Galileo shows his great lust for knowledge (and for food), and nothing will stop him from pursuing his studies. For this reason he steals the Dutch invention of the telescope and passes it off as his own; he needs money for his work and the Venetians want inventions that will help them get rich. Eventually Galileo moves to Florence, where he has more money and time to devote to his studies. However, there he also comes under control of the Church and must be more careful about propagating the Copernican theory. In 1625 Galileo successfully proves to the official Church scientist, Clavius, that the earth is not the center of the world. but the Inquisition forbids him to publish his findings. During the next eight years, Galileo maintains his silence while working on new ideas. When a more enlightened priest, a mathematician, is elected to the papacy as Urban VIII, Galileo believes that the time is ripe to advance his new scientific theories. However, the Grand Inquisitor convinces the Pope that the Church would lose its authority if Galileo were allowed to chart the new solar system. The Inquisition summons Galileo, but the Pope insists that Galileo not be touched, only shown the instruments of torture. Galileo's students, especially his disciple Andrea, are certain that Galileo will not recant. Yet Galileo, who loves the simple pleasures of life, breaks down under pressure. Andrea and the other young scientists became totally disillusioned and leave him.

Next we are given a picture of the older Galileo of 1637, under close watch by the Inquisition. He lives with his daughter, a spinster, who could never marry because her father's heresy made her a poor catch. Galileo seems exclusively interested in wine and food, but when Andrea Sarti arrives on his way to Holland, Galileo gives him a secret copy of the *Discorsi* to smuggle out of the country. Andrea now looks upon his mentor as a hero. Yet Galileo makes it clear that he is not worthy of admiration because he had not planned to make the copy. In fact, his cowardly actions will influence other scientists to bow to the demands of institutional power rather than to serve the people. It is with this knowledge, and with the *Discorsi*, that Andrea takes his leave and crosses the frontier.

Many interpretations of *Galileo* have insisted that the play's greatness depends on its ambiguity. Galileo is not really a criminal but a human being caught up in his passion for the truth and his passion for good living. Yet the play clearly shows that Galileo mistakenly believes it possible to sacrifice one passion for the other. It is obvious that the younger, more courageous Galileo is to be contrasted with the older, more resigned Galileo, living in confinement. This contrast is highlighted in the final meeting between the young Andrea and the old Galileo. Brecht's characters are all drawn to demonstrate how the contradictions of the times influence their lives and actions. The priests are all brilliant men who delight in argument for the sake of argument and not for the sake of uncovering the truth. The lower-class figures—Andrea, his mother, Federzoni—are passionately devoted to Galileo and the experiments he makes for the benefit of mankind. The gestures throughout the play carry the social and political attitudes of each figure, and Galileo ends as a repentant "criminal."

**Gáspár, Margit** (born 1908). Hungarian playwright and translator. Miss Gáspár writes popular comedies touching upon the current political issues of the day in a light, journalistic fashion. Her entertaining plots and skillful dialogues compensate to some extent for her schematic characters. Her best-known plays are *Uj Isten Thébában* (New God in Thebes, 1946) and *Hamletnek nincs igaza* (Hamlet Is Wrong, 1962). She has translated Maugham, Mauriac, and Pirandello into Hungarian.

**Gatti, Armand** (born 1924). French dramatist. Born in Monaco into a family of poor immigrants (his father was a street cleaner), Gatti had a difficult childhood, alternating between school and small jobs. When he was about sixteen, he began trying to write poetry and plays. In 1943 he joined the Resistance, was arrested and condemned to death, then was pardoned and sent to a concentration camp near Hamburg. At the end of the war he was released and became a parachutist. After the war Gatti became a local journalist and then a reporter, working in South America, Cuba, and China. His trip to China, which led him to write an important book on Communist China, also inspired his first published play, *Le Poisson noir* (The Black Fish), which received the Prix Fénéon in 1959 but was not performed until 1964. From then on Gatti devoted himself entirely to the theater and the cinema. His film *L'Enclos* received a prize at Cannes and another in Moscow in 1961.

His first play, chosen for production by Jean Vilar and directed by Jean Négroni in 1959, *Le Crapaud-Buffle* (The Bullfrog), a kind of sketchy allegory dealing with the theme of dictatorship, was a failure. His subsequent plays, performed in Villeurbanne, Lyons, Marseilles, and Toulouse, and sometimes directed by himself, made his reputation as one of the foremost French playwrights in the political and social genre.

Gatti's theater is very often based on his own experiences: for example, his father's life (LA VIE IMAGINAIRE DE L'ÉBOUEUR AUGUSTE G. [The Imaginary Life of the Garbage Collector Auguste G., 1962]), the universe of concentration camps (*L'Enfant-rat* [The Rat Child], published in 1960; *La Deuxième Existence du camp de Tatenberg* [The Second Existence of the Tatenberg Camp, 1962]), and his encounters with guerrillas and revolutionaries (*La Naissance* [Birth] and *La Passion du Général Franco*, 1968). On the whole, and objectively, the theme of his works is that of the victimization that leads or should lead to revolution, in the perspective of a very leftist ideology. Strikes, wars of liberation in the East as well as in South America, and trials such as that of Sacco and Vanzetti (*Chant public devant deux chaises électriques* [Public Song for Two Electric Chairs], 1966) are the subject matter of his aggressive and critical plays.

Gatti's idea was to create a revolutionary dramatic art corresponding to his revolutionary subject matter. Although he has assimilated all the new techniques, he does not at all indulge in the theater of personal neuroses, which other revolutionary playwrights, such as Adamov, try to integrate into their political ideologies. His contribution is essentially that of improving on the Brechtian technique of distanced narration, and complementing it with an extremely complex orchestration of spectacle and sound. The wealth of scenic imagination, the simultaneity of scenes, the different levels of voice, the constant use of visual devices (slides and film), and the brutal juxtaposition of times and places have transformed what might well have seemed mere propaganda into the successful theatricalization of national and international revolutionary ideas.

OTHER PLAYS: *L'Enfant-rat* (The Rat Child, published 1960), *Le Voyage du grand Tchou* (1962), *Chronique d'une planète provisoire* (Chronicles of a Temporary Planet, 1963), *Un Homme seul* (1966), *V comme Vietnam* (V as in Vietnam, 1967), *Les 13 Soleils de la rue Saint-Blaise* (1969).

**Gelber, Jack** (born 1932). American playwright and director. Gelber was born in Chicago and received a bachelor's degree in journalism from the University of Illinois in 1953. His first play, *The Connection,* produced off-Broadway by the Living Theater in 1959, received considerable critical attention, ranging from outraged condemnation to lavish praise; it won an Obie and a number of other awards. It was hip drama about the hip world of heroin, simple enough in situation (a group of addicts wait for their connection to arrive, he does, they have their fix and drift off) but unsettling in its form. The addicts are supposedly participating in the making of a play and a film about addicts, so, as they wait, Jaybird, the scriptwriter, Jim Dunn, the producer, and two photographers try to get the junkies both to be themselves and to fit into a predetermined plot. Like Genet (and Shakespeare), Gelber plays on the nested realities of "real people" playing actors playing "real people" playing actors, and every effort is made to worry the audience that perhaps these are actual addicts before them and that the washroom is not just "backstage" but a place where (as in *The Blacks*) the real crime, the real fix, takes place. The final effect, unlike Pirandello's rather lyrical sleights about illusion and reality, is to leave the audience with the feeling that the play itself may be perilously actual; by the end Jaybird and one of the photographers, formerly square, have taken a fix and the vulnerable audience can only wonder uneasily if any drugs were planted in the tobacco it was urged to buy in the lobby during intermission. Suddenly there seems to be no safety, no exempt place where it is possible just to look and listen.

This "interaction between audience and players," which Gelber has stated is one of his goals, and which has been unsettling to some of his critics, has not been so well achieved in later plays. *The Apple,* produced by the Living Theater in 1961, deals with a New York coffeehouse theater group in the process of trying to produce a play, but despite lines intending to make the "real" audience also the "fictive" audience, there is not the unavoidable involvement created by *The Connection.* Part of the difficulty lies in a phenomenon that is relatively new to drama, the problem of point of view; in *The Apple* and in his next play, *Square in the Eye* (1965), there are sections that exist as subjective experiences within one of the characters (for example, Act II of *The Apple* is Tom's perception of his own death) in such a way that the audience is witness and not participant.

Gelber's first Broadway play, *The Cuban Thing* (1968), failed not because of the numerous bomb scares and the protests of angry exiled Cubans but because the play itself was dramatically and politically turgid.

Gelber has also written the screenplay for the film *The Connection* (1962) and a novel, *On Ice* (1964). He was awarded a Guggenheim Fellowship for creative writing for 1963–64 and another for 1966–67. An off-Broadway Albee, Gelber leaves his admirers wondering if the early promise will be renewed and developed.

**Genet, Jean** (born 1910). French dramatist. Abandoned by his mother, brought up in a state orphanage, and then put into the care of peasants, Jean

Genet was caught stealing at the age of ten and was sent to reform school. He finally escaped, joined the Foreign Legion, then deserted, and proceeded to lead a life of petty crime and imprisonment. It was in prison that he began to write poetry and novels. Jean Cocteau and then Jean-Paul Sartre took Genet under their protection, made his works known in the 1940s, and, through their testimony, managed to keep him out of jail. Genet has had five plays performed. The first, *Les Bonnes* (The Maids), was directed in 1947 by Louis Jouvet, at the same time as Jean Giraudoux's *L'Apollon de Bellac*. It was misunderstood, provoked something of a scandal, and since then Genet, without disowning it, has stated that he considers it the least courageous of his works. His subsequent plays have indeed proved to be increasingly daring and imaginative. *Les* PARAVENTS (The Screens), directed in 1966 by Roger Blin and Jean-Louis Barrault at the Théâtre de France, provoked actual riots because of his treatment of the French Army during a period of colonial war. Since the late 1960s Genet would seem to be neglecting literature in order to devote more of his time to social action and protest in both France and the United States.

In his plays, as in the rest of his works, the world Genet presents is that of the various groups condemned by established society in the name of Good. As he mentions in his autobiographical *Journal d'un voleur,* his sympathy—because of having been abandoned by his mother and because of his prison experiences—is with all those considered criminals by society. The characters in his plays are thus members of those rejected and outlawed groups that are declared guilty, with no appeal possible: murderers, thieves, prostitutes, perverts, blacks, North Africans. Whereas established society claims that its supreme value is Good, the condemned groups, according to Genet, seek their glory in Evil or in a state of abjection so extreme that it becomes as striking as the dignity of upright men. Genet thus portrays a countersociety, parallel to ours but, as it were, the negative of it, with its own laws, hierarchies, and rites, which are the opposite of ours, just as a black mass is the opposite of a real mass. This countersociety is the reflection of established society and exists only in relation to it: the maids are the mirror image of their mistress (*Les Bonnes*), just as the Blacks in LES NÈGRES (The Blacks, 1959) are "black" only because of the Whites. There is a complex relationship of hate and admiration between the two worlds, for each needs the other and is threatened by it. Philosophically, Good and Evil are necessary to one another, each being the inverse image of the other. Genet, of course, deliberately takes the side of Evil. Hence his art consists in giving a positive value, both aesthetic and moral, to what is ordinarily considered as negative: bad taste becomes Beauty; degradation, Glory; treason, a form of Honor, and so on. The objective here is to give a real existence to everything that is condemned and repudiated in the name of Good, and thus to reverse the situation by making the world of Good a paltry, negative reflection of reality, which is so-called Evil.

This philosophical inversion has made it possible for Genet to create highly theatrical dramatic works. The fantastic spectacle of criminals or the oppressed is the parodic mirror image of the spectator's world. When the world of Good is shown onstage, it is represented by caricatural figures of authority: judges, bishops, policemen, governors, generals, queens. Within the dramas, the characters play at going, or really do go, from one world to the other: in *Le Balcon* (The Balcony, 1960), for example, the sexually obsessed who frequent Mme Irma's brothel in order to play at being a bishop or a judge really do become a bishop or a judge after a revolution has taken place.

Certain critics persist in seeing Genet's works as a claim in favor of the oppressed and victims of authority. And, indeed, his plays violently satirize established society. But primarily they paint a portrait of an anti-society condemned to become more and more like the image that society makes of it, and whose members can fulfill themselves only by being worse than that image. Added to this is a personal element: despite all his transgressions of laws and social taboos, the poet Jean Genet never manages to be a hero of Evil. Even in the first play he wrote, *Haute Surveillance* (Deathwatch, produced 1949), Genet portrays himself as the character Lefranc, who, despite the murder he commits, will never belong to the race of great criminals. Genet's world is peopled by two opposed and grandiose races that reflect one another: that of authority and that of the criminal elite. Genet himself, condemned by the former, may have chosen the latter, but he does not have the grace of Evil: He is damned on both sides.

Consequently, in his works, the two societies reflect each other *ad infinitum*, and the final resolution seems to be complete negation—the image of a universe in which there is nothing but reflections and no reality. Mme Irma, owner of a house of illusions, sends the spectators home, at the end of *Le Balcon*, assuring them that at home "everything will be even more false" than in her theatrical brothel.

The rejection of reality in Genet's works must no doubt be seen in this perspective. His characters speak in incredibly literary language, both rich in slang and borrowed in part from the greatest of French literature; his sumptuous or strange settings are highly stylized; the action is akin to fantastic ceremonies and would seem like a parody of exorcisms. All these devices are not so much a kind of "poetry" meant to suggest a hidden reality as they are a deliberate attempt to repudiate the reality of the spectacle and, by the same token, the spectator's reality. Indeed, Genet's great baroque and frightfully luxuriant plays may be compared to mock ceremonies that, with ferocious joy, sing of the annihilation of our world.

**Germany.** In September 1944 because of the destruction of many theaters and the bankruptcy of the Hitler regime, all theaters were closed. From 1933 to 1944 the development of German drama had in any case been at low ebb. Many of the outstanding dramatists, actors, directors, and set designers, who had made Berlin a world center for theater in the 1920s, had either fled Germany or were killed during the war. Drama under the Nazis took the form of propaganda. Most plays became pageants that celebrated the purity and superiority of the Aryan race. With few exceptions, notably Gustaf Gründgens and Heinz Hilpert, German directors interpreted and distorted the classics to serve the political ideology of the Nazis.

In the fall of 1945, the Allied forces permitted the theaters to reopen. Throughout the country performances were held in makeshift theaters until new buildings could be constructed and supplies obtained. Gradually the old repertory system supported by the cities and states was reinstituted. Today, most of the leading theaters (approximately two hundred in East and West Germany) are subsidized by municipalities or states. This situation necessitates a certain amount of official control of employees and programs of the theaters. Consequently, there is a close connection between politics and the theater. Indeed, German theater is not only a moral institution in Schiller's sense of the word—that is, a secular church—but also a political arena. The theaters have become centers where religious, social, economic, and political issues are presented with as much openness as is permitted by the policies of the city and state in which each theater is located. Since Germany has been partitioned into two different states, West Germany (Bundesrepublik Deutschland, B.R.D.) and East Germany (Deutsche Demokratische Republik, D.D.R.), there have been two distinct postwar developments in the German theater which must be considered separately.

*West German drama.* The postwar development in West Germany can be characterized by the trend toward decentralization and pluralism. Berlin had been the theater metropolis, noted especially for the Schlosspark-Theater, now under the direction of Boleslav Barlog. After 1945 other cities developed ensembles of equal caliber. Important companies were the Munich Kammerspiele (under the direction of Hans Schweikart), the Schauspielhaus in Düsseldorf (Gründgens until 1955, then Karl Heinz Stroux), the Schauspielhaus in Bochum (Hans Schalla), the Landestheater in Darmstadt (Gustav Rudolf Sellner), the Deutsche Theater in Göttingen (Hilpert), the Deutsche Schauspielhaus in Hamburg (Gründgens, then Oskar Fritz Schuh and Hans Lietzau), and the Städtischen Bühnen in Frankfurt (Harry Buckwitz). This decentralization is in large part due to the situation of Berlin, which is walled off from the rest of West Germany. It is also due to the fact that the cities and states contribute huge subsidies to local companies. Many cities can boast a large complex of buildings which house stages for theater, opera, ballet, and workshops. In almost every average-sized urban community the cultural complexes have either been rebuilt or renovated in the postwar epoch in grand bourgeois style, and the directors, actors, set designers, stagehands, dancers, and musicians, as well as the administrators, have glorified status as civil servants. Cities compete with one another to distinguish themselves by offering varied and lavish programs in the arts. A well-balanced program for an eleven-month season generally consists in two or three classical plays, the rediscovery of an unusual play of the past, a foreign play, an early twentieth-century play, and a play by a contemporary author. The contemporary and foreign plays are generally somewhat avant-garde, but not too offensive to the bourgeois establishment.

This diet, which is fed, as Brecht would say, in the "culinary theater" for the upper classes—less than 5 per cent of the population attends the heavily subsidized theater—was not possible in the immediate postwar years. They saw instead an invasion of foreign dramas, which made the German stage strangely cosmopolitan. Plays by Wilder, O'Neill, Milller, Williams, Giraudoux, Claudel, Sartre, Anouilh, Lorca, Eliot, Fry, and Priestley, along with the classics (mainly Shakespeare, Goethe, Schiller, Molière, Ibsen, Shaw, Chekhov, and Hauptmann) and the works of two Swiss playwrights, Frisch and Dürrenmatt, dominated the German stage until 1960. The abundance of foreign plays and the diversity resulted from the Allied occupation and the desire on the part of the Germans to look outside their country and to get in step with the "democratic" times. Among the German plays that had particular appeal were those of Kaiser, Toller, Wolf, Brecht, and Wedekind. The popular contemporary plays dealt with the complex situation of the Nazi period, guilt feelings in the postwar epoch, and, in time, with the economic boom and the hypocrisy of the *nouveaux riches*. Carl Zuckmayer's *Des Teufels General* (The Devil's General, 1946) and Günter Weisenborn's *Die Illegalen* (The Illegal Ones, 1946) were endeavors to show that resistance to the Nazis had existed. Wolfgang Borchert's *Draussen vor der Tür* (The Man Outside, 1947) was a moving account of a soldier who returns to his home city after the war and cannot adjust in a society that wants to black out the past. Despite the success of these playwrights, it was quite difficult for younger dramatists to compose works that corresponded to the times: West Germany was an "open society" until 1960, which meant that the modes of behavior and the value system were in a state of flux, and the dramatists had difficulty relating to this flux. It was during this period that cabarets relying on short simple skits, songs, and parodies came into fashion and provided a high form of entertainment for a brief period in Germany. It was also during the 1946–1960 epoch that the parable play came into fashion. Writers in this genre sought to abstract universal forms and values from reality and set them in stories that served as analogies to social situations. The form was favored by many dramatists searching for a way to contend with the West German realities in dramatic form. Richard Hey's *Thymian und Drachentod* (Thymian and the Death of the Dragon, 1955), Hermann Moers' *Zur Zeit der Distelblüte* (At the Time of Thistle Blossoms, 1958), Gert Hofmann's *Der Bürgermeister* (The Mayor, 1958), Tankred Dorst's *Freiheit für Clemens* (Freedom for Clemens, 1961), Siegfried Lenz's *Die Zeit der Schuldlosen* (The Time of the Innocent, 1961), and Karl Wittlinger's *Die Seelenwanderung* (The Wandering of Souls, 1963) are all plays in which symbols and ostensibly universal situations are used to comment on conditions in postwar Germany. Wolfgang Hildesheimer and Günter Grass employed techniques similar to those in the parable play; yet their "absurd" plays of the late 1950s abandon moralism and universality for the particular. Other writers, such as Leopold Ahlsen and Herbert Asmodi, moved in the direction of social realism to deal philosophically with the consequences of the economic miracle in West Germany.

With the production of Martin Walser's *Der Abstecher* (The Side Trip, 1961) followed by his *Eiche und Angorra* (The Oak and the Angora, 1962), a new wave of plays swept over West Germany. These dramas, which showed strong Brechtian influence, attacked socioeconomic conditions in West Germany. Walser's plays are for the most part political parables, as are those of Hans Günter Michelsen, who paints surreal pictures of social and political destitution. Their plays caused only minor ripples in the vast sea of German theater. The tidal waves were stirred up by documentary and historical plays. Heinar Kipphardt, who left East Germany in 1959, wrote a series of documentary dramas, *Der Hund des Generals* (The General's Dog, 1962), *In the Matter of J. Robert Oppenheimer* (1964), and *Joel Brand* (1965), which disclosed links between capitalism and fascism. Rolf Hochhuth brought about two international controversies with his documentary plays *The Deputy* (1963) and *Soldiers* (1967), in which he attacked, respectively, Pope Pius XII and Winston Churchill as representatives of their times, out of touch with their people. Peter Weiss composed a series of unusual history and documentary plays, *Marat/Sade* (1964), *The Investigation* (1965), *The Song of the Lusitanian Bogey* (1967), *Vietnam-Diskurs* (Vietnam Discourse, 1968), and *Trotzki im Exil* (Trotsky in Exile, 1970), which show his movement toward Marxism, not unlike that taken by Brecht. Other documentary plays that have stirred Germany since 1962 include such varied works as Dorst's *Toller* (1968), Günter Walraff's *Nachspiele* (Imitations, 1968), Hans-Georg Behr's *Das himmlische Peloton* (The Heavenly Firing Squad, 1969), and Hans Magnus Enzensberger's *Das Verhör von Habana* (The Havana Inquest, 1970).

There were various reasons for this trend toward documentary dramas that criticize the capitalist forms of social conduct and economic production in Western countries, particularly in West Germany. First and foremost, there was the Eichmann trial of 1961, which brought out the fact that many Nazi criminals were still respectable citizens in West Germany and that the government had been lax in pursuing them. One result was that pressure was placed on West Germany to lengthen the time limit in the statute on war criminals. Many trials followed in the 1960s which were to influence documentary dramatists with regard to setting (the courtroom) and content (parallels between fascism and capitalism). The documentary playwrights were also aided by the presence of Erwin Piscator at the Freie Volksbühne in Berlin. He had been largely responsible for documentary experimentation along Marxist lines in the 1920s, and he continued this work until his death in 1966.

Another reason for the rise of documentary experiments, which aim to make the facts of history speak in contradiction to the position of the establishment, was the growing discontent with the Christian Socialist Union and the Christian Democratic Party, which had ruled Germany under Konrad Adenauer since 1949. While living standards rose enormously in West Germany—thanks in great part to American funds—the quality of life did not alter much. Although West Germany no longer has a Fascist government, many of the men who held high positions under the Hitler regime retained these positions, and disparities between the upper and lower classes became more apparent in the postwar period, as did the anachronistic forms of justice and education. As West Germany became a "closed society"—that is, more stable in its conventional forms—discontent with the authoritarian attitude of the ruling classes grew. Employees demanded more of a voice in the operation of factories, schools, corporations, and theaters.

The theater has been affected in various ways. Writers such as Walser, Kipphardt, Weiss, Hochhuth, and Dorst have been overshadowed by Peter Handke, Hartmut Lange, Martin Sperr, Jochen Ziem, Barzon Brock, Wolfgang Deichsel, Egon Menz, and Gerlind Reinshagen. These younger playwrights, most of whom are members of a collective publishing house, Verlag der Autoren, have written dramas designed to raise political consciousness and to call for social changes. Although not necessarily more gifted than their elders, they are more original and inventive. Handke's plays (see also AUSTRIA) are ingenious attacks on the bourgeois theater as museum. Sperr's modern folk plays, from *Jagdszenen aus Niederbayern* (Hunting Scenes from Lower Bavaria, 1966) to *Koralle Meier* (1970), are dramatic explorations of the Fascism latent in the country folk of southern Germany. Lange's plays range from satirical parables on Stalinism in *Der Hundsprozess* (1964) to a critical examination of Prussian intransigence in *Die Gräfin von Rathenow* (1969).

Along with the radical plays, there have been many changes in the theaters. One of the most interesting and also most radical theaters to emerge into the limelight is the Schaubühne am Halleschen Ufer, in Berlin, which is directed by Peter Stein. Other young directors who have made their mark as innovators are Hans Hollmann, Hans Neugebauer, Claus Peymann, and Hans Neuenfels. Not only have these directors selected political plays to produce, but they have sought to politicize the theater. This movement has disturbed the bourgeois establishment and the boards of trustees who control the theaters. Since the theaters cost an inordinate amount of money to maintain and attendance has declined over the years, there is discontent on both sides. Some directors want to give more control to the actors and stage workers in the course of a production. Others have refused to comply with the radical demands of their underlings. In Düsseldorf, where the liberal director Karl Heinz Stroux has endeavored to bring more political plays into the program, there were student strikes against the premieres and a series of plays that were to celebrate the inauguration of a new cultural complex. This situation developed because only bourgeois dignitaries were invited to the opening nights. At the 1970 conference of the Academy for Performing Arts, two leading directors declined to participate because Harry Buckwitz, formerly a director in Frankfurt, now in Zurich, had been assailed as a former Nazi and had become the center of a political dispute. Moreover, the officers of the academy were constantly challenged regarding the structure of the organization. Discussion groups argued the problems of subsidies, shared responsibility in the theater, socialist directives, and audience participation. There were also discussions of the relevance of the academy itself. Indeed, the postwar development of West German theater, so pluralistic and rich in its origins, has come a long way toward questioning its social relevance. In East Germany, such relevance is demanded of the theater. In West Germany, the relevance lies in the fact that it is ostensibly not demanded.

*East German drama.* Between 1945 and 1949, Russian authorities were in charge of the theaters. More than seventy groups began producing plays that ranged from the classics to works of Wedekind, Toller, Friedrich Wolf, Brecht, Zuckmayer, Odets, Miller, Priestley, Anouilh, Salacrou, and Russian playwrights. The authors and their plays generally expressed a social democratic attitude, and the Russians allowed the theaters considerable freedom in their productions. It was during this period that some of the leading directors, playwrights, actors, and set designers in exile returned to East Germany. Among them were Brecht, Wolf, Erich Engel, Fritz Wisten, Caspar Neher, Helene Weigel, and Wolfgang Langhoff. The most prominent theaters were those in Berlin: the Deutsches Theater, the Volksbühne, and the theater of the Berliner Ensemble, which was organized in 1949 and established in its own Theater am Schiffbauerdamm in 1954.

In 1949 the subsidized theaters were placed under the control of the newly established East German government. As in most Communist countries, the party took measures to censor the production of the plays. The development of the East German theater cannot be understood without taking into consideration the relationship between the state and the theater: It is the express purpose of the East German government to make the stage into an instrument for political, social, and ethical education. Therefore, the government, through its Ministry for Culture (instituted in 1954), issues directives which determine the course of East German writers and theaters. The emphasis is at all times on social realism used to illustrate socialist tenets. Just how real the plays may be depends on the political climate of a particular epoch. In the 1949–50 season that climate was cold. Stalinist influence on the government led to strict regulation of the theaters. This caused some to close and others to cancel or rework productions that deviated from the party program. Even Brecht had many difficulties with the censors. In 1951, for instance, the Central Committee of the Communist Party proclaimed that it would begin a fight against formalism in art and literature. This meant that it favored Stanislavski's psychological and social realism in the theater and looked askance at experiments with form and substance, especially those that were critical of the realities in East Germany. Consequently, most of the productions for a time were either classical plays or East German and Russian historical dramas emphasizing the importance of a socialist tradition.

In 1953 the "thaw" allowed for a change in the cultural politics of the government, and the theaters were given more freedom and control over their schedules and productions. Still, no great changes were evident in the types of dramas performed in East German theaters. Such contemporary playwrights as Heda Zinner, Kuba, and Hans Lucke sought to present historical themes in a socialist sense or else imitated classical dramatists. The problems of developing a new tradition in East Germany were portrayed by the chief dramaturge of the Deutsches Theater, Heinar Kipphardt, in *Shakespeare dringend gesucht* (Shakespeare Urgently Sought, 1952), which attacked both bureaucrats and playwrights for making it difficult to present dramas of quality about social conditions.

In the spring of 1956 a special conference of theater directors and dramaturges was called by the Central Committee of the Communist Party, and the problems which hampered the development of the East German theater were openly discussed. A decision was reached to eliminate the growing bureaucracy in the theater. The result was more experimentation and a turn toward West European plays. Among the East German playwrights who began to receive attention were Harald Hauser, Peter Hacks, Alfred Matusche, Helmut Sakowski, Helmut Baierl, and Heiner and Inge Müller. These writers addressed themselves to the contemporary conditions of workers in factories and farms. They examined such problems as Russian usurpation and control over factories, farm collectivization, and qualitative versus quantitative production. Some varied approaches can be seen in Hauser's *Am Ende der Nacht* (At the End of the Night, 1955), Baierl's *Die Feststellung* (The Evidence, 1957), the Müllers' *Der Lohndrücker* (Undercutting, 1958) and *Die Korrektur* (The Correction, 1958), Sakowski's *Die Entscheidung der Lene Mattke* (The Decision of Lene Mattke, 1959), and Hacks's *Die Sorgen und die Macht* (Troubles and Power, 1960). These playwrights were influenced by two events, the Twentieth Conference of the Communist Party, where a demand was made for more plays with a strict socialist tendency—in other words, didactic plays—and the Bitterfeld Conference of 1959, where playwrights were urged to turn more toward the practical problems in East Germany, to make contact with workers, and adhere more closely to the socialist line. The Bitterfeld Conference in particular had important consequences for the development of East German playwrights. These playwrights can be classified into three groups, Brechtian, doctrinaire, and amateur.

The most talented of the East German dramatists are those who, influenced by Brecht, have tried to go beyond him in developing a new theater of socialist dialectics. They have encountered serious resistance from the government because of this. Peter Hacks was explicitly criticized at the Bitterfeld Conference and eventually dismissed as dramaturge of the Deutsches Theater. The more experimental and openly critical plays of Hacks, Heiner Müller, and Volker Braun cannot be produced. Despite this fact, they have remained committed to the East German socialist experiment and undauntedly continue to write plays that smack of Brecht and dialectics and make the East German functionaries uneasy. Hacks's *Moritz Tassow* (written in 1961, produced in 1965) recalled Brecht's *Galileo* in its depiction of the gargantuan appetite and power of a worker whose energies neither he nor the state seems capable of channeling. This situation is treated similarly in Heiner Müller's *Der Bau* (The Construction, written 1963–1966) and Braun's *Kipper Paul Bauch* (The Dumper Paul Bauch, written 1962–1965). Helmut Baierl also shows a strong resemblance to Brecht in the style and theme of his plays, especially in *Frau Flinz* (1961), which can be compared to *Mother Courage*, and in *Johanna von Döbeln* (1969), which can be likened to *Saint Joan of the Stockyards*. However, Baierl tends to be much more doctrinaire in his conclusions than Brecht, Hacks, Müller, or Braun. The last three have recently turned to Greek themes and German history in practicing their form of Marxist social criticism on the stage. The official censors have not appreciated the zeal with which they have followed the directives of the Bitterfeld Conference in criticizing social conditions in contemporary East Germany.

The censors have been happier about the course taken by such dramatists as Rainer Kerndl, Rolf Schneider, Harald Hauser, Alfred Matusche, Claus Hammel, Friedhold Bauer, Horst Kleineidam, Horst Salomon, and Helmut Sakowski. These writers have taken more doctrinaire steps in portraying realities in East Germany, or they have, in the cases of Schneider, Hammel, Matusche, and Bauer, avoided difficulty with the bureaucrats of culture by dealing with such historical themes as imperialism in Western nations, particularly America. Although these playwrights may be no less gifted than the followers of Brecht—and indeed they too use Brechtian techniques—they adhere to the more dogmatic socialist principle, preached by Lenin, that art should serve the party. The result is that many plays produced by these writers and others verge on propaganda and socialist soap opera. The main themes of the dramas pose questions concerning the new socialist man and the conflict between East and West, which was heightened by the construction of the Berlin Wall in 1961. Some of the more interesting dramas produced by these writers have been Schneider's documentary plays, *Prozess Richard Waverly* (The Trial of Richard Waverly, 1963) and *Prozess Nürnberg* (The Nuremberg Trial, 1967); Kerndl's *Seine Kinder* (His Children, 1963); Hammel's *Um neun Uhr an die Achterbahn* (At Nine by the Roller Coaster, 1964); Bauer's *Baran und die Leute im Dorf* (Baran and the People in the Village, 1967); and Alfred Matusche's *Der Regenwettermann* (The Rainy Weather Man, 1968).

The plays of Sakowski, Kleineidam, and Salomon are marked by naïveté and socialist slogans intended to indoctrinate workers into a socialist system that demands continual self-discipline and sacrifice. These three writers all stem originally from the working class: Sakowski was a forester, Kleineidam a carpenter, Salomon a miner. All their plays were written after 1959, that is, after the Bitterfeld Conference, and they themselves are examples of the third group of playwrights, the amateurs, who at one time or another take on professional status. After 1959, the East German government supported the organization of theaters and operas in factories and farms. There are more than 125 different amateur groups in the country. These groups have not only encouraged and produced talented writers, actors, and directors, but have contributed to new experiments at established theaters, particularly in Halle and Magdeburg. Here the theaters under the direction of Gerhard Wolfram and Horst Schönemann (Halle) and Hans Diether Meves (Magdeburg) have asked workers to criticize and help rewrite scenes of plays that do not correspond to reality as they see it. The emphasis is on a new type of audience participation wherein the proletarian audience is not only the substance of the play but also the creator.

Despite these original efforts and the experiments of such gifted directors as Benno Besson, Werner Freese, Manfred Wekwerth, Konrad Zschiedrich, Wolfram Krempel, and Hans Anselm Perten, recent developments are not encouraging. Attendance in the subsidized theaters, which cater to a new class of petty bourgeoisie within the Communist hierarchy, has fallen. The Berliner Ensemble has not only lost its best director, Manfred Wekwerth, but it has slowly taken the shape of a Brecht museum. The Deutsches Theater lost the director Wolfgang Heinz and some of its leading actors. The many changes of directors and actors in the past few years are caused by pressure from government functionaries who want the theaters to adhere to socialist doctrine and by internal disputes over socialist dramaturgy.

Aside from the original productions of classical plays and those of Brecht, the material produced by East German dramatists leaves a great deal to be desired. They generally portray either mundane problems of the proletarian world that must be in accord with socialist doctrine (not social reality) or historical themes which use traditional techniques to draw parallels with the present. The most interesting plays are those imported either from the East— Czechoslovakia, Poland, Russia—or the West. The plays of Hochhuth, Weiss, and Kipphardt and those of certain American, English, and French authors have had some success. Actually, there is great potential in the theaters of East Germany. Not only have some excellent provincial theaters in Rostock, Magdeburg, Karl-Marx-Stadt, and Gera gained prominence through their experiments and high quality of acting, but the younger playwrights, both the Brechtians and the doctrinaire, have demonstrated a fine mastery of their craft. The main problems with East German theater seems to lie within the theater itself. The government is bent on feeding the public a strict diet of party slogans and socialist ideals. This limits the freedom and creativity of writers and directors so that the theaters cannot become attractive places for proletarian audiences who already know the ABC's of Communism by heart. No one in East Germany disputes that drama should be used as an instrument to help the masses change social conditions and to raise social consciousness. The question that many people would like to debate concerns who should determine what the theater as an instrument should accomplish and how it should work toward socialist ends.

**Gilroy, Frank D.** (born 1925). American playwright. Born and educated through high school in New York City, Gilroy attended Dartmouth College and spent one year at the Yale Drama School. He is primarily a television scriptwriter, but he has had one notable success on Broadway: *The Subject Was Roses*, a naturalistic domestic drama of abiding misunderstanding and isolation. The play opened in 1964 with scanty audiences, did not play to a full house until its 136th performance, yet went on to win the Pulitzer Prize and the Drama Critics Circle Award and to enjoy a two-year run. A film adaptation was issued in 1968. Three other plays by Gilroy have been produced: *Who'll Save the Plowboy?* (1962), winner of an Obie as the best American play of the year, and *That Summer—That Fall* (1967), both sentimental views of domestic problems; and *The Only Game in Town*, which failed on Broadway in 1968.

**Glass Menagerie, The** (1945). A play by Tennessee Williams. It received the New York Drama Critics Circle Award. The play is memory, Tom Wingfield's account of his escape, like his father before him, from a coffin of familial demands. The emotional focus of the play, however, is not Tom but his sister, Laura. Although trapped in a sterile but steady job in a shoe factory to support the family, Tom is able to leave and write poetry if he wants. Laura has no such escape from her living death. The gentleman caller that their mother Amanda insists Tom bring home for Laura serves only to increase the lame girl's sense of her isolation, her sense of being a unicorn, who has no kind. And the more Amanda harps on her own genteel southern popularity, the more her daughter withdraws.

Williams has balanced the play so that Amanda's shrill mothering is not totally offensive. She, too, is caught in a memory play of her own, those lost plantation days that showed how much "she ought to be loved." Even the gentleman caller, Jim O'Connor, is living in a dream of his past glory as a high school baritone and the yearbook prediction that he was bound to succeed in anything he went into. Amanda, Jim, Laura, each has an unreal world, a fragile menagerie of memories or hopes that makes the present gray life bearable. Tom alone has tried actual escape through flight, but he finds himself more faithful than he intended to be: The play and its pathos are, after all, *his* haunting memory. Its quality suggests he has become a poet, but its grief shows that total escape is not possible.

In the production notes, Williams explains his use of screen devices "to give accent to certain values in each scene." These flashed images and words are usually omitted in production. Some, like the image of the blue roses, coupled with recurring music and dim lighting, might effectively increase the dream quality of the play; but others, like the word "Love!" are awkwardly melodramatic.

The play is highly autobiographical. Williams used his own name, Tom, for the narrator; he, too, worked in a shoe factory in St. Louis, where he felt frustrated and trapped. His sister, Rose, had a painful experience in secretarial school and cherished a collection of glass animals; her complete mental break is related to Laura's increasing withdrawal. Although Williams' mother has stated she is not Amanda Wingfield, she too was a southern belle and member of the D.A.R., and she confiscated Williams' copy of *Lady Chatterley's Lover*.

*The Glass Menagerie* was previewed in Chicago in December 1944; it opened in New York in March 1945.

**Goetz, Curt** (1888–1960). German dramatist, actor, and screenwriter. Because of family financial difficulties, Goetz was unable to study medicine, so in 1907 he turned to acting. He became one of the outstanding comedians of the German stage. After World War I he began writing one-act sketches in which he and his wife, Valerie von Martens, played the major roles. Because of their opposition to the Nazi regime, they eventually made their way to Hollywood, where Goetz took a great interest in films. After 1945 he returned to Europe and rewrote some of his cycles of one-act plays into full-length comedies and film scripts. He was most successful with *Das Haus in Montevideo* (1946), a comedy about the hypocrisy of a schoolteacher whose high moral standards weaken when his daughter can inherit a fortune; *Hokuspokus* (1953), made into a satirical film on justice; and *Dr. med. Hiob Prätorius* (1950), a delightful film about a gynecologist who has a fiery, jealous wife. All of Goetz's plays express a *joie de vivre* and are filled with witty characters who complicate their lives.

OTHER PLAYS SINCE 1945: *Die Tote Tante* (The Dead Aunt, 1923, revised as *Das Haus in Montevideo*, 1946), *Miniaturen* (Miniatures, 1958).

**Gombrowicz, Witold** (1905–1969). Polish novelist and dramatist. Gombrowicz was born in Małoszyce and studied law in Warsaw, where his first work, a collection of short stories, was published in 1933. At the outbreak of the second world war, Gombrowicz was in Argentina, where he remained till 1963. On his return to Europe he spent a year in Berlin, at the invitation of the Ford Foundation, then settled in Vence, in the south of France. Before the war Gombrowicz had become famous in Poland for his intellectually stimulating grotesque satirical novel *Ferdydurke*. He continued his writing in a similar vein with the novels *Transatlantic, Pornografia*, and *Cosmos*. No less interesting are his witty, though narcissistic, *Journals*. Gombrowicz was

186

awarded the International Publishers' Prize (the former Prix Formentor) in 1967. Although he spent so many years abroad, his work has had considerable influence on the younger generation of writers and intellectuals in his native country.

Just as Gombrowicz's reputation in fiction rests on a few novels, so in drama he secured an important position as the author of only three plays. The first of these, *Iwona księżniczka Burgunda* (Princess Ivona, written 1935, published 1938), dates from before the war and is an early example of the theater of the absurd. It is in fact a surrealist tragi-farce. Prince Philip's betrothal to a plain, uninteresting, apathetic, sickly girl, Ivona, causes profound disturbance at court, evoking an atmosphere of suspicion, ridicule, and general incongruity. Ivona alone is entirely consistent in her behavior, and this fact in itself exposes the ridiculousness of others and their actions. Ivona's murder is arranged, but this too seems a nonsensical solution, until it can be carried out with semblance of majesty and elegance. The notion that reality consists merely of semblances and cross-views of people about one another is typical of the author.

In his next play, *Ślub* (The Marriage, written 1946, published 1953), Gombrowicz concentrated on the problem of how people "form" one another through their dreams, their actions, and their images of others with whom they are involved. Henry, a young soldier, returns from the war in a dream to find his parents, his fiancée, and his home transformed. His family's deeds, gestures, and words are constantly in a nonsensical flux. At the same time they are exposed to external danger, personified by an aggressive drunkard. Henry and his father try to bring the situation under control. In the process the simple people whom the story concerns become a King, a Queen, a Chief of Police, dignitaries, courtiers, while Henry himself becomes the Prince, and his servant-girl fiancée a Princess. But the hero, who dreams, is also transformed by the outside world created in his dream. As the author said, "everything here creates itself . . . Henry creates the dream, and the dream creates —him. People create one another, and the whole pushes forward towards unknown solutions." Henry deposes his father and becomes King, but also a tyrant. His self-styled marriage ceremony is interrupted by nasty events, which give lie to the fairy-world setting because the modern world is capable of producing only nightmares. Henry's best friend kills himself at his instigation. Henry claims to be innocent, but orders himself to be imprisoned. In their contact, the characters impose on one another a way of behavior, speech, and action; everyone deforms others and is deformed by them. Hence, as the author said, "this drama is above all a drama of Form." Gombrowicz experimented here also with "literary" elements of drama, employing stylized speech (from pseudo-poetry to dialect), parody, and chorus.

At the outset of his last venture into drama, entitled *Operetka* (Operetta, 1966), Gombrowicz stated: "The text of a modern play is less and less meant to be read. It becomes rather a kind of score, which begins to live on the stage, in performance." He selected the form of an "operetta" because "monumental operetta idiocy, hand in hand with monumental pathos of history . . . would be *Operetta's* best presentation on the stage." In fact, the form Gombrowicz chose is mainly parodistic and explodes many stylistic conventions and clichés. The dialogue is fragmented and abounds in inarticulate sounds. The action begins before the first world war and concerns the efforts of the blasé Count Charm, a devotee of dress, to seduce the lovely Albertine, a devotee of undress. Act II presents a great surrealistic ball at the count's castle, culminating in revolution. Act III takes place after the revolution and World War II. In spite of all the cataclysms, Albertine rises in the finale from the coffin where she was hiding and triumphs in her "ever young nakedness, ever naked youth." Of all three of Gombrowicz's plays, *Operetta* shows most clearly his links with traditions of the Polish theater of the absurd, reminding one of the plays of Stanisław Witkiewicz. At the same time it is his most forward-looking play, in the sense of being virtually a scenario for the present-day avant-garde total theater.

**Görgey, Gábor** (born 1929). Hungarian poet, translator, and playwright. Görgey studied German and English at Budapest University, and has published two books of poetry and many translations. His plays are *Komámasszony, hol a stukker?* (The Pistol Shot, 1969), *Rokokó háború* (Rococo War), *Délutáni tea* (Afternoon Tea), and *Népfürdő* (Public Bath). Görgey is a Hungarian pioneer of the "theater of the absurd." His most interesting play, *Komámasszony, hol a stukker?* is a penetrating analysis of the nature of power in which five characters, each representing a definite social group, terrorize each other one by one. Coercion creates a vicious circle; within this circle changes are possible but coercion remains.

**Grass, Günter** (born 1927). West German dramatist, poet, novelist, and sculptor. The unusual and bold contours of Grass's works stem from his attempt to conquer the political tempest of his times. After witnessing the upheavals in the "free city" of Danzig during his youth, Grass was obliged to serve in the German Army at the age of seventeen. In 1946 he was released from an American prisoner of war camp and was employed first as a farmhand and later as a potash miner. Before he was accepted by the Düsseldorf Academy of Fine Arts as a student of sculpture, he worked part time as a stonemason's apprentice and learned the art of carving tombstones. Grass studied sculpture in Düsseldorf until 1952 when he moved to Berlin to work under Karl Hartung. He showed great promise as both a sculptor and a painter and intended to continue along these lines in Paris, which became his home in 1956. However, Grass had already begun experimenting with poetry and playwriting, and between 1956 and 1959 he went through his first phase as a dramatist strongly influenced by the French dramatists of the absurd, Ionesco, Beckett, and Genet.

It is largely due to the fact that Grass's own life has undergone a series of abrupt changes that he is prone to turn the world in his dramatic works upside down. The absurd is normal for Grass, the unusual, usual. The stage is a huge canvas where images are carved to startle spectators, to shock them into seeing the contradictions in their daily routine. In *Hochwasser* (Flood, 1956) a family moves from the bottom floor of a house to the roof to escape rising waters. Everything is in a state of upheaval, and Grass portrays the different reactions that the members of Noah's family have to the flood. The play ends on a banal note, one that is very much in keeping with the major theme of banality. Grass is concerned here about the split between the generations in Germany following World War II. As the waters rise, the banal, older generation, represented by the father and aunt, wants to rescue old, useless articles. They are almost untouched by the chaos, whereas the younger generation is uprooted. Since there is no communication between father and son, they go different ways when the floods subside.

This problem of communication in a period of upheaval is a central motif in Grass's works. It is always part and parcel of the absurd situation in his early plays. In *Die bösen Köche* (The Wicked Cooks, 1956) a count holds the secret recipe for an extraordinary soup, which, actually, is only cabbage soup mixed with some gray substance. Two groups of cooks work frantically to steal the recipe from the count, but he constantly foils them. Eventually he promises them the recipe if Martha, a nurse, will become his wife. The exasperated cooks, who are tired of wild-goose chases, agree to this concession, but on later discovering that the count has forgotten the recipe because of his state of marital bliss, they swear to gain revenge. Ironically, they are left helpless and dumbfounded when the count and Martha commit suicide at the end of the play. One of the cooks admits that the recipe has become "an excuse for running. Nobody wants it any more. It's not a matter of the soup." Indeed, the matter concerns words that might form a recipe for life. Grass has his cooks tumble preposterously throughout five acts to reveal their inability to provide nourishment for themselves and to understand themselves. They seek someone else's words as the key to life, and when they fail to obtain the recipe, they run in fear of themselves. Grass indicates here that man is essentially a bungler when he endeavors to adopt the recipes of others for his own.

In *Onkel, Onkel* (Mister, Mister, 1958) Grass explores the situation of a killer manqué named Bollin, who tries to live up to the press releases and stories of famous killers, yet always bungles the job. Each of his intended victims fearlessly disarms him. A sick girl expresses no surprise when Bollin emerges from under her bed. A forest warden persuades Bollin to help him out of the very trap that Bollin had set for him. An opera singer whom Bollin wants to slaughter in a bathtub convinces him that he has the talent to become a singer, and he flees in fright. Finally, an aging, crippled Bollin is taunted by two children in a park. They terrorize him, take his watch, pen, and revolver, and then shoot him. This is the end of a criminal who cannot commit crimes in a time when crime has become a matter of course.

Two other plays, *Noch zehn Minuten bis Buffalo* (Only Ten Minutes to

Buffalo, 1959) and *Zweiunddreissig Zähne* (Thirty-two Teeth, 1959), deal with a related theme: the paralysis of people who live with illusions about themselves and their times. In the first, a shepherd observes a painter sketching sailships on a meadow and two engineers trying to propel a rusty locomotive to Buffalo. They are hindered by their illusions, and in the end are left behind with them when the shepherd, a realist, climbs into the locomotive and goes off with it. In *Thirty-two Teeth,* a character by the name of Friböse is plagued by a teacher named Purucker, who appears in the most unexpected places to brush Friböse's teeth. Friböse flees to Switzerland and then to America, but he can never escape Purucker, who represents troublesome reality.

Grass's writings are a confrontation with reality, especially with the German past. After writing plays and poems between 1956 and 1959 which deal with the problem of breaking down illusions in order to communicate about reality, Grass turned to the novel and produced three outstanding works, *The Tin Drum* (1959), *Cat and Mouse* (1961), and *Dog Years* (1963). During this time he became more concerned with politics, returned to Germany, and began campaigning for the Social Democratic Party. Consequently his works since 1963 have more of a direct political bent to them. This is particularly true of *Die Plebejer proben den Aufstand* (The Plebeians Rehearse the Uprising, 1966). The play is largely a documentary investigation that examines the tragic flaw of the German people, that is, the virtue necessary for insurrection. Hence, the subtitle "A German Tragedy." To a certain extent, the play also condemns Bertolt Brecht's position during the rebellion of June 17, 1953, in East Berlin. Grass transforms the grand master of political theater into a disillusioned esthete alienated from his own *Verfremdungstechnik* and the conditions of the working class. Brecht is called the boss in the play, and yet the boss is symbolic not only of Brecht but of all those individuals whose involvement with art and science estranges them from society. Incapable of acting for the workers, who revolt against their repressive government, the boss eventually declares himself, and all others who fail to live up to their political promises, guilty of treachery.

Grass conceived his drama with a superb knowledge of Brechtian and Shakespearean dramaturgy and with a remarkable sense of irony. The boss is rehearsing a Marxist version of Shakespeare's *Coriolanus,* which parallels his own situation, when the Berlin workers come and ask him to support their uprising. He in turn uses the Coriolanus play as a Brechtian parable to explain why their rebellion will fail. At times the players speak the Brechtian tongue, but their language is on the whole Shakespearean blank verse, denoting the quality of their political thinking. Grass's purpose in writing his "German Tragedy," as well as the boss's purpose in staging *Coriolanus,* is to illustrate to the masses and liberals how not to plan and carry out an insurrection. By pointing out mistakes, the real demands of a revolution will become apparent.

To read Grass's play about Brecht as a literal condemnation of Brecht or as a thorough analysis of the 1953 workers' uprising limits the meaning of this drama. The immediate past is useful to Grass only in so far as it comments on the present political dilemma in Germany. He provides us with the picture of a doomed rebellion and implies that it fails because the people do not know how to use their power. Not only do they grope helplessly for a means to realize their protest, but the boss also gropes helplessly for the words that will change Shakespeare's *Coriolanus*. Both experiments are unsuccessful because the words of an authoritarian state interfere with the intentions of both the revolutionaries and the playwright. When the language of the people is no longer their own, and when this language cannot reflect manifold possibilities for enriching one's life in society, it loses all real value. It is, in essence, dead. Grass would have all people realize that they are the source of government and the heart of language. If they do not accept and assume this power, they are criminally liable for the crimes perpetrated on them by a foreign body.

In his most recent drama, *Davor* (Before, 1969), based on his novel *Local Anesthetic*, Grass examines the contemporary student protest in West Germany. A seventeen-year-old pupil named Flip Scherbaum wants to burn a dachshund in front of one of the most exclusive hotels in Berlin because he wants to make the Germans aware of the atrocious situation regarding napalm in Vietnam and how it relates to German politics. Scherbaum is supported by his girl friend, Vero Lewand, who is a radical follower of Mao. On the other side, there is Scherbaum's teacher, Starusch, who wants to dissuade Scherbaum, though he admires his protest. Starusch receives advice from his dentist, a pragmatic technocrat, on how to handle Scherbaum. He is also somewhat hampered by his colleague Irmgard Seifert, who wants to overcome the past but wallows in self-recrimination for acts committed in the Nazi period. Despite this, Starusch succeeds, with the help of the dentist's rational arguments, in persuading Scherbaum not to burn the dog but to become editor of the school newspaper. Scherbaum learns that real reforms can only be obtained through systematic argumentation and presentation of the facts.

Grass synchronizes many of the dialogues in the thirteen scenes to show how all action is related in a political sense. The simultaneity of the actions and the debates is, however, too contrived and tends to falsify the real situation of the radical movement in Germany. There are, of course, many ways to interpret this play—as a self-confession, a political treatise, a psychological debate. Whatever the approach may be, Grass's direction as a playwright is quite apparent. He has moved from the absurd to the political drama in an effort to devise new means to convey the importance of confronting the contradictions in reality.

OTHER PLAYS: *Beritten hin und zurück* (Rocking Back and Forth, 1959).

**Great Britain.** The English actors, playwrights, directors, and managers whose careers were interrupted by the second world war returned in 1945 and 1946 to a traditionally conservative profession. Their theatrical system was one possessing many peculiar features, most of them inimical to experiment or innovation of any kind. In the West End of London high rents and rising costs put a premium on caution and the well-tried formula for commercial success, while managements and theater landlords formed an oligarchy of interlocking companies that severely limited the operations of independent producers. A survey in 1946 found a mere sixteen "straight" plays running in London, eight of which were produced by the same management. Outside London a circuit of theaters (many under the ownership of the London managements), when not given over to music hall or the annual Christmas pantomime, was visited by productions awaiting a vacant London theater or by West End successes on tour. In addition, the provinces boasted more than a hundred "repertory" theaters, of which none presented plays alternating in a true repertory system and all but a handful advertised a weekly change of bill, relying on scantily rehearsed versions of standard West End fare to satisfy their audiences. With few exceptions (notably at Birmingham, Liverpool, and Glasgow) the repertory companies had fallen far short of the high promise held out by the repertory movement, which had begun at Manchester in 1907, and had contributed little except a dubiously valuable training for actors to the English theater of the '30s and early '40s.

For many years the under-rehearsed and inadequately financed seasons of Shakespearian drama at the Memorial Theatre, Stratford-on-Avon, had encountered the mounting impatience of the critics, although the appointment of Sir Barry Jackson (founder, director, and patron of the Birmingham Repertory Theatre) as director in 1946 marked the turning point in this company's fortunes and the beginning of its growth to world stature. The Old Vic Company, whose war effort had consisted of a crowded program of provincial tours, had returned to London, where at the New Theatre in 1944 Laurence Olivier's Richard III produced for critic J. C. Trewin "one of the exciting Shakespeare nights of the century." Under the direction of Olivier, Ralph Richardson, and John Burrell, some brilliant performances compensated for the lack of a firm overall policy. In the years before the return of the company in 1950 to its traditional home at the Old Vic Theatre on the South Bank of the Thames (a casualty of wartime bombing), a history of personal disagreements and administrative difficulties was to have a serious effect upon the quality and confidence of this famous company. The old tradition of Shakespearian seasons presented by actor-managers was maintained with high-spirited integrity for a few years by Donald Wolfit, and John Gielgud's glittering seasons at the Haymarket were to be long remembered. But by 1954 England's national dramatist could be absent from the West End stage for an entire season—a sure symptom of the declining vitality of the English theater of the period.

Theater managers, fearful of alienating their audience by an increase in seat prices and ever wary of enterprise or originality, found their natural caution encouraged by two governmental impositions. First, an Entertainment Tax, which drew a levy upon ticket sales without regard to production expenses, dictated an economic policy of immediate success or immediate closure. The exemption of certain companies with an "educational or partly educational" program enabled the Arts Council to cooperate with Tennent Plays (a non-profit-making subsidiary of London's major producing management) in a series of notable productions, but the division between a theater of entertainment and a theater of education was arbitrary and unwelcome. Second, managers fell under the jurisdiction of the Lord Chamberlain, a functionary who combined the management of the royal household with the censorship of stage plays and the licensing of London theaters. In the latter capacity his rigid insistence that the public be safeguarded from fire by the visible presence of an "iron curtain" made the proscenium arch an inescapable feature of the English theater. Scarcely less flexible were his measures as censor to protect the theatergoer from a variety of moral dangers, which ranged from allusions to the heads of friendly states to serious studies of sexual abnormality, thus imposing a restriction upon the stage from which every form of published literature was free.

A flourishing countrywide amateur theater movement contributed little to the health of the professional stage, either by the discovery of new dramatic talent or the creation of an informed and discriminating audience. The movement made a distinctive contribution only to religious verse drama, which included a series of plays, from Christopher Fry's *The Boy With a Cart* (1938) to John Arden's *The Business of Good Government* (1960), written for amateur performance. The dramatic societies of Oxford and Cambridge continued to provide entry to the theatrical profession for a number of notable actors and directors, whose undeniable talents were sometimes marred by precocity or lack of technical expertise. But, despite the scholarly efforts of a dedicated few, the study of drama as a theatrical art rather than a branch of literature had failed to achieve official university recognition, and the links between learning and the theater so successfully forged by William Poel and Harley Granville-Barker seemed in danger of disintegrating.

Dramatists whose work was tailored to the taste of West End audiences could still prosper despite these disadvantages and some, like Noel Coward and Terence Rattigan, built upon reputations they had established before 1940, while writers as diverse as Peter Ustinov and William Douglas Home embarked upon successful postwar careers. But the English commercial system was hostile to novelty, and outside it had grown up what director Norman Marshall has termed "the other theatre," run on precarious budgets and without subsidy by actors and directors devoted to the theater as an art. Before the war, companies playing before a club membership (and thus placing themselves outside the Lord Chamberlain's jurisdiction) in inconvenient and out-of-the-way premises, or in a theater hired for a Sunday-night performance, had served to introduce English audiences to the avant-garde theater of Europe and America as well as to new English writing. In prewar England, writes

Marshall, "a timid and reactionary theatre existed side by side with an immensely vital and progressive group of rebel theatres." After the war, economics, always hostile to these small-scale ventures, bid fair to prohibit them altogether. By 1950 the number of Sunday producing societies had dwindled to six, few of which were active. Of the club theaters only the Arts retained sufficient vigor to contribute to the dramatic revival of the '50s and continue its struggle for survival well into the '6os, when for a time it was to become an experimental outpost of the Royal Shakespeare Company.

It was in fact to take the English theater some fifteen years to come to terms with the postwar world. These years were to see the establishment of state subsidy, on a scale small by European standards but unprecedented in England, the founding of a company at the Royal Court Theatre devoted to the discovery of new playwrights, the revitalization and expansion of the Shakespeare Memorial Theatre, and the creation of a National Theatre Company housing some of the finest acting talents in the world. The commercial theater lost several of its West End homes, and the majority of its suburban and provincial theaters, but emerged strengthened by this concentration of its resources. The weekly repertory companies retreated before the rival attraction of television, to be replaced in time by the promise (if not always the achievement) of a flourishing regional drama that was not merely a pale replica of Shaftesbury Avenue, the center of London's commercial theater. At length new theaters were built, breaking free from the tyranny of the proscenium arch in a variety of experimental forms. Drama found its way into the syllabi of some six universities. Censorship, after a progressive relaxation of its rules, disappeared altogether. Partly as the product and partly as the animating cause of these developments there emerged a number of young and remarkable playwrights who formed a coherent movement only in their determination to release the theater from the genteel understatement of English drawing-room drama.

The months immediately following the end of the war gave little hint of the changes that were to come. Freed from the anxieties and restrictions of wartime, a public hungry for entertainment filled the theaters of London and the provinces. Not yet menaced by the popularity of television, theater managers seemed to have good reason to be complacent and lacked any incentive to depart from their well-tried formulas. Such hope as there was in these years for a dramatic renaissance to come was vested in a movement of verse dramatists, predominantly Christian in inspiration and fostered by the director E. Martin Browne. His season of "poets' plays" at the Mercury Theatre included Ronald Duncan's *This Way to the Tomb* (1945) and Fry's *A Phoenix Too Frequent* (1946). It was Fry, with his colorful situations and dazzling verbal sleight-of-hand, who went on to win overwhelming public success with *The Lady's Not for Burning* (1948), the first of a sparkling succession of "comedies of mood." T. S. Eliot, the anglicized American poet whose *Murder in the Cathedral* (1935) lay at the beginning of the movement for the revival of verse drama, returned to the stage with *The Cocktail Party,* directed by Browne for the Edinburgh Festival (1949), the first of Eliot's three postwar dramas and a play whose ironic adherence to the conventions of drawing-room comedy won puzzled admiration from the critics. The problem of presenting the spiritual experience of the Christian upon the contemporary stage has elicited some of the most interesting dramatic experiments, and some of the finest dramatic language, of the past three decades. But the entire movement was more or less contemporaneous with Eliot's career as a dramatist, and Fry was one of the last major figures in a movement that had its roots in the prewar years and by 1960 had come to seem irrelevant at best to the new problems that dramatists faced. "I don't regard my writing as poetic," stated Ann Jellicoe in that year. "The word 'poetic' nowadays is almost a term of abuse." Nevertheless, the drama of Fry and Eliot, if neglected on today's stage, must take its place along with the work of John Osborne, John Arden, and Harold Pinter in any assessment of contemporary English theater. Placing Fry and the best revivals of the period against a European context, which looked mainly to France for its inspiration and expressed itself in the ballet as much as the literary theater, Peter Brook discovered in the late '40s "a theatre of colour and movement, of fine fabrics, of shadows, of eccentric, cascading words, of leaps of thought and of cunning machines, of lightness and of all forms of mystery and surprise— it was a theatre of a battered Europe that seemed to share one aim—a reaching back towards a memory of lost grace."

The prose drama of the same decade lacked the imaginative brilliance of the verse playwrights or the ballet. Novelist and playwright J. B. Priestley offered the West End playgoer some serious, humane, and thoughtful fare in his postwar plays, and almost alone among dramatists of the period reflected in his work the social conscience that had swept a Labour government into power with a massive majority. Sean O'Casey, another, more militant, socialist living in self-imposed exile in Devon, continued to write. But although the fiery eloquence of his early work was not extinguished and the rhythm and imagery borrowed from the Irish vernacular continued to impart a poetic element to his dramas, the plays of this period lacked the simplicity and immediate force of *Juno and the Paycock* or *The Plough and the Stars* and failed to find the audience they deserved. Only *Red Roses for Me* (1942) had a brief, unsuccessful West End run. A typical popular success of 1947 was William Douglas Home's amusing but trivial *The Chiltern Hundreds,* in which the conventions of drawing-room comedy are uneasily adapted to embrace contemporary politics, while other plays (*Worm's Eye View,* 1945; *Seagulls over Sorrento,* 1950) reduced the experience of the recent war to the status of material for commercial comedy. The new writing of the United States and France, in terms of its immediate effect upon the English stage, was less an influence upon than a substitute for native English drama. The year 1948 saw London productions of Arthur Miller's *All My Sons,* Tennessee Williams' *The Glass Menagerie,* and

Jean-Paul Sartre's *Crime Passionel,* while English dramatists produced two soundly commercial plays—Rattigan's *The Browning Version* and John Dighton's *The Happiest Days of Your Life,* which drew respectively on the sentimental and the farcical sides of that forcing-ground of English emotions, the private school. In the years before the rediscovery of Brecht (a potent influence upon W. H. Auden and Christopher Isherwood in prewar years), attempts to extend the range or significance of the English drama all too often ended in heavy political allegories, of which Peter Ustinov's *Moment of Truth* (1951) and John Whiting's *Marching Song* (1954) provide examples.

In short, the English stage had become, by the early '50s, an intellectual backwater. Its most eloquent and famous condemnation is to be found in Richard Findlater's *The Unholy Trade* (1952). In the age of the hydrogen bomb, he wrote, the English playwright "seems to be primarily concerned with the surface of life as it was lived fifty years ago." His drama "takes its sociology from *Punch,* its politics from British Movietone, its religion from memory." As for the English actor, "unobstrusiveness is still the prime ideal . . . He practices the art of understatement, and reaps an abundant harvest in the nuances of quietness. He acts inside, rather than outside; instead of expressing, he implies; crises are registered in a hesitant cough, the nervous lighting of a cigarette, the relentless stirring of a teaspoon." It was not to be long before public dissatisfaction with the dullness of these wares was spelled out in the box-office returns. The audiences who had queued to fill the theaters immediately after the war now found an alternative attraction. B.B.C. television, established on an experimental basis before the war, resumed transmission on the same limited scale in 1946 and entered a period of expansion in 1949. The independent companies began operations in 1955 and within a few years had a nationwide coverage. In the provinces the public found that their local theater could offer neither the comfort of their own home nor the standard of performance that they soon learned to expect on their television screen. Despite the halving of Entertainment Tax, to be followed by its total abolition in 1957, the '50s saw the beginning of a decline in the weekly repertory and provincial touring systems from which neither was to recover. Almost anything, a hot summer, a cold winter, a royal death, or a coronation, could be blamed for the closure of a few more theaters in the first half of the '50s; in 1957 it was noted that about one hundred theaters had closed in the provinces since 1948.

Although prospects for the theater seemed bleak indeed in the early '50s, the ground for its revival in the second half of the decade had already been prepared. The institution that was to have the most profound effect upon the organization of the theater had begun its operations immediately after the war. Founded in 1940, C.E.M.A. (the Council for the Encouragement of Music and the Arts) had insured that the performing arts remained available to wartime audiences—often creating an appetite for the theater where none had existed before. For the differing needs of peacetime the organization was reconstituted as the Arts Council of Great Britain. From a Treasury Grant of £175,000 spread over all the arts in 1944–45, its budget increased to allow a subsidy of £1,705,609 to the theater alone in 1967–68. Despite its modest beginnings, the significance of the Arts Council was not lost upon the founder-chairman, Lord Keynes. Almost unnoticed, he observed in 1945, "state patronage of the arts has crept in." The bounty of the state has not been matched in England by civic or industrial endowments (although the contribution of individual cities, and most notably Coventry, has been far from negligible) and there can be no doubt that the Arts Council has been the biggest single factor in freeing the theater from its postwar commercial rigidity. The pages of the Arts Council Annual Reports offer an invaluable chronicle of the growth of the subsidized theater as well as some magisterial essays on the philosophy of public patronage.

However, before a permanent alternative to the commercial system had been securely established, it was to festivals of drama and the arts that hopeful audiences traveled. The Edinburgh International Festival was launched in 1947. It was in Edinburgh that T. S. Eliot returned to the theater and an excited Tyrone Guthrie discovered the virtues of the open stage, but in time the official program was to seem less important than the "fringe" of new plays presented by students and young companies of actors in whatever premises they could find. In 1949 the Malvern Festival was revived, but it was never to repeat the successes of its prewar seasons when, directed by Sir Barry Jackson and dedicated to George Bernard Shaw, it had premiered Shavian drama and revived a host of earlier English plays. By the '50s, as well as the season of opera at Glyndebourne and Benjamin Britten's musical Aldeburgh Festival, a host of festivals up and down the country, from Pitlochry (1950) to St. Pancras (1954), presented an annual program which included a greater or smaller amount of drama. In 1962 a new and important event entered the festival calendar with the opening of the Chichester Festival Theatre, and in 1968 the annual student festival of drama (sponsored by the London Sunday Times) changed its regulations to insist that all plays presented must have been hitherto unperformed in England.

Many such festivals owe their origin to the year in which Britain set out to celebrate her national identity before the world. There was a note of defiance, even of unreality, in the mood which, in the year of the Festival of Britain (1951), overtook a country racked by financial crisis and bewildered by the decline of its imperial grandeur. It was hardly surprising that "few contemporary plays of merit emerged for the occasion," as the Arts Council noted after the event; and John Whiting's dark and bitter Saints' Day, offering a foretaste of the irrational violence that was to emerge in the work of Pinter and others later in the decade, passed almost unnoticed despite its award in the Arts Council's Festival of Britain Play Competition. But one event, quite in accord with the spirit of the festival, was to have no little influence upon the drama of later years. In York E. Martin Browne revived, for the first time since their suppression in the reign of Elizabeth I, the York Cycle of Mystery Plays (thereafter to be presented triennially), to demonstrate to scholars and theater workers the power that lay behind the uncomplicated language, the epic sweep of action, and the simplicity of staging in medieval drama.

Thus in the postwar years the festivals offered a less restrictive home to dramatists than the commercial stage. Apart from the verse drama noted above, however, the first hints of an impending break with naturalism, and with the social assumptions that seemed to accompany it upon the English stage, came not so much from new writing as from experimental attempts to dispense with the "picture-frame" staging made inevitable by the proscenium arch. The rigidity of English safety regulations (unchanged since the days of gas lighting) had left directors some distance behind their European and American colleagues, but limited innovation was to prove acceptable after the war. In 1948 John English established the Arena Theatre Company, performing for a limited season each year on a semicircular stage surrounded on three sides by the audience (thus arena staging, in English parlance, is a term rarely applied to theater-in-the-round). The first adaptable theater, designed by Richard Southern for the Drama Department at the University of Bristol, was built in 1951. In the same year the Cockpit Theatre Club was founded in London by Ann Jellicoe to experiment with the open stage. In 1955 the Studio Theatre, under the energetic direction of Stephen Joseph, was formed and played "in the round" at Scarborough, with winter Sunday-night productions in London. The Festival of Britain was responsible for an experiment in theatrical form at the first Mermaid Theatre, erected by Bernard Miles in the garden of his St. John's Wood home, where with the assistance of Shakespearian scholars *The Tempest* was presented in simulated Elizabethan style. The Assembly Hall of the Church of Scotland provided an unlikely home for one of the most fruitful of these early postwar experiments: in 1948 Tyrone Guthrie first produced the sixteenth-century *Satire of the Three Estates* for the Edinburgh Festival on a platform stage surrounded on three sides by the pews and galleries of the Assembly Hall. The new theaters so far described, when they were not small studios for the use of amateurs or students, were temporary affairs or makeshift conversions: The first new professional theater to be built after the war, the Belgrade, Coventry (1958), proved to be a proscenium-arch theater of disappointing and conventional design. The following year saw the opening of the Mermaid Theatre, Puddle Dock; the open stage, designed by C. Walter Hodges, was an imaginative attempt to re-create the principles of Elizabethan staging inside the shell of a bombed city warehouse. In another way the Belgrade and the Mermaid both pointed to the future: by including coffee bars and restaurants, by organizing recitals and discussions, they attempted to keep the theater building alive throughout the day and invest it with a social function beyond the mere production of plays. Tyrone Guthrie's enthusiastic con-

198

version to the cause of the open stage, his imagination fired by the Edinburgh Assembly Hall, set in train a series of events that culminated in 1962 with the opening of the Chichester Festival Theatre, built with a three-sided stage and permanent façade following Guthrie's advice and the precedent he had established at the Festival Theatre, Stratford, Ontario. After years of political controversy Nottingham at last saw a new civic theater open in 1963 with an open, partially adaptable stage and ancillary features including a lively restaurant. Since the opening in 1967 of the Northcott, Exeter and the Octagon, Bolton, both with three-sided stages, a majority of the increasing number of new theaters to be built has incorporated some form of open or adaptable staging. Theater-in-the-round, however, did not find a purposely built home until the opening of the Cockpit Theater in London (1970), its most notable achievements in the '60s having taken place in converted motion-picture theaters at the Pembroke in Croydon (1959–1962) and the Victoria in Stoke on Trent (opened 1963).

Thus the retreat from picture-frame illusion slowly but emphatically became an accepted feature of theater architecture. Playwrights themselves, however decisive their rejection of naturalism, have in the main continued to submit happily to the supposed despotism of the proscenium arch, and few (with Arden the most notable exception) have impressed or implied dissatisfaction with this architectural feature. Only in the most recent years has new writing shown a lively interest in stepping out of the picture frame, and the move has been not toward the epic, rhetorical stage of a Chichester Festival Theatre but to the subterranean intimacy of the avant-garde theater club. But before 1956 (the verse dramatists always excepted) the most notable experimental drama had been written not for the stage but for radio, where the B.B.C. Third Programme offered a haven for minority tastes. Louis MacNeice, Dylan Thomas, and Giles Cooper were all authors of outstanding work for this medium. The stage was less hospitable to new writers. The plays of John Whiting, who may legitimately be regarded as a herald of the new wave of English dramatists, were doomed in the early '50s to commercial failure and scant recognition. And the development of a more flexible, less rigidly commercial theatrical system would have been a small achievement without the regeneration of the conviction that the theater, as an intellectual and social force, was in the vanguard of the arts. By the latter half of the '50s this had been achieved.

The year 1955 in the theater had been unremarkable, the main event being the English premiere of Samuel Beckett's *Waiting for Godot*, three years after the Paris success of *En Attendant Godot*. Although the play caused widespread interest and some controversy, it was regarded at the time more as a curiosity from the Continent than a serious challenger to the prevailing modes of domestic drama. The year 1956, however, was undoubtedly the *annus mirabilis* of the contemporary English theater. In that year a season of plays presented by Paul Scofield and Peter Brook included *Hamlet*, *The Power and the Glory*, and *The Diary of Anne Frank*, and the visit of the Berliner Ensemble with a repertoire that included Brecht's *The Caucasian Chalk Circle* and *Mother Courage*, with Helene Weigel, was to have a lasting effect upon the English theater. But 1956 was primarily the year in which new writing, in a contemporary and relevant idiom, at last became possible. In East London Joan Littlewood's Theatre Workshop Company, dedicated to the politics of the far left, at last attracted public attention with *The Quare Fellow*, the first play of former Irish Republican Army rebel Brendan Behan. In April the English Stage Company, formed under the direction of George Devine with the express purpose of introducing new writers to the stage, opened at the Royal Court Theatre with Angus Wilson's *The Mulberry Bush*, to be followed by Arthur Miller's *The Crucible*. In May came the third play of the season, John Osborne's *Look Back in Anger*.

The first night of *Look Back in Anger* is regarded with justice as the turning point in the fortunes of the postwar English theater, marking the moment when the climate changed from one basically inimical to new writing to one which favored (perhaps too uncritically) the original and the experimental. But John Osborne himself cannot be called the leader of a movement, and the success of *Look Back in Anger* was a symptom rather than a cause of this change. Nor was the English Stage Company the single forcing-ground of the new drama. During the last half of the '50s the plays of John Arden and Ann Jellicoe were presented to audiences at the Royal Court Theatre; Arnold Wesker's *Roots* trilogy was produced with the cooperation of the English Stage Company at the newly opened Belgrade Theatre; and Joan Littlewood's Theatre Workshop developed its distinctive style in Shelagh Delaney's *A Taste of Honey*, Brendan Behan's *The Hostage*, and Frank Norman's *Fings Ain't Wot They Used T'Be*. In the following years the Arts Theatre Club, for a time controlled by the Royal Shakespeare Company, played its part in fostering a variety of new talent. Other dramatists, including Harold Pinter, early in his career, continued to allow their plays to be presented by impresarios working within the commercial system.

Rather than a new movement, then, there was a renewed interest and a sense of excitement in the theater. As the decade closed, the work of writers as diverse as Arnold Wesker, Harold Pinter, and John Arden had reached the stage, among a host of scarcely less talented writers who included John Mortimer, N. F. Simpson, Shelagh Delaney, Ann Jellicoe, Alun Owen, Robert Bolt, and Peter Shaffer. Writers who a few years previously might never have considered writing for the stage now found that this medium offered the opportunity of reaching a lively, immediate, and receptive audience.

The passionate denunciations of the upper-middle-class ethos in Osborne's first play gave a veneer of commitment to social change to the new drama. It seemed to reviewers that the stage had become a platform for angry writers of the left, and the term "kitchen-sink drama" soon came into currency to denote the degree of unadulterated social realism, new to the English stage, which seemed the hallmark of the Osborne generation. But it was more by coincidence than design that four major dramatists, Osborne, Arden, Wesker, and Pinter, and others like Shelagh Delaney who seemed of equal stature at the time, began their careers around the same time with plays in dingy settings whose working-class or lower-middle-class characters seemed to have their way of life summed up in Arden's title *Live Like Pigs*. These writers made their way to the kitchen sink more by way of reaction against the delicate proprieties to which the ear of the English theatergoer had become attuned than as part of a coherent school of social realism. Only Wesker has established himself as a socialist writer first and foremost—and even his writing has moved steadily away from the naturalism with which it began. In Osborne's own work there was little interest in left-wing protest by the time of *Luther* (1961), and Arden, a writer who has assimilated Brechtian theory, has adopted a dramatic stance that rejects engagement with any rigid ideological system. Joan Littlewood's Theatre Workshop, a company which has professed socialism unequivocally, produced from writers such as Brendan Behan, Shelagh Delaney, Frank Norman, and Stephen Lewis an affectionate (and sometimes a sentimental) view of the working classes which left little place for anger against the social system. The rise to prominence of Harold Pinter, whose first full-length play (*The Birthday Party*, 1958) was denied a run by the hostility of first-night reviews, demonstrates that political or social comment is far from being fundamental to the change that has overtaken contemporary drama. In short, attempts to find a common denominator, in dramatic style or intellectual conviction, among the dramatists of the period, is unlikely to succeed. The reality is more complex and the change more fundamental.

In fact the distinguishing mark of this period has been a new freedom—freedom of language, freedom of theme, freedom of dramatic form. Freedom carries its own pitfalls, no less likely to catch the untalented writer than the dangers inherent in the securely plotted, naturalistic drama—though less likely to be damned immediately by reviewers still fumbling for adequate critical standards. But in the best writers liberation from the tongue-tied traditions of postwar naturalistic drama has led to fresh perception and a new theatricality. Thus a new psychological realism is a feature shared by many writers, exploring the byways of sexuality and the instinctive violence that the human animal has carried with him into the twentieth century with a frank honesty free from the circumlocutions and facile moralizing of earlier decades. Here is a feature linking dramatists as diverse as Osborne and Pinter with writers, like Joe Orton and Charles Dyer, whose work has a predominantly farcical tone. An extension of this same element in the theater of the '60s has led to the emergence of writers, among whom Edward Bond and Charles Wood may be numbered, who paint a social and historical canvas animated entirely by the uglier promptings of the human psyche, thus producing a theatrical counterpoint to the dissent of the '60s in its rejection of the liberal, optimistic humanism of the '40s and '50s.

The history of the drama since 1956 has not been one of uninterrupted progress; some years have been as barren of good writing as any before *Look Back in Anger*. The determination to leave no theme untreated has often declined into a meretricious desire to shock; political comment has often been as naïve as it has been ineffectual; the hard-won freedom from the restrictions of drawing-room drama has often manifested itself only in aimless plots, undisciplined dialogue, and inconsistent characterization. Of the dramatists who have made their name in the past twelve years, many, like Robert Bolt, may be assessed ultimately as serious but nevertheless popular commercial dramatists who have availed themselves of the new idiom, while established writers of the caliber of Coward and Rattigan, without abandoning the standards of craftsmanship by which they set so much store, have taken advantage of the freer climate to explore as sensitively as any of the younger writers the hitherto forbidden theme of homosexuality. It is probably true that the overall standard of writing for the stage in 1969 is not far different from that of 1949, but what distinguishes the later drama is a new relevance of the life and language on the stage to that lived and spoken by the vast majority of Englishmen outside the theater. Probably of working-class or lower-middle-class origin, and unlikely to have been educated at a university (among the first wave of new dramatists, only Arden was a graduate), the playwright of today perceives character and relationship without the sophisticated and often artificial assumptions of his predecessors. As likely as not he has himself served an apprenticeship on the stage and his work will have a robust theatrical quality. A new generation of actors portrays the new language and the new gestures of the English theater: A regional accent is no longer a defect to be gently obliterated at drama school, and the art of understatement observed by Richard Findlater has been replaced by a new vigor. In a country still nervously sensitive to class distinction, actors and authors, if not always their audiences, no longer celebrate the tacitly shared suppositions of the upper middle classes.

If, as has been argued, the writers of the past decade cannot be divided neatly into schools, at least some pattern can be discerned in theatrical styles and tastes within the period. It was a period underpinned by the extension of the subsidized sector of the theater and the rapid growth of two major companies. While the overall decline in theater attendance continued in the late '50s, new theater buildings and the expansion of existing companies built up areas of resistance where was fostered a new generation of theatergoers accustomed to a drama that was not in overt competition with motion pictures and television. With Arts Council encouragement, the best of the weekly repertory theaters adopted a policy of running plays two or three weeks, and as standards improved audiences were recaptured. An indication of the changing pattern of patronage was offered in 1964, when the closing of the London Windmill Theatre, after thirty-two years of nonstop revue, was balanced by the opening of theaters run by a university, a drama school, a council-backed repertory company, and the Parks Committee of the London County Council. And by the following year the Arts Council was able to congratulate itself on the provincial revival and the growing acceptance of the concept of the civic theater. Progress in the provinces was matched by the growth in stature of the Shakespeare Memorial Theatre Company (rechristened the Royal Shakespeare Company in 1961). Its steady advance in the '50s under the competent and sometimes inspired direction of Anthony Quayle and Glen Byam Shaw gave way to rapid expansion with the appointment of Peter Hall, then aged twenty-nine, as director in 1960. Declaring that his Stratford actors could develop an adequate style for their Shakespearian performances only if they retained their familiarity with other dramatists, classical and contemporary, Hall leased the Aldwych Theatre as a London base for the company. While Stratford was to concentrate upon Shakespearian productions, the Aldwych was to have a more flexible program that included the possibility of commissioning modern work. Joined by Peter Brook and Michel St. Denis as co-directors, and engaging artists on long-term contracts, Hall was soon able to undertake ambitious projects such as the old Memorial company could never have contemplated, providing an alternative within the subsidized theater to the glittering West End seasons, which actor-managers of the stature of Donald Wolfit or John Gielgud could no longer offer as a commercial proposition. While the Royal Shakespeare Company grew from strength to strength, the Old Vic Company enjoyed only spasmodic successes. The appointment of Sir Laurence Olivier as first director of the Chichester Festival Theatre in 1962 was, it soon became evident, the first step toward building up the nucleus of a company which, with Olivier at its head, was to replace the Old Vic Company with the long-awaited National Theatre Company.

The year 1963 ranks as a runner-up to 1956 in the annals of the postwar theater. A post-Osborne generation of dramatists began to emerge, represented by James Saunders with *Next Time I'll Sing to You* at the New Arts and Charles Wood with *Cockade* at the Royal Court. The flagging fortunes of the Theater Workshop Company were revived by the spectacular success of *Oh What a Lovely War*. The Royal Shakespeare Company at Stratford embarked upon an ambitious cycle of Shakespeare's history plays, under the title of *The Wars of the Roses*, and presented the first of an annual series of international seasons at the Aldwych, which was to bring before the London theatergoer visiting companies including the Comédie Française, the Moscow Art Theater, the Actors Studio of New York, the national theaters of Greece and Israel, and the Umewaka-Hashioka Noh Company of Japan. Never had actors, directors, and writers enjoyed such opportunity for studying the styles, classical and modern, of the international theater as has been offered them in England since 1963. In the provinces, Leicester saw the opening of a new theater, and the Nottingham Playhouse opened its door under the short-lived triumvirate of John Neville, Frank Dunlop, and Peter Ustinov. In Bristol, a company loosely affiliated to the London Old Vic had created a major provincial center for the drama at the Georgian Theatre Royal. It now acquired the Bristol Little Theatre to become the first civic theater operating two separate companies. Overshadowing these events, on October 22, 1963, the National Theatre Company began its life with Peter O'Toole's *Hamlet* in an Old Vic Theatre fresh from four months' renovations. The repertory that followed achieved a level of ensemble playing that probably surpassed anything seen in the British theater since the war, although in the years that followed, the eccentric choice of plays upon which such supreme care and craftsmanship were lavished was increasingly criticized.

Such, in brief, was the background of development in the years that followed the dramatic revival of 1956. On the stage the growing freedom from commercial restraint meant that experiment, backed by an all-important period of adequate rehearsal, was no longer ruled out. If a survey cannot hope to track the passing fashions of the most ephemeral of the arts, at least two clear influences interacting upon writers and directors can be discerned.

The year that saw *Look Back in Anger* was also the year of the Berliner Ensemble's visit, and undoubtedly a powerful force at work in succeeding years was the belated recognition of the theater of Bertolt Brecht. As early as 1957 Brechtian influence can be recognized in the music-hall routines that cut into the action of Osborne's *The Entertainer;* but it was not until the early years of the '60s that a liberation of theatrical style attributable to Brecht became a major feature of contemporary drama and, heralded by the publication of two full-length Brecht studies in English and a flurry of articles and translations in theater journals, imitations of the "epic theater" appeared upon the English stage. In 1960 Robert Bolt's *A Man for All Seasons* was introduced by a "common man," whose ironical comments upon the progress of the play interrupted the flow of historical action. In the following year John Whiting returned to the theater with *The Devils,* an episodic drama of bold and sweeping grandeur produced by Peter Wood for the Royal Shakespeare Company. Later in the same year John Dexter directed Albert Finney in *Luther,* Osborne's first historical drama and one whose staging conventions clearly showed an interest in Brechtian techniques. In 1962 Dexter produced Wesker's *Chips With Everything,* a play in which the author of the *Roots* trilogy made a decisive break with naturalism in favor of a loosely episodic structure balanced by moments of intense physical realism. Brecht's own *The Good Woman of Setzuan* was staged in an ill-fated production by the English Stage Company in 1956; *Galileo* reached the appropriately anti-illusionistic stage of the Mermaid Theatre in 1960, and early in 1962 the Royal Shakespeare Company presented *The Caucasian Chalk Circle* in an honest production by William Gaskill, paying full attention to Brechtian theory. Peter Brook's Stratford production of *King Lear* with Paul Scofield in the title role in November of the same year, with its close attention to the syntax of individual scenes, its costumes with the patina of age upon them, and its rusty thunder sheet in full sight of the audience, suggested to critics that Brechtian theory had new insights to offer upon the Shakespearian stage. But Brook's *Lear* marked the extent as well as the climax of Brechtian domination of the English stage, for, while production techniques continued to show his influence, the fascination that he held for writers proved short-lived. In fact a closer examination of the plays mentioned above would reveal that in none is the influence of Brecht more than superficial. The German dialectician's appeal to reason contrasts strongly with the emotional vigor of the English authors, and only in the work of John Arden, the most academic of the new dramatists, do we find anything approximating the "alienation effect," which (at least in theory) is the profound feature of Brechtian drama. Impatient with the restrictions of naturalism, the playwrights of the early '60s turned to Brecht for the rapid narrative flow of his drama, his unashamed rejection of the theater of illusion, and the muscular precision of his language, which was apparent even in translation.

In Brook's *Lear* the interpretation of the play was borrowed from Jan Kott, the Polish author whose *Shakespeare Our Contemporary* compares Lear with the grotesque characters of Samuel Beckett's dramas. The years 1963 and 1964 marked the swing of the pendulum away from the epic theater of Bertolt Brecht toward the "theater of cruelty" with which the name of Antonin Artaud is associated. Artaud, whose collection of essays *The Theater and Its Double* had to wait until 1958 for publication in an English version, had been a growing influence in the postwar French theater, while his name was hardly known in England or the United States. Like Brecht, Artaud called for the destruction of the theater of illusion and turned to the Orient for an alternative model. But in Artaud's apocalyptic theater there was to be no room for the exercise of the intellect so important to Brecht. Likening the theater to a plague, he expected it to sweep away the "Occidental" vices of order, reason, and morality and restore man to his true and terrible stature. Words were to lose their primacy in the "theater of cruelty" and enactments recalling the rituals of savagery were to take their place. What attracted directors of the '60s was not Artaud's disordered philosophy but the attractive possibility of a "total theater" that his writings presupposed. In the autumn of 1963 Peter Brook and Charles Marowitz, in an experimental group affiliated with the Royal Shakespeare Company, began to explore Artaudian theory in practical exercises. The exploration produced Arden's one-act *Ars Longa, Vita Brevis*, Marowitz's condensed, reshuffled collage of *Hamlet* (with "the entire thing played out in short, discontinuous fragments which appeared like subliminal flashes out of Hamlet's life"), and a much-praised production of Genet's *The Screens*, which mingled Brechtian and supposedly Artaudian devices. The style evolved by this group finally reached the general public in 1964, in *The Persecution and Assassination of Marat as performed by the inmates of the Asylum of Charenton under the direction of the Marquis of Sade*, by Peter Weiss, which in Brook's Aldwych production became a startling portrayal of the grotesque and tragic aspects of madness not always appropriate to the literary text on which it had been grafted. For Brook the virtues of the play lay in its "clash of styles . . . the violence illuminated by the cool flow of thought." Certainly violence was to become the dominant mode in the drama of the mid-1960s. The commercial theater celebrated the success of Joe Orton's *Entertaining Mr. Sloane* (1964) and *Loot* (1966), farces quivering with physical violence, before the author's eerily appropriate death by violence in 1967. The year 1965 saw the discovery of a major new dramatist by the English Stage Company in Edward Bond, whose *Saved* was denied a license by the Lord Chamberlain for the scene of brutal realism in which a group of working-class youths batter a baby to death. The same author's *Early Morning* (1968), also banned by the censor, painted the picture of a Victorian age haunted by cannibalism and casual atrocity. In 1966 Peter Brook again took up the theme of violence, this time against a contemporary political canvas, in the ambiguously titled *US*, a collaborative effort which, despite its four months of rehearsal, appeared to most critics as an incoherent mixture of theatrical styles, but which nevertheless struck a note of authentic anguish in its picture of an intelligentsia powerless and yet somehow guilty before the terror of Vietnam. At the National Theatre John Dexter experimented with Artaudian production techniques in *A Bond Honoured*, adapted from Lope de Vega by John Osborne.

The theme of violence still preoccupied dramatists at the beginning of the '70s. Interest in the extension of forms of consciousness, which had introduced the happening and the mixed-media show to American audiences, and the cultivation of the actor's inner powers to present him as a myth-making figure, alive with magic potency, which had drawn attention to Julian Beck's Living Theater company and Jerzy Grotowski's Teatr Laboratorium, were tendencies whose effect on the mainstream of English drama was already noticeable and seemed to be increasing. But there were other, less spectacular developments within the English theater of the '60s to which the playwrights of the '70s might prove to be equally indebted. Whether influenced by Pirandello, by the English tradition of the "play within a play" which stretches back at least as far as Shakespeare, or by the more immediate influence of Brecht, a number of otherwise very different dramatists share an interest in the reverberations between the artificial world of theatrical performance and the intangible reality which that performance tries to capture. As early as 1957 N. F. Simpson's *A Resounding Tinkle* employed a number of devices to remind the audience that what they were witnessing was not reality but a play performed by actors. In

*The Entertainer* Osborne ingeniously contrasted his hero's domestic life with the forced gaiety of his music-hall routines. In 1963 the theme was developed more fully in *Next Time I'll Sing to You*, James Saunders' subtle exploration of the relationship between actor, author, and dramatic subject in the form of a "play within a play" condemned never to pass beyond the first rehearsals. In the following year Brook's production of *Marat/Sade* exploited the full theatrical potential of the performance given within the play by the "inmates of the Asylum of Charenton." Since that date writers with intentions and abilities as varied as those of Tom Stoppard (*Rosencrantz and Guildenstern Are Dead*, 1967; *The Real Inspector Hound*, 1968), John Bowen (*After the Rain*, 1966), Henry Livings (*The Little Mrs. Foster Show*, 1968), David Halliwell (*K. D. Dufford* . . . 1969), and David Caute (*The Demonstration*, 1969) have used the "play within a play" as a central image in their exposition of the dialectics of truth and illusion.

Equally indebted to the vitality of theatrical imagery has been the development of a specifically English form of "documentary drama," deriving less from Brecht than from the production techniques developed by Joan Littlewood in the Theatre Workshop Company, and owing something to the "living newspapers" of prewar agitprop drama. *Oh What a Lovely War* (1963), by "Theatre Workshop, Charles Chilton, and the members of the original cast," juxtaposed the troop songs of the first world war, delivered in the idiom of a Pierrot show, with fully documented statements delivered by the military leaders, actuality slides presented upon a screen, and a "Newspanel" starkly recording the mounting casualty rate, to provide a theater of objective fact that nevertheless had not dispensed with passionate emotion. In 1964 *Hang Down Your Head and Die*, a program using similar techniques to mount an attack upon capital punishment, devised by David Wright and originating at Oxford University, enjoyed a limited London run. But on the whole the development of this form of theater has been confined to the provinces, most notably under Peter Cheeseman's able direction at the Victoria Theatre, Stoke on Trent. There for some years actors, director, and a resident playwright have collaborated annually to convert historical material into a documentary drama relevant to their regional audiences. Most successful of these dramas has been *The Knotty* (1966), a history of the growth of the North Staffordshire Railway written under workshop conditions while Peter Terson was the theater's resident dramatist. By concentrating upon local history and involving a resident playwright in his enterprise, Cheeseman has created the most distinctive regional theater in England.

By contrast, a feature of the current English theater which should not be overlooked is the renewed vitality of the tradition of naturalism. The season devoted by the English Stage Company to the little-known plays of D. H. Lawrence in 1968 served as a rediscovery of the honest, emotional power of a naturalism that is not restricted to the superficialities of drawing-room drama;

and a number of sensitive dramatists of the '60s, among whom David Storey deserves mention, have chosen to regard the formal requirements of naturalism as a necessary discipline rather than an imposition.

Whatever the future of the English drama is to be, it may be suggested that in the theater, as in other spheres of the intellect, the English have proved empirical and eclectic, suspicious of large theories and complex speculation. There has been no English Sartre, putting forward his convictions with equal facility in plays, novels, and major works of philosophy, and (Eliot excepted) no English parallel to Brecht, backing up his dramatic output with articulate and fully formulated critical theory. The influence of Continental Europe upon English drama is less strong than appearances suggest. John Arden owes as much to the English ballad tradition as to Brecht's verse, as much to the principles of medieval English staging as to Brecht's epic technique. N. F. Simpson may be a dramatist of the absurd in the school of Ionesco, but his work has equally strong affinity with the fantasies of Edward Lear, Lewis Carroll, and the weekly "Goon Shows" broadcast in the '50s. Even Artaud served only to remind writers and directors of the streak of cruelty that runs through Elizabethan and Jacobean drama. "We English," wrote John Osborne in the opening stage direction to A Bond Honoured, "are more violent than we allow ourselves to know. That is why we have the greatest body of dramatic literature in the world." English dramatists of the present day, like Shakespeare and Shaw before them, have been content to ignore the rules to which their more classically-minded Continental contemporaries have submitted, and this, as always, has led to misunderstandings with the critics. Where their predecessors were attacked for not conforming to such rules, contemporary writers have suffered from an academic heavy-handedness that insists upon discovering rules where none exist. Scholars who find deep metaphysical significance in the farces of David Campton or Henry Livings, a wholly consistent world-view in Arden or Osborne, or a fully developed and revolutionary theory of the drama behind the pauses and non sequiturs of Harold Pinter, are almost certainly mistaken. It is the strength of contemporary English dramatic writing at its best, as it is of the actors and directors who interpret it, that it takes its material directly from an experience of life, without the intervention of consciously articulated critical formulas.

Most theatrical developments of the period can similarly be seen to be the fruit of long-standing English ambitions. The National Theatre, when at last it is established in its own home, will fulfill most of the functions foreseen for it by William Archer and Harley Granville-Barker in 1904, surpassing their scheme in some respects but falling short of it in others. The censorship of stage plays, finally abolished in 1969, was an injustice against which George Bernard Shaw had fulminated for half a century. The dissatisfaction with the proscenium arch, in the English context, owes its inspiration to the Shakespearian productions of William Poel (1852–1934), and a direct line can be traced from his pioneering work at the beginning of the century to the opening of the Chichester Festival Theatre in 1962. The stage design of the postwar period, in its move from the light, the detailed, and the naturalistic toward the massive, the conventional, and the symbolically suggestive may claim Gordon Craig, a designer fifty years ahead of his time, as an influence as potent as Brecht. Stratford excepted, regional theaters have made little headway with the true repertory system practiced on the Continent, and have shown little enthusiasm for the touring partnerships frequently advocated by Arts Council administrators. While it is true that, with a few exceptions (theaters at Coventry, Bristol, Nottingham, Stoke on Trent, and the Edinburgh Traverse Theatre), the production of new plays has remained obstinately metropolitan, the best of the regional theaters still follow the formula and ideals of Miss A. E. F. Horniman's Manchester Repertory Theatre (1907–1921). The English Stage Company's lease of the Royal Court Theatre, home of the Vedrenne-Barker seasons in the first quarter of this century, is a reminder of the continuity and high ideals of the tradition to which the new English dramatists, directors, and actors belong. The adequate public subsidy, which has been a decisive factor since the war, has not created a new theater so much as given fresh life to one that had flourished at the beginning of the century but had come dangerously close to extinction through commercial pressure.

For a general appraisal of British theater since 1945 see the following: Norman Marshall, *The Other Theatre* (1947); J. B. Priestley, *Theatre Outlook* (1947); Richard Findlater, *The Unholy Trade* (1952); J. C. Trewin, *Dramatists of Today* (1953); Martin Esslin, *The Theatre of the Absurd* (1961); Kenneth Tynan, *Curtains* (1961); Laurence Kitchin, *Mid-Century Drama* (1960) and *Drama in the Sixties* (1966); John Russell Taylor, *Anger and After: A Guide to the New British Drama* (Revised Edition, 1969), first American edition published as *The Angry Theatre; New British Drama* (1962); J. C. Trewin, *Shakespeare on the English Stage 1900–1964* (1964); Richard Findlater, *Banned! A Review of Theatrical Censorship in Britain* (1967).

Collected articles and interviews may be found in: *Stratford-upon-Avon Studies, 4: Contemporary Theatre*, edited by John Russell Brown and Bernard Harris (1962); *Experimental Drama*, edited by W. A. Armstrong (1963); *The Encore Reader: A Chronicle of the New Drama*, edited by Charles Marowitz, Tom Milne, and Owen Hale (1965); *Theatre at Work* (collected interviews), edited by Charles Marowitz and Simon Trussler (1967); *Twentieth Century Views: Modern British Dramatists*, edited by John Russell Brown (1968). Helpful journals are: *New Theatre* (1945–1949); *Theatre Newsletter* (1945–1952), continued as *Theatre* (1952–1953); *Theatre World* (1945–1965); *Encore* (1953–1965); *Plays and Players* (1953ff.); *New Theatre Magazine* (1959ff.; Vol. VII, No. 3 [1968] has a full index). See also "Special Number on the Theatre," *The Twentieth Century*, Vol. CIX, No. 1008 (February 1961) and "British Theatre 1956–66," *Tulane Drama Review*, Vol. XI, No. 2 (Winter

1966). Basic reference works on the theater in Great Britain include: *Who's Who in the Theatre,* 10th–14th Editions (1947–1967); The Arts Council of Great Britain, *Annual Reports* (1946ff.); *The Stage Year Book* (1949ff.); *Theatre World Annual* (1950ff.).

**Greene, Graham** (born 1904). English novelist and dramatist. Educated at Berkhamsted School (where his father was headmaster) and Balliol College, Oxford, Greene began a career in journalism, serving on the staff of the London *Times* from 1926 to 1930. A childhood that often wavered between boredom and total despair led to a six-month period of psychoanalysis and left its mark on the later novelist and playwright. By 1926 he had adopted the Roman Catholic faith, "with an intellectual if not an emotional belief in Catholic dogma." His first novel appeared in 1929, and before the war he had published *It's a Battlefield* (1934), *A Gun for Sale* (American title, *This Gun for Hire,* 1936), and *Brighton Rock* (1938). The years 1940 and 1941 were spent as literary editor of the weekly *Spectator;* military service in the Intelligence branch of the Foreign Office (1941–1944) was to lend color to such later "entertainments" as *Our Man in Havana* (1958). With the publication of *The Power and the Glory* (1940), *The Heart of the Matter* (American title, *The Labyrinthine Ways,* 1948), and *The End of the Affair* (1951), Greene's career as a novelist of major stature was well advanced. In 1953 *The Living Room* appeared in the West End. Occupying a territory familiar to readers of his novels, this treatment of a young Catholic girl's adulterous affair with an older man that leads from blissful infatuation to a full and painful understanding of the complexities of love and culminates in suicide won praise for its subtle portrayal of character and deftly controlled plot. The setting, a house inhabited by two eccentric sisters who had closed up every room in which a death had occurred, aptly symbolized the play's theme and, without overstepping the boundaries of naturalism, anticipated the notions later to be adopted by the dramatists of the absurd. The apparent miracle that restored James Callifer to life at the expense of a young priest's faith rendered *The Potting Shed* (1957) more susceptible to controversy; but even those who could not accept the intervention of the supernatural could admire Greene's deft contrast of the bland humanism of H. C. Callifer's admirers with the melancholia of the priest without faith and the intensity of James Callifer's search into his forgotten past. *The Complaisant Lover* (1959), a skillful drawing-room comedy whose familiar theme is adultery in prosperous suburbia, and *Carving a Statue* (1964), least successful of Green's plays, complete his dramatic output. Although his plays may never be regarded as more than an appendix to his work as a novelist, they nevertheless provided the commercial West End theater of the '50s with three of its most brilliant and thoughtful successes.

Among the numerous dramatizations of his novels the most remarkable has been *The Power and the Glory,* adapted by Denis Cannan and Pierre Bost (1956). His films include *The Third Man, Our Man in Havana,* and *The*

*Comedians.* He has been awarded the title of Companion of Honour (1966) and numerous literary and academic distinctions. *Graham Greene: Some Critical Considerations* (1963), edited by Robert O. Evans, includes "Graham Greene's Plays: Technique Versus Value" by Jacob H. Adler and a bibliography by Neil Brennan.

OTHER PLAYS: *The Heart of the Matter* (adaptation, with Basil Dean, 1950).

**Gründgens, Gustaf** (1899–1963). German actor, director, and theater manager. Though he never developed his own school of acting nor a particular dramaturgy, Gründgens had a great influence on the German stage during his lifetime. After studying with Louise Dumont in his native city, Düsseldorf, he began acting in Halberstadt, then Kiel, and finally Hamburg. Between 1923 and 1928 Gründgens built his reputation in Hamburg as an actor who possessed a majestic command of character, exquisite grace, and subtle wit. In 1928 he accepted a position with the Deutsches Theater in Berlin and gained fame playing the roles of the dandy and the gentleman gangster. He soon began to direct operas at the Staatsoper and to act in films such as Fritz Lang's *M* and Max Ophüls' *Liebelei*. In 1932 he moved to the Prussian Staatstheater, where he played Mephisto in Goethe's *Faust*, parts I and II. He achieved great renown in this role, which he constantly reincarnated, and he eventually directed the play and made it into a film. Like many German artists of his time, Gründgens was especially intrigued by the Faustian syndrome and its significance for the German people.

During the Hitler regime he stood his ground as manager of the Prussian Staatstheater (1934–1944) and focused his attention on the classics. Gründgens endeavored to use the classics to offset the Nazi ideology and pageant plays, but his achievement was confined to an aesthetic realm. After the war he continued to stress the classical repertory, and his productions of *The Sea Gull, Tasso, Hamlet, Richard III, Don Carlos, Wallenstein, Danton's Death, Miss Julie,* and the *Oresteia* received great acclaim, as did his acting. He managed the Städtische Bühnen in Düsseldorf (1947–1951), the Düsseldorf Schauspielhaus (1951–1955), and the Deutsches Schauspielhaus in Hamburg (1955–1962). Gründgens proved himself to be an adroit manager who reigned supreme over his actors and the bureaucratic forces that subsidized the municipal theaters. His self-discipline as an artist and his total commitment to the classical tradition made him an imposing figure in the contemporary German theater when all sense of tradition and humanity had become distorted. Gründgens published two books, *Wirklichkeit des Theaters* (1953) and *Briefe, Aufsätze, Reden* (1967).

**Gyárfás, Miklós** (born 1915). Hungarian journalist and playwright. Between 1951 and 1956 Gyárfás edited a theatrical review. Since 1951 he has been teaching at the Academy of Theatrical Art in Budapest. His numerous comedies and his plays for radio and television are characterized by a high degree of technical skill but on the whole lack deeper psychological insight. Some of Gyárfás' work shows the influence of J. B. Priestley's drama. His collection *Családi játékok* (Family Games, 1969) includes a television play, *Komédia a tetőn* (Comedy on the Rooftop), which displays Gyárfás' talent for the grotesque and his potential affinities with the "theater of the absurd."

# H

Haavikko, Paavo (born 1931). Finnish playwright and poet. Haavikko has been a businessman and a free-lance writer; since 1967 he has been the literary chief of the Otava Publishing Company. He was the youngest person ever to receive an honorary Ph.D. from the University of Helsinki.

Haavikko is that rare bird a genuine poet. Since the early 1950s, his poems have undergone a continuous process of change and renewal, never following the footsteps of anyone else: They have been imagistic and refined, exuberant with a Baroque-like richness of layers and details, wryly ironic and sarcastic, lyrical and intimate, always personal in their tone, diction, and free rhythm. All of Haavikko's plays, written in prose, deal with historical subjects filtered through his personal concerns. *Münchhausen* (1958) sent its hero to Catherine the Great's court on a political and erotic mission; the density of Haavikko's poetic language made the script a difficult task for the theater. *Nuket* (The Dolls, 1960) is an essay for the stage on Gogol writing *Dead Souls* and keeping company with the fabrications of his own imagination. *Agricola ja kettu* (Agricola and the Fox, 1968) climaxes in the last moments of the Lutheran reformer and founding father of Finnish literature as he returns home from the court of Ivan the Terrible and experiences the anxiety caused by a very Finnish dilemma in power politics between West and East, King Gustavus Vasa and his Russian antagonist. *Brotteruksen perhe* (The Brotterus Family, 1969), set in eighteenth-century Finland, depicts a series of marriages as shrewdly calculated business transactions. With its cool atmosphere and profound disillusionment, its matter-of-fact diction and strictly regulated use of verbal metaphors, the play is typical of Haavikko's style in the late 1960s. He has also written radio and TV plays (for example, *Ylilääkäri* [Physician in Charge, 1966]).

Hacks, Peter (born 1928). East German dramatist and poet. The most talented of the playwrights in East Germany, Hacks is a dedicated Marxist who has endeavored to rewrite history and reveal elements of the class struggle in dramatic form. He first began as a student of the theater in West Germany and in 1951 wrote a doctoral dissertation, *Das Volkstück des Biedermeier* (The Folk Play of the Biedermeier Period). Soon after this he began writing historical plays, which owe a great deal to Brecht's dramaturgy. *Das Volksbuch vom Herzog Ernst* (The Chapbook of Duke Ernest, 1953) is an epic account of Duke Ernest's ascent to the throne of the Holy Roman Empire in the tenth century. Hacks makes it clear that it was not by his innate gifts but by stumbling over people. Actually, Ernest is a mock hero whose adventures in Europe and the Middle East reveal the exploitative motives of the European aristocracy and the real economic reasons behind the "holy" wars. In *Die Eröffnung des indischen Zeitalters* (The Beginning of the Age of India, 1954), Hacks once again focuses on the economic motives that determine the actions of men. Queen Isabella will support Columbus' exploratory journey to India only because she wants gold. On the other hand, Columbus is portrayed as a dedicated scientist-explorer who seeks financial support mainly to carry out his research. Like Brecht's Galileo, he is a man of the Enlightenment living in dark times and forced to make compromises with capitalist powers in order to reach his goal. As a member of the working class, the son of a weaver, his conquests are dedicated to all of humanity. However, after he has put down a mutiny toward the end of his voyage, he realizes that he is ushering in an age of greed for gold and not the golden age. Nevertheless, he feels that his discoveries must be made and placed in the hands of the people and future scientists in the hope that they will use them well.

In essence, Hacks's Columbus play continued raising the questions that Brecht had raised with his Galileo play about the role of the scientist in modern society. And, in order to be closer to Brecht, Hacks moved to East Berlin in 1955, where he became dramaturge at the Deutsches Theater. In 1963 he was dismissed in a dispute with East German bureaucrats. During this time, his most productive period, he wrote his best play, *Die Schlacht bei Lobositz* (The Battle of Lobositz, written 1954, produced 1956), which once again reveals the influence of Brecht's plays—*Schweyk im Zweiten Weltkrieg* (Schweik in World War II) and *Pauken und Trompeten* (an adaptation of George Farquhar's *The Recruiting Officer*). The play takes place during the Seven Years War. A young Swiss powder worker named Braeker is recruited into the Prussian Army by a sly lieutenant named Markoni. Braeker is extremely gullible and loyal to the Prussians. He has no political awareness and does not intend to desert the army like his friends. However, after he learns that Markoni is going to have him killed to win a bet, Braeker realizes the true meaning of Prussian honor and discipline and determines to return to Switzerland. On two occasions he can save Markoni's life, but he decides that the recruiting officer's life is not worth saving. In fact, he is rewarded by the Austrians for deserting the Prussians and retiring to peaceful Switzerland. Hacks uses an epic structure to bring out the gradual development of Braeker's political awareness. In a certain respect, Braeker is a folk hero who learns through the school of hard knocks that the real enemy is the aristocracy, and in his own adroit, rustic manner he avoids being exploited and triumphs in the end.

In another play, *Der Müller von Sanssouci* (The Miller from Sans Souci, 1958), which takes place in the eighteenth century, Hacks also ridicules the Prussian aristocracy. Here the machinations of Frederick II are exposed. He is worried that the people think him too despotic. Therefore, he contrives to steal a miller's property and subject himself to his own laws without really losing what he has stolen. Here the farmer loses his battle but learns what a preposterous and thieving tyrant the king is. In general, Hacks's historical dramas lack tension and are too predictable. He is most effective in drawing folk characters and pitting them in a battle of wits against aristocratic oppressors. He is adept at using language for the characterization of historical personages and folk types, and placing these characters in their proper historical context.

In 1959 Hacks was encouraged by a conference of cultural administrators in Bitterfeld to turn his attention to the present. These "supervisors" of culture desired to see East Germany realized onstage, and Hacks produced *Die Sorgen und die Macht* (Troubles and Power, 1960), which treats production problems in a coal plant and glass factory between 1956 and 1957. Actually the play centers on the Hegelian precept of turning quantity into quality. The coal factory produces a low-grade brick that ruins the machines in the glass factory. This is discovered, and Max Fiodorra, who falls in love with Hede, a worker in the glass factory, pushes for reforms in the coal factory, which is quite rich because of the quantity of coal it produces. Reforms are made, and the coal factory begins to lose money while the glass factory prospers. Eventually a compromise is reached, and the coal factory produces a large quantity of high-grade bricks. Though the romance between Max and Hede adds a false note of sentimentality to the play, it does deal honestly with the problem of competition and production in East Germany—the case was an actual one reported in the newspapers.

In another play dealing with contemporary issues in East Germany, *Moritz Tassow* (written 1961, produced 1965) Hacks writes a takeoff on Goethe's *Tasso*. A swineherd named Moritz Tassow, who is supposed to be a mute, discovers some books about 1945 (obviously the writings of Marx) and gradually learns how to read and speak. He gathers some farmers together to lead a revolution against the landowner Herr von Sack. They dispossess Sack and set up a commune on the estate "Gargantin." The commune allows for free love and a great deal of leisure time to play. Eventually, the party intervenes, and Mattukat, a party member, explains to Tassow that all the farms are to be organized into a system of collectives. A functionary named Blasche replaces Mattukat and puts an end to the commune. Tassow decides to become a writer. As in many recent East German plays, the problem considered here involves the utilization of the creative forces within the individual which demand expression and threaten to split the individual from a socialist society. Hacks has Moritz opposed by two types of party functionaries: Mattukat who has an appreciation of the creative individual and Blasche who operates without understanding. Neither the party nor Moritz resolves the contradictions, and Hacks himself is still seeking ways to develop a social organization that encourages individual creativity.

His most recent efforts have been along the lines of adaptations. He has remodeled works by John Gay (*The Beggar's Opera* in *Polly oder Die Bataille am Bluewater Creek*, 1963), Aristophanes (*Peace* in *Der Frieden*, 1962), H. L. Wagner (*Die Kindermörderin*, 1963), and Meilhac and Halévy (*The Beautiful Helena* in *Die Schöne Helena*, 1964). In each one of these works he endeavors to stress the socialist elements with verse and song. His dry humor owes a great deal to the traditional folk play. Even his *Amphitryon* (1967) resembles more a modern folk play than a classical portrayal of Jupiter's infatuation with Alcmena and the mischievousness and glory of the gods. Hacks's play is a folk farce that exposes the patriarchal and military nature of Amphitryon and places Jupiter in the role of a mediator who demands that Alcmena be loved and appreciated as a woman. The mistaken identities are revealed in a social framework allowing for new consciousness when roles are reversed. The frolic of the play is closely tied to social comment.

Hacks's return to the Greeks, and to history, in *Margarete von Aix*, reflects the difficulties he has encountered in dealing with contemporary problems in East Germany. Since he cannot be as honest or as open as he desires in re-creating the present-day situation onstage, he has resorted to using mythical and historical examples that parallel the present. This is a method that Brecht, his mentor, used with a great deal of success. Hacks, too, is adept at this, and his intention in championing the folk is reflected in the language, characters, and substance of his plays.

OTHER PLAYS: *Der Schuhu und die fliegende Prinzessin* (The Owl and the Flying Princess, written with Uta Birnbaum, 1966), *Omphale* (1970).

**Hair** (1967). Progenitor and best of the "love-rock-musicals." *Hair* was first produced off-Broadway in 1967 by Joseph Papp at the New York Shakespeare Festival Public Theater. The super-media show with its rock music (by Galt MacDermot) and love-and-protest lyrics (by Gerome Ragni and James Rado), its electrified humanity (strobe lights on moving bodies, amplified voices), its colorful beads, fringe, long hair, and Levi's, and above all its happy cast clearly having fun, not "acting" but "being," made the show an instant success. It opened on Broadway in 1968, where nude scenes were added, and spread across the world; after two years the Broadway production was still swinging and the show had been given in at least fourteen foreign countries and, despite attempts at censorship, in almost every major city in the United States, with no abatement of energy. Much of the enthusiasm that makes the show work is due to the fact that local casts, guided usually by members of the original production, adapt the show to local issues and styles. The sense of real community that is so attractive, the hippie thing at its best, is generated by the fact that the cast does feel itself a community: As one of the actors put it, "*Hair* is a way of life and we must lay it on the line for others to see."

**Hall, Peter** (born 1930). English director. After an active amateur career at Cambridge, Hall began his professional work for the theater in 1953. From 1955 to 1956 he was director of the Arts Theatre Club, where the English premiere of Beckett's *Waiting for Godot* was among his productions. In 1960 he was appointed managing director of the Shakespeare Memorial Theatre Company (renamed the Royal Shakespeare Company in 1961). He resigned this post in 1968 but remains a co-director of the company. Under his direction the company entered a period of expansion, acquiring a London home at the Aldwych Theatre and extending the repertory to include the work of other dramatists, classical and contemporary, besides Shakespeare. By engaging actors under long-term contracts, Hall and his co-directors were able to bring more resources to bear upon their productions than could any other companies of the time. In 1962 the company acquired the Arts Theatre Club for a brief period. Among the new works introduced to the stage were Henry Livings' *Nil Carborundum* and David Rudkin's *Afore Night Come*. In 1963 the Aldwych was the home of the first of a series of annual programs of World Theatre that was to bring most of the major theatrical companies of the world to England (see GREAT BRITAIN).

Among the beneficiaries of Hall's direction at the Royal Shakespeare Company were Livings and Harold Pinter. Pinter's play *The Homecoming* (1965) and his double bill *Landscape* and *Silence* (1969) received a meticulous interpretation under Hall's direction. Peter BROOK, who joined the company as co-director in 1962, was able to take advantage of the conditions established by Hall to experiment with a group of actors in the techniques of the "theater of cruelty" (1963) and to devote extended periods of rehearsal to his productions of *Marat/Sade* (1964) and *US* (1966).

Hall's Shakespearian productions for the company included *The Wars of the Roses*, which Hall and John Barton adapted from Shakespeare's history plays and which reached a wide audience on television (1963), and a controversial *Hamlet* starring David Warner (1965). He was appointed director of the National Theatre in succession to Lord Laurence Olivier in 1972.

**Hall, Willis** (born 1929). English dramatist. Born in Leeds and educated there at Cockburn High School, Hall has often been associated with the new dramatists who emerged following Osborne's success in the mid-1950s, but he may be more accurately characterized as a commercial dramatist who has learned much from the style and techniques of the new drama without departing radically from themes traditionally popular in the English theater. His initial success, *The Long and the Short and the Tall* (1959), shows the influence of Osborne's *Look Back in Anger* in the irrepressibly vituperative tirades of Bamforth, the rebellious member of a group of soldiers patrolling the Malayan jungle before the fall of Singapore. In 1960 he began his fruitful partnership with Keith Waterhouse in *Billy Liar*, adapted from Waterhouse's novel of that title. The many plays on which these authors have collaborated since that date exhibit considerable variety, but the majority stick to the successful formula of *Billy Liar*, which combines the traditional themes of North Country comedy with a certain degree of social comment. As well as writing for the stage, Hall has been a prolific author of radio and television plays and has collaborated with Waterhouse on a large number of successful screenplays, which include *Whistle Down the Wind, A Kind of Loving, Billy Liar*, and *Lock Up Your Daughters*.

OTHER PLAYS: *The Royal Astrologers* (1958), *Last Day in Dreamland* and *A Glimpse of the Sea* (two one-act plays, 1959), *Chin-Chin* (adapted from the French of Billetdoux, 1960), *Celebration* (with Waterhouse, 1961), *England, Our England* (revue, with Waterhouse, 1962), *Azouk* (adaptation, with Robin Maugham, 1962), *All Things Bright and Beautiful* (with Waterhouse, 1962), *The Sponge Room* and *Squat Betty* (two one-act plays, with Waterhouse, 1962), *They Called the Bastard Stephen* (with Waterhouse, 1964), *The Gentle Knight* (one act, 1964), *The Love Game* (adaptation, 1964), *Say Who You Are* (with Waterhouse, 1965), *Whoop's-a-Daisy* (with Waterhouse, 1968), *Children's Day* (with Waterhouse, 1968).

**Halliwell, David** (born 1937). English dramatist. His first play, *Little Malcolm and His Struggle Against the Eunuchs* (1965) portrayed the budding spirit of student revolt in a North Country college of art more than a year before the authorities were harassed by authentic revolutionaries on their doorsteps. *Little Malcolm* accurately captures the incoherent and ultimately ineffectual mixture of fantasy, adolescent frustration, and genuine grievance that animates the rebellious Malcolm Scrawdyke and inspires his followers to a comic and yet frightening violence. Halliwell's second important play again displays a North Country man (this time exiled in London), who feeds upon his own rhetoric until the division between dream and reality is blurred, but the violence in *K. D. Dufford . . .* (1969) extended, if it did not exceed, the boundaries of taste acceptable to audiences in the late '60s. *K. D. Dufford Hears K. D. Dufford Ask K. D. Dufford How K. D. Dufford'll Make K. D. Dufford*, as its full title implies, is concerned not so much with a central action as with the process of unconscious interpretation to which an event is subjected as it passes from experience into memory. The action culminating in the brutal murder of a young child is enacted and reenacted on the stage, in alternative versions that represent reality, the imagined and self-indulgent re-creations of the five characters involved, and a commercial dramatization of the same events. "Frequently and intentionally almost too vile to be tolerated," wrote Simon Gray in the *New Statesman*, "[*K. D. Dufford*] is not in the end about child-murder, or even about sex. It is about—indeed, it is a brutally funny demonstration *of*—the cross-infection between the shameful fantasies on which our private selves depend, and the squalid illusions of what we accept as the real world."

OTHER PLAYS: *The Experiment* ("a documentary with humor," with David Calderisi, 1967).

**Hammel, Claus** (born 1932). East German dramatist and journalist. Hammel has combined playwriting with his work as a drama critic for some of the leading magazines and newspapers in East Germany. He has mainly concentrated on adapting novels for the stage, and one of his most interesting plays is his version of Mark Twain's *A Connecticut Yankee in King Arthur's Court*, entitled *Ein Yankee an König Artus' Hof* (1967). Here an American soldier dies in Vietnam. While he is in heaven he is converted to pacifism and granted permission to return to earth to attempt to change society. Once he lands on the earth again, he works for the hamony of all classes by encouraging technological progress and developing a humanitarian outlook. Though his projects have some success, they fail in the end because Western society is not ready for socialism. The Yankee dies a second time.

Most of Hammel's other plays deal with contemporary issues in East Germany. In *Um neun Uhr an der Achterbahn* (At Nine by the Roller Coaster, 1964) he portrays the East-West conflict. Sabine, a young secretary, discovers some time after World War II that her mother lives in West Germany and that she can legally join her. Though she would prefer to remain in East Germany with her foster parents, she wants to test the Communist Party to see how much it would fight for her. The party, however, does not intend to make a decision for her. She goes to the West and is dismayed by the exploitative nature of the people there. At the end of the play, she returns to East Germany, pregnant but willing to face the future as an unwed mother in a socialist society. Though contrived, the play is not a cliché portrayal of the East-West conflict. East comes off better than West, as is to be expected, but the East is not a Utopia. Hammel conveys a sense of the pioneer hardness demanded by the East German State and contrasts it with the decadence of West Germany. The equation does not always work, but Hammel is not concerned as long as the message of his socialist realism reaches his audience.

OTHER PLAYS: *Fischerkinder* (Fisherman's Children, 1962), *Frau Jenny Treibel oder Wo sich Herz zum Herzen find't* (Frau Jenny Treibel, or Where True Hearts Come Together, 1964), *Morgen kommt der Schornsteinfeger* (The Chimney Sweeper Comes Tomorrow, 1967), *Le Faiseur oder Warten auf Godeau* (Le Faiseur or Waiting for Godeau).

**Hampton, Christopher** (born 1948). English dramatist. Hampton was still an Oxford undergraduate when his career as a dramatist began. *When Did You Last See My Mother?* (1966), originally written for a student group and later performed professionally, is a carefully orchestrated chronicle of two schoolboys' plainful expeditions into the heterosexual world. A melodramatic strand to the plot, ending with the death of the mother of one of the boys, was perhaps indicative of the author's youth, but the psychological accuracy in the portrayal of the relationship between the two adolescents, matched by the ironic, self-mocking quality of the dialogue, provided clear evidence of

Hampton's genuine talent. *Total Eclipse* (1968), a dramatic treatment of the relationship between Verlaine and Rimbaud, is a polished study in amorality that consolidates the achievement of his first play. In 1968 Hampton was appointed to the position of resident dramatist at the Royal Court Theatre and has adapted several plays for performance by the English Stage Company. In *The Philanthropist* (1970), a wittily structured comedy in an academic setting, Hampton's gift for subtle, articulate dialogue that hides a wealth of nervous feeling found full play in the study of an ineffectual philologist sheltering from life in a world where words and language have lost their relation to practical reality.

**Handke, Peter** (born 1942). Austrian dramatist, poet, and novelist. Undoubtedly the most original of the younger playwrights in German-speaking countries, Handke is paradoxically also the most traditional. The ideas, situations, and language of his plays are, to be sure, unique and drawn from the peculiar conditions of the 1960s in Austria and Germany. On the other hand, Handke's attack on the banality of middle-class life harks back to the folk satires of the nineteenth-century Austrians Ferdinand Raimund and Johann Nestroy. His intense desire to strip language of its superficial baggage and to expose the emptiness of platitudes and conventions recalls the efforts of the Austrians Hugo von Hofmannsthal, Karl Kraus, and Ödön von Horváth in the first part of the twentieth century.

Handke began writing novels and poetry while studying law at the University of Graz. His two prose narratives *Die Hornissen* (1966) and *Der Hausierer* (1967) show Handke's strong interest in Camus and existentialist philosophy. His first plays, which are called *Sprechstücke* ("Speak Plays"), were written between 1965 and 1967 and are also existential in nature: They are attempts to demolish conventional language, to reduce the accepted forms of speech to nothing so that new forms can be created out of this nothingness. Essentially, then, Handke is a revolutionary playwright, for he sees reified speech patterns as conditioned by a society unaware of how sterile and static it has become. And, he wants to change these patterns.

*Publikumsbeschimpfung* (Offending the Public, written 1965, produced 1966), the best of the *Sprechstücke,* seeks to make the audience aware of its decadent condition by using the audience as the subject matter of the play. Four anonymous speakers appear on stage to welcome the audience. The lights in the theater remain on while the actors divide the lines equally to transmit them to the public. Using rhythms that resemble litanies in the Catholic Church, everyday noises, and the Beatles, the actors tell the spectators that their expectations (those conditioned by the bourgeois luxury theater) will not be fulfilled. There will be no action, no plot. The stage is a stage. The audience is an audience, and the actors onstage begin to make the spectators conscious of themselves by talking about how the audience breathes, smells, looks, and reacts. The audience becomes the subject of the play. Toward the end, the actors announce that the audience will be cursed. All types of curse words are spewed forth by the actors, and finally they close by thanking the spectators for making the show what it was. The curtain falls, then rises, and the actors stand and stare into the audience while applause for the audience is heard over loudspeakers. Handke's play is an attempt to smash the illusions and the rigid forms that hold audiences captive. Here he attacks the traditional audience-actor relationship by exposing the spectator to the senselessness of the theater ritual.

In all of Handke's *Sprechstücke* he tries to raise the consciousness of the spectators. These plays are without images. They present a concept of the world in words. By revealing the meaninglessness of these words and the rituals to which they are attached, Handke moves the spectator to the point of reconsidering his own position in the world. In *Weissagung* (Prophecy, written 1964, produced 1966) four speakers stand on a bare stage repeating similes in the future tense so that the images reveal nothing. The monotony and repetition of the sentences bring out the banality of such stale language, and the spectator is left with an awareness of the humdrum routine of daily life. In *Hilferufe* (Cries of Help, 1967) numerous persons form two groups of speakers. One group proposes clichés to the other group, which is looking for one word. All clichés are rejected with a "no" until the word "help" is proposed. Here Handke is asserting that only the word "help" can express meaning for the individual who wants to be free from a life filled with platitudes and clichés. In *Selbstbezichtigung* (Self-Examination, written 1965, produced 1966) two actors (one male, one female) form a single character "I." The two speakers talk about the childhood of "I" and how "I" became the object of sentences and a series of letters. It is because the speakers of "I" have realized what "I" might become despite social conditioning that they begin a self-accusation. The confession amounts to a series of incidents that could have been avoided if "I" had been more conscious of its individual freedom, its power to make history instead of following the rules of duty as laid down by society. The result: "I am what I have been. I have been as I should have been. I have not become what I should have become. I have not maintained what I should have maintained."

This theme of self-determination is explored in Handke's most important play to date, one that breaks with the pattern of the *Sprechstücke* by placing more emphasis on gesture and pantomine. *Kaspar* (1968), Handke's longest play, is based on a historical event that is the subject of several poems and novels in German literature. Kaspar Hauser, a boy of sixteen, appeared in Nuremberg one day in 1828. He could only speak one sentence in dialect and did not know his name. The people of the city looked after him and taught him how to read and write. Still he could never recollect his past, and five years after his appearance in Nuremberg, he died in a mysterious way. Handke's Kaspar is a clown who stumbles behind the curtains of a disordered stage strewn with various pieces of furniture and clothing. When he finally finds the slit between the curtains, he emerges as though he were being born. He can speak only one sentence: "I want to be a person like somebody else was," and he constantly repeats this sentence as if to make sure that he can hold on to it. After he bumps into the props on stage, four speakers begin to blare at him over a public addresses system. The "Prompters" begin a speech torture designed to make Kaspar lose grip on his only sentence and to initiate him into society. As they instruct him about the rules and regulations of society by pounding sentences into his consciousness, he begins to order the stage and dress in a proper fashion. However, the pressure of the words, which are making Kaspar into an automaton, becomes too much for him. He splits, and other Kaspars appear on stage representing this division. They mimic him and mock him as he continues to follow the conventions of society. Kaspar has been so fully indoctrinated that the prompters are no longer necessary, but eventually he breaks down and closes the play with an outburst of disgust: "Goats and Monkeys!" (Othello's strange exclamation to Lodovico.) Handke's play portrays the negative side of social conditioning in order to reflect the possibilities for resistance to this tide of conformity. He reduces the social norms to banalities and demonstrates that the normal process shatters the personality and makes one into a blubbering fool. The emphasis on this insane condition—the senility of institutional society—is further emphasized when Handke suggests in the stage directions that fragments of speeches by political and religious figures, as well as remarks by poets and writers at official functions, be piped over loudspeakers into the lobby during the intermission. Handke wants to expose the audience to the same speech torture that Kaspar undergoes. Kaspar is not effective in resisting, but his ineffectiveness should be reason for our resistance.

The pantomime in *Kaspar* has been carried one step further in Handke's most recent plays, *Das Mündel will Vormund sein* (The Minor Wants to Be the Guardian, 1968) and *Quodlibet* (1970). In the first, not one word is spoken. The scene is a farmhouse, and the characters, an apprentice (the minor) and the farmer (the guardian), wear masks. Both are clowns. The apprentice is at first intimidated by the farmer, and imitates him. Both go through different routines, the farmer commands the apprentice, and the apprentice follows the commands. It is apparent that the apprentice is not satisfied with his role. After a quarrel, the farmer mysteriously disappears. The audience is never sure what has happened except that the apprentice has changed his clothes and looks like the farmer at the end of the play. Instead of using words as in the *Sprechstücke*, Handke shows here how the banal gestures that represent oppressive conditions must be overcome.

In *Quodlibet*, this pantomime is carried to its utmost extreme. Several figures (a general, a bishop, a dean, a member of the Maltese Cross, a fraternity student, a Chicago gangster, a politician with two bodyguards from the C.I.A., a professional dancing pair, a woman in evening dress with a fan, a woman in a pants suit with a poodle), all dressed lavishly in their official clothes, stroll onto a bare stage and begin to mix with one another. They exchange conversations, generally tidbits, platitudes, clichés. They drop words from their sentences and then use the wrong word. After this, they quote phrases from politicians. These phrases are not addressed to anyone in particular. They are monologues. The figures are now concerned solely with themselves, caress themselves, talk to themselves. Finally, the figures move about quietly and rationalize brutal and violent acts of injustice they have witnessed while the two bodyguards make obscene gestures at one another. The stage gradually becomes dark, and the curtain falls. One is reminded of Marx's phrase that the ruling ideas of any epoch are those of the ruling class. Handke's play is an attempt to expose the ruling figures and their ideas by mimicking their speech and conventions. Throughout all his plays, *Sprechstücke* and pantomimes, Handke is on a quest to rediscover the essence of communication. In effect, his obsession with banality is a concern for humanity.

OTHER PLAYS: *Der Rittüber den Bodensee* (The Ride over Lake Constance, 1970).

**Hanley, William** (born 1931). American playwright. Hanley was born in Ohio, graduated from high school in Bayside, New York (1949), attended Cornell (1950–51), and appeared off-Broadway in the early 1960s as one of several promising new playwrights when his pair of one-acts *Whisper into My Good Ear* and *Mrs. Dally Has a Lover* (1962) won the Vernon Rice Drama Desk Award. His first full-length play, *Conversations in the Dark* (1963), closed after a few days of pre-Broadway tryout in Philadelphia, but *Slow Dance on the Killing Ground*, on Broadway in 1964, proved to be a singularly moving analysis of guilt and violence. Despite the improbability that Glas, fleeing from his collaboration with the Nazis, Randall, fleeing his act of matricide, and Rosie, seeking an abortion, should all come by accident together on the night of Eichmann's execution and should lay bare each other's guilts, and despite Hanley's tendency to overexplain, the play has a simplicity of structure and a complexity of meaning that is strangely convincing. The next year *Mrs. Dally Has a Lover* and *Today Is Independence Day* had a brief run on Broadway. Hanley has also done a television drama, *Flesh and Blood*, which was produced on NBC-TV in January 1968; the tendency here is toward much talk and too much melodrama and represents a regression, not an advance, from the promise of his best play, *Slow Dance on the Killing Ground*.

**Hansberry, Lorraine** (1930–1965). American playwright. Born in Chicago, Miss Hansberry grew up in the Negro Southside. When she was eight her father, a wealthy real estate broker, bought a house in a white neighborhood and with the N.A.A.C.P. fought successfully to the Supreme Court for his family's right to live there. After attending the University of Wisconsin, Miss Hansberry moved to New York City in 1950, married songwriter and music publisher Robert Nemiroff in 1953, and pursued her interest in theater and social questions by beginning to write plays. *A Raisin in the Sun* (1959), about a Negro family's attempt to move into a white neighborhood and the maturation of the man of the family, was a great success on Broadway, won the New York Drama Critics Circle Award, was made into a popular movie, and has frequently been anthologized. In setting out to "write a social drama about Negroes that will be good art" Miss Hansberry succeeded in producing the first Negro play that almost every American saw in one form or another or at least knew about. Her next production, also traditional in form and timely in subject matter, was not so successful. Despite good reviews and the efforts of large numbers of theater people, artists, and friends to keep the play open, *The Sign in Sidney Brustein's Window* (1964) closed after 101 performances, at the same time that Miss Hansberry died from the cancer with which she had been struggling during the months of production. These two plays are too slight to establish Miss Hansberry as an important dramatist, and they are too old-fashioned in form with a tendency toward soap opera; but the attractiveness of her person and the social passion that drives the plays won for her a promising position in the American theater of the 1960s, frustrated by her unfortunate death at the age of thirty-four.

**Happenings.** In the late 1950s and early 1960s small groups of artists in New York City contrived events in which "drama" and "life" could be brought into the closest possible conjunction. Unlike plays, "happenings," as these events are called, have no recognizable form. A group assembles in a loft, at a gallery, or on a street corner and the event begins. How the group responds to the event determines in part the direction the happening may take. Unlike plays, happenings have no existence apart from their momentary celebration; they cannot be repeated or preserved (even though there may be "scripts"); they are not dependent upon words but upon "objects" (whatever properties —including other persons—the contrivers have provided for the participants to play with). A few sentences from Allan Kaprow's article in *Art News* (May 1961) will help illustrate what can happen at a happening: "Suddenly, mushy shapes pop up from the floor and painters slash at curtains dripping with action. A wall of trees tied with colored rags advances on the crowd, scattering everybody, forcing them to leave. There are muslin telephone booths for all with a record player or microphone that tunes you in to everybody else. Coughing, you breathe in noxious fumes, or the smell of hospitals and lemon juice."

These first happenings were elitist, since only a select group contrived them and only a relatively small number of persons participated. But from their spirit have come related phenomena on a larger scale or of a more popular nature: love-ins and be-ins with their costume-parading, body-painting, food-exchanging, and spontaneous game-creating; guerrilla theater with its assault on and attempted engagement of everybody it happens upon; participation sculpture and murals with their invitation to the man in the street to do something with them or to them. Appeal and response: life as drama.

An anthology of scripts by Allan Kaprow, Claes Oldenburg, Robert Whitman, and others has been edited by Michael Kirby under the title *Happenings* (1966).

**Hauser, Harald** (born 1912). East German dramatist, novelist, and journalist. After studying law in Freiburg and Berlin during the 1920s, Hauser journeyed to the Soviet Union in 1931 and was inspired by the socialist experiments. When he returned to Germany, he began working for the Communist Party and in 1933 was forced to flee the country. His years of exile were spent in France, where he fought in the resistance and edited the illegal newspaper *Volk und Vaterland*. Upon returning to Germany in 1945, he settled in Berlin and continued his work as a journalist.

Hauser's plays center on the conflict between individual needs and the demands of society. In *Am Ende der Nacht* (At the End of the Night, 1955) a German engineer, Peter Jenssen, wants to leave a German firm controlled by the Russians because he fears that he will be blamed for the failure of a turbine engine. Eva Brandt, his assistant, convinces him that the Russians are seeking not scapegoats but cooperation. In fact, the head Russian engineer, who is in love with Eva, informs them that the Soviets are going to give complete control to the Germans. The past is to be forgotten. The individual problems, including the love relationships, are common ones that can be solved in a socialist society. This message comes too easy when one considers the immense economic difficulties caused by the Soviets between 1949 and 1955 when they dismantled machines and assumed control over factories in East Germany. Hauser focuses on the problem but renders a cheery picture with a sentimental love story. The same is true of the play *Barbara* (1964), where a woman is again the heroine in a triangle and discourages the man she loves from fleeing to the West when the Berlin Wall (1961) is erected. Hauser's socialism borders on both romance and propaganda, which distills the dramatic conflict in his plays.

OTHER PLAYS: *Prozess Wedding* (The Wedding Trial, 1953), *Im Himmlischen Garten* (In the Heavenly Garden, 1958), *Weisses Blut* (White Blood, 1958), *Häschen Schnurks* (The Novice Schnurks, 1960), *Night Step* (1962).

**Havel, Václav.** See CZECHOSLOVAKIA.

**Hawkes, John** (born 1925). American teacher, novelist, and playwright. Hawkes was born in Stamford, Connecticut, graduated from Harvard (B.A. 1949), and taught English at Harvard from 1955 until 1958; he is now a professor of English at Brown University. Between 1949 and 1964 Hawkes produced seven novels: *Charivari* (1949), *The Cannibal* (1949), *The Beetle Leg* (1951), *The Goose on the Grave* and *The Owl* (in one volume, 1954),

*The Lime Twig* (1961), and *Second Skin* (1964); *Lunar Landscapes* (1969) contains stories and some of the earlier short novels. In 1964–65 he was writer in residence at the Actor's Workshop in San Francisco, where he wrote his first plays, *The Innocent Party* and *The Wax Museum,* published the next year with two later plays, *The Undertaker* and *The Questions.* The sense of faceless menace that pervades the plays and the skill with which Hawkes captures the exact pitch of banal conversation relates his short plays to the work of Ionesco and Pinter, and the lucidity with which he conveys an allusive and complex set of character relationships suggests a first-rate literary talent. Whether he will, with longer and more substantial plays, turn this into a first-rate dramatic talent remains to be seen.

Háy, Gyula (born 1900). Hungarian playwright and translator. The best-known living Hungarian playwright, Háy resided abroad for the greater part of his creative life. In the '20s and early '30s Háy was living in Germany. His first play, the powerful *Isten, császár, paraszt* (God, Emperor, Peasant), was staged there in 1932. A historical drama, permeated by the "analytical" Marxist view of history, *Isten, császár, paraszt* gives a dramatic account of the career of Sigismund of Luxembourg, King of Hungary and Holy Roman Emperor. At the Synod of Konstanz, Sigismund scores a tactical defeat against the Pope, but he cannot save his main adversary, whom he wishes to win over as an ally, John Huss, the Czech reformer. A card-carrying Communist since 1932, Háy took part in the 1934 workers' uprising in Vienna and from 1935 he lived in the Soviet Union. He returned to Hungary after the war and became a professor at the Academy of Theatrical Art in Budapest. He received the Kossuth Prize in 1951. In these years most of Háy's prewar plays were staged in Hungary. They included the internationally renowned *Tiszazug* (To Have and to Hold), a realistic play portraying the inhuman land-hunger of poor peasants in a remote Hungarian village. The plague of "schematism"— Stalinist socialist realism—left its mark on Háy's art. In the first postwar decade he wrote plays such as *Az élet hídja* (The Bridge of Life, 1946), the saga of the construction of Budapest's first new bridge, replete with super-heroic workers and vile bourgeois intriguers. The political changes in Hungary that followed Stalin's death—notably Imre Nagy's first premiership—and Háy's own negative experiences forced him to take another look at social reality. *Varró Gáspár igazsága* (Gáspár Varró's Truth, 1954–55) is a result of his new search for authenticity. In this play the truth of an old swineherd employed on a collective farm clashes with the "higher interests" of party functionaries. The truth of facts, however, emerges triumphant and the play ends on an optimistic note. As one hero declares in the play, "Those who are trying to protect the state from the truth do not believe in the truth of our social order." An ironic epilogue to *Varró Gáspár igazsága* was Háy's imprisonment in 1957 for "anti-State activities." Released in 1960, Háy made a living on translations and it was not until 1964 that a collection of his plays, *Királydrámák*

(Kings' Dramas), could be published. Since 1965 Háy has been living in Switzerland. His post-1956 creative period gave birth to the historical dramas *Mohács* (1958–1960) and *Attila éjszakái* (Attila's Nights, 1961–1963), the satirical play *A ló* (The Horse), and more recently to *A főinkvizitor* (The Chief Inquisitor) and *Apassionata*. *Mohács*, Háy's best historical play since the Sigismund drama, recalls the historical situation leading up to the 1526 battle of Mohács against the Ottoman Turks, which ended independent Hungarian statehood for the next 150 years. The youthful hero of this play, King Lajos, is doomed to failure in his brave efforts, for all internal and international forces are against him. The brunt of Háy's criticism goes against the brutal, ambitious, venal, and vain magnates, Hungary's main gravediggers. *Attila éjszakái* (the first act of which was printed in English in the *Tri-Quarterly*, Spring 1967) is a somewhat loosely constructed, but in parts brilliant, play on the "Scourge of God," who for Háy is a much more humane and intelligent figure than he is for most Western writers and chroniclers. *A ló* (1960, staged in Oxford 1965) is the story of Caligula's horse made consul by order of the emperor and the subsequent horse-worship in Rome; the parallel with another "personality cult" is obvious. *A főinkvizitor* (1968) and *Apassionata* (1969) are devoted to Háy's reckoning with the past. They deal with political conditions in Hungary before and after the 1956 uprising and attack opportunism as the hotbed of slavery. Háy's drama grows out of the realist tradition, though in his most memorable plays realism is peppered with irony. Some of his characters are reminiscent of those of George Bernard Shaw, and his dramatic technique is akin to that of such Western contemporaries as Friedrich Dürrenmatt.

**Heiremans, Luis Alberto** (1928–1964). Chilean dramatist. Heiremans was an actor and playwright of considerable variety. Although he wrote high commedy, psychological drama, and musical comedy—*Esta señorita Trini* (1958), the first Chilean musical, was a great success—Hieremans was preoccupied with the effort to create a theater based on popular traditions, often with strong religious symbolism. *Versos de ciego* (Blind Man's Poems, 1960) focused the quest of the Three Wise Men in present-day rural Chile, employing popular poetic traditions and medieval structure. *El abanderado* (The Standard Bearer, 1962) attempted the same with folklore. In *El Tony chico* (The Little Clown, 1964), he used the quest form to study loneliness and love in a circus clown obsessed by the search for meaning, who is himself Christ-Everyman.

**Hellman, Lillian** (born 1905). American playwright. Miss Hellman was born in New Orleans and spent her childhood there and in New York. She attended New York University and Columbia in the 1920s but did not graduate. She is essentially a successful playwright of the '30s and early '40s: *The Children's Hour* (1934), *Days to Come* (1936), *The Little Foxes* (1939), *Watch on the Rhine* (1941), winner of the New York Drama Critics Circle Award, and *The Searching Wind* (1944) are all characterized by a concern with social issues and personal morality and are executed with a careful traditional craftsmanship. Miss Hellman also wrote a number of screenplays during this period. Her first postwar play, *Another Part of the Forest* (1946), continued her study of the Hubbard Family of *The Little Foxes*. Then with *The Autumn Garden* (1951) the hard edge and sharp vision gave way to a quiet poignancy that many critics compared with Chekhov: arrival and departure, futility and hope, in one enduring house where "most of us lie to ourselves, darling, most of us." *Toys in the Attic* (1960) is, like the earlier work, basically a well-made play, almost Southern Gothic in its concern with incest, possession, and destruction. Since the war Miss Hellman has only these three plays that are entirely her own; the rest are adaptations of novels or other plays. She has also done an edition of Chekhov's letters (1955) and a memoir, *An Unfinished Woman* (1969).

**Hey, Richard** (born 1926). West German dramatist and journalist. Following in the tradition of Dürrenmatt and Frisch, Hey favors parable plays and allegories to comment on actual events in Germany. *Thymian und Drachentod* (Thymian and the Death of the Dragon, 1955), which is similar to Dürrenmatt's *Romulus der Grosse*, is a good example of Hey's dramaturgical work. The setting is a fictitious realm. Thymian, an eccentric king, is rather apathetic about the political situation in his country. His apathy irritates the politicians immensely, for a neighboring, totalitarian country is infiltrating Thymian's government. When a resistance fighter from this country escapes and finds refuge in Thymian's kingdom, he is disillusioned by the king's resigned attitude and the bigotry of the prime minister. By the end of the play he kills himself out of despair. Hey's play is not a tragedy. Like Dürrenmatt, he writes with cynicism to comment on man's comic attempts to reach his ideal world. In *Weh dem, der nicht lügt* (There's Trouble for Anyone Who Doesn't Lie, 1962) he portrays the dilemma of a modern Don Quixote. Hans Hilarius Edler von Kapoffum fights againts a real-estate firm and the film industry to maintain his ideals. In the end he is crushed by the ruthless business world. Hey's dramas are witty and have interesting plots. However, as with most parable plays, the substance of the ideas loses its relevance because the parallels with reality are contrived and ambivalent.

OTHER PLAYS: *Revolutionäre* (Revolutionaries, 1953), *Der Fisch mit dem goldenen Dolch* (The Fish With the Golden Dagger, 1958), *Margaret oder das wahre Leben* (Margaret, or The True Life, 1958), *Lysaiane, oder auf den Flügeln des Abschieds* (Lysaiane, or On the Wings of Departure, 1963).

**Hildesheimer, Wolfgang** (born 1916). German dramatist, painter, novelist, and short-story writer. After spending his youth in Hamburg, Hildesheimer emigrated with his parents in 1934 to Palestine, where he became a carpenter and studied graphics. After this, he moved to London and attended the Central School for Arts and Crafts in order to study painting. When World War II erupted, he became a British Information Officer and later served as an interpreter during the Nuremberg trials. In 1950 he decided to settle in Germany. Like Günter Grass and Peter Weiss, he turned from painting to drama and fiction. After drawing praise for his first collection of short stories, *Lieblos Legenden* (1952), Hildesheimer wrote his first drama, *Der Drachenthron* (The Throne of the Dragon, 1955), which reveals the same irony and wit that characterize his stories. *Der Drachenthron* is a satirical version of the Turandot story. Here the man who solves the puzzle is not a real prince but an intellectual outsider, something of an opportunist, who pretends to be a real prince. However, he does not take over the kingdom but allows a real prince to gain control. The parable here obviously concerns the intellectual who uses his talents for the wrong cause and relinquishes his power for the wrong reasons. The play was revised in 1959 as *Die Eroberung der Prinzessin Turandot* (The Conquest of the Princess Turandot).

The parables that Hildesheimer construes in the plays that follow are not as obvious. In a trilogy, which he calls *"Spiele, in denen es dunkel wird"* (Plays in which it becomes dark), the characters are caricatures of certain types in West Germany, and the situations are absurd. In *Pastorale* (The Pastoral, 1958) a group of people gather on a meadow to make music together, but the music of these senile Philistines amounts to nothing more than decadent business. In *Landschaft mit Figuren* (Landscape With Figures, 1958) a painter does portraits of banal characters. As he works on them, they die, and he sends the paintings to a collector. While he works, he is disturbed by a glazier who installs violet windowpanes in the studio. At the end, the panes break, and the painter is left in light. *Die Uhren* (The Clocks, 1958) is a repetition of the previous play. Here the glazier installs pitch-black panes in the room of a man and woman who, meanwhile, recall their past. A clock salesman arrives and sells them all sort of clocks. By the end of the play, the couple are living in the clocks, where they make ticking noises.

These plays make no sense. Yet Hildesheimer argues that the nonsense is of the essence. The world cannot be deciphered. It is absurd, and the stage can only reflect this absurdity. In *Die Verspätung* (The Delay, 1958) the absurd becomes an abstruse canvas—Hildesheimer conceives scenes like a painter —and yet the texture is richer than in the other plays. Here a professor comes to a town that is falling apart. He is supposedly looking for a Guricht, an extinct bird. The inhabitants of this town (the mayor, a schoolmistress, a coffinmaker, and the woman innkeeper) mock him and argue that his rival Mollendorf has surpassed him in all his endeavors. Yet when a representative arrives on the scene to raise the hopes of these people who are helplessly watching their town decay, the professor reveals that he has influenced the government to allow the town to decay in order to create conditions to attract the Guricht. The representative, who turns out to be Mollendorf, and the others, with the exception of the sleeping coffin-maker, are overcome and leave the town in defeat. Yet the professor, too, is overcome when he learns that the Guricht does not exist. He dies of grief while the coffin-maker mumbles about his past. Hildesheimer has created a remarkable drama about characters who invalidate the search for themselves. No one is certain of what is said or done. Reality is created by the imagination, which in turn denies the created reality. This theme reoccurs in *Nachtstück* (A Night Piece, 1963), in which a nervous man living in a dilapidated villa takes all types of precautions to prevent a robbery. He constantly talks to himself, checks and double-checks to make sure of what he has done from one second to the next. However, all this is to no avail. A burglar breaks into his room. Though the owner of the house manages to catch and bind the burglar, he takes sleeping pills and is knocked out by them. The burglar frees himself and robs the owner of everything. This play continues Hildesheimer's experiments with reality. Here we have the burglar representing an outside world that crashes in on the privacy of a fearful, pill-taking protagonist who cannot combat the outside force despite all his preparations. This would seem to be absurd, and it is absurd. Hildesheimer does not believe that a reality which has become neurotic can be any less neurotic onstage. This places Hildesheimer in a strange situation, for he apparently would like his plays to serve as parables that carry social criticism. It is impossible to deny the social satire in his absurd situations, but most of his ingenious observations are lost in the darkness of his own imagination.

OTHER PLAYS: *Der schiefe Turm von Pisa* (The Leaning Tower of Pisa, 1958), *Mary Stuart* (1969–70). Hildesheimer has also adapted Sheridan's *The Rivals* (1961), Goldoni's *Fathers-in-Law* (1961), Sheridan's *The School for Scandal* (1962), and Shaw's *Saint Joan* (1968).

**Hirche, Peter** (born 1923). West German dramatist. After serving in World War II as a soldier, Hirche held various jobs before he turned to writing full time in 1949. He has concentrated mainly on radio plays, with a great deal of success. His first stage play, *Triumph in tausend Jahren* (A Triumph in a Thousand Years), produced in 1955, satirizes war with the use of the alienation effect. *Die Söhne des Proteus* (The Sons of Proteus, 1962) is a dream play with farcical elements that deals with overcoming the past in Germany. Hirche's plays reveal his close association with radio in depending more on sound than on action, more on clever tricks than on original conceptions.

**Histoire de Vasco** (Vasco, 1956). Six tableaux by Georges Schehadé. The play was first performed on October 15, 1956, at the Schauspielhaus in Zurich, under the direction of Jean-Louis Barrault. When Barrault again staged *Histoire de Vasco* in 1957 in Paris, there was some protest against its being antimilitarist propaganda at a time when France was at war in Algeria. And indeed, on one level, this play is a satire on war and the military mentality. But it is, above all, the adventure of a man of pure and timid heart who discovers his capacity for courage and dies of it.

Around 1850, during a war in some unidentified country, which could be as well in Europe as in South America, General Maravigna, who holds the rank of Mirador, decides to entrust a very dangerous mission to a young and timorous barber, Vasco, who, out of fear, hides in his shop, provoking the disapproval of old men and patriotic widows. The Mirador's choice is based on his theory that the timorous are effective because they have "a sense of nuances." In the forest next to Vasco's village, Marguerite, who lives in an abandoned wagon with her father, César, and some stuffed dogs, sees herself in a dream transformed into a madonna and engaged to a young barber. When she discovers Vasco's existence, he has already been taken away to the lines of battle by Lieutenant Septembre, on orders from the Mirador, without being told the reason for his mission or the dangers he will encounter. César and Marguerite set out to search for him. Vasco, meanwhile, meets up with three of his country's soldiers grotesquely disguised as women. He surprises them by his apparent indifference to danger and his skill as a spy, whereas in fact he is merely unaware of the real situation. He then encounters Marguerite, but she does not discover that he is her "fiancé" until after he has crossed into enemy lines, where he is taken prisoner by three soldiers disguised as chestnut trees. Questioned by the formidable Lieutenant Barberis and Sargeant Caquot, Vasco finally understands the situation and the danger he is in and turns himself into a hero by giving false information to the enemy officers. His bravery will lead to victory for his country but also, as he well knows, to his own execution by the enemy when they find out that he has deceived them. The play ends with César and Marguerite praying and weeping over Vasco's body, to the cawing of crows that had been awaiting his death from the very beginning, and while Lieutenant Septembre, nostalgically recalling his own lost innocence, realizes how bitter the victory really is.

With his little hat, his basket, and his parasol, Vasco—at once shy, innocent, and crafty—recalls the silhouettes of tender clowns and Charlie Chaplin. He embodies the kind of purity that quite simply encompasses heroic sacrifice as well as cowardice. Around that transparent soul unfolds the hilarious and murderous farce of war, in which lying reigns supreme and is symbolized by the ridiculous disguises of the soldiers. The very concise dialogue is cut precisely to fit the action and the spectacle; verbal and scenic images correspond clearly and neatly, and the impression of the whole is that of a fairy tale for adults—at first comic, then tragic—imbued with a very pure inner poetry.

**Hivnor, Robert** (born 1916). American teacher and playwright. Hivnor was born in Zanesville, Ohio; after serving in World War II he taught at the University of Minnesota, where his play *Too Many Thumbs* was first produced in 1948, then later given off-Broadway. This comic biological-philosophical fantasy has as its hero a "brilliant male chimpanzee" who evolves in three acts from beast to being "all head." The process of evolution is reversed in his charmingly poetic play *The Ticklish Acrobat* (produced by the Artist's Theatre in New York, 1954), where an American archaeologist digs through layers of civilization in a Dalmatian village; the comic spirit and form of the play are Shakespearean, a pastoral scene, foolish faults cured by love, substitution in bed, a sense of beneficence and fruitfulness culminating in a double wedding. His play dealing with racial issues, *The Assault Upon Charles Sumner*, is printed in New Directions' *Playbook 2: Plays for a New Theatre* (1966).

**Hobson, Harold** (born 1904). English dramatic critic. Hobson's first appointment as dramatic critic was with the *Christian Science Monitor* (1931). In 1947 he was appointed dramatic critic of the London *Sunday Times*, a post which he has continued to hold since that date. As chief critic of one of England's two high-quality Sunday newspapers, Hobson's trenchant and unpredictable expression of opinion has wielded considerable influence. Generous in his praise but unrelenting in his attack, and sometimes willfully blind to the virtues of a dramatist with whom his sympathies do not lie, he has been involved in frequent controversy. In fact, Hobson's keen appreciation of the theatrical qualities of a play, although it has sometimes deserted him, has played a far more creative role in the development of contemporary English drama than has generally been recognized. Familiar with the French theater, an admirer of Beckett, and one of the earliest and most consistent supporters of Harold Pinter, he showed an awareness of the nature of the change in contemporary dramaturgy as far-reaching as that evidenced in Kenneth Tynan's more publicized acclaim for John Osborne. He has published collected dramatic criticism in *Theatre* (1948) and *Theatre II* (1950), and is the author of *The Theatre Now* (1953) and *The French Theatre of Today* (1953), and editor of the *International Theatre Annual* (1956ff.).

**Hochhuth, Rolf** (born 1931). German dramatist, essayist, and editor. It is surprising that a playwright who is in many respects so provincial and writes in such stilted verse should create international controversies and sensations. Yet this is exactly what Hochhuth has done. Born in a small town in Hesse, Hochhuth joined a large publishing firm after completing his studies and worked as an editor for several years while doing research on his first play, *The Deputy* (*Der Stellvertreter*, 1963). When the documentary epic— playing time estimated to be five and a half hours—was produced in abridged form by Erwin Piscator on February 20, 1963, in Berlin, it caused an international furor. Hochhuth's drama (five acts written in blank verse with a cadence and moral fervor reminiscent of Schiller) is a forceful protest accusing Pope Pius XII of political inaction and intrigue. Essentially, Hochhuth rewrites history to prove that the Pope refused to publish an encyclical condemning the Nazi persecution of the Jews because he was more afraid of the Communists than of the Nazis and wanted to protect the Church's business interests. Hence, the Pope commits himself and the Church to a course of action that is both politically and morally reprehensible. The alternative to the Pope's action is revealed by the young priest Riccardo and the German engineer Gerstein, who endeavor to expose the nature of the concentration camps and to repudiate their own complicity in the Nazi crimes. When the Pope, who rationalizes his actions in euphemistic terms and pious slogans, refuses to speak out against the extermination program, Riccardo brands him a criminal. Representing the true Christian spirit, he accompanies prisoners to Auschwitz, where he debates with the devil Goebbels and eventually meets his death.

Hochhuth's attacks on the Pope, which he documents carefully in the play, have been interpreted by various critics as a German's attempt to balance the account of history. He has even been charged with slander. Yet the charges against Hochhuth miss the mark, for it would be more correct to label him an idealist who is ridden with guilt because people (including himself) are not as humane and moral as they should be. His historical dramas are endeavors to describe what the history books never depict, and he sets up heroic models that provide us with alternative choices for behavior. In his works Hochhuth never shies away from exploring German crimes. His novella *Die Berliner Antigone* (The Berlin Antigone, 1965), which had a dramatic reading in Munich, is an explicit condemnation of the German atrocities under Hitler. As in his previous drama, the action takes place largely in 1943 and deals with a young woman in Berlin who is placed on trial by a Nazi court for hiding the dead body of her traitor brother, which the state had designated for scientific purposes. She, too, is condemned to death by a judge, the father of her fiancé, who operates as a functionary for an inhuman political machine.

As a political writer, Hochhuth protests and abhors the sacrifice of personal integrity to Fascist institutions and their arbitrary laws. He particularly finds that men who are most responsible for making history are more guilty than the institutions they serve. In his second controversial play, *Soldaten: Nekrolog auf Genf* (Soldiers: An Obituary of Geneva, 1967), he once again touched upon a taboo that caused an uproar in England. In fact, the board of governors of the National Theatre refused to grant Hochhuth's play a permit for production, and the debate about this censorship eventually caused the end of the Lord Chamberlain's function as the national censor. The dispute centered on the play's leading figure, Sir Winston Churchill, whom Hochhuth takes to task, with the support of heavy documentation, for his decision to level the city of Dresden on February 13, 1945. Hochhuth uses Churchill in this drama as he did the Pope in *The Deputy:* He is a chief representative of his nation and his times, a maker of history, who has lost contact with the people and consequently with his own sense of humanity. Churchill is opposed by the Bishop of Chichester, Dr. Bell, who demands the cessation of saturation bombing according to the Geneva covenant proposed by the International Red Cross. Churchill cannot defend his position rationally, for he is a romantic with a mission and unaware of the evil in his actions. However, Churchill's personality is not the main issue of this five-act, wordy historical

233

drama. Hochhuth is directly concerned with saturation bombing in general and draws inferences to the bombings in Vietnam. His play takes the form of a medieval morality play arguing for some type of international agreement to protect civilians in time of war.

Hochhuth's *Guerillas* (1970), which he labels a tragedy, is another mammoth documentary production of crime, corruption, and sin. This time America is his target, and this time his moral fervor cannot carry his plot and ideas. Hochhuth takes a United States senator named David Nicolson, a rich industrialist, gives him an Argentinian wife who is a saintly Catholic, and makes them co-conspirators in a plot to take over the United States and institute a program of socialist reforms from the top down. The time is the summer 1968. The scenes are laid in New York, California, South America, jails, luxury apartments, skyscraper offices, the Pentagon, and submarine bases. Nicolson has managed to infiltrate the establishment with his city guerillas and plans to assume control of the United States with a minimum of bloodshed by threatening the government with an atomic submarine attack and guerilla warfare and by using the mass media to his advantage. However, his wife is caught while on a mission and killed in Guatemala, and Stryker, a colonel in the C.I.A., murders Nicolson in New York by throwing him out of a window and making it look like suicide. Throughout the play, Hochhuth continually reminds us that rich lawyers control Congress, that there has never been a proletarian party in America, that 122 families control the 200 largest concerns and banks in America, that the C.I.A. and the F.B.I. are reactionary organizations plotting against liberal and radical leaders in America and elsewhere. He mixes these assertions with fictitious notions about political assassinations in America and his ideas on how a revolution will come about. In doing so, he paints stereotyped portraits of Americans that are obviously copied from popular magazines. The result: a soap opera about a revolution which is both insipid in its conception and reactionary in content. With this play, Hochhuth has broken with his own artistic principles. In an interview with the critic Martin Esslin, he stated: "I do not think that the author of historical plays is entitled to invent vital incidents. In fact, I think that in doing so he would ruin himself artistically." It would appear that Hochhuth will soon find himself in a state of artistic collapse if he continues to write plays like *Guerillas*.

**Hochwälder, Fritz** (born 1911). Austrian dramatist. Hochwälder is one of the few German-speaking dramatists who went into exile during the 1930s and continued to write dramas of high quality. What is even more remarkable is that his plays adhere to the unities of time, place, and action, and his themes are based on traditional Christian socialist ideas. Hochwälder would seem anachronistic in this contemporary era, which thrives on innovation and chaos both in the world and in the theater. Yet there is a certain resilience in Hochwälder's plays, which stems from his ability to appraise the political situation of the times from a realistic and progressive point of view. This view is that of the outsider who has thrived on being out of step with his times.

Born in Vienna, Hochwälder comes from the working class. After attending high school for a short period, he learned the trade of carpenter and took a strong interest in socialist movements. He joined a trade union in the 1920s and eventually became secretary of the union. During this time he educated himself in the field of history and literature and began writing dramas as a hobby. In 1938, when Austria was annexed by the Nazis, Hochwälder fled the country and gained illegal entrance to Switzerland. Since he was prohibited by Swiss law from practicing his trade of carpenter, he turned his hand to playwriting. After producing one unsuccessful play, he wrote *Das heilige Experiment* (The Strong Are Lonely, 1943), a historical drama, which won him international recognition.

Hochwälder's next important play, *Der Flüchtling* (The Refugee, 1945), was derived from an outline given to him by the German dramatist Georg Kaiser, who had helped him in Switzerland. The drama involves a frontier guard in a country occupied by the Germans. He comes to recognize the importance of human freedom in various dialogues with his wife and a refugee. In the end he allows the refugee to escape with his wife by protecting them with his own life. The play reflects some of Hochwälder's own concern while living in Switzerland, and it goes one step further in its political message than *Das heilige Experiment* in presenting an alternative mode of action to Fascism.

After World War II, Hochwälder decided to remain in Switzerland. This decision did not mean that he was cutting himself off from Austria and Germany. On the contrary, his plays have tended to reflect a growing concern about the Nazi past and coming to terms with this past in the present. Until 1954, Hochwälder dealt with this problem in historical and philosophical terms. *Der öffentliche Anklager* (The Public Prosecutor, 1948) and *Donadieu* (1953) are two good examples of Hochwälder's use of history to parallel the present. In *Der öffentliche Anklager*, the setting is Paris during the reign of terror just after the fall of Robespierre. Theresia Tallien, "Notre Dame de Thermidor," induces the public prosecutor Fouquier-Tinville to trump up charges against an anonymous enemy of the people so that she can put an end to the reign of terror. Fouquier-Tinville employs his usual methods of blackmail and intimidation to build his case against the enemy, whom he thinks is Madame Tallien's own husband. However, the actual "criminal" turns out to be himself. He is executed, but the reign of terror will not end because Madame Tallien and her husband are suspicious of one another and will continue to use terror (perhaps against each other) to maintain their own power and security. The reign of terror in France is constantly likened to the Nazi regime in Germany, and Hochwälder's play is actually a classical study of Fascism and its effects on the people. He demonstrates that no relationship based on fear and intimidation can lead to freedom, nor can people who refuse responsibility for their actions (like the public prosecutor and the other functionaries) gain a sense of freedom. In *Donadieu*, Hochwälder turns to the year 1629 and the final collapse of the Huguenot uprising in France. Here the moral and religious tenets of Hochwälder's plays are most pronounced. Donadieu, a Huguenot nobleman, gives shelter to two couriers of King Louis XIII in his fortress in the south of France. He learns from his daughter that one of the couriers, Du Bosc, had murdered Donadieu's wife. Donadieu swears revenge, but the other courier, Lavalette, informs Donadieu that Du Bosc is carrying a proclamation of amnesty for the Huguenots and therefore should not be harmed. Donadieu practices humility and renounces revenge for the safety of his people. Eventually, Du Bosc, who wants to deceive Donadieu, is killed by Lavalette, the spokesman for tolerance and equality. Written at a time when the cold war was spreading in Europe and a witch hunt was taking place in Switzerland, Hochwälder takes a moral position that condemns slaughter and intolerance, no matter what party practices it. He speaks for Christian socialism, and his historical dramas, which are classical in structure, are attempts to separate the audience from their own contemporary situation so that they can reflect impartially upon the dilemmas in which they are immersed.

More recently Hochwälder has focused on present social and political issues, particularly in Austria, and has broken from the classical framework of his historical dramas. In *Der Himbeerpflücker* (The Raspberry-Picker, 1965) he creates a terrible picture of an Austrian village in 1965 that still longs for the Hitler period. The raspberry-picker was the commander of a concentration camp who used to allow the prisoners to pick raspberries and then kill them from long distances with his rifle. The inhabitants of the village were always impressed by the commander, and when they think he has returned to them twenty years later, they are frightened that their own criminal pasts will be exposed and that they will lose money and prestige. At the same time they are awed by him and want to win his favor with huge bribes. In actuality, they have mistaken a thief for the raspberry-picker, and once this fact is disclosed—that is, after they have made fools of themselves—they "courageously" have the thief thrown in jail and mourn the death of the real raspberry-picker, who according to a newspaper account had hanged himself after being captured by the police. Hochwälder uses archetypal folk characters, such as the pompous wheeler-dealer mayor (who also owns the town restaurant), the corrupt town cop, the obsequious but discontented servant, the sex-hungry country girl, the manipulative director of a factory, and the up-and-coming general contractor, to explore the seeds of latent Fascism, which actually flowered during Nazism and which might still flower. Like other Austrian writers, Hermann Broch and Ödön von Horváth in particular, Hochwälder is interested in studying the sadism, superstition, and perversity of country people in relation to capitalist ideology.

In *Der Befehl* (The Order, 1967), Hochwälder once again examines the

Austrian present in relation to the past. This time he deals with the fate of the Austrian police inspector who was responsible for the death of a Jewish girl during the war in Holland—the reference is to the Anne Frank story. The inspector, Mittermayer, has become one of the most respected police officers in Vienna and is ordered to take charge of the investigation concerning the officer who caused the girl's drowning in Amsterdam. As in *Der öffentliche Ankläger*, the prosecutor is also the culprit. Yet here the conflict is different because Mittermayer is aware that he is the culprit and must decide how to bring about justice. He finally reports to the girl's father that he is the murderer. The father, impressed by the officer's decency, cannot believe it and will not recognize Mittermayer as the murderer. Mittermayer finally drowns himself in despair. Hochwälder's play is a careful reconstruction of the past as viewed from the present condition of a man who has worked himself back into a secure and respectable bourgeois position. The short scenes read like a criminal dossier, and ironically the ideal inspector who sees the criminality of the past cannot convince others that a respectable citizen can commit crimes.

Though Hochwälder relies on traditional devices in his dramatic pieces, his portrayals of the political and moral problems that center on the dangers of Fascism and capitalism are extremely accurate and add a dimension to our understanding of contemporary issues. Hochwälder's own integrity as a socialist and moral thinker is reflected in these plays, and as an outsider, he has managed to penetrate to the core of the socioeconomic contradictions that have caused modern man to lose a sense of his self.

OTHER PLAYS SINCE 1945: *Meier Helmbrecht* (1946), *Der Unschuldige* (The Innocent One, 1949), *Virginia* (1951), *Die Herberge* (The Inn, 1956), *Donnerstag* (Thursday, 1959), *Schicksalskomödie* (Comedy of Fate, 1960), *1003* (1963).

**Home, William Douglas** (born 1912). English dramatist. Born in Edinburgh, Home is son of the thirteenth Earl of Home and younger brother of Sir Alec Douglas Home (formerly Lord Home), conservative politician and former Prime Minister. Educated at Eton and New College, Oxford, Home trained as an actor at the Royal Academy of Dramatic Art and worked on the stage before military service; he has continued to appear occasionally in his own plays. During the years immediately following the war, Home was generally regarded as one of the most able dramatists of the decade. While never transcending the limitations that commercial theater of the period placed upon its playwrights, Home demonstrated that artistry and originality were not inevitably alien to the West End stage. His varied style ranged from farcical comedy in *The Chiltern Hundreds* (1947) to romantic historical drama in *The Thistle and the Rose* (1949). The revolution in taste and style that followed Osborne's *Look Back in Anger* diminished the importance of the commercial sector of the theater in which Home's successes had been scored, and rendered his touch less certain. Morally and aesthetically, if not politically, conservative,

237

he found himself unable and perhaps unwilling to take advantage of the opportunities the new climate of opinion offered, and his successes since 1957
have been restricted to the field of light comedy.

Home is the author of several film adaptations and a volume of autobiography, *Half-Term Report* (1954).

OTHER PLAYS SINCE 1945: *Now Barabbas* . . . (1947), *Ambassador Extraordinary* (1948), *Master of Arts* (1949), *Caro William* (1952), *The Bad
Samaritan* (1953), *The Manor of Northstead* (1954), *The Reluctant Debutante*
(1955), *The Iron Duchess* (1957), *Aunt Edwina* (1959), *Up a Gum Tree*
(1960), *The Bad Soldier Smith* (1961), *The Cigarette Girl* (1962), *The Drawing Room Tragedy* (1963), *The Reluctant Peer* and *Two Accounts Rendered*
(double bill, 1964), *Betzi* (1965), *A Friend in Need* (1965), *The Queen's
Highland Servant* (1968), *The Secretary Bird* (1968), *The Jockey club stakes*
(1970).

**Horovitz, Israel** (born 1939). American playwright. Born in Wakefield,
Massachusetts, and educated in Boston, Horovitz studied on a fellowship at
the Royal Academy of Dramatic Art in London (1961–1963). He was the
first American chosen as Playwright-in-Residence with the Royal Shakespeare
Company (1965). Although he has been writing plays for a number of years
(his first play, *The Comeback*, was produced in Boston in 1956), Horovitz
appeared suddenly on the New York scene with four plays in the 1967–68 season: *Line,* an absurdist drama about the little game of "Be First," was given in
a one-act version at the La MaMa Experimental Theatre Club; *It's Called the
Sugar Plum,* a kind of Jules Feiffer cartoon, and *The Indian Wants the Bronx,*
a play of menace cum pathos, shared a double bill at the Astor Place Theatre,
and *Rats* appeared in *Collision Course,* a collection of sketches, at Café Au
Go Go. This remarkable first season brought Horovitz a Rockefeller Fellowship
in Playwriting, the Vernon Rice Drama Desk Award for Distinguished Contribution to off-Broadway, and an Obie, all in 1968. *The Honest-To-God
Schnozzolla* did not do well off-Broadway in the 1968–69 season, but three one-
act plays by Horovitz, Terrence McNally, and Leonard Melfi, collectively entitled *Morning, Noon, and Night,* caused something of a stir on Broadway.
Horovitz' first film, *The Strawberry Statement,* was the 1970 United States
entry to the Cannes Festival as Best Film and Best Screenplay.

Horovitz's debt to Pinter and Albee is clear, though his plays have a
Jewish folk-sentimentality and a concern with explicit social problems that is
present in neither of the other playwrights' works. But his talent is more than
derivative, and he has a knack for strong moments on stage that marks him
among the most promising of the very recent new playwrights.

**Hubay, Miklós** (born 1918). Hungarian playwright and critic. Hubay
studied art history at Budapest University and for some time edited the French-
language review *Nouvelle Revue de Hongrie.* From 1942 to 1948 he lived in
Switzerland. His first play, *Hősök nélkül* (Without Heroes, 1942), was a sharp

analysis of Hungarian upper-middle-class morality, the decay of this morality being one of Hubay's central themes. *Egy magyar nyár* (A Hungarian Summer, 1954) shows that upright prewar intellectuals with reformist ideas had to clash with their conservative environment. Hubay is a very versatile and many-sided writer, who has made successful forays into the domain of film scenarios and opera librettos: Among others he wrote the libretto for *C'est la guerre*, set to music by Emil Petrovics, and the prose text for *Egy szerelem három éjszakája* (Three Nights of a Love, 1961), the first Hungarian musical (the music for this piece was composed by György Ránki and the lyrics were written by István Vas). Hubay's most recent plays, on political themes, are *Késdobálók* and *Csend az ajtó mögött*. His collected plays were published in two volumes: *Hősökkel és hősök nélkül* (With and Without Heroes, 1964–65).

**Hughes, [James] Langston** (1902–1967). American writer. Hughes was born in Joplin, Missouri, graduated from high school in Cleveland, Ohio (1920), attended Columbia College (1921–22), and received a B.A. from Lincoln University (1929). As a leading Negro writer of the Harlem renaissance in the 1930s, Hughes's work—a prodigious output of plays, poems, novels, short stories, song lyrics, lectures—belongs primarily to the period before World War II. Plays and musicals from this period include *Mulatto* (his first professionally produced play, given on Broadway in 1935, the first and only long-run Broadway hit by a Negro playwright), *Little Ham* (Karamu Theatre, Cleveland, 1936), *Joy to My Soul* (Karamu, 1937), *Don't You Want to Be Free?* (Harlem Suitcase Theatre, 1937), *Front Porch* (Karamu, 1939), *Sun Do Move* (Skyloft Players, Chicago, 1942). After the war he wrote book, lyrics, or both for several operas and musicals, beginning with Kurt Weill's musical adaptation of Elmer Rice's *Street Scene* (1947) and including his own *Simply Heavenly* (1957), *Shakespeare in Harlem* (using work by James Weldon Johnson, 1959), *Black Nativity* (1961), *Tambourines to Glory* (1963), and *Jerico Jim Crow* (1964); his one-act play *The Prodigal Son* had a good run off-Broadway in 1965. A useful study of Hughes's place in the American Negro theater is to be found in Loften Mitchell's *Black Drama* (1967).

**Hungary.** The development of Hungarian drama since 1945 is inseparable from the course of political events taking place in Hungary during the same period. Up to 1945 drama had been most influenced by two main traditions associated with the names of Ferenc Herczeg and Ferenc Molnár. In Herczeg's romantic historical plays the emphasis was on emotional actions and grand heroic gestures rather than on the critical exploration of historical reality, while in his lighter plays Herczeg appeared as a chronicler of traditional Hungarian upper-class virtues and vices and a nostalgic admirer of the gentry. Molnár's plays grew out of a middle-class urban consciousness and were written for a distinctly "bourgeois" public, so they were based to a large extent on the conventions of nineteenth-century naturalism. Molnár's closest model was the Viennese Arthur Schnitzler with his "impressionistic naturalism," to which

Molnár added his special brand of half-cynical, half-sentimental humor characteristic of Budapest coffeehouses. Molnár's later successes in New York were attributed to his brilliant technique, witty dialogues, and the inventive stage setting of his often thin or trite plots. Both Herczeg and Molnár had numerous followers in Hungary, yet by the end of the second world war, with the collapse of old Hungary, the social reality upon which their plays rested had disintegrated. The new democratic Hungary wanted a new type of drama capable of a critical examination of social reality. This also had a tradition, though a much suppressed one, in the works of Sándor Bródy, Lajos Bibó, and Lajos Barta, and in the first few years after the war this tradition was continued by the former émigré writers Gyula HÁY and Sándor Gergely, or by those who, like Tibor DÉRY, had been living in a kind of "inner emigration" within Hungary. Apart from the emergence of Háy as a major Hungarian dramatist when his *Isten, császár, paraszt* (God, Emperor, Peasant), first performed in Berlin in 1932, at last reached the Hungarian stage, the salient feature of these years was a critical analysis of the past striving at a full dramatic expression of the moral contradictions inherent in the Horthy regime. Examples of this trend were Déry's *Tükör* (Mirror, 1946) and Gergely's *Vitézek és hősök* (Valiant Soldiers and Heroes). At this point the lack of new Hungarian plays was felt by the theaters, which were staging modern Western plays side by side with Russian classics, new Soviet authors as well as Shakespeare and Molière. The repertory of Hungarian theaters in this period included plays by Thornton Wilder and J. B. Priestley, Arthur Miller, Sartre, and Giraudoux.

Although in the first postwar season one of Sándor Márai's plays was staged, in 1948 this respectable defender of traditional bourgeois values, who had written the drama *A kassai polgárok* (The Burghers of Kassa), left Hungary to take up residence first in Italy and later in the United States. Another writer whose emigration was a loss for the Hungarian theater was Lajos Zilahy, author of many prewar plays, including *Fatornyok* (Wooden Towers, 1943), which was regarded at the time of its production as a psychological drama with definite anti-Fascist undertones. The greatest stigma of this and of the next period was, however, the complete absence from the stage of plays by László NÉMETH, whose prewar social dramas were among the most interesting experiments to transcend the conventions of the gentry-bourgeois world to create a drama for and of the intelligentsia. Németh's years of silence were nevertheless very productive. His historical dramas, written in this period, enriched the repertory of the Hungarian theater a few years later.

From 1949 to 1953, drama was characterized by inner stagnation masked by pseudo-activity. The political and social reasons for this are now widely known. The nationalization of theaters in 1949 could have created better conditions for artistic work. It increased job security for actors and introduced a more rational basis for repertory policy and it brought certain financial benefits for provincial theaters. On the other hand, the bureaucratic reorganization of all theaters following nationalization had some very harmful effects. Repertories were severely curtailed; most Western plays were dropped; the entire avant-garde theater, including Communist authors such as Bertolt Brecht, were rejected as "decadent." As for the style of acting, the naturalistic Stanislavski method was made compulsory in every theater and many leading actors who would not fit in with collective teamwork were not given roles to match their ability. Parallel with the nationalization of theaters, the Communist Party, which assumed complete power in 1949, launched an "ideological offensive" in the field of culture, extolling socialist realism as the *only* creative method to be followed. This Soviet-type socialist realism (sometimes called Zhdanovism after the Soviet spokesman on cultural affairs, Andrei Zhdanov) was first enthusiastically taken up and emulated by a number of artists, including playwrights, but soon it became clear that it would not lead to the hoped for results. This in turn provoked a debate on "schematism." Communist ideologists reproached some writers for "embellishing reality," disregarding the contradiction inherent in their demand for a "truthful" literature. They would not accept a critical picture of reality, and neither could they accept as true an over-romanticized version of reality.

The characteristic art form of the "schematic" period was the collectivization (or production) drama. In the Communist blueprint for a socialist society the collectivization of agriculture had the utmost importance. On the other hand, many Hungarian peasants had acquired land for the first time in their lives in 1945, when the big feudal estates were divided, and they were reluctant to join the collective farm when the collectivization drive began some years later. The drama of the period tried to show the conflict between the forces of the "old" and the "new" in the countryside—the grim, often tragic clashes between man and man, peasant and state—in such a way as to promote the cause of collectivization at the same time. This meant that such dramas had to play down the seriousness of the conflict and had to have a happy ending of some kind. More or less schematic plays about the collectivization of the countryside were written by Ernő Urbán (*Tűzkeresztség*, Baptism of Fire), Pál Szabó (*Nyári zápor*, Summer Tempest), Imre SARKADI (*Út a tanyákról*, Way from the Farms, 1952), and, after 1956, by József DARVAS (*Hajnali tűz*, Fire at Dawn, 1961). The main fault of these plays was the lack of genuine dramatic solutions. Because the characters were nothing but mouthpieces for class views or political attitudes, the conflicts between them smacked of explanations from a Marxist textbook in which the "progressives" win the support of the undecided and the hesitant and defeat the "reactionaries." Simplifications and crude generalizations mar the work at this time even of such a talented playwright as Háy, whose first "production drama," *Az élet hídja* (The Bridge of Life, 1949–1950), was followed by *Erő* (Power), an equally schematic drama of "peace-loving" scientists overcoming the machinations of their colleagues who had sold out to the "imperialists." Naïve belief in the exclusively social tasks of literature made critics attack a play by Miklós Gyárfás that called for building more apartment houses. They pointed out that the author lost perspective of the *main* task of socialist construction, which was to build up heavy industry.

The only way to avoid the traps of schematism, or at least to minimize the danger of false glorification of the present, was to turn toward the past. Hungary's real experiences during World War II were then, and remained for some years to come, a half-forbidden subject. As for the history of the Hungarian Soviet Republic of 1919, even this theme was far from safe, because some Communist leaders who later fell victim to Stalin's purges—for example, Béla Kun—were not yet rehabilitated. In such circumstances Kálmán Sándor's play *A harag napja* (The Day of Wrath), evoking a dramatic confrontation between revolutionary and counterrevolutionary forces in a small town in 1919, can be regarded as a qualified success. Technically it was a step forward, for instead of the pseudo-conflicts of the average production play it presented (not unlike Soviet plays on the revolution and the civil war) a real conflict between strong-willed and unscrupulous heroes. Gyula ILLYÉS, whose *Lélekbúvár* (The Psychologist), a not-too-successful comedy, was staged in 1948, now delved even deeper into the past. His *Ozorai példa* (The Example of Ozora, 1952), a play recalling the heroism of simple village folk in the Hungarian War of Independence of 1848–49, though an interesting innovation in its theme and form, still had some flaws in its dramatic composition. Nevertheless, with this play Illyés bought time and managed to avoid the full political involvement that proved to be disastrous to some of his prewar colleagues. In 1953 he wrote *Fáklyaláng* (Torchflame), another historical play that marked a sharp break with the emptiness, boredom, and false heroism of the socialist realism of the day.

*Fáklyaláng* is a romantic drama culminating in the confrontation of two concepts and of two personalities, Lajos Kossuth and Arthur von Görgey, political and military leaders of the 1848–49 war. The characters are drawn with great economy; attention is concentrated on the powerful dialogue between the two protagonists. *Fáklyaláng*, together with *Dózsa György* (1954, first staged in 1956), is an important achievement in the traditionally well-developed genre of historical drama, even if Illyés did not succeed in making Dózsa's character as central to the second play as that of Kossuth was to the first. As regards the Kossuth-Görgey debate, which is basically the eternal debate between romantics and realists, Illyés' play, ending with Kossuth's moral triumph, had an interesting follow-up in Németh's *Az áruló* (The Traitor, 1954), presenting the same theme from Görgey's point of view, or at least showing more sympathy with this brilliant military leader who came to be regarded by most Hungarians as a traitor to the national cause. These historical plays, as well as some other dramas by Németh and Illyés, enjoy great popularity in Hungary but are handicapped in Western Europe and in the United

States by their references to historical events or personalities familiar to every Hungarian but little known in other countries.

After Stalin's death in 1953 the political situation started improving, and in June 1953 Imre Nagy became Prime Minister of Hungary. Nagy's program, at the time supported by Moscow, tried to eradicate the worst excesses of the 1949–1953 period (usually called the Rákosi era, after Communist Party Secretary Mátyás Rákosi) and managed to infuse a new national purpose into the body politic. The relaxation of party controls and Nagy's encouragement of more open debate gave a new impetus to Hungarian drama. The following three years, in spite of their political ups and downs, were a time full of hope and expectation, a period rich in good lyric poetry and interesting plays.

The first critical ventures that reached the stage were comedies, Ernő Urbán's *Uborkafa* (The Cucumber Tree) and László Sólyom's *Holnapra kiderül* (You'll See Tomorrow). In fact, both were halfhearted satires still conceived in the patterns of the schematic period, which did not disappear overnight but continued to influence dramatists for years. The plays criticized bureaucracy and "wrong administrative methods" without attacking the whole structure of command that made bureaucratic arbitrariness possible. Déry's one-act play *A talpsimogató* (The Sycophant, 1954) was more of a real achievement, even if its criticism was directed against a single target—a spineless careerist of a student churning out vulgarized Marxist phrases at a university seminar. Déry's student, as some critics observed already at that time, was a finished product of the hypocritical, slogan-mongering Rákosi regime.

The social dramas of the "thaw," as the years between 1953 and 1956 are sometimes called, did not bring much new in the critical examination of the past. The only play worth mentioning in this respect was Miklós HUBAY's *Egy magyar nyár* (A Hungarian Summer, 1954), which follows the dramatic pattern set earlier by such dramatists as Németh and Hubay himself. On the other hand, some young writers confronted problems of the present. Although neither Ferenc KARINTHY in *Ezer év* (A Thousand Years, 1955) nor Sarkadi in *Szeptember* (1955) managed to get to the core of the social problems that they set out to investigate, their attempts were significant. Sarkadi's concern now was to evaluate the human factors involved in the collectivization of the countryside. His old peasants understand that the future belongs to the collective farm, but the vision of a better future for their children cannot make good their human loss or prevent the disintegration of the peasant family. (The problem of "collectivization—at what price?" became the recurrent topic of Hungarian films after 1956.)

The most significant event of the Hungarian theater in 1956 was the production of Németh's *Galilei*. Between 1945 and 1956 Németh wrote eight historical plays, none of which reached the stage at that time. Certain Communist policy-makers feared and overestimated Németh's influence on the Hungarian intelligentsia. In these years even classics were feared by the authorities: When in 1955 the National Theater wanted to put on Imre Madách's classic *Az ember tragédiája* (The Tragedy of Man), even this plan was at first thwarted by dogmatic resistance from above. *Galilei* cannot be called a revolutionary drama in any sense; other plays, such as Háy's *Varró Gáspár igazsága* (Gáspár Varró's Truth, 1954–55) and Istvan Gáli's *Szabadsághegy* (Liberty Hill) were more outspoken in their direct protest against the authoritarian practices of the Rákosi regime. Németh's play presented the alternatives of a great scientist accused of heresy by the Inquisition: Should he compromise for the sake of truth or fight and die at the stake in the name of truth? Galilei chooses the first solution, only to realize after meeting young Torricelli that "the fate of science no longer depends on one mind alone, whatever its excellence." This implies the answer—Galilei should not have compromised.

The revolutionary uprising in 1956 was the culmination of a struggle fought between dogmatists and reformists within and outside the party. Its suppression by Soviet troops created a new situation: although the dogmatic Communists were discredited, their services were indispensable to the restoration of the one-party system, whereas the Revisionist and democratic forces— Imre Nagy's supporters—though they enjoyed the overwhelming sympathy of the population, were silenced or imprisoned or escaped to the West. In 1957 the Hungarian Writers' Association was banned and Déry, Háy, and other writers were imprisoned. Although in the spring of 1957 many theaters opened their doors, their work was seriously impeded by the departure of some outstanding actors to the West and by the imprisonment and temporary banning of others. There were also instances of administrative interference; for example, the performances of Németh's *Széchenyi* turned into a national demonstration and were discontinued after a very short run. It would be perhaps no exaggeration to call 1957 one of the bleakest years in the history of the Hungarian theater.

In the following years the situation gradually improved. Former imbalances in the repertory policy of the theaters were corrected by the inclusion of new Western plays in their programs and by revivals of plays by some of the previously less favored authors, including even such "bourgeois" writers as Molnár. Stage directors suddenly discovered the avant-garde theater of the '20s: Brecht, first played without success in 1945, became the hero of a new cult and his plays were staged. Yet the first years after 1956 did not bring major qualitative changes to Hungarian drama. Numerous political plays tried to show the "counterrevolutionary" character of the 1956 uprising on the one hand and the serious mistakes committed by Communists that led to the uprising on the other. These plays, by Darvas and Imre Dobozy, failed because of their conspicuous half-sincerity and their pseudo-solutions. Lajos Mesterházi's *Pesti emberek* (Men of Pest), a panoramic experimental play about the different roads and political stances taken by members of the same generation, did not fare much better. The sentimental attachment of Mesterházi's characters to Budapest could not make up for their schematic unreality. More interesting are the new works of those writers whose attention around 1960 or 1961 turned to individual moral conflicts—conflicts that had always existed and now reappeared with a vengeance in the socialist society. These plays, by Endre ILLÉS, Gábor THURZÓ, and Magda SZABÓ, present an intellectual criticism of such phenomena as careerism, snobbism, or hypocrisy.

The public's expectations now focused on the long-ailing genre of the comedy. After 1956, in sharp contrast with the Rákosi era, people were encouraged to withdraw into their private lives, to keep clear of politics. Not unexpectedly, social demand for light comedies began to soar. It was satisfied by a number of playwrights of varying talents, of whom the most popular were probably Béla Gádor (*Lyuk az életrajzon*, Hole in the Biography), László Tabi (*Különleges világnap* [An Extraordinary World-day] and *Esküvő* [Wedding]), and Klára Fehér (*Nem vagyunk angyalok*, We Are Not Angels). *Egy szerelem három éjszakája* (Three Nights of a Love, 1961), usually referred to as the first Hungarian musical, the highly successful collaboration of a playwright (Hubay) with a poet and a composer, and Németh's *Az utazás* (The Journey, 1962) were among the best achievements of the early '60s. Sarkadi's last plays before his suicide were also an achievement, albeit a paradoxical and tragically incomplete one. Sarkadi, both in his technique and central themes, showed some affinity with French existentialist drama, and although his work was not exempt from structural flaws, it nevertheless demonstrated a sensitivity to the most important moral issues of our age.

Around 1961 the political climate began to show signs of improvement, and by 1963 the Kádár regime firmly established its new line of "reconciliation" with the non-Communist majority of the nation. In such an atmosphere certain questions that had been shelved after 1956 could be raised again. No one has undertaken the total analysis of the Stalinist structure of society upon which the totalitarian mechanism of power rested but at least two writers paid close attention to the degrading, dehumanizing effects of such power: Háy in his comedy *A ló* (The Horse, 1960) and Illyés in *Kegyenc* (The Minion, 1963). Both writers used the simile of imperial Rome. While Háy's satire stressed the fact that alienated power thrives on servility rather than on faith, Illyés' tragedy reflected the inner torments and final collapse of faith in a false legality, the violation of faith by an all-pervasive tyranny. *Különc* (The Eccentric, 1963), another play written by Illyés in this period, was a historical drama of considerable interest, though of a weaker dramatic structure. It was now Háy who proved himself a real master of handling historical material: His *Mohács* (1958–1960) is possibly the best play of his postwar career. This monumental drama, written while Háy was in jail, is the prelude to a great Hungarian tragedy which, however, has momentous implications for the rest of Europe. It is a pessimistic and deeply ironical play, though its irony belongs to history, which will revenge the shortsightedness and egotism of those who would not help King Lajos in his gallant struggle to keep the Turks out of the heart of Europe. Háy's play has a curiously contemporary ring—Hungary's defeat is a proof of Europe's impotence.

It was around 1963 that the first Hungarian experiments in the "theater of the absurd" appeared in print and on the stage. Beckett was staged for the first time in Hungary in 1965. There were two reasons for this delay: The strong romantic-rhetorical and naturalistic traditions of the Hungarian drama hampered experimentation and, furthermore, the authorities displayed a rather suspicious attitude toward this kind of theater. This suspicion was fully manifested in the negative official reaction against Miklós Mészöly's Ablakmosó (Window Cleaner), a modern parable of the intrusive, aggressive nature of power. Neither this nor Mészöly's other play, Bunker (Air-raid Shelter), was entirely successful or a strikingly original achievement. Some years later the genre was continued by younger playwrights, including Gábor GÖRGEY and István EÖRSI, with more emphasis on the absurd nature of everyday conventions. Another play, Tóték (The Tót Family, 1967), by István ÖRKÉNY, is a mixture of grotesque and absurd elements sprouting on the psychological fears and aberrations of the war years.

Another nonrealistic trend in the Hungarian theater is the dramatic fantasy (mesejáték) written for puppets or mythical and legendary figures. Such were some of the prewar plays of Áron Tamási (1897–1967), who in his Ördögölő Józsiás (Josiah the Devil-slayer, 1952) used folk motifs in retelling the tale· of a struggle between Fairyland and the Prince of Devil Kingdom. Tamási's other dramatic attempts are less successful, though the purity and playful inventiveness of his language is widely admired. Fantasies attract poets, and Sándor Weöres, one of the best living Hungarian poets, wrote A holdbéli csónakos (Boatman in the Moon), a lively and adventurous puppet play, and the fantastic tragicomedy Octopus, avagy Szent György és a sárkány históriája (Octopus, or The Story of St. George and the Dragon, 1965), which is based on a fragment of the original Saint George legend. Both plays give full rein to Weöres' unrivaled linguistic imagination, but the plot of Octopus is so involved that its production is likely to give a headache to any stage director.

A particularly promising development of the last few years has been the young prose writers' growing interest in the theater. First, Endre Fejes adapted his Rozsdatemető (Scrap-iron Cemetery) to the stage. This laconic, ironical, and hard-hitting novel, the story of a semi-proletarian petty-bourgeois family throughout the last forty years, was a huge success and, in spite of the fears of critics, its stage adaption managed to keep those elements of the novel that had a special appeal to the public. Gyula Csák, another young prose writer, looked at the drama of the disillusioned Communist believer and spun his play Békesség a bűnösöknek (Peace to the Sinners) out of the moral consequences of a still unsolved political crisis. The interdependence of love and sincerity, love and loyalty to one's ideals, were the themes of the well-received psychological dramas of László Kamondy and Károly Szakonyi. Miklós Hubay's new plays, *Késdobálók* (Knife-throwers) and *Csend az ajtó mögött* (Silence Behind the Door), convincingly demonstrate how political crimes and evasions disrupt the fiber of intimate human relations even years after the event. Recently the Hungarian stage witnessed an interesting experiment with the classical drama form. László Gyurkó in *Szerelmem, Elektra* (Electra, My Love, 1968) follows the classical plot up to the point when Aigisthos is killed; after this event, however, he sees a conflict arising between Orestes and Electra, for Orestes refuses to put his mother to death. He wants peace at all costs and Electra's implacable thirst for revenge finally leaves him no option but to kill his own sister. Although Orestes' final action has only a flimsy psychological motivation, Gyurkó's play is an ambitious attempt to draw a symbolical balance sheet of tyranny and revolutionary retribution that has to be stopped before becoming a new kind of tyranny.

The latest social drama to warrant serious attention is *Festett egek* (Painted Skies), a play about the problems of young married couples by Endre Illés. His young protagonists, mainly intellectuals, are tossed between vague individual ambitions and definite social limitations, often escaping from the pressure of hard realities into a dream world. In spite of its optimistic ending, the play conveys the impression that neither their confused and hectic sex life nor their dream-posturing brings these young people closer to self-realization.

Hungary's theaters are all receiving subvention from the state and the directors as well as the stage directors are officially appointed. Within certain limits, however, each theater has a right to choose its own repertory and to compete with others for larger audiences. After the war the Madách Theater offered the strongest challenge to the National Theater, which was specializing in productions of Hungarian and foreign classics. In recent years the brave repertory policy of the Comedy Theater made it the most popular of Budapest theaters. The Thalia Theater is in the vanguard of theatrical development; its artistic director Károly Kazimir has been successfully staging the plays of Brecht, Kafka, Beckett, and other modern Western and Hungarian authors. Among the provincial theaters, especially Pécs, Szeged, and Debrecen have a high reputation and many new Hungarian plays have their first run in these well-staffed and ambitious theaters.

**Hunter, N. C.** (1908–1971). English dramatist and novelist. Educated at Repton and the Royal Military College, Sandhurst, Hunter took a commission and served for three years in the British Army (1930–1933). He left to begin his career as a playwright. He spent a year as a member of the B.B.C. staff (1938–39) and later saw war service with the Royal Artillery. It was not until 1951 that he achieved a major success with *Waters of the Moon*. Thereafter Hunter built up a substantial reputation as a traditional dramatist in the school of Chekhovian naturalism. Unaffected by the changes in English dramaturgy

# I

Iceman Cometh, The (written in 1939, produced and published 1946). A four-act play by Eugene O'Neill. The title contains the combination of seriousness and comedy, ultimate and immediate, that marks the play as a whole. O'Neill told his friend Dudley Nichols that he meant the archaic verb form to suggest the biblical phrase "Death cometh," and the allusion to the iceman to suggest an old bawdy story with a sexual pun ("a typical Hickey story, of the man who calls upstairs, 'Has the iceman come yet?' and his wife calls back, 'No, but he's breathin' hard.'").

The scene is Harry Hope's saloon (like Jimmy-the-Priest's in New York where O'Neill hung out before he had tuberculosis); the year is 1912 (a time when O'Neill had been close to suicide); the cast of nineteen characters, derelicts and has-beens, a few streetwalkers, escapees of various sorts, two policemen; the theme, illusion versus reality, Ibsen's old problem of whether or not "life lies" are necessary, permissible, tolerable, ultimately fulfilling, or destructive. In these summary elements, the play is simplicity itself; but as the characters interact, and there are often many on stage at the same time, the apparently simple and obvious theme becomes increasingly complex: It is as much a play about sexuality, with death as the pun, as it is a play about death, with sex as the pun (the death of character through drinking and whoring, the "murder" of Parritt's mother, Harry Hope's unacknowledged hatred for his dead wife, all of these ambiguous and frequently fearful attitudes toward women reach a climax in Hickey's own hatred and murder of his intolerably good wife). And it is also a play about politics, causes, and mores in relation to individuality (it is not at all clear at the end of the play whether Parritt's suicide is self-punishment or self-affirmation, whether Hickey's advice to give up illusions is not itself an illusion, leaving Larry, the spectator-radical, more deceived than he was before). In this play, more than in most, the plot does not carry the meaning and no one character or group of characters is spokesman. Ibsen suggested answers to the problem of illusion versus reality; O'Neill creates an illusion (the play itself) and its diversity of character, its tedious length, its frequently banal dialogue has the inconclusiveness of genuine reality, to which death does not give meaning, only termination.

Illés, Endre (born 1902). Hungarian fiction writer, essayist, and playwright. Illés studied medicine at Budapest University but soon embarked on a literary career, becoming a contributor to *Nyugat,* Hungary's best literary periodical, before the war. In recent years he has been a publisher's reader and head of a department at a Budapest publishing house. Apart from essays and short stories, Illés wrote mainly comedies, of which *Hazugok* (Liars, 1948) is considered the best. This play shows the power of slander over people whose whole life is built on deception and lies. In collaboration with István Vas he wrote *Tristan* (1956), a dramatized version of the legend of Tristan and Iseult, and the comedies *Türelmetlen szeretők* (Impatient Lovers, 1960) and *Homokóra* (Hourglass, 1961). The latter play gives an incisive critique of snobbism hiding under the cloak of artistic values. Illés' *Festett egek* (see HUNGARY) deal with young couples. The purity and precision of Illés' language, his intellectual honesty, and his well-observed characters make him one of the leading playwrights on social themes in present-day Hungary.

Illyés, Gyula (born 1902). Hungarian poet, essayist, and playwright. Illyés comes from a family of peasants and workers; his father was a mechanic on a large estate in western Hungary. After the fall of the Hungarian Soviet Republic in 1919, in the activities of which Illyés was marginally involved, he emigrated to Paris. The following years in France were very formative in Illyés' life. He returned to Hungary in 1926 and published his first book of poetry in 1928. Soon afterward his talent was recognized by the influential poet and critic Mihaly Babits, who made him an editor of the literary review *Nyugat.* In the inter-war period Illyés wrote some realist epics and radical lyrical verse, a successful biography of the nineteenth-century Hungarian poet Sándor Petőfi (1936), and a penetrating sociological study of the life of the village poor, *Puszták népe* (People of the Puszta, 1936). The latter book became a landmark in the history of the populist movement of "village explorers," which in subsequent years managed to produce a literary sociological survey of the most backward parts of Hungary. During the war Illyés edited the review *Magyar Csillag.* Because he was known for his consistently anti-Fascist views, he had to go into hiding during the German occupation of Hungary in 1944. After 1945 he played an important part in literary and political life, and until 1948 he edited *Válasz,* an independent literary review. Although between 1948 and 1953 Illyés was twice awarded the Kossuth Prize, Hungary's highest state award, he had deep reservations about the practices of the Communist Rákosi regime. These views were later revealed in his world-famous poem *One Sentence on Tyranny.* Between 1957 and 1960 Illyés chose voluntary silence, but after the release of the imprisoned writers he reappeared in print and during the 1960s published several new collections of verse and essays. A vice-president of the International PEN Club, Illyés is now considered by many to be one of the most important living Hungarian writers. His plays, published in two volumes (*Drámák I–II,* 1969), include historical dramas, plays devoted to topical social issues, and comedies. His historical dramas—with one notable exception, *Kegyenc*—are all on Hungarian national themes, usually focusing on a particularly crucial or problematical moment in Hungarian history. One of these is *Ozorai példa* (The Example of Ozora, 1952), a three-act play, partly in verse, which is a dramatic treatment of an episode of the War of Independence of 1848–49. Another historical drama is the short but greatly compressed *Fáklyaláng* (Torchflame, 1953), which depicts a confrontation between the two leaders of the same national struggle, Lajos Kossuth and Arthur von Görgey, in the last decisive hour before the collapse of Hungarian resistance. Here Illyés proves his exceptional talent for constructing dialogues of great emotional intensity. Although Kossuth has to leave the country, never to return, he grows into a legend, a symbol of liberty in the eyes of the masses. This romantic look at history is tempered and to some extent overcome in Illyés' later historical plays. In *Dózsa György* (1954, first staged in 1956), the saga of the sixteenth-century nobleman, leader of the greatest peasant revolt in Hungary, Dózsa's "national" views are contrasted with the radical "social" views of another leader of the revolt. In *Különc* (The Eccentric, 1963) Illyés sheds light upon the tragic conflict between László Teleki, Kossuth's envoy to Paris and the only Hungarian politician of the age with a "European" vision, with his compromise-oriented, narrowly pragmatic political "followers." Yet Illyés' most interesting historical play is probably his *Kegyenc* (The Minion, 1963), the new and completely rewritten version of a play by the hero of *Különc*, the writer-politician Teleki. Here Illyés shows, through the figure of the Roman patrician Maximus, the favorite courtier and minister of Emperor Valentinianus, that the loyal service of absolute power dehumanizes loyalty and destroys integrity. Maximus' suicide at the end of the play is the admission of his defeat. As for comedies by Illyés, they range from *Lélekbúvár* (The Psychologist, 1948), a satirical treatment of super-Freudism applied to bewildered Hungarian villagers, to *Tüvétevők* (Much Ado for a Needle, 1953) and *Bolhabál* (A Ball of Fleas, 1966), respectively subtitled a "Peasant Comedy" and a popular "Farce." *Malom a Séden* (Mill on the Brook, 1960) is a half-successful attempt to show the Hungarian intelligentsia's moral responsibility for Hungary's role in the last war and the undeniable fact that some form of resistance to the Germans was possible even in those circumstances. *Kegyenc* was translated into French and staged at the Théâtre du Vieux Colombier in Paris in 1965.

Imiona władzy (The Names of Power, 1956). A play consisting of three one-act plays by Jerzy Broszkiewicz. The three plays are united by a common theme: corruption associated with the struggle for political power, as manifested in different historical epochs. The historical background is unobtrusive enough for the plays to be topical. *Klaudiusz* (Claudius), set in the period of the ancient Roman republic, is practically a monologue of consul Claudius. Speaking to Quintus, the other consul, who sits silently with his back to the audience, Claudius justifies his policy of strength, explaining why he had removed Quintus from power—and why he had had him strangled before their conversation began. This last revelation comes as a powerful *coup de théâtre*. The visual austerity of *Claudius* is vividly contrasted with the succeeding play, *Filip*, which is set against the splendor of a Renaissance Spanish court. Opening with a poignant dialogue between the dying King Philip and a great castrato singer who had once paid the price of manhood for the voice he is now losing, the action turns to the question of succession. The most obvious choices are eliminated: The good Prince Juan, popular with the people, does not wish to inherit the throne at the hands of the tyrant, and Prince Hieronymus is too self-confident for the ruling coterie's liking. The choice falls on Prince Philip, who seems a pathetically ridiculous nonentity, but who soon, by sheer imitation of the manner of the old king, now dead, makes the nobles bow before him. In *Stoczternaście* (One-Hundred-Fourteen) a prisoner in a cell of a modern prison who has been falsely condemned is suddenly confronted with the man responsible for his conviction, who is now a prisoner himself. While the imaginary new trial in the cell is taking place, a revolution breaks out and the hero leaves the prison, presumably to assume political power. It is the guard who now locks himself safely up and settles down to his new life.

The three styles adopted by Broszkiewicz for the three acts of his play—that of a political monologue in *Claudius*, of a highfalutin, though ironic, historical drama in *Filip*, and of realistic prison-type dialogue in *One-Hundred-Fourteen*—were eminently suited to their content and enhanced the play's overall impact. The unity of theme moved consistently from false sophistry triumphant over honesty in politics in the first play through the powerlessness of noble intentions when faced with *raisons d'état* in the second to the uneasy revindication of decency in the third. The play's message was generally associated with the political changes in Poland of 1956 and its productions scored uncommon success. As a vivid manifestation of political drama in a novel theatrical form, *The Names of Power* was a unique achievement, which Broszkiewicz was not to repeat in his subsequent output.

**Inadmissible Evidence** (1964). A play by John Osborne. Acclaimed by many critics as Osborne's finest play to date, *Inadmissible Evidence* provides an acutely painful picture of a man moving toward a mental breakdown as well as one of the most taxing roles of the modern theater. The scene is set in the office of Bill Maitland, whose daily life is a frantic search for identity in the inadequate jargon of a solicitor not above bending the law in his client's favor. He is seen fumbling for his headache pills, making crude but successful advances to his receptionist, ringing his mistress incessantly, and monopolizing the time of his senior clerk in his quest for self-assurance. One by one the familiar props of his life fall away. Taxis will no longer stop for him, his old legal associates avoid him, he fails his clients and finds himself deserted by his staff, his casual lovers, and his mistress.

The structure and imagery of the play are dictated by the untidy rhythm of life in a solicitor's office; even the Kafkaesque opening in which Bill Maitland finds himself on trial for some opaquely defined act of obscenity takes its nightmare substance from the lawyer's everyday world. A series of interviews with his clients impinges upon the failings of his own life, and he encounters his objective correlative in the dry legal language of a petition for divorce ("That the respondent is a man of excessive sexual appetite . . ."). A long inquiry into a client's homosexual life, although handled with great sympathy, is the play's one apparent irrelevancy. Maitland's anxious fantasies increase their hold on his mind, and by the end it seems that no one is listening to his telephoned diatribes. He is finally alone, and the nightmare world has reached him.

*Inadmissible Evidence* succeeds more unequivocally than Osborne's earlier dramas because in it his sights are set clear upon their target. Attention is distracted from the powerful and compassionate study of the central character neither by factitious social protest nor (although the play exhibits a modest but assured break with naturalism) by self-conscious experiment with dramatic form. Osborne here displays to best advantage his gift for presenting an unpleasant character—arrogant, self-centered, ungenerously demanding, his speech strident with wounding abuse—who wins the sympathy of the audience, as he attracts his lovers, by reason of an animal intensity of life possessing him. "But," he tells his teen-age daughter in a passionate confrontation, "and this is the but, I still don't think what you're doing will ever even, even, even approach the fibbing, mumping, pinched little worm of energy eating away in this me, of mine, I mean." This "worm of energy" is the vital spark of Osborne's drama, human contact is its battleground, and Bill Maitland's fight to preserve it from extinction gives *Inadmissible Evidence* its tragic quality.

**Incident at Vichy** (1964). A play by Arthur Miller. The scene is Vichy, France, at a place of detention; the year 1942; the dramatic time no longer than the playing time, an uninterrupted hour or hour and a half. The cast of twenty-one characters are men of all ages and walks of life. A German professor, with a degree in racial anthropology, is using French and German police and military to round up suspected Jews; the action of the play takes place in the waiting room, as the prisoners interact with each other and with their captors in their struggle to reckon with the true meaning of the event in which they find themselves.

The businessman, Marchand, of course goes free. The poor and insignificant—a gypsy, a waiter, a boy, an old Jew—have no chance whatsoever. Of the rest, Lebeau, a painter, is willing to speak of the horror they face, but is too weak from starvation to try to escape; Monceau, an actor, refuses to believe there are boxcars and furnaces—much less penis inspection—and feels that his confidence will win him his freedom. Bayard, an electrician, clings stubbornly to a belief that the masses will eventually right the evils of the Nazis (and he denies that the Nazis are 99 per cent ordinary working-class people). But the most important perspectives are those of Leduc, a doctor (psychoanalyst), and Von Berg, an Austrian prince and the only non-Jew among the prisoners. As the two men talk, knowing that Leduc will be killed and Von Berg go free, the prince agonizes over his own exemption; Leduc responds that he does not want Von Berg's guilt but his responsibility. The climax of the play comes as Von Berg, returning from his interview, gives Leduc his pass to freedom, and Leduc accepts the pass, "his hands springing to cover his eyes in the awareness of his own guilt." Leduc escapes, and the play ends as a German major (who had denied that persons any longer exist or that self-sacrifice was any longer possible) and Von Berg stand "forever incomprehensible to one another, looking into each other's eyes"; four new prisoners are brought in.

The play was first performed on December 3, 1964, staged by Harold Clurman for the Repertory Theater of Lincoln Center for the Performing Arts. It has been the subject of considerable critical controversy, much of it centered about its relationship to Hannah Arendt's *Eichmann in Jerusalem: A Report on the Banality of Evil* (1963).

**Inge, William** (born 1913). American playwright. Born and educated through high school in Independence, Kansas (B.A. University of Kansas, 1935), Inge is both a product and a representative of the American Midwest: His plays are traditional in form, their characters unsophisticated, their values and ideals typically middle-American. Although he had been interested in going to New York in search of a career in drama, Inge attended George Peabody College for Teachers (M.A. 1938; his thesis was titled "David Belasco and the Age of Photographic Realism in the American Theatre") and taught English and drama in a high school in Columbus, Kansas (1937–38), and at Stephens College in Missouri (1938–1943). A fortunate meeting with Tennessee Williams, whom he interviewed in 1945 when he was drama critic for the St. Louis *Star Times*, led Inge to write his first play, *Farther Off from Heaven*, which was produced two years later by Williams' friend Margo Jones with her Little Theatre Group in Dallas, Texas.

With the 1950 Broadway production of *Come Back, Little Sheba*, Inge achieved instant success (due in part to the excellent performance of Shirley Booth in the role of Lola). Then followed three other commercial and critical Broadway successes: *Picnic* (1953), awarded the Pulitzer Prize and the Drama Critics Circle Award; *Bus Stop* (1955); and *The Dark at the Top of the Stairs* (1957). The defects of sentimentality already present in these first plays were fully exposed by the less satisfactory plot structures of his later Broadway plays, *A Loss of Roses* (1959), *Natural Affection* (1963), and *Where's Daddy?* (1966). In addition to a number of short plays, some of which were worked up into the full-length pieces already mentioned, Inge has written an original screenplay, *Splendor in the Grass* (awarded an Oscar in 1962), and adapted for the film the novel *All Fall Down* (1962).

Inge tends to write all of his plays as variations on a theme. In *Bus Stop,* for example, he provides various couples, or individuals, who demonstrate some aspect of love: Elma Duckworth and Dr. Lyman play a naïve Juliet and a Romeo manqué; Grace and Carl get together for some necessary sex; Cherie, the promiscuous *"chanteuse,"* and Bo, the virgin cowboy, learn about tenderness and fidelity; and Virgil, alone, gets left out in the cold. Even his most recent play, *Where's Daddy?*, with its promising beginning that suggests it may reach satiric comedy, ends up as a series of illustrations that love requires a sense of self-importance. These and other motifs recur throughout the plays: the young woman who loses her innocence; the adolescent who struggles with his, or her, own sense of identity or independence; the older women tantalized by the virile young man; love and sex as solution to insoluble problems. The greatest weakness of the plays is in the dialogue itself, with its almost comic-strip triteness: It appears to be neither regionally exact nor the language of "real men" heightened nor clever pop art, rather the phrasing and diction are like a very bad foreign guess at middle-American idiom.

Inge's best play, *Come Back, Little Sheba,* avoids or transcends many of these difficulties. Even though the ancillary characters seem like caricatures or simple types—collegiate Marie, athletic Turk, industrious Mrs. Coffman— the central character, Lola, has a pathetic quality that rings absolutely true. Her vacant look, her futile gestures, her whine of wasted life and childish babble all fit together with a series of events that, however sentimental in basic conception, produce an effect that is theatrically convincing and quite moving. Unfortunately, Inge never again realized this talent for domestic desperation. There is one book-length study, *William Inge* by R. Baird Shuman (1965).

**Invasion, L'** (1950). A play in four acts by Arthur Adamov. It was first performed on November 14, 1950, at the Studio des Champs-Elysées, Paris, under the direction of Jean Vilar. Pierre, with the help of his wife, Agnès, and his friend Tradel, is trying to decipher and edit the almost illegible manuscripts of his late brother-in-law, Jean, under the eye of his own Mother. He disagrees over the work with Tradel, who re-creates the text too freely. Completely absorbed in his work, Pierre starts to withdraw into himself. Finally, in despair over the platitudes of the partly restored text, he shuts himself in a closet for two weeks and leaves orders that no one speak to him. When he comes out, he finds that Agnès, encouraged by Mother, has left with an unknown man, "the First Comer," who had arbitrarily come to live with them. Pierre tears Jean's papers to pieces and leaves the stage. At the end of the play Agnès returns and is rejected by Mother, and Tradel, who has come to get the papers to save them from Jean's parents, discovers that Pierre is dead. Mother remains alone.

The virtual illegibility of the manuscripts, the complex and apparently unjustified precision of the characters' strange movements, the oblique dialogue in the manner of Pinter, the unexplained but accepted presence of the First Comer, allusions to a vague political threat from outside, the alarming behavior of the dominating Mother, her laughter and complicity with a mysterious lady friend, and sinister variations in lighting, all go into creating the atmosphere of a rigorous and implacable nightmare. By means of this absurd universe Adamov has represented the progressive alienation of a man haunted by his incapability and a victim, as well, of the misunderstandings created by noncommunication.

Ionesco, Eugène (born 1912). Rumanian-born French dramatist. Born in Slatina, Rumania, of a French mother, Ionesco left for Paris with his parents when he was one year old. After twelve years in France, his family returned to Rumania, where he learned the language. He studied at the University of Bucharest, began his literary career as a poet and critic, worked as a French teacher, and married. Back in France in 1938, with the intention of writing a thesis on sin and death in French poetry (he was never to write it), Ionesco spent the war years in Marseilles. Then in Paris after the war, cut off from Rumanian literary life, he worked as a proofreader in a publishing house. In 1949 he decided to learn English, which gave him the idea for his play The Bald Soprano (La Cantatrice chauve), performed in 1950. Every season from then on Ionesco has had one or several plays performed in avant-garde theaters and also, since 1960, on the big stages. By 1959 his reputation was international: He was guest of honor at the Helsinki Colloquia on the theater, and Rhinocéros was first produced in Düsseldorf. The play was later performed in Paris, as were Le Piéton de l'air (A Stroll in the Air, 1963) and La Soif et la faim (Hunger and Thirst, 1966). An actor on occasion, Ionesco played in an adaptation of Dostoevski's The Possessed in 1951. In January 1970 he was elected a member of the French Academy.

Basic to Ionesco's theater is the astonishment generated by language and its relationship to logic as well as to concrete reality. This triangle of contradictions remains central to all of Ionesco's works. And in this respect, La Cantatrice chauve is perhaps the purest of his plays. Yet there is also the suggestion of an anguish caused by brutal and threatening forces that are clearly explicit, as in La Leçon (The Lesson, 1951): The collapse of language and thought releases an eroticism in the professor that leads to murder. From that play on, Ionesco's works as a whole consist in the depiction of a stifling terror provoked by everything in the world that is absurd and uncontrollable. Both comedy and pathos are created by man's inability to rise above his condition. As Ionesco's plays become increasingly ambitious, specific obsessions become more and more clearly integrated into two great absurd themes: a thirst for the absolute, which leads to the discovery of being and nothingness, both equally unjustified, and a fear of inexplicable death. Ionesco's art consists in embodying that fundamental anguish in a variety of forms, from dreamlike images to intellectual allegories. According to his theory, the invisible must be made visible. The guilt and deterioration of the couple in *Amédée* (1954) are represented respectively as a giant corpse that never stops growing and as mushrooms growing on the floor of their apartment. Oppressive authority, not only social but metaphysical, is embodied as a policeman-father-doctor in *Victimes du devoir* (Victims of Duty, written 1952, produced 1953), as a giant policeman in *Tueur sans gages* (The Killer, 1959), and as a giant and mute monk in *La Soif et la faim*. Exaltation and the feeling of liberation are expressed through stage effects, with the characters literally flying, as at the end of *Amédée* and in *Le Piéton de l'air*. One of Ionesco's best-known devices is scenic proliferation. In *The Chairs* (*Les Chaises*, 1952), *Rhinocéros*, *L'Avenir est dans les œufs* (The Future Is in Eggs, 1958), and the third part of *La Soif et la faim* the intensification of the feeling of helplessness is conveyed by the visible multiplication of objects or characters—an image of the terror provoked both by an overabundance of things and the threat of death. Ironically, in *Exit the King* (*Le Roi se meurt*, 1962) he uses the contrary device and has the world surrounding the main character progressively disappear.

The total effect of an Ionesco play is that of a break with reality. Fantasy is presented with all the characteristics of the normal world, and the normal world is treated as a fantasy. What would ordinarily be astonishing is sometimes accepted unquestioningly, and everyday reality is a reason for astonishment. On the whole, these works are a portrait of mankind as completely out of place in the world, whatever it does and whether it knows it or not.

Ionesco has never hidden the fact that he makes use of personal obsessions, such as the wife-mother who appears in a good number of his plays or fire and flames, a constant motif of terror. Two images that transcend the personal are a kind of oozing dampness (which serves to express the feeling of habit, of resignation to a life nearing death) and free blue space (which quite simply evokes the infinite, freedom, eternal love, festivity). The tragedy of Ionesco's characters is that although they believe they are escaping from the damp prison and reaching that space in which they can breathe, it turns out to be an illusion and remains beyond their possibilities. In *Victimes du devoir*, *Tueur sans gages*, *Le Piéton de l'air*, and *La Soif et la faim* the experience of that space is very short-lived, for the mad hope of happiness and expansion is killed by some frightful discovery or undefinable sin. For example, in *La Piéton de l'air* the hero, at the end of his exalting flight, discovers that at the very heart of the "azure" is the hellish end of a world ravaged by atomic explosions. In *Tueur sans gages* the marvelous radiant city, as opposed to the protagonist's cold, damp room, is in fact the field of action for a monstrous killer.

Ionesco's dramatization of the impossibility of adapting to the world and man's helplessness in the face of the absurd is often very comical. The exaggeration of the characters' clumsiness and astonishment or, on the contrary, of their blindness, the use of a systematic distortion of the platitudes of language, the introduction of vulgar good sense into extraordinary situations, the grotesque nature of certain fantasy effects, the parody of logical reasoning, which leads to nonsense—all, as applied to the lower-middle-class world of today, take on the character of the old, effective devices of farce. Yet the laughter of Ionesco is always accompanied by terror and, as time goes on, is increasingly counterbalanced by pathos. His central character (called Choubert, Jean, and, several times, Bérenger) has lost some of his clownish stiffness, become gifted with lucidity and goodwill, and uses language that is both more lyrical and more parodical. Since Ionesco has taken to making more and more public statements about himself in articles and memoirs, his works may now be considered neoromantic—that is, a personal confession dramatized with all the devices of the new theater, in which he—along with Beckett, Adamov, and others—was a pioneer.

For several years Ionesco has been involved in controversies regarding his confessional theater, and has defended his right to present his own drama and vision without submitting to the ideological demands that his critics wish to impose upon him. From his published discussion with the English critic Kenneth Tynan in 1958 to his aggressive satire of the insincerity of ideologists in *La Soif et la faim,* he has more and more vigorously affirmed that the only real and authentic drama is that of the individual as a prey to his fantasies, his anguish, and what he calls "burning nostalgia." The dispute is a result of the fact that in his plays Ionesco deals with the great problems of the modern world, and that certain critics, who unquestioningly accept the solipsism of other less ambitious or purely poetic playwrights of the absurd, find Ionesco's closed individualism in contradiction to the questions he propounds. In any case, there is no doubt that Ionesco's imagination as a playwright is, if not the most original on the French stage today (Samuel Beckett, who is more rigorous, far surpasses him as both a writer and a philosopher), at least the most richly varied in his mixture of burlesque, pathos, realism, and expressionism.

OTHER PLAYS: *La Jeune Fille à marier* (Maid to Marry, 1953), *Le Maître* (The Leader, 1953), *Jacques ou La Soumission* (Jack, or The Submission, 1955), *Le Tableau* (The Picture, 1955), *L'Impromptu de l'Alma* (Improvisation, or The Shepherd's Chameleon, 1956), *Le Nouveau Locataire* (The New Tenant, 1957), *Scène à quatre* (Foursome, 1959), *Délire à deux, à tant qu'on peut* (Frenzy for Two or More, 1962), *La Lacune* (The Blank, 1966), *Leçons de français pour Américains,* 1966), *Jeux de Massacre* (Carnival Slaughter, or Aunt Sally, 1970); *Le Salon de l'automobile* (The Motor Show, a radioplay, 1952).

**Italy.** Twenty years of Fascist rule had a deadening effect upon Italian drama. Although there was almost an immediate profusion of postwar plays at the end of the second world war, they were largely tirades against fascist oppression, outmoded in style and untheatrical. The government subsidized productions of new plays, but Italians preferred performances of foreign plays, especially those that had been forbidden under the Fascist regime. From 1945 to 1948, foreign plays dominated the repertories of Italian companies. This merely encouraged bad imitations of foreign plays, further evidence of the deterioration of Italian drama. While the neorealistic cinema brilliantly drama-tized the impact of the war and Fascist oppression, the drama foundered for want of a suitable idiom to express the emotional and ideological conflicts of postwar Italy.

The state-subsidized theaters undertook the difficult task of updating the theater and reviving interest in Italian drama. The postwar theater actually began with the establishment of the Piccolo Teatro di Milano (1945), under the direction of Paolo Grassi and Giorgio Strehler. They not only developed one of the most brilliant repertory companies in Europe, but introduced Italy to the works of Bertolt Brecht, whose contributions were to exert a major in-fluence on Italian drama of the '50s and '60s.

Although the repertories of state-subsidized theaters were dominated by foreign plays and Italian classics, there were also productions of new plays by young writers, especially if they had won any of the important government-sponsored drama contests. Naturally, the most successful plays of the '40s were those of already established playwrights such as Ugo Betti and Eduardo de Filippo. Betti, the foremost Italian dramatist since Pirandello, wrote some of his most successful plays during the '40s: *Corruzione al Palazzo di Giustizia* (Corruption in the Palace of Justice, 1944), *L'inchiesta* (The Inquiry, 1945), *L'isola delle capre* (Island of Goats, 1946). Betti dramatized the existential dilemma of modern man existing in an unknowable universe but still possess-ing a strong sense of moral dignity and inner freedom. One of the most power-ful dramas about postwar Italy was De Filippo's *Napoli milionaria* (1945).

*Cristo ha ucciso* (Christ Killed, 1946), by Gian Paolo Callegari (born 1912), is set in a village in Calabria during an annual performance of a Passion play. Callegari's play justifies the desire for revenge sensed by so many helpless victims of Fascist oppression. The brilliant satire *La guerra spiegata ai poveri* (The War Explained to the Poor, 1948) was the work of a new playwright, Ennio Flaiano (born 1910), who was later to collaborate with Federico Fellini in the writing of the films *I vitelloni*, *La strada*, and *Le notti di Cabiria*. One of the most successful writers of prewar Italy, Enzo Duse (born 1901), had several successes in the '40s: *Jou-Jou* (1945), *Sei di Gennaio* (The Sixth of January, 1947), and *Le Zitelle di via Hydar* (The Spinsters of Hydar Street, 1949). Duse was a versatile writer of comedies and dramas; his dialogue was a unique blend of standard Italian and Venetian dialect. The noted author and journalist Massimo Dursi (born 1902) wrote two witty comedies, *Caccia alle lepre* (Hare Hunt, 1948) and *La Giostra* (The Tournament, 1950).

One of the most prolific playwrights of the '40s, Vittorio Calvino (1909–1956), wrote one of his best plays at the end of the decade, *Così ce ne andremo* (Let's Go, 1948). A leading playwright of the '30s, Silvio Giovaninetti (1901–1962), wrote *Ciò che non sai* (What You're Not Aware Of, 1946) and *L'abisso* (The Abyss, 1948). His plays were psychological studies concerned with the proverbial question of illusion and reality. *L'abisso* is a tense drama of a man seeking to escape his terror during an air raid by attempting to seduce an adolescent girl. *Sangue verde* (Green Blood, 1949) is a deliberate attempt at a contemporary Greek tragedy: A scientist in a godless world commits suicide after discovering that his wife is actually his sister. The destructive possibilities of man's scientific achievements were expressed in Riccardo Bacchelli's *L'Alba dell' ultima sera* (The Last Evening's Dawn, 1949), a drama of a scientist who prefers to die rather than reveal the secret of a terrible weapon he has invented.

The '50s began with an interesting play by Valentino Bompiani (born 1898), a philosophical playwright with a keen theatrical sense and a gift for dialogue. Bompiani began his career in 1931 and continued writing for the stage throughout the war years. His *Anche i grassi hanno l'onore* (Even Fat People Have a Sense of Honor, 1950) is a satire of Italy's bourgeoisie. *Albertina* (1948) was a penetrating study of the physical and moral havoc wrought by World War II. *Paura di me* (Afraid of Me, 1953) dramatizes a man's destructive quest for power. In the final scene, the protagonist falls on his knees, asks forgiveness of God, and then flees. He is quickly succeeded by his equally power hungry stepson. The theme is clear: Corruption begets corruption in a never-ending cycle. Bompiani has termed his drama "theater of remorse."

Vincenzo Tieri (1895–1970), a leading writer of romantic comedies, returned to the theater after an absence of seven years with *Maus* (1950), which was followed by *L'ingresso libero* (Free Admission, 1953). Charmingly wicked women and clandestine love affairs were characteristic of Tieri's plots. Another popular comic playwright, Luigi Bonelli (1893–1954), wrote *L'imperatrice in vacanza* (Empress on Vacation, 1953), which concerned the reincarnation of Catherine the Great. Orio Vergani (1899–1960), who had been closely associated with Pirandello (1867–1936) in the '20s, returned to playwriting after an absence of thirteen years with *Sette scalini azzurri* (Seven Blue Steps, 1955) and *Li Ma Tong* (1955). Vergani was among the first playwrights to employ the technique of *racconto a rovescio*, whereby the protagonist functioned also as a spectator, commenting upon the events of the play. *Nora seconda* (1954), by Cesare Giulio Viola (1886–1958), was a moving story of a daughter and mother who find each other after twenty years of separation. However, rather than experiencing immediate joy in their new union, the two women must overcome the obstacles of time and the generation gap. Viola is among the most important Italian dramatists of the period between the two world wars. Although he wrote during a period of intense dramatic experimentation that encompassed the theater of the grotesque, Pirandellism, and surrealism, he remained fundamentally a social realist, strongly influenced by Ibsen.

Stefano Landi (born Stefano Pirandello in 1895), in his *Sacrilegio massimo* (Highest Sacrilege, 1953) and *Visita di mattina* (Morning Visit, 1955), continued to manifest the Pirandellian qualities of his works of the '30s. These were powerful dialectical studies probing the elusive nature of reality. *I Veleni non fanno male* (Poisons Don't Hurt, 1953) was a whimsical comedy in a theater of the grotesque style. Anna Bonacci, one of Italy's few women playwrights, wrote fashionable comedies that were successful even abroad. Her *L'ora della fantasia* (The Dazzling Hour, 1954) is a comedy set in a provincial nineteenth-century English town. The plot concerns a sexually frustrated wife, a romantic prostitute, a London gigolo, and a meddlesome mayor.

During the '50s Diego Fabbri (born 1911) established himself as one of Italy's major dramatists with *Inquisizione* (1950), *Il Seduttore* (The Seducer, 1951), *Processo a Gesù* (Christ on Trial, 1955), and *La bugiarda* (The Lie, 1956). Fabbri's plays are imbued with his strong Catholic convictions: salvation is possible through mutual love and understanding. In *Processo a Gesù*, Fabbri's major work, Christ defends himself in court against his accusers. Christ is found guilty and sentenced to death, exemplifying man's incapacity for love. Vitaliano Brancati (1907–1954), with his bitter attacks on Catholicism and middle-class values, provided a sharp contrast to Fabbri's religiosity. Brancati viewed Italy as a society full of meaningless traditions, hypocrisy, and prejudices. Among his works were *Una donna di casa* (Housewife, 1953) and *Il viaggiatore dello Sleeping Car No. 7 era forse Dio* (Perhaps God Was the Traveler in Sleeping Car Number 7, 1959).

Alberto Moravia (born 1907), one of Italy's leading novelists, began writing actively for the stage in the '50s. He ignored the Brechtian trend of the Italian drama that emphasized spectacle over dialogue and concentrated instead upon refinement of language as the epitome of great drama. *La mascherata* (1958), written during the last ten years of Mussolini's regime, is a bitter denunciation of Fascism. *Beatrice Cenci* (1955), one of his best plays, is an original adaptation of a sixteenth-century tale, emphasizing the decadence of its characters and changing Beatrice from a helpless victim into an aggressive, intelligent women who uses her sexual charms to avenge herself upon her father. Daughter and father are enmeshed in a Freudian love-hate relationship. The play reveals the impossibility of making moral judgments in an age when good and evil are indistinguishable.

Federico Zardi (born 1912) showed himself to be one of Italy's leading satirists: *Emma* (1952), *I tromboni* (The Brass, 1956), and *I Giacobini* (The Jacobins, 1957). *Emma* is the drama of an Italian Mme Bovary with conservative attitudes, a spoof of the questionable allegiance of certain Italian intellectuals to the Communist Party. The tragicomic experience of an upper-middle-class girl seeking truth in an illusory world is dramatized in *I tromboni*. The form and style of the play provide strong evidence of the continuing influence of Pirandello on modern Italian drama.

The novelist Giuseppe Dessí (born 1909) writes plays with episodic plot construction, numerous characters, and frequent changes of time and place: *La giustizia* (Justice, 1959) and *Qui non c'è guerra* (Here There Is No War, 1960). Ezio d'Errico (born 1892) is among Italy's few absurdist playwrights. His *La foresta* (1959) dramatizes the dehumanization of modern society by technology. The inhabitants of this modern concrete forest are all lost souls, eternally trapped, dreaming of liberation. Occasionally the sound of a train is heard passing in the distance A ticket collector, the symbol of death, appears; those whose tickets have expired must die. In *Tempo di cavalette* (Time of the Locusts, 1958) postwar Italy is depicted as a ruined village inhabited by selfish opportunists. The viciousness of the villagers is evidenced when two juvenile delinquents murder Joe, an Italian-American who has returned to his homeland to share his wealth with his former compatriots. Even in death Joe is forgiving, reappearing later as a Christ figure; but the village is doomed. The villagers are all destroyed by a holocaust of locusts. The only survivor is a little boy, a possible hope for a new world. The brilliant play *Un caso clinico* (A Clinical Case, 1953), by the novelist Dino Buzzati (born 1906), is another rare example of an Italian absurdist work.

Luigi Squarzina (1922) was another of the new playwrights of the '50s: *Tre quarti di luna* (A Three-Quarter Moon, 1953), *La romagnola* (The Woman from Romagna, 1959), *La sua parte di storia* (Her Part in History, 1962), and *Cinque giorni al porto* (Five Days at the Port, 1969). Squarzina frequently dramatizes events from contemporary history. *La romagnola* is an epic of the war years in Romagna from June 28, 1940, to April 19, 1945. It comprises thirty episodes interspersed with songs and dances, numerous characters, and a narrator-chorus. The first play of Giovanni Testori (born 1923), *La Maria Brasca* (1960), depicted the bitter struggle for survival of Italy's poor working class. Testori's filmscript for *Rocco and His Brothers* (1961) received wide acclaim. Aldo Nicolaj (born 1920) also criticizes Italy's social inequality. *Gli asini magri* (The Lean Donkeys, 1960) is a bitter picture of factory workers in an industrial city. *Il mondo d'acqua* (The World of Water, 1963) is most characteristic of Nicolaj's drama: realistic dialogue tinged with lyricism, a slightly bitter humor, and a resignation to life's difficulties.

Giuseppe Patroni Griffi (born 1921) and Franco Brusati (born 1922) are Italy's most fashionable playwrights. Patroni Griffi's *D'Amore si muore* (Dying of Love, 1958) and *Anima nera* (Dark Soul, 1960) are studies of Italy's unscrupulous status seekers. *Anima nera* reveals the difficulties of marriage between a young couple of differing social classes. The man's former poverty and troubled background are an inevitable obstacle to the possibility of a successful marriage to this proper middle-class girl. The play is cinematically conceived, with frequent shifting of time and place and memory scenes, all evidence of Patroni Griffi's talent as a film writer. Brusati is an astute critic of Italy's upper middle class. *Il benessere* (The Good Life, 1960), written in conjunction with Fabio Mauri, depicts the bittersweet life of the social elite: their endless pleasure-seeking, insincerity, infidelities, boredom, and self-destruction. At the conclusion of the play Flora, the protagonist, calmly urges a young waiter to suffocate her with a pillow. Brusati's *La fastidiosa* (The Irritating Woman, 1964) reveals the disintegration of a wealthy family, a microcosm of a decaying society.

The social dilemmas of the '60s are further revealed in two plays by Luciano Codignola (born 1920), *Il gesto* (The Gesture, 1961) and *Il giro d'Italia* (A Tour of Italy, 1965). A consummate intellectual and humanist, Codignola believes that reason must prevail if mankind is to survive. *Notti a Milano* (Milanese Nights, 1963), by Carlo Terron (born 1910), exemplifies his intense concern with man's conscious or unconscious deception of himself and others. In recent years the novelist Natalia Ginzburg has been writing for the stage. *La segretaria* (The Secretary, 1967) is a tragicomedy concerning a group of intellectuals who live together in a suburb of Rome. Their lives center around two sad and hopeless women. The generation gap, the impossibility of communication, and the danger of excessive sentimentality are the prevailing themes in *La segretaria.*

Roberto Mazzucco (born 1927) is committed to eliminating the social prejudices endured by Italy's working class. The protagonist of *Un italiano tra noi* (An Italian in Our Midst, 1964) is a sensitive, intelligent, but impoverished southern Italian laborer working for a construction company in Rome. Although cognizant of the humiliations, the agonies, and the compromises life has forced upon him because of his social class, he never understands the social forces that have conditioned his life. The play is an attack upon Italian industrialists who, Mazzucco maintains, exploit the working class and destroy Italy's natural environment.

Carmelo Bene (born 1937), an actor, director, and playwright, is among the leaders of the avant-garde. He has written *Manon* (1965), *Pinocchio* (1966), and *Nostra Signora dei turchi* (Our Lady of the Turks, 1966). In 1966 Bene and Mario Ricci established Beat 72, an experimental theater in Rome. Bene converts popular stories and folk tales into satirical pieces for the stage. In his version of *Pinocchio*, the puppet alone survives; the other characters, symbols of a conventional and hollow society, are all destroyed. Bene's theater is extremely visual, with colorful, exaggerated costumes, macabre characters, and an emphasis upon mimicry and pantomime.

Playwrights such as Bene belong to the *commedia dell'arte* tradition of Italian drama, a nonliterary tradition placing greater emphasis upon the actor and stage spectacle. This is the lifeblood of the Italian theater, for the other major tradition of the Italian drama is a literary one, with a tendency to be excessively philosophical and rhetorical rather than theatrical. It relies on long passages regarding the nature of reality, the meaning of time, the question of identity, and the possibility of salvation. Such drama has little appeal abroad, and not very much even in Italy, yet government-sponsored drama contests, presided over by judges schooled in the literary tradition, continue to encourage such weighty plays.

Eduardo de Filippo (born 1898), one of the world's great actors and vaudeville comedians, is Italy's leading playwright today. This brilliant dramatist and showman steeps his plays in the rich *commedia* tradition of Naples, and his themes and characters have universal appeal. Younger playwrights such as Bene, Mario Fratti (1927), and Dario Fo (1926) also avoid the Italian tendency to philosophize, and strive to convey their themes through vital theatrical images. They experiment with language and introduce strident sounds into their dialogue whenever possible, for they believe that the melodiousness of Italian can be as monotonous as it is beautiful.

In this respect, certain regional dialects make for better dialogue than stage Italian. Some Italians, especially those of the working classes, feel greater emotional involvement in plays written in dialect than in stage Italian, which to them sounds literary and unreal. Dialect theater companies rarely tour. It is extremely difficult to convert dialogue written in dialect into stage Italian, and almost impossible to translate it into a foreign language. In consequence, the world remains ignorant of the rich dramatic material of Italy's dialect theater. The major exception is De Filippo, but it is doubtful as to how successfully his Neapolitan dialogue translates into other languages.

The future of the Italian drama is uncertain. It still suffers from government censorship. Although censorship has officially ended, the government still recognizes Mussolini's concordat with the Vatican forbidding any performances in Rome of plays that would offend against the sacred nature of the Eternal City. There is still control of the repertories of state theaters because of government subsidy. Judges at government-sponsored drama contests screen out plays they consider to be morally or ideologically controversial. Independent theaters, possible havens for experimentation, find it difficult to survive because of crippling taxation.

The wealthier film corporations have always managed to combat censorship, but the theater is not big business in Italy and few dramatists earn their living at playwriting. Despite these difficulties, a number of talented Italians continue to write for the stage. If the government relaxes its controls over state theaters and allows for greater experimentation, the future for the drama may become brighter.

# J

**Jahn, Hans Henny** (1894–1959). German dramatist, novelist, musician, and organ builder. One of the most gifted German artists of the twentieth century, Jahn was also a tragic figure. His quest to overcome the split within himself that was mirrored by the *Doppelgänger* motif in his works ended in suicide. Born in Hamburg, Jahn completed his high school studies just as World War I commenced. He resisted the draft and fled to Norway. Upon his return to Hamburg in 1918, he began writing dramas and studying the organ and church music. His early plays have a religious, mystical atmosphere with characters who are torn by conflicting desires. This atmosphere is also noticeable in Jahn's music and his writings about music. During the 1920s Jahn established a music publishing firm. He also built organs, which were considered to be among the best in Europe. In 1933, on being declared a political risk by the Nazis, he emigrated first to Switzerland, then to Denmark in 1934, where he lived as a farmer. In 1945 he returned to Hamburg.

Jahn's postwar writings reflect the same concern with desolation and disharmony as his early works. His play *Thomas Chatterton* (1956) is most revealing, since it deals with the gifted artist who becomes victimized by his own talents. Jahn makes a plea for society to protect the individual genius both from himself and from the intrusion of unwanted forces. His posthumously published play, *Der staubige Regenbogen* (The Dusty Rainbow, 1961), also picks up this theme in dealing with the tragedy of an atomic physicist. Aside from his postwar plays, Jahn published an important trilogy, *Fluss ohne Ufer* (1949–1960), which explores the links between eroticism, creativity, and perversion, as did his play *Armut, Reichtum, Mensch und Tier* (Poverty, Wealth, Man and Beast, 1948).

OTHER PLAYS SINCE 1945: *Spur des dunklen Engels* (The Trace of the Dark Angel, 1952), *Hier ist ein Neger zu lynchen* (Here Is a Nigger to Lynch, 1957, a revised version of *Strassenecke*, 1931).

**Jardiel Poncela, Enrique** (1901–1952), Spanish dramatist. A steady contributor to humor magazines, a movie scriptwriter, and an impresario, Jardiel Poncela first won a popular following as a novelist. The sum of his theatrical career is eight plays written between 1927 and 1936 and twenty written between 1939 and his death. All were at the time severely condemned by critics,

265

who were unable or unwilling to recognize the novelty of his art. But his attempted renovation of the comic theater through constant technical experimentation, constant violation of normal expectations, was usually appreciated if not always understood by his audiences. Now critics see in *Eloisa está debajo de un almendro* (Eloisa Under an Elm, 1940), for one, the embryo of what might have been a native Spanish "theater of the absurd." It abounds in extravagant situations and labyrinthine confusions, all of which prove at the denouement to answer to an inner logic, a calculated madness. This nonsensical sense, identified if not defined as Jardielesque humor, continues to play an important role in the aesthetics of Miguel Mihura, Víctor Ruiz Iriarte, and José López Rubio. Whether best described as caricature, parody, or farce, the plays elicit a reaction far different from that benign contentment, akin to stupor, induced by the typical Spanish drawing-room comedy.

OTHER PLAYS SINCE 1936: *Los ladrones somos gente honrada* (We're Honest Thieves, 1941), *Madre* (*el drama padre*) (1941), *Los habitantes de la casa deshabitada* (The Inhabitants of a Deserted House, 1942).

**Jellicoe, Ann** (born 1927). English dramatist and director. Born in Middlesborough, Yorkshire, and receiving a North Country education, Ann Jellicoe trained for the stage at the Central School of Speech and Drama, London, where she was awarded the Elsie Fogerty Prize in 1947. She began a career as actress, stage manager, and director in repertory, returning to Central School as a teacher of acting in 1953. In 1951 she founded the Cockpit Theatre Club in London to experiment with the use of the open stage, and there she directed a number of plays. She has directed and collaborated with the directors of her own plays. For a time she ran the Royal Court Theatre's Writers' Group, which explored the use of improvisation and similar creative techniques.

Sharing third prize in the *Observer* 1957 Play Competition, Ann Jellicoe's first play, *The Sport of My Mad Mother*, reflects her interest in the experimental theater. Taking its title from the words of the Hindu hymn "all creation is the sport of my mad mother Kali," it draws on the idiom of a group of teen-age Teddy boys and their girls to create a ritualized pattern of excitement and violence that harks back to the primal mysteries of birth, life, love, and death. The basis of a plot can be discerned in the emergence of one of the girls as the "mad mother" of the title, infused with a magical, savage intensity of life, but it is fruitless—and indeed contrary to the author's expressed aims—to look for any intellectually formulated set of ideas to emerge from action or dialogue. "When I write a play," she has stated, "I am trying to communicate with the audience. I do this by every means in my power—I try to get at them through their eyes, by providing visual action; I try to get at them through their ears, for instance by noises and rhythm . . . I am trying to use every possible effect that the theatre can offer to stir up the audience—to get at them through their emotions." As a consequence the dialogue is more important for its rhythm than its content; patterns of words are repeated endlessly in formulaic fashion, while the action is modulated in a series of rising crescendos more analogous to a musical score than a conventional dramatic plot. A musician who accompanies the action on a range of percussion instruments and converses with the audience reinforces Ann Jellicoe's declared purpose of minimizing the barrier between stage and auditorium. "It is clear from her use of music and dance," wrote critic Kenneth Tynan, "that she knows the direction in which the theatre is moving." In fact, few plays have followed the distinctive style of *The Sport of My Mad Mother*, and its Teddy boy rituals now seem oddly dated. But if the direct influence of the play has been small it still occupies an important place in the history of postwar English drama as an early indication that the revolution sparked by *Look Back in Anger* was less concerned with social protest than with a new quality of vitality in theatrical expression, coupled with a revaluation of the participatory role of the spectator. "The audience," Ann Jellicoe has stated, "is the vital factor in the theatre, more volatile and unpredictable than play or actors, which are, after all, fixed entities."

Unhappily, Ann Jellicoe's second play never reached an audience. Commissioned by the Girl Guide organization for performance at a rally in Wembley Stadium by a cast of eight hundred girls and one hundred boys, *The Rising Generation* (1960) offered an opportunity for bold experimental drama on a monumental scale, but the plot, which included a female conspiracy to eliminate men and expunge them from history, was considered unsuitable and the play was cautiously if not unpredictably rejected.

*The Knack* (1961) is a successful combination of the avant-garde techniques of *The Sport of My Mad Mother* and the familiar material of conventional comedy. Initial objections to its outspoken theme and dialogue overcome, *The Knack* has achieved its due recognition in the accolade of a film version. A frail plot explores the reactions of three young men, "all of us more or less total sexual failures" in Tom's declaration, to the unexpected presence of a girl of plain but engaging simplicity from the provinces. The skill with which Tom, apparently sublimating his drives in frenzied redecoration of his flat, preserves Nancy from Tolen, the omnivorous sexual predator, and gently wakens the timid Colin's interest in the girl provides scope for subtle and occasionally tender observation of character. There is scope, too, in the games devised by Tom to free Colin of his repressions, for excursions in the style of Miss Jellicoe's first play into the world of improvisatory fantasy whose rising excitement conceals an element of violence. "The play," states its author, "is about how you should treat other people, and its form reinforces what it has to say."

Ann Jellicoe has spoken of her interest in symbolism, myth, and ritual (all of which she admits to having used "intuitively" in *The Sport of My Mad Mother*) in terms which reveal the influence of Jungian theory and, perhaps, the limitations to which her technique is subject: "Myths are the bodying forth, in stories, in images, of our longing, conflicts and fears, they give shape to the deepest human urges, often to unspoken, archetypal drives which cannot be formulated wholly in words . . . Ritual is a device we use to give our lives scale and significance, to reassure ourselves as to the importance of our values, to celebrate such values."

Paradoxically, Ann Jellicoe's development as a dramatist has brought her closer to the conventional modes of drama and deprived her work of much of its unusual interest. *Shelley or The Idealist* (1966) is a historical drama with a strong narrative line that, despite some opportunities for experimental production, relies for its effect upon an exploration of Shelley's character and the effect of his fiery social idealism upon the less unworldly aspirations of his wife and lover through the medium of a language alive to delicate shades of nuance and understatement. Albeit subtitled "A Tragicomedy," *Shelley* borrows its structure from a tragic formula that might not have surprised its nineteenth-century protagonist. "Shelley is a tragic hero," writes the dramatist in her preface, "insofar as he was a great man destroyed by his own tragic flaw: his blindness to the frailty of human nature."

An interview with Ann Jellicoe by Jill Pomerance and Michael Anderson appeared in *New Theatre Magazine*, Vol. I, No. 4 (1960). Miss Jellicoe is the author of *Some Unconscious Influences in the Theatre* (1967) and has written a Preface to *Shelley or The Idealist* (1969). Her work is discussed by John Russell Taylor in *Anger and After* (1969).

OTHER PLAYS: *The Giveaway* (1968). Translations: *Rosmersholm* (1959), *The Lady from the Sea* (1961), *The Sea Gull* (1964).

**Jones, LeRoi** (Moslem name: **Ameer Baraka**; born 1934). American poet, playwright, and essayist. Born in Newark, New Jersey, Jones traveled through the world of white success back to a self-chosen black community. He has a B.A. in English from Howard University and did graduate work at Columbia and the New School for Social Research. He was awarded a Whitney Fellowship in 1961 and a Guggenheim in 1964. After a period of social and artistic lionization by white liberals in New York, Jones moved from Greenwich Village to Harlem, where he founded the Black Arts Repertory Theatre in 1965, and then from Harlem to Newark and Spirit House, a black community center and theater group, which he directs in the development of latent African virtues. Jones is also spiritual leader of this Moslem (Kawaida) community.

In addition to a large number of broadsides, Jones has published several volumes of verse: *Preface to a Twenty Volume Suicide Note* (1961), *The Dead Lecturer* (1964), *Black Art* (1966), and *Black Magic* (1969). He has issued three books of essays, contributed poetry and prose to various journals, edited anthologies of black literature, and written one autobiographical novel and one book of short stories.

In 1964 Jones won an Obie for *Dutchman,* which many still consider his best play. In "the subway heaped in modern myth" a white woman provokes and kills a black man; the others in the car dispose of his body and Lula readies herself for her next ritual victim in this endless ride of human damnation. Jones said in a 1964 interview that *Dutchman* "is about the difficulty of becoming a man in America." *The Baptism, The Toilet,* and *The Slave,* produced off-Broadway that same year, continue this theme with a violence in subject matter that becomes even more pronounced in later work.

*Experimental Death Unit # One* (1965), *A Black Mass* (1966), *Great Goodness of Life: A Coon Show* (1967), and *Madheart* (1967) are published together as *Four Black Revolutionary Plays* (1969) and are all animated in one way or another by Jones's axiom that "We must eliminate the white man before we will ever be able to draw a free breath on this planet." In the same volume reference is made to *J-E-L-L-O* (1965), which the publisher refused to print because it attacks a public figure's private life, but which Jones asserts has been seen by more black people than most plays (aside from television productions). He has also published *Arm Yourself or Harm Yourself* (1967).

In his search for "the play that will split the heavens for us . . . called *The Destruction of America*" Jones has since 1965 been writing propaganda drama for restricted audiences, though in 1969 his historical pageant *Slave Ship* was seen off-Broadway and *Great Goodness of Life,* billed as *Black Quartet,* with three plays by other black writers had a New York run and went on national tour in the 1970s. The *leitmotiv* of Jones's current spirit and work is the subtitle to his volume of revolutionary plays: "All Praises to the Black Man."

**Jotuni, Maria [Gustava]** (1880–1943). Finnish playwright and novelist. Jotuni studied literature at the University of Helsinki; her husband, Viljo Tarkiainen, was a professor of Finnish literature. Her classic comedies of love, crisp, aphoristic, and antisentimental, were followed by two posthumous plays published after the war. *Klaus, Louhikon herra* (Klaus, the Lord of Louhikko, 1946) is a tragedy based on a subject from Finnish folk poetry; its tone and large-scale structure remind one of Renaissance drama. *Amerikan morsian* (The Bride from America, 1966) was discovered much later, following the publication of a long and important novel. It is a comedy of marriage, showing the self-centered, adolescent egoism of the middle-aged husband, a shoemaker, as a contrast to the humbleness and wisdom of the wife. Jotuni's late works are a profound protest against inter-war primitivism and worship of power. *Maria Jotunin näytelmät* (1964) by Irmeli Niemi is a study of Jotuni's plays.

# K

**Karinthy, Ferenc** (born 1921). Hungarian playwright, journalist, and fiction writer. A son of the outstanding Hungarian writer Frigyes Karinthy, Ferenc Karinthy studied Hungarian philology in Budapest. His first book, a novel, was published as early as 1943, but it was only after the war that he seriously embarked on a literary career. His narrative talent and genuine, occasionally ribald, humor made his short stories and sketches widely popular. His first play, *Ezer év* (A Thousand Years, 1955), directed public attention to the problem of secret abortions in Hungary. This problem had assumed frightening proportions, partly as a result of Draconic laws that were rescinded a few years later and partly because of society's ignorance on sexual matters. *Budapesti tavasz* (Budapest Spring, 1953–1956) tells of the tragic love affair of a young ex-student deserter and a Jewish girl during the siege of Budapest in 1944; the play ends with the arrival of the Russian troops and the dawn of a new era. Yet Karinthy's most authentic works to date are his one-act plays, published in the collection *Hét játék* (Seven Plays, 1969). These include *Bősendorfer* (Steinway Grand) and *Duna-kanyar* (At the Bend of the Danube), both written in 1966, and the witty *Gőz* (Steam, 1968). These short plays are skillful variations on a single theme, intimate duets in which all possibilities of laughter and surprise are explored. Some of Karinthy's one-act plays were translated into English and performed in Boston in 1969.

**Kartoteka** (The Card Index, 1960). A play by Tadeusz Różewicz. "The play's 'Hero' is of indeterminate age, occupation, and appearance. . . . The play is realistic and takes place in the present. The chair is real. . . ." Thus writes the author about his first play, *Kartoteka,* a work most characteristic of his own dramatic output and of the Polish brand of the theater of the absurd. The play consists of loosely connected scenes in which the "hero" encounters successively a number of stylized characters—among them his relatives, a journalist, a young German girl—who meet him, as it were, in various phases of his life. There is no "real time" and the different periods are treated as present. The "hero's" name changes constantly; he is a contemporary Everyman, challenged by grotesque, farcical, and pathetic figures.

The form of the play is dramatically evocative if we consider that the hero does not leave his room, indeed, his bed, and the room seems to be situated at some symbolic crossroads of space (Warsaw, standing for Poland) and history. The author describes through his "hero" the troubled experiences of his generation, which had lived through the war and the postwar period of transition. The confrontation of the disjointed bits of that past with the realities of the contemporary world, and the representatives of a new generation, imbues the play with considerable dramatic power. It is also a poetic play, related in its diction to Różewicz's own austere "anti-poetic" poetry. *The Card Index* contains also many quotations and parodies of literary styles and has the distinction, like Mrożek's *Tango*, of being at the same time an uproarious comedy and almost a national drama. Under a frivolous surface it is, in fact, one of the most important plays to have been written in Poland since World War II.

**Karvaš, Peter.** See CZECHOSLOVAKIA.

**Kennedy, Adrienne** (born 1931). American playwright. Miss Kennedy was born in Pittsburgh, grew up in Cleveland, and attended Ohio State University. At the age of twenty she began writing and in 1962 joined Edward Albee's Playwrights' Workshop. Her play *The Funny House of a Negro* appeared off-Broadway and was awarded an Obie in 1964. *The Owl Answers,* a one-act play dedicated to Albee, was produced off-Broadway in 1965. *A Rat's Mass* was presented by the Theatre Company of Boston in 1966. *In His Own Write,* an adaptation of John Lennon's book, was produced in London, where Miss Kennedy now lives, by the National Theatre Company in 1967. She has also written the plays *A Lesson in Dead Language* and *A Beast's Story* (off-Broadway, 1969), as well as novels, stories, and poems.

There is a cryptic quality in Miss Kennedy's plays that is both tantalizing and confusing; a deliberate merging of several levels of being so that, unlike the transformations used by Megan Terry, where an actor "plays with a set of quick-changing realities," a character is simultaneously several beings (in *The Owl Answers,* for example, the list of characters includes "SHE who is CLARA PASSMORE who is the VIRGIN MARY who is the BASTARD who is the OWL" and "BASTARD'S BLACK MOTHER who is the REVEREND'S WIFE who is ANNE BOLEYN"); this complexification of character coupled with stylized patterns of action and the frequent use of Catholic religious symbols gives Miss Kennedy's plays the feeling of ritual, pure drama freed from literal representationalism.

**Kerndl, Rainer** (born 1928). East German dramatist, poet, journalist, and critic. After being released from a prisoner of war camp in 1948, Kerndl returned to East Germany and began working as a journalist. During this time he began to write stories and poems and to develop his talent as a drama critic. In 1961 he tried his hand at playwriting and produced his first play, *Schatten eines Mädchens* (Shadows of a Girl). Most of his dramas bring out Germany's Nazi past and seek to deal with the problems of overcoming this past in East Germany. In *Seine Kinder* (His Children, 1963) Karl Sorge, a party organizer, returns to his hometown in order to settle down and determine why certain projects involving an electric plant have not been completed. The time is the present (1960s) and the mistakes of the 1930s and 1940s are recalled to point the way to the solution of both economic and familial problems. In *Die seltsame Reise des Alois Fingerlein* (The Strange Journey of Alois Fingerlein, 1967) a simple farmer undergoes great transformations in the period from World War II to the present. As he travels, he loses his naïveté and becomes more conscious of the class struggle. He is disillusioned by Nazis and capitalists alike and finally finds his place in East Germany. In *Der verratene Rebell* (The Betrayed Rebel, 1968) Kerndl gives a semidocumentary account of the unsuccessful attempt to assassinate Hitler on July 20, 1944. The focus is not so much on Hitler but on the reactionary conspirators who are merely concerned with eliminating Hitler and gaining power, not in changing Germany. Kerndl constantly casts East Germany in the light of a promised land. Though his writing bespeaks a great degree of honesty and social conviction, his honesty borders on puritanism, which obscures the problematical nature of the postwar development in East Germany.

OTHER PLAYS: *Pläydoyer für die Suchenden* (Plea for the Seekers, 1965), *Ich bin einem Mädchen begegnet* (The Girl I met, 1970).

**Kingsley, Sidney** (born 1906). American playwright, director, and producer. Born in New York City, graduated from Cornell (B.A. 1928), Kingsley was a popular prewar playwright, who produced and directed most of his own plays on Broadway. *Men in White* won the Pulitzer Prize and Theatre Club Award in 1933 and was made into a film in 1934; *Dead End* won a second Theatre Club Award in 1935 and was made into a film in 1937; *Ten Million Ghosts* appeared in 1936, *The World We Make* in 1939, and *The Patriots,* winner of the Drama Critics Circle and several other awards, in 1943. Since World War II Kingsley has presented *Detective Story* (1949), winner of the Edgar Allan Poe Award, made into a film in 1951; *Darkness at Noon* (1951), an adaptation of a novel by Arthur Koestler, winner of the Drama Critics Circle Award; and the farce *Lunatics and Lovers* (1954) and *Night Life* (1962), both failures. In most of his work Kingsley relies on a sense of atmosphere generated by realistic re-creation of a particular world—hospitals, slums, police stations, prisons—a vivid milieu that supplies much of the dramatic impact of the play and also constitutes its limitation. The plays are frequently melodramatic in plot and sketchy in characterization; timely issues have made them at first appear more substantial than they later are seen to be. For example, the attack on Stalinist Russia in *Darkness at Noon* seemed starkly realistic to a 1950s audience worried about Communism; a decade or two later the play's sentimentality was more apparent and its interest diminished.

**Kipphardt, Heinar** (born 1922). West German playwright, essayist, novelist, and physician. Though he left East Germany to settle in the West, Kipphardt has maintained his independence as a Marxist writer, and this integrity is reflected in all his works. He began his career while studying medicine in East Berlin. From 1950 to 1959 he worked at the Charité Hospital, while serving as chief dramaturge of the Deutsches Theater. His first play, *Shakespeare dringend gesucht* (Shakespeare Urgently Sought, 1952), records his experiences as a dramaturge. The play is a satire about young dramatists in East Germany who try to pawn off second-rate plays dealing with social problems as topnotch dramas. The comedy is critical not only of the general practice of East German theaters at that time but also of the political hypocrisy of people who do not really believe in socialism. In another play, *Der Aufstieg des Alois Piontek* (The Rise of Alois Piontek, 1956), he portrayed bureaucratic life in East Germany as a farce.

Because of various pressures, Kipphardt decided to move to West Germany in 1959. *Die Stühle des Herrn Smil* (The Chairs of Mr. Smil, 1961), an adaptation of the Russian novel *Twelve Chairs*, by Ilf and Petrov, was produced there. Kipphardt continued his satirical writing in the West by debunking the "new economic policies" of Russia at the end of the 1920s. Kipphardt was concerned not so much with Russian policies as with the corruption and incompetence within the contemporary bureaucratic state.

After the satires, Kipphardt turned to the documentary mode and produced his three most important plays, which have given him the reputation of being West Germany's leading documentary dramatist. Schooled in the Brechtian tradition, Kipphardt works with spare language and hypotactic structures to reconsider the evidence of disputed political cases. In *Der Hund des Generals* (The General's Dog, 1962) he places a German officer on trial for sending an entire regiment of soldiers to their deaths because one of them had accidentally killed his pet dog. Though graphically portrayed, the general's inhumanity is not the main point of the drama. Kipphardt is more concerned with the fact that this general (among others) is a free, respected citizen in West Germany today. The past, according to Kipphardt, has been buried all too quickly by the guilty, and guilt is only felt by the few who have opened themselves to the truth. In his next play, *In the Matter of J. Robert Oppenheimer* (*In der Sache J. Robert Oppenheimer*, 1964), the question of German guilt gives way to the question of universal guilt and responsibility. Here Kipphardt uses the transcripts of the Atomic Energy Commission's investigation committee to show that Oppenheimer as a scientist sacrificed the good of humanity to the interests of an irresponsible state. Like Brecht's Galileo, Oppenheimer eventually repents his past activities and refuses to be further employed as a tool of the American government. Kipphardt's antipathy for devious and inhumane political institutions and their tools is demonstrated also in *Joel Brand: Geschichte eines Geschäfts* (Joel Brand: The History of a Deal, 1965), in which the Eichmann proposition to exchange one million Jews for ten thousand trucks is undermined by the intrigues of petty governmental bureaucrats. In laying bare the hypocritical position of the Americans and English in this documentary drama, Kipphardt does not apologize for the Germans. He bluntly questions the basis of political action and examines the position of minority groups caught in a power struggle between larger nations. In doing so, Kipphardt, who moved from East to West, has come to challenge the claims of the "democratic" West. Recently he has returned to the satirical mode, and in *Die Nacht, in der der Chef geschlachtet wurde* (The Night the Boss Was Slaughtered, 1967) he parodies an average West German couple who dream about fleeing the confines of bourgeois life. Their dreams are nightmare pictures of the wish-fulfillments conditioned by capitalist advertising, and they reflect their crass cultural "ideals." Kipphardt means to bring out the contradictions in bourgeois capitalism, which drain human beings of sensitivity. His latest work is an adaptation of J. R. M. Lenz's *Die Soldaten* (The Soldiers), which makes the contours of Lenz's attack on the military and the bourgeoisie of the eighteenth century much sharper.

**Kleineidam, Horst** (born 1932). East German dramatist. At the close of World War II, Kleineidam began working as a weaver and carpenter in East Germany. In 1952 he decided to go to the West, and he took jobs as a farmhand and miner. It was during this period that he began to write, and, after returning to East Germany in 1958, he studied at the Johannes R. Becher Literaturinstitut and produced some of his plays with amateur groups. Like numerous other young East German dramatists, Kleineidam focuses on problems of the workers and the conditions under which they work. He also incorporates the generation conflict into his plays, which lends them a certain historical importance. In *Von Riesen und Menschen* (About Giants and Humans, 1967), he takes a sentence from Engels for his theme: "The Renaissance needed giants and created them." So it is with the socialist state East Germany. A young dynamic engineer, Ulrich Barhaupt, wants to make experiments and improvements at a factory directed by his father, a more conservative and pragmatic worker. After various quarrels, Ulrich undertakes an experiment that fails. The father magnanimously covers up for the son, and they agree that they must combine experience with originality to make the changes necessary for the development of the factory. The play is grounded in the real conflict in East Germany between young radical technocrats, who insist on quality and change, and conservative bureaucrats, who resist experimentation. Kleineidam's play is weak in that it only hints at the real power struggle inside and outside the party, which has no easy solution.

OTHER PLAYS: *Der Millionenschmidt* (1962).

**Klinger, Kurt** (born 1928). Austrian dramatist, poet, critic, and short-story writer. As it did on many other men of his generation, World War II made a strong impression on Klinger, and his plays reveal an intense desire to strip away the illusions in life in order to attain truth and social justice. After studying at the University of Vienna, Klinger worked as actor, director, and dramaturge in Linz, Düsseldorf, and Frankfurt, and began writing his own plays. In his best drama, *Odysseus muss wieder reisen* (Odysseus Must Travel Again, 1954), he uses motifs from the Greek epic to portray problems of the postwar epoch in Austria and Germany. Here Telemachus rejects the return of his father, Odysseus, defeats him in battle, and sends him on his way because Odysseus represents a generation that understands only patriarchal domination and war. Telemachus intends to bring peace to Ithaca and institute social reforms. Klinger's drama is a classically structured *Heimkehrer* drama, one of the many produced in Austria and Germany that deal with the problems of returning soldiers. Here, unlike the situation in Wolfgang Borchert's *Draussen vor der Tür*, the soldier is rejected because he brings with him a militarism that cannot rebuild society. Klinger also questions the mission of the poet in *Der goldene Käfig* (The Golden Cage, 1955) and argues that real potential can be developed only if self-knowledge is achieved. His most recent work has broken with traditional forms and moves toward surrealism in an effort to find the border line between reality and illusion.

OTHER PLAYS: *Treibjagd auf Menschen* (Manhunt, 1953), *Der Weg ins Nordland* (The Way to the North Country, 1955), *Der Lauf der Welt* (The Course of the World, 1957), *Das kleine Weltkabarett* (The Small World Cabaret, 1958), *La Sera* (1959), *Die neue Wohnung* (The New Apartment, 1959), *Wer die Wahl hat* (Whoever Has the Choice, 1960).

**Kokkonen, Lauri** (born 1918). Finnish playwright. Kokkonen is a school inspector living in Middle Finland. His first plays were sympathetic analyses of present-day village society: *Hopeinen kynttilänjalka* (Silvery Chandelier, 1958) and *Laahus* (Bridal Veil, 1958). *Viimeiset kiusaukset* (The Last Temptations, 1960) presents the life of Paavo Ruotsalainen, a well-known pietistic folk leader and hymn writer, as a series of visions the hero sees on his deathbed. Breaking with the formulas of the usual biographic play, Kokkonen shows conflicts between theory and practice, faith and doubt, in the career of this religious leader. The playwright uses free verse and a speaking and dancing chorus as elements in his boldly stylized and elliptic stage techniques.

**Kopit, Arthur** (born 1937). American playwright. Born in New York City, Kopit attended Harvard University. In his last three years as an undergraduate, he won two playwriting contests and had nine plays produced (six of which he directed). *The Questioning of Nick, Gemini, Don Juan in Texas* (written with Wally Lawrence), *On the Runway of Life You Never Know What's Coming Off Next, Across the River and Into the Jungle, Aubade, Sing to Me Through Open Windows,* and *To Dwell in a Palace of Strangers* were seen in Cambridge, Massachusetts, between 1957 and 1959. The play that he wrote while on a postgraduate traveling fellowship brought him sudden international attention: *Oh Dad, Poor Dad, Mamma's Hung You in the Closet and I'm Feelin' So Sad.* First produced by a group at Harvard in January of 1960, it was given productions in London (1961), New York (1962), and Paris (1963). The tendency toward ebullient parody and rhetorical effervescence

275

that gives *Oh Dad* an adolescent quality (a highly competitive 135 I.Q. type of adolescence) carries over to Kopit's next play produced in New York, *The Day the Whores Came Out to Play Tennis* (1965), which is clever but indicates no advance over his earlier work. Whatever relation Kopit's plays may have to theater of the absurd seems to come from his joy of capering in intellectually modish forms and not from a shared vision. With *Indians* (1969), however, despite its similarity to other grand multimedia productions on Broadway, Kopit gets closer to a style of his own; here, at least, the drama is a complex, not just a joke. Whether all this talent and energy will find something to say remains to be seen.

**Kops, Bernard** (born 1928). English dramatist. A minor but attractive figure among contemporary playwrights, Kops is the son of Jewish working-class parents from London's East End. Leaving school at thirteen he moved from job to job until he began to write, graduating from poems to a novel and ending as a dramatist writing for radio and the stage. The title of the first, and perhaps the most successful, of his plays indicates its aspirations; but more successful than the contrived Shakespearian allusion in *The Hamlet of Stepney Green* (1956) is the shrewdly observed picture of what the author calls "the dying Jewish community of the East End of London" in a sentimental comedy that "laments a world that has passed away." Against a background of lively and spontaneous bursts of song and dance that reminded some critics of traditional Yiddish theater, David Levy, a young and introspective dreamer, vows to avenge his father's death. By a pleasantly ironic twist it is the ghost of the father who encourages reconciliation and persuades the son to return amicably to the family pickled-herring stall. A new stage in Kops's development was marked by *The Dream of Peter Mann* (1961), written while Kops was resident dramatist with the Bristol Old Vic Company. Although the sentimental picture of Jewish life is not abandoned, the dominant element is one of satirical fantasy in an attack upon materialistic values in a world heading for nuclear destruction. *Enter Solly Gold* (1962) successfully returns to the less pretentious themes of his earlier work with the amusing portrait of a likable confidence trickster posing as a rabbi whose dizzying success is halted only when, persuaded that honesty is the best policy, he finds himself abandoned by all those to whom his deceit has brought happiness.

Two later plays, written for radio after a visit to Eastern Europe, are more pessimistic in tone. *Home Sweet Honeycomb* and *The Lemmings* (both 1963) deal in ambitiously symbolic terms with the individual's struggle against the pressures of society and end on a hopeless note. In the former play this struggle is seen in the capitulation of the hero in a world governed by advertising slogans, in which failure to conform is punished instantly by death; in the latter play it takes the form of a headlong, inexplicable rush to destruction. "Instead of a dying community," writes Kops of the theme of his later work, "it has now become the dying of the human race."

**276**

Kops is the author of an autobiography, *The World Is a Wedding*. OTHER PLAYS: *Goodbye, World* (1959), *Change for the Angel* (1960), *Stray Cats and Empty Bottles* (1962).

**Korneichuk, Aleksandr Evdokomovich** (1905–1972). Soviet dramatist. Born in the Ukraine, Korneichuk's early plays, *Na grani* (On the Border, 1929), *Kamenny ostrov* (Island of Stone, 1929), and *Shturm* (Storm, 1931), deal with the struggles against Ukrainian nationalism during the early years of the Soviet regime. *Gibel eskadry* (Destruction of the Squadron, 1933) describes the fate of a Bolshevik Black Sea naval squadron during the civil war. *Platon Krechet* (1934) is a study of the problems of the Soviet intelligentsia. *Bogdan Khmelnitskii* (1939) is a historical epic dealing with the integration of national minorities into the Soviet Union. The latter two plays jointly won a Stalin prize in 1941. *V stepakh Ukrainy* (In the Steppes of the Ukraine, 1941) deals with problems of collective farm life. Korneichuk's war dramas include *Partizany v stepakh Ukrainy* (Partisans in the Steppes of the Ukraine, 1942) and *Front* (The Front, 1942). *Makar Dubrava* (1948), which won a Stalin prize in 1949, concerns a Donets Basin miner and his hopes for the building of Communism after the war. *Kalinovaya roshcha* (The Guelder-rose Grove, 1950), which ridicules sluggards in socialist labor, won a Stalin prize in 1951.

**Kortner, Fritz** (1892–1970). Austrian actor, director, and dramatist. Kortner's career can be divided into two distinct phases: that as an actor until 1949 and that as a director up to his death. He was born in Vienna as Nathan Kohn (he changed his name in 1916) and studied at the renowned Burgtheater. Kortner made his acting debut in 1910 at the National Theater in Mannheim, Germany; the next year he moved to Berlin, where he had small roles at the Deutsches Theater. After this engagement he worked at theaters in Dresden, Vienna, and Hamburg. Kortner finally achieved stature as the leading expressionist actor of his time in 1919 when he played the title role in Ernst Toller's *Die Wandlung*. During the next decade Kortner was primarily active at the Berliner Staatstheater. He continued to develop his expressionist method of acting, which gradually gave way to a realistic mode in such plays as *Hamlet, The Merchant of Venice,* and *Oedipus*. By 1933 Kortner decided to leave Germany, and he emigrated to the United States in 1938, where he acted in various films. When he returned to Germany in 1949, he began to make a new name for himself as a director. Most of his productions involved long and intensive rehearsals. Kortner emphasized realistic detail and precision in an almost Promethean quest for truth onstage. He was most successful with the plays of Strindberg, Shakespeare, Schiller, and Frisch, which he endowed with psychological insights and moral fervor that pertain to contemporary social problems.

PLAYS: *Donauwellen* (The Waves of the Danube, 1949), *Zwiesprache* (Dialogue, 1964).

**Kruczkowski, Leon** (1900–1962). Polish dramatist. Kruczkowski was born in Cracow and after technical studies there worked for a while in the chemical industry, then taught in vocational schools. An active socialist from his youth, he remained connected with the movement of the left throughout his life. In the '30s Kruczkowski won acclaim with historical novels, in which he stressed hitherto neglected social problems. An army officer in the 1939 September campaign, he spent the war years as a prisoner of war in Germany. After the war Kruczkowski engaged in direct political activity. He was vice-minister of Culture and Art (1945–1948) and president of Polish Writers' Union (1949–1956). He was also a deputy to the Seym and, from 1957 until his death, a member of the Council of State. He was awarded the Lenin Prize in 1953.

Kruczkowski's plays are largely political in their content. In his first play, written before the war, *Przygoda z Vaterlandem* (The Adventure with Vaterland, 1938), he warns of the danger of fascism, which he sees as arising directly out of the nationalist feelings inherent in the Germans. Kruczkowski's most famous drama, *Niemcy* (The Germans, 1949), deals directly with the problem of the moral responsibility of the German people for war crimes. An eminent liberal scholar of Göttingen, Professor Sonnenbruch, tries to live with his family through the Nazi period in splendid isolation, but his failure is inevitable when he is faced with his former pupil and assistant, an anti-Nazi, who has escaped from a concentration camp and is trying to find refuge in his house. The professor's family is more directly involved with the war: His son is an officer of the S.S.; his invalid wife a fanatical Nazi; his daughter-in-law enraged against all those who do not support the German cause and embittered by her husband's death at the front and the death of her children in an air raid. The professor's daughter, an artiste, is probably least affected by the moral inertia, or the opportunism, that paralyzes "decent" citizens like her father; it is she who tries to help the assistant. In another play on war themes, *Pierwszy dzień wolności* (The First Day of Freedom, 1959), Kruczkowski showed a group of Polish officers, just liberated from a camp for prisoners of war, who take up quarters in a German home and help a local doctor's family. Human considerations prove insufficient when the town is threatened by stray German Army units and group solidarity has to be reasserted. An issue of the cold war was treated by Kruczkowski in *Juliusz i Ethel* (1953), an anti-American, dramatically successful plea based on the Rosenberg case. He was less successful in two plays on postwar Polish themes: *Odwety* (Retaliations, 1948), an arbitrary indictment of the anti-Communist underground, and *Odwiedziny* (The Visit, 1954), which deals with postwar changes in the Polish countryside. In his last play, ŚMIERĆ GUBERNATORA (Death of the Governor, 1961), Kruczkowski moved successfully toward a new, broader dramatic form and a story not involving any immediate political issues.

A staunch representative of realism in dramatic form, Kruczkowski was regarded as the "official" dramatist of postwar Poland. It would be wrong, however, to dismiss his plays as mere propaganda vehicles. Though prone to equate the proper political attitudes with the right moral motives, and the other way around (which resulted in an oversimplification of issues and a bias, particularly in his plays with a Polish setting), he had a gift for exploring genuinely dramatic situations. His analysis of German problems and character was fair and to the point, doubtless because the connection between politics and moral attitudes was clearly applicable in this context. It is not by chance that his plays with German themes have been widely performed in Germany, both East and West. Perhaps Kruczkowski's most remarkable achievement consisted in reviving politically committed drama and, in his last plays, broadening the concept of it through the use of nonrealistic devices.

OTHER PLAYS SINCE 1945: *Grzech* (Sin, reworked from a play by Stefan Żeromski, 1951).

**Kuba** [pen name of **Kurt Barthel**] (1914–1967). East German dramatist, poet, and film writer. During his youth Kuba worked as a painter and interior decorator. He soon joined the Socialist Party and was forced to flee Germany in 1933 because of his anti-Fascist activities. He lived for a time in Prague, and then in England, where he worked as a farmer and wrote poetry. In 1946 he returned to East Germany and continued to write poetry as well as short stories and journalistic reports. Kuba is best known for his poems and even his two plays are written in verse. *Klaus Störtebecker* is a dramatic ballad celebrating the achievements of a famous German folk hero of the fourteenth century who stole from the rich and gave to the poor. *Terra Incognita* also has folk elements: It recalls the long search for and discovery of oil by thousands of workers on East German soil in 1961. Kuba endeavored to poeticize the pioneer spirit in East Germany. However, the epic form tends to be too unwieldy for his songs of praise.

**Kühnelt, Hans Friedrich** (born 1918). Austrian dramatist and poet. After studying electrical engineering in Austria, Kühnelt moved to Munich, where he took a job as technician with the Bavarian Machine Works. However, he soon became interested in acting and left his position to join the Munich Kammerspiele. World War II interrupted his acting career for several years. In 1946 he resumed his stage work at the Landestheater in Salzburg and also began writing dramas. His prime concern is with the inexplicable nature of the universe and the position of man in regard to technology and automation. In his best play, *Ein Tag mit Edward* (A Day With Edward, 1953), a robot becomes human but then allows himself to be dismantled by the firm that made him. The problems confronting the human race are too much for the machine to handle. Kühnelt does not employ a biting satire but, in most of his plays, fills his humorous social criticism with melancholy. Essentially, his dramas bemoan the pathetic condition of man in the scientific age.

OTHER PLAYS: *Spass muss sein* (There Has to Be Joking, 1947), *Der*

# L

**La MaMa Experimental Theatre Club.** A coffeehouse theater group in New York City. Founded in 1962 as the Café La MaMa by Ellen Stewart, this showcase was to be a place where new plays by new playwrights could be given inexpensive production (about $200) for a few performances by a sympathetic and innovative company of artists. After a series of moves and readjustments occasioned by various city regulations, La MaMa reorganized as a private membership club and settled into its own building a few blocks from its original harassed location in the East Village. Miss Stewart, who works during the day as a fashion designer, has borne most of the expense of the theater herself. Now La MaMa is one of the most significant of the off-off-Broadway groups, both with regard to the playwrights it has fostered (Megan Terry, Rochelle Owens, Sam Shepard, Leonard Melfi, Tom Eyen, Jean-Claude van Itallie, and Lanford Wilson, for example) and the skill of its productions, which, despite limitations of time and money, approach total theater, integrating word, gesture, music, and dance. The La MaMa company is particularly noted for its ensemble body motions, controlled and perfectly coordinated so that "ugly" subjects, like the bestiality and violence in *Futz*, become beautiful theatrical experiences. The La MaMa troupe has made several European tours and many of its plays are available in print.

**Landscape** (1969). A play by Harold Pinter. Denied a license for performance shortly before the abolition of stage censorship, this short play was presented on B.B.C. radio in 1968 before appearing on the stage in a double bill with *Silence*. Like its companion in the double bill, *Landscape* reflects the influence of Samuel Beckett in the reduction of action on stage and communication between its characters to the vanishing point, but its style and structure may also be interpreted as a direct development of Pinter's earlier work. In the kitchen of a country house a man and woman sit on opposite sides of a long kitchen table, speaking intermittently. "Duff refers normally to Beth," directs Pinter, "but does not appear to hear her voice. Beth never looks at Duff, and does not appear to hear his voice." While Beth talks dreamily of a love affair in the distant past, Duff recounts the trivia of his recent experience, apparently undeterred by the failure to arouse his wife's interest. In Pinter's customary style the normal expository techniques of dramatic writing are abandoned. The past events to which the two constantly refer do not illuminate their background so much as form the stuff of their present existence. Beth's tender reverie and her husband's roughness of expression establish the two separate worlds of experience that mark their failure to communicate. But as the play progresses to its climax the importance of a critical moment in their earlier lives does become distinct, although the extent to which the actual facts coincide with their separate memories of them is left for the spectator to judge. The crisis occurred when Duff returned home after a journey with his employer to confess that he had been unfaithful to his wife. ("The girl herself I considered unimportant," he says. "I didn't think it necessary to go into details. I decided against it.") But he has returned to a wife whose ephemeral love affair during his absence has cut her off from him forever. After his momentary aberration Duff's simple life continues to be located in the everyday world of his present experience, while Beth's is rooted in a single moment of time.

With great delicacy Pinter uses a pattern of contrapuntal imagery to link the distant and contrasting worlds of Duff and Beth. As Beth's memory returns to the dunes of the beach where she made love, Duff talks of yesterday's walk "as far as the pond." While she relives a visit to a hotel bar with her lover, Duff recounts an argument over the quality of the beer in his local pub. Pinter's dialogue in *Landscape* seems at first to be composed of arbitrary utterances separated by impregnable silences, but a close analysis of its verbal structure reveals that speech follows speech with an inner necessity comparable to that of the developing action in an Aristotelian well-made play.

Pinter's early plays had been praised by most critics for their essentially theatrical qualities, and by removing action and personal conflict from direct representation on the stage he seemed to many critics to be taking a retrogressive step. But the qualities that marked Pinter's previous work recur in a more subtle form in *Landscape*. The problem of verification, which had previously so preoccupied the dramatist, reappears in Beth's perpetual effort to re-create a past experience. The incursion of unexplained violence is reformulated as an aspect of male sexuality when Duff, at the climax of the play, recalls his return to his wife: "I took the chain off and the thimble, the keys, the scissors slid off it and clattered down. I booted the gong down the hall. The dog came in. I thought you would come to me, I thought you would come into my arms and kiss me, even . . . offer yourself to me. I would have had you in front of the dog, like a man, in the hall, on the stone, banging the gong . . ." The mystery of sexual surrender, which in the plays leading to and including *The Homecoming* (1965) had been expressed by Pinter's interest in the figure of the whore, is transformed into the gentleness of Beth's closing words: "My hand on his rib. (*Pause*) So sweetly the sand over me. Tiny the sand on my skin. (*Pause*) So silent the sky in my eyes. Gently the sound of the tide. (*Pause*) Oh my true love I said."

As Pinter's work developed, the external violence of his earlier plays became internalized, reappearing as an aspect of human psychology. In *Landscape* Pinter carries this process of internalization further than ever before, to produce a work which, so far from being static, vividly dramatizes the essential and irreconcilable conflict between the coarse physicality of man and the tender submissiveness of woman.

**Lange, Hartmut** (born 1937). West German dramatist. Like Heinar Kipphardt before him, Lange left East Germany because he wanted more freedom to write and produce dramas with heavy social and political criticism, and, like Kipphardt, he has maintained a Marxist point of view despite his disillusionment with the socialist experiments in East Germany. Before coming to West Germany in 1965, Lange studied film at the Deutsche Hochschule für Filmkunst in East Berlin and worked at the Deutsches Theater. He adapted and translated plays by Molière, Shakespeare, Jonson, and Yevgeni Schwarz, but none of his own plays were produced. This was most likely due to their witty and candid portrayal of the contradictions and conditions in East Germany. Lange is undoubtedly one of the most talented younger dramatists schooled in the Brechtian tradition who is seeking ways to continue this tradition without harassment.

In *Senftenberger Erzählungen oder die Enteignung* (Stories of Senftenberg, or The Expropriation, written 1960) he juxtaposes twelve scenes in a dialectical exposition about the manipulations of Brack, the owner of a supermarket, who endeavors to undermine the collective enterprise of a factory during a period of economic crisis. Measures are finally taken against Brack the capitalist. His supermarket is expropriated by the state. His store and its supplies are used for socialist purposes. The same problem, individualism versus collectivism, is examined in *Marski* (written 1963, produced 1966), wherein the huge farmer Marski must learn to curb his appetite when he is deserted by his friends whom he had "enslaved" by making them work off loans on his farm. The friends all decide to join a farmer collective and share in the benefits. Marski learns that he cannot handle his farm alone, and his friends prove to him that his gargantuan appetite can be satisfied by the collective. In both *Senftenberger Erzählungen* and *Marski,* Lange reveals an uncanny gift for portraying folk characters. His language is poetic and lively, and he has a remarkable eye for capturing those elements that lead to conflict in a country that is in the process of developing socialist programs. Lange goes one step further than Brecht did in depicting the great potential of individualists who can be trained to serve a socialist cause. He also shows that the needs of the people may somehow force them to work against socialism in moments of desperation. Their appetites must be satisfied and their power channeled so that they do not destroy the development of socialism.

Lange's most ambitious treatment of this theme is a combination of two one-act plays written between 1964 and 1967, *Der Hundsprozess* (The Dog's

Trial) and *Herakles*. The plays are dialectically placed side by side because Lange wants to lash Stalinist totalitarianism and also study the helplessness of Stalin. *Der Hundsprozess* is a didactic parable in seven scenes in which Lange satirizes the Soviet domination of smaller countries. He employs a terse, rhythmic language, a chorus of apes, a political priest subject to fits of frenzy, and a bumbling grand inquisitor, all in an effort to ridicule the Soviet bureaucrats. The bureaucrats trump up charges against Karpantua, the leader of a small country under Soviet control, who wants *real* socialism. In the play the Soviets are called Dshugaschwilists and worship a monstrous portrait of Josef Dshugaschwili (Stalin). The picture is smashed over the head of the grand inquisitor by Karpantua, who refuses to go through the routine of humiliating himself in a show of obsequiousness to the father country. Karpantua is consequently placed on trial. His friends and followers are changed into dogs and he is executed. The mock trial demonstrates the animal brutality of totalitarian regimes. In *Herakles* Lange takes a different approach to Stalinism: Heracles becomes a metaphor for Dshugaschwili. Here Lange portrays a giant who is fed lies, and, because of these lies, he kills innocent youths. Lange focuses on two myths in which Heracles pushes Iphitos from the tower and accidentally kills Eurynomous in a moment of wrath. Heracles is not so much a murderer as he is a victim of his own power. Once again Lange mirrors the gargantuan human being who must learn to control his appetites if he is to contribute toward social development. In each of his plays Lange reflects the human degradation that stems from uncontrolled individualism. He uses both features from the folk play and Brechtian techniques to bring out his concern for the people and their movement toward Communism. In this respect, it should be remembered that his move to West Germany was not a move to capitalism but to greater freedom so that he could develop his political criticism in his dramas. His most recent work, *Die Gräfin von Rathenow* (The Countess von Rathenow, 1969), reveals just how distant he is from the dominant ideology in West Germany. Lange's play is an extraordinary adaptation of Heinrich von Kleist's novella *The Marquise von O.* The setting is Prussia during the Napoleonic Wars. The new theme is the intransigence of the Prussian mind. Lange makes a laughingstock of the Prussian aristocracy by having the Countess, who was raped by some unknown person while unconscious, take a servant for a lover to emancipate herself from her tyrannical father. Though the Countess is apparently innocent, the father has rejected her as a sinner and liar. The hero of the play is a servant, a character invented by Lange, not by Kleist. He accompanies the French Lieutenant Marquis de Beville, who had raped the Countess and wants to repent for his "crime." The servant thinks his master an idiot for respecting the bourgeois code of honor and decency. According to the servant, who constantly addresses the audience as Lange's mouthpiece, the best thing that could have happened to Prussia was exactly the rape of Prussia, which helped break down its feudal system. Lange's play is a comedy; Kleist's novella is a tragicomedy. Lange does not take the aristocratic classes seriously, but his dramas are serious comments on the ruling class in every land.

Lange has translated Shakespeare's *King John* and *Richard III*, Molière's *Tartufe*, and *The Dragon*, by Yevgeni Schwarz.

**Laterna Magica.** See Czechoslovakia.

**Latin America.** In spite of political frontiers and the precarious social, economic, and cultural levels that interfere with effective cultural interchange, the Latin American process is essentially one, with the natural local variations occasioned by peculiar political, ethnic, or geographic considerations. This unitary character is obvious in poetry and prose and, when carefully examined, becomes apparent in theater as well. In spite of regional variations, the theatrical process of Latin America in the twentieth century has a very similar outline from one nation to another. By 1945 the larger metropolitan centers boasted viable commercial seasons and sometimes dramatists of real quality. Lima and Mexico City had a theater tradition dating to the early days of the colonial period; Buenos Aires theater during the first three decades of the century had achieved a substantial degree of artistic and commercial success with the naturalistic regional drama; Havana, Bogotá, and other cities still showed some evidence of what had been a strong regional comic tradition. Virtually every urban complex had active experimental groups, in most cases since the late 1920s.

This does not mean that every metropolitan center had good theater. The commercial fare was too often inferior local versions of French farce or rhetoric in the vein of the Spanish dramatists José Echegaray and Jacinto Benavente. Even the most inventive of dramatists were usually obliged to work within forms and conventions of realistic commercial comedy or melodrama. But exiled Spanish directors and actors had brought a sense of discipline, and the simple fact of the door opening to the world after World War II had a profound effect. University theaters were of increasing importance, and some were becoming the centers of activity and the primary sources of dramatists, actors, directors, and technicians. In Chile, the foundation of the Catholic University drama school and the Theater Institute of the University of Chile (ITUCH) were the chief reasons for the emergence of one of the most impressive Latin American movements. The University Theater group of Mexico was in fact a permanent repertory company serving as liaison and guide for other groups within the various schools, many of which had their own experimental theaters, such as the School of Architecture, which has recently produced notable directors and actors.

An important related factor in postwar development has been the near institutionalization of experimental theater in many areas. Although the experimental movement has slackened critically in the last few years, the result of an overabundance of groups competing for a small theatergoing public and increasing economic pressures, it has been the major factor in Argentina and Uruguay, where it became virtually formalized in the so-called independent movement, with its carefully structured program of training and performance. The Chilean movement has been institutionalized in the universities; in many other areas other types of state support, although sometimes minimal, have made possible types of work which would otherwise have been out of the question.

In spite of such assistance, often the movements, both experimental and commercial, are sporadic, underfinanced, and undertrained. The audience is still largely middle and upper class, entertainment oriented, and highly conservative. Many nations have overt censorship, and artistic freedom is severely limited in other ways. A substantial proportion of productions are of foreign plays, usually guaranteed commercial successes, and efforts at innovation are often hampered by amateurism and bureaucratic indifference, in spite of legislation in most nations calling for a proportion of works by national authors. Against this background, Latin American companies have been doing Latin American plays throughout the world; contests and festivals of various types have mushroomed. There are substantial efforts at getting theater to the provinces, and many dramatists are attempting to develop a theater based on popular elements and folklore. Much of this is heavily political and social; often, it is dramatically weak. But the best Latin American dramatists have a double commitment to artistic excellence and to an examination of the role of Latin America in a rapidly changing world.

As might be expected, the most significant theater activity in Latin America is to be found in Mexico and the major countries of South America— Argentina, Brazil, Chile, Colombia, Cuba, Peru, Uruguay, and Venezuela; Puerto Rico also has an active dramatic life. (See separate articles on these nations.) Few Latin American nations, however, are without some sort of theater, although in many cases it is the sporadic efforts of small groups, often housed and sponsored by schools or civic and cultural organizations. Guatemala has had some precarious activity since 1930, but the lack of a substantial public and a chronically hazardous political atmosphere have prevented any real development. Manuel Galich, now a resident of Cuba, has produced a steady stream of acid satire, often so vitriolic as to be anti-dramatic. Both Galich and the Nobel Prize-winning novelist Miguel Angel Asturias have worked in the theater within the popular tradition and the Indian mythic heritage, but neither has accomplished work of real significance. In other Central American nations the same state prevails. In El Salvador, the Spanish director Edmundo Barbero provided steady leadership, with governmental support since 1952. Walter Beneke, whose diplomatic responsibilities have prevented him from writing more than a few plays, has produced *El paraíso de los imprudentes* (The Paradise of the Unwise, 1955) and *Funeral Home* (1956), which deal with responsibility and freedom in an idiom influenced by

French existentialist theater. In Panama, José de Jesús Martínez is, like Beneke, nearly a one-man theater, although he has resided much in Mexico. His best work is *Juicio final* (Final Judgment, 1962), an example of skill and originality within a framework provided by Beckett. The characteristics of Martínez's theater is its gentleness and humanity; he is an example of what can be done in spite of working very nearly in a vacuum, and under his leadership and that of a few others, the last few years have seen a rapid though still unsteady growth of small drama groups.

Costa Rica has produced two interesting playwrights in Alberto Cañas and Daniel Gallegos. Like most dramatists in the smaller nations, they are uneven, showing the need of training and of interaction with experienced theater people. The remaining nations have little theater except for Ecuador, where Pedro Jorge Vera and Francisco Tobar García have achieved something resembling a steady died of theater, although the level is uneven. Demetrio Aguilera Malta, now a resident of Mexico, has achieved substantial success with rapid, impressionistic one-acters. Ecuador, like Bolivia, Paraguay, and most of Central America, is still very far from having a viable theater.

**Lenz, Siegfried** (born 1926). West German dramatist, novelist, and journalist. Lenz was born in East Prussia and served in the German Navy during World War II. After being released from an English camp for prisoners of war in 1945, he settled in Hamburg and studied literature and philosophy at the university. He also worked for the newspaper *Die Zeit,* and eventually left the university to become one of its editors. After publication of his first novel, *Es waren Habichte in der Luft* (1951), Lenz left the editorial board to devote full time to writing. He is one of the most popular authors in West Germany today. Most of his works show a strong interest in existentialism. Though his dramas are not as successful as his prose works, such as *Deutschstunde* (1968), he has a knack for developing interesting dramatic situations. His first drama, *Die Zeit der Schuldlosen* (The Time of the Innocent, 1961), was a parable play about the problem of confronting guilt. Nine respectable citizens who were responsible for the death of a resistance fighter are called together after a successful *coup d'état* to account for their crime. They are placed in the same situation that they faced when they committed the crime. After one of them takes the guilt upon himself by shooting himself, the citizens are acquitted. But the judge implies that they will all carry their guilt with them. Lenz's most recent play, *Die Augenbinde* (The Blindfold, 1970), is also a parable play; it treats the theme of freedom and confinement. Four men and a woman on an expedition in unexplored territory are captured by a tribe of blind natives. Their freedom can only be obtained if they become blind and join the tribe. Only two of the explorers resist. Though they have made the correct choice for pure freedom, it is questionable at the end of the play whether they will win their freedom. Lenz's parables all concern the contemporary scene. He sees society as taking the form of a prison and

287

questions the individual's potential for breaking down the walls that oppress him and make him, existentially speaking, criminal. Unfortunately, Lenz's characters and situations themselves are confined by the two-dimensional quality of his plays, and his socioexistentialist explorations lead up blind alleys.

OTHER PLAYS: *Das Gesicht* (The Face, 1964).

**Leonard, Hugh** (born 1926). Irish dramatist. A Dubliner whose real name is John Keyes Byrne, Leonard was formerly a civil servant; he now lives in London. His reputation was established with *Stephen D.* (1962), his first play to reach the London stage, which was adapted from James Joyce's *Portrait of the Artist as a Young Man*. Since then many of his plays have been seen in London after first being presented at the Dublin Festival. Witty and yet sensitive, Leonard is a professional dramatist who, despite the satirical overtones in some of his work, relies for his dramatic effects principally upon affectionate observation and contrast of character. He is the author of numerous television plays and has written dramatic criticism regularly for the journal *Plays & Players*.

OTHER PLAYS: *The Big Birthday* (1956), *A Leap in the Dark* (1957), *Madigan's Lock* (1958), *A Walk on the Water* (1960), *The Passion of Peter Ginty* (1961), *Dublin One* (1963), *The Poker Session* (1964), *The Family Way* (1964), *When the Saints Go Cycling In* (1965), *All the Nice People* (*Mick and Mick*) (1966), *The Quick and the Dead* (two one-act plays, 1967), *The Au Pair Man* (1968), *The Patrick Pearse Motel,* (1971).

**Lernet-Holenia, Alexander** (born 1897). Austrian dramatist, novelist, and poet. Despite the fact that he has satirically attacked the empty conventions of Austrian high society in his plays, Lernet-Holenia fought to protect these conventions as an officer in both World Wars. Like most of the Austrian writers born at the end of the nineteenth century, Lernet-Holenia admired the cosmopolitan qualities of the Austrian upper classes but frowned upon their moral decadence. His early works are drawing-room comedies that use expressionist techniques for light social satire. Lernet-Holenia was greatly influenced by Arthur Schnitzler, whom at the same time he parodied. In such works as *Österreichische Komödie* (Austrian Comedy, 1927), *Die Frau des Potiphar* (The Wife of Potiphar, 1934), *Glastüren* (Glass Doors, 1938), and *Die Schwäger des Königs* (The Brothers-in-law of the King, 1958) he employs clever dialogue and embarrassing situations to expose the foibles of characters who yearn to escape reality. In his more classical works, *Demetrius* (1926), *Saul* (1938), *Alkestis* (1938), and *Lepanto* (1938), he depicts the tragic side of the Austrian moral collapse. Since 1945 most of his satires, such as *Das Finanzamt* (The Office of Finance, 1957) and *Das Goldkabinett* (The Gold Cabinet, 1958), have been aimed at debunking petty officials and the growing bureaucracy of daily life. Lernet-Holenia's plays have grace and wit, yet these very elements serve to undermine the poignancy of his social criticism.

OTHER PLAYS SINCE 1945: *Spanische Komödie* (Spanish Comedy, 1949), *Bluff, Radetzky* (1956), *Tohuwalsohu* (1965).

**Leskinen, Lauri** (born 1918). Finnish playwright. Leskinen, a farmer's son, is a schoolteacher in Kuopio, in eastern Finland. His novels and short stories are those of an open-eyed, realistic observer; his ear is sensitive to the nuances of spoken language. His acquaintance with amateur stage activities led him to try his hand as a playwright.

Leskinen is the dramatist of painful resignation. His Chekhovian tragicomedies are mature descriptions of everyday people facing the crises of their lives or the lot of their generation. In *Kunniakuja* (Line in Honor of the Deceased, 1966) a schoolteacher retires on the day his daughter graduates from junior college; in *Muistoparaati* (Memorial Parade, 1968), a group of former frontline soldiers comes together twenty years later. The conflicts between the generations, or between ideals and present-day reality, create ironic situations in which Leskinen's characters do not find a common language. His sympathy is on the side of the humble and the meek; his retired teacher still tries to keep high the tattered flag of idealism, yet senses very well his own comicalness. Without preaching or proclaiming, Leskinen succeeds in smuggling important matters into the village or the small-town microcosm presented on stage.

**Lessing, Doris** (born 1919). English dramatist and novelist. Mrs. Lessing was born in Persia and lived in Southern Rhodesia from 1924 to 1949. She made her reputation as a novelist with works that included *The Grass Is Singing* (1950) and *Five* (1953, awarded the Somerset Maugham Award in 1954). In the late '50s she turned her attention to writing for the stage, achieving a marked success with her second play. Presented by the English Stage Company, *Each His Own Wilderness* (1958) was hailed as an example by an older writer of the drama of social commitment, which seemed at that time the dominant mode of most of the younger writers associated with the company. In fact, the political issues the play introduces are less essential to its success than is the soundly traditional study of personal relationships it presents. Myra Bolton, an attractive middle-class widow involved in the Campaign for Nuclear Disarmament and enjoying a life of sexual freedom, tries to persuade her son to end his dependence upon her and enter the adult world. The son's emotional reliance upon the mother, powerfully and sympathetically represented, is the central feature of the play. Despite the assurance with which Mrs. Lessing handled conventional techniques of naturalism in *Each His Own Wilderness*, the form of her next play was a result of her decision that "naturalism, or, if you like, realism, is the greatest enemy of the theatre." Written in 1958 but not presented on the stage until 1962, *Play With a Tiger* is set among "the rootless, declassed people who live in bed-sitting-rooms or small flats or the cheaper hotel rooms." A seedy ambience on the fringes of the artistic and intellectual world is well established, but the attempt to push the exploration of character further than naturalism will allow, in a series of duologues in which the two main characters give dramatic expression to their childhood and other fantasies, is not wholly successful.

OTHER PLAYS: *Mr. Dollinger* (1958).

**Littlewood, Joan.** English director. Miss Littlewood's career as a director began in the '30s in Manchester, where, with folk singer and dramatist Ewan MacColl, she founded the left-wing Theatre of Action. In 1945 she founded Theatre Workshop, a company committed to the task of presenting classical and modern drama before working-class audiences. Hampered by lack of funds, the company pursued a migratory existence in Manchester, Wales, and elsewhere before finding a permanent home at the Theatre Royal, Stratford, in London's East End, in 1953. The company's reputation grew with productions by Miss Littlewood of *The Good Soldier Schweik* (1954), *Volpone* (1955), and *The Italian Straw Hat* (1955), and in 1956 Theatre Workshop began its contribution to the revival of the English theater with the production of Brendan Behan's *The Quare Fellow*. In a period of intense creativity during the following two years the company was to present, among other new plays, Behan's *The Hostage* (1958), Shelagh Delaney's *A Taste of Honey* (1958), and Frank Norman's *Fings Ain't Wot They Used T'Be* (1959), all sharing a distinctive style which they owed to Miss Littlewood's method of direction. In her hands the author's contribution (sometimes consisting of a mere scenario) was used as a provisional starting point to be developed and expanded in creative improvisation in rehearsal. To intensify the emotional quality of a scene the company would often depart from naturalism, employing techniques drawn from the music-hall tradition that included song, dance, and direct address to the audience.

The resulting plays, infused with a theatrical freshness and vigor that English audiences had rarely experienced since the war, share with Osborne's *Look Back in Anger* the distinction of breaking away from the middle-class banality of the drawing-room drama of the '50s. To many critics it seemed that Theatre Workshop offered a model for the English theater of the future. Its dramatists—Behan from Ireland, Delaney from the industrial north, and Norman and others from Cockney London—were creating a rich and idiomatic language free from the stilted artificiality of their predecessors, while its theatrical style, close to that of the popular drama of earlier ages, seemed capable of attracting new audiences to a theater that had long been a middle-class minority interest. This promise was not wholly fulfilled. Of the two major authors to emerge in this period, Behan did not live to complete another play after *The Hostage* and Shelagh Delaney was not to repeat her initial success. Critics sympathetic to Miss Littlewood's aims have conceded that her audiences were not significantly different in their composition from those who filled the West End theaters. The company itself was faced with a dilemma when the profitable transfer of its successes to the West End destroyed much of the ensemble work so vital to the creative spirit of the company.

In 1961 Joan Littlewood left Theatre Workshop, announcing ambitiously unrealistic plans for a "fun palace" to provide for all the arts in London's

East End. In 1963 she returned to direct *Oh What a Lovely War*, written by "Theatre Workshop, Charles Chilton, and the members of the original cast." This condemnation of war, created out of the troop songs and recorded statements of the leaders in the first world war, proved to be one of Miss Littlewood's most brilliant successes and was to have a lasting influence upon the English theater in the form of the "documentary drama" developed by Peter Cheeseman and others (see GREAT BRITAIN).

Miss Littlewood's attempt to direct a musical in the normal environment of the commercial theater (Lionel Bart's *Twang!!*, 1965) failed spectacularly. In 1967 she ventured into the field of political satire with productions of *MacBird* and the less vindictive *Mrs. Wilson's Diary*. In 1965 and 1966 she worked at the Centre Culturel Internationale, Tunisia. Her contributions are discussed in "Working with Joan," in *Theatre at Work*, edited by Charles Marowitz and Simon Trussler (1967).

**Livings, Henry** (born 1929). English dramatist. Educated at Grammar School in Prestwick and at Liverpool University (which he left after his second year), Livings had completed his military service and held a variety of jobs before beginning a career as an actor with the Century Mobile Theatre in 1954. His first London appearance was at the Theatre Royal, Stratford, in Brendan Behan's *The Quare Fellow* (1956). A television play, *Jack's Horrible Luck*, written in 1958, was produced in 1961, and Livings embarked upon a full-time career as a dramatist. Achieving immediate notoriety with *Stop It Whoever You Are* (1961), a play that included scenes in a factory lavatory and the seduction by a teen-age beauty of an old-age pensioner, followed by his death treated in terms of broad farce, Livings is typical of the writers whose sturdy individuality has invaded the English theater since 1956. His familiarity with a working-class background and his experience on the stage has had a richer influence on his writing than has his formal education. If his drama is undisciplined, it never lacks theatrical vigor. The action of his plays passes into a world of anarchic unreality, but it is unreality given a value by his feeling for the bewildered characters involved—the lavatory attendant in *Stop It Whoever You Are*, the simpleminded radio mechanic in *Big Soft Nellie* (1961, formerly titled *Thacred Nit*), and the National Servicemen of *Nil Carborundum* (1962). Livings' world is one where chaos seethes below the surface; given half a chance his characters unleash their fantasies and a riot of disorder follows. But the workaday world, mechanical and ugly, is never far away, endangering the delicate illusions to which his heroes cling—just as the huge boiler shudders in the background and finally explodes in *Eh?* (1964) while the gentle, confused Val spends his honeymoon and feeds his giant mushrooms on machine oil in the cramped boiler room below. Since *Eh?* the quality of Livings' work has become increasingly uneven; *The Little Mrs. Foster Show* (1968), the most ambitious of his later plays, takes brutality, black and white, in independent Africa as its theme, uncertainly pushing the action forward in a series of revue-style sketches. With his keen eye for the ridiculous, farce has proved Livings' most appropriate medium, but *Kelly's Eye* (1963), a taut, atmospheric piece about the love of a young girl for an older man with murder on his hands, is a powerful and wholly serious work, tender, savage, and tragic.

Fond of fantasy for its own sake and uniting farce with the traditionally incompatible emotion of compassion, Livings has evoked mixed critical reactions. The attempt to find a hidden meaning beneath the surface of his plays has received little encouragement from their author. Taxed in 1963 with the difficulty found in interpreting his plays, he replied, "Once you get on the stage . . . then you are not in fact creating a platform where people have gone to see an attitude, but to see a kind of sacrament. To me, the stage is an altar, it's a religious occupation, religious and artistic, in that you pray to the glory of man on the stage." His plays call for a direct, unreflective response from the audience, and his quality lies in the wild invention of his plots, in his ear for the absurd phrases that emerge from everyday speech, and in the warm understanding and sympathy he extends to the eccentric outcasts of society.

His plays for radio and television include *A Right Crusader, Jim All Alone,* and *There's No Room Here for You for a Start.* An adaptation of *Eh?* has been filmed by Peter Hall, director of the stage version, under the title *Work Is a Four-Letter Word.* An interview with Livings by John Russell Taylor and Tom Milne appeared in *Encore,* Vol. X, No. 4 (1963).

OTHER PLAYS: *The Quick and the Dead Quick* (1961), *The Day Dumbfounded Got His Pylon* (one act, 1965), *Good Grief* (an "entertainment" composed of short plays, 1967), *Honour and Offer* (1969).

**Living Theater.** A theatrical company founded by Julian Beck and his wife, Judith Malina, in New York City in the late 1940s. This pacifist-anarchist, experimental theatrical community had as its purpose "To increase conscious awareness, to stress the sacredness of life, to break down the walls." They began with poetic drama at the Cherry Lane Theatre in the 1951–52 season (plays by Paul Goodman, Gertrude Stein, Bertolt Brecht, García Lorca, Kenneth Rexroth, T. S. Eliot, and Pablo Picasso). When the Fire Department closed the theater, the Becks moved to a loft at 100th Street and Broadway, where from 1954 to 1955 they continued their explorations until the Department of Buildings limited the occupancy to eighteen. By 1959 they were able to open a theater and a school in Greenwich Village and there moved into the improvisational realism (strongly influenced by Artaud) that characterizes their most recent developments. Jack Gelber's *The Connection* and Kenneth Brown's *The Brig* are most representative of this period. After this theater had been closed by the Internal Revenue Service in 1963 and the jailed Becks had served their sentences, the company went permanently to Europe, where they had successfully toured twice before. They continued a celebrated career, living in communal poverty and, like wandering missionaries, continuing to try to effect that early purpose through theatrical experiment and a way of life that had increasingly become one with it. A brilliant, if controversial, reputation preceded their return visit to the United States in 1968, but despite the superb production of *Frankenstein* and the sensational nudity-cum-marching-outdoors of *Paradise Now*, audience enthusiasm generally turned to disappointment as walls of hostility seemed to be erected, not broken down, by the Living Theater. To many of the audience, invited to be participants but carefully kept as spectators, the company seemed to be engaged in an on-going and very exclusive form of group therapy, solipsism rather than theater. In 1970, back in Europe again, the Living Theater broke into three groups of about a dozen persons each and planned to continue along three separate lines of development.

Pierre Biner's *Le Living Theatre* (1968) provides a good history of the group, with lists of performances in Europe and some fine photographs. Julian Beck's essay in *The Brig* (1965) is more accessible, but only covers the American period. Michael Smith's *Theatre Trip* (1969) is a diary of his months with the Living Theater in Europe in 1966.

**Long Day's Journey into Night** (written between 1939 and 1941, produced and published 1956). A four-act play by Eugene O'Neill. Awarded the Pulitzer Prize in 1957, this is O'Neill's masterpiece, the play in which all of his previous experimentations fit together in perfect coordination and simplicity. The style is realistic, observing unities of time and place, exact in setting, listing even the books on the shelves, limiting dialogue and event to what is strictly probable; yet these very realistic details function as symbols: The house, which is not a home, is a family coffin; the single day, with its careful division of acts to correspond to morning's hope, noon's worry, evening's despair, and night's loss, is a symbol of the whole of life, just as the night toward which it moves is death; the books and dialogue, with their range of poetry and philosophy, are themselves symbolic of the human evasions that occur—saying is not being, memories are not life. The play is autobiographical and works out relationships between sons and fathers, sons and mothers, develops the theme of illusion versus reality that is explored in much of O'Neill's other work, but does it with such quiet clarity that the characters are entirely believable in themselves. As James Tyrone, successful matinee idol, demonstrates the parsimony that has alienated him from his sons; as his wife, Mary, returns to morphine; as the elder son, James, continues his dissolute, wrecked life; as Edmund faces his tuberculosis, the love-hate that operates in the family group becomes for each a personal nemesis more convincing than any O'Neill had contrived in earlier plays. It is a long play, but the dramatic effect is one of total coherence, a single vision of tragic fate.

**Look Back in Anger** (1956). A play by John Osborne. The play that introduced a major new dramatist to London audiences and formed a watershed in the history of postwar English drama opened to mixed reviews from the first-night critics. On the following Sunday, however, critic Kenneth Tynan wrote in the *Observer: "Look Back in Anger* presents post-war youth as it really is. . . . I doubt if I could love anyone who did not wish to see *Look Back in Anger*. It is the best young play of its decade." A new movement in the theater had begun; and after a television excerpt had boosted box-office receipts, the production by the newly formed English Stage Company became a popular success, earning its author the *Evening Standard* Award for the most promising playwright of 1956.

As a representative of the frustrated youth of Britain in the '50s Jimmy Porter has not stood the test of time. His problems are too personal, his grievances too particular. As a compulsive human being aflame with wit and invective, whose stabbing desire to hurt overrides his genuine tenderness for his wife, he is a creation for the stage of permanent interest. A graduate from a provincial university with a working-class background, Jimmy has married the daughter of a retired colonel and runs a sweet stall in a Midland industrial town. Their cheaply furnished attic flat is the background against which Jimmy pours out his resentment against his wife, her parents, and the stifling environment in which he lives. Goaded beyond endurance, his wife leaves, to be replaced briefly in bed and at the ironing board by the friend who encouraged her to go. The play ends with Alison's return, after suffering the loss of her child, and the couple achieve an uneasy harmony in a shared fantasy world of bears and squirrels. The plot, in its conception and execution, is not remarkable. The play's originality centers on the dominant character of Jimmy Porter. Accustomed to heroes who practiced the English art of understatement and hid their feelings behind stiff upper lips, critics and theatergoers were taken aback by the virulent and open nastiness of Jimmy's character. Osborne has called the play a "lesson in feeling," and it is emotion, direct, harsh, and unambiguous, that *Look Back in Anger* brought back to a stage muted by a tradition of polite circumlocution. "How I long for a little ordinary human enthusiasm," Jimmy cries to his wife on a torpid Sunday evening. "Just enthusiasm, that's all. I want to hear a warm, thrilling voice cry out Hallelujah!" His celebrated anger seems to feed on the aimless drift of modern life: "There aren't any good, brave causes left." But even this complaint is part of a torrent of resentment against the dominance of his new lover. "Why, why, why," begins the speech, "why do we let these women bleed us to death?" Jimmy's anger has an unequivocally personal motivation; it was born when, as a "small, frightened boy," he sat dumbly at his dying father's bed. "You see, I learnt at an early age what it was to be angry—angry and helpless. And I can never forget it. I knew more about—love . . . betrayal . . . and death when I was ten years old than you will probably know all your life." The anger in this play moves beyond the narrow confines of social protest to touch upon the raw nerves of the human condition.

Although Osborne's "lesson in feeling" is not a socially committed drama in the strict sense of the word, it nevertheless represents a decisive shift in the stance of the English dramatist. Gone is the urbane assumption that the theater presents middle-class characters and their problems to middle-class audiences in polite conversation pieces, and with it the smug suggestion that the English drawing room, preserved almost unchanged from Edwardian days by playwrights and directors, represents a high point of civilization and wit. The success of *Look Back in Anger* enlarged the social scope of contemporary drama as much as it extended its emotional range.

Had the theater of the '50s been less anemic than it was, *Look Back in Anger* would not have become a *cause célèbre*. It is very much an early play in which the author is learning his craft. The management of a sweet stall is a curiously unconvincing occupation for Jimmy Porter and scarcely touches upon his consciousness at all—in contrast to the style in which, in Osborne's later work, the dialogue of an Archie Rice or a Bill Maitland is permeated with the commonplaces of his profession. Porter's speech rhythms are often too carefully contrived to sound impromptu. The bear-and-squirrel fantasy played out by Alison and Jimmy seems merely whimsical beside the exploration of adjacent sexual territory in Osborne's later work. "I daren't pick up a copy of *Look Back* nowadays," confessed Osborne in 1961. "It embarrasses me." But no play was more necessary to the English theater of 1956, and its discovery remains the principal achievement of the English Stage Company. More information about the play may be found in *John Osborne: Look Back in Anger, A Casebook* (1968), edited by John Russell Taylor.

**López Rubio, José** (born 1903). Spanish dramatist. Beginning his literary career in the '20s with short stories and humorous sketches, López Rubio then turned to the theater, collaborating with Enrique Jardiel Poncela and Eduardo Ugarte. He worked on scripts in Hollywood for Twentieth Century Fox and Metro-Goldwyn-Mayer in the '30s, returning to Spain and similar interests in the '40s and to the legitimate theater in the '50s. A celebrated dialoguist, noted for his ingenuity and humor, López Rubio is a serious exponent of what many refuse to take seriously, the "theater of evasion." Uninterested in the circumstantial existence in an everyday world, which the social realists have identified as the sole reality worthy of theatrical concern, López Rubio explores that world created by the psyche to replace what it finds and rejects in its objective surroundings. The resultant interplay of reality and illusion is skillfully manipulated for comic effect. But it is also the source of pathos, for the characters' deviance from normal behavior, their absurd but never grotesque role-playing, is a calculated madness by which they avoid confronting a situation with which they cannot cope. Their consciousness of the fiction of their lives, their interest in their story as story rather than history, makes López Rubio's better plays, *La venda en los ojos* (Blindfold, 1954) most especially, artistically worthwhile in the best Cervantine and Pirandellian tradition.

OTHER PLAYS SINCE 1936: *Alberto* (1949), *Celos del aire* (Idle Jealousy,

1950), *La otra orilla* (The Other Shore, 1954), *Un trono para Cristy* (A Throne for Christy, 1956), *Las manos son inocentes* (Innocent Hands, 1958), *Diana está comunicando* (Diana's Busy, 1960), *Nunca es tarde* (It's Never Too Late, 1964).

**Lowell, Robert** (born 1917). American poet and playwright. Born in Boston, a great-grandnephew of James Russell Lowell and distant cousin of Amy Lowell, Robert Lowell continues this New England family's long tradition of literary distinction. After graduating from Kenyon College (A.B. *summa cum laude*, 1940) and serving a prison term as a conscientious objector in World War II, Lowell began issuing volumes of poems every few years: *Land of Unlikeness* (1944), *Lord Weary's Castle* (1946), *Poems 1938–49* (1950), *The Mills of the Kavanaughs* (1951), *Life Studies* (1959, 1968), *Imitations* (1961), *For the Union Dead* (1964), and *Near the Ocean* (1967). He has also done a number of translations. Among the many awards he has received are the Pulitzer Prize (1947), the Harriet Monroe Poetry Award (1952); the National Book Award (1960), and the Bollingen Poetry Translation Prize (1962).

Lowell began his work in drama with a version of Racine's *Phèdre*, commissioned by Eric Bentley for *The Classic Theatre* (1961). Writing contemporary American verse and focusing on some of his abiding themes (the relationship among character, power, and violence), Lowell remained, despite certain anachronisms, relatively faithful to Racine's play.

With *The Old Glory* Lowell turned to drama of his own. This theater trilogy is based on stories by Nathaniel Hawthorne and a novella by Herman Melville, whose prose narratives provide events and characters which Lowell transforms into verse drama. Although intended as a unit, the three parts of the play have been produced separately (it would, in fact, make a rather long evening in the theater to see all three at once). *My Kinsman, Major Molineux* and *Benito Cereno* were given at the American Place Theatre in 1964, and *Benito Cereno* had a regular off-Broadway run in 1965. *Endecott and the Red Cross*, the first play of the trilogy, was not presented until 1968, this too at the American Place Theatre. The three pieces together explore revolution, power and its consequences, savagery and "civilization," and the ambiguous relation of these to freedom. Flags are used as a unifying symbol throughout: the Red Cross of ruling England, the Rattlesnake proclaiming the colonists' "Don't Tread on Me," and the pirates' skull and crossbones. Each banner is symbolic in some way of a kind of glory, and the problem of the men living in the confused world of particularities is to decide where that abstraction "glory" dwells and how to achieve its height, if indeed such is at all possible or desirable.

The language of *The Old Glory* is poetry, not prose, but this is not a distinction that makes the listening audience uncomfortable; the lines have a felicity in rhythm, a coordination through imagery that is dramatically all to the good. Where the plays suffer is in Lowell's tendency to write long speeches that leave the action static. This is particularly noticeable in the most recent rewriting, the expanded version of *Endecott and the Red Cross*. *Benito Cereno* is theatrically the most successful of the three, partly because of the strong sense of suspense and the more immediate menace that pervades the plot, but also because the character relationships themselves, the ironies of master-slave freeman-rebel, are more directly accessible to an audience than the subtle soul-searchings of an Endecott.

With *Prometheus Bound*, given at the Yale School of Drama in 1967, Lowell once again adapted an existing play and carried further his concern with idea, rather than action. He used prose, rather than Aeschylus' verse, as he explained in the Author's Note, in order to "tone down the poetic eloquence, and shove in any thought that occurred to me and seemed to fit. My idea was for some marriage between the old play and a new one." Thomas Parkinson's *Robert Lowell: A Collection of Critical Essays* (1968) is a useful volume of studies by various critics.

# *M*

**MacLeish, Archibald** (born 1892). American poet, writer, and teacher. Born in Glencoe, Illinois, educated at Yale (A.B. 1915) and Harvard (Ll.B. 1919), MacLeish began his career as an attorney (1920–1923), then went to France to write. After his return to the United States, he served as Librarian of Congress (1939–1944) and in a number of other federal offices during the '40s. From 1949 until 1962, as Boylston Professor of Rhetoric and Oratory at Harvard, he taught courses in poetry and creative writing.

In addition to a large number of volumes of poetry, essays, and addresses, MacLeish has also written several plays, most of them in verse and most intended for radio: *Nobodaddy* (1926), *Panic* (1935), *The Fall of the City* (1938), *The States Talking* (1941), *The Admiral* (1944), *The Trojan Horse* (1952), *This Music Crept by Me upon the Waters* (1953), *J.B.* (1958), *The Secret of Freedom* and *Air Raid* (1961), *Herakles* (1967) (these dates are years of publication). MacLeish also wrote the libretto for a verse ballet *Union Pacific* performed by the Monte Carlo Ballet Russe in Philadelphia in 1934.

Most important of these is the full-length play *J.B.*, a modern version of Job. As in his other plays, MacLeish gives this myth current political relevance; biblical boils are updated to atomic disaster, but the problem remains the same, how does a man face evil? The ancient Semitic story probes a mystery; MacLeish's play tries to provide an answer: love. But unfortunately love is neither logically nor dramatically convincing as a solution in the context of the play. That this verse drama was, in revised form, given a Broadway production (1958) and became a best seller reveals something of the fears and needs of Americans in an increasingly threatened world. In *Herakles* MacLeish further acknowledged this sense of unwitting participation in disaster by use of myth.

MacLeish's work is considered in David Lutyens' *The Creative Encounter* (1960), and he is the subject of a full-length study in S. L. Falk's *Archibald MacLeish* (1966). *A Tribute to Archibald MacLeish* (1966) contains poems and recollections by former students.

**McNally, Terrence** (born 1930). American playwright. McNally grew up in Texas, and received a B.A. in English from Columbia University in 1960 and a Guggenheim Fellowship in 1967. His first play, *And Things That Go Bump in the Night* (1965), was a parable about placating evil with evil, showing a family's effort to insure a "safe place" for itself by ritual destruction of others (a plot with uncomfortable national parallels). It failed on Broadway, but McNally has been instantly and startlingly popular on the experimental circuit. *Next* (Westport, Connecticut, 1967), a grim little anecdote about army induction and our mechanically impersonal society, was quite successful in New York and Boston productions (1969) on a double bill with Elaine May's *Adaptation*. *Morning, Noon, and Night*, three one-act plays by Israel Horovitz, Terrence McNally, and Leonard Melfi, respectively, opened on Broadway in 1968. Despite McNally's subtitle, "A Perverted Comedy," and his "avant-garde" situation of sexual orgy, the play remains basically boulevard comedy. That same year McNally also contributed a sketch to *Collision Course* and produced *Cuba Si! Sweet Eros* (1968) caused the biggest sensation off-Broadway because of its use of total nudity, but, compared with an earlier play also involving an abduction, Murray Schisgal's *Tiger*, this one-act play seems as formless and pointless as a college fraternity skit. McNally has also written for television: *Apple Pie* and *Botticelli* (National Educational Television, 1968).

**Mains sales, Les** (Dirty Hands, 1948). A play by Jean-Paul Sartre. It was first performed on April 2, 1948, at the Théâtre Antoine, Paris, under the direction of Pierre Valde. It comprises seven tableaux, the second to the sixth of which are flashbacks. Hugo Barine has just spent three years in prison, in an imaginary country in Central Europe, for having murdered his wife's lover. Such, in any case, is the official story. Actually, Hoederer, the supposed lover of his wife, was one of the heads of the Communist Party, and Hugo, a young member of the party, had volunteered to assassinate him for political reasons. During wartime, when there was no possible communication with Moscow, Hoederer, thinking it realistic, had taken it upon himself to collaborate with the liberals and the right; that is, in order to save the Communist cause and mankind, he did not hesitate to "dirty his hands." One faction of the party, to which Hugo belonged, considered him a traitor to the cause. But it has now been discovered that Soviet Russia is in favor of a policy such as Hugo's, and the whole party is again taking orders from Moscow. If Hugo killed Hoederer because he believed he was his wife's lover, Hugo may be "retrieved" for the party. If, on the other hand, he killed him because of his political principles, Hugo is now too dangerous for the party and must be done away with.

The five central tableaux of the play deal with the events, meetings, and conversations that led Hugo to kill Hoederer, after managing to become his secretary. An intellectual and rebellious bourgeois, Hugo believes he will find his identity by committing an act dictated by purity of principles, such as the murder of Hoederer. Now Hoederer is the first "real man" Hugo has ever met. Convinced that he is right to be against Hoederer, but attracted by his authenticity and true humanity, Hugo keeps putting off the murder. Meanwhile, Hugo's friends become impatient and try to kill Hoederer with a bomb. Once

Hugo thinks they have lost confidence in him, he feels even more attracted by Hoederer, who suggests helping him emerge from his despondent confusion as a young bourgeois. But Jessica, Hugo's wife, is also attracted by Hoederer, and Hoederer, who is tempted, finally kisses her. Hugo comes upon them unexpectedly at that very moment and shoots Hoederer. Before dying, in order to save Hugo, whom his bodyguards are ready to kill, Hoederer says that he has slept with Jessica and that Hugo shot him out of jealousy.

The possible motives for Hoederer's murder are so intertwined that it is impossible to decide whether Hugo's act was political or prompted by passion (the passion being Hugo's friendship for Hoederer, which was betrayed, not his love for his wife). In the last tableau Hugo has to decide for himself. He chooses to have himself killed by his former friends, by stating that he has shot Hoederer for political reasons. He thus gives Hoederer's death a meaning worthy of the man, for someone like Hoederer dies for his ideas, not for anything vulgar like adultery. At the same time, he defines himself as the man he has always wished to be—a pure revolutionary.

*Les Mains sales* is a very melodramatic play, filled with suspense and sudden twists in the plot. The complexity of the action creates a feeling of complete uncertainty in the spectator concerning the true reason for Hoederer's murder, so that Hugo's free and voluntary choice at the end seems to be the only possible solution. On the level of characterization Sartre's Hugo is a remarkable portrait of a young bourgeois tortured by his inability to really become committed, and, in Hoederer, he has created the figure of a mature, authentic, complex man, both ruthless and profoundly generous, who is perhaps the most fully human and attractive character in all his works.

**Maison d'os, La** (The House of Bones, 1962). A play in six scenes by Roland Dubillard. It was first performed on November 2, 1962, at the Théâtre de Lutèce, Paris, under the direction of Arlette Reinberg. Apparently inspired by a passage from the Goncourts' *Journal*, *La Maison d'os* depicts the solitude of a master who is dying in his huge and complex house, peopled by some forty servants, including a doctor, a priest, and an architect. All the characters are prisoners of their own little worries. The Master is concerned about his health and his diminishing authority; the servants are haunted by their duties, the hierarchical system, the master-slave relationship, and the imminent death of their Master. Each one is doggedly preoccupied with his own practical or philosophical *idée fixe*. Since the idea is generally beyond comprehension or logic, communication with others is difficult, little quarrels become more and more frequent, and a general climate of both exasperation and nonchalance is created. Toward the end of the play one gets the impression that the Master has died. But since he reappears, it is hard to know whether he is really dead or still dying—which, on the other hand, is of no importance.

Every short scene in the play is a little absurd sketch in itself. The characters seem deeply concerned about some activity or some idea that is not always explicit. Each one goes about his business with the earnestness of an ant, but without being able to clearly communicate its nature or significance. If two characters happen to understand each other, they generally do so without enlightening the spectator. As a result, the stage is virtually crawling with life that has no justification outside of pure nonsense.

The language of Dubillard's characters is unique in French theater today. It is theoretically explanatory and demonstrative, but is constantly thwarted by clichés, errors in syntax, and especially the anacolutha of spoken language. Thus what the characters thought they were going to say and what they do say is always out of phase. They consequently resort to empty affirmations, but expressed so vehemently that they admit of no answer. This systematic exaggeration of a realistic way of speaking leads to bringing both language and thought into question in a hilarious way.

The scenes of *La Maison d'os* may be taken in any order at all, so that the director or reader has the right to walk about in the play as if it were a house and may choose to go from the basement to the attic or from the attic to the basement, or since a parallel is drawn between the house and a human body, from organ to organ, as he pleases, witnessing the absurd work of death.

**Manner, Eeva-Liisa** (born 1921). Finnish poet and playwright. Manner has worked for a publishing house and as a free-lance translator and essayist; she lives in Tampere and, for part of the year, in Spain. Her translations include *Romeo and Juliet, The Tempest,* and *Woyzeck.*

*Tämä matka* (This Journey, 1956), a collection of her poems, was a remarkable, change-making achievement: She is a pantheist combining precise observations with an intellectual curiosity and interest in age-old phenomena. *Eros ja Psykhe* (1959), originally written as a radio play, is a delicate love story in free verse, speaking with its metaphors and rhythm rather than with its action. Manner made a new start as a dramatist with her *Uuden vuoden yö* (New Year's Eve, 1965), a bold cross section of a group of middle-aged intellectuals discussing, drinking, and revealing themselves; the harshest and most outspoken lines are given to a young Bohemian poet. This Albee-like chamber play is Manner's best drama so far; *Toukokuun lumi* (The Snow of May, 1967) and *Poltettu oranssi* (Burnt-Out Ocher, 1969), a Freudian and poetic case study, vary the theme of sensitive young girls experiencing disappointment in love at the hands of harsh or unthinking men.

**Marat/Sade** (in full, **The Persecution and Assassination of Jean-Paul Marat as Performed by the Inmates of the Asylum of Charenton under the Direction of the Marquis de Sade [Die Verfolgung und Ermordung Jean Paul Marats dargestellt durch die Schauspielgruppe des Hospizes zu Charenton unter Anleitung des Herrn de Sade,** 1964]). A play by Peter Weiss. There are five versions of the Marat/Sade play, which has been translated into sixteen languages and produced in more than thirty countries. The synopsis here is based on the fifth version, published in 1965, which is the most radical from a political point of view.

The play, set in the bath hall of the asylum in Charenton, is divided into two acts with thirty-three scenes. The director of the asylum, Coulmier, welcomes the audience and sits on the side of the stage with his family on a raised podium. The herald, who comments on the action throughout the play, introduces the patients who will be playing the characters in the drama: Jean-Paul Marat, the great radical, who sits in a bathtub throughout most of the play because he suffers from a skin disease; Simone Evrard, his mistress, who attends him; Charlotte Corday, dissident from Caen, who murders Marat because she feels he is too bloodthirsty; Dupperet, a Girondist, who is a consort of Corday's; Jacques Roux, the radical priest, who inflames the crowd's desire to create a true proletarian revolution; four singers, Curcurucu, Polpoch, Kokol, and Rossignol, who represent the masses; and finally, the Marquis de Sade, who is the writer and director of the play. The time is 1808, and de Sade's drama about Marat's assassination takes place on July 13, 1793. The patients who are not acting in the play sit in the rear on benches attended by nurses. Coulmier explains that he allows de Sade to produce these plays because it is good therapy for the patients. However, when the four singers pay homage to Marat and the Revolution and when Roux's inflammatory remarks about the Napoleonic regime encourage the patients to chant "Who keeps us prisoner/ Who locks us in/we're all normal and we want our freedom," it becomes apparent that Coulmier will actually restrain the behavior of the patients and actors and that the play concerns not only 1793 but also 1808 and the present. The action that follows the opening scenes shows Corday's attempts to assassinate Marat, which end when she kills him with a kitchen knife. The highly varied scenes include discussions of the meaning of the Revolution. Each character takes a stand of some sort, and the herald explains to the audience what is happening. The most important dialogues of the play are those between Marat, who speaks from a tub at the left, and de Sade, who speaks from the right. Between them the action takes place. De Sade takes the individualist's point of view. He is disappointed with the Revolution because it led to uniformity, bureaucracy, and barbarity. Marat justifies the bloodshed of the Revolution by arguing: "We can't begin to build till we've burnt the old building down/ however dreadful that may seem to those/ who lounge in make-believe contentment/ wearing their scruples as protective clothing." De Sade is pictured, along with the bourgeoisie, as a counterrevolutionary who will betray the people, as does Corday by killing Marat. At the other extreme is Roux, who must eventually be put in a straitjacket. His final words addressed to the patients and masses, "When will you learn to see/ When will you learn to take sides/ When will you show them," serve as the motto of the play. During the course of the drama, the patients get out of hand, Coulmier raises objections, the four singers erupt into song, and the herald comments ironically on the importance of maintaining order. In the final scene, the patients become so aroused, demanding revolution and copulation, that they break out into a frenetic dance. Coulmier calls upon the male nurses to suppress the patients.

De Sade laughs triumphantly while Coulmier desperately calls for the curtain to be closed.

Most critics of Weiss's play have argued that the playwright presents a fascinating argument about the meaning and potential of a revolution without providing an answer. And, if there is a winner in the debate, then it is de Sade. Weiss, however, has rejected this interpretation, and certainly a close analysis of the fifth version would show him to be correct. Weiss uses de Sade to write a play about Marat in order to comment on the futility of his position as counter-revolutionary. The political criticism of the play is intended to point out that Marat was ahead of his time in recognizing that the French Revolution favored the bourgeosie. In terms of the framework of the play, it is obvious that the staff of the asylum represent the oppressive system of the bourgeoisie under Napoleon, which de Sade, in particular, realizes must be torn down.

Marat/Sade is based on authentic documents. De Sade in fact was kept imprisoned in the asylum of Charenton from 1801 to 1814, where he produced his plays and sometimes acted in them. Coulmier encouraged such amateur theatricals and often the high society of Paris were invited to attend. Though giving a Marxist interpretation to Marat's situation, Weiss generally remains true to fact. Weiss shows the contradictions in three epochs—1793, 1808, and the present—in order to demonstrate the necessity for revolution. The asylum is used as a symbol for the dominant system of bourgeois capitalist society. The inmates can be free only when they learn who their real enemy is: their bourgeois keepers.

Weiss employs techniques from Brecht's epic theater: notably the alienation effect and the political ballad. But Weiss goes even further than Brecht toward creating a total theater. As the director Peter Brook has observed, Weiss contrasts styles and keeps the audience looking forward and back all the time in order to understand the meaning of the play. This is dialectical theater at its best. Its answer to human dilemma is to raise questions that only we can answer.

**Marcus, Frank** (born 1928). English dramatist. Born in Breslau, Germany, and educated in England, Marcus was formerly an actor, director, and antique dealer. He is now theater critic for the London *Sunday Telegraph*. As a dramatist he first attracted attention with *The Killing of Sister George* (1965), a seriocomic study of an actress whose personal life has become inextricably enmeshed with her role in a long-running radio serial. Marcus showed himself to possess an able gift for parody and social satire, but the play was chiefly remarkable for its frank portrayal of the Lesbian relationship between the two central characters. As critic and author Marcus has continued to champion freedom of expression on the stage, while insisting that entertainment is as valid a function of drama as social or political comment. As dramatist, however, he has not repeated the artistic or commercial success of *The Killing of Sister George*.

OTHER PLAYS: *Minuet for Stuffed Birds* (1950), *The Man Who Bought a Battlefield* (1963), *The Formation Dancers* (1964), *Cleo* (1965), *Studies in the Nude* (1967), *Mrs. Mouse, Are You Within?* (1968), *The Window* (1969).

**Marqués, René** (born 1919). Puerto Rican dramatist. Marqués is committed to the cultural and political independence of his island. His first success, which is repeated each time the play is performed in Puerto Rico, was *La carreta* (The Ox-Cart, 1954), a crushingly naturalistic portrait of a rural hill family which seeks its fortune in the slums of San Juan and New York City but finds that fulfillment in the land of its roots. Later works are more advanced technically but follow the same obsessive theme. *Los soles truncos* (The Truncated Suns, 1958) utilizes various levels of time and illusion to show the cultural shock which dominates the island. In *Un niño azul para esa sombra* (A Blue Child for That Shadow, 1960) this theme is blended with the anguish of the intellectual whose economic needs and human drives are irreconcilable. In *La muerte no entrará en palacio* (Death Shall Not Enter the Palace, not produced), Marqués attempted political tragedy, with uneven results. *La casa sin reloj* (The House Without Clocks, 1961) is in the vein of the absurd in its ironic setting for the theme of the need of communication. Where time had been for Marqués a corrosive force destroying a golden past, he now appears to be saying that we must live within our world: *Carnaval adentro, Carnaval afuera* (Carnival Inside, Carnival Outside, 1963) and *El apartamiento* (1964). *Mariana o el alba* (Mariana, or The Dawn, 1964) marked a surprising turn toward a lyrical, romantic, historical work with a political purpose; *Sacrificio en el Monte Moriah*, not yet staged, presents the biblical theme of Isaac and Sarah as parallel to the situation of Puerto Rico. Marqués' theater is strikingly complex; he is preoccupied with the intangible reality of Puerto Rico and his characters suffer from profound guilt feelings; they are obsessed by the need for sacrifice and atonement.

**Matusche, Alfred** (born 1909). East German dramatist and poet. After completing his studies at the technical university in Leipzig, Matusche began writing plays and poetry for the radio. In 1933 he joined the underground resistance against the Nazis. Most of his works were discovered and destroyed by the Nazis at that time. After World War II, he returned to writing drama for the stage and radio. His cycle of four plays, *Die Dorfstrasse* (The Village Street, 1955), *Nacktes Gras* (Naked Grass, 1958), *Das Lied meines Weges* (The Song of My Way, 1967), and *Der Regenwettermann* (The Rainy Weather Man, 1968), depicts the 1933–1945 period in Germany and the eventual triumph of socialism in East Germany. Matusche uses a terse language to convey the tension of the situation during World War II, when the common people were trapped in a Fascist war but never gave up hope for the future. In *Der Regenwettermann* a German infantryman refuses to carry out an order to shoot Jews in a town in Poland. He eventually commits suicide, but his act enables a Jewish boy to escape the Nazis. That is, a life is preserved in death. Matusche captures the desperate predicament of little people in a war that works against them in all his plays. He sets a mood of hardship that is resolved not by party slogans but by the pragmatism of common people who are bent on survival under any system.

OTHER PLAYS: *Van Gogh* (1966), *Kap der Unruhe* (Cape of Unrest, 1970).

**Mell, Max** (born 1882). Austrian dramatist, poet, translator, and short-story writer. Like two of his close friends, Hugo von Hofmannsthal and Rainer Maria Rilke, Mell was greatly concerned with the disintegration of values and the inadequacy of language in overcoming this breakdown at the turn of the century. Educated at the University of Vienna, Mell began to publish poetry and short stories in 1904. During World War I he served as a soldier at the front. The torment and suffering he experienced from 1916 to 1918 made him turn more to religion for salvation and (like von Hofmannsthal) to the drama for a form to reaffirm his faith in man and God. While other dramatists moved toward atheism, expressionism, and Communism during the 1920s, Mell wrote modern mystery plays that he called *Festspiele*—festive plays or plays to commemorate certain occasions. These dramas are religious parables that are classically structured. They are all written in verse and are intended to offset the chaos of the times by providing pure Christian symbols that are concrete enough to maintain faith in the Judeo-Christian tradition. During the 1930s and 1940s Mell continued to write in this religious vein. Since World War II he has produced three dramas which do not break with his previous work even though he uses legends. Mell seeks to combine folk tradition with Christian tenets. In *Paracelsus* (1964) he portrays the conflict that a doctor (the traditional healer) has with God in an effort to become humble and help his fellow men. The pious quality evident in Mell's works stems from his close attachment to Austrian Catholicism, and he gives expression to his faith in simple, poetic language that calls for the restoration of divine order.

OTHER PLAYS SINCE 1945: *Kriemhilds Rache* (Kriemhilde's Revenge, 1951), *Jeanne d'Arc* (1951).

**Mercer, David** (born 1928). English dramatist. A working-class childhood in Yorkshire was followed by a period in a variety of employments that ended in a nervous breakdown for Mercer with the collapse of his marriage and his failure as a schoolteacher. After psychoanalysis he embarked upon a career as a playwright, first for the medium of television and subsequently for the stage, motivated, in his own words, "through what I recognized about the past—that one had to confront family, class, present situation and everything." The clash of past and present, in social, political, and psychological terms, does indeed form the basic theme of Mercer's dramatic work. His ambitious television trilogy *The Generations* (1961–1963), written for the

B.B.C. and an important landmark in the development of television drama as a serious and significant art form, portrays the relationship between father and son at both a personal and a political level. The dogmatic, working-class socialism of the Yorkshire miner, whose political doctrines were forged in the years of the Depression, encounters the uncertain and troubled conscience of today's young left-wing intellectual, while at the same time the insecurity, alienation, and divided loyalties of a new intelligentsia with a working-class background are perceptively depicted. An increasing emphasis upon psychological rather than social factors in the formation of character can be detected in the successive plays of the trilogy, a development that is continued in Mercer's first stage play, *Ride a Cock Horse* (1965). A successful North Country writer living in London moves between his wife and two lovers in a progress toward schizophrenic collapse, to end cradled symbolically in his father's arms. But the wounding intelligence of the dialogue is not matched by an adequate conflict at a structural level and the play was a critical and commercial failure. In two plays written for the Royal Shakespeare Company Mercer attempted a wider allegorical statement of the breakdown of ordered society. In *The Governor's Lady* (one act, 1965) a colonial administrator's widow shares with the audience a hallucinatory vision of the world she knows and understands reverting to primal savagery, while in the complex and underestimated *Belcher's Luck* (1966) the mutual dependence of master and servant changes, against the setting of an impoverished country estate, to a more subtle and sinister relationship as Victorian certainty gives way to the blurred convictions of the present day. A symbolic pattern of impotent and domineering sexuality infuses both action and dialogue with a rich and recurrent imagery that strengthens the underlying theme.

*After Haggerty*, the first of Mercer's stage plays to arouse considerable critical interest, emphasizes its author's recurrent preoccupation with the figure of the successful writer whose intellectual standing and irreproachably left-wing commitments are at odds with the failure of his human relationships and in particular his inability to come to terms with his own working-class family background. Scenes which cut rapidly from Bernard Link's public lectures on the new British drama to the painful encounters with his father effectively and often wittily establish the complex contradictions in his character. More enigmatic is his relationship with Claire, a brilliantly observed specimen of intelligent and self-lacerating American womanhood and the deserted wife of Haggerty (in whose London flat Link now lives). The influence of the absent Haggerty progressively dominates the couple until the play reaches its macabre conclusion with the arrival of a coffin and the news of Haggerty's death in support of an African guerrilla movement. Although the relationship between Claire and Haggerty in some sense mirrors that between Link and his father, and Haggerty's active revolutionary role seems to contrast with Link's political impotence as a critic, the play lacks a coherent thematic unity and is memorable rather for the vivid honesty of its portrayal of Link, his father, and Claire. *Flint* is an obscurely allegorical comedy in which, as in *Belcher's Luck,* sexual potency becomes a defiant symbol of opposition to the repressions inherent in established order. But Flint, a septuagenarian vicar of the Church of England, is a less convincing figure than Belcher, and despite some Aristophanic moments the play remains a minor *jeu d'esprit.*

Mercer's television plays include, in addition to the trilogy mentioned above, *A Suitable Case for Treatment* (1962), filmed as *Morgan; In Two Minds* (1967), a controversial study of schizophrenia indebted to the theories of Ronald Laing; and *The Parachute* (1968), in which the generational conflict is transferred to Nazi Germany. When his contributions to the stage and television are considered together, Mercer takes his place among the foremost of contemporary English dramatists. A Marxist under the influence of Laing, Mercer has portrayed the interaction of social and internal pressure upon his heroes with great subtlety, and the range and variety of dramatic styles he has successfully adopted indicate plainly that he is not restricted to dramatizing the dilemma of the intellectual with a North Country working-class background. But his outstanding achievement at the present time has been his ability to present, with a masterly use of articulate dialogue, complex and convincing portraits of men and women of high intelligence who owe little or nothing to the upper-middle-class intellectual tradition that dominated the English stage for the first half of this century.

A further group of three plays, *On the Eve of Publication* (1968), *The Cellar and the Almond Tree* (1970), and *Emma's Time* (1970), sets Mercer's most searching and subtle exploration of the left-wing intellectual against a personal and political background that extends from England to Eastern Europe. For their technical assurance as well as for their impressive understanding of the wounding ambiguities of the human psyche, the three plays mark a new phase in Mercer's development as a television dramatist.

Interviews with Mercer have appeared in *Plays and Players* (April 1965) and the London *Times Saturday Review* (February 14, 1970). John Russell Taylor wrote "David Mercer: After Freud and Marx," in *Plays and Players* for May 1970.

**Meri, Veijo** (born 1928). Finnish playwright and novelist. Meri, the son of an army officer, grew up in a milieu saturated with stories about military life and warfare. When he became of age, World War II was over. He never experienced the front himself, yet he has written much about it. He studied history at the University of Helsinki, then worked for a publishing house; since 1959 he has been a free-lance writer.

Meri excels in grotesquely comic, slightly absurd situations in wartime and everyday life. His characters move in a floating, uncontrollable world. His war novel, *Manillaköysi* (Manila Rope, 1957), translated into eleven languages, contains wild inner stories within the main story. The proportion of dialogue in Meri's novels kept growing until he gave in and began adapting them for radio, television, and the theater. His first stage play, *Sotamies Jokinen vihkiloma* (Private Jokinen's Marriage Leave, 1965), starts with scenes of horror on the front, then develops into a picaresque situation behind the front: The antihero has to find a bride, any bride, to justify his leave. *Uhkapeli* (A Game of Chance, 1968) is set in Kaiser Germany during World War I; *Suomen paras näyttelijä* (The Best Actor in Finland, 1969) is an amusing extravaganza about a Bohemian actor mixing his profession with real life. *Nuorempi veli* (The Younger Brother, 1970) gives a panoramic view of the change of life in the Finnish countryside. Meri is a master of dialogue; his characters keep hitting the nail in a curiously comic and oblique way. For the stage he has developed a kind of epic pointillism, proceeding in short, crisp, poignant scenes fit for his picaresque stories and gallows humor. Meri has been a leading figure in Finnish literature since World War II. *Se on kultamaa* (It's a Golden Country, 1969), by Kalevi Haikara, is a study of Meri's novels.

**Mexico.** The year 1950 marks the turning point between the experimental generation of Ulises and Orientación, whose roots were in the 1928 movement, and a younger group, in the best sense pupils of the earlier experimentalists. Xavier Villaurrutia produced some of his best commercial work during the 1940s, but his death in 1950 and Celestino Gorostiza's sporadic contributions in a realistic idiom, left only Rodolfo USIGLI of the older group. Usigli, tenaciously independent of any school, achieved commercial success only in the 1950s with sarcastic Shavian satires, which often achieved box-office success because of their sensationalism: *Jano es una muchacha* (Janus Is a Girl, 1952), *El niño y la niebla* (The Child and the Mist, 1951). Some of these had been written long before, and his best works, *El gesticulador* (1947) and *Corona de sombra* (Crown of Shadows, 1947), continued to cause uproar and to disconcert critics because of their caustic view of the Mexican character, although by the 1960s they were widely recognized as among the finest of Latin American drama. Of late Usigli has written only several one-acters and the final stage of a trilogy begun with *Corona de sombra*, *Corona de luz* (Crown of Light, 1947), an ambiguous interpretation of the legend of the Virgin of Guadalupe.

Chronologically a member of the same group, Salvador Novo had considerable impact as head of the Department of Theater of the National Institute of Fine Arts. During the late 1940s he developed an important program of children's theater, established seasons of Mexican drama, and encouraged younger playwrights. His adaptations for children's theater of *Don Quixote* and Valle Inclán's *Astucia* (Cunning) stimulated his interest, and for the last twenty years Novo has steadily produced works notable for their agility, theatricality, and verbal mastery. Increasingly, Novo's works have treated the psychological survival of the Indian past.

Novo's work for the National Institute of Fine Arts and the stubborn existence of such experimental groups as José de J. Aceves' Proa Grupo, José Ignacio Retes' Linterna Mágica, and Xavier Rojas' Teatro Estudiantil Autónomo were crucial in overcoming the serious theater recession of 1947. Other critical contributions were the foundation of the institute's Drama School, the establishment of the annual regional and national drama contests, and the activity of the National Institute of Social Security in building theaters and stimulating the drama. Out of this activity came a group of dramatists who are among the most significant in Latin America today. The date usually assigned to the new movement is 1950, the date of the premiere of Emilio CARBALLIDO's *Rosalba y los Llaveros,* a delightful comedy of provincial customs, which used this staple form of commercial drama to show that it need not be superficial. After other works in the same style, which are very nearly satires of their own genre, Carballido developed a flexible technical approach that is equally effective in the tragedy *Medusa* (1960), the poignant satire of *El relojero de Córdoba* (The Watchmaker of Cordoba, 1960), or the social orientation of *Yo también hablo de la rosa* (I Also Speak of the Rose, 1966). Luisa Josefina Hernández's earliest plays were realistic portrayals of the frustrations of women in a male-dominated provincial society; she has since tended increasingly toward social satire. Hernández's most recent plays, based on historical and folk materials, are consciously designed as didactic theater. Most of her current work, however, is in the novel.

Sergio Magaña, a member of the same group, writes little but with great variety: the sordid life of urban tenements (*Los signos del Zodíaco,* 1953), the psychology of Montezuma II, and the conflict of guilt and evil in a detective (*El pequeño caso de Jorge Lívido* [The Small Case of Jorge Lívido], 1958), and musical comedy. *Los argonautas* (1967) is a chillingly comic vision of the Spanish conquest. Magaña, a dramatist of great technical ability, is, like Hernández, distracted from the theater by other writing. Carlos Solórzano, like virtually all the members of this group, has abandoned the realism of his early work; Solórzano has evolved toward a total theater centered on the conflict between good and evil (*Las manos de Dios* [The Hands of God], 1956). Recently, Solórzano has written only one-acters, the majority in a dramatic idiom influenced by Camus and Ghelderode. Elena Garro has also written chiefly one-acters, the majority in the late 1950s. Her emphasis on illogical communication and the conflict between levels of illusion illustrates her affinity with the "theater of the absurd," although her style developed independently. Garro of late has devoted himself principally to the novel, and Carballido and Solórzano have also published novels, a telling comment on the economic and artistic difficulties of the Latin American dramatist.

Other playwrights of the same group include Héctor Mendoza, primarily a director, whose delicate treatment of adolescence, *Las cosas simples* (The Simple Things, 1953), is one of the earliest and best treatments of the problem of youth; Jorge Ibargüengoitia, Mexico's best manipulator of black humor; Luis Basurto, a commercial dramatist and author of sensational sentimental dramas; and Wilberto Cantón, whose earlier eclectic line has been abandoned in favor of a conscious program of naturalistic exposé dramas based on real incidents. Few important young writers have as yet emerged, a fact that is due in part to the relative youth of the established writers and in part to the hegemony of the director. Héctor Azar is an imaginative director whose original works demonstrate the great vitality and inventiveness of his approach to theater. Vicente Leñero, a distinguished young novelist, has achieved considerable success in the last two years with an adaptation of his best-selling novel *Los albañiles* (The Builders), and with *Pueblo rechazado* (Rejected People), based on the story of Father Lemercier and the Emmaus commune. Alejandro Jodorowsky, a Chilean who studied with Marcel Marceau, has aroused interest in avant-garde circles with his "Panic Theater," based on happenings and the conception of theater as spontaneous ritual.

**Michel, Georges** (born 1926). French dramatist. Born in Paris, Georges Michel is a clockmaker by profession. In 1960, after ten years of writing plays and novels that were never published, he was discovered by Jean-Paul Sartre and Marguerite Duras. Three of his plays have been performed.

Georges Michel's satirical plays violently attack contemporary society and echo the protest against capitalism of many rebellious young people in the West today. The theme central to these plays is that "aggression" of the adult world, with its false values and good conscience, to which youth is now subjected. In *La Promenade du Dimanche* (The Sunday Walk, 1966) Michel uses the typical Sunday walk of a lower-middle-class French family, during the turmoil following the independence of Algeria, to satirize commonplaces of language, the boredom of daily life, and the bad faith of solid citizens in their indifference to the dangers of complete dehumanization. The child of the family, who tries to ask questions about life's essential problems, is overwhelmed by trite answers from his parents. At the end he is killed by a stray bullet. *L'Agression* (1967) is about a gang of rebellious teen-agers living in a society whose only values are consumer goods. Attacked, solicited, and brainwashed by adults and publicity, they end by yielding to the pressure and playing precisely the same game.

OTHER PLAYS: *Les Jouets* (The Toys, 1964).

**Michelsen, Hans Günter** (born 1920). West German dramatist. After several years in a camp for prisoners of war, Michelsen was released in 1949. These years left a strong impression on him and his plays are all attempts to come to terms with the Nazi past. Most of his characters are either crushed by the past or try to relive the past, which they cannot avoid. In each instance, they go around in circles.

Michelsen is, relatively speaking, a latecomer to the theater. Although he worked for a theater in Trier and a radio station in Munich, it was not until 1963 that his first drama, *Stienz,* was produced. *Stienz* established a pattern that is repeated in all Michelsen's plays. A retired army captain lives in the ruins of an old building with his daughter. He attempts to write his memoirs while Sergeant Stienz, who has remained faithful to him, guards the only entrance to the apartment. Stienz's pacing (like the throbbing of his conscience) disturbs the captain, who cannot get beyond the first page of his memoirs. Eventually he shoots Stienz, but this is in vain because his daughter takes up Stienz's post. In *Lapschiess* (1964) Michelsen has an old man reminisce with a young woman in the ruins of a house. As he reveals his past and suggests that he was actually the lover of the woman's mother, he shoots her. In *Feierabend 1 und 2* (After Work 1 and 2, 1963) a woman who owns a bar begins a relationship with a young man who had murdered his mistress. Their conversations suggest that he will probably murder her, too. In the second part of the play, a young man murders his mother to liberate himself from the confines of a bourgeois household. Each of these plays centers on a past that haunts the characters, and their only course of action seems to be violence. But Michelsen indicates that violence does not free anyone, but is as criminal and disturbing as their previous brutal acts.

This theme is varied somewhat in *Helm* (1965), Michelsen's best play. Helm is a crippled victim of World War II. He meets several ex-officers who were responsible for his mutilation and invites them to his hunting lodge in a gesture of reconciliation. The officers appear at the lodge but do not find Helm. They decide to leave and one by one are shot by Helm, who is taking his revenge on the past. The murders in this play seem more justifiable than those in the previous plays. After the first killing, the officers realize that they will be the objects of a manhunt, and their discussions about the past reveal how little they recognize their guilt for their obvious crimes. Still, it is difficult to determine whether Michelsen believes in revenge as a means to overcome the past. In his latest two plays, *Frau L* and *Planspiel* (Program, 1969), his characters remain desolate in the present because of the past. In *Frau L,* an old woman recalls how she once deceived her husband and ran off with a vagrant. She does most of her talking to a young vagrant, whom she has picked up from the streets and who spends most of his time sleeping. She also confides in a young neighbor woman, who constantly declares how faithful she is to her husband. Toward the end of the play, the young woman decides to run off with the vagrant, and the old woman is left alone. In *Planspiel* an old ex-general tries to relive the war by issuing commands to a vagrant, who plays the role of his adjutant. The general endeavors to rescind a command which had led to the death of Lieutenant von Thorei, his daughter's fiancé. The game ends in the general's breakdown. In the final scene his daughter stands at his grave and carries on a conversation with the dead von Thorei. Michelsen employs a tense, morbid language in all his plays to evoke a past that will not stay dead. His characters are imprisoned by this past, and most of their conversations are monologues that correspond to the circular pattern of the plays. The difficulty with Michelsen's eerie dramas results from the theme he explores; the plays are repetitious and burdened by the past.

OTHER PLAYS: *Drei Akte* (Three Acts, 1965).

**Mihura, Miguel** (born 1905). Spanish dramatist. Mihura wrote his earliest plays in collaboration with his associates on *La codorniz*, the offbeat humor magazine that he himself founded. *Ni pobre ni rico ni todo lo contrario* (Neither Poor nor Rich, nor to the Contrary, 1945, with Tono [Antonio de Lara]) and *El caso de la mujer asesinadita* (The Case of the Assassinated Woman, 1946, with Alvaro de Laiglesia) gave impetus to the revolution in the comic theater heralded by Enrique Jardiel Poncela. There followed *Tres sombreros de copa* (Three Top Hats, 1952), considered by many the best comic play of the contemporary Spanish theater. The "codornizesque" humor of the plays—farce, satire, and caricature when not merely delightful nonsense—breaks with the conventions of high comedy and the comedy of manners, which the playwrights did their best to undermine. Mihura's mastery of the macabre, his forte, is best appreciated in *Carlota* (1957) and *Melocontón en almíbar* (Peaches in Syrup, 1958), parodies of the mysteries of J. B. Priestley and Agatha Christie, so long a part of every theatrical season in Spain. In the midst of chaos, though, Mihura never loses sight of the saving humanity of his characters, ordinary people perplexed by confusions born of their own folly. Consequently, his aesthetics never approaches the extremes of that of N. F. Simpson or the Continental absurdists, playwrights to whom he is frequently compared.

OTHER PLAYS: *Mi adorado Juan* (1956), *Maribel y la estraña familia* (Maribel and the Strange Family, 1959), *El chalet de Madame Renard* (1961), *La bella Dorotea* (1963), *Ninette y un señor de Murcia* (1964), *La decente* (Decency, 1967).

**Miller, Arthur** (born 1915). American playwright. Miller's career has been typical of that of a successful American writer. He served a brief apprenticeship to his craft in his work at the University of Michigan (B.A. 1938) and afterward in various scriptwriting jobs for the Federal Theater Project, CBS, and NBC; suffered the failure of his first play to be produced (*The Man Who Had All the Luck* closed after five performances on Broadway in 1944); went on then to win the 1947 New York Drama Critics Circle Award for *All My Sons* and the Pulitzer Prize for *Death of a Salesman* in 1949; and thereafter, except for the period of his marriage to Marilyn Monroe (1956–1961), regularly offered the public the successful production of a new play every few years.

Most of Miller's important full-length plays focus upon a family relationship counterpointed against a larger society, a personal ethic against a public ethic, and often show the greatness of an individual within his private Eden and his corresponding failure in the world. Despite the use of violent subject matter (witch hunts, duels, suicides, executions, serious betrayals), the action of the plays is usually carried by words, not gestures, speeches that state rather than movements that demonstrate. Intense passions are discussed, analyzed, and categorized by the characters who feel them; conflicts and relationships are remembered and explained. This tendency toward talk and psychologizing gives a quiet tediousness to some of Miller's plays, like The Price (1968), and may severely limit their future interest as theories of human behavior are modified or as plays again become more theatrical.

Miller's best play is still DEATH OF A SALESMAN. Here psychological theories and social problems are not as important as the drama itself. The writer may later explain that the law Willy Loman has broken is "the law of success," but his play, not his essay, is the real clarification of what that means. Like so many fathers in Miller's plays, Willy is a man who has lost his money and his honor, both of which are essential to his preserving intact the myth of his own accomplishment. His honor—defined in his private Eden by the esteem of his sons, especially Biff—was lost in one moment of revelation when Biff found him in a hotel room with "the woman." The loss of money is more gradual, as his sales fall off and, now old, he struggles still to live on commission, until finally the failure reaches completion when he is discarded by the company he had worked for all his life. In the face of this diminution, the intensity of Willy's "human passion to surpass his given bounds" is seen by Miller to be the stuff of tragedy (see his essay "Tragedy and the Common Man" and his Introduction to The Collected Plays, 1957).

Whether or not Death of a Salesman is a modern tragedy, the play succeeds because Miller has taken a significant social situation (selling, not just things but "personality"), located it at its most sensitive point (the need to sell one's own personality not only to strangers in the public world but, more fearfully, to family at home and even to one's self), and developed it through a series of "Private Conversations" that allow for a variety of theatrically interesting moments, with frequent changes in mood and pace, using a language that approaches poetic heights but rings true as the words of ordinary people.

In THE CRUCIBLE (1953) Miller also explores the struggles of a man to find his own integrity amid a welter of "life lies," both those of the community and those of his own making. In this play Miller distances his attack on a contemporary social evil by using historical material, but the parallel that exists between the Salem witch trials of the 1690s and the senatorial witch hunts of the 1950s is unmistakable. (Miller himself was denied a passport to travel in 1954 and questioned by the House Committee on Un-American Activities in 1956.)

In later plays, especially AFTER THE FALL and INCIDENT AT VICHY (both 1964), Miller shifts his argument away from questions of deception and employs what appears to be a new focus in his thought, one that may help locate the cause of deceptions. As Leduc, caught in a Nazi roundup of suspected Jews, comments in *Incident at Vichy:* "I am only angry that I should have been born before the day when man has accepted his own nature: that he is *not* reasonable, that he is full of murder, that his ideals are only the little tax he pays for the right to hate and kill with a clear conscience." The darkness of this vision is balanced by Quentin's realization in *After the Fall* that there is no Eden: "And the wish to kill is never killed, but with some gift of courage one may look into its face when it appears, and with a stroke of love—as to an idiot in the house—forgive it; again and again . . . forever."

Deception and destruction are the preoccupation of Miller's plays, in ordinary American families, in a New England theocratic community, among both recent immigrants and successful sophisticates, between and within ethnic groups. The intention is philosophical, the terms of the investigation are frequently psychological.

Miller has written his plays in a variety of forms: the conventional and predictable well-made play (*All My Sons* and *The Price*); memory play, inside the mind of a central character (*Death of a Salesman,* which had first been titled *The Inside of His Head,* and *After the Fall*) or in the report of an engaged narrator (A VIEW FROM THE BRIDGE; one-act version, 1955; two-act version, 1956); period melodrama (*The Crucible*), and philosophical melodrama (*Incident at Vichy*). He sometimes makes use of national or regional accents to vary character types (New York Jewish in *The Price;* Sicilian in *A View from the Bridge;* Irish and Scandinavian in *A Memory of Two Mondays,* 1955). Miller has used the dramatic techniques popular from Ibsen to Tennessee Williams and used them competently; he has not been an innovator in style.

OTHER PLAYS: adaptation of Ibsen's *An Enemy of the People* (1950).

**Montherlant, Henry de** (born 1896). Born in Paris into a family of aristocrats, Montherlant began to write tales and short plays at the age of ten. During his youth, in addition to his studies, he continued to write and also became proficient in sports, including bullfighting (he killed his first bull at fifteen). The first world war inspired him to write *L'Exil* (1914), a full-length play that was not published until 1929. After being wounded during the war, he went back to literature and sports. In 1920 he finished his first book, *La Relève du matin,* and also gained renown for his skill in soccer and footracing. From 1925 to 1935 he traveled, especially in Spain (where he was wounded by a bull) and North Africa. Having first become known as a novelist, Montherlant, whose *Pasiphaë* (1928) was performed twice in 1938, did not really begin his career as a playwright until 1942, when the Comédie Française staged *La Reine morte* (Queen After Death).

Montherlant's works, which include some thirteen plays, are essentially psychological, in the traditional sense of the word. The purpose of the theater, according to him, is to dissect feelings and passions and to reveal their origins, dynamics, and contradictions. To that extent, his plays are related to French classicism, and some critics have not hesitated to compare Montherlant to the seventeenth-century master of psychological tragedy, Jean Racine.

Montherlant's heroes are presented as superior beings, lucid and strong, and devoted to the highest values: honor, duty, and nobility of soul. Early in the plays they seem to be masters of their situations and of themselves, and, conscious of their superiority, they hold in contempt everything they deem mediocre. Thus, in *La Reine morte*, the King of Portugal, Ferrante, believes that duty comes before any other consideration. He has decided to marry off his son, Pedro, to the Infanta of Navarre, for reasons of state; when he discovers his son's secret marriage to Inès de Castro, he sends him to prison "for mediocrity," because Pedro has forgotten his obligations as a prince, choosing instead to be happy in a human and simple way. In *Fils de personne* (No Man's Son, 1943) and *Demain il fera jour* (Tomorrow the Dawn, 1949) the lawyer Georges Carrion despises his son, Gillou, who—at fourteen in the first play and at seventeen in the second—represents the frivolity, indifference, and irresponsibility that Carrion has rejected in the name of higher moral values. Some critics have interpreted the haughtiness of Montherlant's heroes as a model of behavior, given by a writer whose own morality is individualistic and aristocratic. In fact, by endowing his characters with a higher morality, Montherlant makes their fall or their disintegration more dramatic and thus writes plays that are very similar to traditional tragedy. Certain of his superior heroes, faced with some weakness or mediocrity they wish to eliminate, gradually discover, in the course of the action, their own weakness or bad faith or unacknowledged fears. The aging King Ferrante, in *La Reine morte*, finally has pregnant Inès de Castro killed, not for any higher reason of state, in which he no longer believes, but because of his hatred of life, the future, and even himself. As for Carrion, in *Demain il fera jour*, it is quite simply out of his fear of being persecuted after the Liberation and in order to be able to whitewash himself that he allows his son to join the Resistance, resulting in the young man's death. Other Montherlant heroes become inflexible when faced with an ordeal, persecution, or general baseness, or go all the way in their search for the exceptional and the noble. But then they are led to sacrifice themselves completely and drag others along with them. For example, Alvaro, in *Le Maître de Santiago* (1948), who has always succeeded in remaining above the hypocritical materialism of sixteenth-century Spain, finally surrenders to the mystique of *nada*, nothingness, total renunciation, and involves his daughter in it as well.

Both possibilities—the discovery of a weakness and uncompromising self-sacrifice—are combined in Montherlant's two most successful plays: Port-Royal (1954) and La Ville dont le Prince est un enfant (written 1951, produced 1967).

Montherlant's works are difficult. They are filled with ambiguities, for, like the French "moralists" of the seventeenth century, from Pascal to La

Rochefoucauld, Montherlant considers that human nature consists of ambiguities and contradictions. And, of course, such uncertainties are a source of intense dramatic conflict. Montherlant is also similar to the French classical writers in his conception of realism. For him a play is a mirror of the reality of passions. He thus depicts simple confrontations in which the mechanism of choice, whether free or determined, is expressed in minute detail at every stage of its development: Weary kings are shown in the process of deciding to kill; a father or a lover is shown discovering whether he has renounced his beloved out of true superiority or fear; haughty moralists are gradually faced with their true motives, whether ethical or prompted by passion. Therefore the language must avoid surface realism, and the characters have to express themselves in the precise and analytical style of the French psychological tradition. As a result, Montherlant's prose is as difficult to translate as Racine's poetry. It is cut to fit the inner mechanism of passion and bad faith, as conceived by classical psychology. In other words, the drama of agonized souls is expressed in the purest rhetoric of the French tradition.

The staging of Montherlant's plays sometimes seems to suggest Renaissance (*Malatesta,* 1950) or baroque (*La Reine morte*) luxury. In fact, it is meant to evoke the paroxysms of an inner struggle between moral and immoral exigencies. When Montherlant situates his plays in a conspicuously picturesque period, it is because that period and the heroes he has chosen represent a typical exaggeration of the conflict. Then again, the apparent luxury of certain of his other plays is the frame for an ascetic soul. *Port-Royal* and *La Ville* are fine examples of the basic austerity that gives Montherlant's works their purity.

OTHER PLAYS SINCE 1945: *Celles qu'on prend dans ses bras* (The Women You Take in Your Arms, 1950), *Brocéliande* (1956), *Don Juan* (1958), *Le Cardinal d'Espagne* (1960), *La Guerre civile* (1965).

**Morgan, Charles** (1894–1958). English novelist, critic, and dramatist. After service in the Navy during World War I, Morgan studied at Oxford (1919–1921), where he was president of the Oxford University Dramatic Society. He joined the editorial staff of the London *Times* in 1921 and from 1926 to 1939 was the principal dramatic critic of that newspaper. As a creative writer he will be remembered principally as a novelist whose work includes *Sparkenbroke, The Fountain,* and *The Judge's Story.* Sharing the carefully polished style of the novels, his plays present an essentially humane and optimistic vision of a world in which good rather than evil predominates, seen during a crisis of conscience that culminates in the eventual triumph of virtue and human wisdom. *The Burning Glass* (1953), whose central character has discovered a lens with the capability of devastating a distant country but refuses to allow its use except in dire necessity of war, cogently expresses the author's belief that the possession of excessive power over nature will corrupt the human mind, and was among the earliest of plays to confront English theatergoers with a dramatization of the moral problems posed by the development of nuclear power.

Morgan was the recipient of numerous national and international honors, and the winner of many prizes for his novels. He was also the author of *The Confession*, a play for radio. He wrote an introduction to *The Burning Glass* (1954), and H. C. Duffin has discussed his work in *The Novels and Plays of Charles Morgan* (1959).

OTHER PLAYS SINCE 1945: *The River Line* (adaptation from his novel, 1952).

**Mortimer, John** (born 1923). English dramatist and novelist. Mortimer became a barrister in 1948 after education at Harrow and Oxford and wartime employment as assistant director and scriptwriter in the Crown Film Unit. While working as an attorney he published six novels. His first play, *The Dock Brief* (1955), and his first full-length play, *I Spy* (unstaged), were both first written for radio. Mortimer's plays are distinguished by a fine ear for the nuances of spoken English, and his characteristic dramatic form is comedy, which he has described as "the only thing worth writing in this despairing age, provided the comedy is truly on the side of the lonely, the neglected, the unsuccessful, and plays its part in the war against established rules and against the imposing of an arbitrary code of behaviour upon individual and unpredictable human beings." Mortimer has shown a humane and compassionate gift for dramatizing the illusions with which "the lonely, the neglected, the unsuccessful" disguise their failure. Typical among his characters are Elaine Lee in *The Wrong Side of the Park* (1960; set in "the crumbling, Victorian area of north-west London where I live"), who blames her second husband for what was in fact her own failure during her first marriage, but is slowly and painfully forced by events into an acceptance of the truth; and Sam Turner, who in *Two Stars for Comfort* (1962) bolsters the morale of his hotel's clientele while his marriage founders and his business totters toward bankruptcy. Mortimer's full-length plays, in particular *Two Stars*, suffer from his tendency to allow his minor characters to decline into thinly observed stereotypes, but his writing is rescued from banality by the sensitivity with which he consistently invests his central theme. His knowledge of the English legal scene is used effectively in *The Dock Brief*, the study of an unsuccessful barrister, with which he made his early reputation. *The Judge* (1967) draws upon the same experience, but the play's action, concerning a judge obsessed with his retributive role who visits the town of his childhood to settle a score with his conscience, marks a new departure for Mortimer, for in addition to a remarkable psychological portrait of the central character and a nicely observed treatment of muted vice in the cathedral close, *The Judge* carries allegorical overtones unusual in this dramatist. *A Voyage Round My Father* (1970), originally written for television, has a strong autobiographical element in its portrait of a blind lawyer whose personality dominates the household in which a young man reaches his maturity. With its evocative memories of the Second World War and its keen ear for the nuances of English eccentricity, it proved the most satisfying of Mortimer's full-length plays.

Although Mortimer's emergence as a dramatist in the mid-1950s has caused his name to be linked with the younger playwrights whose work became prominent at the same time (he has contributed to revues and a triple bill in which the work of Harold Pinter has also figured), his own subtle observation of character is set in a more traditional framework and is little influenced by the new stance of the period. So far from looking back in anger, many of his characters, like Crispin in *Collect Your Hand Baggage* (1960), are what the author describes as nostalgic survivals "from the sentimental, hopeful 1940s into the cold, clear, despondent world of today."

His television plays include *Call Me a Liar* (1958) and *David and Broccoli* (1960). Mortimer has written an Introduction to *Three Plays* (1958).

OTHER PLAYS: *The Dock Brief* and *What Shall We Tell Caroline?* (double bill, 1955), *Lunch Hour* (1960), *Come As You Are!* (four one-act plays: *Mill Hill, Bermondsey, Gloucester Road,* and *Marble Arch,* 1970).

**Mother Courage and Her Children** (Mutter Courage und ihre Kinder, written 1939). A play by Bertolt Brecht. As he did with many of his plays, Brecht rewrote the scences of this play to bring out the dehumanizing effects of war and the crude attitudes of the unenlightened proletarians. To a certain extent, he strove for the brutal comic effect of Breughel's paintings. The twelve scenes of his play, which is subtitled "A Chronicle of the Thirty Years War," cover a time span from 1624 to 1636 and take place in Sweden, Poland, and Germany. The central character is Anna Fierling, nicknamed Mother Courage, who appears in the writings of the seventeenth-century German writer H. J. C. von Grimmelshausen. Brecht does no more than borrow the name. His Mother Courage is a wily itinerant trader who follows different camps in order to make profitable deals. She lives off the war and does not understand that it is actually the war that lives off her and people of her kind. She has three children from three different fathers: Eilif, a brave and sometimes much too rash young man; Swiss Cheese, an honest if slow-witted youth; and Kattrin, a good-hearted mute, who has been mentally retarded ever since being hit on the head by a soldier. In the course of the drama, the virtues of the children prove their downfall because they have never been educated to use them to their own advantage and that of their class. Mother Courage is unable to protect them because she is interested in making deals rather than in fighting her real enemies.

One by one Mother Courage loses her children because she is more concerned for her wagon, the symbol of property in the play. Swiss Cheese a paymaster in the Swedish Army, hides the regimental cashbox when the Catholics overrun the camp. Because he is too honest to reveal the hidden money, he is sentenced to death. Mother Courage has an opportunity to save his life by selling her wagon, but she bickers too long about the price. She also fails to see (and perhaps help) Eilif and Kattrin before they die because she becomes involved in trades in nearby towns. In the end, Mother Courage is left alone with her wagon, which she pulls by herself in a harness.

Mother Courage is often portrayed as a Niobe-like heroine who manages to fend for herself despite the odds against her. Yet this type of portrayal misses the mark, for Mother Courage is a pathetic figure consumed by her obsession for property, especially her wagon. She forgoes happiness and the welfare of her children for the sake of property and trade. At one point in the play, the Dutch cook, who has joined her, offers her part-ownership of an inn he has inherited. She refuses, ostensibly because he will not allow her to bring Kattrin. However, it is clear that her real reason for refusing is that she cannot bring herself to give up her wagon and her trade.

Using songs, a wry language, and the alienation technique, Brecht succeeds in portraying a ravaged countryside populated here and there with people at the mercy of the war. Along the trail, Mother Courage is brought into contact with a Protestant minister, who disguises himself as her handyman to escape capture, a prostitute, who works her way into the aristocratic classes through the war, and farmers and soldiers, who act against their own interests to save their skins, which, paradoxically, will cause them to lose their skins. Brecht presents audiences with a topsy-turvy world in the hope that they can draw from the spectacle lessons that will help them set the world aright. Parallels are drawn to World War II, but Brecht sets the war in the seventeenth century so that the audience can distance themselves from the contemporary war and view it objectively.

**Mrożek, Sławomir** (born 1930). Polish dramatist. Mrożek was born in Borzęcin. He studied architecture, painting, and Orientalism, without taking degrees. He first worked on a Cracow newspaper as a writer and cartoonist and soon began to write satirical short stories, of which he has published five collections. He has also published two novels and two books of cartoons. His first play was produced in 1958 and he has since written sixteen more. Apart from their original successes in Poland, his plays have been produced in translations in many countries. Mrożek himself has for some years lived mainly outside Poland, first in Italy and, following his protest against the invasion of Czechoslovakia, has now settled in the West.

Mrożek first made his name as a playwright with crisp, short plays, each of which explored one selected theme to its limits. His first, *Policja* (Police, 1958), untypically for this period almost a full-length play, is based on the only too real assumption that when the last imprisoned revolutionary turns loyal, the institution of the police is threatened with redundancy. The only way to save it is through the sacrifice of a policeman who poses as a revolutionary. In *Męczeństwo Piotra Oheya* (The Martyrdom of Peter Ohey, 1959) an ordinary citizen is sacrificed for reasons of state and has to be hunted down by a visiting maharaja as an imaginary tiger. External pressures are supplemented by Ohey's own feeling of insecurity and fear, coupled with the myth of self-sacrifice. The metaphor of pressures exerted on the individual by society and its vested interests has been reworked in a Kafkaesque direction in *Striptease* (1961), where two simpleminded and opportunistic officials, threatened by a mysterious gigantic hand, vainly try to assert their rights when forced to strip and finally go blindfolded to their doom. In some of Mrożek's plays, impersonal forces are not needed to make life hell, since—though in a different way than in Sartre—other people suffice. In *Na petnym morzu* (At Sea, 1960) three men are adrift on a raft in the middle of the ocean. Two may survive if they eat the third—but which one? To decide, they play a game that reminds one strongly of the politics of the Stalinist era. In *Karol* (Charlie, 1960) an oculist is visited by two men, a grandfather and a grandson, who are looking for a certain Charlie, whom they want to shoot. In order to prove that he is not the man they are looking for, the oculist procures a Charlie for them to shoot. In *Zabawa* (Party, 1962) three bored farmhands break in on a party to find that there is none, so they arrange their own merrymaking, which consists of pointless activities from drinking to dressing up and an attempt at hanging. The play contains elements of a parody on Stanisław Wyspiański's national drama *Wesele* (Wedding, 1901). In a wider sense the play refers to the hopelessness of the human situation and the emptiness of pleasures in our time. In *Czarowna noc* (The Enchanted Night, 1962) two bureaucrats sharing a hotel room on a duty trip regard each other's company as intolerable but preserve a semblance of good manners until a mysterious young woman—an embodiment of their dreams— appears in the night and throws everything out of gear. In a lighter mood Mrożek wrote *Dom na granicy* (Home on the Border 1967)—a metaphor for some ridiculous divisions of our world, using as an example an ordinary household through the middle of which an international frontier line has been drawn; and *Kynolog w rozterce* (Dog-lover in a Dilemma, 1962), in which he shows through a pair of animal lovers how everyone has his particular likes, dislikes, views, and habits, and is ready to combat the preferences of other people to foster his own.

Some of Mrożek's early longer plays had, perhaps, more appeal for his native audiences: *Indyk* (The Turkey, 1960), in which he strongly satirized those traits in their character that prevent Poles from engaging in positive action; and *Śmierć porucznika* (Death of the Lieutenant, 1963), which at the time caused controversy because of his forthright reappraisal of patriotism and certain national myths. There was no doubt, however, about the universal appeal of his full-length play *Tango* (1964) and the plays that followed it. Mrożek has now moved to grand political metaphor in such plays as *Testarium* (1967), a perverse study of a power game and revolution. The Regent asks the Magi to choose the Prophet. Since there are two Prophets, one is eliminated; but the other is accidentally killed and this the people will not tolerate. The heads of the Regent and the Magi are placed on a bench next to that of the Prophet to face the audience. *Poczwórka* (Quartet, 1967) and *Drugie danie* (Second Course, 1968) are two variations on the theme of how certain historical and social patterns reoccur in succeeding generations: loves and hates between, and shared by, sons and fathers, the desires of sex and of power interplaying, authority being questioned, ideals going down the drain, politics compromised through specters of the past, revolt substituted by conformism—all this clad in an imagery that is primarily erotic. Under a delightfully perverse guise Mrożek propounds a thesis even more skeptical than that of TANGO: that the whole basis of social existence in our culture is corroded by an irremediable malaise.

Mrożek's *Wacław* (1970) is a political parable "in 77 scenes" about a shipwrecked slave named Vatzlav who sees in his misadventure a chance to make good. The country in which he lands is ruled by a bloodsucker—in the literal sense—Mr. Bat. Bat and his lady are deposed by rebels purporting to act on behalf of somewhat bewildered masses. The opportunist ex-slave antihero tries to succeed at any price by fawning on the representatives of different social forces, even offering to become a bear and be hunted, if necessary. His efforts lead to nothing: Having come full circle, he manages to escape from the rebels' executioner and makes for another shore. But will he succeed? The characters in the play represent recognizable social groups and attitudes, also archetypal figures from mythology, including the Genius and his daughter, Justine (Justice), who is made to expose herself publicly and is raped, and Oedipus Rex, whose new punishment for old crimes is to be buggered by soldiers. *Wacław* is a farcical morality play, witty, cynical and disillusioned. Perhaps, however, it leaves an uneasy hope in the final image of Vatzlav reluctantly carrying in his arms Justine's baby, whom he has just saved from drowning, into the unknown future.

One of the most original Polish writers, Mrożek is a leading exponent of the "grotesque view of life." The action of his plays is rationally developed from absurd assumptions to their logical conclusions. But often the assumptions are not as absurd as they seem: Standing at a bus stop, or sitting in a restaurant in many a country, one can easily encounter situations that make one think of Mrożek as a strict realist. If he brings his situations to their ultimate conclusions, it is to point out his skeptical moral, to confront man with himself in order to make him draw definite, though not very happy, conclusions. For Mrożek's sharp, sometimes macabre, sense of humor accompanies a rather pessimistic outlook on life and makes him closely akin to the leading dramatists of the European theater of the absurd. But besides being a European, he is also a national playwright, firmly, though perversely, planted in the Polish dramatic tradition.

OTHER PLAYS: *Woda* (Water, 1967), a monologue for radio.

**Müller, Heiner** (born 1929). East German dramatist and journalist. After receiving his high school diploma in 1945, Müller worked in a book firm and then entered the field of journalism. In 1954 he assumed the editorship of a monthly magazine, and four years later moved to the Maxim Gorki Theater, where he gained the experience to help his development as one of the most gifted East German dramatists.

Müller's plays are largely concerned with workers and their attitude toward their work as they prepare the way toward social progress. His first drama, *Der Lohndrücker* (Undercutting, 1958), dealt rather openly with the poor conditions in the factories during 1948 and the morale of the workers, who shirk their responsibility because the returns for extra output are low. One worker undercuts the others by extending himself and proving that production can be improved. Müller demonstrates how workers have to learn to sacrifice their immediate interests and develop pride in the socialist state despite its weaknesses in the early stage. His short scenes move dialectically toward a conclusion that recognizes the need of collective efforts to make socialism work. In *Die Korrektur* (The Correction, 1958), which Müller wrote in collaboration with his wife, Inge, the period is 1956, and here the problem for the workers is somewhat different. Instead of developing a new attitude toward their work, the workers must learn to reach a more understanding relationship with each other and the leader of the brigade so that they can be useful in the development of socialism. Finally, in *Der Bau* (The Construction, written 1963–1966), Müller uses an epic structure to portray the conflict of theoreticians with pragmatic workers. The brigade at a firm rebels against the men who sit at desks. The workers have no use for red tape and ethics and will use whatever devices available to help them get their job done. By hook or crook they intend to succeed. This type of thinking and working is capitalistic, and the party secretary comes to deal with the workers. He is successful in convincing them that planning can be combined with spontaneity and calculation with vitality so that they will follow the new proposals for higher productivity. Still, the major conflict involving working methods versus theory is unresolved at the end. Müller's play has not been produced in East Germany because of its open criticism, and he has resorted to writing adaptations of various classical plays. Even here it is interesting that he turns to the problem of the worker in support of the worker versus bureaucracy. In *Herakles 5* (written 1964–65) Müller deals with the fifth labor of Heracles, the removal of dung from the stables of Augeas. Despite the dirty job and the opposition of both Zeus and Augeas, the clownlike Heracles manages to clean the stables, and he is applauded by the Thebans as he moves on to his next labor. Obviously, Heracles represents the workers in East Germany who are confronted by bureaucrats and institutions that hinder their work and their efforts to establish socialism in practice. Müller's remarkable experiments with the drama attempt to serve this socialism, but they have not won him the favor of the party.

OTHER PLAYS: *Die Umsiedlerin oder das Leben auf dem Lande* (The Change of Home, or Life in the Country, written 1956–1961, produced 1961),

*Zehn Tage, die die Welt erschütterten* (Ten Days That Shook the World, 1957), *Philoket* (Philoctetes, written 1958–1966, produced 1968), *Ödipus, Tyrann* (1966), *Prometheus* (1969), *Horatier* (The Horatii, 1969), a translation of Shakespeare's *As You Like It* (1968), *Horizonte* (Horizons, 1970), *Die Weiberkomödie* (The Comedy of Women, 1970, based on a radio play by Inge Müller).

**Muñiz, Carlos** (born 1927). Spanish dramatist. Muñiz identifies himself with Lauro Olmo and Ricardo Rodríguez Buded, exponents of the "committed" social theater. Unlike them, however, he as frequently looks to individual as to societal flaws for the causes of human failure, the *leitmotiv* of his plays. *El grillo* (The Cricket, 1957) is a realistic portrayal of a failure, relentlessly probing his debilitating mediocrity, revealing the void of an existence he himself tries to fill with a torrent of words, sounds without substance. *El tintero* (The Inkwell, 1961) reworks the theme, but here the technique is expressionistic, and the causes of failure lie beyond human understanding, much less control. Increasingly alone in a dehumanized world, bewildered by a labyrinthine bureaucracy, the symbol of modern society, the protagonist in his search for meaning suffers the anguish born of recognition of the absurd. Such fare, by now passé in the literature of other countries, puts Muñiz in the vanguard of dramatic experimentation in Spain.

OTHER PLAYS: *Telarañas* (Cobwebs, 1955), *Las viejas difíciles* (The Old Women, 1966).

# N

**Naughton, Bill** (born 1910). English dramatist. One of the older beneficiaries of the new dramatic movement, Naughton was born in Ireland and grew up in Bolton, Lancashire. For many years he was a manual laborer, working as truck driver, weaver, and coal-bagger. In the '50s he began writing for radio and television, and in a series of radio documentary dramas swiftly established his talent for the accurate portrayal of working-class life in London and the North Country. Transferring his abilities to writing for the stage, Naughton emerged as a playwright of wide human sympathies with a vigorous feeling for comedy that insured the popular success of his work.

PLAYS: *All in Good Time* (1963), *Alfie* (1963), *Spring and Port Wine* (1964), *Annie and Fanny* (1967).

**Nègres, Les** (The Blacks, 1959). A one-act play by Jean Genet. It was first performed on October 28, 1959, at the Théâtre de Lutèce, Paris, under the direction of Roger Blin. *Les Nègres,* which Genet called "a clown show," is more a parodic ceremony than a play. In front of an audience that must be white (if there are no Whites, a white dummy must be placed in the audience), a troupe of black actors, who claim to work at other jobs outside the theater, divide into two groups. One group, consisting of Village, Archibald, Vertu, Félicité, and so forth, wearing extravagant evening dress, is going to play at being Blacks, at times with spontaneity, at times parodying and exaggerating the idea that the Whites have of them. The other group, made up of some of their anonymous friends, wears grotesque white masks, representing the white colonial authorities: a queen, a missionary-bishop, a governor, a judge, and a manservant; this group is going to perform on a platform above the stage and, facing the white audience, will be a caricatural mirror image of it.

The ceremony is comprised of two movements: the reconstruction of the rape and murder of a white woman, whose coffin is onstage under a sheet, and the symbolic conviction and annihilation of the Whites. Village is given the role of the murderer, and he plays it with difficulty and in anguish, hesitating between the written text of the ceremony and his own improvisations because of his love for the actress Vertu. To embody the white woman, the director, Archibald, chooses Diouf, who in real life is a priest. He is given a white mask representing a jolly fat woman: Village tells how he seduced the woman;

Village and Diouf disappear behind a screen. The masked characters on the platform, who make up the Court, and who, in a burlesque manner, show their indignation at the crime, decide to depart for Africa to judge it. They leave the platform, and as they arrive onstage, they discover that under the sheet, instead of a coffin, are merely two chairs. Next, there is a scene in which the Queen and the Negress Félicité confront one another, symbolizing Europe and Africa, and in which the White Masks are jeered at and threatened. The scene is interrupted by the arrival of a Black called Ville de Saint-Nazaire, who announces the execution of one of their people who was a traitor, and the departure of another Black for Africa, where he plans to organize the rebellion. The actors of the Court, who had removed their masks, put them on again for the symbolic annihilation of the Whites: Slaughtered one after another, they are sent to Hell.

The ceremony of *Les Nègres* is a mocking fraud. No White has been raped and killed, but that is one of the crimes that the Whites imagine committed by the Blacks, and the game consists in parodying and ridiculing the white imagination. In fact, the real action takes place outside the theater: the traitor's execution and the organizing of the rebellion. Indeed, the only point of the ceremony was to divert the Whites' attention from the true action by ridiculing them. Genet would seem to be saying that the Blacks can free themselves of the image the Whites have of them only by exaggerating that image and carrying to the extreme their negritude and the crimes imagined by the Whites. On the other hand, the Whites need the Negroes and the grotesque image the Negroes have of the Whites. This reciprocal relationship is doubtless more characteristic of Genet's vision than of the racial situation itself. The tone of the play is violent and full of hate, sarcasm, and very high lyricism.

**Németh, László** (born 1901). Hungarian writer and playwright. Németh's father was a grammar-school teacher at Nagybánya (now in Rumania), but the family moved to Budapest before the first world war and it was there that Németh completed his secondary education. He studied medicine and dentistry and until 1942 worked as a school doctor. Between 1945 and 1950 he taught in a grammar school at Hódmezővásárhely in southeast Hungary; since 1950 he has lived alternatively in Budapest and at Sajkód, a village at Lake Balaton. Németh's literary career began in 1925, when he won the short-story competition of the literary review *Nyugat*. He remained a contributor to this review until 1932, when personal differences with the editor led him to found his own periodical *Tanú* (Witness). It was in *Tanú* (1932–1936) that Németh published some of his best essays, which were later collected and published in *A minőség forradalma* (The Revolution of Quality, 1940). By the '40s Németh had become the most influential ideologist of the populist movement. His non-Marxist socialist views are sometimes referred to as the ideology of the "Third Road." Németh advocated a society of small communities of producers and stressed the special significance of intellectuals in a socialism of "quality," as well as the positive role of national traditions in the construction of a new society. Although his elitist populism was not exempt from certain misconceptions, the long ban imposed upon his original works after the war was unjustifiable. He resumed publishing in 1954, and in 1957 he was awarded the Kossuth Prize. The publication of his collected works began in 1969. Németh's creative talent left its mark on all literary genres, with the exception of poetry. His best novels are *Égető Eszter*, *Gyász* (Mourning), and *Iszony* (Repulsion); the last was translated into English. As a playwright Németh has been very productive, though some of his dramas are better read than performed. His plays can be divided, by and large, into two groups, historical and social. The social dramas, in which Németh's technique shows the influence of Ibsen, are variations on the same central theme: the intellectual hero fails in his pursuit of Utopia, for his family and social environment lack understanding of his ambitious plans. *Szörnyeteg* (The Monster, 1953), the story of an unsuccessful break-out attempt of a historian whose truthfulness is an obstacle in the way of "normal" human relations, continues this theme, but *Nagy család* (The Big Family, 1963) ends on a more optimistic note: perhaps it is possible to create some kind of a community that can live and work together in harmony. *Az utazás* (The Journey, 1962), one of Németh's most controversial plays, is a comedy. Its hero is an elderly, small-town schoolteacher of geography, long slighted and ignored by the regime, who is suddenly given a free trip to the Soviet Union. Upon his return his impressions, made public in the local press, are misinterpreted both by the local anti-Communist intelligentsia and by dogmatic party functionaries. This comedy could easily turn into tragedy, such is the incomprehension of the opposing camps, each conformist in its own way. In Németh's view the conflict between outstanding reformers and society is often inevitable, for the outstanding individual creates a temporary imbalance. Such conflicts are the core of Németh's historical plays, whether on Hungarian or foreign historical figures. Németh's Hungarian heroes are talented individuals who are not appreciated by their society, as in *Misztótfalusi Kis Miklós* and *Apáczai*, or who mount desperate revolts against the ready-made roles that society tries to force upon them, as in *Széchenyi*, *Petőfi Mezőberényben*, and *A két Bolyai*. Most of these plays are "monodramas," with the main conflict enacted more within the soul of the protagonist than between himself and other, equally important characters. Németh's dramas with foreign heroes—*VII. Gergely* (Gregory VII), *Husz János*, *Galilei*, *II. József* (Joseph II), *Gandhi halála*—are in some respect less didactic and "monodramatic" than are those on Hungarian themes. *Husz János* (John Huss, 1948) takes place at the Synod of Konstanz, thus forming an interesting parallel with Gyula Háy's play on the same theme; though Németh's language is expressive and the logic of his arguments is powerful, too meticulous fidelity to historical facts mars the dramatic structure of the play. *Galilei* (1953, first performed in 1956) is probably Németh's best play. Galileo perjures himself because he is convinced that his death would be an irretrievable loss for science, but in the fourth act he realizes that his work will be carried on regardless of his personal survival. Act IV, translated into English by Ilona Duczynska and Karl Polányi, was published in *The Plough and the Pen* (London 1963).

**Neville, Edgar** (born 1900). Spanish dramatist. A lawyer, Neville early turned to diplomatic and consular work. Frequent leaves of absence from governmental positions have enabled him to follow as well a cinematographic career, resulting in some twenty films and twenty-five scripts. Neville is the first to admit that his is a "theater of evasion," his the nostalgic yearning for a lost spiritual elegance of one who undergoes with discomfort the modern experience. A humorist, he finds his forte in romantic comedy, aways sentimental, sometimes maudlin, never without grace and wit. After the early *Margarita y los hombres* (Margarita and Men, 1934), his best-known play is *El baile* (The Dance, 1952), which traces the love *in vita* and *in morte* of a man and his best friend for the same woman. That *El baile* was one of the greatest postwar box-office successes indicates that Neville's gentle aesthetics, notwithstanding its studied anachronism, both fulfills the theatrical expectations and meets the vital needs of not a few of his contemporaries.

OTHER PLAYS SINCE 1936: *Veinte añitos* (Only Twenty Years Old, 1954), *Alta fidelidad* (High Fidelity, 1957), *Prohibido en otoño* (Prohibited in August, 1957), *La vida en un hilo* (Life Hangs by a Thread, 1959).

**Nicholson, Norman** (born 1914). English poet, dramatist, and critic. Born and educated in Cumberland, Nicholson wrote his first play for E. Martin Browne, who presented it in his series of "poets' plays" at the Mercury Theatre. His second play (on a post-nuclear theme) was commissioned by the Little Theatre Guild. Christian allegories drawing upon the speech and imagery of his native Cumberland, his plays have enjoyed some popularity among amateur societies (he has stated that his own theatrical experience was learned in "the tin-roofed Sunday school, with a tiny stage and homemade curtains"). His failure to make his mark upon the professional stage, despite his qualities as a poet, may be ascribed partly to the declining popularity of the movement for religious verse drama and partly to the faults which Richard Findlater has defined as "his parochialism and lack of stage experience." He has written volumes of verse, criticism, and works on the topography of the Lake District. Nicholson's work is discussed by Richard Findlater in *The Unholy Trade* (1952).

PLAYS: *The Old Man of the Mountain* (1946), *Prophesy to the Wind* (1950), *A Match for the Devil* (1955), *Birth by Drowning* (1960).

**Night of the Iguana, The** (1961). A play by Tennessee Williams. It won the New York Drama Critics Circle Award. A "rather rustic and very bohemian" hotel in Mexico is the scene where, in 1940, several bizzare groups meet: Shannon, a defrocked Episcopal priest now serving as a tourist guide to some fussy female Baptist teachers from Texas; Hannah Jelkes, virginal and artistic, wandering the world with her nonagenarian grandfather, "the world's oldest living and practicing poet"; Maxine, the unbuttoned and recently widowed proprietress of the hotel with her seraglio of young Mexican houseboys; the Fahrenkopfs, a family of pink and gold, nakedly angelic Nazis, with martial march and earthy laugh. The play is focused on Shannon, who is tormented by his sexual desires and his absent God. He is at the end of his rope, near a second emotional breakdown. Maxine wants to possess him, the Baptist ladies want to destroy him, only Hannah has something to give him: love that has nothing to do with sex and help that has nothing to do with possession.

There are two important symbols in the play, the ancient poet and the iguana. With all his senses failing him, the poet is striving to produce his final poem. When that is completed, in the last moments of the play, he dies, not destroyed but himself complete. The iguana, on the other hand, has been caught by violence and tied with a rope, to be fattened for eating. It struggles to escape. Shannon, impelled by Hannah, frees the iguana—"a little act of grace"—and life triumphs over death. Both of these symbolic events, death and life, have been achieved by man, not God (Shannon frees the iguana "because God won't do it"). And although Shannon goes off, himself captive to Maxine, the dangers and evils in his world are now individual and finite. No threatening God of the Thunders; in fact, as Hannah's response to the poet's death shows, "There's no one." The night referred to in the title is a dark night of the soul teaching Shannon that there is life and there is death, each in its own way difficult and fulfilling, dangerous but not malevolent.

**Norman, Frank** (born 1931). English dramatist and novelist. A Londoner from the East End, Norman was one of the dramatists to contribute to the success of Joan Littlewood's Theatre Workshop in the latter half of the '50s. With music by Lionel Bart, Norman's first play, *Fings Ain't Wot They Used T'Be* (1959), a nostalgic extravaganza of low life in Cockney London, took shape in rehearsal as a collaborative effort of author, actors, and director. That Norman's talents are not confined to improvisatory ventures of this sort was demonstrated decisively by *Insideout* (1969), an unsentimental and bitterly realistic picture of prison life.

OTHER PLAYS: *A Kayf Up West* (with music by Stanley Myers, 1964).

**Norway.** There is a certain irony in the fact that Norwegian playwrights should find Bertolt Brecht's ideas provocative, for his career was briefly intertwined with that of Nordahl Grieg (1902–1943), Norway's most important writer and playwright in this century. It was as a "counter" to Grieg's play about the Paris Commune of 1871, *Nederlaget* (The Defeat, 1937), that Brecht wrote *Die Tage der Commune* (The Days of the Commune). Grieg's tragic death in a wartime plane crash dashed hopes for a renaissance in Norwegian drama, and two decades elapsed before another playwright of real fire appeared: Jens Bjørneboe (born 1920), with his Brechtian *Til lykke med dagen* (Congratulations! 1965).

The writers of Grieg's generation who have written for the theater (with few exceptions, Scandinavian writers for the theater today are poets, novelists, critics, or performers first, and playwrights second) have pursued a course of deliberate departure from realism, perhaps as a reaction to the realistic tradition of the 1920s and 1930s that seemed to spring up naturally in the long shadow cast by Ibsen.

A number of these authors have written in *nynorsk,* or *Landsmål,* which evolved from certain provincial dialects and in the mid-nineteenth century was established as the nation's second official language. The subject matter of their plays has included affirmations of the traditional values of rural life and examinations of the implications of the German occupation, both themes treated, more often than not, in a lyric, symbolic, or expressionistic manner. In *Christophorus* (Saint Christopher 1948) by Tore Ørjasætter (1886–1968), a man tries to come to grips with the evil in himself, which is personified in a *Doppelgänger. Den lange bryllupsreisa* (The Long Honeymoon, 1949), by the same author, is a passion play about a man forced to answer to a freedom fighter for his failure to act during the war. The lyricist Tarje Vesaas (1897–1970), credited with writing the first Norwegian anti-war play, *Ultimatum,* in 1932, wrote about the wartime underground movement in *Morgonvinden* (The Morning Wind, 1947). Praised for his evocative dialogue and his symbolism,Vesaas has been compared with Maeterlinck. His *Bleikeplassen* (The Bleaching Place, written 1946, produced 1953), an expressionistic play about a laundering establishment, has a touching character, Krister, whose aspirations to purity are manifested in a desire to die in a clean white shirt. Aslau Vaa (1889–1965), one of the finest poets of her generation, wrote movingly about her home, the valley of Telemark, which is also the home of Tarjei Vesaas. Two of her plays are rich with imagery of peasant life in the Middle Ages: *Tjugendagen* (The Twentieth Day, 1947) and *Munkeklokka* (Monk's Bell, 1950).

Tormod Skagestad (born 1920) has played a multiple role in the development of *nynorsk* drama: as a playwright; as the director-manager of Oslo's Det Norsk Teatret, which since 1913 has been dedicated to the production of *nynorsk* plays; and as the controversial translator of Ibsen's plays into *nynorsk.* The theme of his best-known play, *Byen ved havet* (The Town by the Sea, 1962), is the need for individuals to speak out against the threat of extinction in an atomic age even when such an action disturbs the tranquillity of the society around them.

Among the older writers who have established some reputation as dramatists in *Riksmål,* the other official Norwegian language, are Johan Borgen (born 1902), Ernst Orvil (born 1898), Hans Heiberg (born 1904), and Odd Eidem (born 1913). The central theme in Borgen's expressionistic play *Eventyr* (Adventure, 1949) is a popular one in Scandinavia: the tragicomic plight of the poet trying to find a place in a commercial society. "What else can a poet do," asks Borgen's protagonist, "other than proclaim his wretchedness/so that all the fools die—of self-knowledge." Attitudes toward the war are reflected in Heiberg's *Minnefesten* (The Memorial Celebration, 1946) and Orvil's *Skudd under månen* (Shot Under the Moon, 1961). In Heiberg's play a man thought to have perished in the war returns home and embarrasses a group of people gathered in his memory by exposing their hypocrisy. Orvil's play, as critic Olav Dalgard has suggested, is an effective dramatization of the disturbing self-confrontations Norwegians were forced to endure. The central character says: "The war was a concentration of the evil in us, and of the good. . . . I still sense the shadows in my blood." Eidem, known primarily as a theater critic, has written two historical plays that have attracted some attention: *Spillet om Bly-Petter* (The Play for Lead-Peter, 1947), about the helplessness of a cowed proletarian in conflict with insensitive, repressive members of the upper classes, and *Guds gjöglere* (God's Performers, 1960), about the deposal of the last Catholic bishop of Norway.

Without question, the important event in Norwegian drama in the 1960s was the debut of Jens BJØRNEBOE. An established polemical poet and novelist, Bjørneboe introduced Brechtian-style theater to Norway and shocked audiences with his *Congratulations!*, an attack on the inadequacies of the Norwegian penal system. This was followed by *Fugleelskerne* (The Bird Lovers, 1966), about Germany's second invasion of Europe in the same generation: the economic invasion. Another hopeful sign was the production of *Gitrene* (Cages, 1966), written by Finn Carling (born 1925), a symbolic play set in a zoo, in which the characters are alternately animals and humans and have biblical names. Alienation is the central theme: Isaac returns from the dead and confronts his killer—Abraham, the animal and the father he did not know. Isaac's mistake was in reaching out, in opening the cage between the beast and the man, failing to realize that "Solicitude knows no bounds, provided that there are bars that separate us." In 1967 Georg Johannesen (born 1931) presented a provocative satirical revue, *Kassandra*, "a comedy in three parts about Cassandra, who acts as judge in legal proceedings between God and Satan." Johannesen's play was further evidence that a revival may be under way in Norwegian drama.

Useful studies of drama in Norway are to be found in Harald Beyer, *A History of Norwegian Literature*, edited and translated by Einar Haugen (1956), and *Theatre in Norway*, a special issue of *World Theatre*, No. 4 (1964).

# O

**Obaldia, René de** (born 1918). French dramatist. Son of the Panamanian consul in Hong Kong and a Frenchwoman, and brought up by a Chinese nurse, Obaldia, after having been rather unsuccessful at school, decided to become a writer. His career was interrupted by the war, during which he was a prisoner in Germany. He finally achieved some renown in 1949 when his poem *Midi* was awarded a prize. A novelist as well, he received the Prix de l'Humour Noir in 1956 for his *Fugue à Waterloo* and the Prix Combat in 1959 for *Le Centenaire*. His first dramatic works were impromptus written to amuse the guests at the Centre Culturel de Royaumont, of which he was associate director from 1949 to 1952. It was not until 1956 that those impromptus were staged in Paris. In 1960, after a public reading of *Genousie*, Jean Vilar decided to have it performed at the Théâtre Récamier of the Théâtre National Populaire. Since then Obaldia has become established as one of the most imaginative humorists today, yet more in the vein of Boulevard theater than of the avant-garde.

Obaldia's plays are often very wordy developments of a whimsical idea. In *Genousie* time stops for the space of a love story (which proceeds from love at first sight to ecstasy to murder) between a young poet and a woman who doesn't understand French and speaks the language of her imaginary country, Genousie. *Le Satyre de la Villette* (The Satyr of La Villette, 1963), a play that shocked certain critics by its comical frivolity, deals with the attraction —sometimes unacknowledged, occasionally leading to rape—of mature men for twelve-year-old girls. *Le Général inconnu* (The Unknown General, 1964) presents the adventure of a science-fiction general accused of high treason and married to a wife who spends her life peeling potatoes. *Du Vent dans les branches de sassafras* (Wind in the Sassafras Branches, 1965) is a "chamber Western"—that is, a parody of American Westerns on a small stage.

Obaldia, whose humor is often superficial and facile, combines in his plays a flow of lyricism and satirical allusions to contemporary fads or customs: science fiction, television, the social life of pseudo-intellectuals, and the like. The mixture is sometimes really comical—for example, the presence of a real horned and poetic satyr in the modern world of television and Lolitas (*Le Satyre de la Villette*) or a prostitute in the Wild West telling the story of an Indian attack in classical Alexandrines (*Du Vent*).

OTHER PLAYS: *Le Défunt* (The Deceased, 1958), *Sept Impromptus à loisir* (Seven Impromptus for Leisure, 1956–1961), *L' Air du large,* (Sea Air, 1962), *Le Cosmonaute agricole* (The Farming Astronaut, 1965).

Obaldia has written three radio plays: *Le Damné* (The Damned, 1962), *Les Larmes de l'aveugle* (The Blindman's Tears, 1964), and *Urbi et Orbi* (1967).

O'Casey, Sean (1880–1964). Irish dramatist. Born in a Dublin tenement and largely self-educated, O'Casey worked as a laborer before his career as a dramatist began. The most outstanding playwright to be discovered by the Abbey Theatre, Dublin, in the years immediately following Irish independence, he established himself with *The Shadow of a Gunman* (1922), *Juno and the Paycock* (1925), and *The Plough and the Stars* (1926) as a dramatist writing within the naturalistic tradition. Drawing on his personal experience of the Irish struggle for freedom, the language of his plays nevertheless came close to poetry with a heightened use of the rhythms and idioms of his native Ireland; and his plots, by sensitive contrast of character and skillfully presented confrontation of revolutionary ideals with the mixed motivations of everyday life, touched upon universal themes. In *Juno and the Paycock* O'Casey gave the Abbey Theatre its most popular play in twenty years; *The Plough and the Stars,* dealing, in O'Casey's characteristic mixture of satire and realism, with the 1916 Easter Rebellion, proved offensive to Irish susceptibilities and caused a riot at its first Dublin performance in 1926. From that year O'Casey made his home in England. The break with his native country became more complete when *The Silver Tassie* (1929), largely on the prompting of W. B. Yeats, was rejected for performance by the Abbey Theatre. The bold formal experiments of this bitter commentary upon the exploited heroism of World War I surprised and disappointed those who had come to look upon O'Casey as an untutored genius from the working classes, whose plays echoed the life and language he had observed in the Dublin slums; but the play has stood the test of time and is now regarded as one of the few works from England to rank with the experimental drama of Russia, Europe, and the United States during the same decade.

For the next thirty years O'Casey continued to write, in spite of hostility from his own country and neglect on the English stage. His anticlerical, left-wing sympathies endeared him neither to a country increasingly dominated by the Catholic Church nor to a theatrical system dependent for success upon the response of middle-class audiences. But, although he was never to reach the heights of his earlier dramas, the plays written during the '40s and '50s deserve greater attention perhaps than they have received. Whether by bringing everyday reality into unexpected contact with the supernatural, as in *Cock-a-Doodle Dandy* (1949), or by the depiction of imaginary political upheavals in a contemporary Ireland, as in *The Star Turns Red* (1940) or *Red Roses for Me* (1942), O'Casey continued to affirm the values of energy, love, and generosity exemplified by youth against the life-denying forces of commerce and a bigoted church. His feeling for the rhythm of Irish dialect remained unimpaired, and his use of music and dance contributed to the poetic mood created in the plays, while the abrupt incursion of death into their action reinforced the urgency of O'Casey's theme and sometimes conflicted with the element of whimsical sentiment from which his writing is not entirely free.

Controversial to the end, O'Casey lived to see his last play withdrawn from the Dublin Theatre Festival after objections from the archbishop of that city, although in *The Drums of Father Ned* (1960) the dramatist's attack upon the dominance of the church and the petty divisions that have denied Ireland her heritage are tempered with a degree of charity unusual for O'Casey. The picture of the young people in whose hands the future must lie, free from the folly of their elders and in league with the anarchic vitality of the mysterious Father Ned, is a moving testimony to the spirit that animated the dramatist during a career of almost forty years.

Generous in friendship and outspoken in controversy, O'Casey fought courageously against ill health and stubbornly rejected offers of national and academic honors. He found himself out of sympathy with the despairing tone that sounds through much of modern literature, and with characteristic zest he rejected the pessimistic viewpoint he discovered in Beckett's *Waiting for Godot*. He wrote six volumes of autobiography and many occasional essays on the theater and other subjects. He is the subject of a number of biographies, including David Krause, *Sean O'Casey, The Man and His Work* (1960); Saros Cowasjee, *Sean O'Casey, The Man Behind His Plays* (1963) and *O'Casey* (1966); W. A. Armstrong, *Sean O'Casey* (1967); Ronald Ayling, editor, *Sean O'Casey: Modern Judgments* (1969), with fuller bibliography.

OTHER PLAYS SINCE 1945: *Purple Dust* (1945), *Oak Leaves and Lavender* (1946), *Time to Go, Bed-time Story*, and *Hall of Healing* (1951), *The Bishop's Bonfire* (1955), *Pictures in the Hallway* (adaptation, 1956), *I Knock at the Door* (adaptation, 1956).

**Odets, Clifford** (1906–1963). American playwright and film writer. A charter member of the Group Theatre in 1930, Odets was a representative playwright of the theater of social consciousness and protest that flourished in the Depression decade before World War II. His *Waiting for Lefty* (1935) is a classic of agitprop drama and was widely popular throughout the United States as well as on Broadway, where even fat capitalists were brought to their feet shouting "Strike!" along with the characters in the play. *Awake and Sing!* (1935), like most of Odets' plays, is built around a family situation that reveals him as a forerunner of Arthur Miller; the accuracy of his dialogue and his conjunction of myth with homely realism relate him to Tennessee Williams.

In the late '30s Odets went to Hollywood, for financial reasons, to write for films, and though he tried to keep up his connection with the New York theater scene, his later plays for the Group Theatre—*Rocket to the Moon*

(1939) and *Night Music* (1940)—were failures. Nor are the plays written after the dissolution of the Group Theatre distinguished: *Clash by Night* (1942), *The Big Knife* (1949), *The Country Girl* (1950), and *The Flowering Peach* (1954). The later plays, like the early ones, are usually well structured, center around a family situation, are often in urban middle-class Jewish idiom, and have some sort of social or political message, but the Marxist passion had cooled and hope, somehow, seemed wanting in comfortable California.

In 1964 a musical was made from *Golden Boy*, Odets' most successful play, produced by the Group Theatre in 1937. Aside from this adaptation, whatever current interest there is in Odets is academic. A useful sketch of Odets in the '30s is to be found in Group Theatre director Harold Clurman's *The Fervent Years* (1945) and Gerald Rabkin's *Drama and Commitment* (1964).

**Off-Broadway.** In use at least since the mid-1930s, the term "off-Broadway" actually describes a phenomenon that had an earlier beginning. Since 1915, when the Washington Square Players and the Provincetown Players began a new theater movement in New York's Greenwich Village, that area has fostered a theatrical alternative to Broadway. In the postwar '40s another renaissance began, less experimental than that of 1915 or that of 1931 but dedicated to good production of good plays in intimate staging. It offered an opportunity to playwrights whose works were unacceptable on Broadway or had failed there, and provided them with a stepping-stone to more established commercial success. By 1960 there were thirty off-Broadway theaters (the most distinguished and most influential of which was the Circle in the Square) producing more plays each season than Broadway, reviving neglected plays by great writers such as O'Neill, and fostering a new wave of playwrights such as Edward Albee, Jack Gelber, and, a few years later, LeRoi Jones. By 1970 off-Broadway had come, through expansion and commercial success, to seem more and more like Broadway, despite the smaller theaters. The real alternative to Broadway had become OFF-OFF-BROADWAY.

**Off-Off-Broadway.** In the late 1950s the term "off-off-Broadway" began to be used to describe the experimental theaters springing up in New York City as alternatives to OFF-BROADWAY. Unlike the commercial theater off-Broadway, the off-off-Broadway theater is often located in coffeehouses, cabarets, churches, warehouses, or other low-rent off-beat places. Productions are of original works and are inexpensive; usually those involved are paid nothing or only a token amount. Tickets are often replaced by audience "membership fees" or donations. More than merely an available stage, the theater is often the home of a company of writers, actors, and production artists united by a certain permanence in participation and a common philosophy of experimentation, often in rebellion against prevailing styles. Most important of these groups, some of which are now defunct, are the American Place Theatre, the LA MAMA EXPERIMENTAL THEATRE CLUB, Caffè Cino, the

Judson Poets' Theater, the LIVING THEATER, the New Lafayette Theatre, the OPEN THEATRE, the Performance Group, and Theatre Genesis.

**Olmo, Lauro** (born 1923). Spanish dramatist. Self-educated, Olmo published poems, short stories, and novels before turning to the theater. His plays follow the formulas of the social theater established since Antonio Buero Vallejo's *Historia de una escalera* (1949). The playwright seeks to awaken the social consciousness of a dormant bourgeoisie by documenting the sordid details of the mediocre lives of working-class protagonists beset by personal, circumstantial, and societal failings. In both *La camisa* (The Shirt, 1962), his most celebrated play, and *English Spoken* (1968), the characters struggle against a social ambient in which emigration, dishonesty, or failure are the only alternatives in the quest for a livelihood. *La pechuga de la sardina* (The Sardine's Breast, 1963) is reminiscent of García Lorca's *La casa de Bernarda Alba* in its portrayal of women alone in a suffocating, sexually charged atmosphere, hostile to their psychic and physical needs. *El cuerpo* (The Body, 1966) deviates from the formulas in that it is an intensive study, almost "esperpentic" in its deformation of the probable, of but one character and his phobias. Olmo has also published, under the generic title *Teatro infantil* (1969), some excellent pieces for the children's theater.

**Olsen, Ernst Bruun.** See BRUUN OLSEN, Ernst.

**Olsson, Hagar** (born 1893). Finnish playwright. Olsson is a remarkable and many-sided writer from the inter-war years. Her *Rövaren och jungfrun* (The Bandit and the Maiden, 1944) includes elements of contemporary criticism transposed into a setting during the famine year 1868. Egoism and helpfulness, brutality and pity are contrasted within an atmosphere marked by superstition and the presence of death. *Kärlekens död* (The Death of Love, 1952) is a post-expressionistic fairy play, an echo of Olsson's more purely expressionistic phase in the late 1920s. A "Doctor," half quack half magician, visits a home for the aged and gives relief to its inhabitants, a group of living dead. This simple plot is interwoven with fine threads of poetry, satire, and comedy.

**O'Neill, Eugene [Gladstone]** (1888–1953). American playwright. A happy combination of unhappy experiences helped shape the life of one of the twentieth century's greatest playwrights. Born in a hotel room in New York's theatrical district, Broadway, nursed in the wings and dressing rooms of theaters across the country, O'Neill had no stable childhood, no regular home; as he told a reporter in 1932, he started life as a trouper. The sense of insecurity that early rootlessness can induce was compounded by the necessity of his being sent away to school, though even this was irregular. He later remembered with great bitterness being alone at Christmas when the other boarders went home to their families while his was on the road. His older brother's irresponsibility and profligacy and his mother's addiction to morphine deprived the boy of much that the surety of strong and certain personal bonds might have provided. And finally his father became an object of open hatred. James O'Neill was a fine actor-manager who spent his professional life in a popular and financially successful melodramatic adaptation of Alexandre Dumas' novel *The Count of Monte Cristo.* Eugene learned a great deal about theater from helping with productions of this play, and as a boy he thrilled with excitement over his father's performance, but as a young man he began to realize the play's essential mediocrity and saw his father's career as a prostitution of talent for the sake of money. There were many arguments over money and their climax came when O'Neill blamed his father's parsimony for his mother's addiction and for his own relegation to a state rather than a private sanatorium when he had turberculosis in 1912. These animosities became the subject of a later play, LONG DAY'S JOURNEY INTO NIGHT.

The six-month illness was beneficial. In the few years before its advent, O'Neill had gotten himself suspended from Princeton in 1907, entered into a brief marriage in 1909, and fled its consequences by prospecting for gold in Central America. Malaria, poverty, and dissipation as a seaman in South America and on New York's waterfront brought on the tuberculosis; enforced rest brought him time to read, the Greek tragic poets and Strindberg especially, and the resolve to be a playwright. A year in George Pierce Baker's famous playwriting seminar at Harvard (1914–15) and a fortunate meeting with an avant-garde theatrical group, the Provincetown Players, set O'Neill on the way of success.

His early work was with powerful, naturalistic one-acters, frequently using the sea as milieu and as symbol, like the four plays in the cycle *S.S. Glencairn* (1916–1918). The tragic ironies that are so much a part of O'Neill's vision are present in these short pieces and in his first full-length play, *Beyond the Horizon,* for which he won the Pulitzer Prize in 1920, and in *Anna Christie* (1921). Correlations with Greek tragedy become obvious in *Desire Under the Elms* (1924) and the trilogy *Mourning Becomes Electra* (1931). Always experimenting with form, both literary and theatrical, O'Neill also wrote in expressionistic (*The Emperor Jones,* 1920) and romantic-symbolic (*Marco Millions,* 1928) modes, and in various combinations of these (*The Hairy Ape,* 1922). He is a master of the one-act structure (*Hughie,* 1965), the full-length play (*Long Day's Journey into Night,* 1956), and the play-as-novel (*Strange Interlude,* 1928). Highly aware of the visual, as well as the verbal, effect of a production, he experimented with masks (*Lazarus Laughed,* 1928) and double images (*Days Without End,* 1934); in all his plays setting is of the greatest importance (the house, for example, in *Mourning Becomes Electra*), and so too is the physical relationship among actors (the pietà tableau in *A Moon for the Misbegotten,* 1947).

By 1936, when O'Neill was awarded the Nobel Prize, he had already made a major contribution to modern drama. There followed a decade of silence during which, in ill health and often low spirits, he lived and wrote in seclusion under the beneficent care of his third wife, Carlotta Monterey. Then with the Broadway production of THE ICEMAN COMETH (written in 1939, produced in 1946) O'Neill began a second period of achievement that has extended beyond his death in 1953. A Moon for the Misbegotten (written in 1943) was a failure in its out-of-town tryout in 1947 and was withdrawn, the last play that O'Neill wrote and the last production in which he had any voice. Long Day's Journey into Night (written between 1939 and 1941) was produced on Broadway in 1956, a brilliant success that won O'Neill posthumously his fourth Pulitzer Prize. A Moon for the Misbegotten was produced in New York the next year, followed by A TOUCH OF THE POET in 1958, the only completed play in the cycle of an American family destroyed by greed, to be titled A Tale of Possessors Self-Dispossessed. Another unfinished play in this cycle, More Stately Mansions, which O'Neill had worked on between 1935 and 1941, was produced in Stockholm at the Royal Dramatic Theatre in 1962 and on Broadway in 1967. These postwar productions alone would place O'Neill in the first rank of American playwrights, whose vitality was made possible by his experimental work.

The standard editions of O'Neill's plays are The Complete Plays of Eugene O'Neill (1934–35), in twelve volumes, and The Plays of Eugene O'Neill (1946), in three volumes. Manuscripts and papers are in the O'Neill Collection at Yale. The most recent corrected list of the plays, giving years of writing, first production, and publication is in Timo Tiusanen's O'Neill's Scenic Images (1968), a useful examination of the plays in theatrical terms. The definitive biography is Arthur and Barbara Gelb's O'Neill (1962). There are some thirty book-length studies of O'Neill's work and countless articles in theatrical and scholarly journals.

**Open Theatre.** An experimental workshop in New York City for playwrights, actors, directors, and other artists involved in dramatic production. Led by a former member of the Living Theater, Joseph Chaikin, this workshop profits from the method of communal exploration and improvisation originated by the older group. Since the mid-1960s the Open Theatre has served as an off-off-Broadway seedbed for playwrights such as Megan Terry, Jean-Claude Van Itallie, Maria Irene Fornes, and Michael Smith, whose plays have then moved on to regular off-off-Broadway and off-Broadway runs. Best known of these are Miss Terry's Viet Rock and Van Itallie's America Hurrah. Nonverbal communication, theater games, and TRANSFORMATIONS are among the exploratory techniques used by the Open Theatre, which is indebted, through the influence of the Living Theater, to the theories of Artaud. Of the many experimental companies in the United States in 1970, this seemed the most skillful and the most promising.

**Örkény, István** (born 1912). Hungarian writer and playwright. Orkény studied chemical engineering at the Technical University of Budapest. His first stories were published in the prewar left-wing review Szép Szó. After the war he worked as dramatic adviser at various Budapest theaters. He is widely known as an author of short, poignant sketches and bizarre, somewhat surrealistic stories published in the collections *Jeruzsálem hercegnője* (Princess of Jerusalem) and *Nászutasok a légypapiron* (Newlyweds Stuck in Flypaper). Örkény's first play on a war theme, *Voronyezs* (1948), has never been staged and is practically unknown. His play *Tóték* (The Tót Family, 1967), an adaptation of his own formidable story of the same title, portrays the sufferings during the war of a docile family terrorized by a paranoid army officer on leave. The family believes that their son's welfare may depend on this officer, but cannot endure his unusual demands. The play abounds in grotesque situations but the plot is too thinly spread for a full-length comedy.

**Orton, Joe** (1933–1967). English dramatist. Born in Leicester, Orton left school at sixteen and two years later went to the Royal Academy of Dramatic Art. His varied career included a spell in jail and ended in a violent death. His first play, *The Ruffian on the Stair*, which was written for radio, was staged only in the late '60s. Despite his adoption by the English Stage Company, which presented *The Ruffian on the Stair* on a double bill with *The Erpingham Camp* under the title *Crimes of Passion* in 1967 at the Royal Court Theatre, Orton must rank primarily as a dramatist who discovered and brilliantly exploited the commercial possibilities of black comedy. His full-length plays dealt in violence, corruption, and extravagantly perverse sexual misdemeanors, but these themes were rendered as inoffensive to the theatergoers of the '60s as was adultery to Georges Feydeau's audiences by the disarming amorality of the skilled farce writer. The breakneck precision of his plots was matched by the unique quality of his dialogue. With prim obstinacy his characters struggled with clichés as they might have with unfamiliar, and sometimes unsuitable, formal dress. "I'd rather witness a birth than a death any day," observes McLeavy in *Loot*. "Though the risks involved are greater." It is imprudent to suggest how so individual a talent might have developed. The posthumously staged *What the Butler Saw* (1969) represents a falling-off from the comic invention of *Loot*, but the revolutionary holiday-makers of *The Erpingham Camp* provide some astute if oblique comments on the nature of authority, rebellion, and public violence. Orton was the author of two television plays.

"The Late and Lamented Joe Orton," an article by John Russell Taylor, appeared in *Plays and Players* for October 1970.

OTHER PLAYS: *Entertaining Mr. Sloane* (London Critics' "Variety" Award as the Best Play of the Year, 1964).

**Osborne, John** (born 1929). English dramatist. Osborne has described his parents as members of the "impoverished middle class." He was born in London and, after his father's death in 1941, he spent some time in a "rather cheap boarding school," leaving it in 1946 to take up journalistic work on trade magazines. His career in the theater began in 1948 as an actor, and later as an actor-manager, in the commercial repertory system, working mainly at seaside resorts. Two early plays appeared outside London: *The Devil Inside Him* (written with Stella Linden) was staged in 1950, and in the following year *Personal Enemy* (written with Anthony Creighton) was presented after censorship of a homosexual strand in the plot had rendered the script (in the producer's words) "largely unintelligible." Collaboration with the same author produced *Epitaph for George Dillon*, written before *Look Back in Anger* but revised for its first production at the Royal Court Theatre in 1958 and transferred, after further rewriting, to the West End later in the same year. The play, about an unsuccessful actor and would-be playwright who trades in his artistic ideals for mediocrity in the suburbs, is competent but unremarkable; but if it can be assumed that Osborne himself was largely responsible for the speeches of George Dillon, it is in this role that the authentic voice of an Osborne hero first makes itself heard, strident and self-centered, a mixture of petulance and mordant humor.

In May of 1956 Osborne made his London debut as an actor at the Royal Court Theatre with the company that had accepted *Look Back in Anger*. He played several minor roles there in that and the following year before virtually abandoning his career as an actor.

On May 8, 1956, LOOK BACK IN ANGER, presented by the English Stage Company, received its first night at the Royal Court Theatre, in a performance that was arguably the most important single event in the history of postwar English drama. Two catchphrases soon found their way into the jargon of the '50s. Osborne, it was said, belonged to a school of "angry young men" speaking for the youthful dissidents of mid-century Tory England (Colin Wilson, author of *The Outsider*, and novelists John Wain and Kingsley Amis were enrolled as fellow members). It was not much longer before the term "kitchen-sink drama" was coined to describe the genre to which *Look Back in Anger* seemed to belong—a new brand of social realism that looked without flinching at the squalid conditions of lower-middle- and working-class households. Alison's interminable sessions at the ironing board seemed an archetypal expression of this new mode of dramaturgy; Jimmy Porter's cry "There aren't any good, brave causes left" seemed to bespeak the rebellious confusion of the new movement. If Osborne's subsequent career as a playwright has done nothing else, it has demonstrated plainly that he is not a dramatist of the kitchen sink, and confirmed that his work affiliates him to no political group, however loosely defined. While his stature as a dramatist has increased, his role as a leader of revivified socialism has been shown to be an artificial one thrust upon him by the critics.

THE ENTERTAINER, in 1957, with Laurence Olivier as the hero whose tragedy is spelled out in the age-old patter of the music-hall comedian, proved an immediate success. Like *Look Back in Anger*, it was a play that on the surface seemed to have been generated in an outburst of anger against

339

the system (Archie Rice loses a son in the Suez campaign), but it can be seen with the benefit of hindsight to be a remarkably acute psychological study of an individual who remains unmistakably Osborne's creation. The next few years marked a disappointing stage in Osborne's progress. The year 1958 saw the production of the early work *Epitaph for George Dillon*, and in 1959 Osborne's only attempt at a musical, *The World of Paul Slickey* (another refurbishing of something written before *Look Back in Anger*), was produced. The uniformly hostile critical reaction to this sprawling and humorless satire, based loosely on the activities of a gossip columnist involved with a family of supercilious aristocrats, injured Osborne deeply and fostered in him a resentment of the role of the press, which was made doubly acrimonious by the unwarrantable intrusion of certain newspapers upon his private life a year or so later.

In November 1960 the television play *A Subject of Scandal and Concern* did something to redeem Osborne's reputation; in 1961 he returned to critical favor with *Luther*. The influence of Brecht, which had already made its presence felt in the music-hall scenes of *The Entertainer* and in the role of the narrator in his television play, was apparent in the episodic structure and staging conventions of *Luther*. The historical theme, however, was handled in a far from Brechtian manner and Osborne's Martin Luther was an impressive addition to his eloquent gallery of emotional, volatile heroes whose impact upon the audience is immediate and direct.

Two one-act plays followed at the Royal Court in 1962 under the title of *Plays for England*. *The Blood of the Bambergs*, apparently occasioned by the excitement surrounding the wedding of Princess Margaret, is a petulant satire of little permanent interest; *Under Plain Cover* has rather more to commend it. *Sunday Times* critic Harold Hobson wrote that it "brings Genet into England," but this portrait of two happily married clothes fetishists, who thrill at the mention of "knickers" and act out their sadomasochistic fantasies in appropriate costume before tumbling into bed, lacks the compulsion of *The Maids* or *The Balcony*. In addition, the play's construction is strained by the introduction of a journalist who, discovering the pair to be brother and sister, breaks up the ménage for the publicity value of his disclosure. What made the play remarkable at the time (as Kenneth Tynan observed), and offered a foretaste of the feast of permissiveness that was to follow later in the decade, was the author's refusal to regret or condemn the extravagant perversions so cheerfully enjoyed by his incestuous couple.

More than two years intervened before the appearance in 1964 of IN-ADMISSIBLE EVIDENCE, one of Osborne's most impressive achievements to date. The central character, Bill Maitland, ill at ease in the progressive '60s and cynical about the qualities of modern youth, alarmed those critics who still insisted on seeing in Osborne's heroes a projection of the dramatist's own personality and beliefs; but Maitland's language and attitudes accurately reflect the atmosphere of the solicitor's office in which he works and his polemics reveal a consistency of characterization rather than the author's own viewpoint. Technically, although structural imperfections are not lacking, *Inadmissible Evidence* represents an advance upon Osborne's previous work: Maitland's breakdown is convincingly and economically developed in a plot uncluttered with extraneous actions.

A *Patriot for Me*, refused a license for public performance on the grounds of its free treatment of homosexuality, was presented before a "club membership" audience (exempt from the Lord Chamberlain's jurisdiction) at the Royal Court Theatre in 1965, involving author and management in financial loss but winning the *Evening Standard* Award for the best play of the year. The decadent milieu of the Austro-Hungarian Empire at the turn of the century is well captured in this drama of a homosexual officer blackmailed into the betrayal of his country. Redl's slow discovery of his abnormality, subtly and sensitively presented, demonstrated that Osborne can employ the art of understatement as well as the rhetoric of passion when occasion demands. The "drag ball" in Act II, which achieved immediate notoriety, has been criticized as an unnecessary scene introduced for sensational effect but *New Statesman* critic Ronald Bryden found it the play's "centre, its validation, the image from which all else takes perspective and completeness."

Less successful in its exploration of sexual eccentricity was *A Bond Honoured*, presented by the National Theatre in 1966. It is difficult to see what prompted Kenneth Tynan, in the capacity of literary manager for the National Theatre, to ask Osborne for his adaptation of Lope de Vega's *La Fianza Satisfecha* (a play about the power of Christian redemption to save the most extreme of sinners) except its undercurrent of senseless violence coupled with brother-sister incest (to which Osborne gratuitously added mother-rape). John Dexter's stylized production, conceived during a period of growing interest in Artaud's "theater of cruelty," attracted favorable comment, although the adaptation itself was almost universally condemned and must be regarded as one of the most misconceived of Osborne's theatrical ventures.

Two of his most recent plays, *Time Present* and *The Hotel in Amsterdam*, both presented at the Royal Court Theatre in 1968, have returned to the study of contemporary English characters and have abandoned experiments in dramatic form. *Time Present* introduces Osborne's first female protagonist, an actress in her mid-thirties whose vaguely Lesbian friendship with a socialist politician comes to grief during the crisis of her father's death and her own pregnancy. Despite a lack of action, the emotional tone of the play is tightly controlled and a remarkably sharp portrait emerges of the tense, bitchy, hypercritical Pamela, equally impatient of the modish young swingers of the '60s and her earnest, do-gooder parliamentary friend. *The Hotel in Amsterdam* too is a play of mood rather than action, although the suicide of K. L., the film tycoon dominant in the lives of the little group in the hotel drawing room, imposes a formal unity missing in *Time Present*. Nevertheless until the end *The Hotel in Amsterdam* is the most restful of Osborne's plays, the tension that is always present in his work smoldering fitfully behind the small talk of Laurie and his friends, united by their conspiracy to give K. L. the slip for a whole weekend. It is a fragile, brief period of relaxation and in the character of Laurie we glimpse a new element of tenderness in his confession of love for Annie.

With Tony Richardson, Osborne founded Woodfall Films in 1958, and thus shares the credit for having introduced the work of contemporary dramatists and novelists to motion-picture audiences without the artistic distortions usually caused by commercial pressure. In 1965 he directed Charles Wood's *Meals on Wheels* at the Royal Court Theatre, and in 1968 he took the major role in David Mercer's television play *The Parachute*.

Without doubt Osborne is a major dramatist, but his work does not fit neatly into any critical category. His early plays seemed to be those of a writer committed to social change, and there are signs that Osborne himself accepted this evaluation of his work. He is sensitive to the world around him and responds passionately and immediately to the issues of the day; but he is too much of an individualist to care for the orthodoxy of socialist or revolutionary doctrine. Mixed with the contempt for modern mediocrity in *Look Back in Anger* and the scorn for the bungling imperialism of the Suez campaign in *The Entertainer* is a nostalgia for vanished splendor that creates a certain bond between Jimmy Porter and Alison's father, "one of those sturdy old plants left over from the Edwardian wilderness," and invests old Billy Rice with a stature his son never achieves. Tranquility recollected in emotion is Osborne's contribution to aesthetics. His later characters, railing enviously against the hippy scene and insulating themselves from the commonplace world with their wealth, confirm rather than reverse the tendencies of his early drama.

Osborne cannot be called a formal innovator. His interest in Brecht and Artaud has made only a superficial mark on his dramaturgy, and despite the techniques displayed in the music-hall scenes of *The Entertainer* or the Kafkaesque trial scene that opens *Inadmissible Evidence,* he remains a naturalist at heart. Ironically, the playwright who started a movement by carrying the drama into the dingy atmosphere of a Midlands bed-sitting room has ended by setting two of his most recent plays in a London luxury apartment and an expensive foreign hotel, the old stamping grounds of pre-Osborne drama.

Even within the limitations of the naturalistic play Osborne is impatient of the niceties of his craft. Among his persistent faults may be numbered heavy-handed exposition, plots bolstered up with excessive and often melodramatic action and, conversely, a tendency for the major confrontations and conflicts between his characters to be kept off the stage. His minor characters, even in his later plays, often remain shadowy nonentities eclipsed by the heroes to whom they act as foils, while the action of his dramas is rarely carried through to a consistent and satisfactory conclusion. But it is easy, in enumerating Osborne's faults, to overlook his great achievements. His plays, for all their adherence to the well-trodden paths of naturalism, are magnificently theatrical. His writing has the quality that demands, and in all his major works has received, a performance that taxes the actor to his utmost limits. No dramatist writing since the war has offered a comparable succession of brilliant roles to the English actor, from Kenneth Haigh and Laurence Olivier in his first two plays to Jill Bennett and Paul Scofield in his two most recent. Like Shaw, Osborne has revitalized the English theater by his command of the oldest and most vital weapon in the dramatist's armory, language. His gift is for rhetoric, clear, articulate, and springing from the heart; his characters are at their best when, their tongues loosened by anger or alcohol, they give passionate vent to their emotion, often helped by the very indiscipline of their creator's straggling plots. Osborne's rhetoric is dramatically satisfying insofar as each of his characters speaks a language that is private to himself, using an idiosyncratic imagery blended of his personal experience and private obsessions. Osborne began with the portrait of a frustrated young intellectual of working-class origins and has progressed to that of a writer in his forties whose success has brought him little peace of mind ("I work my drawers off," says Laurie, "and get written off twice a year as not fulfilling my early promise by some Philistine squirt drumming up copy"), and clearly the situations of Osborne's characters reflect his own experience. But to regard them merely as facets of Osborne himself is to overlook the immense scope of his dramatic creations, ranging from the agonized intensity of religious feeling in Martin Luther to the repressed homosexuality of Lieutenant Redl.

Osborne described *Look Back in Anger* as a "lesson in feeling," and, although their rhetoric feeds on ideas, what unites Osborne's characters is precisely the depth of feeling they communicate to an audience. Most of Osborne's characters are unpleasant; when they make contact they hurt; but they possess a vitality, a quality that Bill Maitland in *Inadmissible Evidence* calls a "fibbing, mumping, pinched little worm of energy," that commands a reluctant sympathy. The generous honesty of Osborne's examination of the human psyche and its motives, finding its satisfaction far from the realm of reason, in sexual aberration or the infliction of pain, has made him a dramatist as typical of the second half of the twentieth century as Pinter or Ionesco.

In 1964 Osborne received the Academy of Motion Picture Arts and Sciences' Oscar award for his screenplay of *Tom Jones*. He is the subject of a number of studies, including Ronald Hayman's *John Osborne* (1968) and Martin Banham's *Osborne* (1969). His work is discussed in the following: Kenneth Tynan, "The Angry Young Movement," in *Curtains* (1961); John Russell Taylor, editor, *John Osborne: Look Back in Anger, A Casebook*

(1968); and Simon Trussler, *The Plays of John Osborne* (1969), with a fuller bibliography.

**Owen, Alun** (born 1926). English dramatist. Born in North Wales, Owen moved with his parents to Liverpool at the age of eight. His career as an actor began in 1942, and until 1959 he worked in the theater, in television, and in films. He began writing verse at an early age, and *Two Sons*, his first play for radio, was broadcast in 1957. *The Rough and Ready Lot* (1959), his first play to reach the stage, concerns a group of mercenary officers involved in a revolution in nineteenth-century South America. When a route is blocked by a monastery sacred to the Catholic faith, conflict between Catholic, Protestant, and atheist breaks out and ends in violence and death. With its strong situation reflected in vigorous dialogue and sharply individualized characters the play attracted attention as an example of the new realism made possible by the success of *Look Back in Anger*. More characteristic, however, of Owen's subsequent work was *Progress to the Park* (1959), a loosely structured picture of life among a group of young friends in contemporary Liverpool. The main strand of the plot, which concerns the unsuccessful love affair of a Protestant boy with a Catholic girl, pinpoints Owen's concern for the religious divisions that are a prominent feature of the city. With the eloquence of his race, Teifion, a Welsh Liverpudlian embarking upon a career as a writer, acts as the author's mouthpiece in condemning the narrow bigotry that has molded his friends.

The style of *Progress to the Park* was developed in three plays for television, *No Trams to Lime Street*, *After the Funeral*, and *Lena, Oh My Lena*, all evocative explorations of characters, whether English or Welsh, whose personalities have been molded by their Liverpool background. After the success of these plays Owen continued to write for television, moving away from the Liverpool format, with which he had established a solid reputation, toward a variety of dramatic forms, ranging from the nonrealistic symbolism of *The Rose Affair* to the political setting of *You Can't Win 'Em All*, and including a number of frankly "commercial" entertainment thrillers.

In his return to the stage with *A Little Winter Love* (1963), Owen produced a mature and often moving study of the love affair between a Welsh poet-lecturer and the wife of his superior, a soulless American academic administrator. This soundly constructed piece, with its astutely observed gallery of academic types, proved that Owen's developing abilities were by no means in conflict with the demands of the more serious West End playgoer. Much of Owen's dramatic output since that date (including *Maggie May*, a Liverpool musical on which Owen collaborated with Lionel Bart, 1964) has been tailored with professional competence for commercial success.

Owen's career is one of the most consistently successful among the writers for the English stage who have emerged since *Look Back in Anger*. His Liverpool-Welsh background has enabled him to impart a lyrical, passionate, and yet realistic flavor to the dialogue of the emotional scenes in which

ıe excels. Few contemporary dramatists in England have been able to rival
Owen in his ability to create expressive and wholly convincing exchanges be-
ween men and women at decisive moments of love, hatred, or envy. The
;ocial realism and working-class or lower-middle-class settings of his earlier
)lays suggested that he was influenced by the movement initiated by Osborne.
An examination of his career from a later vantage point suggests that it might
ıot have been very different had Osborne never written for the stage: his
:alent, although vigorous and independent, is most at home in the scenes and
;ituations which have always been attractive to theatergoers.

Owen has written contributions to a television comedy series and the
screenplay of *The Criminal* (1960) and the Beatles' film *A Hard Day's Night*
(1964). His work is discussed by John Russell Taylor in *Anger and After*
(1969).

OTHER PLAYS: *The Game* (*The Loser* and *The Winner*, 1965), *The Goose*
(1967), *There'll Be Some Changes Made* (1969).

**Owens, Rochelle** (born 1936). American poet and playwright. Miss
Owens was born in New York City and lives there now with her husband, who
is also a poet. She has contributed to *Four Young Lady Poets* (1962), edited
by LeRoi Jones, and *A Controversy of Poets* (1965). Her play *The String Game*
was published by the Judson Poets' Theatre in 1965; her volume of poems
*Salt and Core* was issued in 1968. In 1965 she was awarded a Rockefeller
grant for playwriting; in 1968 she was a fellow in the Yale-ABC Playwriting
Program at the Yale University School of Drama. Her most widely known
play, *Futz*, was given at the La MaMa Experimental Theatre Club in 1967
and the next year in a regular off-Broadway run won that season's Obie Award
for the best play; a delicate truth about the bestiality of violence emerged
from the poetry of this stark hillbilly parable. Later plays have somehow missed
the aesthetic refinement of *Futz*; experiments like *Beclch* (1968) and *Homo*
and *The Queen of Greece* (1969) show that Miss Owens is still finding her
way as poet-playwright.

# P

**Paravents, Les** (The Screens, 1966). A play in seventeen tableaux by Jean Genet. First performed on April 16, 1966, at the Odéon-Théâtre de France, Paris, under the direction of Roger Blin, *Les Paravents* is Genet's longest and most complex play. It has more than eighty characters (some actors have to play several parts) and theoretically should be performed outdoors in a hilly landscape. On stage the setting for it consists of superimposed platforms. For each tableau a number of screens—either white or painted in violent colors—are brought onto the platforms to suggest, in an unreal way, the various places involved in the action. In the last tableau the stage has four levels, and nine screens mark the boundaries of a village square, a grocery, a brothel, a house, and, on the highest level, the realm of the Dead.

Although much of the activity is not clearly defined, there are two main lines of action: on the one hand, the rebellion of an Arab collectivity against the colonists who exploit them; on the other, young Saïd's willful descent into an increasingly profound abjection, which leads to his complete annihilation.

Saïd, his mother, and his wife, Leila (who is so ugly that her face is always masked with a hood), are the poorest and most oppressed of the Arab population. Saïd's choice—with the help of his mother, who constantly sings the glory of their poverty and abjection—consists in carrying to the extreme the unhappiness and evil imposed on them by their oppressors. Saïd tries to embody and transcend the colonists' image of the Arab as a liar, a thief, a murderer, and a traitor. However, the people's rebellion breaks out. Plantations are burned, guerrillas fight the European soldiers, murders begin to multiply. Various groups of characters represent the European oppressors: soldiers of the Foreign Legion, colonists, and stereotyped figures such as a vamp, an academician, and a banker. Genet universalizes the image of colonial oppression by mixing up nationalities (English, Belgian, French) and by creating a jumble of periods (for example, modern soldiers, but an 1840-vintage judge, banker, and general). The rebels are inspired by a woman, Kadidja, who, even after having been killed, continues to be the mouthpiece not only of the rebellion but of the Evil that "impregnates" it. Saïd goes to an even greater extreme than the others in pursuing Evil: He comes to betray his own people.

346

In the last tableau most of the main characters are assembled and ironically reconciled to each other in the realm of the Dead. They are awaiting Saïd. In the world of the living the Arab forces are victorious and have replaced the oppressive society of the colonists with another society that is just as organized. Saïd, whom the most poverty-stricken Arabs consider their "flag," is killed by the Arab forces, who are promoting a new order. But he never arrives in the realm of the Dead that the spectator sees on stage: He has gone beyond, into nothingness. For Genet, an annihilation that complete, caused by a refusal to compromise with any type of Good—and thus a rigorous renunciation—is the equivalent of saintliness.

The play is rich in substance because of the complex interaction within each group and among the groups. Each one is a fantastic small world in itself, peopled with extreme, monstrous, or grotesque creatures. One of the most striking groups is that of the brothel, reigned over by the great prostitute Warda—a place where the other activities converge and are sifted out through violent eroticism, and where everything becomes sublimated through a complicated and illusory ritual. In addition to the prostitutes and their customers, the trio Saïd-his mother-Leila, as they progress toward total renunciation; the Foreign Legion soldiers, led by a Lieutenant-Sergeant couple who are bound to each other by a homosexual mirror-play of reflections; and the farcical colonists—all represent the classes of heroes (adored or detested), saints, and ridiculous enemies that people Genet's imagination, reflecting each other and indulging in a dialectical battle *ad infinitum*, to that point of annihilation that Genet calls glory.

*Les Paravents* is written in a language characteristic of Genet, consisting of the most striking images, a constant tension between the sumptuousness of the words and the horror or muck of what they designate, and a mixture of the noblest French and the strongest slang. The unreality of that mixture, which causes the spectator's head to swim, makes the play into a huge verbal phantasmagoria, comparable to a black mass in an anti-world. On the visual level as well, the whole ceremony is phantasmagoric: Every character is torn from reality by his costume or makeup, and every screen is less a "setting" than a kind of seedy and barbarous sanctuary before which the rites of abjection, power, eroticism, and murder are performed. In that respect, one of the most powerful scenes of the play is the one in which the rebels, called together by Kadidja, with fierce hatred, paint on the white screens that take up the entire stage the bloody crimes they have just committed.

After one relatively calm performance, *Les Paravents* provoked several riots at the Théâtre de France. The murder onstage of French soldiers, scatological scenes performed between French flags, and the systematic derision of colonization and the army were, very shortly after the Algerian war, considered by certain groups of veterans and patriots as unbearable insults. And in fact, the play, in its language and spectacle, is a call to violent rebellion against the established authorities, as well as glorification of crime and of evil in general. But it must also be understood as a hymn to misery and as a great poem in action, in which Genet invents a new beauty and a new saintliness.

**Paso, Alfonso** (born 1926). Spanish dramatist. Son of a famous actress and a playwright who bestowed some 380 pieces on the Spanish stage, married to the daughter of Enrique Jardiel Poncela, the great comic playwright, Paso is above all else a man of the theater. He already has some one hundred plays to his credit, not infrequently opening four or five a season. His one-act plays of the late 1940s were done under the auspices of the highly experimental Arte Nuevo group. The macabre humor of his comedy-mysteries— *Usted puede ser un asesino* (You Can Be an Assassin, 1958) is one of the best —leads critics to compare him to the revolutionists of the comic theater, Miguel Mihura and Jardiel Poncela. Exponents of the social theater claim kinship with *Los pobrecitos* (The Poor, 1957) and *La boda de la chica* (The Wedding, 1960). But in the last analysis it is Paso's bourgeois comedies based on clever manipulation of character, situation, and dialogue, potboilers whose sole purpose is to entertain and to aid a healthy digestion, that endear him to impresarios and audiences alike. The fact that he often begins rehearsals of Act I before Acts II and III are written does not inspire confidence in the perdurability of the greater part of his dramatic production.

OTHER PLAYS: *No se dice adiós, sino hasta luego* (Not Goodbye, but Till Later, 1953), *Cuarenta y ocho horas de felicidad* (Forty-eight Hours of Happiness, 1956), *El canto de la cigarra* (The Song of the Locust, 1958), *Cuidado con las personas formales* (Watch Out for Serious People, 1960), *Cosas de papá y mamá* (1960), *La corbata* (The Tie, 1963), *Desde Isabel, con amor* (From Isabel With Love, 1967).

**Pemán, José María** (born 1897). Spanish dramatist. Poet, orator, publicist, and world traveler, Pemán has always been active in politics. He is a member and was once director of the Royal Academy. With the early *Cuando las cortes de Cádiz* (1934) and the postwar *Metternich* (1942), historical dramas in verse, Pemán proved himself a worthy disciple of Eduardo Marquina (1879–1946), who perfected the genre. His later prose plays combine realistic representation of manners and morals and social commentary, a style culminating in *Callados como muertos* (As Still as Death, 1952). Pemán's interest in the everyday problems of the bourgeoisie does not place him in the vanguard of the European theater, but it does guarantee him continued commercial success. His free versions, reworkings really, of Greek and Roman tragedies (*Oedipus, Antigone, Electra,* and Seneca's *Thyestes*) may well prove to be his most enduring contribution to the Spanish stage.

OTHER PLAYS SINCE 1936: *Ella no se mete en nada* (She's No Busybody, 1941), *La casa* (1946), *Entre el no y el sí* (Between No and Yes, 1951), *Los tres etcéteras de don Simón* (1958), *La coqueta y don Simón* (1960), *Los monos gritan al amanecer* (Monkeys Scream at Dawn, 1963).

**Peru.** Before World War II Peru scarcely had a theater. Isolated figures such as Juan Ríos, Percy Gibson Parra, and Bernardo Roca Rey had struggled with uneven success. Much of the relative success of the movement since 1950 is due to the work of Sebastián Salazar Bondy, poet, essayist, and author of a number of plays on Peruvian history and social problems. His studies of moral decay (*Algo que quiere morir* [Something That Wishes to Die], 1951) and the spiritual ruin of a family (*No hay isla feliz* [There Is No Happy Island], 1954) are both dramatically effective and filled with controlled rage at the system which permits such abuses. He showed his versatility in *El fabricante de deudas* (The Inventor of Debts, 1962), a delightful satire on entrepreneurism, and other works. Salazar Bondy's early death in 1964 was a severe loss to his country's theater. The senior dramatist in Peru today is Enrique Solari Swayne, whose *Collacocha* (1956), a somewhat rhetorical, realistic drama of the building of the Transandean tunnel, achieved international success. His later plays—*La mazorca* (The Ear of Corn, 1966), *Ayax Telamonio* (1968)—share the social context and verbalism, but have not achieved the success of *Collacocha*.

Peru boasts a number of highly promising dramatists who are moving in a variety of formal directions. Sarina Helfgott is highly imaginative, and in *El verdugo* (The Executioner, 1966), based on the Eichmann trial, she achieves the needed discipline. Julio Ortega has done interesting work influenced in part by Beckett, and in the exploration of dramatic possibilities of the pantomime and blackout. Julio Ramón Ribeyro, working within traditional realism, and Elena Portocarrero, in the vein of *commedia dell'arte* and the traditional farce, are established figures, and Alonso Alegría emerged in 1969 with *El cruce sobre el Niágara* (The Crossing of Niagara), a tense drama of individual courage and mutual need.

**Pinget, Robert** (born 1920). French dramatist and painter. At first a painter, Pinget began his literary career in 1950. His works are mostly novels, the earliest of which—such as *Graal Flibuste* (1957)—are characterized by their satiric tone and, above all, by a very rich and whimsical imagination. From *Le Fiston* (1959) on, the novel served Pinget as a means to question the reality of the world and the past, and he thus became an exponent of the "new novel," along with Alain Robbe-Grillet, Michel Butor, Claude Simon, Nathalie Sarraute, and Marguerite Duras.

Pinget's plays are derived from his novels or parts of his novels. *Lettre morte* (Dead Letter, 1960), for example, is a scenic adaptation of *Le Fiston*. The main character of the play, Levert, is a father awaiting a letter from his son, who has taken off without leaving an address. He goes on and on about his distress in rambling conversations with a bartender, actors on tour, a postman—people who find his poor little story banal or make fun of it. The bartender himself deserted his father; the actors are performing in a play entitled *The Prodigal Son;* the postman knows of a similar case of a father's grief. The play goes around in circles, giving the impression of a grayish, absurd, hopeless world, and one ends by doubting the reality of even the departed son and the past evoked by Levert.

Pinget is often rather similar to Beckett, whose *All That Fall* he translated into French. Somewhat like certain of Beckett's characters (in *Endgame* or *Play*, for example), those of Pinget painfully try to reconstruct or even create, through language, a reality or a past that continues to elude them. The hero of *L'Hypothèse* (The Hypothesis, 1966) attempts to explain what happened to a manuscript and to describe its contents, but finds that he is contradicted and ridiculed by his own image, which is projected onto a giant screen and gives the facts in quite a different way. In *La Manivelle* (1962) two old people recall their common past, but end up altogether contradicting each other. This radio play was translated by Samuel Beckett as *The Old Tune*.

OTHER PLAYS: *Architruc* (1962).

**Ping-Pong, Le** (1955). A play in two parts and twelve scenes by Arthur Adamov. It was first performed on March 2, 1955, at the Théâtre des Noctambules, Paris, under the direction of Jacques Mauclair. At the Café de l'Espérance, under the eye of the cashier Madame Duranty, two young men, Arthur and Victor, are fascinated by their games at the pinball machine. They are joined by a young and elegant Bohemian, Monsieur Roger, as well as by a man who collects the money from the pinball machine, Sutter, and a girl, Annette. The lives of this group of five characters revolve entirely around the machine and the company that manufactures it, called the Consortium and directed by "the Old Man," alias Monsieur Constantin. When Madame Duranty's pinball machine breaks down, she goes from job to job (manager of public baths, then of a dancing school) while waiting despairingly for her machine to be repaired. Annette, an usher in a movie theater, then a shoe salesgirl, then a manicurist, dreams of working for the Consortium as a "scout." Monsieur Roger becomes the Old Man's nonchalant and absolutely inefficient secretary. As for Arthur, he involves his friend Victor in plans for perfecting and complicating the machine—plans that the Old Man sometimes accepts and sometimes rejects. Time goes by and the situation deteriorates: Victor gives up his plans and becomes a doctor; the Consortium has serious economic difficulties; the Old Man grows senile and dies; Annette, too, dies; Sutter leaves for America. In the last scene we find Arthur and Victor both at the age of seventy. They are playing ping-pong. Gradually they manage to simplify the game to the point of getting rid of the net and the rackets, and finally even ignoring the table. During a last wild and free game Victor collapses from a heart attack.

*Le Ping-Pong* was a turning point in Adamov's career as a playwright—a transition from theater of the absurd to a theater of social criticism. The pinball machine, by imposing its rules on the characters, also imposes its own obsessive language on them, dehumanizes them, and sends them bounding unpredictably from one job to another and from one relationship to another, like its balls. In the last scene the pinball machine has been obliterated by ping-pong, and the game of ping-pong itself is finally repudiated. Clearly, the pinball machine is the symbol of a consumer product, apparently meant for pleasure, which causes man's unhappiness by becoming the object of economic machinations. The chief victim of the operation is Arthur, a creative and poetic young man, diverted from true creation by the wheelings and dealings of the Consortium.

**Pinter, Harold** (born 1930). English dramatist. The son of a tailor in the East End of London, Pinter was educated at Hackney Downs Grammar School and trained for the stage at the Royal Academy of Dramatic Art and the Central School of Drama. Under the stage name of David Baron he acted in provincial repertory from 1949 to 1957, working between engagements as a waiter, dishwasher, and door-to-door salesman. He has from time to time acted in and directed productions of his own plays. Before his first play Pinter had already written what he calls "hundreds of poems and short pieces of prose," of which about a dozen were published, and an unpublished novel that provided material for his radio play *The Dwarfs*. Pinter's career as a playwright began in relative obscurity in 1957, when *The Room*, a one-act play, was hurriedly written for performance by students in the Drama Department at Bristol University. THE BIRTHDAY PARTY, his first full-length play, was a commercial failure the following year. From this unpromising foundation Pinter has built up an international reputation that places him at the forefront of contemporary English dramatists and has stimulated, in critic and theatergoer alike, a major reassessment of the relationship between dramatist, play, and audience. Pinter's role as an innovator has been frequently stressed: less emphasis has been placed on the steady personal development in theme and style that can be traced in his work and which invests the later plays with a quality quite different from that of the earlier work upon which most discussion of Pinter's technique has been based.

*The Room* and *The Birthday Party*, together with the one-act play *The Dumb Waiter* (written in 1957, although not performed until 1960), share a formula that earned them the epithet of "comedy of menace" (first applied by David Campton to his own work in 1957). In each play the room in which the action is set forms a temporary haven of security for a character besieged and eventually destroyed by the unexplained hostility of an outsider. In *The Room*, a woman is visited by a blind Negro; after he is brutally and inexplicably killed by her husband, she loses her own sight. Meg's lodger in *The Birthday Party* is carried away, cowed into speechlessness, by two visitors to her shabby boardinghouse. In *The Dumb Waiter* orders for ever more exotic meals are passed down the "dumb waiter" to the basement of an empty house where two professional murderers await their next assignment. It was not so much the surreal nature of the action that puzzled Pinter's earliest audiences as the dramatic mode employed in its presentation. Pinter refuses to suggest, by skillful exposition or subtle display of character, that the dramatist has a superior knowledge of his creations for the stage, or that a significant scheme will emerge from their actions; his audience is no more privileged than the man who overhears the conversation of strangers in the street. The sequence of events that, in the Western tradition of drama, gradually unfolds a pattern of action with Aristotelian clarity is lacking in Pinter. Indeed, by making his characters contradict assertions made only a few moments previously, Pinter deliberately denies the possibility of such a coherent scheme. Nor have the many attempts to wrest a symbolic meaning from the action of the plays met with encouragement from the author. He has described the genesis of *The Room:* "I went into a room one day and saw a couple of people in it . . . . I started off with this picture of two people and let them carry on from there." With equal insistence he has ascribed the origin of *The Birthday Party* to a study of characters observed in a lodging house during his life as a touring actor. But paradoxically these plays in which action and dialogue are apparently arbitrary prove to possess a superb formal structure. Pinter has few equals in the art of preparing for a climax by subtle variations in tone and tension. While causation and relationship remained obscure in Pinter's early drama, the abrupt and inconsequential patterns of everyday speech were captured with unfailing skill. Rarely has the ambiguous nature of human communication been so acutely and wittily expressed as in the obsessive and rhythmic patterns of Harold Pinter's dialogue. It is the clash between the surreal, unfamiliar nature of the action and the instantly recognizable, exact realism of the dialogue that imparts a unique flavor to Pinter's work.

A *Slight Ache* (a one-act play broadcast in 1959, staged in 1961) follows a pattern similar to that of the earlier plays in its portrait of the effect, at first unnerving and finally overwhelming, of a match-seller who stations himself without explanation in the lane outside a couple's country house. But it marks a development in the role of the mysterious intruder, for the match-seller's presence exacerbates tensions that already exist between husband and wife, and after his invitation into the house the unbroken silence he maintains acts as a catalyst bringing the couple's unspoken thoughts to the surface. Thus a journey to the interior can be traced from the gratuitous mystification of his first short play, through *The Birthday Party*, where the arrival of Goldberg and McCann is more organically related to the fears and inadequacies displayed by Stanley in the opening scenes, to the more consistently developed psychological emphasis of A *Slight Ache.*

These early plays established Pinter, among a growing minority of admirers, as a master of the theatrical equivalent of the close-up shot, seizing on a moment of violence or undefined horror, glimpsed in immediate sharpness against a background that remained opaquely out of focus. It was in *The Caretaker* (1960) that Pinter first achieved popular success, in a play that dispensed altogether with the mysterious strangers of his earlier work. This study of a tramp's shifting and uneasy temporary relationship with two brothers nevertheless bears the hallmarks of its author in the unexplained circumstances of the two brothers, the brilliant accuracy of the dialogue, and the doubt whether any statement, from the tramp's claim that his name is assumed and his "papers" are in Sidcup to Aston's plans to build a shed in the garden, can be taken at face value. Aston's long, acutely painful, account at the conclusion of the second act of his treatment for a mental disorder seems to supply a clue to his ambivalent attitude toward the tramp, but Pinter himself has declared that "it isn't necessary to conclude that everything Aston says about his experiences in the mental hospital is true." Attempts have been made to find a consistent explanation, at a symbolic as well as a psychological level, of the alternating friendliness and menace of the two brothers toward the confused tramp Davies, but the work defies interpretation of this order and, using the techniques of the earlier plays with greater subtlety, calls for a direct, unreflective response from its audience.

Early in 1960 *The Birthday Party* was presented on television and "for days," writes an enthusiastic critic, "one could hear people in buses and canteens eagerly discussing the play as a maddening but deeply disturbing experience." Within three years Pinter's startling and complex talent had been generally recognized and a new and ugly word, "Pinteresque," entered the English language to describe the kind of situation and, more especially, of dialogue mirrored in his plays.

*A Night Out*, produced successively on radio, television, and the stage (1960), is a more naturalistic piece about a son's relationship with a domineering mother and the sexual difficulties encountered by the youth. *The Dwarfs*, although staged in 1963, is primarily a radio play (first broadcast in 1960) based on Pinter's unpublished novel and exploring the mind of a man whose hallucinatory world is peopled by the dwarfs of the title; it has been called one of his most personal statements. Another television play, *Night School*, was broadcast in 1960.

In *The Collection* (1962) and *The Lover* (1963), both one-act plays that were televised before they were staged, Pinter entered upon an exploration of sexual themes foreshadowed in *A Slight Ache* and *Night Out* and culminating in *The Homecoming*. *The Collection* centers upon one of Pinter's favorite topics, the question of verification. A husband's attempt to discover whether a young fashion designer slept with his wife exposes a complex set of heterosexual and homosexual relationships between four characters, but leaves the question unanswered and indeed suggests that the true version of the story, if there is one to be found, has no more validity than any of the alternative versions put forward in the course of the action. "There are no hard distinctions," Pinter had written in 1960, "between what is real and what is unreal, nor between what is true and what is false. The thing is not necessarily either true or false; it can be both true and false. The assumption that to verify what has happened and what is happening presents few problems I take to be inaccurate." In *The Lover* the gulf between illusion and reality is deliberately bridged by a suburban couple. A husband who leaves for work in the morning regularly returns in the afternoon to visit his wife in the guise of a lover while she acts the part of a casual pickup. The play ends with the apparent suppression of the couple's life as husband and wife in favor of the fantasy roles. The disturbing excitement of sexual encounter also forms the subject of two television plays, *Tea Party* (1965) and *The Basement* (1967, written for production as a film).

Pinter's third full-length play *The Homecoming* (1965), which provoked varying critical reactions and won the New York Drama Critics Circle Award, can best be understood as a further development of the author's interest in the unpredictable, disruptive power of erotic attraction, which takes the place of the mysterious intruders of the earlier plays. *The Homecoming* achieves its taut atmosphere, its undercurrent of suppressed violence and its glittering, enigmatic dialogue without recourse to externalized menace. The coolly accepted proposal that Ruth, introduced to her husband's family on a fleeting visit from the States, should remain behind "as a kind of guest," a sexual partner shared between her brothers-in-law and father-in-law, earning her keep by a nightly stint of prostitution, is presented with as little explication as the eruption of physical violence in the earlier plays, and uses greater subtlety to provoke a similar sense of deep-seated unease on the part of the audience. An additional feature of *The Homecoming* is that the action is set within a complex set of family relationships. The family of father, brother, and three sons is bound together by constant reference to the mother of the family, now dead, spoken of sometimes as a paragon of virtue and sometimes as a whore. Obliquely the suggestion is made that Ruth arrives in this male household to take up the ambivalent role vacated by the mother. Is Ruth a nymphomaniac, and was she a total stranger to this family before her arrival as Ted's wife? Has she, in fact, understood and accepted the terms of the agreement? Why does her husband acquiesce in the scheme? True to his earlier technique, Pinter offers no answer. "A character on the stage," he wrote in 1960, "who can present no convincing argument or information as to his past experience, his present behaviour or his aspirations, nor give a comprehensive analysis of his motives, is as legitimate and as worthy of attention as one who, alarmingly, can do all these things. The more acute the experience the less articulate its expression." Although a notable feature of Pinter's development has been the introduction of ever more articulate characters, the central experience and motivation of those characters remains impenetrable.

Pinter has confessed in an interview to the increasing difficulty he has found in writing for the stage, and it was 1969 before any new work by this author reached the stage (the production of *Landscape*, which was broadcast in 1968, was delayed until the impending abolition of stage censorship had come into effect). *Night* is a brief and gentle duologue contributed to a West End entertainment entitled *Mixed Doubles;* more substantial are the one-act plays LANDSCAPE and *Silence* (produced on a double bill). In each play what seems a sharp break with the style of his earlier work can be seen upon closer analysis to be a further refinement of Pinter's characteristic techniques and preoccupations. The use of motionless actors whose speeches are not so much an exchange of dialogue as a series of alternating monologues reflects the influence of Beckett's later plays, but the themes woven into the texture of these exchanges are expressive of the difficulty of communicating a version of the past, and of the independence of a cherished memory from the world of verifiable facts, which were prominent in much of Pinter's previous work. The obscurity of his characters' past and the sensitive immediacy of their present experience are combined in a typical manner, and the overt violence of sexual aggression and surrender that marked *The Homecoming* has been transmuted into a compassionate understanding of male and female psychology. The almost total lack of contact between the *dramatis personae* gives these plays a superficially static appearance; in fact a subtle rhythm controlled by a delicate counterpoint of recurrent imagery achieves the same effects as the more obvious structural devices of his earlier plays and does much to substantiate the claim that it is Pinter, rather than Fry or Eliot, who has restored poetic drama to the postwar English stage.

Despite his insistence on the traditional nature of his dramatic technique, Pinter must be regarded as the most original of the English dramatists to have emerged since 1956, and it would be unwise to attempt a final assessment of a writer who has departed so radically from the customary formulas of his chosen medium. He comes from a Jewish family in the East End of London, and has stated that as a child after the war he encountered violence "in quite an extreme form" from neo-Fascist groups. Violence has remained a constant theme in his writing, and the emphasis on the indissoluble strength of the family bond (particularly noticeable in *The Homecoming*) may owe a great deal to the influence of Jewish family life. But unlike Arnold Wesker, a writer with a background similar to his own, Pinter has remained distrustful of ideological commitment, stating that propaganda on the stage forces characters "into fixed and artificial postures." What literary influences can be detected in his work stem from twentieth-century novelists rather than dramatists, and he is indebted to the novels as much as the plays of the writers whose influence he most readily acknowledges. "Beckett and Kafka stayed with me the most," he has said of his early reading—"I think Beckett is the best prose writer living." But while the influence of these and other writers can certainly be detected, and the popularity of his work outside England can be ascribed in part to his affinity with a European tradition of literature, it must not be forgotten that Pinter is an actor whose works are primarily written for the stage. The precise theatrical effect of his plays has remained unique, despite the many imitations his success has encouraged, and it has stubbornly resisted critical definition.

The puzzling nature of Pinter's writing has attracted a good deal of academic attention, much of it wide of the mark. Perhaps the most valuable insight is offered by the critic Walter Kerr, who has claimed that Pinter is "the only man working in the theater today who writes existential plays existentially." Of the dozens of writers dramatizing existential theories "none but Harold Pinter," he has suggested, "has taken the fundamental proposition seriously enough to present his plays in the new existential sequence." Pinter's characters have no identity beyond that which they define for themselves in the very action of the play: each new action is a further definition of identity that nevertheless leaves the next action intransigently unpredictable. Nor does the action of his drama reverberate with larger meaning. While Beckett's tramps may reflect a metaphysical notion of life's futility as they await Godot's arrival, Davies' forlorn hope of retrieving his papers in Sidcup is wholly devoid of larger symbolism.

It seems clear that Pinter himself entertains no such intellectually formulated notions of his position as a writer. His own comments, as revealed in interviews, suggest an intuitive approach controlled by a preoccupation with form. "As far as I'm concerned," he said in 1961, "my characters and I inhabit the same world. The only difference between them and me is that they don't arrange and select." Although he has abandoned the customary props of exposition and revelation, the rhythm of his plays is orchestrated with minute attention to detail, indications of pauses and momentary hesitations punctuating the text like rests in a musical score. "For me," he has stated, "everything has to do with shape, structure, and overall unity." Whatever Pinter's own disavowals, however, the kind of response his plays demand may be called "existential" in that his audience is called upon to experience, in all its uniqueness, an individual emotion, a sudden action, or an unexpected phrase, without speculation upon its significance, relevance, or coherence within a wider pattern of things. The sizable theatergoing public that is now prepared to accept his work within these novel terms of reference stands as some indication of his achievement.

Pinter's adaptations of the novels of other writers for the screen have been much admired: They include *The Servant, Accident,* and *The Pumpkin Eater.* He has also written a screen version of *The Caretaker.* Included in his output are a number of revue sketches, written around 1959, called by their author "plays in miniature" and reproducing, in a few pages of dialogue, all the characteristics of his major works. The actress Vivien Merchant, whom he married in 1956, has premiered most of his female roles. An interview with Pinter by Harry Thompson appeared in *New Theatre Magazine,* Vol. II, No. 2 (1961); Lawrence M. Bensky also published an interview in *Theatre at Work* (1967), edited by Charles Marowitz and Simon Trussler. Pinter has been the subject of several books, among them Walter Kerr's *Columbia Essays on Modern Writers No. 27: Harold Pinter* (1967), Ronald Hayman's *Harold Pinter* (1968), and John Russell Taylor's *Writers and Their Work No. 212: Harold Pinter* (1969). His work has also been discussed by John Russell Brown in "Dialogue in Pinter and Others" in *Modern British Dramatists* (1968; edited by Brown), by Martin Esslin in *The Theatre of the Absurd* (1961). *The Homecoming: A Casebook* (1969) was edited by John Lahr. Esslin published a full-length critical discussion, *The Peopled Wound: The Plays of Harold Pinter*, in 1970.

OTHER PLAYS: *Old Times* (1971).

**Piscator, Erwin** (1893–1966). German director and theater manager. Though he was born into a family that had produced a long line of Protestant ministers, Piscator did not continue the tradition. Instead he transformed the theater into a political church with his "protestant" fervor. This fervor was directed toward social change, and he sought to develop theatrical techniques and a dramaturgy that would correspond to Marxist tenets. This was, however, not the case early in his career. Piscator was first strongly influenced by the spectacular expressionist devices of Max Reinhardt, and he was not committed to politics while acting at the Munich Hoftheater before World War I. However, his experiences in the war transformed him into a political radical.

From 1920 to 1924 he formed two theater groups, the Tribunal Theater (1920–21) in Königsberg and the Proletarisches Theater (1923–24) in Berlin, which endeavored to appeal to workers and actually played in gathering places of the workers. In 1924 Piscator was engaged by the Volksbühne (People's Theater) in Berlin, and he continued to produce plays that agitated for political change. Piscator used such dramas as Alfons Paquet's *Fahnen* and *Sturmflut*, Gorky's *A Night's Lodging*, and Schiller's *The Robbers* to stress the need for revolution. In each of these productions Piscator used documentary techniques such as film projections, loudspeakers, photographs, posters, and news reports to lend the plays a sense of authenticity and immediacy.

Because of his radical politics, Piscator was obliged to leave the Volksbühne in 1927, and he decided to start his own theater once again at the Nollendorfplatz in Berlin. He persisted in his experiments and produced several important plays with revolutionary technical means: Ernst Toller's *Hoppla, Wir Leben* was staged with interludes on film; Tolstoi's *Rasputin* was played on a stage that gave the appearance of a globe and symbolized the earth; Hašek's *The Good Soldier Schweik* was performed on a conveyor belt with slides and screens by George Grosz. Piscator worked closely with the leading political dramatists of his time, including Brecht, Felix Gasbarra, Walter Mehring, Ernst Toller, and Friedrich Wolf. He used the epic theater to create a *Totaltheater*, in which all possible means of production were employed collectively and in a historical sense to stage plays designed to move the audience to change conditions in society. Piscator was most interested in substantive questions

357

that revealed social contradictions. His own theater lasted only one year. Nevertheless, he continued to work at other theaters in Berlin, experimenting with epic and documentary techniques.

In 1931 Piscator traveled to Moscow where he directed at the International Theatre for a brief period. When Hitler gained control of Germany in 1933, Piscator was forced to work outside the country permanently. In 1936 he traveled to New York to adapt Theodore Dreiser's *An American Tragedy* into *The Case of Clyde Griffiths*. He then returned to Paris, where he worked until 1939. With the outbreak of World War II, Piscator departed again for New York and directed the Dramatic Workshop of the New School for Social Research until 1951. While in New York, Piscator adapted Robert Penn Warren's *All the King's Men* and Tolstoi's *War and Peace,* always placing great emphasis on the political content of the works. Aside from these adaptations, he also produced numerous other plays and trained American actors with the hope of establishing a political theater in America. However, the probes of Senator Joseph R. McCarthy disillusioned him, and he returned in 1951 to West Germany, where he was invited to direct plays ranging from the classical to the contemporary. In 1962 he became general manager of the Freie Volksbühne in Berlin. Here he had a great impact on the development of the documentary drama. He personally directed the first productions of Rolf Hochhuth's *The Deputy* (1963), Heinar Kipphardt's *In the Matter of J. Robert Oppenheimer* (1964), and Peter Weiss's *The Investigation* (1965). Until his death in 1966, Piscator fought for a theater that would develop the political consciousness of the audience. His book, *Das politische Theater* (1929, revised 1964), and his collected essays reveal his great concern in social problems and his desire to change society along Communist lines. His concern and desire were essentially religious in nature and demonstrate his ties to his Protestant background. Perhaps this is the reason why Piscator's political theater never achieved the effect he desired. His politics turned the theater into a secular church, and this church functioned as a bourgeois institution that adumbrated his politics.

**Pogodin, Nikolai Fyodorovich** (pen name of N. F. **Stukalov;** born 1900). Soviet dramatist. Born at Gundorovskaya-on-the-Don, Pogodin began a career as a journalist in 1920, eventually becoming a special correspondent for *Pravda.* His travels throughout the Soviet Union provided him with material for his early plays: *Temp* (Tempo, 1928–29), dealing with industrial construction during the first Five-Year Plan; *Poema o topore* (Poem of the Ax, 1930), concerning the discovery of stainless steel; and *Moy drug* (My Friend, 1932), outlining problems of the transformation to socialism in Russia. *Aristokraty* (Aristocrats, 1934) describes the rehabilitation of former criminals by means of forced labor on the White-Baltic Sea canal. *Chelovek c ruzhyom* (Man With a Gun, 1937), for which Pogodin received a Stalin Prize in 1941, was the first of a trilogy of plays about Lenin. The other parts of the trilogy are

*Kremlevskie kuranty* (Kremlin Chimes, 1941) and *Tretya, pateticheskaya* (The Third, Pathetic, 1955). In the latter play the connection of Stalin, who died in 1953, with Lenin is minimized. *Missurysky vals* (Missouri Waltz, 1950) was an anti-American play, which centered its attack on President Truman. *Sonet Petrarki* (Petrarch's Sonnet, 1956) ignores political themes, concentrating on the anguish of an adulterous love affair.

Poland. Early Polish drama was comparatively insignificant in quantity and quality and followed roughly the pattern of drama in Western Europe, though on a smaller scale and with less originality. In the nineteenth century the great Romantic poets—Adam Mickiewicz (1798–1855), Juliusz Słowacki (1809–1849), and Zygmunt Krasiński (1812–1859)—created poetic drama of European importance. Its intense patriotic and moral content, and its loose, panoramic form, which held immense possibilities for imaginative theatrical treatment, found their continuation in the Young Poland Movement, notably in the work of Stanisław Wyspiański (1869–1907), Poland's greatest poetic dramatist and theater visionary of this century. This trend in Polish drama, continued by playwrights of lesser talent, has always been in the foreground, if only because present-day dramatists keep reacting to it and the problems posed by it, through argument, paraphrase, and parody. The nineteenth century was also the major source of Polish comedy, particularly in the work of Aleksander Fredro (1793–1876), and later of naturalistic and psychological drama, cultivated by such writers as Jan August Kisielewski (1876–1918), Gabriela Zapolska (1860–1921), and Tadeusz Rittner (1873–1921). This trend, enriched through the treatment of new social and ideological problems in the work of such writers as Stefan Żeromski (1864–1925), became the other main source of tradition and a model for much new drama of the postwar years.

The period between the two world wars, which for Poland was a time not only of newly regained independence, but also of political uncertainty and of unsolved social problems, was in many ways a period of transition. Dramatic output in this period was plentiful. Poetic drama was continued by Karol Hubert Rostworowski (1877–1938), psychological drama by Zofia Nałkowska (1885–1954). There was a feminist group of playwrights, headed by Maria Morozowicz-Szczepkowska (1889–1968), and a socially radical group of Communist poet-playwrights, of whom the most representative were Bruno Jasieński (1901–42) and Witold Wandurski (1891–1937). Adolf Nowaczyński (Neuwert) (1876–1944), author of historical dramas, and Wacław Grubiński (born 1883), who wrote light, drawing-room comedies, were typical of the right-wing writers. There was also a sophisticated, "scientific" comedy, whose exponents were Bruno Winawer (1883–1944) and Antoni Cwojdziński (born 1896). The dominant tendencies of the inter-war drama were to a certain extent continued in the early years after World War II.

The war itself, with its havoc of destruction and holocaust in human lives, with the humiliations of the Nazi occupation, was a profound shock for artists and playwrights, as for all the nation. For the nearly six years between 1939 and 1945 open theater life of any importance did not exist. Many dramatists, actors, and directors were killed, imprisoned, or dispersed abroad. Nevertheless activity did not come to a standstill. Plays were written to be produced as soon as the war ended; even playwriting competitions were organized clandestinely. Some performances took place in secret. Apart from established writers continuing their activity, new talents emerged. Unfortunately a number of them did not survive the war and their participation in the Resistance or the Warsaw Rising of 1944, and only single promising plays bear witness to the lost potential of such writers as Andrzej Trzebiński (1922–1943), with his *Aby podnieść różę* (To Pick Up Rose); Tadeusz Gajcy (1922–1944), author of *Homer i Orchidea* (Homer and Orchid); and Krzysztof Baczyński (1921–1944), who wrote *Dramat* (Drama). Most of these young writers were poets and the heightened sensitivity of poetry that characterizes their plays was to be taken up, a decade later, by their contemporaries or somewhat younger colleagues.

The immediate postwar years, 1945 to 1948, however, were dominated by the older generation of dramatists who, in their different ways, tried first of all to give expression to their wartime experiences and relate them to the postwar reality, so different from the world they had known before. In this vein Jerzy SZANIAWSKI (1886–1970) scored his only postwar success with DWA TEATRY (The Two Theaters, 1946). Ludwik Hieronim Morstin (1886–1966), a humanist and classical scholar, followed his prewar success, *Obrona Ksantypy* (The Defense of Xanthippe, 1938), with other plays taken from mythology and ancient history, which he presented as relevant today. In *Penelopa* (1945) he gave an updated variant of a husband returning from the war after a long absence. His *Kleopatra* (1954) is a disillusioned study of a woman of character almost turning defeat into triumph, but losing her stake through the irony of fate and the faithlessness of men. Morstin's prolific postwar output included a number of plays written in the '50s on themes from Polish and foreign history; some on contemporary subjects were executed in his last years. Traditional and unadventurous in their form, his plays abounded in noble sentiments and good-natured optimism, and for this reason appealed to audiences. Jarosław Iwaszkiewicz (born 1894), well known for his poems, short stories, and novels, followed his prewar stage successes, particularly a play about Chopin, *Lato w Nohant* (Summer at Nohant, 1936) with a contemporary play dealing vaguely with postwar reconstruction as exemplified by events in a small town, *Odbudowa Błędomierza* (The Reconstruction of Błędomierz, 1958). In the late '50s he produced another biographical play, *Wesele pana Balzaca* (The Wedding of Balzac, 1959), in a similar traditional vein. In his only other postwar play, *Kosmogonia* (Cosmogony, 1967), Iwaszkiewicz reverts to the tradition of somewhat whimsical psychological drama in the style of Szaniawski, though the melodramatic suicide of a young artist in contemporary setting has its roots in the events of the war.

The first postwar years saw the emergence of a group of Catholic playwrights who tried to reconcile the horrors of the war and the occupation—the subject of many of their plays—with the workings of Providence. Wojciech Bąk (1907–1961), a poet, wrote a number of plays before the second world war, but perhaps his most significant work is his postwar historical verse drama *Upadek Kartaginy* (The Fall of Carthage, 1967), in which events of ancient history are shown as topically relevant today. The most outstanding dramatist in the Catholic group is Jerzy ZAWIEYSKI (1902–1969), whose great popularity in the '40s was the direct result of his tackling the moral problems of the time with genuine passion and with reluctance to adopt easy solutions. Most of his plays surpassed the confines of a sectarian label. An equally prolific writer, also classed as "Catholic," is Roman Brandstaetter (born 1906), a poet and essayist, author of more than twenty plays in verse and prose, historical and modern. Though among his plays are some with religious subjects, such as *Teatr świętego Franciszka* (The Theater of Saint Francis, 1948), or an occasional work on a classical theme, such as *Odys płaczący* (The Weeping Odysseus, 1956), Brandstaetter became particularly well known for his biographical dramas. His early success, a play on the life of Rembrandt, *Powrót syna marnotrawnego* (Return of the Prodigal, 1948), was followed by plays taken from the lives of Copernicus (1953), King Stanislas Augustus (1955), the Napoleonic soldier Sułkowski (1952), the actor Bogusławski (1951), and the poet Mickiewicz (1953). The same period brought, among other plays, *Ludzie z martwej winnicy* (Men from a Dead Vineyard, 1949), set in Spain during the Napoleonic occupation, and *Dramat księżycowy* (The Moon Drama, 1954), concerned with the popular uprising against Ferdinand II, king of Naples. Among Brandstaetter's most successful plays are three that deal with the second world war. *Upadek kamiennego domu* (Fall of the House of Stone, 1950) shows the remote effects of guilt on an Italian composer who had not helped a Polish architect about to fall into the hands of the Gestapo. *Dzień gniewu* (The Day of Wrath, 1962), an austere drama in blank verse set in a monastery in a Nazi-occupied European country, presents a confrontation between the prior and his onetime seminarist friend, now an S.S. major in charge of an extermination campaign against the Jews. In strong contrast with these plays is *Zmierzch demonów* (Twilight of the Demons, 1964), a play in verse concerned with the last few days of the Third Reich and its leaders, set in a conference room of Hitler's bunker. This unusual *tour de force* involves grotesque, satire, journalistic reporting, and highly stylized comment. Of Brandstaetter's many styles and subjects, the straightforward approach worked best. It is exemplified by *Milczenie* (Silence, 1956), a human drama of a disillusioned Marxist writer beset by political pressures in the Stalinist Poland of 1951.

The work of the writers mentioned thus far was in most cases unmarked by those ideological pressures shaping Polish literature and drama in the years 1949 to 1955 that are embodied in the term "socialist realism." A national festival of Soviet drama was held in 1949 to teach Polish dramatists, through the example of their Soviet colleagues, how to deal with modern problems and relate them to contemporary life, and how to depict the new socialist man. In 1951 the Festival of New Polish Drama was launched: Bourgeois themes and ideas had disappeared and the new socialist realist theater was declared officially born. Propaganda in the form of so-called "productivity plays" was fostered, theater was to be "the noblest of agitators." Writers who were interested in the dramatic conflicts of people rather than in the interplay of social forces wrote plays that were not produced, or tried to escape to historical subjects. The officially acceptable plays gave a picture of the new reality and showed factories, village common rooms, building estates, full of worker-stakhanovites—but, contrary to the expectations of the party bosses, they were not free of glaring defects. Their plots were monotonous, characters were presented in black and white opposites, and lifeless and unconvincingly depicted problems were resolved by artificial happy endings. The work of the majority of the playwrights of this period did not survive the altered situation that came later with the so-called "thaw"—the process of liberalization brought about by the death of Stalin and the political changes that followed—and can be dealt with but briefly.

The doyen of leftist playwrights, Leon KRUCZKOWSKI (1900–1962), fared best, because he was endowed with talent, had conviction in the cause he served, and, except in a couple of his minor plays, was able to transcend the limitations imposed on the artist in this period. This hardly applied to minor practitioners of the genre, which was subdivided into three main streams. There were the productivity plays proper, dealing mainly with either industrial or agricultural enterprises, occasionally with construction projects or hospitals. Another group of socialist realist plays dealt with international issues connected with the cold war. Western imperialism and capitalist abuses were exposed in such plays as Kruczkowski's *Juliusz i Ethel* (1953) and Adam Tarn's *Zwykła sprawa* (A Common Case, 1950), perhaps one of the more successful works of this kind. The third category of socialist realist plays dealt with the second world war from an angle acceptable in the Stalinist period. In this category plays on subjects such as the Warsaw Rising, or Polish participation in the war under any aegis other than the Soviet, were conspicuous by their absence.

Few socialist realist playwrights achieved any lasting importance or popularity. Jerzy Lutowski (born 1923), a relatively successful dramatist of the mid-1950s, wrote some productivity plays, *Kret* (The Mole, 1955), *Sprawa rodzinna* (A Family Matter, 1955)—but also a play on the Silesian Rising of 1921, *Wzgórze 35* (Hill 35, 1951). Perhaps most interesting—because of the contrast between them—are his two plays which concern his own profession, that of a medical doctor. Whereas *Próba sił* (Trial of Strength, 1950) is a black-and-white denunciation of criminal reactionary forces disrupting life in a clinic, exposed in an exemplary manner, *Ostry dyżur* (The Middle of the Operation, 1956) is a product of the political "thaw." In dealing with an anti-Communist doctor who has to operate on the party boss responsible for his persecution, Lutowski considers the question of professional ethics and exposes the rigidity of party officials in the Stalinist period of "personality cult." In the late '50s and in the '60s Lutowski produced only a comedy and a dramatic triptych on the subject of freedom.

Another line of Polish drama, the historical play, prospered in the late '40s and up to the mid-1950s mainly as an alternative to the stultifying themes of socialist realism rather than as one of its aspects. The same is true of plays on classical subjects, though they could be treated politically. An example is *Ocalenie Antygony* (The Rescue of Antigone, 1954), by Krystyna Berwińska (born 1919), which ends with a successful popular revolt against the tyrant Creon. Progressive elements in history were invariably stressed. Nonetheless the prime advantage in writing a historical play lay in escaping from the limited and unsafe contemporary subjects. In this particular period this was as true of Morstin and Brandstaetter as of other practitioners. Though some plays dealt with foreign subjects, the emphasis was on native history, particularly the lives of famous artists and poets, as well as on the national uprisings against oppressors. Typical of the first category are the plays of Wacław Kubacki (born 1907)—*Rzymska wiosna* (The Roman Spring, 1955), dealing with an episode in the life of Mickiewicz, and *Krzyk jarzębiny* (The Cry of Rowan, 1949), based on a real life incident made famous in Polish Romantic literature. Kubacki also wrote *Jakobińskie gniazdo* (The Jacobins' Nest, 1955), a play that was concerned with the events of Kościuszko's insurrection of 1794. Among the more successful historical writers of the period were Halina Auderska (born 1904) and Aleksander Maliszewski (born 1901). Auderska was at her best in her play *Rzeczpospolita zapłaci* (The Commonwealth Will Pay, 1954), dealing with Andrzej Frycz Modrzewski, the eminent political writer and secretary to King Sigismund Augustus in the sixteenth century. Maliszewski wrote a popular play, *Droga do Czarnolasu* (The Road to Czarnolas, 1953), about another of this king's secretaries, the great Renaissance poet Jan Kochanowski, and a play about the young Mickiewicz, *Ballady i romanse* (Ballads and Romances, 1955).

The historical plays, performed alongside the classics, had their part in relieving the tedium of productivity plays, and they diminished in number with the advent of the "thaw," which brought new problems and called for a new approach to drama. Perhaps the earliest kind of drama to emerge in the mid-1950s was the comedy. A lighthearted comedy, with a twinge of satire, was admissible even in the socialist realist period, as Zdzisław Skowroński (1909–1969) and Józef Słotwiński (born 1908) proved in the five plays they wrote together in the years 1949 to 1954. Notably in *Imieniny pana dyrektora* (The Director's Nameday, 1954) the productivity play was in effect parodied. Skowroński was soon to write, on his own, a more serious play, *Maturzyści* (The Graduates, 1955), describing the far from satisfactory situation in a school virtually tyrannized by the Communist youth organization. Another exponent of satirical comedy in a rather light vein was Jerzy Jurandot (born 1911), author of *Takie czasy* (Such Times, 1955), another productivity play parody. Comedy for pure entertainment made its appearance in the mid-1950s in the plays of Artur Marya Swinarski (1900–1965). His comedies, based on mythological, biblical, and historical subjects, were witty and daring. Among the best known is his *Trojan Trilogy,* comprising *Achilles i panny* (Achilles and the Maidens, 1956), *Złota wieża* (The Golden Tower, 1958), and *Epilog w Egipcie* (Epilogue in Egypt, 1958). His other plays include *Ararat* (1956) and *Powrót Alcesty* (Alcestis Comes Back, 1958), and two serious historical plays, *Źródło pod aniołami* (The Well Under the Angels, 1959) and *Sześciu z Calais* (Six Men of Calais, 1958).

By an ironic twist of circumstance, the most popular political comedy of the post-"thaw" period had been written as early as 1944, though it was first performed only in 1956: *Święto Winkelrida* (Winkelried's Feast) by Jerzy Andrzejewski (born 1909) and Jerzy Zagórski (born 1907). Set in a rather mythical Switzerland and conceived as a satire on the Establishment of the Right, the play suddenly became perfectly applicable to the Stalinist Establishment of the Left and uproariously demolished its taboos. With the settling down of political passions aroused by the bloodless anti-Stalinist revolution of 1956, comedy shifted to social allegory, as exemplified by the plays of Jerzy BROSZKIEWICZ (born 1922), and even to philosophical allegory, seemingly obscure but never far from vital current problems. This can be seen most clearly in the work of Leszek Kołakowski (born 1927), the brilliant Marxist philosopher who, deprived of his chair at Warsaw University after the student riots of 1968, became a Senior Fellow at All Souls, Oxford. In his *Wygnanie z raju* (The Expulsion from Eden, 1961), a highly modern version of Paradise set up as a bureaucratic police state produces results similar to those of the biblical original, except that Adam and Eve prefer their ultimate exile to the luxurious slavery of Eden. *System księdza Jensena albo Wejście i Wyjście* (The System of Jensen the Priest, or Entry and Exit, 1965), set in a mysterious dentist's waiting room, presents a philosophical comment on political systems and on bureaucracy.

Kołakowski's plays come close to the theater of the absurd. The appearance of Western influences in the mid-1950s, with productions of work by Ionesco and other exponents of the genre, stimulated its growth, but the Polish theater of the absurd has roots deep in the native dramatic tradition and has certain characteristics of its own. Its origins go back to the elements of grotesque in the dramas of the great Romantic and neo-Romantic dramatists.

Already before the second world war, Stanisław Ignacy WITKIEWICZ (1885–1939) and Witold GOMBROWICZ (1905–1969) had produced work that put them in the first rank of European absurdists even before the term was invented, and even though they had to wait decades for recognition. In the years 1946 to 1950 an eminent lyric poet, Konstanty Ildefons Gałczyński (1905–1953), wrote a cycle of more than one hundred and sixty mini-playlets, entitled *Teatrzyk "Zielona gęś"* (The "Green Goose" Little Theater). These tiny grotesques, based on surrealist metaphor and abstract humor, contained all the elements of the Polish brand of the theater of the absurd and were a kind of missing link between their predecessors and the drama that followed. Instead of exposing the absurdity of life in general, the Polish absurdists directed their detailed attention to the particular Polish aberrations in mores, the discrepancies between wishes and real possibilities and the pressure of adverse external circumstances, economic as well as political. Sławomir MROŻEK (born 1930), whose first play was produced in 1958; Tadeusz RÓŻEWICZ (born 1921), who made his debut as a dramatist in 1960, and Witkiewicz, whose collected edition of plays was posthumously published in 1962, all employed complex and very different dramatic forms. They have been Poland's most important contribution to world drama in the last quarter century.

Close to the theater of the absurd stands a group of poet-playwrights. In the mid-1950s Miron Białoszewski (born 1922) produced in his own little avant-garde theater short plays that combined linguistic games with the debunking of historic and ideological clichés, as in *Wyprawy krzyżowe* (The Crusades, 1955). Another poet, Jarosław Marek Rymkiewicz (born 1935), produced a play in verse, *Król w szafie* (A King in the Wardrobe, 1960), an absurdist evocation of a phantom monarchist past, followed by *Lekcja anatomii profesora Tulpa* (Professor Tulp's Anatomy Lesson, 1964), in which the corpse in Rembrandt's famous picture comes to life and reenacts his awesome past. Rymkiewicz's latest work, *Król Miesopust* (King Carnival, 1970), is a witty farce of the absurd in verse, closely akin to the plays of Gombrowicz with its mythical king and queen who, betrothed to each other, prefer to couple with rough peasants and change places in a perverse merry-go-round turning full circle. One of the most important poet-playwrights is Tymoteusz Karpowicz (born 1921), who in his early plays touched on the psychological thriller in *Wracamy późno do domu* (We're Coming Home Late, 1958) and *Wszędzie są studnie* (There Are Wells Everywhere, 1960) and in a costume play with a moral, *Zielone rękawice* (The Green Gloves, 1960), before he found his genre in surrealist plays. In *Dziwny pasażer* (The Strange Passenger, 1964) a passenger goes around town in a taxi on an odd quest for his long lost past and identity only to find that the past has been buried under the trifling matters of everyday life. In *Kiedy ktoś zapuka* (Stranger at the Door, 1967) strange knocks on the doors of people living in a block of flats lead to the outburst of imprisoned tensions, neuroses, and suspicions culminating in a dramatic climax.

In *Jego mała dziewczynka* (His Little Girl, 1963) the director of a toy-manufacturing concern visits a mysterious correspondent dissatisfied with his products and in the course of these visits encounters his past fears and trespasses, but also hope. In Karpowicz's later plays—*Przerwa w podróży* (An Interrupted Journey, 1967), *Czterech nocnych stróżów* (Four Night Watchmen, 1967), and *Człowiek z absolutnym węchem* (The Man With a Perfect Sense of Smell, 1967)—his poetic metaphors on the plight of modern man tend to become complex almost to the point of obscurity. Some poets have used metaphor for subjects of science fiction. One of the best plays of this kind, with philosophical ambitions, is *Ekspedycja* (Expedition, 1966), by Artur Międzyrzecki (born 1922). One should also mention *Kreator* (1962), by Witold Wirpsza (born 1918), a parodistic comedy on the Promethean myth: The bureaucratized Prometheus of today creates not people but paper fiction.

One of a group of poets writing in a more straightforward manner, Bohdan Drozdowski (born 1931), although the author of a surrealist play, *Klatka* (The Cage, 1962), is best known for his strongly realist plays. *Ballada polska* (The Polish Ballad, 1964) deals with an aspect of the Warsaw Rising of 1944; *Ostatni brat* (The Last Brother, 1960) with the civil war that followed the establishment of Communist regime after the second world war. Drozdowski's most popular play, *Kondukt* (The Funeral Convoy, 1960), traces the relations and conflicts among several representatives of different social groups in present-day Poland. They are involved in transporting the body of a young miner to his native village on foot because the truck carrying the body has broken down. More "poetic" and reflective is Zbigniew Herbert (born 1924), the author of four short plays, of which two deal with classical themes. *Jaskinia filozofów* (The Philosophers' Den, 1956) reinterprets the imprisonment and death of Socrates in the light of modern political experiences. In *Rekonstrukcja poety* (Reconstruction of a Poet, 1960) the author uses the example of Homer to contrast the essence of poetic creation, as experienced by the poet himself, with the myths and misinterpretations of professional commentators. In his two plays with a modern setting, Herbert shows up the blind cruelty inherent in human relationships. In *Drugi pokój* (The Other Room, 1958) a young couple wait for an old woman next door to die so that they can take over her room. In *Lalek* (1961) it is a journalist who is watching and reporting on a local boy's death in a drunken brawl in a small, stagnant provincial town. Stanisław Grochowiak (born 1934), another outstanding poet and the author of half a dozen excellent radio plays, has also written some stage plays. *Szachy* (Chess, 1961) is a perversely nostalgic comment on the passing of the old feudal world with the end of the German occupation in 1945. *Chłopcy* (The Boys, 1964), a realistic, biting picture of life in an old people's home run by rather exacting nuns, reveals complexes of the inmates as well as of the staff. *Król IV* (King IV, 1963) presents a grotesque, disillusioned view of political power: In a dilapidated kingdom, ineffectual conspirators bungle the attempt to assassinate an equally ineffectual king. He takes a long time to die, while they prepare to go into exile for fear of a neighbor king, Fortinbras, who may or may not invade. This pastiche of *Hamlet* also caricatures some real situations from recent history. The most recent newcomer in the sizable group of poets turned dramatists is Ernest Bryll (born 1935), whose first play, *Rzecz listopadowa* (The November Thing, 1968), was a deliberate attempt to draw on the tradition of national poetic drama and revive the form to suit modern problems. More poetic than dramatic in its structure, it presents a wide panorama of modern Poland against the background of Remembrance (All Souls') Day, attended by a foreigner of Polish origin. Bryll's satirical bite and ability to get to the core of national complexes was put to further use in his *Kurdesz* (The Feasting Song, 1969), a play written in the same free vein, with a gallery of recognizable types. The story line concerns a visit of a war hero, now a high dignitary, to his native village. In between his highly charged political plays, Bryll surprised his public with a traditional Christmas play, *Po górach, po chmurach* (Round the Mountains, Round the Clouds, 1968), and another stylized play about old-time High Tatra brigands, *Na szkle malowane* (Painted on Glass, 1969).

Plays on social themes, veering between satire and entertainment, have dominated in the last decade. Older writers did their best to keep up with new problems. Anatol Stern (1899–1968), yet another poet, produced a pessimistic last play, *Rzeźnia* (The Slaughterhouse, 1967), in which the title signifies an image of the world. Michał Choromański (born 1904) followed his *Cztery sztuki bez znaczenia* (Four Plays Without a Meaning, 1959)—the best of which dealt with war and occupation—with *Largactil* (1961), a modern morality play. Marian Promiński (1908–1971) began as a novelist and became a prolific playwright after 1957. His first play, a surrealist drama on the theme of wartime Resistance, *Sąd nie śpi* (The Court Is Not Resting, 1957), was followed by plays on subjects as diversified as the politics of ancient Rome in *Romulus i Remus* (1966), problems of high-pressured jet pilots in the modern Polish Air Force in *Niski pułap* (Low Ceiling, 1965), naturalistically treated village life in *Dawna przykra sprawa* (The Old Nasty Affair, 1962), and an alumni reunion in *Zjazd koleżeński* (The School Reunion, 1965), as well as metaphorically treated cave exploration, *W jaskini albo Kosmogonia* (In the Cave, or Cosmogony, 1963), and cosmic flights in a thriller, *Rakieta Thunderbolt* (The Thunderbolt Rocket, 1958).

The bulk of dramatic output, however, was produced by the middle and younger generation. Some writers have already been mentioned from the generation born in the '20s. Another, Marek Domański (born 1921), wrote a farce on the "scientific" approach to marriage in *Zawsze nieznany ląd* (Always an Unknown Land, 1967), and also a popular "neo-productivity play" in reverse, *Ktoś nowy* (Somebody New, 1964). Satire on modern society in eleventh-century guise is to be found in Władysław Orłowski's "stage parable"

*Sprawiedliwość w Kioto* (Justice in Kyoto, 1961). Orłowski (born 1922) has also written a play that deals with a search for the cause of a plane crash during a routine flight, *Piąty lot* (The Fifth Flight, 1965). Krzysztof Gruszczyński (born 1925) has written a thriller concerning an accidental intruder in the American nuclear arsenal, *Wielki Bobby* (Big Bobby, 1960). Jerzy Przeździecki (born 1927) scored a success with a contemporary play about an ex-sports champion's frustrating life as a beach attendant at a sea resort, *Garść piasku* (A Handful of Sand, 1963). Aleksander Ścibor-Rylski (born 1928) has made his specialty ingenious small-cast plays on marital and sex problems: *Bliski nieznajomy* (The Close Stranger, 1968) and *Rodeo* (1969). Janusz Krasiński (born 1928), known for the "angry realism" of his prose, is a diverse playwright among whose work is a black prison comedy, *Czapa* (Death in Installments, 1965), and two somewhat surrealist thrillers, *Wkrótce nadejdą bracia* (Brothers Will Come Soon, 1967) and *Filip z prawdą w oczach* (Philip With Truth in His Eyes, 1968). A group of writers of the generation of the '30s began their careers in the mid-1950s by writing satiric sketches and songs for the Warsaw Student Theater of Satire and later turned to playwriting. They include Agnieszka Osiecka (born 1936), Andrzej Jarecki (born 1933), and Jarosław Abramow (born 1933). Abramow, in particular, scored a number of successes with satirical plays on aspects of life in contemporary Poland: *Duże jasne* (A Mug of Beer, 1962, written with Jarecki), *Anioł na dworcu* (Angel at a Railroad Station, 1964), and *Derby w pałacu* (Derby at the Palace, 1966). But his latest play, *Ucieczka z wielkich bulwarów* (Escape from the *Grands Boulevards*, 1969), is surprisingly set among the Paris clochards, with a thrilling finale at an experimental clinic. It poses some interesting questions about the sociability of men and is a proof of a considerable extension of the author's scope. Another writer of this generation, Jerzy Krzysztoń (born 1931), a novelist and short-story writer and author of a number of radio plays, has also written some stage plays. He deals with modern youth in *Rodzina pechowców* (The Ill-luck Family, 1958) and with the generation gap in *Rocznica Mercedesa* (The Mercedes Anniversary, 1962). His best achievement, *Towarzysz N.* (Comrade N., 1965), is almost a modern version of Gogol's *The Inspector General,* without the inspector. The arrival of a mysterious young man who is thought to be a high official sent to investigate, even though he just walks around smiling without asking any questions, throws a provincial town into turmoil. Everyone, from the mayor and other dignitaries to the weathercock on the town-hall tower, is most upset. All the local intrigues and dishonest deals are exposed, and disaster seems inevitable until a poem published in a newspaper with the stranger's photograph reveals that he is only a poet.

In the '60s also some younger talents emerged, with a marked difference of approach from their somewhat older contemporaries. Ireneusz Iredyński was born in the late '30s and therefore is hardly able to remember the second world war, yet he gives in his *Jasełka-moderne* (A Modern Nativity Play,

1962) a surrealist view of the concentration camp. A troupe of actors, ordered to perform a Christmas play, actually "become" the characters they portray. The play is imbued with a macabre quality of the theater of cruelty. Iredyński, who is also known as a poet and fiction writer, continued in the same vein with *Żegnaj Judaszu* (Farewell, Judas, 1965). Maciej Zenon Bordowicz (born 1941), a poet, theater director, and actor, won a Warsaw first-play competition for his dramatic essay on small-town frustrations, *Idący o poranku* (Walking in the Morning, 1964). He followed it with a number of powerful plays that combine psychological insight, strong realism, and a sense of menace: *Jam Session* (1965), a study of aging parents with a child crippled in an accident; *Psalmy* (Psalms, 1965), in which the accounts of unspecified ex-underground thugs are settled through mental and physical tortures in a theater of cruelty manner, with biblical evocations; *Akty* (Acts, 1967), which depicts tough goings-on in a hostel of mine-builders, with some Pinteresque episodes; and *Non Stop* (1968), an almost surrealist play based on a real account of two old women who barricaded themselves in their apartment at the end of the second world war and stayed there for many years, waiting for the "Bolsheviks" to leave the country. Another young writer to win the Warsaw first-play competition was Krzysztof Choiński (born 1940). The winning play was *Krucjata* (Expedition, 1961) a modern, psychoanalytic version of the myth of Iphigenia, who is sacrificed to fulfill Calchas' sadistic desires. Choiński followed it with *Nocna opowieść* (A Night's Tale, 1963), a psychological thriller set in modern Poland. In recounting the experiences of a group of people forced to spend a night in a mountain hostel at the mercy of a gang, the play illustrates the differing moral attitudes in the face of brutal force. The plays that followed—a television comedy, *Cedrowy dwór* (Cedar Mansion, 1963) and *Alarm* (1966), a stage play—did not fulfill Choiński's brilliant early promise. The latter play, a virtual monologue of a Nazi specter terrorizing a woman, is an ambitious but oversimplified essay in mental and physical cruelty.

Drama suitable for present-day "total theater" originated in Poland (if one excepts the earlier attempts of Witkiewicz and Gombrowicz) with *Przyczynek do teorii uczłowieczenia w procesie edukacji* (A Contribution to the Theory of Humanizing in the Process of Education, 1965), a play by Andrzej Bonarski (born 1932). Bonarski, a novelist and physics professor, composed here an extended parable about the education of a humanoid, from simple language to the most advanced use of philosophy and poetry, culminating in disillusionment. The text is more like a scenario, with ample scope for mime, improvisation, audio devices, and audience involvement—altogether a *tour de force* of avant-garde drama. A versatile writer, Bonarski is also the author of *Antygona* (1966), a topical version of the classic play set in a modern black African state, and of a daring sex comedy set in a girls' school, *Panienki* (The Young Ladies, 1968).

The tendency to experiment in total theater by combining physical action with an abundance of not always consequential dialogue has been the more frequent in Poland in recent years. In a powerful first play, *Paternoster* (1969), Helmut Kajzar, an experimental theater director born in the '40s, presented a kind of dream about a young man's return from the big world to his native village. He employs an idiom inspired by Gombrowicz's *Marriage*, adopting the principle of relativity of characters and events, disjointed dialogue, inarticulate sounds, and archetypal images. He developed his style further in *Rycerz Andrzej* (Andrew the Knight, 1970), a totally disillusioned view of a young man's education in life's iniquities, or on the loss of innocence. There is similar inventiveness in the work of a slightly older writer, Tomasz Łubieński. After writing two short playlets, published respectively in 1959 and 1964, he came forward with a full-length play, *Zegary* (The Clocks, 1968), a most ingenious combination of physical action with exuberant, "orgiastic" dialogue that does not refrain from using linguistic stereotypes and a pastiche of nineteenth-century usage. The story concerns a Napoleonic hero turned vicious chief of police, but the action takes place in his old age, when he has sunk into obscurity. Time is relative, scenes from various periods in his life interchange constantly, as do the characters, and Gombrowiczian inspiration is clearly visible. But Łubieński's originality consists in making his merry-go-round of sex and politics work not just through words but through physical action. He has, however, set the theater a difficult task.

From different and quite unique premises spring the experiments of Jerzy Grotowski (born 1933) as adaptor of dramatic texts for his own Theater Laboratory, where the body of the actor is virtually the substitute for literature. The austerity of the "poor theater" leaves no room for abundance of dialogue. It is significant, however, that Grotowski has adapted almost exclusively the great classics, and one might argue that he remained true to them in spirit however extensively he cut the text and altered the externals— for instance, by transferring the action of Wyspiański's *Acropolis* from the Cathedral at the Royal Castle in Cracow to a Nazi concentration camp. For this reason, however original Grotowski is as a theater director, his working scenarios based on other authors' texts cannot be considered his own plays in the strict sense of the word, except perhaps for *Apocalypsis cum figuris* (1969), his production-scenario constructed imaginatively from excerpts of the Bible and the writings of Dostoevski, T. S. Eliot, and Simone Weil.

On the whole, the quarter century 1945 to 1970 has been a rich and varied period in Polish drama, with more writers than ever before active in the field and a few acquiring international status. The spontaneous growth in the first few years after the second world war was interrupted by the enforced episode of socialist realism in the period 1949 to 1955, but it has continued since then in many directions and styles. This growth has been assisted by the possibilities of staging at more than one hundred professional theaters, of production in radio and television, and of publication in book form and in the excellent

Warsaw monthly *Dialog*, established in 1956. Paradoxically, even the existence of censorship, executed with varying intensity and somewhat dubious efficiency but not unnaturally resented by writers, has contributed to the richness of styles in Polish drama by forcing playwrights to deviate from straightforward statement in the direction of parable and other nonrealist forms. But even though Polish theater may at this time be dominated by the director and the stage designer, the dramatic text has retained its traditionally high importance.

**Pörtner, Paul** (born 1925). West German dramatist, essayist, novelist, and translator. Upon his return from the Western Front and his recovery from an injury, Pörtner began to work as an assistant director in Wuppertal. In 1949 he formed his own theater group in Remscheid. His first play, *Mensch Meier oder Das Glücksrad* (The Man Meier, or Fortune's Wheel, 1959), shows Pörtner's interest in existentialism. Meier is the average citizen who goes through his daily routine without realizing how excruciating it actually is. This routine is broken when his commuter train fails to move one day. He then moves from situation to situation that makes him aware of how much his life is determined by petty bureaucracy. At the end of the play, the vicious cycle of his daily routine begins again, but Meier is aware of his suffering and eventually will have to do something about his anguish. Pörtner's next play, *Variationen für zwei Schauspieler* (Variations for Two Actors, 1960), also deals with routines, yet here he is concerned with all the possible alternatives that will allow people to communicate with one another. Hs most recent plays are much more experimental and show the influence of Frénaud, Jarry, Tardieu, and Beckett, all writers whom he has translated. Pörtner concentrates on what he calls *Mitspiele* or "Play-Alongs." His aim is to move spectators to participate in the play and perhaps heighten their own awareness. In *Scherenschnitt* (The Silhouette, 1963) Pörtner asks the audience to guess who the murderer is and plays the audience's version before he has his own performed. In this way, both versions can be compared and make the audience ponder its choice. His other plays also call for some form of audience participation. Although they sometimes display interesting theatrical and therapeutic techniques, they have thus far not proved to be outstanding plays. Ironically, his original experimentation imposes limits that confine the free play of the author's imagination and text.

OTHER PLAYS: *Sophie Imperator* (1962), *Entscheiden Sie sich* (Decide for Yourself, 1964), *Spielautomat* (The Toy Automaton), *Test* (1970).

**Port-Royal** (1954). A one-act play by Henry de Montherlant. It was first performed on December 8, 1954, at the Comédie Française, under the direction of Jean Meyer. On August 21, 1664, the Archbishop Beaumont de Péréfixe decided that the nuns at the monastery of Port-Royal, who refused to sign a "formulary" condemning five alleged Jansenist statements, would be deprived of the sacraments. On August 26, faced with the nuns' persistent insubordination, he exiled twelve of them to other convents, thus destroying the unity of the religious community. In this play, one of the tensest and most austere of his works, Montherlant telescoped the two days into one, emphasized the moral agony and psychological conflicts of the persecuted nuns, and managed not to complicate the picture with theological discussions.

For a long time the nuns at Port-Royal have been subjected to pressure from the ecclesiastical and royal authorities. One of them, Sister Flavie, seems to take sides with the authorities. Another, Sister Françoise, considers the quarrel a waste of time, diverting them from their prayers. Sister Angélique, the sub-prioress, apparently unswerving, is in fact weary of it all and frightened. She confesses to Mother Agnès, indirectly, that she has begun to be assailed by doubt because of God's silence regarding the persecutions to which Port-Royal and Jansenism have been subjected for more than twenty years. The Archbishop, on a last visit to Port-Royal to persuade the nuns to sign the formulary condemning certain Jansenist ideas, is once again confronted with their refusal. Overcome with rage, he forbids the nuns access to the sacraments and announces that twelve of them will be sent to other convents and replaced by nuns of other orders that are obedient to the Church and King. This new persecution has a kind of miraculous effect on Sister Françoise, who stands up to the Archbishop and defends the purity of Jansenist Christianity against the compromises of the Church. On the other hand, Sister Angélique, who is one of the twelve singled out to be exiled, declares that Sister Flavie has been spying on them and has denounced them to the Archbishop. Sister Flavie then speaks in praise of submission to duty; she finds her own peace in blind obedience to ecclesiastical authority. As for Sister Angélique, she is terrified at the idea of what awaits her in the new convent. In the next to the last scene—the climax of the play—while Sister Françoise, who will remain at Port-Royal, has acquired new strength and faith, Sister Angélique leaves, tormented by doubts about herself, about her ability to resist the temptation of signing, and about her faith. The play ends with the arrival of the twelve new nuns.

Although all the characters are complex and dramatic, the play is dominated by Sister Angélique, who belongs to the family of Port-Royal reformers and identifies with the destiny of the place and its spirit. But all the events of the play are ordeals that shake her convictions. We thus witness the agony of a great soul assailed by moral poison and doubt, resulting in devastation and leading to the "gates of darkness." In contrast, Sister Françoise is led, by the same events, to strength and light.

Theatrically, the play is spectacular. In the sober setting of the monastery parlor, one at first sees only the nuns, all in gray habits crossed with red. A striking contrast is produced in the middle of the play by the arrival of the Archbishop, his attendants, and police officers, all in their colorful, luxurious costumes, which, according to Montherlant, makes them resemble magnificent insects. At the end, night falls on Port-Royal with the arrival of the twelve nuns of the Visitation, dressed in black.

**Portugal.** Portuguese drama since World War II is the province of but a few cognoscenti. The first impression of a visitor to Lisbon is that the genre is alive and well: Theaters are not scarce, titles are plentiful and change with regularity. But appearances deceive. The fare is predominantly musical comedies, revues, and translations, the latter replacing rather than supplementing indigenous productions. When a serious Portuguese play does appear, usually in a subsidized theater, it is by a classic, not a contemporary, playwright. Production costs and rigorous censorship have made rare the staging of an original play by a living Portuguese author. One effect has been the creation, not by choice but of necessity, of what has been called an Armchair Theater. Playwrights see their plays, and those of their contemporaries, only in print, and consequently are unfamiliar with the vagaries of actual production, the limitations as well as the possibilities that the physical properties of the living stage reveal. Another effect has been the failure of all but a handful of those who look only to the stage for their livelihood. Thus the drama has become a genre into which successful novelists and poets make an occasional foray. Best known among these are José Almada Negreiros, Joaquim Paço d'Arcos, Miguel Torga, whose *Mar* (Sea) is something of a modern classic, and José Régio, known for intellectual plays, such as *Jacob e o anjo* (Jacob and the Angel) and *A salvação do mundo* (The Salvation of the World). Torga and Régio show, perhaps, the greatest range. Bernardo Santareno and Luís Francisco Rebelo are two who have managed to devote themselves almost exclusively to the theater. The former, whose art is best appreciated in *O lugre* (The Lugger) and *A promessa* (The Promise), is the Portuguese García Lorca. The latter has spent his professional career studying and propagating Portuguese drama in review, critique, anthology, and example, but his work still has not transcended the peninsula. The roster is lengthened, though by no means completed, by reference to *Forja,* the rural tragedy by Alves Redol; the social dramas of middle-class life by Ramada Curto, Henrique Galvão, and João Gaspar Simões; the verse tragedy *O Indesejado* (The Unwanted) by Jorge de Sena, and works by Romeu Correia, Carlos Selvagem, Alfredo Cortês, João Pedro de Andrade, and Luís de Stau Monteiro. More recent are A. Portela Filho, A. Sobral, Fiama H. P. Brandão, J. E. Sasportes, and Maria Teresa Horta.

Among useful works on Portuguese theater are the following: Hernâni Cidade, "Portuguese Literature in the Last 25 Years: The Novel and Theater," *Books Abroad,* Vol. XXVIII (1954); Gerald M. Moser, "Portuguese Literature in Recent Years," *Modern Language Journal,* Vol. XLIV (1960), Vol. XLVI (1962), Vol. XLVII (1963), and "Portuguese Writers of This Century," *Hispania,* Vol. L (1967); Luís Francisco Rebelo, *Teatro português do romantismo aos nossos dias* (Lisbon 1959, anthology to appear in twelve fascicules), *Imagens do teatro contemporâneo* (Lisbon 1961), *Teatro portugués contemporáneo* (Madrid 1962), "Panorama del moderno teatro portugués," *Primer Acto,* No. 34 (1962), and *História do teatro português* (Lisbon 1968), and W. H. Roberts, "Portuguese Théâtre de Fauteuil, 1945–1955," *Hispania,* Vol. XL (1957).

**Priestley, J. B.** (born 1894). English dramatist. A Yorkshireman, educated at Bradford and Trinity Hall, Cambridge, Priestley rejected an academic career in favor of the profession of literature. His reputation as a novelist was firmly established with the popular success of *The Good Companions* (1929). It was by way of an adaptation of this novel that his work for the stage began. Since 1931 he has written more than thirty plays, involving himself in the management of many of them, while continuing an active career as novelist, essayist, and broadcaster. If not all of his prolific output is of equal merit, Priestley at his most satisfying combines a zestful energy and an insatiable intellectual curiosity with an intense conviction of man's responsibility toward his fellow beings. During the late '30s and the '40s Priestley was generally accepted as the outstanding serious dramatist writing in prose for the English stage. His more ambitious plays, sometimes unsuited for the pressures of the English commercial theater, often achieved greater recognition abroad than at home.

Naturalism was the dominant mode of the English stage during the period of his major achievement and many of his plays, from the broad Yorkshire comedy *When We Are Married* to the Chekhovian study of provincial academic life in *The Linden Tree,* fit comfortably into the naturalistic framework. "The older I get," he has observed, "the better I understand the part played in my life and writing by early influences. Politically and socially I am a radical; culturally I am a conservative. I really belong to the avant-garde of the 1880s . . ." But elsewhere Priestley has balanced this partial truth with the justifiable claim that he has "always fretted and conspired against downright naturalism." In contrast to the bluff rationalism that leads inevitably to socialism and is his most obvious characteristic, Priestley has shown an intense interest in the theory, deriving from P. D. Ouspensky and J. W. Dunne, that man can step briefly outside the inexorable onward march of time. *Dangerous Corner* (1932), *Time and the Conways* (1937), and *I Have Been Here Before* (1937) rely for their effect on illuminating the present by a glimpse of the future or by some alternative version of the events being played out on stage. *Johnson Over Jordan* (1939), a critical and commercial failure whose merits were to be a subject of controversy for years to come, owes something to the expressionist movement in its employment of music, ballet, and masked, allegorical characters to create "a biographical-morality play in which the usual chronological treatment is abandoned for a timeless dream-examination of a man's life." In *They Came to a City* (1943), a play which successfully captured the contemporary spirit of urgency for social change once the war should end, the dramatist again escaped from the restrictions of natural chronology by translating his characters, at some crisis in their lives, to an unknown city where their reactions to its Utopian life-style provided a reflection upon their personalities in the everyday world.

But while, in these and other plays, Priestley chafed against the trappings of naturalism, the language of his characters remained prosaically tied to the conventions of drawing-room drama, lacking either the stark realism of Osborne and his successors or the polished cadences of an Eliot or an Arden. Those of his plays which are most ambitious technically are not among his most successful. Although in the Old Vic production of 1946 it was no more than a partial success with the public, the more modest device in *An Inspector Calls*, in which the relentless questioning of a mysterious police inspector reveals the skeletons lurking in the well-stocked cupboards of a complacent Edwardian household, displays Priestley's concern for humane behavior at every personal and social level more impressively than *Johnson Over Jordan*.

Priestley's wartime broadcasts, when the influence of radio was at its height in England, established him as spokesman for the mood of social conscience that arose out of a newly forged national unity, and his primacy as a dramatist coincided with this mood. In 1947 the words of Professor Linden in *The Linden Tree* expressed cogently the aspirations of those who had elected a postwar socialist government: "Call us drab and dismal, if you like, and tell us we don't know how to cook our food or wear our clothes—but for Heaven's sake, recognize that we're trying to do something that is as extraordinary and wonderful as it's difficult—to have a revolution for once without the Terror, without looting mobs and secret police, sudden arrests, mass suicides and executions, without setting in motion that vast pendulum of violence which can decimate three generations before it comes to a standstill."

Although J. B. Priestley was the foremost spokesman for socialism upon the English stage in the '40s and early '50s, his broad-based, tolerant sympathies had little appeal for the more strident and impatient voices of the later '50s and '60s, and he can scarcely be regarded as a forerunner of the drama that has emerged since *Look Back in Anger*. Since 1956 his own most successful work has been an adaptation of Iris Murdoch's novel *A Severed Head* (1963), in which he collaborated with the author. But it is sometimes easy to underestimate the achievement of a writer who deliberately rejects the complicated special language of philosophical or literary theory in favor of plain speaking, and J. B. Priestley's drama must be accorded a significant place in the history of twentieth-century English theater.

Priestley has written introductions to the plays appearing in the three-volume work *Plays* (1948–1950) and *The Art of the Dramatist, A Lecture* (1957). He is the subject of three biographies: Ivor Brown's *J. B. Priestley* (1957), David Hughes's *J. B. Priestley, An Informal Study of His Work* (1958), and Gareth Lloyd Evans' *J. B. Priestley—The Dramatist* (1964).

OTHER PLAYS SINCE 1945: *Ever Since Paradise* (1947), *The Golden Fleece* (1948), *Home Is Tomorrow* (1948), *Summer Day's Dream* (1949), *Bright Shadow* (1950), *Dragon's Mouth* (with Jacquetta Hawkes, 1952), *Treasure on Pelican* (1952), *Private Rooms* (1953), *Mother's Day* (1953), *The White Countess* (with Jacquetta Hawkes, 1954), *A Glass of Bitter* (1954),

*Mr. Kettle and Mrs. Moon* (1955), *The Golden Entry* (1955), *Take the Fool Away* (1956), *These Our Actors* (1956), *The Thirty-First of June* (1957), *The Glass Cage* (1957), *The Pavilion of Masks* (1963).

**Puerto Rico.** Modern theater in Puerto Rico traces its roots to Emilio Belaval's Areyto group (1940–1942), an outgrowth of the broad awakening of Puerto Rican cultural consciousness in the late 1930s. A substantial number of the plays of the 1940s and 1950s were heavily social in tone and naturalistic in style, as a response to the extreme economic problems of the island. The First Puerto Rican Drama Festival of 1958, an annual event that has become a highlight of drama in Puerto Rico, marked an emergence to a more cosmopolitan approach. Belaval was one of the principal authors during the 1940s and 1950s, with intellectual works which satirically attack the closed modern Occidental world. The most effective regular dramatists are Manual Méndez Ballester, René MARQUÉS, Francisco Arriví, and Luis Rafael Sánchez. Méndez Ballester, a survivor of the awakening of 1938, created a series of naturalistic rural thesis plays; since then, he has essayed formal tragedy, the dissolution of the family in New York's Barrio Latino, and a variety of other thematic and formal variations. In *El milagro* (The Miracle, 1958) he created a complex dialogue regarded by some as an answer to Beckett's irreligious philosophy, and *La feria* (The Fair, 1963) is a symbolic assault on dehumanized mechanized society.

Marqués and Arriví are of an intermediate generation. The former is the best known of Puerto Rican dramatists, and his work has been performed internationally. *La carreta* (The Ox-Cart, 1954) is a naturalistic view of the disaster of a mountain family which emigrates to San Juan and ultimately to New York; it is the most popular work of Puerto Rican drama. Marqués' best work is in the vein of complex, imaginative, symbolic drama rooted in the problems of his people: *Los soles truncos* (The Truncated Suns, 1958) and *Un niño azul para esa sombra* (A Blue Child for That Shadow, 1960). He has continued to experiment constantly; *La muerte no entrará en palacio* (Death Shall Not Enter the Palace), as yet unperformed, is an attempt at a political tragedy; *La casa sin reloj* (The House Without Clocks, 1961) is an ironic comedy on the nature of man within time and our guilt for our world. He has since worked with highly stylized symbolic drama, a deliberate glorification of a national heroine in *Mariana a el alba* (Mariana, or The Dawn, 1964), and a reinterpretation of the biblical myth of Abraham and Sarah, *Sacrificio en el Monte Moriah* (1969).

Arriví is the chief animator of the festivals and one of the principal reasons for the existence of theater in Puerto Rico. His plays are characterized by an obsessive treatment of the schizophrenic role of the artist in Puerto Rican society; this has developed increasingly into an examination of social problems. Arriví's best works are those which examine the spiritual self-mutilation of those Puerto Ricans unable or unwilling to accept their double European and

African heritage: *Bolero y plena* (1956), *Vejigantes* (1958), *Sirena* (1959). One of the major advantages of Arriví's theater is his skill with lighting and staging, as can be seen in the highly controversial political satire, *Coctel de Don Nadie* (Mr. Nobody's Cocktail Party, 1964). Like Marqués, Arriví is deeply concerned with the erosion of Puerto Rican ways of life and the increasing Americanization of the island. This theme is constant in Puerto Rican drama; it is visible in the works of Pedro Juan Soto, better known as a novelist, and Luis Rafael Sánchez, best of the younger playwrights and heavily influenced by Marqués.

# Q

Quoat-Quoat (1946). A play in two scenes by Jacques Audiberti. It was first performed on January 28, 1946, at the Théâtre de la Gaîté Montparnasse, Paris, under the direction of André Reybaz. Originally written in the form of a Platonic dialogue, *Quoat-Quoat* was not intended for the stage. It was nevertheless chosen for staging by André Reybaz and Catherine Toth. During the Second Empire a young and shy archaeologist, Amédée, is on a ship bound for Mexico, believing that he is entrusted by the government with the job of discovering a hidden treasure. On board he falls in love with the captain's daughter, whom he manages to involve in an adventure "outside the Catholic hand of God" and under the protection of the obscure Mexican divinity Quoat-Quoat. But it happens that there is a rule aboard according to which it is forbidden, under penalty of death, for government secret agents to pay court to the women. Amédée is therefore condemned to death by the captain. When it is discovered that Amédée is not the agent but merely being used to divert attention from the real agent, a woman from Bordeaux, he is freed. However, he heroically decides to have himself killed anyway. The captain, whom we gradually discover to be God the Father, and from whose domination Amédée is trying to escape, is weary of his own rules and of his passengers. He is preparing to destroy his ship (in other words, his creation) as the curtain falls.

Around this allegory of the rebellion of innocence against the absurdity of divine creation, Audiberti has written a series of exuberant scenes, alternatively burlesque and lyrical, cruel and tender, and filled with long monologues teeming with comical and vigorous images. Two scenes are particularly amusing: the one in which a wild Mexican woman tries to extract Amédée's secret of the hidden treasure, and that in which Amédée exchanges personalities with the *gendarme* who is holding him prisoner. The scene in which Amédée and the captain's daughter imagine their love and their discovery of Quoat-Quoat and the treasure, while being full of fun, is also one of the best examples of Audiberti's incantatory imagination.

Ridiculed by some of the public in 1946, the play was performed again in 1968 with great success.

# R

**Rattigan, Terence** (born 1911). English dramatist. A promising scholar at Harrow and Trinity College, Oxford, Rattigan left the university before taking a degree to follow his chosen career as a playwright. *French Without Tears* (1936) established him at once at the head of his profession with a record run of 1,049 performances. Since *Flare Path* (1942) his career has been one of almost unbroken success. Unashamedly a dramatist who measures achievement in terms of the popularity of his plays in the commercial theater, Rattigan is a past master of the English variation of the well-made play. "I believe sloppy construction, untidy technique, and lack of craftsmanship to be grave faults," he has written, "the more grave in that they may, with nothing more than industrious application, be so easily avoided." Without the brittle wit of a Coward in his comedies or the burning rhetoric of an Osborne is his serious dramas, Rattigan has a gift for deft, unpretentious dialogue that makes its inescapable impact through perfect timing. Of his early comedies he has claimed that "far from being aimless and vapid displays of juvenile high spirits, they were put together with the utmost care and craftsmanship; that the absence of epigrams, literary phrasing, and verbal wit was deliberate, and was not only not a vice but was in fact a virtue."

Rattigan's drama, with its public-school heroes and tacit acceptance of the social and political standards of the upper middle classes, exemplified everything against which the young dramatists of the 1950s found themselves in revolt. But Rattigan is a far from trivial playwright, and his reputation has not been destroyed by the arrival of Osborne, Pinter, and Arden. The excellence he has displayed from the beginning in the technicalities of play construction has concealed his progress from the shallow characterization of *French Without Tears* and the patriotic tear-jerking of *Flare Path* to the psychological accuracy of his later writing. *The Browning Version*, which was produced on a double bill with *Harlequinade* under the title *Playbill* in 1948, is a penetrating study of the effect of faded idealism and frustrated ambition upon an aging schoolmaster and his wife. It marked a new depth of feeling in Rattigan's work and won the Ellen Terry Award. Thereafter Rattigan's major success has lain in the slow revelation of private emotions: frustrated love in *The Deep Blue Sea* (1952), loneliness in the two plays set in a residential hotel comprising *Separate Tables*

(*The Window Table* and *Table Number Seven,* 1953), and, taking advantage of a relaxation of censorship, homosexuality in *Ross* (1960). There is much that is conventional in Rattigan's writing, but the economical simplicity of his dialogue, characterization, and dramatic structure is a result of deliberate discipline and not poverty of the imagination, and demonstrates the strength as well as the limitations of the English well-made play.

In the preface to the second volume of his collected plays (1963), the playwright rashly characterized the playgoer whose tastes he tried to please as "a nice, respectable, middle-class, middle-aged, maiden lady, with time on her hands and the money to help her pass it . . . She is, in short, a hopeless lowbrow." "Aunt Edna," as Rattigan named this figure, soon achieved notoriety as a symbol of everything that seemed wrong with the English theatergoer of the '50s, much as Rattigan himself was taken to stand for everything that was wrong with dramatic writing. In the preface to his third volume of plays, Rattigan shrewdly defended his position by arguing that writers of Osborne's generation have continued to cater, in their own way, to the same Aunt Edna.

Rattigan is the author of a number of films and has adapted many of his own plays for the screen; his television plays include *The Final Test* and *Heart to Heart* (1962), and *Nelson* (1966). It was with an adaptation of the last-named television script, dealing with the last three months in the life of Nelson and Lady Hamilton, that Rattigan succesfully returned to the London stage in 1970 after seven years' absence. Rattigan served during the war as an air gunner in the R.A.F. Rattigan published *The Collected Plays,* in three volumes (1963–64). John Russell Taylor discusses his work in *The Rise and Fall of the Well-Made Play* (1967).

OTHER PLAYS SINCE 1945: *The Winslow Boy* (the Ellen Terry Award, 1946), *Adventure Story* (1949), *Who Is Sylvia?* (1950), *The Sleeping Prince* (1953), *Variation on a Theme* (1958), *Joie de Vivre* (a musical version of *French Without Tears,* 1960), *Man and Boy* (1963), *A Bequest to the Nation* (1970).

**Ribman, Ronald** (born 1932). American playwright. Born in New York City, graduated from the University of Pittsburgh (Ph.D. 1963), Ribman taught English at a midwestern college for one year; he has been a full-time writer since 1963. *Harry, Noon and Night,* a black comedy about power and domination, was produced at the American Place Theatre in 1965, followed in 1966 by *The Journey of the Fifth Horse,* a psychological study of evasion and recognition based in part on Turgenev's story *Diary of a Superfluous Man, Journey* was awarded an Obie for the best off-Broadway play of the season In 1966 Ribman was also awarded a grant from the Rockefeller Foundation *The Ceremony of Innocence,* using the life of Ethelred the Unready to suggest criticism of current political situations, was first presented at the American Place Theatre in 1968. Three short plays billed as *Passing through from*

*Exotic Places* were given off-Broadway in 1969. None of Ribman's plays has had a long run. *The Final War of Olly Winter*, a drama about the war in Vietnam written expressly for television, won wide critical acclaim after its presentation on CBS Playhouse in 1967; a handsome reprint of the script with many pictures has been issued by CBS.

**Richardson, Jack** (born 1935). American playwright and drama critic. Born and educated in New York City, Richardson graduated from Columbia University with a B.A. in philosophy (1957) and then did some graduate work at the University of Munich. Even though he soon switched from scholarship to playwriting, his work keeps an academic quality. *The Prodigal*, his first and perhaps best play, produced off-Broadway in 1960, is a reworking of the *Oresteia* done with a consciousness of literary context, not only of Greek drama but also of contemporary philosophical playwrights such as Sartre and Giraudoux. It is the idea that animates the play, not the characters, and certainly not the dialogue, which tends to be stilted and undifferentiated. Like Shaw, Richardson (through Orestes) comments on the need for a better world and the impossibility of this species of mankind to effect anything more creative than "justice," balancing death with death. Unfortunately, Richardson does not have Shaw's wit, so that his next play, *Gallows Humor* (1961), also produced off-Broadway, is very ponderous comedy; once again it is the intellectual perspicuity of the idea that is of interest, not its dramatization. After a literary, allusive (and unnecessary) prologue, two short acts demonstrate the lure and the danger of "disorder" and the rigidities of society, life in death and death in life. The need for control, for ordered certainties, that is in part the subject of this play, and of the novel *The Prison Life of Harris Filmore* (1963), seems unfortunately to affect Richardson's writing, making it appear argument rather than experience, intellect with no exuberance or spontaneity. Two other plays, *Lorenzo* (1963) and *Xmas in Las Vegas* (1965), failed on Broadway. *As Happy As Kings* was done at New Theatre Workshop in 1968.

**Rifbjerg, Klaus** (born 1931). Danish playwright, poet, film writer, novelist, and critic. An energetic, controversial writer, sometimes referred to as the *enfant terrible* of Danish literature in the 1960s, Rifbjerg made his debut as a poet with the collection *Under vejr med mig selv* (On the Track of Myself) in 1956, and by the end of the 1960s had more than thirty books to his credit. He began his career in the theater in the early 1960s, working with various collaborators on a series of satirical musical revues, the main themes of which were a distaste for the commercialism rampant in postwar Denmark and a criticism of the Social Democratic Party for failing to lead the nation toward the goal of a democratic socialist society.

Rifbjerg first came to the attention of a larger Scandinavian theater public when his *Udviklingar* (Developments), a "play for four jazz musicians, four actors, and a small theater," was selected by Ingmar Bergman to be premiered at Stockholm's Royal Dramatic Theater in 1965. In 1966 the Danish Royal

Theater presented a successful production of Rifbjerg's *Hvad en mand har brug for* (What a Man Needs), a Pirandello-like drama, with music by Ole Schmidt, in which a man wanders into an empty theater and has a series of encounters (whether real or imaginary is left ambiguous) with his mistress and members of his family. In the course of the action he discovers that worldly success has not given purpose to his life. A *commedia dell'arte* theatricality dominates the play *Voks* (Wax, 1968), in which the characters, unable to maintain their identities and to mature ("wax") into adults, change their roles constantly. Later plays include *Tørresnoren* (The Clothesline, 1969) and *År* (Years, 1970), the latter a reexamination of conventional Danish attitudes toward the German occupation.

**Rislakki, Ensio** (born 1896). Finnish playwright. Rislakki, a journalist, a columnist, and an editor, traveled widely and has published several travel books, among them *Tuolla puolen Limpopon* (Behind Limpopo, 1952), based on his experiences in Africa. Using the pen name Valentin, he has written a group of serious comedies, unsentimental and masculine. His typical heroes are on the surface harsh, inhibited, and hard-boiled, yet they are also sensitive, boys not quite grown up. He has an alert eye for parody and pastiche. Rislakki's plays include a historical comedy of merit, *Rakas Wenander* (Dear Wenander, 1946), and a description of student life, *Ruma Elsa* (Homely Elsa, 1949), which later became a musical. His most remarkable achievement is *Musta Saara* (Black Saara, 1957), an early analysis of the racial problems in Africa, exceptional in its subject matter and in its tough portrayal of a loveless missionary in the middle of a physical and mental desert.

**Rodríguez Buded, Ricardo.** Spanish dramatist. Rodríguez Buded's *La madriguera* (The Warren, 1960), like Antonio Buero Vallejo's *Historia de una escalera* and Lauro Olmo's *La camisa*, other works important to the development of the social theater in Spain, is a play in which the multiple protagonists are subservient to the circumstances of their existence. Within the suffocating confines of a lower-class rooming house transpire the insignificant details of lives without meaning. The sordid ambience itself is the true protagonist of the play. The intent, and that of the social theater in general, is to confront the audience with a societal reality, objectively represented, which will elicit pity and sympathy and, ultimately, awaken a dormant social consciousness. *El charlatán* (1962), with a much reduced *dramatis personae* and a lighter tone, seems more in keeping with the traditional comedy of manners. A family languishing in complacent inertia is offered fresh insight and new alternatives by an audacious house painter. But here, too, what some would judge but an interesting story more or less verisimilarly told, is, by the author's assertion, "a reality which mirrors wider horizons," a microscopic revelation of the tediousness of the world of the proletariat.

**Roi se meurt, Le** (Exit the King, 1962). A play in one act by Eugène Ionesco. It was first performed on December 15, 1962, at the Théâtre de l'Alliance Française, Paris, under the direction of Jacques Mauclair. King Bérenger I is dying. He has about an hour and a half left to live—that is, just the time of the performance. He is helped, during his last moments, by his doctor, a cleaning woman, a guard, and his two wives, Queen Marguerite and Queen Marie. There are many signs of his impending death: aging, aches and pains, the fact that he frequently falls. His end is also represented by the progessive destruction of his kingdom: Its population is disappearing, its borders are narrowing, the very ground is sinking into bottomless chasms. At first Bérenger does not want to believe that he is dying. "Why was I born, if it was not forever?" Then, with the help of Queen Marie, he tries to rebel, to survive through an effort of will. But his world continues to diminish: The guard, the cleaning woman, and even Marie disappear. Queen Marguerite teaches him to give up his memories, his own body, and his very being. She too then disappears. At the end of the play, on an absolutely empty stage, the king on his throne fades out as well, and when the curtain falls, nothing remains but a gray light.

Bérenger is both any individual surprised by his own death and demanding a reprieve because he realizes he has forgotten how to live, and all humanity. Indeed, Bérenger has invented everything from fire to atomic fission; he is Homer and he is Shakespeare. Whether an individual or humanity, the only reality, everything considered, is death; the rest is nothing but vanity. This play, in which Ionesco uses the devices of the theater of the absurd, has at the same time a very rigorous structure and more pathos than most of his plays. The anguish of death, the realization of being condemned, with no appeal possible, and one's distress when faced with the inefficacy of rebellion are expressed forcefully and simply. By means of the progressive disappearance of secondary characters and the vision of a kingdom that is gradually annihilated, Ionesco has constructed a striking allegory of the fact that for every man the world exists only insofar as he lives. *Le Roi se meurt* is thus the work most characteristic of Ionesco's despondent solipsism.

**Roots.** A trilogy by Arnold Wesker comprising *Chicken Soup With Barley* (1958), *Roots* (1959), and *I'm Talking About Jerusalem* (1960). Some discrepancies in chronology and other minor details provide evidence that this trilogy was not conceived as a whole from the beginning. Each of the plays is complete in itself and the first two, if not all three, can be read or performed without reference to the others. But taken together, the three plays represent the fullest expression of the socialist experience in prosperous postwar England. A dramatist of human feeling rather than political theory, Wesker follows the fortunes of the Kahns, a Jewish émigré family in the East End of London, over a period of more than twenty years, in which the natural pattern of life over two generations is as important as the historical background. *Chicken Soup With Barley* covers the years from 1936 to 1956, in which the growing isolation of Sarah Kahn, the dominant figure in this play, is echoed in the decline of the Communist Party in England. Beginning with the growing unity of a party united against the threat of Fascism, the play ends with the despair and confusion that split the party after the Soviet invasion of Hungary. Like much of Wesker's work, the play employs a double perspective. The inevitable processes of life, as age and illness encroach upon family and friends, dulling the optimism and idealism of youth, control the structure of the play as much as any of the major historical events. The moral weakness of Harry Kahn, exemplified by his petty theft from his wife's purse in the first act and his refusal to fight illness at the end, is as great a test of Sarah's humanist faith as is the spectacle of Soviet brutality, and to their son, Ronnie, as he passes from youth into manhood, the decline of his father is as appalling as the news from Hungary. Among the minor characters, Monty Blatt's development from a belligerent militant to a successful small-business man anxious to live down his political past is as much due to a universal trait of human nature as it is to his indignant condemnation of the Soviet oppression of the Jews. Equally explicable in terms of his own character is Dave Simmonds' conversion from a hero of the Spanish Civil War to someone with no illusions about working-class heroism. Sarah alone continues to cling with primitive faith to her simple dogma. "You have to start with love," she tells Monty in the first act. "How can you talk about socialism otherwise?" By the end, in the moving confrontation of mother and son after Hungary, she is close to admitting that her sustaining belief flies in the face of reason and experience. "Please, Ronnie," she pleads, "don't let me finish this life thinking I lived for nothing . . . . You've got to care, you've got to care or you'll die."

While *Chicken Soup With Barley* deals with the socialist experience from the viewpoint of the committed party member, *Roots* is set by contrast among the unthinking, apolitical majority. Beatie Bryant, a young woman who has fallen in love with Ronnie Kahn and plans to marry him, returns from London to prepare for a meeting between Ronnie and her family of Norfolk farm workers. Filled with his missionary fervor, she attempts to impart to her family something of Ronnie's political vitality and intellectual interests. It is only in the final scene, when she learns that he has ended their relationship, that the full extent of her failure to enter Ronnie's intellectual world is made clear. The borrowed words with which she had harangued her family had been learned parrot-fashion from Ronnie, and she confesses her inability to adapt herself to his life-style. But this moment of humiliation is to be her spiritual awakening: As she condemns the apathy and cultural exploitation of the working classes that have created a barrier between her and Ronnie, she finds for the first time that she is speaking and thinking for herself. "It does work," she cries in wonderment, "it's happening to me, I can feel it's happened, I'm beginning, on my own two feet—I'm beginning . . . "

The action of *Roots* spans a mere two weeks. The dull routine of the Bryant household is not subject to the slow erosion of ideals and political faith that accounts for the extended time schemes of the first and last plays of the trilogy. The play thus comes close to the structure of traditional naturalistic drama, but it breaks new ground in the English theater by depicting the poverty and cultural deprivation of rural life with unremitting realism. In Beatie Bryant, battling against the stultifying influence of this environment with a poignant sense of the life she and her family have missed, Wesker created one of his most successful characters and convinced many critics that naturalism infused with a new sense of social commitment was to be the dominant feature in the reviving fortunes of the English theater. But Wesker himself was to move away from strict naturalism after the *Roots* trilogy, and his humanistic socialism was to seem outmoded in the theater of the '60s.

*I'm Talking About Jerusalem* returns to the Kahn family itself. Without the faith in the ultimate perfectibility of society that sustained Sarah Kahn, her daughter, Ada, leaves home to help her husband assert his independence of the values of industrial civilization. Dave Simmonds' attempt to make a living as a craftsman in a remote Norfolk cottage is naïvely unrealistic, but its failure is due as much to deficiencies within himself as to society's rejection of his work. He is guilty of an unnecessary theft from his employer and reveals a selfish craving for admiration: "Ten years I spent here trying to carve out a satisfactory life for my wife and kids and on every side we've had opposition. From the cynics, the locals, the family. Everyone was choking with their experience of life and wanted to hand it on. Who came forward with a word of encouragement? Who said we maybe had a little guts? Who offered one tiny word of praise?" Having seen their ideals fail in society at large, Dave and Ada have to face the difficult truth that they will not find them in themselves. For Ronnie Kahn, too, the couple's return to the city is a personal defeat: "I don't understand what's happened to you two. I used to watch you and boast about you. Well, thank God, I thought, it works! But look at us now, now it's all of us." The play ends on a note of bitter realism as Ronnie is forced to accept that he cannot look to Dave for "our new vision."

The *Roots* trilogy contains most of the features that characterize Wesker's writing. Most obvious is the vitality of his characters, unashamedly reveling in the sheer physical delight offered by work, talk, food, and the enjoyment of art. Related to this is his feeling for the importance of communication. Ronnie's insistent claim that words are "bridges" from person to person is echoed throughout the trilogy. Sarah's growing isolation is expressed in the failure first of her husband and then of her daughter, Ada, to talk openly with her. One of the major weaknesses of the Bryant family is their inability to discuss their problems together. Equally clear is Wesker's refusal to separate political feeling from human experience. Sarah Kahn's political strength is another facet of the human warmth she displays so abundantly all her life. Beatie Bryant's awakening to her cultural deprivation comes from the shock of her rejection by Ronnie. Dave and Ada Simmonds suffer a series of bitter personal experiences before they learn that their retreat from society is founded on false premises. Wesker's view of life is one whose high points are lived out in speech and action, and his achievement in the *Roots* trilogy is to have communicated this sense of life in direct expression on the stage.

The emotional exuberance so vividly expressed in Wesker's writing has sometimes caused him to be dismissed as a naïvely romantic thinker, but this is to do less than justice to the subtlety with which he places his characters in perspective. The Bryant family, despite their narrow existence, have a genuine understanding and tolerance of human nature that is a match for Beatie's secondhand intellectual theories. Nor does Wesker condemn the figures who desert Sarah or break down Dave's and Ada's determination. Conversely, Wesker has been called a disillusioned socialist by those who see a rejection of Communism in Ronnie's outburst in *Chicken Soup* and despair at the failure of socialism in Beatie Bryant's inability to convert her family or in the Simmonds' return to the city. This is an interpretation that Wesker himself has passionately rejected, and with reason. The trilogy asserts the necessity for political and personal ideals and the supreme difficulty of maintaining such ideals in the everyday world, and his appraisal of the socialist experience in inevitable conflict with human nature is marked by honesty, courage, and realism.

**Różewicz, Tadeusz** (born 1921). Polish poet and dramatist. Różewicz was born in Radomsko. During World War II he worked as a private tutor, a laborer, and a town hall messenger, and in 1944 he published his first volume of poems. After the war Różewicz studied art history at Cracow University. He soon became one of the most prolific and outstanding Polish poets. He has also written short stories and film scenarios. Różewicz won a number of prizes, including the State Prize for Literature, First Class, in 1966. In a form related to the prewar avant-garde, Różewicz expressed through his poetry the problems of his time with a sharp and moving directness.

When, about 1960, Różewicz directed his attention to drama, he used some of his poetic devices. The rhythm and construction of his dialogue and monologue are those of poetry. And yet, disenchanted with the word, he is far from attributing to it an absolute value and, in accord with modern tendencies, regards the author's contribution as only one of the elements that create a performance. In the directions to one of his plays, *Śmieszny staruszek* (The Funny Old Man, 1964), he writes: "This is the scenario of a play. Out of this one must make the play." In Różewicz's plays reality, disjointed like pieces in a jigsaw, reassembles itself to form a biting comment on man's maladjustment in contemporary society, on the evils of the society, and on the world itself. His plays show a close affinity with the theater of the absurd, already firmly established in his first play, KARTOTEKA (The Card Index, 1960). An indefatigable experimenter, he searches constantly for new forms, though he never loses sight of the overall importance of the problems tackled.

In *Grupa Laokoona* (The Group of Laocoon, 1961), through amusing, disjointed, banal conversations of random groups of characters, Różewicz builds up the picture of a decadent, fragmented civilization and of the crisis of human values, with the famous sculpture of the title serving as a metaphor of a world in the mortal throes of nihilism. In *Świadkowie albo Nasza mała stabilizacja* (The Witnesses, 1962), again on a seemingly simple basis of three dialogues— a man and a woman reciting a poem, a husband and wife talking about every-day occurrences, two men chatting at a café table—the insecurity, cruelty, and stupidity of man and the malaise of our civilization are penetratingly analyzed. In *Wyszedł z domu* (Gone Out, 1964), a father strays from his routine journey home and slips on a banana skin, an accident that affects his mental powers. When he eventually turns up with his head bandaged, his wife tries to jolt him from his state of amnesia and indifference by means of verbal "shocks." But it becomes obvious that the husband is much happier in his state of childish innocence than as the head of a rather sordid family. The ostensibly conventional plot provides the author with a framework for excursions into grotesquely expressed social criticism. *The Funny Old Man* is an impressive study of old age, of human loneliness and helplessness, worked out in a virtually unbroken monologue spoken in self-defense by an old gentleman on trial for molesting little girls.

*Akt przerywany* (The Interrupted Act, 1964) reflects Różewicz's dissatisfaction with all existing dramatic forms and is an example of anti-theater in almost pure form. The play consists mainly of stage directions and the author's reflections on tendencies in modern theater, on the various possible ways— or rather the impossibility—of composing a play in our time. The reflections are illustrated by scenes in which various dramatic conventions are explored and exploded. It is interesting to note that this ironically "anti-theatrical" piece has proved quite effective on the stage. Not as effective, though, as *Stara kobieta wysiaduje* (The Old Woman Broods, 1968), a grotesquely apocalyptic vision of the end of the world in a heap of rubbish, in which everything and everyone is being buried with relentless and systematic inevitability. The old woman of the title is the ancient fertility symbol—with a dried up womb. *The Old Woman Broods* is, perhaps, the author's most pessimistic work and, through its ambivalence of meanings and its synthesis of the tragic with the comic, seems to complete a phase in his dramatic writing.

OTHER PLAYS: *Spaghetti i miecz* (Spaghetti and the Sword, 1964), *Moja córeczka* (My Little Daughter, a film scenario adapted for the stage, 1966).

**Rudkin, David** (born 1936). English dramatist. Rudkin's theatrical reputation rests upon one play. He alternated between writing and musical composition as a youth, and after graduation from university became a music teacher. His sporadic interest in playwriting received encouragement when a short radio play was accepted by the B.B.C.; his next dramatic work was *Afore Night Come*. Appearing as it did in 1962, the play occupies an important position in the shift from the largely social preoccupations of the English theater in the '50s toward the emphasis upon violence that was to characterize the latter half of the '60s. Set in the heart of the English countryside during the fruit-picking season, *Afore Night Come* culminates in the ritual murder of an Irish tramp by the orchard workers. The slow revelation of the dark superstitions that lurk beneath the placid surface of contemporary rustic life is handled with great subtlety, and the mounting tension as the play progresses toward its climax is masterly. Without leaving a level of almost documentary realism, Rudkin consciously or unconsciously creates a gallery of archetypal figures—the wandering tramp-scapegoat, the wise lunatic, the intellectual humbled by irrational forces. But the sacrifice that is central to the play is scarcely credible as a feature of contemporary English life, and the play succeeds as an atmospheric *tour de force* rather than an acceptable statement of the human predicament. Critic John Russell Taylor points to its affinity with the work of Algernon Blackwood or Arthur Machen rather than with that of Genet.

Since *Afore Night Come* Rudkin has continued to teach music as well as write. He has produced a number of television plays, film scripts, translations, and the book of a ballet (*Sun into Darkness,* 1963). An interview with Rudkin appeared in *Encore,* Vol. XI, No. 4 (1964).

**Ruiz Iriarte, Víctor** (born 1912). Spanish dramatist. A dilettante artist devoted to literature but only moderately successful as a journalist and critic, it was not until the 1940s that Ruiz Iriarte's long interest in the theater bore fruit. He is now a member of the International Institute of the Theater and director of the Sociedad General de Autores de España. Since *Un día en la gloria* (One Heavenly Day) appeared in 1943, no season has been complete without a comedy by Ruiz Iriarte. His early and possibly still best plays, *El landó de seis caballos* (The Six-Horse Landau, 1950) and *El gran minué* (The Great Minuet, 1950), are fantasies in which his idea of the theater as a medium of joy, playfulness, tenderness, and understanding finds full expression. Later plays deal more with the everyday problems of the bourgeoisie, but fantasy still predominates. His dramatic formula, in fact, is best described as one in which the need for love and consequent companionship and security, its fulfillment thwarted by false social standards, is met by recourse to illusion or deception, a final return to reality necessitating a working compromise between truth and fiction. The knack of never exceeding the bounds of palatability, which limit sentiment and pathos, has enabled Ruiz Iriarte to continue to satisfy his audiences' expectations of drawing-room comedy.

OTHER PLAYS: *El puente de los suicidas* (Suicide Bridge, 1944), *Juego de niños* (Child's Play, 1952), *Esta noche es la víspera* (On the Eve of Tomorrow, 1958), *El Carrusell* (1964), *Un paraguas bajo la lluvia* (An Umbrella Under the Rain, 1965), *La muchacha del sombrerito rosa* (The Girl With the Red Hat, 1967), *Historia de un adulterio* (1969).

# S

**Sakowski, Helmut** (born 1924). East German dramatist and journalist. Sakowski began working as a forester in the early 1940s and was then drafted into the army. After he was released from a prisoner of war camp in 1946, he studied forestry in Stollberg. Four years later he went to work in the national department of forestry. During the 1950s he turned his hand to writing stories and plays for television and the stage. Most of his works concern the development of the individual, who must learn to see his goal in the collective rather than in isolation. Practically all his dramas deal with the role of the emancipated woman in the new socialist state. Her fulfillment is not derived from any particular relationship with one man but in her relationship to the socialist state. Sakowski combines folk elements with doctrine in well-made plays that are often too contrived to be credible.

PLAYS: *Die Entscheidung der Lene Mattke* (The Decision of Lene Mattke, 1959), *Steine im Weg* (Stones in the Way, 1962), *Weiberzwist und Liebeslist* (A Woman's Quarrel and the Ruse of Love, 1961), *Sommer in Heidkau* (Summer in Heidkau, 1966), *Wege übers Land* (Ways over the country, 1969).

**Salacrou, Armand** (born 1899). French dramatist. Born in Rouen, Salacrou studied both medicine and philosophy. At first divided between Communism and surrealism, he nevertheless made a fortune in advertising, which he satirized in his comedy *Poof* (published 1947, produced 1950), yet which allowed him to devote himself entirely to the theater. His works have earned him such respect from his fellow playwrights that he was recently elected president of La Société des Auteurs et Compositeurs Dramatiques.

Salacrou's reputation was established with his first ten plays, written before the war—particularly *L'Inconnue d'Arras* (The Unknown Woman of Arras, 1935), *La Terre est ronde* (1938), and *Histoire de rire* (When the Music Stops, 1939). After a period of silence during the years of the Nazi occupation, his *Les Fiancés du Havre* (The Fiancés from Le Havre, 1944) was performed at the Comédie Française shortly after the liberation of Paris. The most important work written by Salacrou directly after the war was *Les Nuits de la colère* (Nights of Anger, 1946), a play constructed in flashback form, which deals with the Resistance, the political wait-and-see policy, and the moral conflicts provoked by such stands and their consequences. Most of his subsequent plays take place in French bourgeois circles, sometimes in Normandy (especially Le Havre). While on a certain level they are satires of those circles, they transcend traditional satire to the extent that the characters are haunted by death, the absence of God, and problems of time. Often the subject matter is very comical: *L'Archipel Lenoir* (The Lenoir Archipelago, 1947) deals with a family that decides, in order to save their reputation and their financial interests, to kill the grandfather, who is guilty of having raped a young girl; in *Une Femme trop honnête* (An Overly Respectable Woman, 1956) the heroine chooses to have her husband killed in order to purify her life by eliminating her remorse at having taken a lover; in *Sens interdit* (Wrong Direction, 1952) time is reversed and the characters are born old, have love affairs as they grow younger, and die babies. The tone of other plays is more serious. *Dieu le savait!* (God Knew It! 1950), for example, is the portrayal of a Le Havre family's distress and confusion sometime after their town had been bombed out and they are confronted with painful discoveries about some of their pasts.

While Salacrou's dialogue and the structure of certain of his scenes are closely related to the traditional naturalist theater, his characters' feelings and ideas show philosophical concerns typical of the mid-twentieth century. Burlesque or moving, his plays are permeated with profound anguish provoked by the absurdity of life, the silence of the cosmic universe, the incoherence of human behavior, and the contradiction between man's freedom and universal determinism. Time plays an essential role in any inquiry into man's condition, and most of Salacrou's plays deal with the question either in the form of flashbacks or through the unexpected arrival of characters who had been thought to have vanished forever: Bitter disclosure follows upon bitter disclosure and results in regrets, uncertainties, and painful conclusions regarding man's fate. The originality of Salacrou's tone derives from the fact that as a leftist and former member of the Communist Party, he is constantly torn between the optimism of the left, which leads to action, and the pessmism of the absurd, which leads to the loss of all hope.

In 1961, with *Boulevard Durand,* Salacrou tried his hand at writing a documentary play based on an actual trial held in Le Havre in 1910, involving a strike leader. This historico-epic reconstruction is related to a new tendency in modern theater: the didactic dramatization of revolutionary struggles, pointing up the heroism, suffering, and mistakes of those who have actually participated in such historical events.

OTHER PLAYS SINCE 1945: *Le Soldat et la sorcière* (The Soldier and the Witch, 1945), *Pourquoi pas moi?* (Why Not Me?, 1950), *Les Invités du Bon Dieu* (Guests of the Good Lord, 1953), *Le Miroir* (1956), *Comme les chardons* (1964).

**Salom, Jaime** (born 1925). Spanish dramatist. Salom is a practicing ophthalmologist. His theatrical career dates from the receipt in 1948 of the Teatro Español Universitario prize for student playwrights. He is a highly versatile playwright. *Culpables* (The Guilty, 1961) is a mystery. So too is *Falta de pruebas* (Lack of Evidence, 1964), but with the pretentions of a thesis play. *Juegos de invierno* (Winter Games, 1964), *Parchis Party* (1965), and *Espejo para dos mujeres* (A Mirror for Two Women, 1965) are comedies. *El baúl de los disfraces* (The Trunk of Masks, 1964), one of his more successful plays, is indeed a mixed bag, by the playwright's own admission, passing "from high comedy through vaudeville to drama and perhaps tragedy," though the latter claim is debatable. Its theme, the successive roles man adopts in the course of his life, is a favorite not only of Salom but of the "theater of evasion" in general. However, it is on the basis of his more recent serious dramas, *La casa de las chivas* (Goat House, 1969), and *Los delfines* (The Dauphins, 1969), that critics grant Salom his place in the contemporary theater. The former play depicts the temptations of the world, the flesh, and the devil in an atmosphere in which normal social and psychological restraints are loosened. A group of soldiers is billeted by an old man and his two daughters during the last days of the Civil War. The technique is realistic, the presentation of the conflicting emotions as frank as the Spanish stage allows. More impressive technically is Salom's excursion into the theater of ideas, *Los delfines,* a generational study which details the transfer of power in a capitalistic society awakening to its social obligations. Realistic scenes alternate with direct narration on a nonrepresentational stage in the attempt to achieve both theatrical and didactic efficaciousness.

OTHER PLAYS: *El mensaje* (The Message, 1955), *Verde esmeralda* (Emerald Green, 1960).

**Salomon, Horst** (born 1929). East German dramatist, poet, and journalist. Salomon worked in a youth organization until 1950 and then switched to mining. During this period of his life he began writing and was eventually sent to the Johannes R. Becher Literaturinstitut in Leipzig to study drama. He dramatized his experiences in the mines in an effort to contribute to social realism. One of his plays, *Katzengold* (Cat's Gold, 1964), deals with a conflict between the generations over the development of the mines. The hero of the play, Piontek, an old miner, who is sensitive to the radical ideas of the young miners, is able to hold conflicts in check by providing strong leadership and directing the vigor of the young into useful channels. The play itself had to be rewritten several times to suit the social precepts of East German censors. Salomon's difficulties with bureaucracy are reflected in *Der Lorbass* (1967). Here a young man named Harald Schmieder, an inventor with the nickname Lorbass, who does not know how to put his talents to use, makes a mechanical dog and leads an unconventional life. Once again, an older member of the community recognizes the failings in the older generation which cause Lorbass' alienation. After Lorbass proves his mettle by taking the blame for an accident in a firm, he is recognized as a young man with integrity and ingenuity and is encouraged to continue working on his weird inventions—this time for the benefit of society. Salomon's play works toward a new form of proletarian comedy. Yet the treatment of the proletarian problem reminds one of the well-made petty bourgeois comedy of the nineteenth century.

OTHER PLAYS: *Vortrieb* (Propulsion, 1961–62).

**Sarkadi, Imre** (1921–1961). Hungarian writer and playwright. Sarkadi studied pharmacy and law, worked as a printer, a journalist, a schoolteacher, a dramatic adviser at a theater, and, for a short time, as a factory hand. He wrote four plays and several film scenarios, of which *Körhinta* (Merry-go-Round, 1956) won him international recognition. In 1955 he was awarded the Kossuth Prize. He committed suicide. *Út a tanyákról* (Way from the Farms, 1952) and *Szeptember* (1955) are plays about the collectivization of the countryside, abounding in emotional conflicts and highly dramatic clashes between advocates and opponents of collectivization. His two plays written after 1956 show the disintegration of moral norms in the new society: *Oszlopos Simeon* (Simeon Stylites, 1960) is about an artist addicted to alcohol who chooses "ascetic nihilism" as a way of life; *Elveszett paradicsom* (Paradise Lost, 1961), Sarkadi's last play, is the personal tragedy of a doctor who finds the girl he loves soon after he had committed a crime which will probably land him in jail. The great social conflicts of the '50s gave way in Sarkadi's later dramas to self-tormenting individualism with existentialist undertones.

**Sartre, Jean-Paul** (born 1905). French dramatist. Born in Paris into the bourgeoisie, Sartre spent his adolescence in La Rochelle. He entered the Ecole Normale Supérieure in 1925 and passed his *agrégation* in philosophy in 1928. While teaching in Le Havre and Paris before the war, he wrote essays on philosophy, one novel (*La Nausée*, 1938), and a collection of short stories (*Le Mur*, 1939). Sartre discovered theater after he had been taken prisoner in 1940, when he wrote and directed a play with his fellow prisoners in the *stalag*. Once freed, he went back to teaching in Paris and continued until the end of the war. In 1943 he reached a relatively large public with his play *Les Mouches* (The Flies) and became one of the foremost French philosophers with the publication of *L'Etre et le néant*. Indeed, at the time of the liberation, he was already considered a likely successor to the great prewar thinkers and writers. From then on he devoted himself not only to literature and philosophy but to social and political action. He was awarded the Nobel Prize for Literature in 1964, but refused it for political reasons. Director of the review *Les Temps Modernes*, which he founded in 1945; traveler and reporter, in the United States, Cuba, and China; novelist (*Les Chemins de la liberté*, 1945–1950); philosopher (*Critique de la raison dialectique*, 1960); political essayist and literary critic, Sartre has also had some ten of his plays produced and has written two film scripts.

Sartre's plays are based on his philosophy, existentialism, and reflect his intellectual evolution. Yet they do not require a detailed knowledge of existentialism to be understood. They are, above all, dramas built around situations in which the characters are forced to question their very being, as well as the reasons for and the value of their acts, and discover, at the price of violent action, their freedom and their responsibility. The characters make these discoveries through their relationships with other people and, most of all, in the context of social and political action. Since, for Sartre, existence is unjustified, men are "condemned" to be free, and life has no real meaning other than what men give it, his plays about man's condition reveal all the traps involved and are finally tragic.

In his first play, Les Mouches, Sartre used the Greek myth of Orestes and Electra, which had already been reworked by Giraudoux in Electre (1937). But whereas Giraudoux's characters are in the process of fulfilling their own essences—that is, fulfilling possibilities fixed in advance—Sartre's characters, on the contrary, create their own fates by discovering that nothing is fixed and that everything depends on their freely chosen acts. Oreste, in Sartre's play, is a young esthete with no ties—therefore altogether "available." But that availability is a kind of nothingness. Here, Sartre's stand is opposed to the uncommitted freedom of such prewar writers as André Gide. For Sartre, in order to emerge from nothingness, one must take the risk of lucidly committing oneself and assuming one's freedom. His reasons for commitment are moral: Oreste kills his mother and her lover in order to free the people of Argos from false guilt, which was making them the slaves of the authorities and the gods. After the killing, Oreste assumes the responsibility for his crime and is thus truly a heroic liberator. Right in the middle of the Nazi occupation, when the Vichy government was trying to convince the French that their oppression was deserved because of their collective guilt, Sartre's play strikingly revealed the inauthenticity of such an idea and showed that men are subjected to their fates only when they accept bad faith. Any man of good faith may freely try to invent an act that will liberate himself and the others along with him. Les Mouches, under the mask of a Greek legend, was obviously a means for rejecting the pessimism resulting from France's defeat, as well as a call to rebellion. On a deeper level it was the affirmation of the fact that, whatever happens, men are always the creators of their own fates.

In the spring of 1944 Sartre's Huis-Clos (No Exit) was performed. By imagining three dead people condemned to live for eternity in the same room in hell, Sartre was able to show characters who are incapable of transforming their lives by any new acts. All that any one of them can do is to ask the other two to reassure him about the meaning of his life. Thus Sartre, in dissecting their relationships, dramatizes the constant torture represented by the resistance, aggressivity, or submission of others.

The meaning of life, freedom, relationships with others, and the extreme acts by which individuals become committed have remained the themes central to Sartre's works since the war. But these themes are never treated abstractly. They are revealed and pointed up in contemporary situations: the Resistance and torture in *Morts sans sépultures* (The Victors, 1946); white supremacy in the South of the United States in *La Putain respectueuse* (The Respectful Prostitute, 1946); the tragedy of a young bourgeois faced with revolutionary politics in LES MAINS SALES (Dirty Hands, 1948); the problems of good and evil in a revolutionary and godless world in LE DIABLE ET LE BON DIEU (The Devil and the Good Lord, 1951); a satire of anti-Communist journalism in *Nekrassov* (1955); and torture, as well as Germany's recovery, in LES SÉQUESTRÉS D'ALTONA (The Condemned of Altona, 1959).

Although rather conventional in form, Sartre's dramatic techniques are very varied, ranging from naturalism (*Les Mains sales*) to the historical fresco (*Le Diable et le Bon Dieu*) or the satiric revue (*Nekrassov*). His plays make up a "theater of ideas" in modern terms, which is successful because the ideas are concretized in dramatic acts whose violence and serious import recall the extreme situations of the world today.

OTHER PLAYS SINCE 1945: *L'Engrenage* (In Mesh, 1969). Sartre adapted *Kean*, by Alexandre Dumas père, in 1953 and Euripides' *Les Troyennes* in 1965.

**Sastre, Alfonso** (born 1926). Spanish dramatist. Sastre is one of the most influential playwrights of the contemporary Spanish theater. Yet since 1954 only five of his plays have been staged by professional companies in Madrid. The opening of *Escuadra hacia la muerte* (Death Squad, 1953) was widely acclaimed as one of the most important events of the postwar theater, but it was allowed a run of only three performances. Sastre has identified capricious censorship, timid impresarios, and a public taste debased by melodrama and boulevard comedy as the causes of the difficulties he has met in the pursuit of his career, and against them he has directed a torrent of words. In the *autocríticas* that precede the printed editions of the plays (the only form in which many of those plays can be known); in the manifestos that marked the founding of the Teatro de Agitación Social in 1950 and the Grupo de Teatro Realista in 1960; and in the critical studies *Drama y sociedad* (1956) and *Anatomía del realismo* (1965), he has predicated the urgency of the untrammeled exploration of a tragic theater based on the realistic representation—revelation, really—of man in his true existential situation. His themes are those of the "committed" theater: justice, guilt, responsibility, freedom. *Escuadra hacia la muerte* is a metaphysical statement on man in a hostile universe. *Muerte en el barrio* (A Death in the Neighborhood) and *En la red* (Dragnet, 1961) study man in society; *La mordaza* (The Gag, 1954), man en famille. In *La cornada* (The Goring, 1960), man preys on man in an anthropophagous relationship evocative of the myth of Saturn. *La sangre de Dios* (The Blood of God) is an analysis of faith and the absurd in terms borrowed from Kierkegaard's elaboration in *Fear and Trembling* of the story of Abraham and Isaac. Man's subjective experience of time is the theme of *El cuervo* (The Raven, 1957). Technically, Sastre's studies in time are the most innovative aspect of his theater. *Ana Kleiber*, a three-act restatement of the earlier one-act *Cargamento de sueños* (Burden of Dreams), a modern *auto sacramental*, works variations on the vagaries of telling and showing, stage time and audience time, and presentation, representation, and re-presentation. After seven years of far from voluntary absence, Sastre again opened an original play in Madrid in 1967, *Oficio de tinieblas* (Mass of Mourning). Though of difficult access, the plays of Alfonso Sastre, like those of Antonio Buero Vallejo, his only serious rival in the tragic theater, keep the contemporary Spanish stage from being the sad, trivial, stunted thing he himself frequently calls it.

OTHER PLAYS: *Ha sonado la muerte* (Death Sounds), *Uranio 235*, *Comedia sonámbula* (A Somnambulistic Play), *Asalto nocturno* (Night Assault), *Prólogo patético*, *El pan de todos* (Our Daily Bread), *Guillermo Tell tiene los ojos tristes* (William Tell Has Sad Eyes), *Tierra roja* (Red Earth).

**Saunders, James** (born 1925). English dramatist. A Londoner and graduate of Southampton University, Saunders was a chemistry teacher before he began to make his name as a dramatist with a succession of one-act plays in which the influence of Ionesco was clearly discernible. His full-length play *Next Time I'll Sing to You*, first staged in 1962 and presented in a revised version in the following year, marks the successful evolution of a more personal and distinctive style. Taking its inspiration from Raleigh Trevelyan's account, in *A Hermit Disclosed*, of the solitary life of a twentieth-century Essex villager, the play presents four varied characters who gather together nightly to explore the hermit's character under a would-be playwright's direction; but their performance expresses only the impossibility of discovering the truth of another's life, let alone of re-creating it in dramatic form. Their performance, repeated nightly, with even apparent departures from the script forming part of a larger structure, is a subtle deployment of the device of the play-within-a-play, which turns the dramatic experience itself into a metaphorical approach to the question posed by the author within the play: "Who or what is it that is so obsessed with me that he makes it necessary for me to live out my long life in this dank slowly-decaying cell to no apparent purpose? Or am I only the *reflection* of an obsession, the remains of an abandoned experiment, abandoned and forgotten . . . ?" Carefully balancing excursions into dazzling rhetoric against passages of delicate humor, Saunders invests his play with the atmospheric unity of a poem, bound together by imagery and recurrent phrases rather than developing action. The play was a co-winner of the *Evening Standard* Award to the most promising playwright of 1963.

*A Scent of Flowers* (1964) displays a similar departure from conventional dramatic techniques, although the subject, the conflict between a girl's love for a married man and her faith as a Catholic, is treated more directly. The ethereal presence of Zoe at her own funeral, living again through the crises of her own short life and the betrayals of her well-meaning family, is handled with a combination of humor and sensitivity, while the constant oscillation of the action between past and present is a meaningful and unselfconscious device illuminating the anguished experience that culminates in suicide.

Saunders has written for radio and television; his one-act play *Neighbours* (1964) is a naturalistic picture of loneliness harassed by sexual and racial tension.

OTHER PLAYS: *Moonshine* (1955), *Alas, Poor Fred* (one act, 1959), *The Ark* (1959), *Committal, Barnstable,* and *Return to a City* (three one-act plays, 1960), *A Slight Accident* (one act, 1961), *Double Double* (1962), *The Pedagogue* (one act, 1963), *Who Was Hilary Maconochie?* (one act, 1963), *The Italian Girl* (adaptation, with Iris Murdoch, 1967), *The Borage Pigeon Affair* (1969), *The Travails of Sancho Panza* (a play for children, 1969).

**Saved** (1965). A play by Edward Bond. Denied a license by the Lord Chamberlain, but performed under conditions of dubious legality by the English Stage Company, *Saved* outraged many critics but found Sir Laurence Olivier among its supporters. A play that remains controversial, *Saved* is less remarkable for the scenes to which the censor objected than for the merciless picture it draws of cultural and emotional deprivation among the contemporary working classes. Scenes of unrelieved domestic squalor and dialogue restricted to monosyllabic exchanges of gnomic and ungrammatical brevity create an impression of stunted and inarticulate personalities whose behavior never rises above the level of animal instinct. In a succession of episodic scenes the play follows the fortunes of Len, a working-class youth who takes lodgings with a family after a sexual encounter with the daughter. In a household where the mother and father never speak and the daughter, Pam, neglects her illegitimate child, left crying ceaselessly offstage; Len mutely tries to regain the affection of Pam, who is now infatuated with another youth. In a scene that quickly attained notoriety, Pam deserts her child in a park. Fred, the boy with whom she is vainly infatuated, and a gang of other youths in search of excitement smear its face in excrement and batter it to death. A conviction for manslaughter follows for Fred, but after his return from jail it is made clear that he will continue to disregard her. Events in Pam's household come to a head when Len, making tentative advances to Pam's mother while he mends a hole in her stocking, is interrupted by the father, and years of silence are broken in a quarrel of squalid brutality. The play closes with no apparent resolution: in total silence Len repairs a chair that was broken during the quarrel. A plot that could easily have degenerated into unconscious humor is saved by the unremitting force of Bond's writing. The spectator is appalled not so much by the events in the play as by the lack of moral vision in the participants. Never once does Fred express any remorse at the death of the infant, and neither Pam nor her family feel any revulsion for the murderers.

**396**

The mental horizons of these characters are limited to the dull acceptance of food, work, and sex. Whether or not Bond's picture of brutalized social life as a background to outbreaks of senseless violence is a true reflection of human nature, the harsh consistency of his portrait is an artistic achievement of considerable dimensions.

The reader searches in vain for any expression of a sense of the degradation of their existence from the characters of the play, or any hint from the author that the society he depicts might have been otherwise than it is. Yet Bond describes the play as "almost irresponsibly optimistic." Len, he asserts, is naturally good and remains so in spite of everything. Some vestiges of moral concern can be dimly discerned in Len's confusion at the spectacle of Pam's silent parents, and his incoherent attempts to persuade the girl to take some interest in her child. His action in repairing the chair in the final scene is explained as a gesture of faith in humanity. "The play ends in a silent social stalemate," writes Bond, "but if the spectator thinks this is pessimistic that is because he has not learned to clutch at straws."

Bond's sincerity in his assertion that it is cultural and emotional deprivation in society that creates the moral emptiness of his characters need not be questioned. Yet this assertion is not embodied in the play, and the impression of human nature that emerges is one of bleak pessimism. In effect, Bond represents the coming together of two important and separate elements in the theater of the previous decade. While Beckett, Ionesco, and the early Pinter had depicted a world of metaphysical despair, irrational violence, and the failure of language, they deliberately cut themselves off by anti-naturalistic devices from direct social comment. On the other hand the writers with a sense of political commitment, most notably Wesker, retained a more optimistic faith in the traditionally humanist values of socialism. By transferring the world of unreason to a recognizable context of family and society, Bond united these two streams in a play with much of the emotional force, and some of the inconsistencies, of the revolutionary political movements of the late '60s.

**Scandinavia.** The highest accolade the Scandinavians use to characterize outstanding achievement, whether in sports or in the arts and sciences, is "world-class"—a clear indication that the achievement has made an impact outside the country or region of its origin. It is something of a miracle that these small countries (with a total population in 1970 of less than that of New York State: eighteen million) produced two "world-class" playwrights in the nineteenth century, two pillars of the modern theater—Ibsen and Strindberg—but it is also notable that in the decades following the second world war there have been an impressive number of Scandinavian writers who have used the theater to stage the problems and conflicts of their day imaginatively and expressively.

Though each Scandinavian country is determinedly independent in outlook, they share a common cultural heritage, and there are contemporary themes that have currency in the drama of all three countries.

The implications of World War II and the cold war are common themes in the plays from the 1940s and 1950s, but they appear also in those written in the 1960s and 1970s. Whereas the Norwegian and Danish writers in the early 1940s tended to ask questions such as "What did *you* do in the war?" younger writers have used the war as a means for exploring larger questions about changing concepts of heroism and self-sacrifice. The Swedes have a different perspective of the period. Perhaps because of their country's long-standing neutral position in world affairs, they have tended to emphasize the frustration of being helpless spectators in the arena of power-bloc struggles. Today, among Scandinavian intellectuals generally, there is widespread hostility toward all partisanship in the East-West conflict, an attitude of "a plague o' both your houses."

A theme of increasing importance in the mid-1960s was the sense of despair over the growing strength of dehumanizing forces in the industrialized countries, a despair related in part to the theme of anxiety in modern world literature as exemplified by Kafka, and in part to a disenchantment with the way the welfare states have developed over the past three decades. Leftist intellectuals have accused the Scandinavian Social Democratic Parties of betraying their ideological missions to create truly democratic societies in which citizens would be sophisticated enough to resist the corrupting influences of materialism. In plays, novels, and poems, the basic assumptions of the "consumer society" are attacked, particularly the right of producers to use the mass media to manipulate public taste and opinion and thus accelerate the dehumanizing process.

One response to the growing materialism has been a renewal of interest in political theater, especially in satirical musical dramas or revues, some produced by commercial and state theaters and some by "group theater" experiments. The "group" (*gruppteater*) movement is supported by actors, directors, and playwrights who are critical of the large, artistically and/or politically conservative state theatrical institutions. They have sought to create a more relevant kind of theater in which political, social, and cultural problems can be given expressive dramatic form through the collective enterprise of small, dedicated groups of artists. By the end of the 1960s the achievements of these group theaters were sufficiently impressive to justify a prediction that they might become the most significant theatrical phenomenon of the next decade.

One indication of the viability of the movement is the variety of points of departure. At the Gothenburg Municipal Theater in Sweden a group organized by actor-playwright Kent Andersson from among members of the permanent ensemble produced several successful political satires. At Stockholm's Pistol-teatern satirical playwright-producer Pi Lind established a reputation as an inventive pioneer in the use of mixed media. And in Denmark, director Eugenio Barba made a minor theatrical mecca of the tiny town of Holstebro, in Jutland, through the successful tours of his Odin Teatret. Barba's approach differs from that of the others in having a comprehensive artistic point of departure rather than a dominantly political one: the revolutionary ideas of Jerzy Grotowski, the director of the Polish Laboratory Theater.

If it is too early to foresee what effect Grotowski will have on the development of drama in Scandinavia, it is not difficult to measure the impact already made, both direct and indirect, by two other foreign sources: Bertolt Brecht and the theater of the absurd.

Brecht's influence can be traced in works that are widely separated from each other along the political spectrum: from Ernst BRUUN OLSEN's lively, predominantly good-natured Bal i den Borgerlige (Ball at the Country Club, 1966) in Denmark, to Jens BJØRNEBOE's bitter Fugleelskerne (The Bird Lovers, 1966) in Norway, to Arvo Salo's and Kaj Chydenius's explosive, pro-Communist Lappo-operan (The Lappo Opera, 1966), which was Finnish in origin but toured successfully throughout Scandinavia. In each instance a mixture of music and bold, presentational drama was used to point up the evils of capitalism and sting audiences into sharper social awareness. One must not, of course, overemphasize the importance of Brecht's inspiration. The Swedish playwright Lars FORSSELL has complained that "the moment you write a play with songs in it . . . you are accused of being influenced by Brecht, especially by people who cannot conceive that you might very well have been influenced by Shakespeare."

Although plays by Beckett and Ionesco have been produced successfully in Scandinavia, the absurdists have affected dramatists there more indirectly than directly. Harold Pinter, for example, has been an important model for the promising young Danish playwright Leif Petersen.

Despite the successes of individual experimental groups, the lion's share of government subsidies in the Scandinavian countries goes to the established state theaters, a practice that has provoked outcries of indignation from playwrights who see themselves cut off from an important outlet in which to practice and perfect their art. But aspiring playwrights are not without recourse. In each country the state radio service has a well-established drama program for both radio and television, providing satisfactory if not generous opportunities for budding talents. Several dozen playwrights have begun or furthered their careers in this way. (See also DENMARK, FINLAND, NORWAY, SWEDEN.)

Schehadé, Georges (born 1910). Lebanese playwright. Born in Alexandria, Egypt, of French-educated Lebanese parents, Schehadé studied in Paris, received a degree in law, and became secretary-general of the Ecole Supérieure des Lettres in Beirut. He gained some renown with his poems, which were published as a collection, Les Poésies, in 1952. When in 1951 the Georges Vitaly Company staged his first play, Monsieur Bob'le, which he had written long before, the public and critics were divided between those who saw the work as a renaissance of poetic theater and those who considered it a lot of empty talk—shapeless, obscure, and pretentious. Supported by established poets (Supervielle, Michaux, Char, and Breton), Schehadé went on writing and turned out six plays.

Schehadé's works contrast sharply with all the rest of the postwar new theater. His plays are dramatized, humorous, and poignant tales—terse, vigorous, and subtle—with an imagery both naïve and mannered, and devoid of the aggressive violence and nightmarish symbolism that characterizes most contemporary theater. Moreover, the language itself—instead of disintegrating, as in most of the theater of the absurd—fulfills a poetic function and serves to reveal the richly varied and secret world of bewitching and comical correspondences.

Central to Schehadé's plays, which are peopled with a large number of touching, burlesque, or grotesquely dangerous characters, is the pure and innocent hero—a poet or a saint—who is obviously in contact with profound truths, which he tries to understand more clearly or preserves by means of his language and acts. Schehadé's first play is the most optimistic in this respect: Monsieur Bob'le manages to convey to those around him his mysterious harmony with a universe of happiness. In *La Soirée des proverbes* (An Evening of Proverbs, 1954) and in HISTOIRE DE VASCO (Vasco, 1956) the adventure of purity goes wrong and the plays end in tragedy. The hero of *La Soirée*, young Argengeorge, finds himself among comic and hateful characters who are symbolic of old age, with all their bitterness, lies, and hypocrisy, and is finally shot by his double, the hunter Alexis, who is the image of the aged Argengeorge. In *Les Violettes* (Violets, written 1960; produced 1966) poetry, happiness, and innocence are destroyed by the atomic craze. The both poignant and comical charm of these plays, in which the basic conflict seems to be elementary, derives from the constant suggestion—beneath a surface of surrealist farce—of a mysterious universe that is neither psychological nor absurd, but appears to be the true paradise of the soul—a precarious paradise, glimpsed by only a few, and which may be lost but sometimes found at the price of extremely complex ordeals.

OTHER PLAYS: *Le Voyage* (1961), *L'Emigré de Brisbane* (Back from Brisbane, 1968).

**Schisgal, Murray** (born 1926). American playwright. Born in New York City, Schisgal graduated from Brooklyn Law School (LL.B. 1953). During his two years of working in a law office in Manhattan and three years of teaching English at James Fenimore Cooper Junior High School in East Harlem, Schisgal wrote novels and plays. In 1960 the British Drama League produced three one-act plays—*The Typists, The Postman* (retitled *The Tiger*), and *A Simple Kind of Love Story;* a longer play, *Ducks and Lovers,* was produced in London in 1961. The double bill of *The Typists* and *The Tiger* was very successful in New York in 1963 and on tour in Argentina, Australia,

Europe, Israel, and South Africa. *Knit One, Purl Two* was presented in Boston in 1963. *Luv,* another extraordinarily successful play, opened in London in 1963 and New York in 1964. *Jimmy Shine* was produced in New York in 1968 for a short run.

All of this work is comedy bordering on farce, black humor, and absurdity, but with enough pathos to appeal to large audiences. The first plays, including some unproduced pieces published in *Fragments, Windows and Other Plays* (1965), make use of Pinter's pattern or two or three characters in a single enclosed place (though in *Luv* the scene is a bridge); where in Pinter's work the overhanging menace is unidentified, in Schisgal's plays it is clearly labeled and spoofed: despair, false comfort, the Freudian scapegoat, love and sex, mechanical society. *Jimmy Shine* is a more complex play in having a larger cast (more than twenty), a more involved plot with flashback scenes, and a less obvious statement. Twelve years after *Look Back in Anger* (1956), Jimmy Shine seems a wiser and more contemplative Jimmy Porter, and the vaudeville moments are reminiscent of Osborne's *The Entertainer.*

**Schneider, Rolf** (born 1932). East German dramatist, novelist, and journalist. Schneider is one of the most versatile writers in East Germany. After studying literature at the Martin Luther University in Halle, he became editor of the cultural and political journal *Aufbau.* In 1958 he left this post to concentrate on writing radio plays and novels. His first stage play, *Godefroys,* was produced in 1962. This drama shows Schneider's predeliction for the trial as a framework for his plays. *Godefroys* deals with the final decline of a bourgeois industrialist family in 1944. This family, led by the father, contributed to the rise of Nazism, and Schneider places it on trial in scenes that reveal the criminal and self-destructive nature of the members of the family. In *Prozess Richard Waverly* (The Trial of Richard Waverly, 1963), Schneider moves to the American scene to present a semidocumentary account dealing with the Hiroshima pilot Claude Eatherley, who accused the United States of murder in dropping the atomic bomb in Japan. Though the original 1961 trial found Eatherley mentally disturbed, Schneider's trial, which is partially based on the original transcripts, endeavors to try the jury, the U.S. Air Force, and the American judicial system. Eatherley is given the name Waverly, and Schneider shows that Waverly's brother, Charles, who brings charges of insanity against Waverly, is supported by the Air Force, which wants to intimidate and incarcerate Waverly because he has been publishing stories about Hiroshima and showing that the United States had various alternatives to the atomic bomb. In the course of the trial, Schneider demonstrates how the Air Force persecutes Waverly and how the judicial system allows for bigotry in the South. The hero of the drama is actually not Waverly but his lawyer, Doc Anderson, who realizes that the Air Force is afraid of Waverly because he knows the truth, and that the truth can attract other people who might form a new faction within America. In *Prozess Nürnberg* (The Nuremberg

Trial, 1967) Schneider once again concerns himself with America. His documentary play is based on the forty-two volumes of the protocol of the Nuremberg international military tribunal and G. M. Gilbert's *Nuremberg Diary*. Schneider reconstructs the trial in five scenes with a prologue and epilogue, placing his emphasis on the conspiracy between the industrialists and the military as those who contributed most to the rise of Hitler. Each of the accused (Göring, Rundstedt, Milch, Keitel, Speer, Schacht, and Streicher) endeavors to lie about his personal responsibility, but their lies are exposed by the facts, as are the socioeconomic forces that led to fascism in Germany. Schneider has the American judge justify the Nuremberg trial as correct procedure against political criminality, and in this way he implies that the present-day tribunals that condemn America's war crimes in Vietnam are also justified. Schneider has turned more to the documentary mode in response to the mood and demands of the people. He sees the documentary as a form commensurate with the times. Though Schneider places the facts in an interesting framework—that is, the trial—he does not endow the facts with a new, vital nature. His strength as a dramatist is in his craftsmanship, not in his poetry. He is a master of the well-made socialist play.

OTHER PLAYS: *Der Mann aus England* (The Man from England, 1962), *Dieb und König* (Thief and King, 1966).

**Schreyvogl, Friedrich** (born 1899). Austrian dramatist, director, essayist, novelist, and poet. After studying political science at the University of Vienna and receiving his doctorate in 1922, Schreyvogl concentrated all his energies on developing his talents as a dramatist. He had already produced two plays as a student, and though he never developed into a great dramatist, he did go on to become one of the most influential men in Austrian theater circles. From 1923 until 1933, he was one of the editors of two important monthlies, *Das Abendland* and *Der Gral*. In the 1930s he taught drama at the Reinhardt Seminar in Vienna and was also the head of the Österreichische Länderbühne. During this time he also wrote numerous plays with strong religious overtones. After World War II he worked closely with the Theater in der Josefstadt and the Burgtheater in Vienna, and in 1959 he became the chief dramaturge of the Burgtheater. Most of Schreyvogl's dramas are well-made plays that call for a return to Catholicism. The majority of his writings either deal with religious motifs or recount Austrian history. Schreyvogl warns against the dangers of nationalism in his plays. He sees the true Austrian tradition as embedded in a humanitarian Catholicism, which can unite the disparate elements of Central Europe. Most of his plays since 1945 have tried to revive this tradition but they are limited by their traditional frameworks.

PLAYS SINCE 1945: *Der Liebhaber* (The Lover, 1951), *Die Nacht liegt hinter uns* (The Night Is Behind Us, 1952), *Der weisse Mantel* (The White Coat, 1952), *Die Versuchung des Tasso* (The Temptation of Tasso, 1955),

*Eine Stunde vor Tag* (An Hour Before Daybreak, 1956), *Ton und Licht* (Tone and Light, 1960), *Der Gott darf nicht sterben* (God May Not Die, 1961), *Ich liebe eine Göttin* (I Love a Goodess, 1961).

**Schwarz, Helmut** (born 1928). Austrian dramatist and director. After obtaining his doctorate in theater at the University of Vienna, Schwarz became a director and worked at various theaters in Vienna. In 1951 he became a reader at the Burgtheater and eventually a director. Since 1960 he has headed the Reinhardt Seminar. As a playwright, Schwarz continues the strong theater tradition of Austrian Catholic socialism. He addresses himself to contemporary issues and uses both the revue and *reportage* as forms to discuss these issues on the stage. *Seine letzte Berufung* (His Final Mission, 1953) analyzes the role of France in contemporary Europe. The *Arbeiterpriester* (Priest of the Workers, 1954) focuses on the conscience of the individual in a police state. *Aushängeschild* (The Certified Sign, 1959) gives an account of a Communist functionary who finds his way back to Christianity. Though Schwarz has begun to use symbolism in his most recent plays, the moral fervor of his own conscience and his realistic attitude shape the substance of his dramas.

OTHER PLAYS: *Brücken* (Bridges, 1947), *Das sind wir* (That's Us, 1948), *Ein Mann fällt aus den Wolken* (A Man Falls from the Clouds, 1949), *Menschen in Not* (Men in Need, 1950), *Die Beförderung* (The Promotion, 1960), *Im Aschenregen* (The Rain of Ashes, 1962), *Das Fehlurteil* (The Wrong Judgment, 1966).

**Séquestrés d'Altona, Les** (The Condemned of Altona, 1959), play in five acts by Jean-Paul Sartre. It was first performed on September 23, 1959, at the Théâtre de la Renaissance, Paris, under the direction of François Darbon. *Les Séquestrés d'Altona* is the most complex of Sartre's plays. The action, which takes place in Altona, Germany, near Hamburg, revolves around Frantz von Gerlach, who has lived as a recluse in his room since the end of World War II. The only person he allows in is his sister, Leni, who is in love with him, and with whom he is having an incestuous relationship. Closed in his room, Frantz keeps alive the idea that Germany, defeated in 1945, is in a state of frightful destitution and close to disintegrating altogether because of the state of oppression in which it is kept by the Allies. Leni has confirmed this illusion of his. Frantz spends his time at a tape recorder, transcribing his impressions of this century and addressing his comments to the "Crabs"—that is, to the creatures who will have replaced man in the thirtieth century and who will be his judges.

The play begins with Frantz's father, one of the biggest German industrialists, telling his two other children, Leni and Werner, as well as Werner's wife, Johanna, that he is dying of cancer and has only six months to live. He makes Werner swear that he will go on living in the Altona house to protect Frantz in case his presence there is discovered, for Frantz is accused of having tried to murder an American officer in 1946. To avoid the scandal of a trial and the dishonor of a conviction, the father has made the outside world believe that his son went to Argentina and then died there.

Johanna rebels against her husband's solemn promise, which makes them prisoners of the sinister house, and decides to do everything she can to get into Frantz's room so that she can persuade him to emerge and thus free them. For his part, the father, who has not seen Frantz since 1946, is ready to become her ally if she can arrange a meeting for him with his son. Leni, of course, is opposed to this. She does not want to share her brother, for how, then, will she be able to encourage him in his seclusion and his madness?

Johanna manages to get into Frantz's room and gradually begins to accept his madness. Moreover, they are attracted to each other and recognize each other as creatures of the same species. Frantz confesses to Johanna that he feels guilty about not having done enough while a lieutenant during the war to assure his country's victory. Most particularly, he did not allow the torture of some Russian peasants, whose information might have saved his men. Johanna readily forgives him this. However, Frantz's confession is a lie. And Leni, to get Frantz back from Johanna, finally tells him that, in fact, Germany is the most prosperous country in Western Europe, and informs Johanna that Frantz was the "butcher of Smolensk" and himself a torturer. Horrified, Johanna forsakes Frantz. And Frantz, whose illusion has been shattered, and knowing that aside from his sister no one would accept him for what he is, decides to see his father and be judged by him. The fifth act of the play is in large part taken up with the dialogue of the father and son, during which they take stock of their relationship and their mutual fates. In 1941, in order to save his son, the father had denounced a rabbi who had escaped from a concentration camp, with the result that the rabbi's throat was cut under the eyes of Frantz, who was reduced to helplessness by four policemen. It was to get rid of that feeling of helplessness that Frantz became a "butcher" later on. He then cut himself off from the world to take refuge in the illusion of Germany's destruction, for a prosperous Germany would have meant that his crimes had been useless and even instrumental in delaying the defeat that had been so providential for Germany. As for the father, his power is in fact an illusion, for he is dominated by his own gigantic organization. Indeed, since both of them are guilty and unjustified, there is nothing left for them to do but die. As they drive off intending to commit suicide in the car, Frantz's tape recorder is on and his voice is describing the "taste" of our century, in which man and the beast that is man's worst enemy are one and the same.

Central to this play is Sartre's obsession with torture, and there is an obvious similarity here between the torture that took place in Nazi Germany and that of the French during the Algerian war. But more generally, Sartre has dramatized the distinctive characteristics of our world today—its violence and contradictions—a frightful game in which the loser wins, and which has prompted Sartre to wonder, in anguish, how it will be judged by history. Moreover, around the lies of Leni and the father, Frantz's intentional "madness," and the performance of Johanna (who had once been an actress), Sartre develops, from all points of view, his conception of bad faith, as well as the hellish circle of relationships with others that he had already dramatized in *Huis-Clos* (No Exit) in 1944.

**Serjeant Musgrave's Dance** (1959). A play by John Arden. Although preceded by two full-length plays, *Serjeant Musgrave's Dance* was the first of Arden's works to attract public attention, much of it at first unfavorable, and it is now recognized as one of the major achievements of this uneven writer. Called by its author "a realistic, but not a naturalistic, play," it portrays a group of four English deserters from an imaginary colonial war in the late nineteenth century, who arrive in a remote North Country mining town with the ostensible purpose of conducting a recruiting campaign. In fact their leader is a half-crazed religious fanatic who has persuaded his three companions to join him in a dramatic gesture against the violence of war. At a meeting in the public square they reveal the corpse of a soldier from the town whose murder led to a vicious reprisal by the British troops. (In 1959 the intentional parallel with recent events in British-occupied Cyprus was clear.) It is at this point that Arden's characteristic reluctance to take an obvious moral stand is revealed. Musgrave's plan, now made clear for the first time, is as indefensible as the violence he opposes. According to his grim logic, "and Logic is to me the mechanism of God," the multiplying history of reprisals and counter-reprisals must be repeated. "Join along with my madness, friend," he appeals. "I brought it back to England but I've brought the cure too—to turn it on them that sent it out of this country." His appalled companion Attercliffe turns against him, and disaster is averted by the arrival of a troop of Dragoons. It was Arden's apparently ambivalent attitude toward violence that produced the accusations of obscurity leveled against the play. In an introduction the dramatist claims that a study of the roles of the women and of Attercliffe will reveal his own viewpoint. "Complete pacifism is a very hard doctrine," he writes, "and if this play appears to advocate it with perhaps some timidity, it is probably because I am naturally a very timid man—and also because I know that if I am hit I very easily hit back: and I do not care to preach too confidently what I am not sure I can practice."

With a close attention to structure that is sometimes missing in his later work, Arden effectively links the minor characters to the main plot. In a town cut off by heavy snows and affected by industrial dispute, the arrival of a group of soldiers polarizes the conflicting interests of the miners and those in league with their employers. The involvement of the two women in the action of the play is important to its development, and the death of one of Musgrave's followers in a brawl foreshadows the group's ambiguous attitude toward violence. The thaw that heralds the arrival of the Dragoons aptly symbolizes the end of Musgrave's brief hold over the town.

*Serjeant Musgrave's Dance* is an important precursor of the move from naturalism that developed in the English theater of the '60s. The language, austere and yet idiomatic, employs imagery reflected in visual terms on the stage, linking the recurrent theme of blood with the scarlet tunics of the soldiers and the wintry blackness of the mining town with the cold steel of Musgrave's Gatling gun. As in all his drama, Arden offers an oblique commentary on the action in the ballads, drawing on the language and rhythms of popular poetry, which alternate with the spoken dialogue. The climax of the play, in which the deserters level a Gatling gun at the crowd while a skeleton in military tunic is hoisted aloft and Musgrave executes his demoniac dance of death, provides a composite theatrical image of unusual intensity.

*Serjeant Musgrave's Dance* is not a perfect play. Arden's language was to develop to greater maturity in his later work, and he was to employ staging conventions outside the tradition of naturalism with greater subtlety and assurance. There is a certain imbalance between Musgrave's fanaticism and the "moral" that the dramatist asserts may be found in the play, and Arden's double-edged sympathies were to have greater dramatic point in some of his later work, most effectively in *Armstrong's Last Goodnight*.

**Shaffer, Peter** (born 1926). English dramatist. Born in London, Shaffer worked as a coal miner (1944–1947) before proceeding to Trinity College, Cambridge. He found employment for a time as a librarian in New York and later with a London firm of music publishers. He began his career as a dramatist in television (*The Salt Land*, 1955; *Balance of Terror*, 1957). Shaffer is a writer as remarkable for his range as for his quality. *Five Finger Exercise* (1958) is a sympathetic portrait of confused adolescence, conventional in structure and in its upper-middle-class setting, but undeniably a play of the late '50s in the qualities that took its audiences by storm: the intensity and emotional accuracy of its portrayal of the overpowering relationship between mother and son. The play won the *Evening Standard* Award for the best play of the year and the New York Drama Critics Circle Award for the best foreign play of 1959–60. *The Private Ear* and *The Public Eye*, two one-act plays (the first sentimental and the second farcical) presented in a double bill in 1962, are recognizably from the pen of the author of *Five Finger Exercise*. *The Royal Hunt of the Sun* (written before 1962 but not staged until 1964) marks a radical stylistic departure in a full-scale historical treatment of the conquest of Peru of which the author wrote: "My hope was always to realise on stage a kind of 'total' theatre, involving not only words but rites, mimes, masks and magics. . . . It is a director's piece, a pantomimist's piece, a musician's piece, and of course an actor's piece, almost as much as it is an author's." First presented under John Dexter's direction at Chichester, it is one of the rare modern plays in which the opportunities offered by the open stage have been grasped. The one-act *Black Comedy,* presented by the same director for the National Theatre in the following year, is perhaps the most successful farce written since the war. To a classical formula of mistaken identities, rival candidates for the hero's love, and a tangled scheme of unexpected arrivals timed with split-second precision, Shaffer adds the Oriental convention of presenting scenes supposedly occurring in pitch darkness under full stage lighting, with an ingenuity that contributes brilliantly to the sharply visualized physical quality of the action onstage.

*The Royal Hunt of the Sun,* Shaffer's most ambitious play, was acclaimed for its imaginative assimilation of Brechtian techniques. But the language is not grounded upon an imagery adequate to the boldly nonnaturalistic style of the play, and the presentation of the sardonic, isolated *persona* of Pizarro, culminating in the betrayal of his intense, uneasy friendship with the Inca god-king Atahualpa, is a conventional character study of the reluctant atheist in search of new gods, which, it might be argued, is not organically linked to the theatrical devices that have earned the play its reputation. Shaffer's most sustained success, from *Five Finger Exercise* to his most recent one-act play *The White Liars* (1968), has lain outside the political, historical themes associated with the name of Brecht, in his sensitive explorations of the psychology of loneliness, isolation, and sexual inexperience or unhappiness, with the hint of homosexuality delicately caught in the nuances of everyday speech.

His screenplays include *The Lord of the Flies.*

OTHER PLAYS: *The Merry Roosters Panto* (with Joan Littlewood and Theatre Workshop, 1963), *A Warning Game* (one act, 1967), *The Battle of Shrivings* (1970).

**Shaw, Robert** (born 1927). English actor and author. Born in Lancashire and educated in Truro, Cornwall, Shaw is the son of a doctor. He studied for the theater at the Royal Academy of Dramatic Art and first appeared on the stage at the Shakespeare Memorial Theatre in 1949. Since then he has taken many parts in Shakespearian and modern drama with that company, the English Stage Company, and in the commercial theater; he has also acted in films and on television. He has written a number of novels (among which *The Sun Doctor* was awarded the Hawthornden Prize in 1959) as well as plays for television. *The Man in the Glass Booth* (1967), adapted from his novel of the same title, owes its inspiration to the Eichmann trial: The Jewish race is symbolically implicated in the guilt of Fascist Germany when the war criminal accused in an Israeli "show trial" is himself revealed as a Jew. This exposition of the morbid and sadomasochistic interest of the Jews in the psychology of Fascism leaves some fundamental questions unanswered, but in its gradual revelation of the insanity of the central character, in its picture of the gnawing unease that lies behind his friendly Jewish humor, and in the atmospheric quality of the trial scene, it reveals its author as a dramatist of considerable power.

OTHER PLAYS: *Off the Mainland* (1957).

**Shepard, Sam** (born 1943). American playwright. Born in Fort Madison, Illinois, raised just outside Los Angeles, Shepard became an actor, worked his way to New York, and began writing plays in conjunction with various off-off-Broadway theater groups. Produced between 1965 and 1968 were *Cowboys* and *Rock Garden* (Theatre Genesis), *Up to Thursday* and *4-H Club* (Theatre '65), *Dog* and *Rocking Chair* (La MaMa), *Icarus's Mother* (Caffè Cino), *Red Cross* (Judson Poets' Theater), *Fourteen Hundred Thousand* (Firehouse Theatre, Minneapolis), *Chicago* (Theatre Genesis), *Melodrama Play* (La MaMa), *La Turista* (American Place Theatre, 1967), *Forensic and the Navigators* (Theatre Genesis). From this experimental circuit, with occasional second productions in off-Broadway theaters, Shepard moved to the attention of a larger audience with a month's engagement of his *Operation Sidewinder* at New York's Repertory Theater of Lincoln Center in 1970.

Shepard's plays are like metaphors hanging in a void: the bathroomless bathtub in *Chicago*, the stark white set of *Red Cross*, the book case in *Fourteen Hundred Thousand* are isolated visual analogues of the action, which is itself strikingly like, and yet unlike, an event in "real life." *Icarus's Mother*, for example, uses the simple event of some people on a Fourth of July picnic, the dialogue an American equivalent of Pinter's unexplained banality; yet the play is dense with interconnections between classic myth and modern menace without ever making any of these connections explicit or even clear. The audience cannot "identify" or genuinely "recognize" what is happening in the play, and in this experience of uncertainty lies its "meaning."

**Sherriff, R. C.** (born 1896). English dramatist. Sherriff was commissioned and saw active service during World War I, after which he began a career as an insurance official. He had been writing plays for performance by an amateur dramatic society for some years before *Journey's End*, his first play to be performed professionally, appeared upon the stage in 1928. It was with this study of the strain of life in the trenches, unpretentious, yet deeply moving, that his reputation was made. The play has been performed in every European language. Sherriff was never to repeat the phenomenal success of *Journey's End* with his later plays. Fond of celebrating the quiet values of suburban England, he must be judged a dramatist of competence rather than originality. He is the author of several novels and numerous screenplays, which include *Goodbye, Mr. Chips* and *The Dam Busters*. He has written a volume of autobiography, *No Leading Lady* (1968).

OTHER PLAYS SINCE 1945: *Miss Mabel* (1948), *Home at Seven* (1950), *The White Carnation* (1953), *The Long Sunset* (1955), *The Telescope* (1957), *A Shred of Evidence* (1960), *Johnny the Priest* (musical version of *The Telescope*, 1960).

**Simon, [Marvin] Neil** (born 1927). American playwright. Simon was born in New York City and attended New York University for a year before beginning to write for television in 1948. After ten years of TV scripts and sketches for revues, he and his brother, Daniel, wrote *Come Blow Your Horn*, presented on Broadway in 1961. This was the beginning of a series of Broadway hits for Neil Simon, for the most part comedies of witty individual lines and sentimental-romantic situations: *Barefoot in the Park* (1963), *The Odd Couple* (1965), *Sweet Charity* (1966), *The Star-Spangled Girl* (1966), *Plaza Suite* (1968), *Promises, Promises* (1969), and *The Last of the Red Hot Lovers* (1970). The earnings from these plays and from film rights have been in the millions, and Simon is reputed to be financially the most successful playwright of all time.

**Simonov, Konstantin Mikhailovich** (born 1915). Soviet dramatist and novelist. Born in Petrograd (later Leningrad), Simonov graduated from the Gorky Literary Institute in Moscow in 1938. His first play was *Obyknovennaya istoriya* (An Ordinary Story, 1940), later retitled *Istoriya odnoy lyubvi* (The Story of One Love). The war against the Japanese in Mongolia in the late 1930s was the subject of his second play, *Paren iz nashego goroda* (A Lad from Our Town, 1941). During World War II Simonov was a war correspondent for the newspaper *Krasnaya zvezda* (Red Star). His play *Russkie lyudi* (The Russian People, published in *Pravda* in July 1942) describes the Russian nation girding for war against the Nazis. Simonov's novel *Dni i nochi* (Days and Nights, 1943–44), which was adapted for the stage in 1946 by A. Viner, celebrated the heroic defense of Stalingrad. His plays *Russky vopros* (The Russian Question, 1946) and *Chuzhaya ten* (The Foreign Shadow, 1949) are anti-American dramas.

**Simpson, N. F.** (born 1919). English dramatist. Born and educated in London, Simpson took a degree at London University and entered the teaching profession. He first became known as a dramatist when *A Resounding Tinkle* was awarded third prize in the *Observer* play competition of 1957 and was presented (in a shortened version) by the English Stage Company. With the success of *One Way Pendulum* (1959) his distinctive style attained some popularity with a wider public. Simpson has been more variously estimated than most of the avant-garde English dramatists who attracted the attention of critics in the late '50s: He has been called both "a more powerful social critic than any of the social realists" and a dramatist whose work "rapidly loses its charms in a life-and-death struggle with the law of diminishing returns." The distinguishing feature of Simpson's dramaturgy lies in the relentlessly stolid manner in which his characters abandon everyday logic in the prosaic surroundings of English suburbia. In *One Way Pendulum* Arthur Groomkirby builds up his savings by feeding coins into his own parking meters, while his son vainly attempts to train a collection of "speak-your-weight" machines to sing the "Hallelujah Chorus." In the second act a symbolic trial with all the trappings of English legal procedure takes place in the Groomkirby household. In the first version of the earlier *A Resounding Tinkle* a plot with similar overtones of surrealism is set in a more self-conscious framework that includes interruptions from the supposed author of the piece and ends with a mockingly observed parody of a critical discussion of the play itself. The attraction of the play, however, lies more in the fantastic conversation of the appropriately named family of Paradocks than in the somewhat obscure commentary upon the nature of reality and dramatic illusion provided by these secondary features. His one-act play *The Hole* (1958) was quick to achieve critical favor for its study of the varied reactions of passers-by to a hole in the street, while *The Cresta Run* (1965) is a parody of the conventional spy thriller that rarely rises above the pedestrian.

The quality of Simpson's work varies considerably; at his best he has shown himself a brilliantly funny and original writer for the stage, but whether his meticulously timed cascades of non sequiturs can be said to make any significant commentary upon the human condition is more open to doubt. Although the attempt has been made to link him with the European tradition of the absurd, it is difficult to point to more than a superficial resemblance of his work to Ionesco's. His antecedents are to be found in the English tradition of nonsensical fantasy exemplified in Lewis Carroll, Edward Lear, and the radio "Goon Show" of the early '50s. Simpson's work demonstrates the pitfalls that await the writer whose basic weapon is the paradox. The pleasure of watching the assumptions of everyday reality collapse soon palls if the artist has no alternative vision with which to replace it, and it is the lack of any such alternative vision that invests Simpson's plays with a static quality that prevents them from reaching the first rank. Simpson's work is discussed by Martin Esslin in *The Theatre of the Absurd* (1961) and by John Russell Taylor in *Anger and After* (1969).

Simpson has contributed sketches to revues, adapted *One Way Pendulum* for the screen, and written scripts for a satirical television series "The World in Ferment."

OTHER PLAYS: *The Form* (one act, 1961).

Śmierć gubernatora (Death of the Governor, 1961). A play by Leon Kruczkowski. Though based on an idea from a short story by Leonid Andreyev, "The Governor" (1906), it is an independent drama, with an undefined geographical and historical setting. The characters of the play are representatives of established institutions and classes opposed to the emerging social forces. At the top of the ladder stands the Governor, who by the virtue of his office is meant to protect the interests of the ruling class. The play deals with the exercise of political power. In an emergency, the Governor orders the police to shoot at the crowd storming his residence, then logically and courageously accepts the moral consequences. A farsighted man, he sees the evils of the system he represents, and foresees its eventual collapse. He also foresees his own death at the hands of revolutionaries—and survives it when a condemned revolutionary whom he has freed accidentally dies in his stead.

Reappearing after his ceremonious funeral, the Governor is virtually rejected by his family and collaborators, and withdraws into the background, at last free to exist for himself, and to be himself, but in a world where there is no place for him.

If in *Śmierć gubernatora* Kruczkowski did not provide an answer to the question of the consequences of a political crime, he did provide nonetheless an unequivocal answer to the question of the consequences of power. Strangely enough, this is not a political play, but a kind of morality play. The former socialist realist abandoned veristic detail and introduced a narrator, who both comments on the action and engages in discussions with the hero. Lonely walks of the Governor, seeking a confrontation with his people—meetings with schoolgirls in a park, with workers in a bar, with a prisoner in the death cell, and with gravediggers philosophizing over his grave—provide a good reason for introducing a number of short, loosely connected scenes that acquire a dramatic power from the urgent search of a finished man trying to rediscover his lost self. In his last play Kruczkowski tried to create a universally valid metaphor instead of a partisan plea. At least in part he succeeded.

**Soif et la faim, La** (Hunger and Thirst, 1966). A play in three episodes by Eugène Ionesco. It was first performed on February 28, 1966, at the Comédie Française, under the direction of Jean-Marie Serreau. The first episode of *La Soif et la faim*, called "Flight," takes place in a damp, gloomy apartment that is gradually sinking into the ground. Jean and his wife, Marie-Madeleine, used to live there and, in spite of her husband's wishes, Marie-Madeleine has brought him back there, along with their baby, Marthe. Jean complains about the horror of the place and its dampness. He is suffocating there—he who dreams of the sun and pure air. Very maternally, Marie-Madeleine insists that the apartment is peaceful and safe, that they must resign themselves to it, and that their happiness lies in the isolation of their love. But for Jean the place is a sign of sinking into death. After two concrete manifestations of his obsessions (the appearance of a mad old aunt who, in fact, is dead, and the image in a mirror of a woman fighting flames whom he does not have the courage to save), Jean begins to talk to himself and gradually decides to flee that prison where death and remorse lie in wait for him. Marie-Madeleine, who persists in believing in the happiness of a quiet life based on their love, will not accept the possibility of Jean's disappearing forever, for "he cannot tear the love out of his heart." In fact, after a long game of hide-and-seek, Jean tears out his heart and places a bloodstained branch of wild roses on the table. Then he disappears. Marie-Madeleine, resigned, starts to rock her baby in the empty apartment. As the episode ends, the back of the stage set is transformed into a marvelous sunny garden, the symbol of Marie-Madeleine's love, which Jean was unable to perceive.

In Episode II, "The Date," the curtain goes up on a large terrace suspended in air, surrounded by mountains and under a gray sky. When Jean arrives, the sky becomes blue and luminous. Jean begins a conversation with two identical guards from a neighboring museum. He explains that he has a date with a young woman and is overflowing with happiness. Time passes and the young woman does not show up. Questioned by the guards, Jean realizes that he has trouble recalling details about the date and cannot manage to describe the young woman precisely. His joy turns to anguish—the anguish of absence and emptiness. After admitting to the guards that he finds it impossible to understand the contradiction between the reality of absence and his anticipation of the young woman's presence, he leaves in search of her. The two guards, themselves only thirsty for wine and hungry for soup, also leave the terrace to enjoy their meal.

The third episode, entitled "Black Masses at the Friendly Inn," is the longest and most complex. The setting represents the large hall of what Ionesco calls "a kind of monastery-barracks-prison." Characters called "brothers" and dressed as monks are awaiting Jean. When he arrives, weary, famished, and thirsty after his long wanderings, the "monks," led by Brother Tarabas, give him generous supplies of food and drink. Then they ask him questions about his travels, which are in fact a test. The brothers know what Jean should have seen: wonders such as "the knight out of the past, asleep standing up in his armor," "temples in the air," or "crystal wolves." But Jean has seen only people, houses, and trees, the things of daily life, and ends by repeating the same simple words. Although Jean's responses to the test were hardly satisfactory, Brother Tarabas decides to offer Jean some entertainment: Two clowns, Tripp and Brechtoll, are each put into a cage. Tripp believes in God, and Brechtoll is an atheistic materialist. Deprived of food, the two clowns at first refuse to deny their faiths in order to procure some. Hours and days go by, while Tarabas and the "monks" torture the two clowns by making them smell the soup. Finally, Brechtoll breaks down and recites the "Pater Noster," and Tripp denies the existence of God. After this didactic spectacle, Jean prepares to leave, but is courteously, though firmly, prevented. He must pay for his food and lodging. As the back of the stage set is transformed into the garden of Episode I, with Marie-Madeleine and Marthe, who is now fifteen, Jean—dressed as a monk—is forced to serve soup to a very large group of famished monks. The play ends with a chorus chanting, at an accelerated speed, the number of working hours Jean still owes, while he goes on mechanically serving, faster and faster, the monks who are at table.

The entire play takes place in an atmosphere of frustration and the strangeness of bad dreams. From beginning to end, Jean's goodwill and aspirations are constantly thwarted by a sense of guilt and by implied threats. He himself is stricken with a romantic malady, which he calls "ardent nostalgia," and which prevents him from accepting his wife's love. The first episode symbolizes his terror of death; the second, the failure of his search for absolute happiness; the third, his being oppressed by the society he rejoins

—a society that aims only at depersonalizing him, and in which ideologies are illusory faiths, since they do not stand up to the test of physical hunger and thirst. In short, *La Soif et la faim*, the story of an individual quest, is an allegory, both "absurd" and lyrical, of the inability to be happy either seeking one's ideals or living in man's society.

**Soviet Union.** Soviet drama, like all of Soviet art and literature since the 1930s, has been inextricably involved with politics. With its view of art as a political instrument and medium of propaganda, the Soviet Communist Party has seen to it that ideological considerations remain of prime importance in Soviet culture. The history of this culture since World War II is one of an alternation between rigid and less stringent controls of artists by the party and of a fluctuation in the degree to which ideological or artistic factors affect works of art.

The cooling of relations between the Soviet Union and the West at the end of World War II had a direct effect on Soviet literature and drama. During the war years, control of writers and theaters had been relaxed. Touring companies and theaters behind the lines were relatively free to choose repertories, which consisted mostly of war plays, prewar dramas with patriotic themes, and Russian classics. This situation changed decisively in 1946, with the beginning of the anti-Western campaign. In August 1946 the Central Committee of the Communist Party issued a decree that ordered dramatists to concentrate on contemporary themes, specifically anti-Western themes.

The clamping of controls on theaters was part of a general increase of party supervision in all the arts. The leader of the campaign was Andrei Zhdanov (1896–1948), a member of the Central Committee. Zhdanov called for a return to socialist realism and reminded writers that "Soviet literature is the most advanced, progressive, and revolutionary literature of the world and Soviet writers have to attack the degenerate, decadent bourgeois culture." Well-known writers, such as the poetess Anna Akhmatova and the satirist Mikhail Zoshchenko, were publicly castigated by Zhdanov for their short-comings in this respect.

Although all forms of art were rigidly supervised, the theater was watched especially closely because of its importance as a medium for mass propaganda. Obedient Soviet dramatists heeded the party's command and produced plays in which the capitalist world was unfavorably compared to the Communist world, or which contrasted the so-called progressive and reactionary elements in Western society. A few plays, such as *Velikie gni* (Great Days, 1946), by Nikolai Virta, had British society as their targets. For the most part, however, anti-Western meant anti-American. Konstantin Simonov's *Russky vopros* (The Russian Question, 1946), one of the more popular anti-American plays, showed what one of the characters called "the two Americas." Harry Smith, a progressive New York newspaper reporter, opposes Macpherson, a warmongering, imperialistic publisher. Smith muses that for a long time he was "naïve enough to think that there was but one America." Now he knows, he says, that there are two—"the America of Hearst" and "the America of Abraham Lincoln, the America of Roosevelt." In *Chuzhaya ten* (The Foreign Shadow, 1949) Simonov depicts evil American scientists who convert a disease-curing discovery of a Soviet scientist into a destructive weapon.

Racial prejudice in the United States was also a popular subject at the time. One of these plays, *Deep Are the Roots*, by James Gow and Arnaud d'Usseau, originated in the United States. It was produced in New York in September 1945, and then was translated into Russian and staged in Moscow in May 1947. A Russian version of *Uncle Tom's Cabin*, by A. Brushtein, was produced in 1948. This play, along with V. A. Lyubimova's *Snezhok* (Snowball, 1948), which portrayed racial discrimination in American schools, became a standard in the repertories of Soviet children's theaters.

The imperialistic tendencies of American politicians was also a favorite topic through the early 1950s. Boris Lavrenyov's *Golos Ameriki* (Voice of America), a winner of a Stalin prize in 1949, shows a fictional American senator, Herbert D. Wheeler of Alabama, who proclaims that it is America's destiny to rule the world. The playwrights Nikolai POGODIN and Anatoly Surov used the names of living American political leaders, especially that of President Harry Truman, in their indictments of United States imperialism. Both Pogodin's *Missurysky vals* (Missouri Waltz, 1949) and Surov's *Zemlyak prezidenta* (The Mad Haberdasher, 1949) had Democratic Party bosses in Kansas City, Missouri, as their targets, and Surov's play claimed an alliance between American politicians and the Nazis.

Details sometimes revealed that the authors of anti-American plays knew little about what they condemned. In T. Solodar's *Malchik iz Marseli* (The Boy from Marseilles, 1951), the ship S.S. *Caroline Truman*, which is reputed to transport diseased food from the United States to Europe, is said to be named after Truman's daughter, whose real name, of course, is Margaret. In A. Yakobson's *Angel-khranitel iz Nebraski* (Guardian Angel from Nebraska, 1952), the American villain, Theodore Nathan Truman, a cultural ambassador to Norway, teaches the Norwegians the secrets of the Yo-Yo. The romanticized gangsters in Pogodin's *Missouri Waltz* look as if they had been lifted from American crime films.

Another common theme in the early 1950s was that of foreign, particularly American, intervention during Russia's civil war of 1918–1920. In 1952 Nikolai Nikitin's novel *Aurora Borealis*, which dealt with the defeat of American and Japanese troops in the Far East in 1919, was staged as a play. L. Rudy's *Slava etikh gney nikogda ne umryot* (The Glory of These Days Will Never Die) and M. Maksimov's *My nikogda ne zabudem* (We Shall Never Forget) castigated Americans for attempting to destroy the nascent Soviet regime. These plays were produced during the period when Soviet propaganda organs were accusing the United States of intervening in the Korean conflict.

Anti-Western plays were not the only fare offered Soviet theatergoers. At least three other themes were almost as prevalent on Soviet stages through the early 1950s. The experience of the war was treated in Aleksandr Kron's *Ofitser flota* (Officer of the Fleet, 1945), with its setting in Leningrad during the German blockade of 1941. A. Viner's adaptation of Konstantin Simonov's war novel *Dni i nochi* (Days and Nights) was produced by the Moscow Art Theater in 1946, as was Boris Chirskov's *Pobediteley* (Victors). One of the more popular war dramas was Aleksandr Fadeev's *Molodaya gvardiya* (Young Guard), an adaptation of his novel. The stage version was produced in 1947 and eventually toured all the theaters of the Soviet Union. Praise of Stalin's military genius and its importance for Soviet victory figured largely in Virta's *Great Days* and Arkady Perventsov's *Yuzhny uzel* (Southern Junction, 1946).

Exaltation of Stalin constituted another major theme during this period. G. Hakhutsrishvili depicted Stalin's early years and career in two plays, *Yunost vozhdya* (The Leader's Youth) and *Voskhodit solntse* (The Sun Rises, 1951). *Prolog* (Prologue, 1952), by Aleksandr Shtein, dealt with Stalin's role in the 1905 revolution.

Another popular theme was the struggle to introduce improvements in industry and agriculture. Usually these plays pitted honest, bright innovators against routine-bound conservatives who opposed change. Surov's *Daleko ot Stalingrada* (Far from Stalingrad, 1946) showed such a conflict in a wartime aviation factory in the Urals. *Osoboe mnenie* (A Personal Opinion, 1949), by S. Klebanov and A. Maryamov, and *Khleb nash nasushchny* (Our Daily Bread, 1950), by Virta, dealt with similar problems in Soviet agriculture.

The trouble with most of the plays through the early 1950s was that their themes were dull, their dramatic conflicts unreal or unconvincing, and their productions theatrically unexciting. Dramatists were hampered by the so-called "no-conflict theory," which prohibited them from showing sharp conflicts in Soviet society on the supposition that in a socialist society there were no clashes of interest. Since the late 1930s the canonical method of theatrical production was the realistic technique developed by Konstantin Stanislavski in the Moscow Art Theater. Stanislavski's striving for a total illusion of reality in the theater was suited for presentation of works of socialist realism. In 1934 the doctrine of socialist realism was propounded as the official Soviet artistic method. Directors and playwrights who rejected realism soon began to be expelled from Soviet theater. One of the major victims was the director Vsevolod Meyerhold, who had worked under Stanislavski at the Moscow Art Theater for a brief time. In contrast to Stanislavski's photographic realism, Meyerhold's concept of theater was of a place where the difference of art from life was stressed. In 1902 Meyerhold left the Moscow Art Theater and worked in various theaters in Moscow, Petersburg, and the provinces until he founded his own theater in Moscow in 1920. Meyerhold's expressionistic experiments ended in 1937 with his arrest. He is believed to have died in a Soviet prison in 1940. Meyerhold's wife, the actress Zinaida Raikh, was found murdered shortly after his arrest. Meyerhold's influence was to reenter Soviet theater almost twenty years later with the work of Nikolai Okhlopkov, a former colleague of Meyerhold's, and with the production of the works of Bertolt Brecht, on whom Meyerhold's ideas seem to have exerted an influence.

Other supporters of an anti-realistic mode of theater were Evgeni Vakhtangov and Aleksandr Tairov. Vakhtangov had also worked with Stanislavski at the Moscow Art Theater. In 1920 he set up his own theater at the Moscow Art's Third Studio and headed it until his death in 1923. In 1926 the Third Studio was renamed the Vakhtangov Theater. Tairov founded the Kamerny (Chamber) Theater in 1914 and remained there until his death in 1950, although he was replaced as artistic director in 1946. Tairov was responsible for bringing many works of Western playwrights into the Soviet repertory, including those of George Bernard Shaw, Eugene O'Neill, and, in 1930, Bertolt Brecht, with a production of *The Threepenny Opera*. As foreign works fell into disfavor Tairov was forced to produce more Russian works. In 1946, shortly before his dismissal as artistic director of the Kamerny, he produced a bold version of Chekhov's *The Sea Gull*. Tairov used the conversations between the young writer Treplyev and the old writer Trigorin to make an implicit criticism of realism, broadly hinting that socialist realism was being called into question. The play did not have a long run.

The generally poor quality of post-1945 Soviet drama drew complaints even from such a highly placed party official as Georgi Malenkov, a member of the Central Committee and Soviet Premier from 1953 to 1955. In late 1952 Malenkov noted that too many Soviet plays were simply trash. There was little hope for change, however, as long as Stalin was in power.

One of the last blows delivered by Stalin to Soviet culture before his death was the "anti-cosmopolitan campaign," which began in 1949. The attacks on "rootless cosmopolitans" (those who were guilty of excessive interest in Western culture and who did not evince proper Soviet attitudes and sympathies) had anti-Semitic overtones. Many of the cosmopolitans who were exposed in the Soviet press were Jews. Shortly before the attacks began in the press, Solomon Mikhoels, the great Yiddish actor, was killed in Minsk under mysterious circumstances. One rumor was that he was attacked and murdered by hoodlums; another was that he had been run over by a truck. There was also a rumor that Mikhoels' death had been ordered by Lavrenti Beria, Stalin's secret police chief. During the campaign Tairov's Kamerny Theater was closed.

The culmination of the anti-cosmopolitan campaign was the "doctors' plot," which was publicized in January 1953. A number of Kremlin doctors, most of whom were Jews, were arrested and charged with conspiring to murder Soviet officials at the instigation of American and British Intelligence agents. Stalin's death in March 1953 ended the campaign against the cosmopolitans and the doctors. In April 1953 the Soviet Union announced that all the doctors had been released from custody.

Even before Khrushchev's denunciation of Stalin at the twentieth Party Congress in 1956 there was a noticeable relaxation in Soviet drama. An unusual outspokenness was perceptible in Leonid Zorin's *Gosti* (The Guests, 1954), which portrayed the conflict between an old Bolshevik and his son, a member of the new class of officials who had arisen during Stalin's reign. The father characterizes his son as one of the "rank-conscious aristocrats, greedy and conceited, remote from the people." Aleksandr Korneichuk's *Krylya* (Wings, 1954) dealt with the "cult of the individual" in his delineation of a provincial administrator. There was a similar theme in Aleksandr Shtein's *Personalnoe delo* (A Personal Case, 1954). At Moscow's Satire Theater Vladimir Pluchek staged Vladimir Mayakovsky's two comedies *Klop* (The Bedbug, 1928) and *Banya* (The Bathhouse, 1930), which had long been banned from the Soviet repertory because of their satirical attacks on Communist society. Ilya Ehrenburg's novel *Ottepel* (The Thaw), published in 1954, labeled the coming era of relative freedom.

Khrushchev's anti-Stalin speech in February 1956 ushered in the most liberated period in Soviet culture since the early 1930s. Writers took full advantage of the opportunity to speak out as they had not been able to do before and to treat themes that were formerly taboo. Samuil Alyoshin's *Odna* (Alone), produced at the Vakhtangov Theater in 1956, caused a sensation because of its sympathetic treatment of a purely personal problem, the question of divorce. Nikolai Pogodin's *Sonet Petrarki* (Petrarch's Sonnet, 1956), which dealt with an adulterous love affair, also treated its subject as something private, apart from Communist Party concerns. Z. Paperny's *Genya and Sonya* (1956) parodied the typical Soviet play based on socialist realism and ridiculed the hackneyed Soviet dramatic themes of industrial production and collective farm life.

Another measure of the relaxation in Soviet theater was the production of dramatic adaptations of the works of Fëdor Dostoevski, the nineteenth-century novelist whose reactionary political views and concentration on religious themes had been displeasing to Soviet cultural authorities. Although acknowledged worldwide as one of Russia's great classical writers, he had been virtually ignored in the Soviet Union. During 1956, the seventy-fifth anniversary of Dostoevski's death, the traditional attention paid to the occasion by new editions and productions of an author's work included stage versions of six Dostoevski works: *The Brothers Karamazov* at the Moscow Art Theater, *The Village of Stepanchikovo* at the Maly Theater, *The Idiot* at the Vakhtangov Theater, *The Gambler* at the Pushkin Drama Theater, *The Insulted and Injured* at the Leningrad Komsomol Theater, and *Uncle's Dream* at the Leningrad Comedy Theater and the Moscow Cine-Theater.

Conservatives in Soviet culture were upset by the liberal trends in the arts. The reactionary tide grew stronger after the Hungarian uprising in October 1956. Liberals continued, however, to assert their views. In November 1956 a meeting of the Moscow Union of Writers debated conditions in drama, especially the "no-conflict theory." The party, as usual, had the last word. In the summer of 1957, Khrushchev issued a proclamation entitled "For Close Ties Between Literature and Art and the Life of the People," which reminded Soviet artists of their duty to propagate Marxism-Leninism.

In the fall of 1958 the publication in the West of Boris Pasternak's novel *Dr. Zhivago* and the awarding of the Nobel Prize to Pasternak stirred another storm. Soviet officialdom was outraged and for a time Pasternak was threatened with expulsion from his native land. Khrushchev took the occasion of the Congress of the Union of Soviet Writers in May 1959 to warn writers that the party would continue to observe them closely. Despite such surveillance, Soviet theater was to remain freer than it had been at any time between the mid-1930s and 1953. Directors and dramatists who had been outlawed were able to resume work. Young directors and playwrights with experimental tendencies appeared. An increasing number of foreign plays appeared on Soviet stages. Soviet playwrights were able to treat a much wider variety of themes than had been possible during the Stalin years.

Nikolai Okhlopkov, who had been banned from Soviet theater along with Meyerhold and others in the 1930s, resumed directing at the Vakhtangov Theater in Moscow. One of his most successful productions was a stage version of Isaac Babel's cycle of stories *Red Cavalry*, which had been attacked in the late 1920s as a slander on the Red Army. (Babel had been arrested in 1939 and had died in prison in 1941.) Okhlopkov also produced Brecht's *Mother Courage* and versions of Shakespeare's *Hamlet* and Euripides' *Medea* in a style similar to that of Meyerhold's productions. Okhlopkov was among the most innovative of Soviet directors until his death in 1966.

Nikolai Akimov, who had worked with Vakhtangov in the 1930s, became director of the new Leningrad Comedy Theater. Akimov's productions of *Goly korol* (The Naked King), *Drakon* (The Dragon), and *Ten* (The Shadow) —three plays by Evgeny Shvarts—revealed to Soviet playgoers a major dramatic talent within their midst. Shvarts, who died in 1958, had been known chiefly as a film scenarist (he wrote the scenario for the excellent Soviet film of *Don Quixote*) and a writer of children's stories and plays. Shvarts' three adult plays, or fairy tales for adults, make sharp comments about the banality of political tyranny.

New directors who added artistic quality and excitement to Soviet theater appeared in the late 1950s. Oleg Efremov, a student at the acting school of Moscow Art Theater, formed a company in 1957 with a group of fellow students that became one of the most popular avant-garde theaters in the Soviet Union, the Contemporary (Sovremennik) Theater. Efremov's theater was the first to stage such Western plays as John Osborne's *Look Back in Anger*, Edward Albee's *The Ballad of the Sad Café*, and Eugene Ionesco's *Rhinoceros*. At about the same time that the Contemporary Theater was being formed, Georgi Tovstonogov was appointed director of the Leningrad Gorky

Theater. Tovstonogov helped popularize Brecht by producing an excellent version of *Arturo Ui*. Like Shvarts and another prominent director, Anatoli Efros (head of the Leningrad Komsomol Theater), Tovstonogov got his theatrical experience by working at the Central Children's Theater in Moscow.

Classical Western dramatists, such as Shakespeare, Molière, and Beaumarchais, had always been popular in the Soviet Union (although productions of foreign works were frowned on during the Zhdanov years), as had such contemporaries as George Bernard Shaw. Modern Western playwrights, who had been unknown to Soviet audiences, began to be produced from the late 1950s onward. Soviet playgoers were introduced to the works of Jean Anouilh, Arthur Miller, Tennessee Williams, Friedrich Dürrenmatt, and Jean-Paul Sartre, as well as those of Brecht, Osborne, Albee, and Ionesco. The work of Samuel Beckett, who has been described by one Soviet critic as "famous for his gloom and pessimism," is still proscribed at this writing, although one scholarly monograph on Beckett has been published.

Works by older, established playwrights, such as Vsevolod VISHNEVSKY and Nikolai Pogodin continued to be produced during the late 1950s. Vishnevsky's *Optimicheskaya tragediya* (Optimistic Tragedy), a story of heroic sacrifice during the Revolution, originally written in 1932, received a stirring new production by Tovstonogov at the Gorky Theater. *Tretya, pateticheskaya* (The Third, Pathetic), the last part of Pogodin's trilogy on Lenin, was produced by the Moscow Art Theater in 1958.

Among younger playwrights, the names of Alexei Arbuzov, Victor Rozov, and Aleksandr Volodin were becoming well known in the early 1960s. Their works were not exceptionally original or striking, but they were an improvement over the turgid, politically oriented productions of the Stalin years. Arbuzov's *Irkutskaya istoriya* (The Irkutsk Story), produced by Nikolai Okhlopkov, had been described as a Soviet version of Thornton Wilder's *Our Town*, with a Greek chorus replacing Wilder's narrator-commentator. Rozov's work, including *Neravny boy* (Unequal Battle), *Pered uzhinom* (Before Dinner), and *V den svadby* (Wedding Day, produced by Anatoli Efros at the Komsomol Theater in 1964), has been likened to that of Chekhov in its attempt to extract poetry from the trivial everyday aspects of life. Rozov's play *Vechno zhivie* (Eternally Living) was the basis for the popular Soviet film *The Cranes Are Flying*, which depicted the personal ravages of World War II in Russia. The plays of Volodin are chiefly concerned with the private tragedies of ordinary human beings and are, like Rozov's work, likened to those of Chekhov. Among Volodin's more successful dramas are *Pyat vecherov* (Five Evenings), *Starshaya sestra* (The Elder Sister), and *Naznachenie* (The Appointment), all of which have been produced at Efremov's Contemporary Theater, as have many of Rozov's plays.

In the late 1960s two other interesting playwrights made their debuts. Eduard Radzinsky, a theatrical producer's son, had his first success with *Sto chetyre stranitsa o lyubvi* (104 Pages About Love), the story of a stormy love affair between two modern Soviet youths, a physicist and an airline stewardess. The play was included in repertories of both Efros' Komsomol Theater and Tovstonogov's Gorky Theater. Another play by Radzinsky, *Snimaya film* (Making a Movie), produced by Efros at the Komsomol, deals with the author's problems with censorship when he was working as a screenwriter. Vassily Aksyonov, whose novel *Zvezdny bilet* (A Ticket to the Stars, 1961) dealt with the lives and aspirations of a group of apolitical Soviet teenagers, entered drama with *Vsegda v prodazhe* (Always on Sale). Aksyonov calls the play a "satirical fantasy" about Soviet society. The production of Aksyonov's play by Efremov at the Contemporary Theater uses masks, songs, chants, abstract sets, and lighting in much the same way as do avant-garde theaters in the West.

The same kinds of effects are seen more often at a theater founded in 1964 in Moscow, the Taganka Theater (officially called the Theater of Drama and Comedy, but usually referred to by the name of its suburban Moscow location). The theater was established by Yuri Lyubimov, formerly an actor at the Vakhtangov Theater. Lyubimov's student production of Brecht's *Good Woman of Setzuan* was so successful that he was given his own theater. Besides his stagings of Brecht's work, Lyubimov's most striking productions have been adaptations of John Reed's historical account of the Revolution, *Ten Days That Shook the World,* and of *Antimiry* (Antiworlds), a cycle of poems by the young Soviet poet Andrei Voznesensky.

Adaptations of works not intended for the theater have been produced also by Vladimir Pluchek at the Moscow Satire Theater. Pluchek has directed stage versions of the work of two Soviet satirists of the 1920s, Ilya Ilf and Evgeny Petrov's (Y. P. Katayev) novel *Dvenadtsat stulev* (The Twelve Chairs) and Petrov's novel *Zoloty telyonok* (The Little Golden Calf). He has also staged *Tyorkin na tom svete* (Tyorkin in the Other World), a long poem by Aleksandr Tvardovsky. At the Komsomol Theater, Anatoli Efros was planning an adaptation of *Odin den' Ivana Denisovicha* (One Day in the Life of Ivan Denisovich), Aleksandr Solzhenitsyn's novel about life in a Siberian prison camp, before Solzhenitsyn fell afoul of the authorities. The large number of adaptations cannot be attributed solely to the scarcity of good contemporary playwrights. Stage versions of Russian novels and poems have long been a tradition in Soviet theater. Even the staid and conventional Moscow Art Theater has its versions of Leo Tolstoi's novel *Anna Karenina* and of Nikolai Gogol's comic masterpiece *Dead Souls.*

The restaging of established classics has also attracted Soviet directors. Georgi Tovstonogov's new production of *Gore ot urna* (Woe from Wit), an early nineteenth-century Russian classic by Aleksandr Griboedov, was one of the more controversial new stagings, principally because of its stress on the isolation of the artist from society, contrary to official Soviet views of the artist as a social engineer. Even more furor was created by Anatoli Efros' productions in 1967–68 of two Chekhov plays, *The Sea Gull* and *The Three Sisters*. Efros' sin against the traditional Moscow Art Theater method of presenting Chekhov was not in doing away with the realistic setting of the plays, for Georgi Tovstonogov had already done that in an earlier production of *The Three Sisters*. Instead, Efros changed the emphases and moods of the plays, transforming the usual placid melancholy of Chekhov productions into a bitter, frenetic atmosphere. One critic charged that Efros' treatment of Chekhov was a decadent one, equally distant from Chekhov and from the contemporary theater (presumably the contemporary Soviet theater). Another critic, whose response to Efros' work was published the same day, took a more balanced view, stating that it was difficult to give up such a long-standing theatrical tradition as the time-honored Chekhovian production developed at the Moscow Art Theater. The critic said that while Chekhov as presented by Efros was perhaps upsetting and that Soviet playgoers were not yet accustomed to it, the productions should not be dismissed hastily. "You will probably leave the production with a heavy heart," said the critic. "But perhaps the burden ought not always be lifted from our hearts when the subject is the meaning of life."

Efros' productions of Chekhov and reactions to them suggest two important facts about Soviet theater at the present time. First, there are elements in Soviet theater that are willing to experiment, or to accept experiment, with new techniques and new attitudes toward drama, even to such seemingly untouchable classics as Stanislavskian versions of Chekhov. Second, there are forces in Soviet theater that are anxious to adhere to tradition and to thwart any attempt at change. The dichotomy between innovators and traditionalists is not clearly one between the younger and the older generations. Among directors in the innovators' camp—Efros of the Komsomol Theater, Efremov of the Contemporary, Lyubimov of the Taganka, and Tovstonogov of the Gorky—are men in their forties and fifties. Even within the innovators' camp there are differences of opinion. Tovstonogov has expressed doubt about the effects on acting of the kind of theater being developed at the Taganka, where the director uses the actor as an instrument to achieve the effects he wants. The same kind of doubt has been stated by Efremov. Both Tovstonogov and Efremov have reached the same conclusions about a solution to the problem—a combination of the expressive, director-controlled techniques of Meyerhold and the realistic, actor-centered methods of Stanislavski. It is possible to refer openly to Meyerhold now. A two-volume edition of his writings on theater was published in 1968.

The fact that there are divisions and discussions in Soviet theater is a hopeful sign and a far cry from the monolithic, deadening "no-conflict theory" that prevailed in the theater until 1953. Such relative freedom has continued in spite of the change of regime in 1964 with the deposition of Khrushchev, and in spite of the trials of the poet Josef Brodsky in 1964 and of the writers Andrei Sinyavsky and Yuli Daniel in 1966. In the past such trials would have been followed by a firm tightening of controls in all the arts. The effect of the expulsion, in 1969, of Aleksandr Solzhenitsyn from the Union of Soviet Writers is still to be seen. A sudden ascendancy of reactionaries in Soviet culture is always possible. Such a decisive shift, however, has not taken place since 1956.

As things now stand in Soviet theater, there are more traditional elements (among them may be included the work and outlook dominant in the Moscow Art Theater, the Maly Theater, the Vakhtangov theater, and the Mossoviet theater) and more innovative elements (including the Contemporary, the Taganka, the Komsomol, and the Gorky theaters), with some theaters such as the Satire Theater and the Comedy Theater seeming to be in an intermediate area. The direction any of these theaters takes will not depend entirely on the director in charge. More than anything else, given the official Soviet view of art as a political activity, drama in Russia will depend on political conditions and pressures. In this respect, nothing has changed since Stalin.

**Spain.** The Civil War (1936–1939) ravaged the theater in Spain, but it did not cease to exist. In Madrid, Rafael Alberti (born 1902) founded Nueva Escena, the best of the Republican theaters, and Max Aub (born 1903) was active in Barcelona and Valencia. On the Nationalist side, José María PEMÁN (born 1897) and Juan Ignacio Luca de Tena (born 1897) did patriotic pieces; Gonzalo Torrente Ballester (born 1910) wrote perhaps the best play of the war years, *El viaje del joven Tobías* (The Journey of Young Tobias); and Adolfo Torrado (1904–1958) garnered consistent audience approval with an outpouring, unchecked until the late '40s, of sentimental melodramas. By the end of the war, though, there was little cause for optimism. Gone were the two most promising young playwrights, Federico García Lorca (1899–1936) and Alejandro CASONA (1903–1965), one dead, the other in exile. In exile, too, were Jacinto Grau (1877–1958), Aub, Alberti, Pedro Salinas (1892–1951), and Ramón J. Sender (born 1902). Ready to resume production as if nothing had happened was a moribund but tenacious old guard whose fare was the depiction of a typical Spain which may once have been, but which now bore no relation to the reality of a prostrate Spain, spectator to a world at war.

The regional comedies of the brothers Álvarez Quintero, in spite of the death of Serafín (1871–1938), continued until the death of Joaquín (1873–1944) to delight seemingly insatiable audiences with the picturesque manners and morals of Andalucía. Eduardo Marquina (1879–1946) resumed production of historical dramas in verse, and the long popular *sainetes* of Carlos Arniches (1866–1943) still crowded the boards years after his death. Finally, Jacinto Benavente (1866–1954), having attained in the teens an importance recognized in 1922 by the Nobel Prize, dominated the Spanish stage with his formulaic comedies of manners, though nothing he did after the war contributed to his stature. There were some playwrights ready to continue careers barely begun at the outbreak of hostilities. Both José María Pemán and Joaquín CALVO SOTELO (born 1905) wrote serious dramas—as serious, that is, as a bourgeois audience would permit—sometimes telling indictments of *peccata minuta* which never called into queston the divine right of the bourgeoisie to inherit the earth. Though both are still before the public, Calvo Sotelo has not surpassed *La muralla* (The Wall, 1954), and Pemán is remembered for *Callados como muertos* (As Still as Death, 1952). Both also cultivate the comedy of manners, and Pemán has done a number of free translations of classical tragedies, which may well prove to be his most important contribution to the Spanish theater.

More exciting during the immediate postwar years was the comic theater of Enrique JARDIEL PONCELA (1901–1952). Nonsense, confusion, absurdity, non sequiturs—these were but some of the elements he combined in farce, caricature, satire, and parody to undermine the conventions of the bourgeois comedy. The late '40s and early '50s saw the justification of Jardiel's innovative techniques, best appreciated in *Eloisa está debajo de un almendro* (Eloisa Under an Elm, 1940), with the triumph of the "new comedy." *Tres sombreros de copa* (Three Top Hats, 1952) by Miguel MIHURA (born 1905), *El landó de seis caballos* (The Six-Horse Landau, 1950) by Víctor RUIZ IRIARTE (born 1912), *Alberto* (1949) by José LÓPEZ RUBIO (born 1903), and, in a somewhat different vein, *El baile* (The Dance, 1952) by Edgar NEVILLE (born 1900) accustomed audiences to a theater based on the untrammeled play of fantasy and illusion and the humor of the unexpected. The formulas are few. A character displays a madness, a deviation from normal behavior, whose very existence he refuses to acknowledge; or he perpetrates a deception, often foolish or madcap. They prove ultimately to be a calculated madness, a pious deception, that permit the protagonist and other characters to avoid a situation with which they cannot cope—thus, the most frequently pejorative appellation of "theater of evasion." Often the characters suffer only innocently and ingenuously the chaos born of human folly. But never are theirs the everyday problems of the workaday world, never the vital preoccupations of the bourgeoisie, much less of the proletariat. Mihura's forte is the macabre humor of the comedy-mystery. Neville invites escape into a prewar *belle époque* lovingly evoked in sentimental comedies. López Rubio is at his best in plays such as *La venda en los ojos* (Blindfold, 1954), which explore the interplay of reality and illusion, fiction and history. Ruiz Iriarte's theater is one of joy and tenderness, lately closer to traditional drawing-room comedy than the fantasy plays of his earlier career. In fact, none of the comic playwrights maintained the earlier spirit of comic innovation. All settled for a more predictable, gentler humor capable of aiding a healthy digestion, and the possibility of a native "theater of the absurd" disappeared. But whatever reservations critics may have, it remains a fact that in the '50s the new comedy ceded ground only slowly to the social theater, and audiences have still not tired of it.

More serious things were happening in the late '40s. In 1945, Alfonso

SASTRE (born 1926) and Alfonso PASO (born 1926), to name but two who went on to establish permanent reputations, collaborated in the founding of Arte Nuevo, an experimental group dedicated to the rejuvenation of the theater through the staging of translations and original works of unestablished playwrights. Paso subsequently went his own way. Having perfected the techniques of the new comedy and the formulas of the bourgeois comedy, he has settled for popular applause. More than one hundred of his plays have already received more than their share of accolades. The '60s saw four and five of his comedies opening every season, and his guaranteed box-office appeal crowded many of the names of the '50s off the stage. No one questions the blessing, but many consider the cure worse than the ill. Sastre, on the other hand, has been unwavering in his devotion to a theater uncompromised by capricious censors, timid impresarios, or unappreciative audiences unused to serious drama. Though few of his plays have been produced, his influence, especially on the young, has been substantial since *Escuadra hacia la muerte* (Death Squad, 1953). *La mordaza* (The Gag, 1954), *En la red* (Dragnet, 1961), and the as-yet-unstaged *Muerte en el barrio* (Death in the Neighborhood) are centered on the themes now associated with the work of the existentialists: justice, responsibility, guilt, liberty. His social intent leads him to prefer the techniques of realism to those of expressionism for the sake of didactic efficaciousness, but *Ana Kleiber* and *El cuervo* (The Raven, 1957), as well as the earlier one-act *Cargamento de sueños* (Burden of Dreams), reveal Sastre the experimentalist. Through numerous manifestos and critical essays and exchanges, Sastre has sought to awaken his Spanish audience to the possibilities of a tragic theater committed to social reform. But in spite of his priority and his continuing activity in the groups Teatro de Agitación Social and Grupo de Teatro Realista, the social theater per se is most indebted, at least for its form, to Antonio BUERO VALLEJO (born 1916), the only other playwright of equal seriousness and stature in Spain today.

The 1949 production of Buero's *Historia de una escalera* (The Stairway) is probably the most important single event in the history of the postwar Spanish theater. Coming when audiences knew only the bourgeois comedy and melodrama and the theater of evasion—not to mention the *astracán, zarzuela,* and folkloric revues, sub-theater all—it was unique in its depiction in uncompromisingly realistic terms of the lives of the proletariat. The play traces the successive failures of three generations of four families to better their lot. The stairway of the tenement in which the insignificant details of their lives transpire comes to symbolize the closed horizons of their universe. The intent is to awaken through the pity and sympathy elicited by their bleak fate, perhaps of their own making but unacceptable nevertheless, the dormant social consciousness of the bourgeoisie. The *leitmotiv* of Buero's later plays, more existentially than socially oriented, is man's search for truth about himself and his situation. His symbols, most appropriate in one who espouses the continuing validity of classical tragedy, are light and darkness, vision and blindness, most rewardingly developed in *En la ardiente oscuridad* (In the Flaming Darkness, 1950) and *El concierto de San Ovidio* (1962).

There are, of course, other names of the '40s and '50s. Juan Ignacio Luca de Tena solidified a career begun before the war with successes such as *El condor sin alas* (The Wingless Condor, 1953), *¿Dónde vas, Alfonso XII?* (1957), and *¿Dónde vas, triste de ti?* (1959). Active too were Claudio de la Torre (born 1898); Luis Fernández Ardavín (1891–1962), a favorite of prewar audiences; Alvaro de Laiglesia (born 1912); and Antonio de Lara or "Tono" (born 1896); these latter two were collaborators of Mihura on the stage and in the pages of *La codorniz*, the magazine whose mad humor contributed to the development of the techniques of the new comedy. José Giménez Arnau (born 1912), better known as a novelist but nevertheless a steady contributor to the stage, initiated his career with *Murió hace quince años* (Dead Fifteen Years, 1952). But in retrospect, these names pale before those of three younger men whose appearance on the scene coincided with the turn of the decade— Lauro OLMO, Ricardo RODRÍGUEZ BUDED, and Carlos MUÑIZ, all of whom were born during the 1920s. They are at the core of the social theater, having made their own the formulas of Buero's *Historia de una escalera:* the realistic depiction of the wasted lives of multiple protagonists trapped in an ambient which permits of no escape.

Olmo's *La camisa* (The Shirt, 1962) and *English Spoken* (1968) reveal the plight of a proletariat unable to earn a decent wage, whose sole alternatives are dishonor, emigration, or failure. Buded's *La madriguera* (The Warren, 1960) dwells on the trivial details of the lives of the occupants of a shabby boardinghouse and the nerve-shredding encounters which the suffocating atmosphere only aggravates. Muñiz's *El grillo* (The Cricket, 1957) deals in strident tones with the frustrations of the white-collar worker unable to rise from mediocrity. All is frustration, failure, despair, hopelessness. The possibility of success is never more than a false hope clung to out of custom, expediency, or self-delusion. Man's fate may in some cases be the result of personal failings, but never does it seem that an individual's actions are even moderately efficacious in the determining environment. Each playwright has proved able to break the mold of the social theater on the level of either theme or technique. Muñiz's *El tintero* (The Inkwell, 1961) is an expressionistic reworking of the theme of *El grillo* raised to a metaphysical level. Buded's *El charlatán* (1962) is more like the traditional comedy of manners, though with social intent. And Olmo's *El cuerpo* (The Body, 1966) is a tragicomedy à la Valle Inclán, which subjects the reality of *machismo* to the deformation of the close-up lens.

Two other playwrights established themselves in the early '60s, Jaime SALOM (born 1925) and Juan José ALONSO MILLÁN (born 1936). The former is highly versatile, writing mysteries, comedies, and farces. But more important are his recent serious efforts *La casa de las chivas* (Goat House, 1969), a Civil War piece, and *Los delfines* (The Dauphins, 1969), a generational study whose theme is the role of conscience in a capitalistic society. Alonso Millán continues the work of the new comedy. His forte is the comedy-mystery of the arsenic-and-old-lace variety. The works of a handful of new playwrights have also begun to appear sporadically on the Madrid stage. They have not yet proved their perdurability, but their works have enriched the theater of the '60s. Eduardo Criado's *Cuando las nubes cambian de nariz* (When the Clouds Change Noses, 1961) is a burlesque, fantasy play. Alfredo Mañas electrified audiences with a Romeo and Juliet play in a gypsy setting, *Historia de los Tarantos* (1962). A neo-popularist musical drama, it legitimizes the folkloric stage, which for decades has been condemned by the critics as unworthy of serious consideration. José Martín Recuerda's *Las salvajes en Puente San Gil* (The Savage Women of Puente San Gil, 1963) has as its theme the appearance of a road company in the provinces and the resultant clash of cosmopolitan and traditional values. A commonly exploited situation on the Spanish stage—Alonso Millán finds in it a font of warm, gentle humor in *La vil seducción* (The Seduction, 1967); Mihura makes of it absurd farce in *Tres sombreros de copa*—Recuerda infuses it with uncommon tension, making of it one of the most searing, cathartic experiences of recent years. The hysterical pitch of his revelation of hypocrisy, envy, hatred, and evil in players and townspeople alike is abated only to allow them to reveal their sordid mediocrity. An "esperpentic" drama, reality is revealed through the distortion of reality, human nature is bared through dehumanization. Antonio Gala's *Los verdes campos de Eden* (The Green Fields of Eden, 1963) is a redemption play in which realistic and expressionistic scenes alternate in the presentation of actions suffused with Christian symbolism without ever lapsing into stylized allegory. Marcial Suárez's *Las monedas de Heliogábalo* (The Coins of Heliogabalus, 1965), like Camus's *Caligula*, is a study in tyranny. Finally, José Ruibal is active in the "underground" theater, contributing short pieces to be staged in cafés before small, involved audiences.

But the most important theatrical events of the '60s involved authors of other decades. For the first time since the Civil War, audiences could see on the stage García Lorca's rural tragedies, *Bodas de sangre* (Blood Wedding), *Yerma*, and *La casa de Bernarda Alba*. The plays of Miguel de Unamuno (1864–1936) and Ramón del Valle Inclán (1870–1936), never widely accepted nor understood during their lifetime, were "rediscovered." The latter's aesthetic of the *esperpento*, by his own definition reality reflected and distorted in a concave mirror, proved the most influential. Finally, renewed interest in the work of Alejandro CASONA received impetus from his return from exile, and his plays dominated the boards during the first half of the decade. The 1964–65 season alone saw four of his plays running simultaneously in Madrid. Though fantasy and illusion are at the heart of his theater, it is not escapist. Rather, in plays such as *La sirena varada* (The Beached Siren, 1934), *La dama del alba* (Lady of the Dawn, 1944), and *La barca sin pescador* (The Boat Without a Fisherman, 1945), fundamental human problems are explored in a context unrestricted by the limitations of space and time of the realistic theater. There remain but those on the periphery of the Spanish stage proper. Fernando ARRABAL (born 1932), an absurdist, has an international reputation, but his work is little known in Spain. And though it can be argued that his themes are Hispanic, his choices of country of residency and language do make him a French playwright. Manuel de Pedrolo (born 1918), whose plays are limited to Catalan-speaking audiences, is also associated with theater of the absurd. The political allegories of José Ruibal, Antonio Martínez Ballesteros, and José María Bellido are available in translation only in journals such as *First Scene* and *Modern International Drama*. Given their unfavorable evaluation of the regime, it is unlikely that they will be soon before Spanish audiences.

Since 1949, Federico Carlos Sainz de Robles has selected the five or six outstanding plays of each season for inclusion in *Teatro Español* (Madrid). Each volume contains as well complete bibliographical information on the entire season. Nearly everything else written since the Civil War, plus many translations and classical pieces, is available in the now more than 650 volumes of *Colección Teatro* (Madrid). Among useful works of criticism are the following: Jean Paul Borel, *Théâtre de l'impossible* (Neuchâtel 1959); *Drama Critique*, Vol. IX (Spring 1966), special issue on Spanish theater includes Enrique Ruiz Fornell, "The Spanish Theater in the Last 25 Years"; F. García Pavón, *Teatro social en España* (Madrid 1962); José Gordón, *Teatro experimental español* (Madrid 1965); Juan Guerrero Zamora, *Historia del teatro contemporáneo*, 4 volumes (Barcelona 1961–1967); Alfredo Marqueríe, *Veinte años de teatro en España* (Madrid 1959); Domingo Pérez Minik, *Debates sobre el teatro español contemporáneo* (Santa Cruz de Tenerife 1953) and *Teatro europeo contemporáneo* (Madrid 1961); I. Soldevila Durante, "Sobre el teatro español de los últimos 25 años," *Cuadernos americanos*, Vol. XXII, No. 126; *El teatro. Enciclopedia del arte escénico* (Barcelona 1958); Gonzalo Torrente Ballester, *Teatro español contemporáneo* (Madrid 1957); Angel Valbuena Prat, *Historia del teatro español* (Barcelona 1956).

**Sperr, Martin** (born 1944). West German dramatist, actor, and director. One of the most gifted of the younger German dramatists, Sperr grew up in Bavaria, which serves as the background of most of his plays. After completing his high school education, he studied at the Reinhardt Seminar in Vienna and then worked at theaters in Wiesbaden and Bremen. In 1967 he began working in association with the Munich Kammerspiele. Sperr's plays all deal with latent Fascist tendencies in the country folk of southern Germany. They are modern folk plays, which seek in a realistic manner to capture the essence of the peasant mentality in order to explain the oppressive and lurid conditions in the

427

villages and towns. In *Jagdszenen aus Niederbayern* (Hunting Scenes from Lower Bavaria, 1966), the village community drives the "village idiot" to suicide and a homosexual to murder while maintaining a veneer of bourgeois respectability. In *Landshuter Erzählungen* (Stories about Landshut, 1967) Sperr once again focuses on the hypocrisy and intolerance of country people. This time he makes the setting a Bavarian town about 1958, the time of Germany's "economic miracle." In seventeen short scenes, each of which contains a story in itself, Sperr portrays the competition between two construction firms ruthlessly seeking to drive each other into bankruptcy. Behind the scenes, so to speak, there is the "idyllic" love story of a young man and woman, whose fathers own the two different firms and cause them difficulties. Here Sperr reverses and parodies this motif in superb fashion, as he does many other conventional bourgeois motifs. The young man, Sorm, loves the young woman, Sieglinde, but makes her pregnant only because he wants to create a conglomerate out of the two firms. Since his own father stands in his way, he murders him. The funeral is then celebrated with a mock wake. The workers who helped Sorm and his father-in-law bring about the new monopoly are cheated and will continue to be exploited. Sperr brings out the sadism, ruthlessness, and greed of small people who are afraid to face themselves and their weaknesses. Instead they constantly seek scapegoats and cover up their atrocious crimes by adhering to outward forms of decency and piety. In order to explain the connections with Fascism, Sperr goes further back into history in his play *Koralle Meier* (1970). The time is 1938–1940; the setting, a small Bavarian town, not unlike Dachau, which has a concentration camp on the outskirts. The motto is taken from Brecht: "The womb from which that crawled is still fruitful," suggesting that Fascism is still possible today. Sperr's story explains why this is so. Koralle Meier, the town's honorable and beloved whore, decides to become respectable by opening up a vegetable store. This causes trouble because her store will be competition for businesses run by the baker and the mayor. Discovering that she has helped some Jews to escape the country by lending them money, they have her shipped to the concentration camp outside the town. She is saved by one of her old customers, a high-ranking Nazi official. When she returns to the town, she tries to get even with the mayor, but her tactics are too naïve. Once again she is sent to the concentration camp, and this time she is shot. Here again Sperr shows how the obsession with profit and the hypocrisy about social and ethical norms creates a breed of men who can easily serve a Fascist system. Sperr does not experiment much with forms and language. He is more interested in archetypal phenomena in realistic settings.

OTHER PLAYS: *Dunkler Bock* (Dark Bock Beer, 1968), *Münchner Freiheit* (Munich Freedom, 1970).

**Stoppard, Tom** (born 1937). English dramatist. Born in Central Europe, Stoppard moved with his parents to England as a young boy. Educated in

Nottingham and Yorkshire, he began a career in journalism with the local press in Bristol (1954–1960) and then moved to free-lance journalism (1960–1963). His first play for radio was broadcast in 1964, and his first television play in 1966. *Rosencrantz and Guildenstern Are Dead*, which entered the repertory of the National Theatre in 1967, aptly caught the mood of the late '60s in its mixture of wit, sentiment, theatrical inventiveness, and apparent profundity. In Stoppard's play the action of *Hamlet* is assumed to be unrolling behind the scenes and impinges upon the life of the two doomed and insignificant courtiers as a disjointed succession of frightening and inexplicable threats to their existence. By changing the perspective of Shakespeare's play to show that events take their significance from the viewpoint of the observer, and by dramatizing the desperate attempts of Rosencrantz and Guildenstern to impose a meaningful pattern upon the welter of action that is sweeping them on to inevitable destruction, Stoppard seemed to many critics to have created a brilliant metaphor for the role of destiny in the life of twentieth-century man. The influence of Beckett's *Waiting for Godot* is discernible in the frantic conversational gambits of Rosencrantz and Guildenstern; but in the final analysis it is not the echo of existential despair from this and other sources that gives the play its distinctive quality, but the wit and originality of both dialogue and *mise-en-scène*. The play won the John Whiting Award in 1967, the *Evening Standard* Award for the most promising playwright of 1968, and the Tony and the New York Drama Critics Circle awards for the best play of 1968.

The success of *Rosencrantz and Guildenstern* led to the reworking for the stage of two works first broadcast on television and radio respectively: *Enter a Free Man* (1968) and *Albert's Bridge* (1968) may be described as partially successful attempts to mingle genuine human feeling with scenes in the absurdist style. *The Real Inspector Hound* (1968), less pretentious than *Rosencrantz and Guildenstern* but no less original, presents another dialectical confrontation of the illusory, predetermined world of the stage with the more puzzling structure of "reality." The inexplicable progress of two theater critics from commentators to participants in a stage thriller, and their eventual fate as victims of a rival critic, masquerading as the stage detective of the title, may fail to present a coherent world-view but it is a deeply satisfying exercise in metaphysical ingenuity and a delightful parody both of the worn conventions of the stage thriller and of the critics' standard reactions to such a work.

Stoppard has published a novel and a volume of short stories. John Russell Taylor discusses the dramatist in "Tom Stoppard: Structure and Intellect," in *Plays and Players* (July 1970).

OTHER PLAYS: *After Magritte* (one act, 1970), *Jumpers* (1972).

**Storey, David** (born 1923). English novelist and dramatist. The son of a Yorkshire miner, Storey was educated at Wakefield Grammar School and signed a contract as a Rugby League footballer for Leeds at the age of seventeen. It was not long before he had abandoned his career as a professional footballer to enroll as a full-time student at the Slade School of Fine Art, London. He became a schoolteacher and began to write novels while working in the East End of London, finally achieving publication with his eighth, *This Sporting Life* (1960). The experience of working with director Lindsay Anderson on the film of this novel stimulated in Storey what he has called "the realization that there must be an inner texture to spoken dialogue" over and above "realistic chat." It is this principle which is sensitively realized in his dramaturgy. Although he had visited the theater scarcely more than a dozen times when his first play was staged, his work reveals a strong formal sense of theatrical tradition and a mastery of the subtle demands of naturalism. His first play, *The Restoration of Arnold Middleton* (1966), is a sympathetic study of a schoolteacher during a period of mental crisis. *In Celebration* (1969) is a moving but unsentimental portrait of a North Country family, which captures the unspoken tensions, rivalry, and affection that exist between working-class parents and their successful children. *The Contractor* (1969), which takes up a subject that Storey first used in his novel *Radcliffe* (1963), is a vivid piece of naturalism whose mood and rhythm is evoked by the construction and removal of a marquee for a wedding reception. A pattern of expectation, celebration, and resumption of normal life is established by the arrival and departure of the contractor's men, and the play is as much a study of the workmen who erect the tent as it is of the family marriage. The two themes are linked by the fact that Ewbank, the contractor of the title, is the owner of the firm erecting the tent for his daughter's wedding. The insecurity of his private life and especially the failure of his relationship with his son are reflected in the weaknesses of the men he employs. The influence of Chekhov upon *The Contractor* is clearly considerable, and yet the sympathetic assurance with which Storey handles the language and psychology of workingmen marks a new stage in the naturalistic tradition of the postwar English theater.

In *Home* (1970) Storey departed from the immediately recognizable social context of his earlier plays into more unusual territory. The inconsequential triteness of the dialogue and the total lack of any developing action are the superficial expression, not of the day-to-day inadequacy and failures of family or working life, but of the total blankness of existence in a mental home. With touching consideration for each other's frailty, two middle-aged men pass the day by exchanging the empty forms of polite conversation and by engaging shyly in social contact with two women patients whose robust coarseness is a foil to their own gentle sadness. *Home* is an almost classic example of the power of naturalistic drama to evoke sympathy for its characters entirely through an unspoken "sub-text" that runs contrary to the dialogue. It confirms Storey's position among the handful of writers who have used the growing freedom of the dramatist not to break away from conventional forms but to impose a new strength and discipline upon them.

Storey's essay "Discussion on Contemporary Theatre," appeared in *New*

*Theatre* Magazine, Vol. VII, No. 2 (1967); John Russell Taylor wrote "David Storey: Novelist into Dramatist," in *Plays and Players* (June 1970).

**Streetcar Named Desire, A** (1947). A play by Tennessee Williams. It received both the New York Drama Critics Circle Award and the Pulitzer Prize. Blanche DuBois arrives to stay with her younger sister, Stella, at Elysian Fields, a poor section of New Orleans. Blanche's moth-like delicacy and her aging southern charm clash with the violent virility of Stella's Polish-American husband, Stanley Kowalski. In the months from spring to autumn, while Blanche stays in the two-room apartment with the younger couple, it becomes clear that she is mentally disturbed: her anguish over the lost family plantation (diminished by "epic fornications"), her haunting memories of her dead husband (a fragile boy who committed suicide when she taunted him for his homosexuality), her desperate attempts to snare Mitch with sexless seduction (ruined by discovery of her years of promiscuity), her furtive drinking, her long hours in the bath, her inappropriate finery and hysterical flirtation. Blanche is appalled by Stanley's bestiality, but her attempts to get Stella to leave him provide no real threat to the intense sexual bond between the married couple. The physical attraction and cultural hatred that has existed between Blanche and Stanley explodes into action when Stella is in the hospital having her baby and Stanley rapes Blanche. This rape, plus her harsh rejection by Mitch, pushes Blanche from desperate self-delusion into serious disorientation. Stella, who says she could not continue to live with Stanley if Blanche's story of rape is true, has her sister committed to a state mental institution. The final moments of the play show Blanche leaving on the arm of the doctor, who has momentarily dropped his impersonality to act the gallant gentleman, and Stella, in anguish over what she has done to her sister, weeping passionately in the arms of the man she could not live without.

In a moment of lucid insight early in the play, Blanche states that the opposite of death is desire. Her madness is her entrance into the death that has been devouring all the residents of the family plantation. A ride on a street-car named Desire has brought her to Elysian Fields, but inability to cope with sexuality has destroyed her. Stanley is a man who crudely knows desire and violent passions; he lives, but unthinkingly. Between them stands Stella, who has left the plantation for survival. She has Blanche's sensitivity coupled with stability and common sense; yet she is bound to Stanley by a passion strong enough to deny the brutal rape. The intellectual values of the play balance among these three characters, but the dramatic sympathies are clearly with Blanche. Despite the final embrace of Stella and Stanley, Blanche's fate suggests that, tragically, desire is not as strong as death.

Williams has used a "Blue Piano" to express the spirit of life in the play, and continually indicates various moods that the music is to express.

The play was first presented in New York on December 3, 1947, under the direction of Elia Kazan. It has subsequently been made into a film and translated into many languages; it remains one of Williams' finest plays

**Strittmatter, Erwin** (born 1912). East German dramatist, novelist, and journalist. Strittmatter is one of the "old" men of letters in East Germany In his youth he worked as a baker, waiter, and chauffeur while participating in the activities of a socialist organization. During World War II he was a soldier, and at one point deserted from the army. In 1945 he began working for a newspaper and writing stories. His reputation as a writer has been built largely on his novels (especially *Ole Bienkopp*, 1963), which are rooted in the folk tradition. This is also true of his plays, which also lean heavily on Brecht's epic devices. In *Die Holländerbraut* (The Bride of the Dutchman 1961) Strittmatter covers the period from 1944 to 1946 and depicts the fate of a young worker, Hanna Tainz, who is seduced by an aristocratic landowner named Heinrich. He refuses to marry her, and, when she becomes pregnant, the blame is placed on a Dutchman. Both Hanna and the Dutchman are incarcerated by the Nazis. After the war, she becomes mayor of the town and is seduced a second time by Heinrich, who has returned from the war and has supposedly mended his ways. However, this time Hanna sees through his exploitative nature and reports him to the authorities to save the newly established farm collective. Actually, there are strong elements of the bourgeois tragedy in this folk play, but they are converted into a "new" drama involving social and socialist problems in East Germany. Strittmatter is didactic but not doctrinaire, and his portrayal of the farmers and their problems in the 1944–1946 period are accurate reflections of socioeconomic conditions.

OTHER PLAYS: *Katzgraben* (1953).

**Sweden.** More than a half-century after Strindberg's death the evidence of his legacy to Swedish drama and theater continues to mount. It is perhaps most apparent in the work of admirers like Pär Lagerkvist, Stig Dagerman, and Ingmar Bergman; in the earnest, often somber expressionistic style and in the brooding search for answers to great moral and ethical questions. But it is also an influential factor in the lively controversies over the relative importance of art and politics that are regular features of the Swedish theater scene Strindberg, always a contentious public figure himself, helped to set the pattern for the controversies, primarily with the caustic, provocative social criticism and satire in his novels and short stories from the 1880s, but also with his repeated exhortation that the literature of the future be less an apolitical product of the imagination and more an anti-Establishment documentary accumulation of facts and ideas. Today the Swedish literary scene is crowded with essays, plays, and novels by radicals who are critical of the cold, bureaucratic humanitarianism that afflicts the welfare state and of the failure of the ruling Social Democratic Party to discourage the spread of dehumanizing commercialism.

Still another aspect of Strindberg's influence can be found in the plays of Lars FORSSELL (born 1928), probably the most important Swedish playwright of the mid-century. Like his predecessor, Forssell is deeply interested in the tragicomic implications of isolation and loneliness and has developed this theme successfully in a variety of dramatic styles and genres: fantasy, realism, historical drama, and surrealistic verse drama.

There is a second legacy that Swedish writers share. As citizens of a country that has remained neutral for more than 150 years, many have felt an obligation to be more than bystanders and have sought to act as consciences to the world, pointing out the absurdities and dangers of power-bloc conflicts and censuring the continuing political and economic exploitation of the under-developed countries, whether by capitalists or Communists. At the same time, the Swedes are aware of the presumptuousness of their position, recognizing that their country, as an affluent industrial state, often profits by the same economic imperialism that its citizens condemn. This ambivalent sense of responsibility may explain why Swedish writers frequently seem obsessed either by a commitment to international peace and understanding that is almost messianic or by a self-criticism that is almost masochistic.

In the late 1940s the response of novelist-playwright Pär Lagerkvist (born 1891) to the chaotic world situation was reflected in two plays: De vises sten (The Philosopher's Stone, 1947), dealing with the moral implications of a search for scientific knowledge and power that uses ends to justify means, and Låt människan leva (Let Man Live, 1949), an oratorio in which a group of martyrs from history present their stories in a series of tableaux. The novelist-playwright Stig DAGERMAN (1923–1954) wrote movingly of Swedish attitudes toward the second world war in Skuggan av Mart (The Shadow of Mart, 1948), in which a young man feels bitter because the family earned money from a factory run for the Germans while his brother fought and died as a freedom fighter. The futility of power-bloc bickering was the theme of a first play by Werner ASPENSTRÖM (born 1918), Platsen är inhöljd i rök (The Place Is Wrapped in Smoke, 1948). Two giants are so preoccupied with establishing procedures for a meeting to settle their differences that they fail to heed a warning that the world is on the brink of destruction.

Sara Lidman (born 1923), a provincial novelist who had a brief but interesting career as a dramatist in the mid-1950s, has a sense of commitment that marks her as a representative figure in Swedish letters. She has written with compassion of the shortcomings of the Swedish welfare state, journeyed abroad to examine and criticize the racist policies of South Africa, and worked with Bertrand Russell against United States involvement in Southeast Asia. The central characters in both Job Klockmakares dotter (Job Klockmakare's Daughter, 1954) and Aina (1956) are women of humble origin who search for love to give their lives meaning. Aina's mother is a civil servant who has progressive political ideas but little time to return her daughter's affection. Implicit in the play, as critic Lars Bäckström has observed, is criticism of "impersonal, idealistic, large-scale social planning in which there is no place for purely individual love and consideration."

A very different spirit was introduced with Lars Forssell's first full-length

play, *Kröningen* (The Coronation, 1956), a reworking of the Alcestis legend
A sophisticated neoclassical lyric poet, Forssell includes Molière, T. S. Eliot
and Ezra Pound among his literary forebears. Early in his career, Forssell was
a contributor to satirical revues, a genre as popular in Sweden as in Denmark
Up until the mid-1960s the emphasis in Swedish revues, even when the theme
were political, was on light comedy. The popular *O vilken härlig fred* (Oh
What a Lovely Peace, 1966), by Hasse Alfredson and Tage Danielson, for
example, poked fun at the Swedes' tendency to be self-conscious and defensive
about their neutralism, but the satire in the revue did not cut deeply. Much
sharper and more controversial were productions staged at Stockholm'
Pistolteatern, a small experimental theater established in 1964 in connection
with the "happenings" movement by director-playwrights Pi Lind (born
1936) and Staffan Olzon (born 1937), and Swedish-American painter-play
wright Öyvind Fahlström (born 1928). Lively, brash, vulgar, and irreverent
the Pistolteatern specializes in the use of mixed media to present political
satire, frequently with a Dadaist flavor. In Fahlström's *Hammarskjöld om Gu*
(Hammarskjöld on God, 1966) extracts from the writings of the late Secre
tary-General of the United Nations were flashed on a screen while a young
actress demonstrated some rather bizarre breast-feeding techniques and loud
speakers blared excerpts from the sound tracks of Greta Garbo films.

An important experiment in political theater was conducted in the spring
of 1967 when the administration of the Gothenburg Municipal Theater per
mitted director Lennart Hjulström and six actors from the ensemble to work
together for three months, improvising upon and elaborating an original script
*Flotten* (The Raft), by one of the members of the group, actor-playwrigh
Kent Andersson (born 1933). In this allegorical musical satire the vessel
of the title represents the Swedish social-democratic welfare state and the
passengers are citizens who are skeptical that they will ever reach their
supposed destination, the Isle of Bliss.

*Flotten* was greeted with enthusiasm by critics and audiences alike, and
Andersson used the same production approach for two other plays: *Hemme*
(The Home, 1967), written with playwright Bengt Bratt (born 1937), and
*Sandlådan* (The Sandbox, 1969). Both works were produced successfully in
Denmark as well as in Sweden. The old people's home that is the setting for
*Hemmet* is another metaphor for welfare-state Sweden, a humanitarian rathe
than humane place where the occupants have everything they need excep
love and a feeling of identity. One of the characters sings:

For him who is homeless in spirit
The Home is an empty idea.

In *Sandlådan* the children and parents who move through the playground
setting reveal in their thoughts and actions some of the misconceptions tha
Andersson interprets as pervasive in modern Sweden, especially the notion tha

children can be programmed like computers and taught to be insensitive to the hypocrisy and impersonality of a "democratic upbringing."

The work of the Kent Andersson group has been in the mainstream of European and American theatrical experimentation in the 1960s. It was one of many organizations to treat the dramatic text as a scenario to be molded and shaped through the improvisations of a small, closely-knit group of theater artists into a production in which setting, costumes, and makeup are simple and suggestive and each performer is expected to play a number of roles. It remains to be seen whether group theater experimentation will influence the essentially conservative institutional structure of the Swedish subsidized theater. In any case, Andersson and his collaborators have demonstrated effectively that it is possible to present successful political theater by making an audience uneasy instead of smugly self-righteous, by challenging its prejudices instead of flattering them.

Comic-satirical revues were not the only form of political theater in post-war Sweden. *Kvinnorna från Shanghai* (Women from Shanghai, 1967), by Tore Zetterholm (born 1915), has the moralistic tone and fable-like quality of a Brechtian *Lehrstück*. This play with music is a sympathetic, factual, if also sentimental account of how the Communists put an end to the longtime exploitations of Chinese female labor by foreign capitalists. Less partisanly political was a play by Mats Ödeen (born 1937), *Flickan i kulturhuset* (The Girl in the Cultural House, 1969), the theme of which is that, despite the liberal attitudes toward women's liberation that prevail in Sweden, a married woman there can lead as exploited and depersonalized a life as any housewife in a more capitalistic society.

The threat of depersonalization and dehumanization in the space age is the theme of the opera *Aniara* (1959) and the one-act play *Robotbas* (Robot Base, 1966). *Aniara,* originally a verse-epic allegory written by poet-novelist Harry Martinson (born 1904) and then adapted for the stage in collaboration with poet Eric Lindegren (1910–1968) and composer Karl-Birger Blomdahl (1916–1968), is a grim and moving piece about the fate of some eight thousand passengers aboard a spaceship that gets lost in outer space while attempting to escape the atomic destruction of the world. An underground missile station is the setting for *Robotbas,* a black comedy by novelist Sven Delblanc (born 1931). The two men who operate the robot base are so subordinate to the unseen authority who speaks to them over a loudspeaker that they are told when to engage in sexual activities with the young lady who has been provided for this purpose.

Although political theater was a burning issue in Sweden in the 1950s and 1960s, it did not dominate the theater repertory entirely. The affluence and high production standards of the subsidized state and city theaters offered to a variety of native playwrights opportunities that were unequaled elsewhere in Scandinavia or even in most of Europe. Among those to use these opportunities to good advantage were the novelists Björn-Erik Höijer (born 1907) and Vilhelm Moberg (born 1896); Erland Josephson (born 1923), an actor and managing director of the Royal Dramatic Theater; poet Sandro Key-Åberg (born 1922); author Bo Sköld (born 1924); and stage director Staffan Roos (born 1943).

Höijer and Moberg have written of the special problems of their home provinces, respectively, Norrbotten, above the Arctic Circle, and Småland, in the south near Denmark. Höijer's most effective play is *Isak Juntti hade många söner* (Isak Juntti Had Many Sons, 1954), a penetrating psychological study of the sexual and religious problems of the inhabitants of the wastelands of the North. Moberg's *Din stund på jorden* (Your Time on Earth, 1967) is one of a series of earnest but sentimental plays and novels in which he has explored the lives of Swedes who emigrated to the United States. Josephson, well known to admirers of Ingmar Bergman films, is an intelligent, articulate writer who has achieved some success with plays, such as the bitter comedy *Sällskaps lek* (Party Game, 1955). Sandro Key-Åberg's *O* (1965), a collection of witty, satirical sketches, was staged in experimental theaters in London and New York after its Swedish premiere. *Min kära är en ros* (My Love Is a Rose, 1962), a play about hot rodders and the generation gap, won critical acclaim for its author, Bo Sköld, but he has yet to fulfill his early promise. The Royal Dramatic Theater production of Staffan Roos' first play, *Cirkus Madigan* (1967), was another demonstration of the effectiveness of group theater improvisations.

A useful source of information on drama in Sweden is Alrik Gustafsson's *A History of Danish Literature* (1958).

**Switzerland.** In many respects, the Nazi era was a boon for Swiss theater. Beginning in 1933, many German and Austrian actors, directors, and dramatists found refuge in Switzerland. Most of them worked at the ZURICH SCHAUSPIEL-HAUS. Under the supervision of Oskar Wälterlin (1938–1961), this theater reached new heights in its production of classical and modern plays. It was here that Brecht's *Mother Courage, The Good Woman of Setzuan,* and *Galileo* received their first performances. It was here also that Max Frisch and Friedrich Dürrenmatt had their start.

When one speaks of Swiss drama, one generally means Frisch and Dürrenmatt. Yet in many respects these two dramatists have transcended the provinciality of their country and have written world dramas. Frisch has written important political parables—*Nun singen sie wieder* (Now They Are Singing Again, 1945), *Die Chinesische Mauer* (The Chinese Wall, 1946), *Don Juan oder die Liebe zur Geometrie* (Don Juan, or The Love of Geometry, 1952), *Biedermann und die Brandstifter* (The Firebugs, 1958), and *Andorra* (1961)—which are strongly influenced by Brecht and at the same time question Brecht's thesis that the theater can lead to change in social conditions. Dürrenmatt is more interested in the possibilities of comedy and farce to reflect the impossibility of determining the outcome of a sociopolitical situation. His major works, *Romulus der Grosse* (Romulus the Great, 1949), *The Marriage of Mr. Mississippi* (1952), *The Visit* (1955), *The Physicists* (1961), and *Der Meteor* (1966), pose theological questions in paradoxes that are difficult to answer. Frisch is more a political pragmatist with a bent toward Marxism; Dürrenmatt is a moralist with a tendency toward Christian existentialism. Both are critical of Swiss society but see Switzerland in their plays as a microcosmic reflection of the world—particularly of the Western world. Their most recent plays and statements about drama show that they are having difficulty in coming to terms with this world and its institutions, which seem to be falling apart.

Swiss theater is comparatively speaking a stable institution. Aside from various private theaters and cabarets, which house commercial comedies and melodramas, the cantons and cities subsidize sizable repertory companies. There are fine ensembles in Basel, Geneva, and Saint Gallen, as well as in Zurich. The French and Italian theaters of Switzerland have not been as successful as the German theaters, which were helped by the German and Austrian refugees who came to Switzerland in the war years. All of the theaters tend to have a well-balanced program of classics and modern plays. With the exception of Maria von Ostfelden's Theater an der Winkelweise in Zurich, there are very few small experimental groups. In 1964 "Expo," a festival of one-act plays, was held in Lausanne to exhibit works by some of the younger Swiss dramatists, and some older ones other than Frisch and Dürrenmatt. Among the playwrights of note are Otto F. Walter, Walter M. Diggelmann, Higo Loetscher, Hans Rudolf Hilty, Max Schmid, and Herbert Meier (German); Robert Pinget, Louis Gaulis, Walter Weideli, Fernand Berset, and Henri Deblüe (French); Reto Roedel and Gino Semadeni (Italian). Up to the present, none of these writers except Pinget has distinguished himself on the international scene. Nevertheless, they have all been active, and the more recent movements in the Swiss theater may give rise to some interesting developments. Both Zurich and Basel have experienced small rebellions over the appointment and deportment of certain directors. Among the younger playwrights, directors, actors, and stagehands, there is a demand for more control over the productions of the theaters. Though Swiss theater is far from cracking its respectable bourgeois seams, there are signs that the companies are moving into an experimental phase and seeking to acquire social relevance.

**Szabó, Magda** (born 1917). Hungarian novelist and playwright. Miss Szabó was born and educated in Debrecen, where she took a degree at Debrecen University in Latin and Hungarian. She was a grammar-school teacher during the war; after 1945 she published two books of poetry and in 1957 made a successful debut as a prose writer. Since then she has published several novels, which are widely read in Hungary and have been translated into most European languages. In her dramas—*Kigyómarás* (Snakebite, 1960) and *Leleplezés* (Unveiling, 1962)—as in her novels, she grapples with individual moral problems. Most of her characters have provincial middle-class origins or backgrounds; their social norms, reinforced by Calvinism or Marxist convictions, drive them to bitter confrontations with truth, which they passionately accept in order to pass judgment upon themselves or others.

**Szaniawski, Jerzy** (1886–1970). Polish dramatist. Szaniawski was born in Zegrzynek, educated in Warsaw and in Switzerland, where he studied literature, art, and agriculture. His first play was produced in 1917, followed by a dozen others till the outbreak of World War II. He also wrote some plays for radio, a few collections of short stories, and a volume of memoirs. Szaniawski was awarded the State Literary Prize in 1930; he was elected a member of the Polish Academy of Letters in 1933. During the war he spent some months in a Nazi prison. In 1946 his first postwar play, *Dwa teatry* (The Two Theaters), was produced. In the same year Szaniawski was nominated as a member of the State Theater Council.

Szaniawski's most productive years were those between the two World Wars; the post World War II period brought only three full-length and two one-act plays. Nevertheless, his position as the dean of Polish dramatists was established after World War II—1947 was the all-time record year for the productions of his plays—and his play *The Two Theaters* became the most popular Polish drama since the war. In his writing Szaniawski continued partly the tradition of Tadeusz Rittner (1873–1921). His was a psychological drama of subtle undertones, atmosphere charged with emotion, poetic mood, and lofty moral tone. In his plays—of which *Papierowy kochanek* (The Paper Lover, 1920), *Ptak* (The Bird, 1923), *Żeglarz* (The Sailor, 1925), *Adwokat i róże* (Lawyer and the Roses, 1929), *Most* (The Bridge, 1933), *Kowal, pieniądze i gwiazdy* (The Blacksmith, Money, and the Stars, 1948) were the most successful—he tried to incorporate the world of dreams into reality, using apt, though simple, dramatic techniques. In *The Two Theaters* he also invoked the recent experiences of his country. Although his immediate popularity may have waned in the last decade, his high place in the history of Polish drama is assured.

OTHER PLAYS SINCE 1945: *Chłopiec latający* (The Flying Boy, written 1949, produced 1958), *Łuczniczka* (The Lady Archer, 1959), *Dziewięć lat* (Nine Years, 1960).

**Szewcy** (The Shoemakers, written 1931–1934, published 1948, first performed 1957). A play by Stanisław Ignacy Witkiewicz, subtitled "A Theoretical Play With 'Songs' in Three Acts." A master cobbler, Sajetan, and his two apprentices are entangled in philosophical and sociopolitical discussions with the bourgeois prosecutor Robert Scurvy and, together with him, are involved in a curious emotional-erotic-intellectual love-hate relationship with Princess Irina Vsyevolodovna Zbereznitska-Podberezka. A Fascist revolution lands the shoemakers and the princess in prison at Scurvy's mercy. Then the situation is reversed: When the socialist revolution succeeds, Scurvy is chained like a dog to a tree trunk. There follows a parodistic debunking of the belief of the early twentieth-century dramatist Stanisław Wyspiański that the union of the intelligentsia and the peasants could bring about a national and social revival. It is not only the peasants, however, whose "mission" fails. The socialist revolution, led by the idealistic self-made leader, the master cobbler, does not achieve success through the liberation of sexual and social activity, and is superseded by an ominous secret power: the bureaucrats and the technocrats of a new totalitarian brand, represented by a robotic Hyperworkoid and two party officials, whose cynical dialogue ends the play.

The Shoemakers, Witkiewicz's last play, written after a break of more than six years, is very complex in its semantic texture and intellectual proposition. Witkiewicz engages here (to quote his translators D. C. Gerould and C. S. Durer) in a "direct assault on the world around him by means of a fantastic hodgepodge of political and philosophical arguments, rhetoric, literary parody, comments on his friends, jokes in mock Russian, invented insults and obscenities, imaginary menus, and frightening prophecies of disaster." This visionary play is a thorough study of the bankruptcy of various social and political systems and an analysis of individual frustrations and boredom. The decay of capitalism, followed by the rise of Fascism and later still by the Marxist-type revolution, which turns into its own caricature, is brilliantly visualized through a series of striking and disturbing metaphors, as well as surrealist juxtapositions. Its topicality can be judged by the fact that its first production, as late as 1957, was stopped after one performance and the play has remained mainly a property of student theater.

# T

Tango (1964). A play by Sławomir Mrożek. This first full-length play by a master of short and miniature plays became an instant success in the author's own country and, perhaps, the best-known postwar Polish play abroad. Reasons for this are not hard to find. *Tango* is composed like a "well-made play," but deals with ideas rather than personal problems, ideas whose topicality and universal appeal cannot be doubted.

The house of the Stomil family is in a state of decay. All values have toppled, yesterday's rebellions against conventions of the past have fossilized into a new "order" of chaos. A young idealistic intellectual named Arthur, disgusted with his family's sloppy way of life—an obvious result of the older generation's having broken with past social and moral conventions—enlists the support of one of its representatives, Uncle Eugene, and a somewhat half-hearted agreement of his young bride-to-be in order to break the impasse and renew the family—and the world. This means converting the household, including his father, a démodé avant-garde writer, to his lofty ideas of social order and "life with a meaning." He tries to renew form rather than substance. Enmeshed in pragmatism, he tidies up clothes, performs traditional ceremonies, plans a formal white wedding. His great aim is eventually "to create a system in which rebellion will be joined with order and nothingness with existence" and thus to "destroy contradiction." But this Utopian synthesis is dissipated into "words, words, words," as one of the characters in *Tango*, echoing Hamlet, comments on Arthur's program. Arthur proves an ineffectual leader, and his death at the hands of the unscrupulous butler-thug, Eddie, followed by the latter's strong (Fascist?) regime, is the inevitable outcome.

*Tango* is a contemporary morality play, full of paradoxes, syllogisms, and witty satire. It abounds with echoes of Vitrac, Ionesco, and Gombrowicz, but is still typical of Mrożek in its analysis of the logic of the intellectual's failure and defeat when confronted with the stark reality of social life and power politics. It would be unwise, however, to see in *Tango* merely a topical play, whose details are allusions to definite events of recent history. Mrożek continues the traditional themes of Polish romantic and neoromantic dramatists in an updated manner. Whereas the rebels of romantic drama believed in the power of the word to prevail over chaos, restore their country's freedom, and repair the state of the world under the guidance of divine justice, Mrożek does not. Having eliminated the highfalutin style of his literary models and reduced the setting from cosmic dimensions to the enclosed confines of the Stomil house, Mrożek has brought the problems of national romantic drama closer to modern sensitivity. The main difference, however, lies in the lack of faith: in God and in the word. Mrożek's hero is unromanticized and antiheroic; his words are empty words, his rebellion limited, under the empty sky, to a power game, or rather, to playing at having power. Mrożek has crammed the problem of a world that is corroded from within by its own decay and threatened from without by gangsters into the walls of a house lived in by people of three generations, who represent a number of differing attitudes. By reducing the problem, he has made it more concrete; by making it typical, he has striven to make it universal. Naturally, *Tango*, because it is not a psychological play, is apt to be more popular in countries whose tradition of drama is not limited to personal problems of individuals, but permits a play of ideas to be understood and appreciated as well.

**Terry, Megan** (born 1932). American playwright. Miss Terry was born in Seattle, received a B.A. at the University of Washington, was awarded a fellowship to Yale and a grant in playwriting from the Rockefeller Foundation. Her "Folk War Movie" *Viet Rock* (1964) was first presented at the La MaMa Experimental Theatre Club, then, revised for a larger area, at Yale and in a regular run in New York City; it has played in Norway, Sweden, Denmark, Germany, Italy, Mexico, Japan, and a number of other countries. As a founding member of the Open Theatre, Miss Terry is basically innovative and her work is usually performed by experimental groups, such as La MaMa, Open Theatre, and Firehouse Theatre, or by avant-garde university drama departments: *In the Gloaming, O My Darling* (1965), *Calm Down, Mother* (1965), *Comings and Goings* (1966), *Ex-Miss Copper Queen on a Set of Pills* (1966), *Keep Tightly Closed in a Cool, Dry Place* (1966), *Jack-Jack* (1967), *People vs. Ranchman* (1967), *Key Is on the Bottom* (1968), *The Magic Realists* (1968), *Massachusetts Trust* (1968), *The Tommy Allen Show* (1969), *Approaching Simone* (1970). Miss Terry has also done two television plays, *Home* (1968) and *One More Little Drinkie* (1969), both on National Educational Television. In the Production Notes to *Viet Rock* Miss Terry states that the play grew out of improvisation and urges that "the visual images here are more important than the words"; statements like these and "There are as many ways to approach this play as there are combinations of four people who might involve themselves in it" (in the Production Notes for *Keep Tightly Closed*) indicate the attitudes through which Miss Terry approaches her experiments in technique and her subject matter, which is often concerned with political-psychological explorations of violence.

**Terson, Peter** (born 1932). English dramatist. Terson worked as a sports instructor in a small village in the Vale of Evesham. His dramatic abilities were discovered by Peter Cheeseman, director of the Victoria Theatre, Stoke on Trent. Terson joined the company of that theater as resident dramatist, remaining there until 1969. As well as contributing to the "documentary" dramas on local themes presented by that company, Terson wrote a series of plays set in the Midland Vale of Evesham that revealed a fertile and original talent. Catching the rhythms of rustic rhetoric with a skill occasionally reminiscent of Pinter's, Terson was able to create a mysterious and sinister landscape with a few bold theatrical strokes. In *A Night to Make the Angels Weep* (1964) Terson charted the stormy currents that flow beneath the placid surface of English country life, neatly implicating three sets of characters in a chain of events that ends in violent death. In *The Mighty Reservoy* (1964), perhaps the most powerful of this series, the theme is the destruction of the city dweller by forces he scarcely understands. As a demented watchman prepares to sacrifice his half-willing victim to the "needs, needs as must be settled" of the giant reservoir he guards, Terson builds his play up to a climax suggestive of the pattern of ritual.

This prolific dramatist thrives on the collaboration of actors, and in 1967 he began to contribute an annual play to the repertory of England's National Youth Theatre. *Zigger-Zagger* (1967), *The Apprentices* (1968), *Fuzz* (1969) are plays ideally suited to the energy and developing talents of the large and youthful cast that this company possesses, and Terson intelligently exploited the opportunity for a theatrical study of mass emotions—among the frenzied supporters of a local football team in *Zigger-Zagger* and the tribal rituals of the factory yard in *The Apprentices.*

Terson's lively and inventive dialogue, tailored to the needs of the company for which he is working, reveals his gift for spontaneity, but in some of his plays, at least, the actions of his wild, anarchic characters are contained within a firm and careful dramatic structure. Through the very nature of his commissions he has not been able to achieve the critical recognition of more metropolitan dramatists, but this unconventional writer is nevertheless among the most interesting to have made his mark in the '60s.

OTHER PLAYS: *All Honour Mr. Todd* (1966), *The Knotty* (documentary, 1966), *The Ballad of the Artificial Mash* (1967), *Mooney and His Caravans* (1968), *The Adventures of Gervase Becket, or The Man Who Changed Places* (a play for children, 1969), *Spring-Heeled Jack* (1970), *The Samaritan* (1971).

**Tervapää, Juhani.** Pseudonym of Hella WUOLIJOKI.

**Theater of cruelty.** See Antonin ARTAUD.

**Theater on the Balustrade.** See CZECHOSLOVAKIA.

**Thomas, Gwyn** (born 1913). Welsh dramatist. Educated in Wales, at Oxford, and at the University of Madrid, Thomas was a schoolmaster before embarking upon a career as writer and broadcaster. A vivid imagination, a prolific wit, and a memory of prewar socialism in the mining valleys of South

Wales had combined to establish Thomas among the contributors to the humorous weekly *Punch* before *The Keep* was staged in 1961. The same qualities were to flavor his dramatic writing. This comedy, a study of a family anchored in the provincialism of contemporary Wales capable of very little except a spontaneous flow of hilarious rhetoric, remains his most successful play. It was a co-winner of the *Evening Standard* Award to the most promising playwright of the year. In his two later and more ambitious pieces the author's disregard for dramatic structure and characterization is more apparent. He is the author of a number of television plays.

OTHER PLAYS: *Loud Organs* (musical, 1962), *Jackie the Jumper* (1963).

**Thurzó, Gábor** (born 1912). Hungarian writer and playwright. Before the war Thurzó worked for Catholic reviews and published several novels and collections of short stories. After 1945 he became dramatic adviser to various theaters and wrote film scenarios. After 1961 he worked for Hungarian Television. Thurzó considers himself a "bourgeois" writer and, not unexpectedly, his central theme is the decay and moral disintegration of the bourgeois world. His first two plays, *Záróra* (Closing Time) and *Hátsó ajtó* (Back Door), both written in 1963, are nevertheless devoted to abuses within the socialist system, such as careerism, hypocrisy, and political opportunism. *Záróra* was strongly criticized for the "new schematism" of its characters. His third play, *Az ördög ügyvédje* (Devil's Advocate, 1968), won more critical acclaim. It is the story of a clerical investigation, taking place during the last war, which aims to find out whether or not to start canonization proceedings for a young Hungarian Catholic of saintly virtues. Although it becomes clear that there are hardly any facts to justify canonization, the proceedings will be started nevertheless in order to give a propaganda victory to the Hungarian Church.

**Topol, Josef.** See CZECHOSLOVAKIA.

**Touch of the Poet, A** (written between 1935 and 1942, first produced and published in 1957). A four-act play by Eugene O'Neill. This is the only completed play in a projected cycle of eleven plays dealing with the corruption of power and money in a nineteenth-century American family, the Harfords. The title of the whole cycle was to be *A Tale of Possessors Self-Dispossessed.* In this play Sara Melody, daughter of an Irish immigrant, witnesses her father's clash with Yankee aristocracy and his subsequent humiliation and reawakening to his true nature, learns from her mother something of the totality (and danger) of love, and succeeds in winning Simon Harford, favorite son of a wealthy New England businessman and his emotionally possessive wife. Although the title phrase is applied most obviously to Simon and Melody, Sara's father, the women in the play embody it, too. Simon has a touch of the poet in that he is an idealist, leaving his father's successful business to live simply and write a tract on a selfless society. Melody is touched with Byronism, wearing his major's uniform from the English army and remembering his battles in Spain even though in his present circumstances he is only a poor, drunken innkeeper. His wife, Nora, has the same poetic tendency to absolutize; her love must be total and selfless or else her life has no meaning. And even Deborah, Simon's mother, is a maker of fictive worlds, dreaming herself mistress to the king of France, a total *femme fatale* (this tendency is shown more in a subsequent play, the unfinished *More Stately Mansions*).

Melody's gusty role as playboy of the Yankee world is the best part of the play; Sara's triumph and her own battling with illusion is less convincing because the object of her personal desires and ambitions is never on stage and seems to exist more as an idea or goal than as a person.

**Transformation.** A type of dramatic improvisation. This dramatic technique, now used by a number of experimental theater groups, is described by Peter Feldman of the Open Theatre as "an improvisation in which the established realities or 'given circumstances' (the Method phrase) of the scene change several times during the course of the action. What may change are character and/or situation and/or time and/or objectives, etc. Whatever realities are established at the beginning are destroyed after a few minutes and replaced by others. Then these are in turn destroyed and replaced. These changes occur swiftly and *almost without transition,* until the audience's dependence upon any fixed reality is called into question." Not merely an "acting stunt," this device is intended to question, dramatically, the very nature of reality, identity, and "the finitude of character." (Quoted from Production Notes in Megan Terry's *Viet Rock and Other Plays,* 1967.)

**Travers, Ben** (born 1886). English dramatist. Although he continued to write in the postwar period, the reputation of this dramatist will rest upon his early farces, in particular *A Cuckoo in the Nest* (1925), *Rookery Nook* (1926), and *Thark* (1927), which were presented at the Aldwych Theatre, London, as vehicles for such actors as Ralph Lynn, Robertson Hare, and Mary Brough. They may be considered as classic examples of twentieth-century English farce, which rejects the relish gained from sexual intrigue by the French masters of the genre in favor of a no-less-skillfully plotted picture of burgeoning confusion and final chaos among a gallery of English characters of exaggerated but recognizable eccentricity. Travers is also the author of numerous novels and screenplays, and of *Vale of Laughter* (1957), a volume of autobiography.

OTHER PLAYS SINCE 1945: *Outrageous Fortune* (1947), *Wild Horses* (1952), *Nun's Veiling* (revised version of *O Mistress Mine* [1936], 1953).

**Turja, Ilmari** (born 1901). Finnish playwright. Turja took a law degree before turning to journalism; he worked as the editor-in-chief of several magazines, including *Suomen Kuvalehti* (1936–1951). In 1970 he still published a regular weekly column. He has traveled widely and produced collections of comic stories and travel books. During the war years he served as an information officer in the headquarters of the Finnish Army.

Turja's *Särkelä itte* (Särkelä Himself, 1944) is a classic comedy that is often revived. Its two central characters, an energetic self-made businessman and a shrewd commoner, are thoroughly Finnish in their ways of speaking and thinking. *Päämajassa* (In the Headquarters, 1965) won instant success with its documentary portrayal of Field Marshal Mannerheim, commander of the Finnish Army, and his closest men in the nearly catastrophic final phase of the war. *Sotamiehen kunnia* (A Soldier's Honor, 1970) is a critical examination of the execution of a deserter at the front. Turja has an ear for epigrammatic phrasing and folk humor; his viewpoints, based on his long experience as a journalist, are strong and individual.

**Turner, David** (born 1927). English dramatist. A Midlander of working-class origin, born in Birmingham, where he still lives, Turner became a school-teacher after graduation from Birmingham University and turned to writing only at the age of twenty-seven. Encouraged by his initial success in writing for radio and television, he left the teaching profession to become a scriptwriter for the radio series *The Archers*. After several plays for radio and television he began writing for the stage in 1960. Of his briskly professional plays, which range in style from social allegory (*The Antique Shop*, 1963) to episodic historical drama (*Bottomley*, 1965), only *Semi-Detached* (1962) has achieved success outside the Midlands. A chronicle of the suburban Midway family's devious schemes to clamber up a few rungs of the lower-middle-class social ladder, *Semi-Detached* is triumphantly modeled on the Jonsonian comedy of humors. The intricately contrived plot conforms to the classical unities, and the shrewdly exaggerated observation of the language and social mores of Midland suburbia has much of the wit and some of the cruelty of Jonson himself. The Midway family are portrayed in a style that is somewhere between caricature and social realism, and Turner neither condemns nor endorses the ruthless materialism which deploys culture and marriage as pawns in the grand strategy of social advancement.

Turner has continued to write for radio and television, and has earned a reputation as a skillful adapter of novels for serialized TV presentation. During 1970 his version of Sartre's trilogy of novels *Roads to Freedom* was serialized by the British Broadcasting Corporation. His work for the stage is discussed by John Russell Taylor in *Anger and After* (1969).

OTHER PLAYS: *The Bedmakers* (1962), *Quick, Quick, Slow* (a musical, 1969).

**Tynan, Kenneth** (born 1927). English dramatic critic. After graduating from Oxford University, Tynan worked briefly as a director in the professional theater before taking up his first appointment as dramatic critic with the London weekly *Spectator* (1951–52). His influence upon public opinion reached its height during the earlier of his two periods as dramatic critic for the London Sunday *Observer* (1954–1958 and 1960–1963). It was in 1956 that his enthusiastic support of Osborne's *Look Back in Anger* as "the best young play of its decade" helped to create a turning point in the postwar

**445**

English theater. For a time he became a spokesman for the "angry young men" of the left whose mark was discerned in most branches of literature and thought. The two intervening years were spent in the United States as dramatic critic of the *New Yorker* (1958–1960). Tynan has also contributed film criticism and a regular column of opinion and comment to the *Observer*. In 1963 he was appointed literary manager of the newly formed National Theatre Company, and in that capacity he commissioned *A Bond Honoured* (1966) from John Osborne and became involved in controversy with the governors of the theater when they refused permission to a production of Rolf Hochhuth's *The Soldiers* (1967). Tynan later formed an independent company which staged the play commercially. In 1969 he gained some notoriety as deviser of *Oh! Calcutta!*

Tynan has played an ambiguous role in the development of contemporary English drama. Undoubtedly it was he more than any other critic who drew attention to the significance of Osborne's first play, insisting on a return to social relevance as the key to the revival of English dramaturgy and engaging in a celebrated controversy with Ionesco on this very point; but his stance as a committed critic of the left does not stand close scrutiny. His elegant style displays the flamboyance and sometimes the exhibitionism of an esthete with little concern for moral or political considerations, and his criticism is more valuable for the fastidious skill with which he records a performance or a *mise-en-scène* than for his literary judgments upon new English drama. The latter part of his career has been marked by similar contradictions, his influence upon the capricious repertory of the National Theatre appearing barely discernible, and the decadent eroticism of *Oh! Calcutta* proving a disappointing culmination of his energetic espousal of the cause of free expression on the stage. The most important of Tynan's criticism is collected in *Curtains* (1961) and *Tynan Right and Left* (1967).

# U

**United States.** Despite expansion of the means of communication and travel after World War II and the increased cosmopolitanism of the nation as a whole, New York City remained the undisputed center of theatrical activity in the United States. With few exceptions, playwrights who succeeded, financially or artistically, were born in New York or lived there for a significant portion of their careers. And the fixed point for this center was a magic place called Broadway: Smash hits occurred *on* Broadway (or critics lamented another miserable season), skillful innovations triumphed *off*-Broadway (or critics lamented that off-Broadway was becoming just like Broadway), and avant-garde experiments exploded *off-off*-Broadway (though no one was quite sure yet what all that would mean). Even the permanent theaters being established outside New York came to be labeled "beyond Broadway."

This Broadway fixation reveals something of utmost importance about the American theater itself and about the response of participants to it: an expectation that great drama ought to be written, produced, and appreciated in the United States and a corresponding embarrassment and disappointment that it is not. And so Broadway remained as a symbol, something to be "on" or "off" depending whether "great" is valued monetarily or aesthetically. The fact that Broadway had been declining commercially since the late 1920s— fewer theaters available, fewer productions per season—only added an ironic element to this ambivalent expectation/disappointment of the American critic and theatergoer. The unpleasant truth is that there are no great American playwrights, never have been (though there are and have been a few good ones), and that by and large most theatrical successes are inexplicable a few years later. The twenty-five years after World War II were not a period of high achievement on the American stage, but they were no worse than the century before and did boast the names of the two or three best American playwrights as well as the hope for a better future.

War years are never good for drama. In 1939 Howard Lindsay and Russell Crouse's *Life with Father* began a record-breaking run on Broadway (a record that has been surpassed only by the decade-long off-Broadway run of *The Fantasticks* in the 1960s). This sort of light formula-comedy persisted throughout the 1940s, along with a number of plays dealing with the war or related issues. Lillian Hellman's *Watch on the Rhine* (1941) and *The Searching Wind* (1944) attacked Fascism; Sidney Kingsley's *The Patriots* (1942) championed democracy. Thornton Wilder's philosophic comedy *The Skin of Our Teeth* (1942) explored the human meaning of physical disaster. James Gow and Arnaud d'Usseau in *Deep Are the Roots* (1945) and Arthur Laurents in *The Home of the Brave* (1945) preached against prejudice as anti-democratic. A number of adaptations, too, filled out the entertainment bills: S. N. Behrman's version of Franz Werfel's *Jacobowsky and the Colonel* (1944), for example, and Paul Osborn's dramatization of John Hersey's novel *A Bell for Adano* (1944). One of the most dramatically serious attempts of the 1940s was the revival of poetic drama. Unfortunately, the best poet to try was not adept at theater (the power of Robinson Jeffers' *Medea* [1947] was due to the performance of Judith Anderson and not to any intrinsic theatricality of the play itself, which is essentially closet drama) and the man of the theater who tried was a miserable poet (Maxwell Anderson's *Anne of a Thousand Days* [1948] and *Joan of Lorraine* [1946] had successful Broadway runs despite the verse). But the last season of the war years, 1944–45, saw two new plays—Arthur Miller's *The Man Who Had All the Luck* and Tennessee Williams' *The Glass Menagerie*—by playwrights who were to become the dominant voices in postwar American theater.

Although Miller's first play failed, his next production, *All My Sons* (on the theme of war-profiteering and self-deception), won the New York Drama Critics Circle Award in 1947. With *Death of a Salesman* (awarded the Pulitzer Prize in 1949) Miller was established as the playwright who, it was hoped, would bring greatness to the American theater through the cerebral genre of modern tragedy. His running mate, Tennessee Williams, winning the New York Drama Critics Circle Award in 1945 for *The Glass Menagerie* and in 1948 for *A Streetcar Named Desire*, would celebrate the flesh and bring the power of myth and of passion to the American stage. Between these two playwrights, perhaps a renaissance.

In the early 1950s Miller continued to produce, but Williams pulled ahead with an extraordinary show of serious and aesthetically quite controversial plays: *The Rose Tattoo* (1951), *Camino Real* (1953), *Cat on a Hot Tin Roof* (1955), *Orpheus Descending* (1957), *Suddenly Last Summer* (1958), *Sweet Bird of Youth* (1959). There was hope, too, in the emergence of two new playwrights of promise, William Inge and Robert Anderson, the arrival of an obviously great and seminal play from abroad, Samuel Beckett's *Waiting for Godot*, and the establishment of a series of off-Broadway theaters, like the Phoenix and Circle in the Square, and off-off-Broadway experimental groups, like the Living Theater and Caffè Cino. Inge and Anderson soon faded, Beckett's play went unappreciated on Broadway in 1956 and again in 1957 (though Edward Albee was to rise from its ashes). But the theater groups thrived, and there, in the late '50s and into the '60s, the real strength of American drama seemed to lie, not in individual dramatists.

The one great exception was, of course, Eugene O'Neill, whose post-humous career encouraged the theater public to believe that there was at least one first-rate native playwright. In 1946 O'Neill had broken a decade of silence with the production of *The Iceman Cometh;* the play was not a commercial success on Broadway, and *A Moon for the Misbegotten* failed in its out-of-town tryout in 1947. O'Neill did not live to see the brilliant productions of his plays by José Quintero, beginning with *The Iceman Cometh* at the Circle in the Square in 1956 and reaching a peak of dramatic accomplishment with *Long Day's Journey into Night* on Broadway that same year. There followed a second chance for *A Moon for the Misbegotten* in 1957, *A Touch of the Poet in* 1958, and, in Stockholm at the Royal Dramatic Theater, *More Stately Mansions* in 1962. The critical uncertainties that had shadowed O'Neill's achievement since his winning of the Nobel Prize in 1936 were dissipated in the 1950s, and his place as genius of the American theater was assured.

The sense of theater-community that began to develop in the 1950s is reminiscent of that spirit in other periods of dramatic achievement: the teens and '20s with their Washington Square Players, Provincetown Players, and Theatre Guild, the '30s with its Group Theatre and Federal Theater Project. More communal than any other art form, theater needed and will probably always need a company of artists not only for the production of plays but also for the fostering of playwrights. Among the first postwar groups to band together with a common goal and a common philosophy was the Living Theater of Julian Beck and Judith Malina, which became the most vital experimental group of the '50s, giving birth to new playwrights like Jack Gelber, whose *The Connection* (1959) was one of their most celebrated productions, and indirectly to other companies like the Open Theatre, whose director, Joseph Chaikin, had been a member of the Living Theater before its exile to Europe in 1963. The development of the Living Theater during the 1960s has been toward theater as a way of life, with the company seen as a family, its members living and sharing physically and psychically, just as for a short period members of the Provincetown Players and the Group Theatre had done. Those earlier groups ended because of separate paths taken by some of their members, as did the Living Theater in 1970. Whether other new groups would be able to balance the communality of art with the communality of life and nurture both remained to be seen. Not only economic efficiency was at stake, but the very element that makes people seek out theater in the first place: the desire to experience and recognize meaning in community with others. To the extent that twentieth-century Americans are deprived of this kind of experience in the usual human loci of family, religion, philosophy, and politics, the more will they need it from social arts like drama.

In addition to the rise of the intimate and somewhat elitist off-off-Broadway groups in the late '50s, there was also a movement to broaden the audience base by providing free public theater. Most notable of these attempts was the foundation of the New York Shakespeare Festival, directed by

Joseph Papp, which gave its first summer performances in Central Park in 1957 and a decade later expanded to a full winter season, with very inexpensive tickets, in its permanent complex of theaters in the elegant old Astor Library. Indoors and out, there is a real sense of festival about this theater for the people, where not coincidentally the internationally famous "love-rock-musical" *Hair* (1967) originated.

This effort toward community became even more pronounced in the 1960s. Suddenly there were dozens of small theater companies in coffeehouses, warehouse lofts, and churches, all over New York City, doing low-cost, experimental productions for what was in many cases a membership audience (at the American Place Theatre, for example, or the La MaMa Experimental Theatre Club) or a neighborhood audience (Theatre Genesis). This diverse phenomenon was labeled off-off-Broadway and took its place as frontier leader of the American theater, producing some of the most interesting new playwrights (Ed Bullins, LeRoi Jones, Robert Lowell, Megan Terry, Jean-Claude Van Itallie). Outside New York there was a corresponding increase in the number of permanent resident theaters established (the Theatre Company of Boston, the Firehouse Theatre in Minneapolis, the Center Theatre Group in Los Angeles, to name only a few) and some very significant attempts to bring theater to people who have no theater (the Free Southern Theatre, as well as various urban programs for plays, free and alfresco).

One of the most unusual events in the '60s was the emergence of a black revolutionary theater. Its leader, LeRoi Jones, had been a successful new young writer in the early 1960s; the off-Broadway and off-off-Broadway stages were open to his plays and produced *Dutchman, The Baptism, The Toilet,* and *The Slave* in 1964. But in 1965 Jones moved from Greenwich Village to Harlem, where he founded the Black Arts Repertory Theatre, and thence to Newark, New Jersey, his home, where he established a black community center called Spirit House. Since then Jones's plays have been militantly black and beautiful, produced usually for black audiences and serving to inspire a whole new group of black playwrights (chief among them Ed Bullins) whose purpose is to forge a new black art and inculcate pride in a people humiliated by subjection and prejudice.

Although the United States had not yet produced its great American playwright, the '60s, like the two decades preceding it, had one or two hopeful possibilities and some severe disappointments. Although Tennessee Williams had been producing regularly, he did not get beyond his early promise. *Period of Adjustment* (1960) was dully domestic; *The Night of the Iguana* (1961) and *The Milk Train Doesn't Stop Here Anymore* (1964) had some of his distinctive power, but were turgid; *The Seven Descents of Myrtle* (1968) and *In the Bar of a Tokyo Hotel* (1969) quietly failed. But Williams' partner from the '40s, Arthur Miller, made something of a comeback in the '60s. After eight years of silence Miller produced *After the Fall* (1964) and *Incident at*

*Vichy* (1964), both plays wrestling with problems of guilt and responsibility, issues close enough to Miller's own life and the lives of the audience to generate considerable interest. With *The Price* (1968) Miller returned to the conventional form of his first successful play, *All My Sons,* and to the themes of deception and destruction that haunt all of his work. Except for the introduction of a comic character, *The Price* showed nothing new in Miller, no advance, and a disappointed public wondered if this promising talent, too, would evaporate.

The strongest hope of the '60s was Edward Albee. With the off-Broadway success of *The Zoo Story* (1960), Albee was suddenly established as a new young playwright having great dramatic skill, both in structure and in language, and, even more wonderful, with something important to say. The encounter of Jerry and Peter—the zoo story that is both told and lived—was recognized as a parable about violence in the heart of civilization, the ambivalence of love and hate, the longing for and fear of communion. Everything about the play worked, its technical and thematic relation to European theater of the absurd was clear, and soon freshmen in college English classes all over the country were studying Albee along with Shakespeare and Shaw. Albee's next plays were equally well executed one-acters: *The Death of Bessie Smith* (1960), *The Sandbox* (1960), and *The American Dream* (1961). But it was with his first full-length play that he reinforced his position as the most promising new playwright: *Who's Afraid of Virginia Woolf?* was an extraordinary success on Broadway in 1962 in one of those rare productions where box-office popularity and serious dramatic achievement meet. With his usual skill, Albee turned an absolutely recognizable and very particularly realistic situation into universal myth, and the American public was fascinated. But with his next original play, *Tiny Alice* (1964), myth-making ran amok and a puzzled audience backed away. It seemed as if Albee, straining for profundity, was smothering meaning with symbolism. This pretentious play was flanked by a series of other disappointments: *The Ballad of the Sad Café* (1963), *Malcolm* (1966), *A Delicate Balance* (1966), and *Everything in the Garden* (1967). Although these last two plays showed something of a revival of Albee's talent, they were still only commercially competent entertainment. With *Box* and *Quotations from Chairman Mao Tse-tung* (1968), Albee returned to his early experimental absurdist manner. And critics wondered if this was yet another talented playwright, like Jack Richardson and Jack Gelber, unable to get beyond the first act of a career.

By the end of the 1960s there was as yet no first-rate American playwright, except possibly Eugene O'Neill. But there was a good seedbed: numerous experimental companies of all kinds flourished as talented and ambitious theater people grouped together for an escalation of possibilities. There were no restrictions, nothing that was not allowed on the stage (short, it seemed, of actual murder and, perhaps, actual sexual intercourse). New

451

and unknown playwrights were published in inexpensive paperback editions available anywhere in the country. Even Broadway seemed to be using all the resources of theater in multimedia productions. In 1969 the talent, the energy, the means existed for an exciting theater fostering fine playwrights; what the 1970s would do with it all remained to be seen.

For American drama since World War II a useful listing of plays and information relevant to production as well as abbreviated texts of the ten best plays is to be found in the Burns Mantle Yearbooks, *The Best Plays of 19—*, published each year to cover the previous theater season in New York and, more briefly, the rest of the United States and parts of Europe. *Theatre World* provides a similar annual analysis of information and includes a large number of photographs. *The Biographical Encyclopaedia and Who's Who of the American Theatre* (1966), edited by Walter Rigdon, is a mine of information, marred, unfortunately, by frequent errors in dates. *The Oxford Companion to the Theatre* (3rd edition 1967), edited by Phyllis Hartnoll, and *The Reader's Encyclopedia of World Drama* (1969), edited by John Gassner and Edward Quinn, contain important entries on American drama. The best collection of primary materials is the theater collection of the New York Public Library, now located in a special building at Lincoln Center for the Performing Arts. Jack Poggi's *Theatre in America: The Impact of Economic Forces, 1870–1967* (1968), Emory Lewis' *Stages: The Fifty-year Childhood of the American Theatre* (1969), and Julius Novick's *Beyond Broadway: The Quest for Permanent Theatres* (1968) are three of many specialized studies. Gerald Weales brings systematic information and balanced judgment to his two volumes of history and analysis: *American Drama Since World War II* (1962) and *The Jumping-Off Place: American Drama in the 1960's* (1969). Criticisms of specific plays, playwrights, and general discussions of the state of the American theater may be found in various books by Eric Bentley, Robert Brustein, Alan S. Downer, John Gassner, Martin Gottfried, Walter Kerr, and others.

**Uruguay.** Uruguayan theater has traditionally been closely related to the Argentine, and many of the major figures of Argentine theater are of Uruguayan origin. The break of political relations between the two nations in 1945 and the subsequent ban on Argentine drama groups voyaging to Montevideo forced Uruguay to develop its own theater. The founding of the Comedia Nacional in 1947, the first resident company in the country's history, led to a regular season, the establishment of the Municipal School of Dramatic Arts, and a series of tours to the interior of the country. Less formal but more important were the independent theaters, an outgrowth of the Argentine system, which led to a remarkable burgeoning during the late 1950s and early 1960s. Since about 1961, there has been a slackening of activity, the result of an excessive number of groups; the problems of uncertain artistic levels and extreme economic competition have been exacerbated by extreme inflation and other economic and political strains.

Carlos Maggi became known in the late 1950s for a series of ironic, irreverent works, including *La trastienda* (The Back Room, 1958) and *La biblioteca* (The Library, 1956); they are sometimes wistful, sometimes biting assessments of Uruguayan life. The grotesque vision implicit in his work has become increasingly marked, and in *El patio de la Torcaza* (The Dove's Patio, 1968) the earlier works are seen to be stages in a development which here erupts in a work of intense vision into the ugliness underlying daily life. In *El patio de la Torcaza*, Maggi achieved the synthesis of contemporary vision and traditional form which Argentine and Uruguayan dramatists have been seeking. Mario Benedetti, best known as a novelist, has written two plays in which Pirandello's influence has been important.

Uruguay boasts at present a substantial number of younger dramatists, none of whom has as yet demonstrated the capacity of Maggi. Two of the best are Híber Conteris and Mauricio Rosencof. Rosencof is sometimes betrayed by his social commitment, which in works such as *Las ranas* (The Frogs, 1961) led him to create an unrelieved panorama of social ills. In later works, especially *La valija* (The Suitcase, 1964), he has shown technical advancement and more subtlety. Conteris is best known for *El asesinato de Malcolm X* (The Murder of Malcolm X, 1967), a powerful work probably influenced by Rolf Hochhuth.

**Usigli, Rodolfo** (born 1903). Mexican dramatist. Although Usigli was a contemporary and friend of the members of the Ulises and Orientación experimental groups, he has remained stubbornly apart while devoting himself to a theater of moral satire. Sardonic but deeply human, Usigli is essentially a Shavian moralist, and follows Shaw's custom of writing long polemical prologues and epilogues. All his work shows his unmistakable stamp; even *Alcestes* (written 1936; unproduced) is typical in its shaping of the Molière theme in a Mexican mold. The two most important tendencies in Usigli's work are the psychopathological and the criticism of national characteristics. Usigli's intransigence, his insistence on portraying the Mexican as Usigli sees him, explain the lengthy period which has often intervened between the writing and production of his works, as well as the critical enmity which has greeted them.

Usigli's greatest commerical successes have been sensational: *El niño y la niebla* (The Child and the Mist, written 1936, produced 1951) treated murder and insanity; *Jano es una muchacha* (Janus Is a Girl, 1952) examines the hypocrisy of the double standard in flamboyant fashion. Although the critical and the pathological lines coexist in most of Usigli's work, he is best in the former, for example in *Medio tono* (Half-Tone, 1937), a study of the dissolution of the middle-class family resulting from exaggerated economic ambition. His best works are *El gesticulador* (written 1937, staged 1947) and *Corona de sombra* (Crown of Shadow, written 1943, produced 1947). The former attacks the perversion of the ideals of the Revolution of 1910 and the gesturing, the hypocrisy, of political leaders. *Corona de sombra*, which uses an untypical anti-chronological sequence, interprets the fleeting empire of

Carlotta and Maximilian in what the author calls its anti-historical truth: the significance of the empire for Mexico's later history, rather than ephemeral fact. Usigli is also the author of important studies of the Mexican drama and the art of playwriting: *México en el teatro* (1932), *Caminos del teatro en México* (1933), and *Itinerario del autor dramático* (1941).

**Ustinov, Peter** (born 1921). English dramatist, actor, and director. Ustinov is the son of Russian émigré parents. After schooling at Westminster, he studied for the stage under Michel St. Denis at the London Theatre Studio. He first appeared on the stage in 1938, and thereafter acted in revue and repertory until joining the army in 1942. His first plays appeared during the war years; after the war he continued to act, direct, and write plays. He first entered motion pictures in 1940 and has been author, producer, director, and actor in that medium. His talents as a mimic and raconteur have reached a wide audience on radio and television. In 1963 he briefly held the post of co-director at the new Nottingham Playhouse.

Ustinov's earliest work revealed a distinctive talent, which excelled in the sympathetic portrayal of eccentrics half-aware of the ridiculous posture they strike in the eyes of the world. His cosmopolitan background is used to good effect in his portraits of the nostalgic Russian émigré community (*House of Regrets*, 1942) and the family imprisoned by its military tradition (*The Banbury Nose*, 1944). The wide-ranging interests of the dramatist are made evident in the variety of subjects he has tackled, which include the human qualities revealed in an ineffectual country priest (*The Indifferent Shepherd*, 1948), the harsh realities of power politics (*The Moment of Truth*, 1951), and a novel view of the generation gap (*Halfway up the Tree*, 1967). A recurrent theme in his work, from *The Banbury Nose* to *Photo Finish* (1962) and *Halfway up the Tree*, has been the repeated appearance of a family characteristic in successive generations, matched by the changes in the individual as he is affected by the processes of time. In *Photo Finish* an octogenarian author miraculously encounters three other versions of himself at successive stages of his life, and the quartet take a privileged view of the mistakes and successes of three generations. The charismatic nature of extreme old age holds a fascination for Ustinov, perhaps most successfully represented in the character of Matthew D'Urt in *No Sign of the Dove* (1953), a figure "in his early hundreds" who acts as a latter-day Noah in this elaborate but unpretentious allegory of man's capacity for self-destruction.

Although his plays often depart from strict naturalism to include an element of whimsical fantasy, Ustinov remains unmoved by the experiments in dramatic form that have affected the stage in the postwar years. He has stated that he will not write in the style of the theater of the absurd "because I don't believe many big themes can be tackled with that technique." Despite his obvious claim to be considered as a dramatist of ideas, his most satisfying plays have been comedies of a fantastic cast, where the author can give full rein to his gift for the telling phrase that betrays a national foible (*The Love of Four Colonels*, 1951) or the ironic gesture that punctures national dignity (*Romanoff and Juliet*, 1956). The latter play, in which romance brings confusion to the rival embassies of the two super-powers in the smallest country in Europe, shows Ustinov's gifts at their happiest. The play won the *Evening Standard* Award for the best play of the year.

Ustinov's mercurial genius blends a Russian feeling for atmosphere with an English sense of the incongruous. The latter may be detected in his observation that he finds it "extremely amusing to go into the shower bath after a game of tennis and see a man with no clothes on but wearing an expression as if he were dressed," while he has admitted to a Russian influence "in that the Russian literary tradition was the first important one which didn't have its roots in any concept of the classical; from the beginning of Russian literature there are elements of comedy and tragedy hopelessly and irrevocably entangled." Ustinov has written an introduction to *Five Plays* (1965); Geoffrey Willans has written a biography, *Peter Ustinov* (1957).

OTHER PLAYS SINCE 1945: *The Tragedy of Good Intentions* (1945), *Frenzy* (adaptation, 1948), *The Man in the Raincoat* (1950), *High Balcony* (1952), *The Empty Chair* (1956), *Paris Not So Gay* (1958), *The Life in My Hands* (1963), *The Unknown Soldier and His Wife* (1968).

# V

Va donc chez Törpe (Chez Torpe, 1961). A four-act play by François Billetdoux. First performed on September 26, 1961, at the Liège Festival in Belgium, under the direction of Antoine Bourseillier, it opened in Paris two days later at the Studio des Champs-Elysées. In an inn in Central Europe, owned by Ursula Törpe, five clients have committed suicide in the space of a few weeks. A police inspector, called in by Ursula, sets about investigating this series of suicides. Ursula counts on the inspector to free her of her clients, who come from the four corners of Europe and consist of some ten people who are weary of life and of themselves. Indeed, they are all candidates for suicide, for whom Ursula serves as a catalyst. The inspector's rational and systematic inquiry at first leads him to total incomprehension of the situation. Gradually, however, he probes deeply into the personality of Ursula, who admits that she is guilty of everything and anything just to put an end to the present state of things. Greedy for life, she scorns her pitiful clients, and her inability to help them—even when she sleeps with them—is precisely what drives them to suicide; not only that, but she takes advantage of the situation by arranging that they make her their heir. Confronted with the inspector's indignation, she defies him to give her clients a new taste for life. The inspector then calls them together, provokes them into confessing their miseries, and tries to bring them out of their complacent world-weariness. His tactics lead to yet another suicide. He therefore decides to close the inn and send all the clients home under supervision. Ursula, in any case, has already sold the inn. She suggests that the inspector become her partner in order to "wake up" the town by building factories and day nurseries. After having refused to allow a last client to enter the inn, Ursula and the inspector spend the night together.

The play's center of interest is the confrontation of the inspector, a methodical civil servant, and Ursula, a free and strong woman trapped by the weak who need her and whom she can only lead to suicide. The general atmosphere of the play is strange, borders on the absurd, and sometimes recalls the works of Kafka. Although rather unsettling, Va donc chez Törpe has its very humorous moments (the scenes depicting the love affair between the inspector and his secretary, Opportune, for example) and manages, by means of a comical ending, to sidestep despair.

**Valentin.** Pseudonym of Ensio RISLAKKI.

**Van Itallie, Jean-Claude** (born 1936). American playwright. Van Itallie was born in Brussels, Belgium, and was brought by his family to the United States in 1940; he grew up in Great Neck on Long Island, attended Deerfield Academy, graduated from Harvard in 1958, and moved to Greenwich Village, where he writes public affairs scripts for television and works with various off-off-Broadway theater groups. Since 1963 he has had plays produced by a number of experimental companies, such as The La MaMa Experimental Theatre Club, Caffè Cino, and the Open Theatre; among these are *War, Dreams, It's Almost Like Being, Where Is de Queen?, I'm Really Here, Thoughts on the Instant of Greeting a Friend on the Street,* and *The Serpent.* Best known of Van Itallie's work is the very popular *America Hurrah* (1966), three one-act plays which ran off-Broadway for over a year and have been produced in several foreign countries. In these plays the pernicious "illusion of eternal safety and universal happiness" that Van Itallie finds in the heart of the American suburbs, where he lived as a child after fleeing the German invasion of Belgium, is attacked by the exposition of an underlying violence in three major areas of "the American way of life": work (*Interview*), entertainment (*TV*), and travel (*Motel*). As a member of the Open Theatre, Van Itallie writes in a style that makes use of the various dramatic exercises of that group, especially transformations, where actors without warning or "reason" shift from role to role. In *Interview,* for example, four men and four women play what is in effect an entire city. The purpose is not efficiency in casting but rather to suggest that in this dehumanized situation people are interchangeable parts of a machine. Much of Van Itallie's work is available in paperback collections of off-off-Broadway theater.

**Vauthier, Jean** (born 1910). Belgian-born French dramatist. Vauthier spent his childhood in Portugal and studied in Bordeaux. He had at first intended to be a painter, but later switched to playwriting. Bada, the character around which his dramatic works are centered, had been created by him, he says, in 1947. But it was not until Vauthier became known for his work on the Arras Festival of 1951 that his first play, CAPITAINE BADA (1952), was performed. He has written seven plays and one film script, *Les Abysses* (1963).

Vauthier's works are characterized by a deluge of words and an almost invariable atmosphere of paroxysm. Whether at grips with one or several women (*Capitaine Bada; Les Prodiges* [The Marvels], 1959), or in search of an imaginatively creative past (*Le Personnage combattant* [The Fighting Character], 1956), or caught up in an Elizabethan-type revenge tragedy (*Sang, fête théâtrale* [Blood, a Theatrical Festival], 1970), Vauthier's heroes, often called Bada, try desperately to attain salvation or self-fulfillment. Their means to this end are long, exasperated analyses, a good deal of shrieking, and bursts of burlesque activity.

Their exasperation, the result of inner torture and the frenzy of their language, alternates between the grotesque and the sublimely tragic. Essentially, these characters are monstrous egotists, altogether absorbed in their resentment against everything that stands in the way of their plans for salvation: their own impotence, the resignation of others—especially women— and the world of objects, all of which, explicitly or metaphorically, represent the poet at grips with the illusions, difficulties, and frustrations of the creative act.

Vauthier's art may be compared to both music and bullfighting: His plays are composed like frantic oratorios, with the movement regulated as in a ballet, during which the characters try to reach a moment of truth, an exorcism, or the death blow.

OTHER PLAYS: *La Nouvelle Mandragore* (The New Mandrake, 1952), *L'Impromptu d'Arras* (1953), *Le Rêveur* (The Dreamer, 1961).

**Venezuela.** Venezuela began to awaken from its slumber in the field of drama in 1950. The influence of the Uruguayan director Horacio Peterson and the Argentine actress Juana Sujo were strengthened by the foundation in 1954 of the Venezuelan Theater Foundation, a coalition of experimental groups. The three national drama festivals of 1959, 1961, and 1966 were extremely important in focusing activity, and today there are many young writers and a substantial number of experimental groups, each with its own specialty. There is a special coloration to the Venezuelan movement as a result of the nation's internal political difficulties and a wave of terrorism, all of which has found expression in the theater.

The three most important playwrights are César Rengifo, Román Chalbaud, and Isaac Chocrón. Rengifo is preoccupied with social inequity and moral ambiguity; his earliest works were Marxist realism, followed by a pronounced Brechtian influence. Now seeking greater formal complexity, Rengifo at his best achieves a sense of sweep and depth, but his work is often dangerously close to the political pamphlet. Chalbaud is sometimes more empathic than Rengifo, and his works have provoked great controversy. Chalbaud's defenders attribute his problems with censorship to his extreme political attitudes; his detractors point to his insistence on scabrous themes. *Requiem para un eclipse* (1959) and *Sagrado y obsceno* (1961) utilized the themes of innocence and vice as vehicles for political and social denunciation. Chalbaud is at his best in such works as *La quema de Judas* (The Burning of Judas, 1964), where his political insistence is controlled and his characters surprisingly human.

A common theme for all three playwrights is the need for communication on an immediate human level. This is, for example the theme of Chocrón's *Mónica y el florentino* (1959). The best of the three, Chocrón is capable of drawing excellent dramas out of the solitude and failure of people who cannot act from love (*El quinto infierno* [The Fifth Hell], 1961), or of creating a work of total theater (*Asia y lejano oriente* [Asia and the Far East], 1966), or of experimenting with open forms (*Tric Trac*, 1967). Like Chalbaud and Rengifo, Chocrón is a "committed" author; unlike them, he achieves a theatrical integration of commitment and art.

Among other dramatists, the most important are José Ignacio Cabrujas, basically social in his orientation, Rodolfo Santana Salas, Gilberto Pinto, Elizabeth Schön, who prefers subjective fantasy, and Manuel Trujillo, whose social content is expressed formally in the idiom of the absurd. At the moment, the Venezuelan movement is one of the most vigorous in terms of the large number of active young dramatists who give promise for the future.

**Vian, Boris** (1920–1959). French dramatist. Born in Ville d'Avray, near Versailles, Vian prepared to enter the Ecole Centrale, an engineering school. As a teen-ager, however, he had developed a taste for jazz and, in spite of a serious heart condition, had learned to play the trumpet. After the war, he performed with several groups in the *caves* of St.-Germain-des-Prés. His writings, some still unpublished, are extremely varied: poems, songs, short stories, criticism, novels, translations, librettos, scenarios, and four plays. He died in 1959 of a heart attack while watching the showing of a film drawn from his novel *J'irai cracher sur vos tombes*.

During his lifetime Boris Vian was known, above all, in the world of St.-Germain-des-Près, and in 1946 was a regular contributor, with his "Chronique du Menteur," to Jean-Paul Sartre's monthly *Les Temps Modernes*. He became more widely known almost uniquely because of the scandal created by *J'irai cracher sur vos tombes* (published in 1946 under the pseudonym Vernon Sullivan), a sadistic parody of the American novel, which was banned in 1949 for immorality. During the '60s Vian's works were discovered by scholars and by French youth. In 1963 his last novel, *L'Ecume des jours*, was reissued and sold 150,000 copies in five years. Recent studies and articles on Vian have made him into a kind of myth and have shown him to be one of the most fascinating literary figures of the postwar period.

Vian's works, often very tender, are permeated with " 'pataphysics"—that is, an anarchical and humoristic vision of the world, which derives from Alfred Jarry. This nonconformity is most particularly apparent in *L'Equarrisage pour tous* (The Knacker's ABC, 1944), a burlesque and nonsensical play about the Allies' landing in 1944, and in *Le Goûter des généraux* (The Generals' Tea Party, 1965), in which military leaders behave like children, create a war to amuse themselves, and end by all committing suicide during a game of Russian roulette.

Vian's best play is *Les Bâtisseurs d'empire* (The Empire Builders), in three acts, first performed by the Théâtre National Populaire on December 22, 1959, a few months after his death. From act to act the spectator witnesses the flight of a family threatened by mysterious invaders. As the family climbs from apartment to apartment, each smaller than the last, it too grows smaller, until in Act III only the father is left, accompanied by a vaguely human creature, ugly and bloody, covered with bandages—the "schmürz." During the entire play the silent schmürz has no function other than to receive blows from the members of the family. The schmürz dies right before the end of the play, just as the invaders are about to enter the apartment—and they, perhaps, are schmürzes. This play is one of the best postwar theatrical metaphors of the anguish of death, the shrinking of the possibilities of life with the passing of time, and the absurd threats which, from within or without, weigh upon man. The schmürz is a striking invention, a sufficiently concrete yet vague symbol of a general malaise that provokes our hatred and our unhappiness.

OTHER PLAYS: *Le Dernier des Métiers* (The Lowest of Jobs, 1964).

**Vidal, Gore** (born 1925). American novelist and scriptwriter. Vidal was born at West Point, New York, where his father was an army instructor in aeronautics, and graduated from Phillips Exeter Academy (1943). He won some attention after World War II as a clever, slightly shocking new novelist. Among his novels are *Williwaw* (1946), *In a Yellow Wood* (1947), *The City and the Pillar* (1948), *The Season of Comfort* (1949), *A Search for the King* (1950), *Dark Green, Bright Red* (1950), *The Judgment of Paris* (1952), *Messiah* (1954), *Julian* (1964), *Washington, D.C.* (1967), and *Myra Breckinridge* (1968). He also has a book of short stories, *A Thirsty Evil* (1956), two books of essays, *Rocking the Boat* (1962) and *Reflections upon a Sinking Ship* (1969). He has written a number of TV plays (he was awarded the Edgar Allan Poe Award for TV in 1955) and several screenplays (*The Catered Affair* in 1956, *I Accuse!* in 1958, *The Scapegoat* and, with Tennessee Williams, *Suddenly Last Summer* in 1959). He has done four plays for the stage. *Visit to a Small Planet*, an expansion of his 1955 TV play, was a success on Broadway in 1957, a science-fiction comedy reminiscent of J. B. Priestley's time fantasies, rather clumsily anti-war in its easy satire of Earthlings. This was followed in 1960 by *The Best Man*, a play about politics, and in 1962 by an adaptation of Düerrenmatt's play *Romulus*. In 1968 *Weekend* had a brief run on Broadway. Vidal is by admission a novelist who writes scripts for a living.

**Vie imaginaire de l'éboueur Auguste G., La** (The Imaginary Life of the Garbage Collector Auguste G., 1962). A play in four parts by Armand Gatti. First performed, with the initial G in the title changed to "Geai," on February 16, 1962, at the Théâtre de la Cité, Villeurbanne, it was directed by Jacques Rosner. Inspired by the childhood and subsequent life of the writer's father, this complex play is built around the death of a forty-six-year-old garbage collector, wounded during a strike in the suburbs of a large city in the 1930s. The garbage collector, Auguste G., relives his childhood, his war years, his loves, and his marriage, deforming them in his imagination. He even pictures himself still alive at the age of sixty, watching a film being made by his son Christian. The film, which tells about his heroic life and death as a revolutionary worker, has certain episodes that are not only being filmed but are also a part of reality.

Times in this play have been systematically juxtaposed. On stage there are six "acting spaces" in different colors. In the main one, which is black, Auguste G. is dying. In the others, at the very same time, one sees Auguste G. at nine, at twenty-one, at thirty, and at an imaginary sixty. Around the protagonist at these six stages of his life are some thirty main characters and an indeterminate number of extras. The present and the past, reality and possibility, are constantly interfering with one another. Life in a cosmopolitan and poverty-stricken suburb, with its struggles, suicides, and brawls, is symbolized by a fantastic dance marathon led by an orchestra of the local Riot Police. The establishment is embodied in the White Baron, who has the power to put down the strike as well as to prohibit Christian's film.

By scenically setting up a conflict between the real and the imaginary, the subjective and the objective, the despair of the present and hope for the future, Gatti has managed to transform a document on the poor into spectacular theater. With no indulgence for man's behavior, Gatti explores it by means of dialogue in counterpoint and makes it into one moment in the dialectic of revolution, which he represents as a both realistic and fantastic kind of circus. Thus, through a scenic synthesis of time and place, he illustrates, in his own way, the revolutionary formula according to which "a life is worth nothing, but nothing is worth a life" (Malraux).

Ville dont le prince est un enfant, La (The City Whose Prince Is a Child, 1967). A three-act play by Henry de Montherlant. It was first performed on December 8, 1967, at the Théâtre Michel, Paris, under the direction of Jean Meyer. Published in 1951, this play, with its biblical title (Ecclesiastes 10:16), was not authorized by Montherlant to be performed until 1967 because of the extreme delicacy of the subject matter. In a Catholic school near Paris, one of the masters, Abbé de Pradts, has called young Serge Sandrier, aged fourteen, to his office. He demands that Sandrier, whom he has taken under his protection, terminate all friendly relations with a pupil in a higher class, André Sevrais, who is over sixteen and who he fears has a bad influence on Sandrier. Sevrais then comes to Abbé de Pradts to suggest that he will change the tenor of his intense friendship with Sandrier and do everything in his power to improve the younger boy, who is a bad student and undisciplined. Pradts agrees, and the two boys make a date to meet in a shack nearby in order to discuss the style of their new relationship. Act II takes place in the shack. Sevrais is ready to devote himself completely to his new mission. In order to seal their friendship, they mix their blood. When they suddenly see Abbé de Pradts arriving, Sandrier panics and hides in a corner. The Abbé finds him and decides that the meeting of the two boys is a sign of Sevrais' deception and the grave dangers of their relationship. In Act III Sevrais learns that he has been expelled from school. Moreover, the Abbé demands that he never see Sandrier again. Sevrais, agonized, nevertheless agrees to the sacrifice. The school Superior comes to discuss the explusion with Abbé de Pradts, who justifies it by declaring that it was meant for the good of all: Sandrier had to be saved, and Sevrais' soul would be strengthened by his painful sacrifice. When he hears the children's choir singing offstage, the Abbé is surprised that he cannot make out Sandrier's voice. The Superior informs him that Sandrier also has been expelled and that he has already left the school. Abbé de Pradts is shattered by grief. Thus the Superior understands that the Abbé's attachment to Sandrier, rather than that of a priest to a soul he must form and save, is a very human passion. The Abbé will sacrifice himself, as he forced Sevrais to do, in order to find the prodigious love that is directed not to the creature but to the Creator, and next to which "all the rest is nothing."

The dramatic interest of La Ville is based upon the ambiguity of a priest's spiritual paternity. In the case of Abbé de Pradts, his lofty morals and the demands of his religion are undermined by a poison—the very poison he believes he has perceived in the sentimental friendship between Sevrais and Sandrier. The tragic irony of the play, which is highly characteristic of Montherlant's works, lies in the fact that, at the end, the Abbé discovers within himself the precise weakness for which he had condemned Sevrais.

Many critics consider La Ville the best of Montherlant's plays, first because, in dealing with a subject that might have been scandalous, Montherlant produced a tragedy of self-sacrifice and self-knowledge, and second because the play is written and composed with rigor and purity—indeed, with the simplicity and directness characteristic of French classical tragedy.

**Virta, Nikolai Evgenievich** (born 1906). Soviet dramatist. Born in Tambov, Virta worked as a shepherd and as a village clerk before becoming a journalist in 1923. His first play, Moy drug polkovnik (My Friend the Colonel, 1942), was based on his observations at the front during World War II. Velikie gni (Great Days, 1947) and Zagovor obrechyonnykh (Conspiracy of the Doomed, 1947–48) treated the anti-Western themes popular in the late 1940s. Khleb nash nasushchny (Our Daily Bread, 1947) depicted life on a collective farm. The three latter plays all won Stalin prizes. Virta had a leading role in enunciating the "no-conflict theory" in Soviet drama, which stated that social conflicts could not exist in a socialist society and should therefore not be included in Soviet plays.

**Vishnevsky, Vsevolod Vitalevich** (1900–1951). Soviet dramatist and novelist. Vishnevsky took part in the October 1917 Bolshevik revolution in Petrograd (later Leningrad) and fought in the civil war from 1918 to 1920. His career as a dramatist began with Sud nad Kronshtadskimi myatezhnikami (The Trial of the Kronstadt Mutineers, 1923), dealing with the revolt against Bolshevik rule in March 1921 by Red Navy sailors at the Kronstadt naval base. His other plays include: Pervaya konnaya (First Cavalry, 1929), based on his experiences in the civil war; Posledny reshitelny (The Final Decisive, 1931) and Optimicheskaya tragediya (Optimistic Tragedy, 1932), both dramas of the struggle against opponents of the young Bolshevik regime; U sten Leningrada (At the Walls of Leningrad, 1943), about the wartime siege of Leningrad; and Nezabyvaemy 1919-y (Unforgettable 1919, 1949), which lauded Stalin's role in the Bolshevik revolution and won a Stalin prize in 1950.

Visit, The (Der Besuch der alten Dame, 1956). A tragicomedy in three acts by Friedrich Dürrenmatt. The major theme in all of Dürrenmatt's plays has centered around man's quest for justice. Here he turns this noble quest into a manhunt which ends in revenge. Ironically, this travesty of justice gives rise to a sense of outrage, which in turn provokes the audience to think about the relative basis of justice.

The play begins at the railroad station of the town Güllen somewhere in Central Europe. The setting and the name of the town are important. The station is a decrepit shack, and the buildings in the background are equally run-down. Güllen, which means "liquid manure" in German, is nothing but a dung heap. The men in front of the shack discuss the enigmatic decline of the town's fortunes, and they look forward to the arrival of Mme Claire Zachanassian, the richest woman in the world, in the hope that she can help them. She had left Güllen forty-five years ago, and the townspeople are preparing a grand welcome to show their love for her. Alfred Ill, owner of the general store, who was once Claire's lover, has been selected by the town dignitaries to wine and dine her so that she will contribute some of her millions to the reconstruction of Güllen. If Ill succeeds, he will become the next mayor, and Ill is confident that he will succeed if everything goes according to plan. However, the "laws of nature" are upset when the express train makes an unannounced stop and Claire Zachanassian suddenly appears. Her figure alone provides a sharp contrast to the poverty-stricken people of Güllen. She is a sixty-three-year-old redhead dressed to kill. She is adorned with a pearl necklace, enormous gold spangles, and artificial limbs. In addition, there is her entourage, which also contradicts all the laws of nature. The group consists of the butler, Boby, about eighty years old, wearing dark glasses; Moby, Claire's doting seventh husband, dressed in an angler's outfit; Roby and Toby, two huge, gum-chewing gangsters, who carry Claire in a sedan chair; Koby and Loby, two blind eunuchs who speak in unison; and various servants who bear a black panther in a cage and a black coffin.

Claire Zachanassian responds graciously to the clumsy efforts of the surprised townspeople and even calls Ill by his old nickname, "black panther." It would seem that Claire is favorably disposed toward Ill and the townspeople. However, Claire's remarks have double meanings. Ill is in actuality no longer Claire's black panther, and yet he will soon become her black panther again— to be hunted and killed. This hunt is only anticipated in the opening scene. After the welcome celebration, Claire guides Ill to Konrad's Village Wood where they used to make love. They reminisce about their youth, and the reminiscence turns into a grotesque love scene with Ill trying to bring back their love but succeeding only in kissing Claire's artificial hand.

Claire has had numerous accidents since her departure from Güllen, and she has in the interim been stitched together as a "new woman," an awesome, synthetic, crude creature, who has returned to the scene of her first "accident" to demand justice. This purpose is disclosed to a congregation of people: Güllen will receive one billion dollars, five hundred million for the town and five hundred million to be shared among each family. One condition: She wants to buy justice. Her butler Boby reveals himself to be the former Chief Justice Courtly, who had arbitrated a paternity claim involving Ill and Claire forty-five years ago. At that time, Ill denied paternity and called upon two witnesses, Louis Perch and Jacob Chicken, who swore they had slept with Claire. These two now step forward as the blind eunuchs Koby and Loby, and claim that Ill bribed them to swear a false oath. They have been punished by Claire with blindness and castration. Boby now asks Claire what happened to her baby. She states that it died a year after she had given birth, at which time she became a prostitute. Now she demands justice, and her justice is one billion dollars for Güllen if someone kills Ill. The mayor rejects Claire's offer in the name of the citizens of Güllen and humanity. He asserts that they would rather be poor than to have blood on their hands. Claire's response: "I'll wait."

Act II begins in Ill's general store. As the townspeople enter and charge their purchases to their accounts, Ill gradually becomes aware that they are all wearing new shoes and they are all banking on his death. Across from the general store in the Golden Apostle Hotel, Claire Zachanassian bides her time by preparing for her marriage with husband number eight and by expediting her business affairs with firms throughout the world. Ill demands that the police arrest Claire for inciting to kill, but the policeman rationalizes the situation. When he receives a phone call about Claire's black panther, which is on the loose, the policeman loads his rifle to recapture it. Ill realizes that he is the real object of the hunt, and soon the entire town begins to stalk him. Ill pleads for help, but the priest can only advise him to flee after the real panther is shot. Like the panther, Ill is hounded by his hunters, the townspeople, who encircle him at the railroad station and prevent his escape. Ill realizes that he is lost.

Act III begins in a barn. Claire Zachanassian has just completed her eighth marriage and has retired to the barn for peace and quiet. The schoolmaster and the doctor come to Claire and plead Güllen's case in the name of humanity. They do not want to kill Ill. They are convinced that the town's business would flourish again if they had the proper credit and financing. However, Claire reveals that she purposely bought these business firms and caused their bankruptcy. As far as humanity is concerned, she states: "Feeling for humanity, gentlemen, is cut for the purse of an ordinary millionaire; with financial resources like mine you can afford a new world order. The world turned me into a whore. I shall turn the world into a brothel." Indeed, Ill has recognized that Claire will succeed, and he has withdrawn to prepare himself for the execution, which will be celebrated as a ritual by the town. The hunt has been successful; a sacrifice will be made to the gods. Reporters come to Güllen for the great event, and the town bustles with newborn activity. Ill

464

has accepted his guilt and has decided to abide by a decision to be reached at a public meeting concerned with his fate. The mayor wants him to commit suicide, but Ill refuses: "I conquered my fear. Alone. It was hard, and now it's done. There is no turning back. You *must* judge me now. I shall accept your judgment whatever it may be. For me it will be justice; what it will be for you, I do not know." Before the meeting, Ill takes a drive with his family in their new car and then meets Claire once again at Konrad's Village Wood. Ill acknowledges that he has accepted his sentence and that his meaningless life will end. Claire admits that her love for him grew into an evil thing because it could not live or die. After this, Ill attends the public meeting, which is broadcast to the world. Under the cover of accepting Claire Zachanassian's donation of one billion dollars to Güllen for the sake of justice, the townspeople vote to give Ill his due. The reporters, cameramen, and majority of the audience leave the auditorium, and Ill is surrounded by the town dignitaries. Finally, the gym teacher strangles Ill, and the doctor pronounces him dead—of a heart attack. Claire Zachanassian comes to collect the corpse and writes out a check for the town. The play ends with the men and women of Güllen dressed in dark suits and evening gowns forming a chorus similar to one in a Greek tragedy. They sing a hymn of praise to Claire and God for restoring fortune and prosperous times to Güllen while Claire departs on a train bearing the black coffin with Ill's corpse.

Ill's murder transforms him into a symbol of justice. In fact, the entire play concerns transformation and justice. Dürrenmatt portrays justice as man-made, and he also sees that man is conditioned by socioeconomic factors. His play is not about the evil nature of small people but about the mutability and weakness of all people. Ill was not the only one guilty of driving Claire to prostitution. It was the entire town, and this is proven by the way the townspeople continue to prostitute themselves. If prostitution is the prime manner of human intercourse, then revenge is the only kind of satisfaction man can reap. Justice is impossible, and Dürrenmatt stresses the collective guilt of mankind in contributing to this situation.

In a later play, *The Physicists*, he stated: "Whatever concerns all can only be solved by all." *The Visit* offers no solution to the problem of attaining justice because the townspeople want to gain profit for themselves individually, and in so doing, they deplete their own natural resources. They must sell themselves to the highest bidder like prostitutes. Here the highest bidder is Claire Zachanassian, the crassest reflection of themselves.

The language and structure of the play serve to heighten the contrast between justice and revenge, between humanity and barbarism. The grotesque figures, the contradictions in the behavior and speech of the people, and their wretchedness in their wretched setting are part of a world turned upside down. The distortions in the action and setting mirror the moral turpitude of a town that has prostituted itself, a town that has fallen apart. The breakdown is,

# W

**Waiting for Godot** (*En Attendant Godot,* 1953). A two-act play by Samuel Beckett. It was first performed on January 5, 1953, at the Théâtre Babylone, Paris, under the direction of Roger Blin. The reaction to *En Attendant Godot* in 1953 was very mixed, for most of the public found that it did not correspond to what is ordinarily called a play and was baffled by the mixture of clownish tricks and metaphysical implications. Now it is one of the most renowned plays of the second half of the twentieth century; it attracts audiences of all ages and all classes; it has been performed throughout the Western world and behind the Iron Curtain; and it had great success with the prisoners at San Quentin (November 19, 1957).

The action—or, rather, the absence of any action—takes place on a country road, in a flat and bare landscape, next to a small bare tree. The two main characters are listed in the program as Estragon and Vladimir, but they call each other Gogo and Didi. They are both tramps wearing costumes that recall the way Charlie Chaplin's "Little Man" was dressed early in the twentieth century: large shoes, bowler hats. Vladimir is the more intellectual of the two: He wonders about their pasts and their relationship as friends. Estragon is concerned only about his present state—most particularly his shoes, which hurt his feet and which he has trouble taking off. Not that Vladimir doesn't also have his little afflictions: There are vermin in his hat, and he has great and painful difficulty in urinating. But one of his main concerns at the beginning of the play is the discrepancy in the Gospel in which only one of the evangelists says that one of the two thieves crucified with Jesus was saved. The reason the tramps remain near the tree, conversing, is that, as Vladimir puts it, they are "waiting for Godot," who apparently has promised them work and protection. But are they waiting in the right place? Is it the right day? Have they ever come to this place before? These questions trouble Vladimir but tire Estragon. To pass the time, Estragon suggests that they hang themselves from the tree; but they decide to give up this plan, because if one of them happened to survive, he would remain alone. So they had just better wait for Godot. Their conversation is interrupted by the spectacular arrival on-stage of Pozzo and his slave, Lucky, bound to his master by a long rope attached to his neck. Pozzo is dressed like a kind of gentleman farmer, holding a whip, and Lucky, like a valet, carrying a suitcase, a basket, and a folding chair, and wearing a bowler hat. At first the tramps think Pozzo may be Godot. Pompous and domineering, he consents to consider the tramps as human beings and decides to stop for a moment. At first touched by Lucky, who they think is being treated inhumanly, the tramps begin to feel differently when Lucky gives Estragon a swift kick and Pozzo claims to suffer because of his slave. Pozzo, doing everything he can to become the center of attraction, gives a theatrical description of twilight, which is, in fact, an image of the death that awaits us all. The tramps' attention is diverted to Lucky when they learn that he is able to dance and to think. But whereas in the past Lucky had danced jigs and fandangos, he now merely breaks out into painful contortions, recalling those of a man caught in a net. When Pozzo orders him to think, which he can do only with his hat on, Lucky launches into a very long and apparently meaningless monologue concerned with some distant, white-bearded God and the "fading away" of man in spite of science and sports. Delivered without interruption, and more and more mechanically, the speech makes the other three characters suffer to such a degree that they throw themselves on Lucky and make him stop by removing his hat. Pozzo then decides to continue on his way and trots off the stage, snapping his whip and preceded by Lucky, who is still at the end of a rope. The two tramps wonder whether they had not already met Pozzo and Lucky. Toward the end of the act a young boy appears and announces that Godot will not come that evening but will surely be there tomorrow. Questioned by Vladimir, the boy gives some information on how Godot treats him. The act ends with night falling and the moon rising almost instantaneously, and with Gogo and Didi exchanging vague recollections of their life together. They decide to leave the place for the night—but remain motionless.

According to the printed text, Act II takes place the next day. Yet the tree onstage is now covered with leaves. Vladimir is more nervous; Estragon has trouble remembering the events of Act I and doubts that they happened the day before. While waiting for Godot, their words and restless activities become more and more insignificant. Estragon has an increasing desire to sleep, and Vladimir rocks him. They indulge in clownish distractions and insult each other to pass the time. A one point they get panic-stricken, thinking they are surrounded. Suddenly they call for God's pity, which Estragon wants ex-clusively for himself. Immediately afterward, Pozzo and Lucky reappear. Pozzo is now blind and the rope is much shorter. They no sooner enter than both characters sink to the ground and are incapable of getting up. After long deliberation and having been promised money by Pozzo, Gogo and Didi decide to help them. But they also fall down, first Didi, then Gogo. They get up after much hesitation and help Pozzo to do the same. He is unable to enlighten the tramps as to what happened the day before, but tells them that Lucky is mute. The question "Since when?" makes no sense to Pozzo; for him everything—birth and death—happens on the same day, at the same moment. Once they leave, Estragon feels even sleepier, while Vladimir reflects on Pozzo's words. Enter the young boy of Act I, again announcing that Godot will not come that evening. We learn that Godot has a white beard. Night falls and the moon rises instantaneously. Gogo and Didi decide to hang themselves with the rope that serves as Estragon's belt. The rope breaks. They decide to hang themselves the next day—unless Godot comes. The act ends with the same lines as did Act I: "*Vladimir.* Well, shall we go? *Estragon.* Yes, let's go." And they do not move.

The absence of any action, in the traditional sense of the word, gives great importance to the characters' slightest gestures and comments. Everything stands out against the emptiness at the heart of the play, but so is everything reduced to insignificance: eating a carrot, picking up a shoe, discussing the Bible, trying to hang oneself, and so forth. The use of vaudeville business (the pantomime of exchanging hats or shoes, for example) is thus both comical and despairing, for it reduces the so-called serious activities of life to the level of a grotesque routine. In the state of unfulfilled waiting, nothing one does while waiting has any value in itself. And this state is clearly the same as that of waiting in a world where God is announced but never comes. In this play the matter at hand is less the nonexistence of God than his absence. That "God" is the root of Godot is obvious; the allusion to Christ and the thieves confirms the playwright's metaphysical intentions; and the young boy may be compared to an angel, but one who brings bad news. However, more broadly, this white-bearded Godot is an image of whatever men happen to be waiting for and which never comes—in daily life as in metaphysical life. In this world reduced to insignificance by the absence of whatever is awaited, events are repeated but at the same time worsen. The distress and boredom in Act II are the same as in Act I but intensified, as are the few specific personality traits of the characters. This gradual deterioration concerns not only the metaphysical world but also society and history: It is one of the meanings of the master-slave couple, Pozzo and Lucky, who are increasingly bound to each other and increasingly powerless. The play is also a poetic meditation on time, which is both interminable in a state of waiting and reduced to the moment when one thinks of birth and death; in either case it is experienced tragically and leads to absolute confusion.

Essentially related to the theater of the absurd, *En Attendant Godot* has nevertheless retained certain of the so-called "human" elements of traditional theater. Gogo's lethargy, childish caprices, and longing to return to the womb, Didi's bursts of dignity and protective affection, and the mixture of tenderness, reciprocal need, and rejection in both characters make them three-dimensional, however sketchy their natures.

Purely on the level of form, *Godot* has great beauty. Although it is filled with allusions to a whole culture (the Bible, Greek tragedy, Dante, James

Joyce), those allusions are totally assimilated into the clear flow of the play. The dialogue is simple and precise; indeed, certain exchanges of the two tramps recall the counterpoint of two instruments answering each other in the twilight of a world that never stops ending.

**Walser, Martin** (born 1927). West German dramatist, novelist, and essayist. Like many of his contemporaries, Walser has been greatly influenced by Brecht. Yet it is not only Brecht who stamps his works, but Kafka, who served as the subject of his doctoral dissertation at the University of Tübingen. In all his plays and novels, Walser reveals a predilection for the parable and the allegory. His foremost concern is to make the private public in a political sense. Hence, he is constantly seeking new ways to portray family problems that reflect contradictions in society as a whole.

Walser's first play, *Der Abstecher* (The Side Trip, 1961), deals with a rich businessman, Hubert, who suddenly decides to visit his former mistress, Frieda, while on a business trip. He hopes that he can relive warm memories, but Frieda is married to a locomotive engineer named Erich. She criticizes Hubert for abandoning her in a cowardly fashion, and Erich supports her. Hubert, however, talks his way out of the dilemma and convinces Erich in a "man to man" talk that he never meant to harm Frieda. The play is framed by a prologue and epilogue that involve two discussions with Hubert and his chauffeur Berthold, who as a human being wants to criticize his employer but as an employee restrains himself. The situation here is reminiscent of Brecht's *Herr Puntila und sein Knecht Matti*, but the revolutionary content is lacking. Walser simply paints a negative picture of people wallowing in their cowardice. Walser's most significant play, *Eiche und Angorra* (The Oak and the Angora, 1962), is also a "negative version" of a Brecht play, *Der brave Soldat Schweyk im zweiten Weltkrieg*. Walser labels the play a "German chronicle." In a series of scenes dating from 1945 to the present, he depicts the development of Alois, who is caught in a process of deterioration. Alois is always a step behind his times. When others have become Nazis, he is still a Communist. When others have become good democrats, he is still a Nazi. This retardation has led to Alois' castration by the Nazis in a concentration camp. After his release from prison, he saves his town from destruction and in the postwar era wants nothing more than to join the men's singing club as countertenor and raise Angora rabbits with Jewish names. Gorbach, the corpulent and intimidating mayor of the town, constantly manipulates Alois for his own gain. Either he uses Alois' voice to win singing competitions, or he sends Alois to mental institutions to cure his backward ideological thinking, which embarrasses the town. In the final act, Alois is not permitted to sing for the men's club because his voice as a castrato brings back memories of the Nazi past. In defiance, he kills his Angora rabbits and hangs their furs on a flagpole. At the play's close Alois is sent to another asylum and his wife, who has become an alcoholic, is sent for a cure. Walser's play is not only a grotesque portrayal of the Philistine life, but, as he says, of the Fascist and capitalist systems. The actions of the characters in the play reveal their attempts to adapt to the ideological and social standards that determine their lives. The respected citizen's ability to conform and adapt as shown by the actions of Gorbach is in actuality no different from Alois' inability to move with the times. Both are victimized by the state. They never overcome the past but regress.

In most of his plays Walser stresses the importance of overcoming the past by exposing the futility and frustration of little men's lives in the present. In *Überlebensgross, Herr Krott* (More Than Life-Size, Mr. Krott, 1964) he portrays a huge, fat businessman as he sits on the terrace of his luxurious house. As his two mistresses and other characters appear on the scene, he tries to conquer his boredom by provoking his subordinates into rebellion. However, not one of the people or organizations with which he deals will provide him the pleasure of rebellion, and he is left in a state of despair. In *Der schwarze Schwann* (The Black Swan, 1964) the twenty-year-old son of a doctor who runs a mental institution confronts his father with crimes committed in a concentration camp during World War II. In doing this, he also confronts himself and others. Like a German postwar Hamlet, he cannot piece the world together, and he eventually hangs himself.

Walser's most recent plays have become less blatantly political. Nevertheless, his criticism of private habits is always motivated in a political sense. In *Die Zimmerschlacht* (The Battle in the Room, 1967), a married couple, Trude and Felix Fürst, forty-eight years old, prepare to go out for the evening. While they are getting dressed, they bicker and fight. Using lies to protect themselves, they eventually tear at the truth. In the second act, fifteen years later, they are in a similar situation but more adept at playing the war game. The battle is intended to expose the petty and desperate nature of their lives, and at the same time to reveal the lies that allow them to continue living. Walser realizes that human beings need lies and illusions, even though they are aware of the truth. They are victims of social and political determination, and as such, they are not despicable, but, as in Edward Albee's *Who's Afraid of Virginia Woolf?*, heroically pathetic. Though Walser's drama about private life can be compared with Albee's play, they are basically different. Walser understands awareness and neurosis as a reflection of political conditioning, while Albee harks back to Freud. In effect, both playwrights are critics of the sickness stemming from bourgeois society in the late capitalist stage.

OTHER PLAYS: *Welche Farbe hat das Morgenrot* (What Color Does Dawn Have, 1969), *Das Kinderspiel* (The Children's Game, 1970).

**Waterhouse, Keith** (born 1929). English novelist and dramatist. Born and educated in Leeds, Waterhouse worked as a journalist in that city and London from 1950 to 1958. He is a novelist whose works include *There Is a Happy Land* (1957), *Billy Liar* (1959), *Jubb* (1963), and *The Bucket Shop* (1968). In 1960 his partnership with dramatist Willis HALL began with an adaptation for the stage of *Billy Liar*. Since that date these two Leeds writers have collaborated on a number of successful works for the stage and screen, predominantly comedies with a North Country setting and an element of social comment.

**Weigel, Helene** (1900–1971). German actress and director. Born in Vienna, Miss Weigel began studying theater as an actress during her high school years, despite the opposition of her parents. After World War I she moved to Germany and acted in the cities of Frankfurt and Berlin. While rehearsing *Drums in the Night* at the Deutsches Theater in 1925, she met Bertolt Brecht, who admired her great natural ability on the stage. They found a great deal in common and were married in 1928. Miss Weigel starred in Brecht's productions of *A Man's a Man* (1926) and *The Mother* (1932) and performed in numerous other plays. In 1933 she accompanied Brecht in emigration and rarely appeared on stage. Two of her notable performances were the lead roles in *The Rifles of Señora Carrar* (1937) and *Fear and Misery of the Third Reich* (1938) in Paris. In 1948 she returned to Europe with Brecht, and the following year she helped him establish the Berliner Ensemble in East Berlin. Since her husband's death in 1956, she has continued to be one of the leading forces in the company. During the postwar period Miss Weigel achieved fame with her portrayal of Anna Fierling in *Mother Courage*, the governor's wife in *The Caucasian Chalk Circle*, Mrs. Luckerniddle in *Saint Joan of the Stockyards*, and Volumnia in Brecht's adaptation of *Coriolanus*. Most of Brecht's chief female figures have been embodied by Helene Weigel the actress, and each of these figures is a sovereign and resolute character whose life is entwined with a revolutionary movement. Miss Weigel's greatness as an actress sprang from her unique awareness of the woman's role in social struggles and how to convey the meaning of this role to audiences. It was this perspicacity that enabled her to develop Brecht's alienation technique and dialectics in acting to near perfection.

**Weingarten, Romain** (born 1926). French dramatist. Born in Paris of a Polish father and a Breton mother, Weingarten studied philosophy at the Sorbonne, then tried his hand at painting, and finally decided to devote himself to poetry, both in cabarets and in the theater, as writer, actor, and director. His first play, *Akara*, had only three performances in 1948. Ionesco later declared that he considered it one of the first important plays of the new theater. *Les Nourrices* (The Wet Nurses), in 1961, was no more successful. However, *L'Eté* (Summer)—first performed in Germany in 1965, then in Paris in November 1966—established Weingarten as a true poet of the theater.

Weingarten is clearly haunted by cats, which for him evoke a world of more or less nightmarish dreams. In *Akara* the cat is the symbolic victim of persecution. In *L'Eté* two cats (acted by men without masks or costumes) play with two children: a girl who dreams of love and an idiot boy who is able to converse with them. For six days and nights, one summer, the two cats and the two children are witnesses to the love affair of two adults who never appear on stage. Not really understanding what the adventure is all about, being animals or innocent children, the four characters react each in his own way, comically or touchingly. The comic scenes (quarrels between the two cats, the love of one of the cats for a fly named Manon) alternate with the touching moments (the painful lucidity of the idiot, the girl's distress when the lovers separate). *L'Eté* is in fact one of the strangest and most delicate plays of postwar poetic theater in France.

OTHER PLAYS: *Le Pain sec* (Dry Bread, 1967), *Alice aux Jardins du Luxembourg* (1970).

Weisenborn, Günther (1902–1969). German dramatist, novelist, essayist, and screenwriter. One of the most influential dramatists and most interesting political figures in Germany during the twentieth century, Weisenborn has never received the recognition due him on the international scene. He began writing dramas while still studying medicine and German literature at the University of Bonn. His first play, *U-Boot S 4* (Submarine S 4, 1928), a tragedy about six American sailors trapped in a submarine, was a resounding success. Weisenborn moved to Berlin, where he wrote *Die Arbeiter von Jersey* (The Workers of Jersey) in 1930 and collaborated with Brecht on *Die Mutter* (1931), an adaptation of Gorki's novel. Because of his opposition to the Nazi regime, Weisenborn's works were banned in Germany, and for a while he traveled in the Americas. During this period he wrote plays under a pseudonym in the hope of contributing to the anti-Fascist cause. In 1937 he returned to Germany to fight in the resistance movement. He was arrested by the Nazis is 1942 and incarcerated until 1945. After being freed by the Russians, Weisenborn made his way back to Berlin, where he founded the Hebbel-Theater along with Karl-Heinz Martin. In 1946 he produced *Die Illegalen* (The Illegal Ones), which painted one of the first pictures of a German underground group fighting the Nazis. His next significant drama was *Ballade vom Eulenspiegel, vom Federle und von der dicken Pompanne* (The Ballad of Eulenspiegel, Federle, and Fat Pompanne, 1949). Here Weisenborn took material from German legend, used elements from Brecht's epic theater, and transformed the traditional rogue Eulenspiegel into a radical fighter. Weisenborn also edited a magazine entitled *Eulenspiegel*, which was to serve a revolutionary cause. In 1951 Weisenborn was appointed chief dramaturge at the Hamburger Kammerspiele. He worked with playwrights, directors, and actors to find new dramatic forms. It was for this purpose that Weisenborn helped found the organization Deutsche Akademie der darstellenden Künste (German Academy of Performing Arts). During the 1950s and 1960s Weisenborn was drawn more and more to historical and documentary dramas. The *Göttinger Kantate* (1958) is a "documentary revue in the form of an oratorio" about the dangers of atomic and nuclear weapons. *Die Familie von Nevada* (The

Family from Nevada, 1958, revised as *Die Familie von Makabah,* 1961) is a historical portrayal of the problems involved in atomic research. *Unternehmen Walküre 44* (The Valkurie Undertaking of '44, 1966) is a documentary account of the attempt by officers to assassinate Hitler on July 20, 1944. Most of Weisenborn's dramas center on sociopolitical problems. Like Brecht, he believed in a theater that might help change conditions and make people aware of how they can build a socialist society. Though not the poet Brecht was, Weisenborn was a skilled craftsman and employed a clipped, dynamic language well suited to the characters he portrayed. His contributions to the German theater, however, go beyond his plays. He was an innovator in every sense of the word, and maintained a remarkable integrity while fighting at the forefront in Germany and in the German theater.

OTHER PLAYS SINCE 1945: *Babel* (1946), *Drei ehrenwerte Herren* (Three Honorable Men, 1951), *Die Spanische Hochzeit* (The Spanish Wedding, 1952), *Zwei Engel steigen aus* (Two Angels Climb Out, 1955), *Lofter oder das verlorene Gesicht* (Lofter, or The Lost Face, 1956), *15 Schnüre Geld* (Fifteen Strings of Money, 1959), *Li-Lifan* (1963), *Flachsmann als Erzieher* (Flachsmann as Educator, 1968).

**Weiss, Peter** (born 1916). German dramatist, painter, film director, and journalist. Forced into exile by the Nazis in 1934, Weiss was not at first aware of the horrors of Fascism and how it would affect his life. In fact, his main concern was with his own talents as a painter, and he was indifferent to the political crisis in Europe. During the 1930s he studied painting in Prague and London and experimented with various mannerist modes of portrayal. In 1939 he emigrated to Stockholm, where his father had opened a factory. Gradually he turned his attention toward making films and writing novels in Swedish. His development as an artist is recorded in a series of autobiographical novels, which have been translated into English: *Der Schatten des Körpers des Kutschers* (The Shadow of the Coachman's Body, 1961), *Abschied von den Eltern* (Leavetaking, 1961), *Fluchtpunkt* (Vanishing Point, 1962). These novels are significant because they reflect the change in Weiss's political consciousness and also his change in style. As Weiss broke from the bourgeois ties of his family and realized that this rebellion was connected with the political protest against Fascism and capitalism, his writing began to shun vague symbolism and became more concrete. This break can be noted also in comparing Weiss's plays written before 1962 with his later political dramas.

*Der Turm* (The Tower, 1948) reveals the strong influence of Kafka, in particular the short story "Das Urteil" (The Judgment). Pablo, a young escape artist, returns to the tower (the circus and also an obvious phallic symbol) where he once did a balancing act and suffered under oppressive conditions. At first Pablo denies his identity and wants to prove that he has grown and mastered a new art form. As escape artist, he allows himself to be bound, and, in the process of trying to undo the ropes, hangs himself. The play is a symbolic piece about freedom and rebellion, and it indicates in a self-indulgent manner how the umbilical cord of the family cannot be broken until the individual has gained a complete sense of his own freedom. In *Die Versicherung* (The Insurance, 1952), Weiss is even more surrealistic: His play is a grotesque parody of the bourgeois inclinations of a police chief, Alfons, who wants to insure himself against catastrophes and revolutions. His decision is made during a soiree at his house when everything is turned upside down. The second scene takes place in the clinic of Dr. Kübel, who had promised to treat the complaints of the people at the party. These people become Dr. Kübel's patients or victims, and his clinic comes to resemble a concentration camp. In the nineteen scenes that follow, Leo, a revolutionary, strangles the family dog, Pluto, in order to steal Erna, the wife of Alfons, and then, after seducing her, discards her in an ash can. Kübel tortures his patients. Alfons, who has been consoled by Hulda, the maid, goes to the barbershop, where his hair is dyed and his mustache cut. After this, his own policemen do not recognize him, and he is arrested and jailed. At the end of the farce, with a revolution in full swing, two workers promenade to the humming tune of sewing machines. Weiss's farcical nightmare exposes the animality and brutality of bourgeois conventions. That is, anarchy and irrationality, kept in order and insured by the ruling class, break through their seams, and the ruling class is destroyed by its own contradictions. Yet the bizarre scenes, which are reminiscent of the Marx Brothers' and Charlie Chaplin's slapstick films, are difficult to stage and their anarchy works against the ideology implicit in them.

In two other plays, written between 1962 and 1963, Weiss shows his fondness for surrealism and the grotesque. In *Nacht mit Gästen* (Night with Guests, 1963), a *Moritat* (ballad play), two children watch their mother and father killed by intruders because of gold. The father is accidentally murdered by a stranger who, coming to warn the family of a robber, mistakes the father for one. The mother is knifed by the real robber. Then the robber and the stranger fight over the gold. Meanwhile, the children open the chest and discover only carrots. They take some to eat and flee while the two men continue fighting. Because of the singsong rhythm of the words, the perspective of the play is that of the children, and their detachment from the incidents they observe is almost more horrifying than the horrors themselves. Weiss uses *Knittelvers* (doggerel) and ballads to attain a simplicity of style and clarity of view while presenting grotesque and terrifying events. In *Wie dem Herrn Mockinpott das Leiden ausgetrieben wird* (How the Pain Was Driven Out of Mister Mockinpott, 1963–1967), he stresses the political nature of certain brutal events. The bumbling, clownish Mockinpott is inexplicably arrested one day while on his way to buy the morning newspaper. Although he has committed no crime, he must bribe the lawyer and the police to gain his freedom. Seeking the cause of his false arrest, he visits his wife, who deceives him; his employer, who fires him; a doctor, who mistreats him; and the government, which confuses him. His pain grows, and he eventually goes to God, who is dressed in a tuxedo and smokes a cigar. When Mockinpott complains about his pain, God demands respect and offers nothing in return. In the end Mockinpott realizes that the inequities from which he suffers result from the existing social system, which he must deny. He no longer moves about like a clown but moves off gracefully on his own. The play is similar to Brecht's *Mann ist Mann*. Mockinpott, whose misery is mocked by singing angels in every scene, is remade into a man when he understands the political reasons for his misery. He is helped forward by the proletarian clown Hans Wurst, who comments ironically on the action of the play. Weiss's didactic drama uses the motif of the clown as in his earlier plays, but here he is more intent on bringing out the political message of the drama. This didacticism has been characteristic of his writing since 1963.

Although most critics tend to disregard the didacticism in Weiss's most famous play, *Die Verfolgung und Ermordung Jean-Paul Marats dargestellt durch die Schauspielgruppe des Hospizes zu Charenton unter Anleitung des Herrn de Sade* (*The Persecution and Assassination of Jean-Paul Marat as Performed by the Inmates of the Asylum of Charenton under the Direction of the Marquis de Sade*, known as *Marat/Sade*, 1964), it is most apparent that Weiss makes an important transition from the unhistorical to the historical, from the apolitical to the political. The play is an attack on the bourgeois class in three epochs: 1793, 1808, and the present. Weiss draws parallels between the debates of Marat and Sade, disputes about the revolution and society, and conditions in Europe today. The madhouse Charenton is, in fact, likened to contemporary Europe. Weiss is fond of images that recall concentration camps, and the revolutionary play-acting, which centers on Charlotte Corday's murder of Marat, and the debates between Marat and Sade lead to a revolt by the patients against the keepers of the asylum. It is against these Philistine upholders of the status quo (and in a sense against the audience) that Weiss vents his anger. This is also the case in *Die Ermittlung* (The Investigation, 1965), which marks his first full documentary presentation of a historical situation with strong Marxist overtones. Here Weiss, who writes most of his plays in verse, transforms a trial against the Auschwitz murderers into a prosecution of present-day Germans who deny knowing about the concentration camps and operate in a system that stimulates them to obliterate the past. By means of staging—the accused sometimes sit with the audience—Weiss confronts contemporary society with charges of criminal negligence and exploitation.

Weiss continued his Marxist approach to contemporary history in a semi-documentary play entitled *Gesang vom lusitanischen Popanz* (The Song of the Lusitanian Bogey, 1967), an attack on the imperialist rulers of Angola. Using music and documents, Weiss recalls the history of Portuguese exploitation in Angola before the native rebellion of March 15, 1961. He compares the situation in Angola to Fascism in Germany and racism in South Africa and the United States. Though Weiss's *Song* is about depressing conditions, it strikes a note of hope in depicting the struggle for freedom of the natives. When bogeymen claim the right to fight for progress by suppressing and "civilizing" undeveloped peoples by force, then there is, as Weiss sees it, no alternative for these peoples but to rebel against the imperialists.

This call for rebellion is clearly stated in another historical drama that contains political manifestos apparent in the title: *Diskurs über die Vorgeschichte und den Verlauf des lang andauernden Befreiungskrieges in Viet Nam als Beispiel für die Notwendigkeit des bewaffneten Kampfes der Unterdrückten gegen ihre Unterdrücker sowie über die Versuche der Vereinigten Staaten von Amerika die Grundlage der Revolution zu vernichten* (*Discourse on the Historical Background and the Course of the Continuous Struggle for Liberation in Viet Nam as an Example of the Necessity for Armed Warfare by the Oppressed against Their Oppressors and Furthermore on the Attempts of the United States of America to Annihilate the Basic Principles of the Revolution*, 1968). Using anonymous actors who constantly switch roles—a technique he employed successfully in *The Song of the Lusitanian Bogey*—Weiss demonstrates in eleven stages the struggles of the Vietnamese people from 500 B.C. to the present conflict. The epic production is an interesting Marxist analysis of Vietnamese history, but the conflicts are stripped bare of their complex contradictions so that the play becomes nothing more than a political pamphlet.

In *Trotzki im Exil* (Trotsky in Exile, 1970), Weiss turns to prose and social realism to examine the rise and fall of Leon Trotsky. In two acts and fifteen scenes, he stages a chronological account of Trotsky's life, employing flashbacks and a dialectical juxtaposition of scenes to argue that Trotsky was the real heir of Lenin and that despite his assassination in 1943, his international Marxism will eventually triumph over Stalinism. The play is filled with political debates about revolutionary tactics and philosophy. Many of the discussions pertain to contemporary issues, and Weiss purposely uses the play as a format to discuss his own revolutionary position. He sees the present revolution beginning again with the students, as it had at the onset of the century, and becoming international in nature, with the revolutionary party leading the proletariat and allowing for freedom of expression and production. Weiss's play is in many respects a fascinating portrait of Trotsky, rash in his youth, always courageous, and tireless in his old age, rarely thinking about himself but about the socialist cause. Still, the drama is too wordy and hampered by its argumentation in favor of Trotsky. Interestingly, it has been rejected in the Communist countries because of its leanings and accepted with qualifications in the West. Weiss apparently wrote the play as a challenge to both East and West. He has taken a stand as an international Marxist, one who continues his exile, though he would in reality like to end it.

**Wekwerth, Manfred** (born 1929). East German director. After working with various amateur groups, Wekwerth joined the Berliner Ensemble and began assisting Bertolt Brecht. In 1953 he was engaged to direct *The Mother* in Vienna, and after 1954 he gradually became one of the leading directors of the Berliner Ensemble. When Brecht died in 1955, Wekwerth assumed an important role in the directorate of the theater and endeavored to develop Brechtian dramaturgy, placing great emphasis on the alienation technique and dialectics. He has encouraged young East German dramatists, such as Helmut Baierl, whose play *Frau Flinz* he directed in 1961. Wekwerth has also written two important books dealing with drama and the work of the Berliner Ensemble: *Theater in Veränderung* (1960) and *Notate* (1967). He recently resigned from the Berliner Ensemble and has been engaged in developing another theater, the Volksbühne, in Berlin.

**Wesker, Arnold** (born 1932). English dramatist. After wartime evacuation from the East End of London, Wesker, the son of Jewish émigré parents, returned to finish his schooling in Hackney and then took up a variety of employments, which included furniture-making, carpentry, and work as a plumber's mate and kitchen porter. From 1950 to 1952 he served with the R.A.F. On his return to civilian life Wesker acquired the trade of pastrycook, which he followed for four years in Norwich, London, and Paris. Most aspects of the dramatist's early life and experiences find some reflection in his plays. It was not until 1957 that Wesker abandoned his full-time profession to follow a short course at the London School of Film Technique, and while there began writing, initially for the screen and later for the stage.

Wesker is among the dramatists whose early work was fostered by the English Stage Company. His first play, *Chicken Soup With Barley* (1958), was produced under their auspices at Coventry, and proved to be the first of three plays that eventually took shape as the *Roots* trilogy, a saga of the life of the Kahn family spanning more than twenty years. General recognition of Wesker's qualities as a dramatist dates from Joan Plowright's performance as Beatie Bryant in Roots (1959), the second play of the trilogy, which won the *Evening Standard* Award for the most promising playwright of 1960. Some inconsistencies in style and structure do not prevent this ambitious trilogy from displaying the features that have established Wesker as a leading but controversial figure among Britain's postwar dramatists. A socialist whose commitment is fundamental to his artistic as well as his political life, Wesker only rarely allows his doctrinaire beliefs to distort his view of humanity. The tension and conflict in his drama—not least in the *Roots* trilogy—spring from a contrast between the socialist view of man as a being capable of perfection and the actualities of human existence. In fact, Wesker's early work was widely regarded at the time as ushering in a new period of unflinching realism that portrayed the working classes as anything but the idealized heroes of the class war. With something of the anguish with which conventional religious beliefs were reconsidered after Darwin's *Origin of Species,* Wesker reappraises socialism in the light of the Hungarian experience and the materialism of Britain in the '50s, and maintains his principles as an article of deep-seated faith rather than of rational dialectics. The slow erosion of socialist ideals exposed to history and human weakness gives a shape to the lengthy time spans of *Chicken Soup With Barley* and *I'm Talking About Jerusalem* (1960), the concluding play of the trilogy, while there is virtual unity of time in *Roots*, where the Bryant family's static and apolitical existence is a foil to Beatie's vibrant discovery of herself after her lover has left her.

*The Kitchen*, written during the same period, was first presented in a one-act version (1959), then revived as a full-length play (1961), and subsequently filmed. "The world might have been a stage for Shakespeare," wrote Wesker in an introduction to the play, "but to me it is a kitchen, where people come and go and cannot stay long enough to understand each other, and friendships, loves, and enmities are forgotten as quickly as they are made." And indeed the restaurant kitchen of the play's setting is a microcosm of Wesker's world, in which the preparation and delivery of food (represented in a skillful blend of realism and stylized devices) is an ugly drudgery turning chefs and waitresses into fevered automata. "When the world is filled with kitchens you get pigs," says a young Jewish pastrycook to drive home Wesker's point that capitalism blights the human spirit. "I can't dream in a kitchen!" cries the idealist Peter, and it is he who brings the play to a melodramatic conclusion, running berserk with a chopper and slashing his wrists. "Why does everybody sabotage me, Frank?" asks the restaurant owner sadly. "I give work, I pay well, yes? They eat what they want, don't they? I don't know what more to give a man." And the play ends with his repeated question "What is there more? What is there more?"

If Wesker's symbolism in *The Kitchen* is obvious to the point of apparent naïveté, his interpretation of the socialist doctrine is one that persistently refuses to regard human beings as mere ciphers. In *The Kitchen*, as in his other plays, there are undercurrents of sensitivity that in the hands of a sympathetic director yield far more subtlety than a cursory reading would suggest.

"You have to start with love. How can you talk about socialism otherwise?" asks Sarah in *Chicken Soup With Barley*, and the message that pervades Wesker's work is not so much the need for socialism as the need for a socialism animated by the warmth and passion of human feeling, for a life to be lived with a new intensity. In this richer world a capacity for the enjoyment of the arts takes an important place. The last scene of *Roots* includes a passionate denunciation of the commercialization of the arts, which denies the majority their cultural heritage, and the foundation, in 1961, of Centre Forty-Two was intended by Wesker as a practical expression of the same philosophy. At the expense of abandoning his own writing for a time, Wesker devoted his energies to this movement, named after a Trades Union Congress resolution calling for T.U.C. subsidy of the arts on a massive scale. "There is nothing wrong with rock 'n' roll," he had said in 1958, "there is only something wrong with it every day." Predictably enough, the nationwide cultural awakening of the proletariat did not follow upon a T.U.C. resolution in its favor, and it soon became evident that Centre Forty-Two had failed to command the support needed for success. After six doubtfully effective Arts Festivals its activities were more modestly confined to the management of the Round House, a Victorian railway engine repair shop which was converted into a large, attractive theater. Wesker's involvement with the management of the Round House ended in 1970.

The preoccupations that underlie Wesker's involvement with Centre Forty-Two are in fact explored more sensitively and realistically in his two plays *Chips With Everything* (1962) and *Their Very Own and Golden City* (1964) than in some of his idealistic pronouncements as director of the project. (A third work completed during the period, *The Nottingham Captain,* is a documentary treatment of the Luddite riots of 1817, presented at the Centre's festivals in 1962.) *Chips With Everything* marked Wesker's break with naturalism in favor of a loose, episodic structure with superficially Brechtian trappings. An R.A.F. training station before the abolition of National Service is the setting, which offers a view of the power structure of the country at large, while the play records a priggish Pip Thompson's progress from upper-class dissident organizing revolt among the other ranks to turncoat "absorbed in English society." A brilliant production by John Dexter won instant recognition for the play, which nevertheless lays itself open to criticism for the author's untypically schematic treatment of character. If the portrayal of the officers sometimes verges upon hostile caricature, the facility with which a squad of recruits, on a prompting from Pip, breaks into the rendering of a little-known revolutionary song is equally far from observed truth. But Wesker's fault is not so much that he has allowed his political persuasions to cloud his view of character, as that he has failed to assimilate completely his newly adopted dramatic techniques. Wesker's emotional view of socialism as a force rooted in personal experience is out of sympathy with the intellectual edge of Brechtian dialectics, and consequently his attempt to make social comment by way of an "alienation technique" jars on the fundamental basis of his writing. More than compensating for these distortions is the honesty with which the author presents the failure of Pip's short-lived attempt to restore to the recruits the culture that is their heritage. For Wesker socialist doctrines are no mere intellectual formulations, but testing grounds of character and intention. "The Labour Movement is choked with bad mannered, arrogant little rebels who enjoy kicking stubborn parents in the teeth," says Jake Latham in *Their Very Own and Golden City.* "Revolutionaries is what we want—they spend less time rebelling against what's past and give their energy to the vision ahead." Pip's inadequate motives once laid bare, it is clear that he is a rebel in this sense and not a revolutionary, and his removal to join the establishment is automatic. Thus the play is not, as it is often taken to be, a simple illustration of the social thinking that lies behind the Centre Forty-Two movement, but an imaginative perception of the tragic difficulties facing such an enterprise. *Chips With Everything* contains some of its author's finest and most powerful writing. Its most expressive moments crystallize in a series of images that exist for the stage rather than the written text: the rising excitement while the recruits at the N.A.A.F.I. Christmas party are persuaded to decline the Wing Commander's patronizing request for "a dirty recitation, or a pop song" and join in the singing of "The Cutty Wren"; Pip's capitulation as he finally plunges his bayonet, screaming into the practice dummy; the silent coal-stealing scene, and the savage irony of the final passing-out parade.

The play with which Wesker ended his self-imposed withdrawal from writing, *Their Very Own and Golden City*, has been widely interpreted as a document of disillusion arising from the author's experience as director of Centre Forty-Two. A study of the play against the context of Wesker's earlier dramatic work reveals that, although it doubtless draws upon Wesker's personal experience in connection with the project, it takes up themes that have preoccupied the author since his earliest work for the stage, treating them with a depth, maturity, and easy command of form that make it a milestone in Wesker's advancing status as a dramatist. Characteristically the growth and decline of a man's visionary enthusiasm provides the structural *raison d'être* for this chronicle of the socialist architect Andrew Cobham's ill-fated Utopian schemes. The episodic plot is carefully organized into a dramatic unity that presents the growth of Cobham's brainchild in a double perspective, related within history to the fortunes of the socialist faith and in personal terms to the natural and inevitable processes of life. That essential tenet of socialist faith, the possibility of change, is matched against a cyclic pattern of youth, maturity, and age that repeats itself in every individual. An entirely adequate and personal nonnaturalistic style is employed with an easy assurance that is missing from *Chips With Everything,* and a portrait of a whole society emerges without the stylistic confusion that marred the earlier play. The question that lies at the heart of the play is posed by Jake Latham, the old Trades Union leader: "Is it better to risk defeat in defence of a principle or to hang on with compromises?" Andrew Cobham's dilemma is that his vision inevitably involves him in compromise. "If I'd come to you," he says to his followers, "with brave declarations and the cry of an easy Utopia would you have believed that? . . . The alternative was that complete revolution we all used to talk about, but there is no situation that is revolutionary, is there? There is no revolutionary situation! . . . Six Golden Cities could lay the foundations for a new way of life for all society—that's a lie, but that's the lie we're going to perpetuate, with our fingers crossed." His "perpetuation of a lie" builds a painful gulf between himself and his wife and severs the ties with his former comrades. In Wesker's earlier plays personal failings and weaknesses had undermined his heroes' idealistic viewpoints; in the more complex action of *Their Very Own and Golden City* adherence to an ideal itself involves Andrew Cobham in compromise and the failure of his personal relationships; his life follows a pattern of self-imposed destruction in the tragic manner.

*Their Very Own and Golden City* is written from the standpoint of a militant socialist facing up squarely to the actual conditions of the contemporary world, and passages of ideological debate assume the audience's sympathy and concern for the socialist movement. By contrast *The Four Seasons* (1965), written during the same period, omits all reference to the existence of a society outside the four walls of the play's setting. Adam and Beatrice pursue their love affair through a sequence of four scenes that echoes the seasonal cycle of nature. The author writes that the play "sets out to explore only the essentials of a relationship with deliberately little recourse to explanation or background; but, the dialogue is heightened, the form highly stylized and the metaphor of the play simple; there lay the dangers both for understanding and performing the work." In fact the play's cold reception was not entirely due to a failure to understand it. The "heightened dialogue" is often drab and sometimes pretentious, illustrating the difficulties in the way of a modern dramatist who tries to achieve a poetic language while neglecting the vigor of contemporary idiom, and it remains difficult to become sympathetically engaged with two characters who are sparse abstractions without (as Wesker stresses) possessing any deep allegorical or symbolic significance. Like all of Wesker's work it possesses nevertheless the virtues of sincerity, passion, and energy. Aware that it marked a new departure in his writing, Wesker has declared that *The Four Seasons* (dedicated to the revolutionaries of Cuba) does not mark an abandonment of his political stance: "If compassion and teaching the possibility of change are two of the many effects of art, a third is this: to remind and reassure people that they are not alone not only in their attempts to build a better world but in their private pains and confusions also . . . *The Four Seasons* was written because I believe the absence of love diminishes and distorts all action."

*The Friends* (1970) abandons the abstract mode of *The Four Seasons* and returns to a style approximating the naturalism of the early Wesker. Esther, a woman in her thirties, dies of leukemia. Central to the play is the effect of her death upon her brothers and friends. In the first act Esther lies dying in bed; the second is dominated by the presence of her corpse. The play is a sombre one in which the everpresent reality of pain and death imparts a new and desperate intensity to the themes with which all Wesker's work is concerned: the clash between personal relationships and social ideals, the urgent need to face the truth in honest speech and action, the search for self-fulfillment through art and knowledge, and the emptiness of life without love. In Wesker's typical fashion, the sense of despair and personal inadequacy created by Esther's death is linked with a wider confusion over the role of socialism in contemporary history. Confronting these characters is the knowledge that the very values which give meaning to their revolutionary aspirations are a product of "bourgeois" culture. It requires no little sympathy with Wesker's preoccupations to follow the heated arguments around the deathbed concerning the guilty contradictions inherent in the possession of beautiful furniture by committed socialists, and nothing short of an act of faith to accept the final scene, in which the corpse of Esther is propped in a chair while the group pays homage to her as the only true revolutionary among them.

Wesker is an embattled controversialist who has been jailed in connection with his anti-nuclear activities. His earliest work seemed to identify him with a group of socialist dramatists of predominantly working-class origins. By the time of *Their Very Own and Golden City*, however, he was the only major English dramatist of his generation whose commitment to the left remained the most important aspect of his writing. Wesker's socialism has always been fundamental to his drama, while in a sense dramatic enactment has played an important part in his view of life. The socialist scheme for mankind, in Wesker's eyes, is without meaning unless seen at the personal, individual level. Ideas begin and end with people, in the pain and confusion of their private lives. Hence the attraction of the stage for Wesker; he has put the theater before any other medium, not for any deeply reasoned theories about the nature of realism on the stage, but simply because for him life must be lived on an emotional, physical level if it is to be lived at all. Only in the theater can ideas be wedded intimately enough to the passions and made inseparable from the voice that speaks them. Only in the theater can he convey his exhilarated belief in life as an active, three-dimensional process, enjoyed on the stage and shared by an audience. This belief is projected in the game of "Look-I'm-Alive" in *I'm Talking About Jerusalem*, in the coal-stealing scene from *Chips With Everything*, and in the miraculous apple-strudel actually prepared during the summer scene in *The Four Seasons* ("Actors learn to fence—why not to cook?" asks Wesker). Arnold Wesker's stage does not present a slice of life accurately observed, so much as a sense of life physically communicated. His romanticism is not the product of too simple an analysis of society, but a courageous assertion of man's value and vitality.

He is the author of the television play *Menace* (1963). His essay "Let Battle Commence!" appeared in *The Encore Reader* (1965), edited by Charles Marowitz, Tom Milne, and Owen Hale. He has been the subject of a number of interviews, among them: with Jill Pomerance in *New Theatre Magazine*, Vol. I, No. 3 (1960); "Centre 42" in *Encore*, Vol. IX, No. 3 (1962); and Simon Trussler in *Theatre at Work* (1967), edited by Marowitz and Trussler. His work has been discussed in the following: "Drama With a Message: Arnold Wesker" by Laurence Kitchin in *Modern British Dramatists* (1968), edited by John Russell Brown; "The Biggest Aunt Sally of Them All" (Centre 42) by Geoffrey Reeves in *Encore*, Vol. X, No. 1 (1963); "Arnold Wesker's Mission" by John Garforth in *The Encore Reader;* and "Arnold Wesker: The

Last Humanist?" by Michael Anderson in *New Theatre Magazine,* Vol. VIII, No. 3 (1968). Ronald Hayman has written a study of the dramatist, *Arnold Wesker* (1969). Wesker himself wrote *Fears of Fragmentation* (1970).

**Whiting, John** (1917–1963). English dramatist. Whiting was educated at public school and trained as an actor at the Royal Academy of Dramatic Art. After military service in the army he acted in repertory, mainly in Harrogate and York. *Conditions of Agreement,* written shortly after the war, was not performed on the stage until, in 1965, a shortened version staged in Bristol impressed critics with dialogue and situations anticipating the work of Harold Pinter. *A Penny for a Song,* directed by Peter Brook in 1951, had only a short West End run (revivals have met with greater success). Later in the same year *Saint's Day* (most of which had been written in 1948) was awarded first prize in a competition organized by the Arts Council to mark the Festival of Britain. Presented at the Arts Theatre Club, it came under savage attack from the critics but was vigorously defended in the correspondence columns of the London *Times* by Tyrone Guthrie, Peter Brook, and others connected with the theater. *Marching Song* (1954) was to prove no more successful; *The Gates of Summer* (1956) did not survive a pre-London tour. After this discouraging reception of his work Whiting withdrew from the theater to make his living writing screenplays, until invited by Peter Hall to dramatize the history of Urbain Grandier from Aldous Huxley's *The Devils of Loudun.* Presented at the Aldwych Theatre in 1961 *The Devils* was the first commissioned work presented by the Royal Shakespeare Company and an immediate success. His one-act play *No Why* was staged posthumously in 1965. Whiting's early death deprived the theater of a remarkable writer at the height of his powers, who had received popular recognition only after years of neglect.

The uncompromising pessimism of Whiting's outlook may have contributed more to the failure of his early work than is generally recognized. Perhaps it has been too readily assumed that the qualities of *Saint's Day* and *Marching Song* would have won wider recognition had they not come before the revolution in taste following *Look Back in Anger.* They are dark, difficult plays, without a glimmer of faith in humanity. Both reflect the bitter experience of the last war, in the unleashing of senseless, nihilistic violence in *Saint's Day* and the general who becomes the scapegoat of a defeated nation in *Marching Song;* but they are overloaded with heavy and obscure symbolism and suffer at times from stiff, literary dialogue. Odd scenes provide flashes of great theatrical intensity, and *Saint's Day* in particular foreshadows Pinter in the irrationally shifting alliances between the three central characters, the ill-defined menace of their servant, John Winters, and the sudden eruption of animal savagery with the arrival of the three escaped soldiers. *A Penny for a Song,* by contrast, is a play of luminous clarity. An England threatened by Napoleon provides the setting for a dramatic contrast of attitudes toward war.

Central to the play is the growing understanding between Edward Sterne, committed to traveling through Europe denouncing war, and the urbane cynicism of Hallam Matthews, while the foolish aspect of war is reflected in the childish enthusiasms of the eccentric Bellboys brothers. This tautly constructed play, with *coups de théâtre* succeeding one another at breakneck pace, has the surface qualities of farce but the underlying bitterness of all Whiting's work: the courses of action chosen by Edward and Hallam are equally counsels of despair. Nevertheless, *A Penny for a Song* was said by its author to have been "written at a time of great personal happiness," and this no doubt is responsible for the felicity of invention that sets off this play from the rest of his work. With the exception of *A Penny for a Song* and *The Gates of Summer*, the theme that runs through Whiting's work is self-destruction. His heroes are displayed in a bleak, pitiless light while they become half-willing accomplices in their own comfortless death. In the world presented in Whiting's plays the ultimate prop of man's faith in his own species is annihilated. In *Marching Song* the distant shepherd's song that restored Rupert Forster's will to live in his prison cell is discovered to be only "the goatherd's expression of love—to his goats. The songs don't make sense." A similar sense of the futility of existence ends *The Devils*, as the crowd fights for scraps of Grandier's body to use as charms.

The rapid, episodic flow of *The Devils* may owe more to Whiting's experience in writing for films than to any specific theatrical influence, although English interest in Brecht's epic theater was at its height in 1961. The dialogue, strong and natural, marks an advance on Whiting's previous writing and the characters represent a panoramic view of mankind without the overt symbolism that marred his earlier work. The sewerman, fishing in human ordure and providing a sardonic commentary on the action, fits naturally into the scheme of the whole. The mass hysteria of the nuns of St. Ursula's convent, who allow themselves to believe that they are possessed by devils under the control of Grandier, is a powerful theme employed to great theatrical effect, but the play may be said to lack a focal point in that Jeanne, prioress of the convent, has no contact outside her imagination with her tormentor, the libertine Father Grandier. *The Devils* displays skill, strength, and subtlety in the interplay of personal and political motives that encompass Grandier's downfall but, perhaps because it is so clearly based on Huxley's study, it fails to communicate a sense of personal commitment to the issues involved.

As well as numerous screenplays, Whiting was the author of four plays for radio and a one-act television play, *A Walk in the Desert*, staged in 1964. Whiting's works have been published in three volumes, *The Collected Plays* (1969). He also published "From My Diary," which appeared in *The Twentieth Century*, Vol. CIX, No. 1008 (February 1961); his criticism is collected in *John Whiting on Theatre* (1966), edited by Alan Ross. An interview by Tom Milne and Clive Goodwin appeared in *Theatre at Work* (1967), edited by Charles Marowitz and Simon Trussler. Trussler also published an article, "The Plays of John Whiting," in the *Tulane Drama Review*, Vol. XI, No. 2 (Winter 1966). Ronald Hayman has published a study, *John Whiting* (1969), with further bibliography.

**Who's Afraid of Virginia Woolf?** (1962). A play by Edward Albee. It won New York Drama Critics Circle and Tony awards. Albee has taken a simple children's song and extended it to its adult equivalent: danger treated like a game, fear handled with bravado. But for both the child and the sophisticated adult, buried in that rhetorical question is a real one, who *is* afraid of the big bad wolf?

The vicious maneuvers of George and Martha after they return home from a faculty party reveal their feelings. As their guests, a young couple called Nick and Honey, get caught in the cross fire, the nature and extent of that feeling becomes evident. It is fear for personal survival, at whatever cost. The silly little bride, Honey, gets sick easily because she is afraid to have children, afraid to be hurt. Her athletic husband is willing to play whatever games are necessary—like Hump the Hostess, who in this case happens to be the college president's daughter—in order to get ahead professionally. Martha, still voluptuous at fifty-two, has always been afraid that she is not lovable and needs to lacerate her husband verbally and emotionally to punish him for being so stupid as to content himself with her. George, the defeated history professor, carries with him a story—truth or illusion?—that he has accidentally killed both his father and his mother, a power for destruction that makes cooperative violence his only way to love.

But the play at no point functions as a clinical abstraction. By means of piercingly accurate dialogue and situation, Albee makes his characters live through a real period of "Fun and Games," "Walpurgisnacht," and finally "The Exorcism," as he has entitled the three acts. When the imaginary son, the only kind of child George and Martha have been able to have, is "killed" by George in a moment of revenge, then language and dramatic emotion shift from bitchy intensity to quiet revelation of the desperate fear that has been there all along, underneath the noise and the dueling. When Martha has spent her anger, against the background of George's chanting Latin liturgy for the dead, and the "innocents," Nick and Honey, have gone, the older couple is left alone, really alone for the first time since their son was "invented" twenty-one years before. The scene is played "very softly, very slowly" as George sings the altered children's song "Who's afraid of Virginia Woolf. . . ." and Martha answers, perhaps for the first time with a pitiful honesty, "I . . . am . . . George . . . I . . . am . . ."

The play was first presented October 13, 1962, and ran for two years on Broadway. When it was denied the Pulitzer Prize, two members of the committee resigned in protest. In 1966 a very popular film was made following Albee's original script quite closely.

**Wilder, Thornton [Niven]** (born 1897). American playwright and novelist. Born in Madison, Wisconsin, educated in public and private schools in the United States and China (where his father was American consul general), Wilder graduated from Yale (B.A. 1920) and Princeton (M.A. 1926). He was a teacher and housemaster at Lawrenceville Academy in New Jersey for several years. A national lecture tour in 1928 began a long period of his lecturing and serving on various cultural commissions.

Wilder's first novel and first play appeared in 1926. He has continued to write in both genres, winning three Pulitzer Prizes, for his novel *The Bridge of San Luis Rey* (1927) and for the plays *Our Town* (1938) and *The Skin of Our Teeth* (1942). Wilder has written a number of one-act plays, simple and colloquial in diction, usually dealing with ordinary people in ordinary events, always from a perspective that reveals the extraordinary within the ordinary, the metaphysical within the mundane. In these and in his full-length plays he has experimented with form, often on a bare stage, and with using a philosophical and psychological, rather than a strictly chronological and spatial arrangement of events. *The Skin of Our Teeth*, for example, portrays five thousand years of the history of man and is related to James Joyce's *Finnegans Wake*, portions of which Wilder has memorized. He regards the theater "as the greatest of all art forms" and relates it to celebrations and festivals, not to naturalistic imitations.

Since World War II Wilder's theatrical productivity has noticeably diminished. *The Matchmaker* was successfully produced in 1954 (and provided the story for the endlessly popular musical *Hello, Dolly!*), but it was not a new play, rather a revision of *The Merchant of Yonkers* (1938). *A Life in the Sun*, based on the Alcestis legend, was given at the Edinburgh Festival in 1955 but was never done in the United States. His last work to be seen in New York was *Plays for Bleecker Street* (given at Circle in the Square on Bleecker Street in 1962); these three one-act plays are part of a larger plan to write fourteen plays, one each on the seven deadly sins and the seven ages of man. A novel, *The Eighth Day*, appeared in 1967.

There are a number of books in various languages on Wilder's work as a whole; the only full-length study of the plays in English is *The Plays of Thornton Wilder* (1967) by Donald Haberman. Useful, though not up to date, is Jerome Edelstein's *A Bibliographical Checklist of the Writings of Thornton Wilder* (1959).

**Williams, Emlyn** (born 1905). Welsh actor, dramatist, and director. Born in North Wales and educated at Holywell County School and Oxford, where he was a member of the Oxford University Dramatic Society, Williams began his acting career in 1927. Since that date he has achieved distinction as an actor on stage and in films, and as a director, often acting in and directing his own plays. Aptly characterized by critic J. C. Trewin as the "voice of the Theatre Theatrical, with a Welsh accent," Williams achieved his major work as a dramatist before the war. In such thrillers as *A Murder Has Been Arranged* (1930) and *Night Must Fall* (1935) he exploited to the full the possibilities of the prewar commerical theater; in such plays as *The Corn Is Green* (1938) he successfully attempted a deeper portraiture of character. After the war his solo performances in the character of Charles Dickens (1951) and the Welsh poet Dylan Thomas (1955), using only material written by those authors, held audiences spellbound and initiated what was to prove a popular genre of the contemporary theater. Williams is the author of *George* (1961), a volume of autobiography.

OTHER PLAYS SINCE 1945: *The Wind of Heaven* (1945), *Trespass* (1947), *Accolade* (1950), *Someone Waiting* (1953), *Pen Don* (1953), *Beth* (1958), *The Master Builder* (adaptation, 1965).

**Williams, Tennessee** [given name, **Thomas Lanier**] (born 1911). American playwright. Williams was born in Columbus, Mississippi, on March 26, 1911, second of three children of Edwina Dakin and Cornelius Williams. In the increasing estrangement between his father, a traveling shoe salesman, and his mother, a "gracious lady" of the impoverished South, young Tom grew to hate the rough insensitive man and found his mother, sister, and maternal grandparents his emotional stay. The typewriter Mrs. Williams gave him after their move from her parents' home to the first home she had with her husband (in St. Louis in 1918) was a refuge for him from increasing paternal conflict. He wrote and won prizes, both at school and in slick national magazines; his father continued to try to bully him out of this "sissified" occupation. In these same unpleasant years of puberty, his beloved sister, Rose, began the withdrawal that culminated in her intense mental suffering and lifelong institutionalization. (For his mother's perspective on this period of development, see her book *Remember Me to Tom.*)

After graduating from high school in 1929, Williams attended the University of Missouri for three years, but dropped out because of the financial pressures of the Depression; he worked for three years at a shoe company (the "living death" which he described in THE GLASS MENAGERIE), suffered a breakdown of some kind in 1935, and spent the summer recuperating with his grandparents. It was at this time that he began seriously to write plays and he continued writing the next year at Washington University (St. Louis) in fruitful collaboration with a dramatic group called The Mummers. Dropped from Washington University in 1937, Williams graduated from the University of Iowa in 1938.

Through a vagabond period of traveling and writing, Williams was supported by small amounts of money sent him from his faithful grandmother and finally by grants obtained for him from various foundations by Audrey Wood, who had become his agent after he won the Group Theatre contest in 1939 with some one-act plays titled *American Blues*. This aid and recognition brought Williams his first opportunity for major production: *Battle of Angels* was produced by the Theatre Guild in Boston, December 30, 1940. The play was a failure (Williams worked at rewriting this play for seventeen years; it was finally completed as *Orpheus Descending* in 1957), but that did not interfere with his productivity. Short plays were presented by various groups and were published in almost every volume of *The Best Short Plays* between 1940 and 1945.

With *The Glass Menagerie* (1945) Williams was established as an important contemporary American playwright. He produced a long play every year or two for twenty-five years, and won New York Drama Critics Circle Awards for *The Glass Menagerie* (1945), A STREETCAR NAMED DESIRE (1947), CAT ON A HOT TIN ROOF (1955), and THE NIGHT OF THE IGUANA (1961); *Streetcar* and *Cat* also won Pulitzer Prizes.

Despite varieties of subject matter and tone in Williams' work, there is a single preoccupation that stands out sharply when the work is seen as a whole. In its most shocking image, this preoccupation is presented as Sebastian's vision of God in *Suddenly Last Summer* (1958): "And the sand all alive, all alive, as the hatched sea-turtles made their dash for the sea, while the birds hovered and swooped to attack and hovered and—swooped to attack! They were diving down on the hatched sea-turtles, turning them over to expose their soft undersides, tearing the undersides open and rending and eating their flesh. Sebastian guessed that possibly only a hundredth of one percent of their number would escape to the sea. . . ." It is this wild scramble to escape, it is the impossible odds that preoccupy Williams. The rather obvious psychosexual paradigms that recur throughout his work are only analogies, not primarily social but cosmic. The excisions that occur—castration, abortion—are images of what must be done in order to survive in a hostile universe. Catherine, who witnessed Sebastian's terrible death, must be lobotomized, have the truth cut out of her mind, if she is to have any peace at all. Yet, thus "castrated," she will be like the sea-turtle cannibalized by predatory birds. The voluntary equivalents of lobotomy, castration, and abortion are what society demands; for the individual they are living death. Many of Williams' characters are among those who try to escape. None succeeds totally. Williams has no vision of what that sea of safety is like; he knows its blackened beach very well.

Often the character who makes a run for it is a poet of one kind or another. *The Glass Menagerie* is too autobiographical for Tom Wingfield's plight at that stage to be anything worse than haunting memories; whatever his fate, he has not yet reached it or envisioned it. But Blanche DuBois (in *Streetcar*), Val Xavier (in *Orpheus Descending*), and Chance Wayne (in *Sweet Bird of Youth*, 1959) have all had their sensitive underbellies rent by the carnivores of their respective worlds. Even Brick (in *Cat*), though hardly poetic, is a kind of prima donna athlete, fugitive from the mores of his father's—and his wife's—world.

Plays like *Cat* and *The Rose Tattoo* (1951) are interesting for their suggestion of an alternative to flight. Maggie, unlike the aborted Heavenly, is trying to conceive; and Big Daddy, unlike the actor whose chances are waning, is planning to win. Both characters have a vitality that is attractive or at least impressive. But regardless of their ultimate fate, they are on the side of the birds, not the turtles, a dubious alternative.

The Rose Tattoo could have presented a viable alternative to Sebastian's ugly image of God. Serafina's comic pursuit of erotic glory is uncomplicated and earthy; no Venus flytrap she. She loves totally, she mourns totally (Williams wrote the part for Anna Magnani). Her madonna is neither frustrated cat nor manipulating big daddy, but a warm deity who smiles on lovemaking every night for twelve years, each time as if it were the first time. But something goes wrong toward the end of the play; the comedy sours. Serafina, in contrast with her daughter, Rosa, whose love is also erotic, suddenly seems too much of a buffoon, too old and too fat. The scene where her new lover, Alvaro, hovers in admiration over the sleeping form of Rosa, reduces Serafina to the grotesque, a phoenix who ought to retire. Williams dramatically will not let the happy flesh be redemptive; no escape that way, just a distracting tickle.

Later plays make very explicit that another word for "God" is "death." (Ever since a strange seizure as an adolescent, Williams has been irrationally fearful of heart attack and death.) Virtually all of his plays are concerned with death in one form or another. The Glass Menagerie has its living death, both for Laura in her difference and for Tom in the "coffin" of family ties. In The Rose Tattoo choice of death or life is the clear alternative. Christ's highway of missions, the Camino Real (1953), is serviced by street cleaners who are demons of death. Orpheus makes his descent into the underworld and never returns to the land of life. The sweet bird of youth is inescapably threatened by the predator age, just as innocence is destroyed by experience. Even Period of Adjustment (1960), Williams' only social comedy, deals with couples coupling over a chasm. But since The Night of the Iguana Williams seems to be attempting a more hopeful attitude toward death, to suggest, perhaps, an alternative to Sebastian's image of God. This is clearest in The Milk Train Doesn't Stop Here Anymore (1964). Here Williams' earlier poet figure seems more successful an escapee. Unlike Val, Chris is not destroyed by the sterilizing demands of society (poor, yes, and attacked by dogs, still he follows his vocation); unlike Cash, another aging playboy, in Sweet Bird of Youth, he has not sold out to the birds in order to survive. By staying with elderly persons until their death, Chris has earned for himself the title "Angel of Death": the God this Christopher carries is not the ugly slaughter of Sebastian's vision; Chris brings his aged friends through death, not merely to death. He makes it possible for them to die honestly, with their jewels off. But Chris himself, the survivor, is not an entirely hopeful character. He has moved from a static art form to a dynamic one, from the fixed order of poetry to the constantly shifting relationships of mobiles. His gift to the dying Mrs. Goforth is a mobile entitled "The Earth Is a Wheel in a Great Big Gambling Casino," which suggests at least cosmic indifference to individual fate, if not the hunger of Sebastian's birds. His next structure will suggest the sound of the sea that rushes unceasingly against that beach from which so few escape. In 1968 Williams produced *Kingdom of Earth* (*The Seven Descents of Myrtle*), a play that deals with a female Orpheus who may manage to make her escape from death, though the result is ambiguous.

Although he is one of the most significant postwar playwrights, Williams has always been an uneven writer. His ear for dialogue is excellent when he deals with southern characters of all sorts; other types frequently sound artificial. What he has to say controls the shape the play takes, but he often does not trust his audience and has recourse to reinforcing gimmicks, like the screen device in *The Glass Menagerie,* or to sensational effects, like the oral sex act in *The Seven Descents of Myrtle.* The strength of Williams' plays comes always from the coherence given them by the passion of the characters; they fail to the extent that those characters are dramatically unconvincing.

A number of short plays appear in the 1953 edition of *27 Wagons Full of Cotton and Other One-Act Plays.* Also noteworthy are *I Rise in Flame, Cried the Phoenix* (published 1951), a play about D. H. Lawrence, and *Lord Byron's Love Letter* (published 1955), a libretto for a one-act opera. Williams wrote the screenplays for the films of *A Streetcar Named Desire* (1951) and *Baby Doll* (1956). He is also the author of *The Roman Spring of Mrs. Stone* (1950), a novel dealing with ideas explored in *Sweet Bird of Youth. One Arm, and Other Stories* (1948, 1954), *Hard Candy* (1954, 1959), and *The Knightly Quest* (1967) contain preliminary studies of characters, plots, ideas, and themes that Williams utilized in later plays. Williams has also published a volume of poetry, *In the Winter of Cities* (1956, 1964), and written a number of essays printed in magazines and newspapers and prefaces to his own work and that of other writers. There are eight or nine book-length studies of Williams' work in English, two or three in foreign languages.

OTHER PLAYS SINCE 1945: *You Touched Me!* (1945), written with Donald Windham; *Summer and Smoke* (1948), *Slapstick Tragedy* (1966), *The Two Character Play* (London, 1967), *In the Bar of a Tokyo Hotel* (1969).

**Witkiewicz, Stanisław Ignacy** [pen name Witkacy] (1885–1939). Polish dramatist. Witkiewicz was born in Warsaw and brought up in Zakopane. In 1904–05 he studied painting at the Academy of Fine Arts in Cracow, then traveled in Western Europe. He took part in an expedition to Australia and New Guinea with the anthropologist Bronisław Malinowski. He returned to Europe at the outbreak of the first world war in 1914, fought as an infantry officer in the Russian Army and was decorated for bravery with the order of St. Anne. At the outbreak of Revolution he was elected commissar by his soldiers. Witkiewicz returned to Poland in 1918 and settled in Zakopane. He wrote some forty-eight plays, most of them between 1918 and 1926. Of these eighteen are lost. He also wrote three novels and a number of philosophical tracts and critical works, among them *Teatr* (*An Introduction to the Theory of Pure Form in the Theater*), in which he expounded his theory of drama. Few of his plays were performed in the period between the two World Wars, but his work has acquired considerable popularity in the last decade. A collected edition of his plays was published in Warsaw in 1962 and productions throughout the country have been mounting steadily. Thus, notwithstanding the fact that he himself died before the period covered by this handbook—he committed suicide at the outbreak of World War II—his work, virtually unknown and unpublished in his lifetime, has now been appreciated for the first time.

Witkiewicz's plays, seemingly fantastic in their plots and action, contained grotesque and disturbing visions of events soon to overcome the world. Having experienced the Russian Revolution at first hand, he had few illusions about the future. A catastrophist, he was convinced of the impending doom of European civilization and culture, and this outlook colored most of his work. In *Kurka wodna* (The Water Hen, 1921) he presented a study of character relationships developed while living under the threat of external upheaval. In a characteristic Witkiewicz finale, the father of the now defunct hero of the play settles down to a game of cards with some runaway financiers while the Revolution is raging and the world around them is falling to pieces to the accompaniment of shooting and explosions. There is an air of futility of individual endeavor in the face of irresistible social forces. But the effectiveness of the latter too is questioned in Witkiewicz's last play, SzEWCY (The Shoemakers, written 1931–1934, produced 1957). Witkiewicz excelled in penetrating studies of totalitarianism and dictators in such plays as *Gyubal Wahazar* (1921). He was also obsessed with "mafias" or "secret governments." Of the works on this theme, *Oni* (They, 1920) is, perhaps, the most significant because it combines his political premonitions with his fears about the future of art. The blissful life of erotic, artistic, and gastronomic experiments led by the connoisseur of art Balandach and his mistress Spika, an actress, is rudely interrupted by the intrusion of a gang, whose purpose is to destroy all arts as an obstacle to the realization of a fully automatized, impersonal society. "They" are led by the founder of a new religion of Absolute Automatism, and include a leading financier, a hellish colonel, and other degenerates. They are the "secret real government." Despite Balandach's defiance, his exquisite art gallery is ruthlessly destroyed. Spika, forced to appear in a "*farce dell'arte*"—a new theater form preparatory to complete abolition of drama—is murdered by her frenzied acting partner, but it is Balandach whom they charge with her death.

One of Witkiewicz's most incisive plays is *Matka* (The Mother, 1924), which combines an attack on the psychological theater of Strindberg and Ibsen (there are parodistic references to *Ghosts* and *The Ghost Sonata*) with an ironic comment on present or potential society. The Mother has to work hard at her knitting in order to support her indolent son, Leon, who sponges on her with his fiancée, Sophia, of a similar disposition. Leon's dream is to abolish the social instinct that oppresses mankind by promoting individual antisocial actions on a mass scale. In Act II Mother, now an alcoholic and a morphine addict, lives in luxury thanks to Leon's and Sophia's industriousness. When it is revealed that Leon has gained his wealth by pimping and spying, and Sophia by being a society whore, Mother collapses and dies. Leon and Sophia bemoan her loss in an orgy of cocaine. After the almost naturalistic first two acts, Act III breaks the convention in the direction of "pure form." Leon's dead father appears together with Mother aged twenty-three, and it turns out that the old Mother who died was a dummy. Leon shoots Sophia's father and lovers. The others leave, but Leon is assaulted by half a dozen workers, who have suddenly appeared; they dispose of him in a specially constructed machine.

In his playwriting, Witkiewicz soon outgrew early modernist influences, though he retained to a certain extent the use of expressionist techniques. His plays comprise a wide range of subjects and forms. He himself provided something like a theoretical guidance for the understanding of the plays, a theory of "pure form," not unlike the theories that Clive Bell and Roger Fry worked out at about the same time in connection with the visual arts. In Witkiewicz's theory of pure form in the theater, he postulated a then new mode of theatrical experience and "a new kind of play which will be liberated from the confines of imitating life and instead make a synthesis of all the elements of the theater —sound, setting, gesture, dialogue—for purely formal ends. Freed from the demands of consistent psychology and logic, the dramatist will be able to use his materials as the musician uses notes and the modern painter colors and shapes. The meaning of such a work lies in its internal construction, not in the discursive content of its subject matter" (Daniel C. Gerould and C. S. Durer, Introduction to *The Madman and the Nun and Other Plays* by S. I. Witkiewicz). This theory, reminding one of the now popular total theater and mixed-media experiments, was in Witkiewicz's day so novel that even the author did not wholly succeed in putting it into practice on a big scale. Among the elements of it that did pervade his plays was the great concern over color arrangements in stage design and costumes and the use of inarticulate sounds, then quite unusual. In the visual aspects he was aided by his talent and experience as a portrait painter, with a striking capacity for color combinations, inspired, as some think, by his use of narcotics. The theater of pure form was to be nonliterary, but it was nonetheless based on a definite philosophical theory. Its pivot was the plurality of realities, often incompatible with one another, which, when portrayed within the boundaries of the same play, will give an overall impression of incongruity and metaphysical strangeness of existence. In Witkiewicz's plays parody and pastiche mingle with philosophical discussion, followed by unusual scenic situations. The dialogue abounds in humor, often of the macabre kind, and for sheer theatrical inventiveness it is hard to find an author who would surpass him. For example, the action of *Szalona lokomotywa* (The Crazy Locomotive, 1923) takes place in a moving railway engine. Two aristocratic criminals hide from the police by posing as engineers; somewhat unbalanced, and in love with a "demonic" woman, they work themselves into a frenzy and their engine into a tremendous pace and pressure, resulting in a spectacular railway smash. Although all Witkiewicz's plays are immensely theatrical, the subject matter of some is easier and makes them more readily acceptable to the general audience. Among these are such plays as *W małym dworku* (In a Small Country House, 1921), a kind of ghost play, and *Wariat i zakonnica* (Madman and the Nun, 1923), a satire on the then fashionable Freudian theory and a forerunner of modern grotesque. Half of Witkiewicz's extant dramatic output is now available in excellent English translations, which should facilitate the appreciation of this important writer, a precursor of modern trends in drama, notably the European theater of the absurd.

EXTANT PLAYS: *Biedny chłopiec* (The Poor Boy, 1893), *Karaluchy* (Cockroaches, 1893), *Komedie z życia rodzinnego* (Comic Scenes from Family Life, 1893), *Król i złodziej* (The King and the Thief, 1893), *Księżniczka Magdalena czyli natrętny książę* (Princess Magdalena, or The Overinsistent Prince, 1893), *Menażeria czyli wybryk słonia* (Menagerie, or The Elephant's Prank, 1893), *Odważna księżniczka* (The Brave Princess, 1893), *Maciej Korbowa i Bellatrix* (Matthew Korbova and Bellatrix, 1918), *Pragmatyści* (The Pragmatists, 1919), *Tumor Mózgowicz* (Tumor Brainard, 1920), *Mister Price, czyli Bzik tropikalny* (Mister Price, or Tropical Madness, written with Eugenia Dunin-Borkowska, 1920), *Nowe wyzwolenie* (The New Deliverance, 1920), *Niepodległość trójkątów* (The Independence of Triangles, 1921), *Metafizyka dwugłowego cielęcia* (Metaphysics of the Two-Headed Çalf, 1921), *Straszliwy wychowawca* (The Terrible Tutor, 1921), *Bezimienne dzieło* (The Anonymous Work, 1921), *Negatyw szkicu* (Negative of a Sketch, 1921), *Mątwa, czyli hyrkaniczny światopogląd* (The Cuttlefish, or The Hyrcanic Worldview, 1922), *Nadobnisie i koczkodany, czyli zielona pigułka* (Sluts and Butterflies, or The Green Pill, 1922), *Jan Maciej Karol Wścieklica* (John Matthew Charles Hellcat, 1922), *Janulka, córka Fizdejki* (Janulka, Daughter of Fizdejko, 1923), *Sonata Belzebuba, czyli prawdziwe zdarzenie w Mordowarze* (The Beelzebub Sonata, or What Really Happened at Mordowar, 1925).

**Wittlinger, Karl** (born 1922). West German dramatist and director. After returning from a French camp for prisoners of war in 1946, Wittlinger studied drama in Freiburg and received his doctorate in 1950. He then trained as a director and formed his own troupe of traveling actors, which continued until 1953. By 1956 he achieved great success with his comedy *Kennen Sie die Milchstrasse?* (Do You Know the Milky Way?), one of the German plays most often performed in the postwar era. The drama involves a supposedly dead soldier who returns from the war. Too honest and naïve to live in the reconstruction society, he lands in a mental institute, where he fights for his identity with a doctor who also experiences his suffering. In another one of Wittlinger's successful plays, *Die Seelenwanderung* (The Wandering of Souls, 1963), he once again focused on two characters, who in this case represent two lost souls. Bum and Axel are two vagabonds, one rather pushy, the other sensitive. Bum pushes his way to the top by pawning his soul in a Germany that produces the "economic miracle," while Axel remains on the bottom. The audience is treated to songs and social parodies that are clever but lack finesse and depth. Wittlinger is essentially a craftsman. Most of his works have been written for television. They tend to be light comedies which use slick dialogue in unusual situations. Wittlinger criticizes social aspects of West Germany in comedies without much bite.

OTHER PLAYS: *Der Himmel der Besiegten* (The Heaven of the Vanquished, 1954), *Junge Liebe auf Besuch* (Young Love on a Visit, 1954), *Kinder des Schattens* (Children of the Shadow, 1957), *Trümmergarten* (The Garden of Ruins, 1957), *Lazarus* (1958), *Zwei rechts, zwei links* (Two to the Right, Two to the Left, 1960), *Zum Frühstück zwei Männer* (Two Men for Breakfast, 1963), *Corinne und der Seebär* (Corinne and the Walrus, 1965), *Tante mit Schuss* (The Aunt Packs a Gun, 1968).

**Wolf, Friedrich** (1888–1953). German dramatist, doctor, and essayist. One of the foremost German expressionists, Wolf came to drama after beginning a career as a doctor. He turned toward socialism after World War I, and it was during the 1920s and 1930s that he wrote his best plays: *Der arme Konrad* (Poor Conrad, 1924) about the Peasant War; *Zyankali* (Potassium Cyanide, 1929) about the laws against abortion; *Die Matrosen von Cattaro* (The Sailors of Cattaro, 1930) about a sailors' mutiny against inhumane treatment; and *Professor Mamlock* (1935) about anti-Semitism. All these plays attack social injustices and criticize oppressive conditions in Germany. Because of Wolf's opposition to the Hitler regime, he was compelled to flee the country and made his way to France, the United States, Scandinavia, and finally Russia. In 1945 he returned to East Germany, where he continued to write plays of social realism that focus on political problems. Of his late works, *Beaumarchais oder die Geburt des Figaro* (Beaumarchais, or The Birth of Figaro, 1946) is his most important. It portrays a Beaumarchais who shies away from revolutionary bloodshed, though he has attacked the aristocratic society in his comedies. Wolf believed that art was a weapon to be used for the benefit of the masses in the class struggle. His critique of Beaumarchais was at the same time a critique of writers who do not strive to raise the political consciousness of their audiences. Wolf himself was a dedicated Communist who never tired of serving the socialist cause in his writings. His works have had a great influence on dramatists in East Germany.

OTHER PLAYS SINCE 1945: *Doktor Lilli Wanner* (1945), *Was der Mensch sät* (As a Man Soweth, 1945), *Patrioten* (Patriots, 1946), *Die letzte Probe*

(The Last Rehearsal, 1947), *Die Nachtschwalbe* (The Night Swallow, 1948), *Wie die Tiere des Waldes* (Like the Beasts of the Woods, 1948), *Aufbruch* (Explosion, 1949), *Bürgermeister Anna* (Mayoress Anna, 1950), *So fing es an* (That's How It Started, 1950), *Thomas Muentzer* (1953).

**Wood, Charles** (born 1932). English dramatist. One of the playwrights who gave the English theater of the '6os its distinctive tone, Wood was born into a theatrical family and had worked as a scriptwriter for radio before his group of three one-act plays under the title of *Cockade* appeared on the stage in 1963. Of the trio *John Thomas* is a slight but violent piece touching upon racial tension and personal inadequacy, while in *Prisoner and Escort* and *Spare* Wood's preoccupation with the psychology of the military mind emerges more clearly. *Prisoner and Escort* is a sharply realistic study of casual cruelty: Two soldiers escorting a prisoner to a military jail meet and bully a young girl, their crude banter changing to genuine malice when they discover her boyfriend is a Negro. *Spare*, by contrast, is an eerie fantasy that explores the essence of warfare in the surrealistic setting of a military museum. In both plays the language of the soldier, with its rhythmic combination of veiled obscenity and professional jargon, provides the main vehicle for Wood's insight into the mixture of cruelty, fear, and frustrated sexuality that animates the fighting man. In these plays the left-wing social protest to which many critics had pointed as the fundamental feature of the new English drama is in unmistakable retreat before a harsher point of view that sees warfare and racial prejudice as the products of darkly ineradicable urges of the human psyche. A vestige of conventional protest (unconvincing in its general context) remains in the character of the convicted soldier in *Prisoner and Escort*, guilty of a hopeless gesture against rising German militarism.

In his next two plays Wood moved away from a military setting. *Meals on Wheels* (1965) was an undisciplined venture into social satire. In *Fill the Stage With Happy Hours* (1966) Wood's gift for accurate dialogue successfully evoked the backstage atmosphere of a seedy provincial theater in which a theatrical family dogged by illness and thwarted ambition plays out its private melodrama.

With *Dingo* (1967) Wood produced what many critics considered his finest play. Set in the North African desert during the second world war, it attacks the rhetoric of heroism by contrasting it with the brutality and confusion that constitute the reality of war. A surrealistic plot is combined with dialogue that mercilessly echoes the obscenities of the lower ranks and the inanities of their leaders. A concert party in the desert becomes an image for the campaign as a whole, and the comic who is master of ceremonies on the "Tails up and Lick 'em show," with a patronizing mixture of smut and patriotic exhortation, symbolizes the ugly absurdity of war itself. Not content with an abstract picture, Wood caricatured the actual figures of Churchill and Montgomery, and the play was denied a public performance until the abolition of censorship. The attack upon personages of recent history laid Wood open to charges of petulance and bad taste, while by obscuring the question of the justification of the war against Nazi Germany he presented a distorted view of his theme. But the artistic validity of the play lies not in its interpretation of historical events, but in the language and dramatic imagery that seemed to many critics more vitally incisive than anything to have preceded it on the postwar English stage.

*H, or Monologues at Front of Burning Cities* (1969), Wood's next work for the stage, places the theme of *Dingo* within a more distant historical setting. General Havelock's relief of Lucknow during the Indian Mutiny of 1857 is dramatized with a mixture of eloquent rhetoric and impressive physical stagecraft that sharply juxtaposes the heroic ideals and the sordid futility of military action. An undisciplined plot obscures the play's argument and for most critics the work was a disappointment after the expectations created by *Dingo*. With a gift for the creation of dialogue that sometimes overcomes his sense of proportion, Wood is at his best in painting a vividly impressionistic canvas such as is found in *Spare* or *Dingo*, but is often less successful in structuring his work into a coherent whole.

OTHER PLAYS: *Don't Make Me Laugh* (one act, 1965), *A Bit of a Holiday* (1969), *Veterans* (1972).

Wood has written for television and motion pictures; the most substantial of his screenplays are *Help!, How I won The War,* and *The Charge of the Light Brigade.*

**Wouk, Herman** (born 1915). American novelist, scriptwriter, and playwright. Wouk was born in New York City and received a B.A. from Columbia University in 1934. In the '30s and early '40s he wrote for radio. Since the mid-1940s he has been a successful novelist; all of his novels have been major book-club choices and many of them have been adapted as films: *Aurora Dawn* (1947), *The City Boy* (1948), *The Caine Mutiny* (1951), *Marjorie Morningstar* (1955), *Youngblood Hawke* (1961), and *Don't Stop the Carnival* (1965). Of his three Broadway plays—*The Traitor* (1949), *The Caine Mutiny Court-Martial* (1954), and *Nature's Way* (1957)—only one is of any importance: Based on his Pulitzer Prize-winning novel, *The Caine Mutiny Court-Martial* was a sensational success on the stage and as a film with its display of a perverse mind and its manipulation of moral questions related to war and personal responsibility.

**Wünsche, Konrad** (born 1920). West German dramatist and poet. Upon completion of his studies at the university, Wünsche settled down in the Rhineland to teach at a high school. He first began writing dramas in the early 1960s. His plays demonstrate his passion for experimentation and his interest in musical composition. His first two plays, *Über den Gartenzaun* (Over the Garden Fence, 1962) and *Vor der Klagemauer* (Before the Wailing Wall, 1962), are poetic parables—sad songs over unfulfilled lives. His next play, perhaps his best, *Der Unbelehrbare* (The Incorrigible One, 1963), borrows elements from the drawing-room comedy and the play of the absurd. The setting is the turn of the century in a plush bourgeois home. The father of a family, who has been poisoned, rises from the dead to urge his son Paul to avenge his death. However, Paul fends him off, as well as the other members of the family. He does not want to be implicated in their sick games. In the end, he himself takes poison and dies a theatrical death. Here again, Wünsche structures his drama according to musical forms, so that the play is highly stylized. One of his most recent plays, *Gegendemonstration* (Counter Demonstration, 1969), an adaptation from his radio play, also shows to what extent Wünsche places emphasis on tonal qualities in his plays. A group of tourists in a foreign city observe a procession they do not understand. They utter typical tourist clichés about the procession, but the procession suddenly turns into a street demonstration, and the tourists themselves become involved in a battle they do not comprehend. The stress here is on lack of communication and acoustic signals that express social attitudes. Wünsche's strict dramatic compositions aim toward using sound to point out subtle differentiations among the situations of people who swim in a world of ambiguity.

OTHER PLAYS: *Les Adieux oder Die Schlacht bei Stötteritz* (Les Adieux, or The Battle of Stötteritz, 1964), *Jerusalem, Jerusalem* (1966), *Dramaturgische Kommandos* (Dramaturgical Commands, 1969).

**Wuolijoki, Hella** (1886–1954). Finnish playwright. Wuolijoki was born in Estonia as Hella Maria Murrik, the daughter of a lawyer. She had a rich and varied life, as a student of literature and folk poetry (M.A. 1908), the owner of a farmhouse, a radical politician and a businesswoman, Brecht's protectress and literary collaborator during his stay in Finland (1940–41). After the war she was general manager of Finnish Radio.

Under the pen name Juhani Tervapää, Wuolijoki wrote in 1936 the first of a cycle of five remarkable plays dealing with the changing fate of Niskavuori, a farmhouse in the center of Finland. The last two of these plays were performed in 1953: *Niskavuoren Heta* and *Entäs nyt, Niskavuori?* (Heta from Niskavuori, What Now, Niskavuori?). The cycle as a whole has its core the monumental, stony figure of the old proprietress, a matriarch keeping the house and family together. Her daughter-in-law Ilona, a radical teacher, is in harmony with Wuolijoki's social views and the open and active way of life that she favored and practiced herself. Heta is the representative of false pride and narrow prejudices; as a rule, the female characters are more prominent than the male. The last play in the cycle shows the new start that was to be made in postwar Finland. There are several films based on this cycle.

Starting from Wuolijoki's subject matter and earlier play, she and Brecht wrote their own versions of the same story. The results were *Iso-Heikkilän isäntä ja hänen renkinsä Kalle* (1947) and *Herr Puntila und sein Knecht*

*Matti* (Herr Puntila and His Man, Matti, 1948). Both scripts center on a big farmer, benevolent when drunk, beastly in his rare moments of sobriety. Brecht's play and a few of his poems include elements of soft lyricism inspired by the nature of Finland; at the same time, however, he gave a sharper edge to the social message of the fable.

The life and works of Wuolijoki meet at a certain point: She was a great storyteller, a woman of quick-flying fantasy, yet also a businesswoman with a firm grasp of realities. Her characters are clearly seen and close to nature; her eye was alert to social changes; her realism is of an agile kind. The conflicts in her plays are developed in a purposeful way. Wuolijoki's last works also include radio plays and volumes of memoirs.

# Z

Zawieyski, Jerzy (1902–1969). Polish novelist and dramatist. Zawieyski was born in Radogoszcz and educated in Łódź. He studied philosophy and art history at Warsaw, Wilno, and Paris universities. For three years he was an actor in the Reduta company. He lived in Paris in the years 1929 to 1933 and in the '30s traveled extensively in Europe and Africa. He made his literary debut with a novel in 1932 and his first play was produced two years later. A socialist and pacifist in his views at first, he gravitated toward Catholicism. His outlook was strengthened during the years of the second world war, which he spent in Warsaw, engaged in the literary, theatrical, and educational activities of the anti-Nazi underground. He came into prominence in the years immediately following the end of the war. Forced out of print and off the stage during the Stalinist repression around 1950, he resumed active life on Gomułka's accession to power in 1956. He returned to the editorial boards of two Catholic periodicals, and was elected president of the Club of Catholic Intelligentsia (a post that he held until his death) and vice president of the Polish Writers' Union. In 1957 he was elected deputy to the Seym and a member of the Council of State, which position he resigned in protest over the repressive measures by the authorities after the student riots in March 1968.

Although Zawieyski was the author of six novels and nine volumes of short stories, essays, journals, and poetic prose, he was best known to the general public for his plays, of which he wrote twenty-seven. Their subjects were drawn from the Bible (Job, Joseph, David, and Pilate), ancient Greece (Socrates, Tyrtaeus, Orestes, and Heracles), Tudor England (*Miecz obosieczny* [The Double-Edged Sword, 1957], a drama about Sir Thomas More), Polish history (*Masław*, 1945), and wartime Polish experiences and the aftermath of war. Among his contemporary plays there is a delightful comedy on Stalinist bureaucracy, *Arkadia* (c. 1956); a serious drama dealing with the Algerian struggle for independence, *Wicher z pustyni* (Wind from the Desert, 1959); a moving dramatic poem set in Vietnam, *Lai znaczy jaśmin* (Lai Means Jasmine, 1961); as well as a somewhat fantastic philosophical comedy set in the Canadian Rockies, *Ziemia nie jest jedyna* (The Earth Is Not Unique, 1960).

Whatever their setting or period, Zawieyski's plays deal with one essential theme: man and his often hopeless, but never pointless, struggle for his own integrity and for freedom from tyranny, political, social, and religious. Though labeled a Catholic writer, he avoided subservience to dogma and often adopted a humanist standpoint. His favorite theme involved a one-man protest against the demands and prejudices of society. He treated this theme literally to start with in such plays as *Sokrates* (1950) and *The Double-Edged Sword,* and metaphorically in a witty late play, *Protest* (1963), based on a theme from Herman Melville's story "Bartleby the Scrivener," about a clerk's refusal to leave the office in which he works and the disturbance his decision creates for the people around him, even leading to murder.

In their form, Zawieyski's plays underwent a great development from the traditional style of his early period to the experimental techniques in which he freely indulged after 1956. The most typical of these is *Maski Marii Dominiki* (The Masks of Mary Dominique, 1957), a poetic play with symbolic characters and even the device of an Egyptian tapestry come to life. Mary Dominique, an embodiment of the irrational, imaginative, revolutionary drives of humanity, is put on trial by the down-to-earth forces of reason. Though finally acquitted, she dies tormented in a desperate effort to break through her loneliness and be understood by the common people. Like almost all the plays aiming at a symbolic presentation of the human condition, *The Masks* is ambiguous and impossible to summarize. In *Idziemy do wujka* (We Are Going to See Uncle, 1964), Zawieyski probed into the relativity of truths about past experience through a confrontation between two generations. He felt most at ease, though, in straightforward plays, whose tone varies from a very serious approach to moral problems in the earlier works—for example, *Rozdroże miłości* (Crossroads of Love, 1945), in which a murder and a suicide committed in the past are affecting people's present through relentless searching of consciences, in the manner of Mauriac—to the witty, good-natured approach exemplified in the late comedies. An example of the latter is *The Earth Is Not Unique,* in which a group of strangers is thrown together in a remote mountain spot while army units search the area for mysterious objects that have reportedly landed there. The play provided the author with the opportunity for amusing and sharp comment on our society in an idiom reminiscent of Christopher Fry. Though not really an innovator, Zawieyski commanded respect through the seriousness of purpose, accomplished technique, and impeccable style of his wide-ranging dramatic output.

OTHER PLAYS SINCE 1945: *Mąż doskonały* (The Perfect Man, 1945), *Ocalenie Jakuba* (The Deliverance of Jacob, 1947), *Dzień sądu* (The Day of Judgment, 1947), *Miłość Anny* (The Love of Anna, 1948), *Pieśń o nadziei* (The Song of Hope, 1949), *Lament Orestesa* (The Lament of Orestes, 1951), *Niezwyciężony Herakles* (The Invincible Heracles, 1952), *Tyrteusz* (Tyrtaeus, 1955), *Wysoka ściana* (The High Wall, 1956), *Każdy* (Everyman, 1957),

*Rzeka niedoli* (The River of Misery, 1957), *Pożegnanie z Salomeą* (Farewell to Salomea, 1961).

**Zinner, Heda** (born 1907). East German dramatist, poet, and novelist. Born in Vienna, Zinner studied acting at the Schauspielakademie there. In 1924 she moved to Germany and acted at various theaters. Toward the end of the 1920s, in Berlin, she began writing verse. She joined the Communist Party. In 1933 she was forced to emigrate and eventually made her way to the Soviet Union, where she worked for the radio and various newspapers. At the end of the war she returned to East Berlin, where she has concentrated on writing popular history plays. Essentially she endeavors to rewrite history according to a socialist tradition. In *Teufelskreis* (The Devil's Circle, 1953) she represents the burning of the Reichstag in 1933 in living newspaper style, emphasizing the Nazi plot. In *General Landt* (1957) she opposes Carl Zuckmayer's concept of the noble Prussian general by concentrating on the tradition of Prussian militarism. Zinner's plays smack of a dull journalism that fails to report complex events in an interesting fashion.

OTHER PLAYS: *Caféhaus Payer* (1945), *Spiel ins Leben* (Play in Life, 1951), *Der Mann mit dem Vogel* (The Man with the Bird, 1952), *Die Lutzöwer* (1955), *Die Fischer von Niezow* (The Fishermen of Niezow, 1960), *Leistungskontrolle* (Achievement Control, 1960), *Ravensbrücker Ballade* (1961).

**Zuckmayer, Carl** (born 1896). German dramatist, novelist, screenwriter, and poet. One of the few playwrights of the older generation who has been successful since 1945, Zuckmayer has striven to keep abreast with the times, which have not always been kind to him. Born in the Rhineland that serves as the background for his early folk plays, Zuckmayer served in the German Army during World War I. After the war, he studied natural sciences at the universities of Frankfurt and Heidelberg. Then in 1920 he moved to Berlin, where his first play, *Kreuzweg* (Crossroads), about a peasant uprising, was produced. During the next few years he worked at various theaters and was a dramaturge in Kiel for a short period. In 1924 he was employed, along with Bertolt Brecht and Erich Engel, by the Deutsches Theater in Berlin. Soon afterward his first outstanding play, *Der fröhliche Weinberg* (The Merry Vineyard, 1925), was produced. Like most of his best early productions, the work is a folk play set in the Rhineland. It concerns the rich owner of a vineyard named Gunderloch, who insists that his daughter Klärchen marry a man who can prove his virility, since he himself had married a sterile woman and was therefore "compelled" to have an illegitimate child—Klärchen. After a series of hilarious situations in which the characters try to hide their true affections, Klärchen reveals that she is in love with a sailor instead of her official fiancé, a student, and the father confesses his love for his housekeeper. The zest for life shown by the characters of the play is brought out by Zuckmayer's superb command of colloquial language and his ability to portray milieus that fit the situation. This is also evident in his other great success of this period, *Der*

*Hauptmann von Koepenick* (The Captain from Koepenick, 1931). Here Zuckmayer took an event that occurred in Berlin at the turn of the century and made it into a type of folk tale. In it he attacked both the rigid and outmoded penal system and Prussian militarism. He particularly ridiculed the German adoration of the uniform, anticipating the ridiculous but terrifying capitulation to it with the rise of Hitlerism in 1933.

Zuckmayer himself had to flee this Hitlerism. He made his way first to Austria, then, in 1938, to the United States, where he lived as a farmer in Vermont from 1940 to 1946. It was there that he wrote his most famous postwar play, *Des Teufels General* (The Devil's General, 1946). This three-act drama concerns Harras, the commander-in-chief of the German Luftwaffe, who in 1941 is put under pressure because new planes are being sabotaged in factories under his charge and causing the death of their pilots. Harras is an extraordinarily gifted and outspoken man, a critic of the Nazi regime, who has remained loyal to the government because of his love for flying. After he is imprisoned and interrogated by the Nazis, who know that he has helped Jews and other enemies of the regime, Harras is given a time limit to find the saboteurs or else be executed himself. He works continuously with his chief engineer, Oderbruch, only to come to the conclusion that his engineer is the saboteur. When Oderbruch, a man of great integrity, explains his opposition to the Nazis, Harras realizes that he himself has been doing the work of the devil. He decides not to report Oderbruch to the Nazis but commits suicide in a defective plane. Though Zuckmayer renders a remarkably accurate picture of the times and uses the Nazi and military jargon with great facility, the portrait of Harras is much too positive and idealistic. Zuckmayer realized this and revised the play in 1961; yet the play still tends to be too simplistic in its politics and serves as an apology for the noble Prussian soldier who was forced to demean himself before the Nazis.

Most of Zuckmayer's postwar plays have the same weakness: They are superficial reports about timely events and verge on melodrama. Zuckmayer has abandoned the folk play for sociopolitical dramas, which take a humanitarian stand and are well made but lack the incisive political ideas that would make them more important than contemporary weekly magazines. *Der Gesang im Feuerofen* (The Song in the Fiery Furnace, 1950) contains much of the idealism present in *Des Teufels General*. The setting is occupied France in 1943. In this surrealistic play a narrator tells the story of how a French resistance group is betrayed by one of its members. They are burned to death in a château on Christmas eve by the Nazis. The traitor is captured after the war and punished. Here Zuckmayer attempts to focus on the question of guilt and innocence in a period of chaos. In *Das kalte Licht* (The Cold Light, 1955) he undertakes to answer the moral question of the scientist's commitment to his nation, as have other playwrights, such as Brecht, Dürrenmatt, and Kipphardt. Basing the play partially on the Klaus Fuchs case, Zuckmayer concludes that it is perfectly correct for America to develop such a weapon as the atomic bomb and morally reprehensible for a scientist to give the formula to the other side in order to create a balance of power. In *Das Leben des Horace A. W. Tabor* (1964), Zuckmayer presents the rise and fall of the nineteenth-century American who became a king of the silver mines in Colorado and a senator. Here he is fascinated by the potential of a small man. The parallels he sees between the legend of the American West and the social problems in America today seem to be taken too much from American Westerns.

Zuckmayer has retained his superb craftsmanship in the postwar years. He knows how to create atmosphere and use colorful dialogue. However, his postwar plays, which have left the realm of the folk play, try to be too fashionable and too relevant. In returning to Europe in 1946, Zuckmayer unfortunately did not return to his roots as a dramatist. He has, indeed, recaptured a sense of drama, but his dramas have not recaptured the more complex drama of life.

OTHER PLAYS SINCE 1945: *Barbara Blomberg* (1949), *Ulla Winblad* (1952), *Der trunkene Herkules* (The Drunken Hercules, 1957), *Die Uhr schlägt eins* (The Clock Strikes One, 1961).

**Zurich Schauspielhaus** or **Zürcher Schauspielhaus.** A theater built on the Heimplatz in Zurich in 1921. Originally called the Zürcher Pfauentheater, it was bought by the Berlin businessman Franz Wenzler, then sold in 1926 to the Rieser brothers, who changed its name to Schauspielhaus AG. There was nothing extraordinary about the ensemble, and if it had not been for the advent of the Nazi regime in Germany and Austria, it might have remained an average provincial theater. However, in 1938 Oskar Wälterlin became chief director of the theater and invited some of the leading German and Austrian actors to take refuge there from the Nazis. Among the leading actors who worked with Wälterlin were Maria Becker, Therese Giehse, Ernst Ginsberg, Erwin Kalser, Kurt Horwitz, Karl Paryla, Ernst Schroeder, and Wolfgang Langhoff. Along with Wälterlin, Leopold Lindtberg directed plays, which included those of Brecht, Camus, Claudel, Kaiser, Hochwälder, Sartre, the classical playwrights, and later the works of Frisch and Dürrenmatt. It was the Zurich Schauspielhaus that kept the great stream of German critical drama alive in exile. The reputation of the Schauspielhaus has not declined since the war. After Wälterlin's death in 1961, he was followed by Kurt Hirschfeld (1961–1964), Peter Löffler (1964–1970), and Harry Buckwitz, all outstanding directors. The Schauspielhaus is noted for its unusually cosmopolitan programs and its ability to anticipate trends in the theater. Like most German-speaking theaters in recent times, it has been moving toward questioning the function of the theater in society and the inner structure of the theater itself.

**Zusanek, Harald** (born 1922). Austrian dramatist and screenwriter. Before the outbreak of World War II, Zusanek studied philosophy, history, and art at the universities of Vienna and Munich. After serving as a soldier in the Austrian Army, he attended the Reinhardt Seminar in Vienna. In 1947 he left the Seminar to found the Voralberger Landestheater. At first he was mainly interested in directing plays, but he gradually began working on his own scripts. After an attempt at producing a Prometheus triology, he wrote *Warum gräbst du, Centurio?* (Why Are You Digging, Centurion? 1949), which dealt with the collapse of the Roman Empire. Most of Zusanek's plays are historical in content and classical in structure. Zusanek is concerned with portraying the historical moment in relation to the past, and he sees the present as a mask that covers the historical process as it moves in either decline or progress. He is particularly interested in the biological decay of a civilization and the position man takes when confronted with this phenomenon. In one of his best plays, *Die Strasse nach Cavarcere* (The Road to Cavarcere, 1952), he uses the Po River floods of 1951 as a symbolic event to indicate the end of the world. He studies the reactions of typical characters in a small town named Ogniluogo ("Everywhere") when they learn that the flood is coming. Zusanek reveals how the respected people of the town worry about their own skins and become brutal while the drifters and outsiders take on a new heroic and humane aspect. The play is too well-made and didactic to carry its message: Life will be reborn in death. Nevertheless, Zusanek has an eye for portraying intriguing folk characters with complex personalities. He also conveys a sense of the great anxiety of postwar Europe in this play and in others such as *Jean von der Tonne* (Jean of Tonne, 1954), *Die dritte Front* (The Third Front, 1956), and *Piazza* (1959). Zusanek argues that meaning lies in meaninglessness and purpose in purposelessness. He endeavors to incorporate Christian precepts into an existentialist view of the world, and in his adaptation of Calderón's *The World Theater* (1963, as *Das Welttheater*), he uses pantomime to express the necessity of fulfilling spiritual needs in opposition to man's lust for power.

OTHER PLAYS: *Henriette Dupont* (1950), *Bettlerin Europa* (The Beggar Europe, 1953), *Des anderen Kleid* (The Other's Dress, 1954), *Kinderspielplatz* (The Children's Playground), *Schloss in Europa* (The Castle in Europe, 1961).